D1270854

CANON CHRISTOPHER

CANON CHRISTOPHER

of St. Aldate's, Oxford

by

J. S. REYNOLDS, B.Litt., M.A.
Rector of Besselsleigh and Vicar of Dry Sandford
with Cothill, Berkshire

"He that winneth souls is wise."
Proverbs 11. 30.

This biography owes its origin to the late
W. H. GRIFFITH THOMAS, D.D.,
Principal of Wycliffe Hall, Oxford, 1905–10

THE ABBEY PRESS
ABINGDON
1967

By the same author:

THE EVANGELICALS AT OXFORD 1735–1871
A Record of an Unchronicled Movement

Printed in England at
THE ABBEY PRESS - ABINGDON
BERKSHIRE

To the Memory of

MARY HENRIETTA REYNOLDS

1856 – 1949

to whom also it was given

to show to a succeeding generation

what was the faith of their fathers

Contents

Bookplate of A. M. W. Christopher

PREFACE

OVER fifty years have passed since Canon Christopher vacated by death his honorary stall at Christ Church, Oxford, and more than sixty years have elapsed since he resigned his benefice of St. Aldate's in that city. Comparatively few remain who recall his memory. Most of those for whom his name has some meaning think mainly of the last period of his parochial ministry or even of his restricted activity in retirement. Almost inevitably they picture an ageing patriarch, with a large and prominent ear-trumpet. As inevitably, in the absence of a biography, his place in the history of Oxford and of the church has been minimised. It is hoped that the pages which follow may thus justify themselves. But it is perhaps of interest, as it is certainly desirable, to explain how they came to be written.

That the image of Christopher's apostolic devotion has been reduced to a somewhat tenuous legend was not the fault of W. H. Griffith Thomas, who, while serving as the Canon's curate, read for a degree at the university of which he afterwards became a doctor of divinity. Dr. Griffith Thomas — although primarily a theologian — began to collect material for a biography during the Canon's lifetime. In this he had his old rector's tolerant co-operation. Returning to Oxford as Principal of Wycliffe Hall in the year of the Canon's retirement to Norham Road nearby, he was able to add to his cherished store of information. Soon after the Canon's ninetieth birthday, and again after his death two years later, Dr. Griffith Thomas appealed for supplementary evidence of Christopher's worth, which flowed in steadily in the form of personal recollections and testimonies. But Dr. Griffith Thomas had meanwhile gone to live in Canada; and a year later the First World War broke out. Nevertheless by 1917 a typescript was ready for his English publisher. But it was considered too long, too loosely woven, and too diffuse. In the event a much abridged version appeared, during 1920, as a series of articles in *The Churchman*. Four years later Dr. Griffith Thomas died in the United States. For the next twenty-five years the typescript was preserved by his widow; and from her it passed, through the good offices of a mutual friend, into the hands of another would-be biographer of the Canon, the present writer.

On Mrs. Griffith Thomas's death, in 1953, at Lafayette, Louisiana, most of the original material, and many of the Canon's letters, with other papers relating to evangelical affairs at Oxford in the nineteenth century, came to light; and these, too, were sent to England for use in compiling this book. Mrs. E. H. Gillespie, Dr. Griffith Thomas's daughter, — on whom, when an infant in his arms, the Canon called down God's blessing, — has given them freely, subject only to the rightful recognition of her father's part in the work. It is no exaggeration at all to say that without the material which Dr. Griffith Thomas collected at a time when it was available, this biography could scarcely have been attempted half a century later. It has, indeed, been necessary to write the whole afresh; and it has been possible to use sources to which Dr. Griffith Thomas either could not easily have had access from the other side of the Atlantic — for example, the episcopal visitation returns for the relevant period — or which were not available at all — as for instance Captain Seton-Christopher's history of his family, published in 1933. The opportunity has been taken to refer to certain episodes and facts connected with the Canon's life, which had either escaped Dr. Griffith Thomas's notice, or were unrecognised or unsought by him. Some of these — such as the Oxford Convention of 1874 — were of no little importance. Others, for example the results of an examination of the invaluable service registers of St. Aldate's, threw light on generalisations which had become misleading as the years went by. Naturally, therefore, the author of the biography as it now stands must take full responsibility for all criticisms this book will encounter.

Certain of these may, perhaps, be forestalled. The chapter on Christopher's four years in India has not had the benefit of direct help from Calcutta. But in view of the short and comparatively incidental character of this period in the Canon's life, it may be thought that the account given is sufficient. The essential facts are believed to have been included. It will be for an historian of La Martinière, Calcutta, to elaborate on what has been written. Again, it has not been possible to work through all the weekly issues of *The Oxford Times, The Oxford Chronicle,* and *Jackson's Oxford Journal* for the years 1859 to 1913 in order to disinter every reference to Canon Christopher, though many such are certainly enshrined there. The demands of parish life even in the country inevitably protract the compilation of a book requiring much detailed research, and do not permit such a further expenditure of time. Nor would it have seemed in the present case altogether justified. These newspapers have been drawn on frequently, though not exhaustively; and in this respect also it is hoped that an adequate picture results, with no serious omissions. Further, to load a book which is intended to be of interest to a number of general readers with other than explanatory footnotes, has seemed inadvisable. All references to sources will therefore be found in Appendix IV. Even distracting numerals in the text have been eschewed, and the author trusts that those who wish for evidence will weigh the visual advantages of this policy against the occasional labour of counting lines. In a narrative composed over a period of ten years, it is difficult to eliminate all unevenness of texture, whether of literary or factual treatment. Where traces of these are noticeable, the author can only plead, though without complete conviction, the passage of time, and diverse preoccupations. Some relevant materials, as well as a number of small errors, were inevitably discovered too late for insertion or correction in the main body of the work. The additional information and necessary emendations may be sought in Appendix VII.

A biographer must needs try to place the subject of his labours in a family setting. In the case of Canon Christopher, his immediate relations were so numerous that it would not be surprising if the reader thought their degrees of kinship somewhat puzzling. The author has therefore compiled a pedigree, to be found at the end of the book, from which he hopes the several connections of individuals mentioned can be discerned without difficulty. It may be well to add that the Christopher armorial bearings were granted at an unhappy period in the development of heraldic science. The representation of them on the dust-jacket accords with the artistic interpretations of the earlier nineteenth century. The coat-of-arms impressed on the binding is derived from a drawing supplied by the College of Arms in 1962.

PREFACE

Publication of this biography has been made possible, as a tribute to the memory of Canon Christopher, by a very generous subvention on the part of one who loved him, and whose continued enthusiasm has unfailingly supported the project. Without such financial aid, so ambitious a memorial to a parish clergyman, whose public image has naturally diminished with the course of time, could not have been raised. The purchase price of one guinea bears little relation to the cost of production, having been kept low intentionally, so that the book should be within the range of all those who might wish to study it. Author and reader alike have much cause for gratitude.

Canon Christopher was one of the truest saints of God. Any believer bold enough to write about him must soon be aware that he is treading on sacred ground. Yet the detachment of an historically-minded biographer naturally encourages a more impartial appraisal of his career than would have seemed fitting, even if it had been possible, in 1917. Chiefly for this reason, it is perhaps not altogether unfortunate that the Canon's life may only now be reviewed, when the quality of his character and the value of his work, in human terms, can be more accurately assessed. The passage of fifty-three years since 1913 brings us marginally to the right side of a point where, according to a standard recognised by many historians, a definitive biography may be more confidently attempted.

J.S.R.

Dry Sandford, Berkshire
10 March 1966

ACKNOWLEDGEMENTS

The number of those who have helped appreciably in the investigations required for writing this book, more particularly during the past twelve years, though not legion, has become decidedly large. This is true even before remembering to include in thanks contributors who over fifty years ago provided Dr. Griffith Thomas with recollections now sprinkled throughout its pages. To their memory, and to the majority of those at present or recently living, I can only, for lack of space, express in general terms my gratitude for kindly assistance in illuminating the narrative or fitting some small part of Canon Christopher's life-story into a precise position. I regret that I cannot mention all by name.

There remain those who have in different ways allowed me to put them to considerable trouble, to whom my own obligations, and those of at least some readers, are such that I cannot but allude to them individually. To my very great indebtedness to the late Dr. W. H. Griffith Thomas, and to his daughter, Mrs. E. H. Gillespie, I have already had occasion to refer in the Preface.

The Christopher family have been most generous in interest and facilities. The late Miss Eleanor Christopher, the Canon's granddaughter, formerly Principal of St. Hild's College, Durham, Miss M. C. L. Christopher, his great-granddaughter, Colonel J. R. C. Christopher, D.S.O., R.A. (Ret.), representing the branch to which the Canon's wife, herself a Christopher, belonged, and Mr. J. D. Christopher, the head of the senior line, have enabled me to enrich this account, in some degree with information, but more especially with illustrations taken from miniatures and contemporary photographs in their possession.

The present Rector of St. Aldate's, Oxford, the Revd. O. K. de la T. de Berry, has given me free access to his parochial records, a permission often willingly implemented by his vergers, the late Mr. W. A. Scholes, and Mr. H. E. Gooch. For the use of other parish books, I am indebted to Mr. F. H. Gibbens, churchwarden of St. Aldate's. The Vicar of St. Matthew's, Grandpont, Canon D. K. Stather Hunt, allowed me to inspect documents relating to his church during Christopher's incumbency, and in this connection I benefitted from the assistance of Miss C. M. Plumb, the last

Headmistress of Grandpont School. Canon R. H. Chambers, when Vicar of St. John's, Richmond, initiated me into the history and buildings of his parish.

The owners, in most cases inhabitants, of houses once lived in by Canon Christopher, have been most tolerant in permitting inspection, verification (especially where the latter involved examining their title-deeds), and ultimately, photographing. Thus to Mr. T. V. Mounstephen of Pendennis, Downend, to Dr. and Mrs. Shaw of Morton House, Chiswick, to Dr. and Mrs. Ian Fergusson of Tudor Place, Richmond, to Mrs. Graves-Morris of Eastbourne, in respect of 68, Banbury Road, Oxford, and to the former Director of the Maison Française, Oxford — Professor H. Fluchère — for admission to 4, Norham Road, I am particularly grateful. Latterly the agents for 14, Coram Street, Bloomsbury, Messrs. Douglas Kershaw & Co., kindly facilitated entry to Christopher's probable birthplace, hitherto inaccessible.

My account of Christopher's years in India owes not a little to Lt. Col. W. E. Andrews, O.B.E., of New Milton, formerly Headmaster of La Martinière, Lucknow, to whom I am especially indebted for the illustration of La Martinière, Calcutta, and to the late Sir Patrick Cadell, C.S.I., C.I.E., whose knowledge of nineteenth century India I learnt to appreciate when he was a member of my congregation at Besselsleigh.

All the time, there has been the invaluable operational background of the Bodleian Library. I may refer with particular gratitude to Dr. D. M. Barratt of the Department of Western Manuscripts, who has charge of the Oxford diocesan archives.

In paying a well-deserved tribute to the public library service, I remember especially the activity of Mr. P. E. Morris, Borough Librarian of Bexley, in connection with Hall Place as a school, and Mr. M. J. Foster, now of Marylebone Public Library, when Reference Librarian at Richmond; likewise of the Reference Librarian at Oxford City Library, Miss M. Nichols, and her former assistant, Miss E. C. Davies.

The Archivist of the Church Missionary Society, Miss R. A. Keen, the Deputy Librarian of the British and Foreign Bible Society, Miss

G. E. Coldham, — mainly in connection with Christopher correspondence in their custody, — and the Archivist of the Society for the Propagation of the Gospel, Miss C. Merion, have been most helpful and patient. To the Directors of Messrs. Coutts & Co., and their archivist, Miss M. V. Stokes, I am obliged, with the consent of the Christopher family, for information relating to Canon Christopher's financial resources.

To particular ladies and gentlemen, I am especially indebted for help with individual items: to Miss A. N. Reeve, Senior Assistant Archivist, Greater London Record Office, in regard to Canon Christopher's place of baptism; to Mr. F. K. Jones, Assistant Archivist of Jesus College, Cambridge, for unravelling the exiguous though curiously complicated evidence relating to Christopher as a scholar on that foundation; to Dr. M. R. Toynbee, F.S.A., of Oxford, for guidance in the early history of Park Town; to Mr. B. Surtees Raine of Gainford, co. Durham, for extracts from the diary of his father, the Revd. T. S. Raine; to Dr. D. R. Porter, formerly Headmaster of Mount Hermon, U.S.A., and recently churchwarden of Besselsleigh, for assistance in elucidating Christopher's Canadian and American tour; to Capt. G. C. Gardner, M.B.E., C.A., for access to scarce, early printed material relating to the Church Army; to Mr. P. S. Spokes, F.S.A., Sheriff of Oxford, for drawing my attention to a manuscript of part of the printed memorial presented to Canon Christopher in 1884; and to Mr. H. D. W. Lees of Lowestoft for the loan of the only copy I know of Christopher's *In Memoriam. Thomas Augustus Nash.*

A few individuals have kindly lent or given me a small number of the Canon's letters, notably the exceptionally long one preserved by the Rt. Revd. F. E. Lunt, Bishop of Stepney, formerly rector of St. Aldate's.

All seventeen chapters have been helpfully scrutinised by my friends Dr. A. B. Emden, F.B.A., formerly Principal of St. Edmund Hall, and Dr. J. D. Walsh, Fellow of Jesus College, Oxford. A family friend of many years, the late Revd. G. Foster-Carter, Canon Christopher's successor as rector of St. Aldate's, examined with particular care the story from 1894 onwards, which came within his own recollection, as well as kindly providing a copy of his lively but now inaccessible article on the Canon, written in 1913. Mr. Foster-Carter's recent death at the age of 90 has meant that — like Bishop Handley Moule (to whom he had been chaplain) in the case of his biography of Charles Simeon of Holy Trinity, Cambridge, and the latter's successor Canon Carus — I cannot, as I had hoped, place this volume in his hands. Death has also lately removed my former rector, to whom I was curate, Canon R. R. Martin, sometime Rector of St. Martin's and All Saints, Vicar of St. Michael's-at-the-North Gate, Chaplain at New College, and Rural Dean of Oxford, who however had likewise, from the critical vantage point of his extensive acquaintance with Oxford history, perused my text. The Revd. F. S. Cragg, another previous rector of St. Aldate's, has kindly read it in his retirement. It is fair to add that I have not followed quite invariably the suggestions of these learned and reverend gentlemen.

My friend Mr. John Horden has given generously of his time in advising me about the form of the lists of Christopher's works and letters, which constitute Appendices V and VI respectively; also about the composition of the list of illustrations, the shape of the index, and numerous points of detail.

I have acknowledged separately, in the list of illustrations, my degree of indebtedness to each person or body who has enabled me to make as complete as possible a visual record of Canon Christopher's life and associations. Several illustrations which I was anxious to procure have been obtained at considerable cost of time and effort on the part of total strangers, notably Mrs. Eastwood of Beaconsfield, in the case of St. Aldates' Old Rectory, and Miss E. M. Foss of Japan, in that of Bishop Poole. The reproductions owe much to the patient and excellent work of two photographers, Mr. J. Furley-Lewis of Kensington, who took great trouble, and Mr. J. W. Thomas of Headington, whose Oxford photography is widely acclaimed. Their contributions are distinguished and acknowledged at the end of the list of illustrations.

The design of the book has benefitted from the advice of Mrs. Rose Harley. The decorative portions of the dust-jacket are the work of

Mrs. G. M. Spriggs of Dry Sandford, who bore with my detailed suggestions while using her artistic skill to full effect. At a vital stage, another parishioner, Miss E. Deane, kindly typed much of the manuscript, when it was urgently needed. Latterly, Miss Felicity Boddington has diligently searched the index for errors of transcription and alphabetical order.

For patience with an author, the Abbey Press must take a prominent place in the annals of book production. Without their kindly forebearance, this work would not have emerged as complete or as accurately shaped as it may be, and probably it would not have emerged at all. I must especially thank Mr. J. H. Hooke for undertaking publication, Mr. J. T. Cullen for his able, stimulating and unwearied oversight, and Mr. J. F. Gale as a meticulous compositor, particularly in revising galley proofs.

To all those, named and unnamed, who have been instrumental in forwarding this biography, I sincerely offer my warmest thanks.

J.S.R.

Illustrations

ILLUSTRATIONS

ILLUSTRATIONS

ILLUSTRATIONS

Nos. 1, 3, 4, 6, 8, 9, 14, 15, 17, 18, 20, 21, 22, 23, 24, 25, 26, 27, 29, 30, 31, 39, 40, 46, 47, 50, 51, 54, 55, 56, 57, 59, 60, 61, 62, 63, 66, 67, 68, 69, 70, 72, 75, 77, 78, 80, 81, 82, 83, 84, and bookplate, p. iv, are from photographs by Mr. J. Furley-Lewis, 145, Cromwell Road, London, S.W.7.

Nos. 7, 28, 33, 34, 36, 37, 38, 43, 44, 49, 65, 79 are from photographs by Mr. J. W. Thomas, hon.M.A.Oxon., of Thomas-Photos, 1, Collingwood Close, Headington, Oxford.

"Next to the consideration of the HOLY SCRIPTURES, no study is so useful and profitable as that of BIOGRAPHY."

The Comprehensive Dictionary of Biography (1860), p.v.

Chapter I

Early Years

1820 - 1839

"A FAITHFUL RECORD of the life of a man who lived by faith in the Son of God, who loved us and gave Himself for us, is good food for the soul. It refreshes and stimulates the Christian to read of one who, as a living branch in 'the True Vine,' brought forth 'the fruits of righteousness, which are by Jesus Christ, to the glory and praise of God.' " These words, written by Canon Christopher in reference to a memoir which he himself had edited, form a no less fitting introduction to his own biography. "The lives of such men," he goes on, "should not be allowed to drop out of sight. They are precious as examples, — they are full of encouragement, — they illustrate the grace of God, — they adorn the doctrine of God our Saviour, — they shew the results of receiving the Gospel not in word only, but also in power and in the Holy Ghost. Our Lord says to His people, 'Let your light so shine before men that they may see your good works, and glorify your Father which is in heaven.' Is it not a duty to keep shining, by means of a memoir, the light of an eminent departed servant of God, who, through living by faith in the Lord Jesus, abounded in 'the work of the Lord' ?"

Sentiments such as these entwine the heart of the long and ample tradition of evangelical biography. The same compulsion actuated the commemorative sermons of the nineteenth and earlier centuries, moving Thomas Scott 'the Commentator' to preach in 1808 a discourse entitled *The Duty and Advantage of remembering Deceased Ministers,* which Canon Smyth has told us he would have been inclined to adopt as a sub-title to his Birkbeck Lectures (published as *Simeon and Church Order* in 1940), since the history of the evangelical revival is in a considerable measure a history of personalities. It is perhaps hardly necessary to add that spiritual leadership and devotion are not essentially associated with special prominence in the visible church. As with other schools of thought, many of the greatest names in the evangelical movement — Simeon and Scott among them — are of men who lived out all their days as plain parish clergymen. This was partly because as true adherents of historic evangelicalism they placed uncompromising allegiance to 'the doctrines of grace,' and considerations of principle, before all else. Some were men of outstanding intellectual distinction. Others were more remarkable for their long sustained influence and self-sacrifice, for their willingness to preach the gospel in season and out of season, and for their active support of all kinds of evangelical enterprise. Such was Canon Christopher. For forty-six years he toiled in a poor Oxford parish, exercising at once loving pastoral care over his parishioners and for the many undergraduates who attended his church. He might well have looked for advancement in another walk of life. He chose the narrow path of Christian duty and service, whereby, unquestionably, countless souls were led to God. In the closing words of *The Times*' obituary notice, ". . . it will be long before Oxford will see his like again."

Christopher was born in London during the first year of the reign of King George IV, on 20 August 1820. As far as is known, the event took place at 14, Coram Street, Bloomsbury, where his parents were then living. In those days, Great Coram Street, as it was called until 1900, was considered in a fashionable neighbourhood, but during the later nineteenth century its reputation declined. Thackeray, who lived next door at number 13 twenty years after Christopher's birth, wrote of an Irish reading room he visited: " Not Palmyra — not the Russell Institution in Great Coram-street — present more melancholy appearances of faded greatness . . ." The Russell Literary Institution, across the road from number 13, has disappeared altogether, but in this respect its mantle has fallen on other parts of the street. Nevertheless number 14, in a terrace of eighteenth century houses, retains an air of distinction and character. Some years later the London address of Christopher's family became 41, Great Ormond Street, an attractive early eighteenth century house, not far from Coram Street, now used by the Great Ormond Street Children's Hospital; but in 1833 this was given up. It is unlikely, as will appear, that Christopher remembered living either in it or at 14, Great Coram Street. He was baptised 'Alfred Millard William.'[1] 'Alfred' was a name then becoming popular. 'Millard' was the surname of his aunt Caroline, to whose care he was committed in boyhood. 'William' was the name of his paternal grandfather. Captain William Christopher, though he died in 1797, was an important figure in the family history. Even so, at a time when more than one Christian name had only recently become common, three was unusual, and perhaps indicative of a conscious pride of pedigree.

For the Christopher family were minor gentry, probably of yeoman origin, claiming descent in unbroken succession from John Christopher, who ranked as a gentleman in the reign of King Henry VIII, and died in 1589. He was a small landed proprietor at Billingham, county Durham, a village near Stockton-on-Tees now almost submerged by industrial development. The Christophers remained in the north country for two hundred and fifty years. During the seventeenth century two branches made their appearance as far south as Worcestershire and Lincolnshire. In the male line, the latter became extinct in the person of Sir Robert Christopher of Alford, who had fought for King Charles I.

Towards the close of the seventeenth century, the Durham family, to which Alfred Christopher belonged, acquired by inheritance a neighbouring property, partly on the boundary with Yorkshire, around Norton, where Bernard Gilpin, 'the Apostle of the North', had resigned the vicarage for conscience' sake in 1556[2]. In 1690 the Revd. Thomas Rudd became Vicar. As curate of Stockton from 1663 to 1712, he was responsible for the erection of its parish church, for which he is said to have secured Sir Christopher Wren as architect on the score of a family relationship. Canon Christopher was a great-great-great-grandson of Rudd, who was father of Thomas

[1]His place of birth and baptism are discussed in Appendix I.

[2]Canon T. R. Scott, a respected vicar from 1890 to 1924, was a great-grandson of Thomas Scott 'the Commentator'.

Rudd the Durham antiquary. The estate devolved upon Captain William Christopher, an explorer well known in his day. As commodore of the Hudson's Bay Company's fleet, he took a leading part in charting the outline of the Arctic coast of North America, and in efforts to trace the North-West Passage. The version of the Christopher coat-of-arms granted to his son George Christopher, Alfred's father, in 1824, takes its distinctive charges — a beaver and a chart of Chesterfield's Inlet, with an anchor incorporated in the crest — from this association.[1]

William Christopher was a personal friend of Captain Cook (who was a native of Marton, five miles from Norton, across the Yorkshire border) and is said to have accompanied him on his last voyage round the world. His exertions brought a substantial fortune. In 1756 he married Ann Tatham, second cousin of the celebrated wit (and Lord Chief Justice) Lord Alvanley, herself a lady of parts. Their eldest son, John Christopher of Crook Hall, near Durham, was progenitor of a line of lawyers who have since lived for more than a generation in Berkshire. Owing to a disagreement between him and his father, Captain Christopher's landed property went to John's brother George. This included the summer residence of the family at Grangefield, by Stockton, and a much larger house on the higher ground looking towards the Cleveland Hills, which was subsequently pulled down.

In 1800 George Christopher married Isabella Ashington, whose uncle, Commander Henry Ashington, was sixty years in the Royal Navy. By her he had seven sons and seven daughters. In 1813, before the younger children (Alfred was the twelfth child) were born, their father sold the family estate, having already, by 1806, moved to the neighbourhood of London. (A hundred years later, 1913 — Alfred died in the spring — was known at Cambridge as 'Ashington's year,' when H. S. D. Ashington of King's, a great-grandson of Mrs. George Christopher's brother Henry, won three of the five events successfully competed for by Cambridge in the university athletic sports.) Two of George's brothers, Henry and Thomas, also left the north. The youngest, Thomas, married in

[1]A contemporary engraving appeared among the arms of subscribers, depicted in the concluding pages of the third volume, to Berry's *Encyclopaedia Heraldica.* It was this coat, and not that hitherto used by the family, which descended to Alfred Christopher.

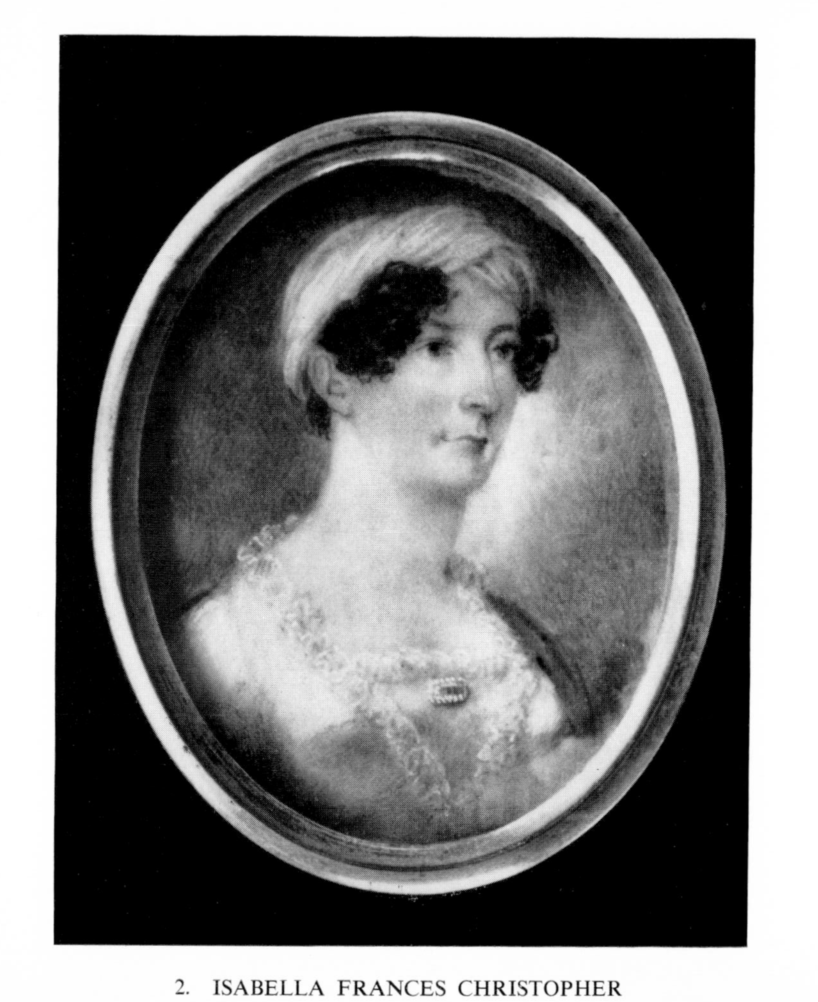

2. ISABELLA FRANCES CHRISTOPHER
1781–1836

3. GEORGE CHRISTOPHER
1779–1861

Parents of A. M. W. Christopher

4. 14, CORAM STREET, BLOOMSBURY, LONDON, 1962
Probable birthplace of A. M. W. Christopher, 1820
His home 1820–22. Demolished 1966

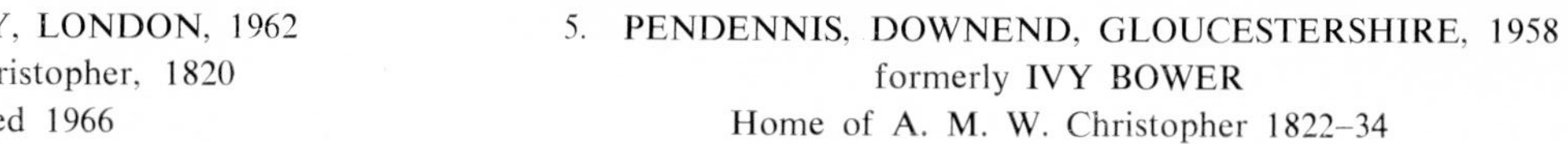

5. PENDENNIS, DOWNEND, GLOUCESTERSHIRE, 1958
formerly IVY BOWER
Home of A. M. W. Christopher 1822–34

1806 Sarah Seton, daughter of James Seton of Oldfold Manor, Hadley, in Middlesex. Their second daughter Maria became Alfred Christopher's wife, and one of their sons, Commander Wilmot Christopher, was a popular naval hero of the 'forties.

Caroline Christopher, only surviving daughter of Captain William Christopher, remained a spinster until 1818, when at the age of forty-one she married Thomas Millard, formerly of Bristol, but since 1815 of Downend, Gloucestershire, a man thirteen years her junior. There was no issue, and in 1822 they virtually adopted the infant Alfred, who was a godson to one of them. George Christopher had not yet taken a house in Chiswick, where he lived until his death in 1861, and where he was already receiving letters by 1827. Nor was his wife yet afflicted by the illness to which she succumbed in 1836; but her sister-in-law and a relatively rich husband were able to prevail on her to part with one of her numerous offspring. In 1822 a younger son Leonard was born. Though subsequently his favourite brother, the arrival of the new baby made young Alfred unhappy in the nursery. Caroline Millard, who was staying with his parents at the time, thus found it easier to press her request. The child was to remain in the care of his aunt and uncle for twelve formative years.

The practice of commencing a biography with an account of antecedents has sometimes been derided. But duly modified, it remains an essential introduction to the life of any man or woman, and in the case of Alfred Christopher for three reasons especially. First he came of a family of strong naval and military associations. Though not pugnacious, he was a fighter born; and this natural aptitude, when combined with the graces of faith, stood him in good stead during fifty-four years of spiritual endeavour in Oxford. Secondly, he was a gentleman by birth and breeding. This was a matter of special consequence in Victorian England, and not least in Victorian Oxford, where it was an important advantage that the leading evangelical incumbent throughout the greater part of the Queen's reign, could not be dismissed, whatever he chose to do, as one who did not know better. Christopher's upbringing, general outlook, and manners were in fact conveniently similar to those of the majority of the undergraduates among whom he was to work, and he found himself on terms of social equality with many of the principal dons. Thirdly, and unexpectedly, we learn that although Alfred Christopher was a member of a large family of brothers and sisters, and owed much to two of them, his childhood was more solitary than that of many an only boy or girl. " The child is father of the man." Christopher was destined to spend the greater part of his life cut off by deafness from the world around him. But he had already learned to live in great measure alone; and those who marvelled at his forbearance with his infirmity often did not realise that he had been prepared from infancy for such a hardship. Moreover he had profited from the lessons of solitude. Thrown to a large extent on his own resources, he developed a sturdy independence of mind and body.

Carried off into Gloucestershire, in his uncle's household at Downend, then a hamlet in the parish of Mangotsfield, now almost entirely built over, some five miles from Bristol, Christopher lived until he was almost fourteen. The house is that known as Pendennis, formerly Pendenny, a comfortable stone-built homestead of ten or twelve rooms standing in two acres of garden. Originally two cottages, it was considerably enlarged and made into one house in the first half of the eighteenth century. Called by Thomas Millard 'Ivy Bower' — parts of it are still clad in thick ivy — it remained Millard property for many years. Until the final six months the lad was not sent to school; and as it happened that there were hardly any boys of his own age and kind in the neighbourhood, he had no other sources of youthful companionship. Occasionally he played with Stephen Cave of Cleve Hill, a small country house later much enlarged and now pulled down. Like Christopher, in after years he was " loving, and capable." A few months younger than Christopher, Cave passed on to Harrow and Balliol. As member for Shoreham, he became a minor politician, and is commemorated by a tablet in Downend church. Another occasional playmate was William Stenson of Bourton-on-the-Water, whom nearly sixty years later Christopher baptised on his deathbed. His father, Dr. Nathaniel Stenson, sometimes stayed with the Millards. The doctor was a baptist, and in this connection, as a nonconformist, made an early impression on young Alfred's mind: " How well I remember the length of his exposition after breakfast when I was a little boy at my aunt's at Downend. Yet I liked him . . ." Millard himself appears, from his will, to have been a churchman.

Sometimes the monotony of life was relieved by visits to or from relations. In 1826, when he was six years old, young Alfred made a pleasant excursion in the company of his aunt to stay with the widow of his uncle Thomas Christopher, who was living on Hadley Common, near Barnet. While there he delighted in the company of his young cousins. He went with Maria and Caroline to Ramsgate, where, happy beyond measure, he played with them on the sands. One day Maria noticed another little girl, accompanied by her mother; and seeing that the child's shoe-lace was untied, she called attention to this and immediately stooped down and fastened it. The lady with her was the Duchess of Kent, and the little girl, Princess Alexandrina Victoria, destined to become the living symbol of the era in which Alfred Christopher exercised most of his ministry. In after life Maria often recalled with pleasure this early memory of her sovereign. Five years later, accompanied by her sister Janet, Maria visited Downend. Alfred always remembered Janet, a young lady of twenty-one, trying to teach her younger sister to sing the warlike song "Oh, give me but my Arab steed", and scolding her because she did not open her mouth widely enough; for he gallantly took Maria's part, and drew Janet's wrath upon himself, a championship which was perhaps not unrelated to the fact that the younger girl became his wife.

Caroline Millard had great faith in simple remedies which she dispensed to the poor; armed with these she doctored them with notable effect. Alfred also received his share. "I really loved my dear Aunt," he wrote long afterwards, but "I believe that she had some sort of idea that she could purge everything bad out of my constitution . . . except original sin. She was too pious to make any mistake about that." Occasionally Alfred was punished for things he had not done. ("If *I* did not do it, *who* did?") He refused to believe that one of the younger servants was responsible. Anyway, he was able to add, the naughty things he in fact did were not found out, and sometimes he was "*very, very* naughty."

Thomas Millard lived as a modest country gentleman. He was still only thirty-two when Alfred came to reside at Downend. Millard had an unusual taste for mathematics, and this he imparted to his nephew, who at the age of eleven had mastered Euclid and delighted in algebra. There came a day when, before breakfast, he found he could appreciate a proposition of Euclid which he had supposed no one in the world could really understand. One of the boy's morning pleasures, we are told, was to race his uncle in solving mathematical problems. From this it might seem that young Christopher was precociously priggish; but there is no other sign of such a trait. So strong was Millard's concern for his interest that many years later he left several thousand pounds to Trinity College, Oxford, for the study of mathematical science. To his "Uncle Millard's partiality for mathematics," Christopher was wont to ascribe, in the providence of God, all the positions which he himself subsequently held. The same beneficent influence he was fond of tracing, link by link, in the lives of others.

The most fascinating books, however, to many boys have to do with wars and battles. Young Alfred Christopher was not exceptional, and everything of that kind which he could lay hold upon he eagerly enjoyed. This evidently implied serious reading, for we learn that the histories of Hume and Smollett were among his treasures — as also, however, was Johnson's *Lives of the Poets* — and that a history of the American War of Independence was another favourite. He wished to be a soldier. A book which greatly encouraged this desire was *The Life of John Shipp,* an orphan in a parish workhouse, who entered the army as a drummer boy, became a sergeant, and led four 'forlorn hopes' at the first and unsuccessful siege of Bhurtpore. It was a true story, and Christopher was enthralled. He imagined himself involved in all kinds of military situations and hair-breadth escapes. This taste he was able to 'improve' while at thirteen, as a day scholar for a few months at a small school in Downend, he worked away at Caesar's *Gallic War*.

In 1831 Christopher had some experience of action, when, in the year before the Reform Bill became law, the military were called out to quell the radical rioters at Bristol. One of the most vivid of his boyhood recollections was that " the glare of three jails, two sides of Queen's [*sic*] Square, and the Bishop's Palace all blazing at the same time seemed quite near to us. The triumphant mob had set the buildings on fire . . ." Shortly afterwards, Major Digby Mackworth, later the fourth baronet and a prominent evangelical layman, took command, charged the crowd resolutely, and broke their resistance. The Mayor of Bristol, Charles Pinney, " in after years . . .

6. CAROLINE MILLARD
1777–1845
Aunt of A. M. W. Christopher

7. THOMAS MILLARD
1790–1871
Husband of Caroline Millard

8. MORTON HOUSE, CHISWICK MALL, MIDDLESEX, 1962

Home of A. M. W. Christopher 1834–44

a warm friend of the Church Missionary Society," who lived to entertain Christopher a quarter of a century later, and his chaplain Thomas Curme, subsequently, as Vicar of Sandford St. Martin in north Oxfordshire, a dear friend of Christopher's, had a narrow escape through the roof of the Mansion House. Alfred was taken into Bristol to see the ruins. Two houses in Queen Square, where the Mansion House lately stood, had been saved, one by a determined occupant with a pair of pistols, the other by a cook with a spit. Another small spectator was Charles Kingsley, later the well-known broad churchman; a year older than Christopher, he had recently been sent to a school at Clifton. Downend was near the colliery district of Kingswood, associated with George Whitefield and John Wesley, and Christopher remembered a gang of colliers coming to his uncle's house soon after the riots, " hoping to frighten him into giving them money. But, as he was not easily frightened, they did not succeed." A thief who disturbed Millard on one occasion was later sentenced to seven years' penal servitude at Botany Bay.

Bristol at this time was an evangelical stronghold. The long reign of Thomas Biddulph of St. James's, considered by Henry Budd as " virtually Bishop of Bristol," had not yet drawn to its close. Downend itself was later associated with Alfred Peache, founder of St. John's Hall, Highbury (now the London College of Divinity, at Northwood), and of the Peache Patronage Trust, who was incumbent of Mangotsfield for fifteen years before becoming Vicar of Downend in 1874. Rather earlier, a figure congenial to Christopher on other grounds, W. G. Grace, son of the Downend doctor, had learned to play cricket in the neighbourhood. Thomas Lathbury, historian of convocation, became curate of Mangotsfield in 1831.

It does not appear that Alfred Christopher was appreciably influenced by evangelical teaching during his sojourn in the west country. But he was acquainted with John Foster the essayist, who lived in a neighbouring village, and who until 1821 had been baptist minister at Downend. At Ivy Bower Sunday was observed with a high degree of strictness, which in later life Christopher, though a strong sabbatarian, recognised as unwise. "When I was a child I used to look on a Sunday afternoon as a pile of catechisms, hymns, and text books, out of each of which I had to learn something, with dismay and depression. It was some time before I could begin. I used to be unhappy on Saturday because the next day would be Sunday." He added an interesting comment. "But these things are changed now. Children are more considered," a remark which suggests that consideration for the young as later understood began in the era which has often been regarded as conspicuous for its absence.

After his short preliminary experience of school life, Alfred returned to his parents at Morton House, Chiswick. History is silent as to why at this stage he left his uncle and aunt. Doubtless it was natural enough that he should rejoin his own family circle when his elder brothers and sisters were fully grown. Alfred's father, with whom he now lived for the first time was, somewhat by contrast to Millard, a keen sportsman, devoted to fishing, hunting, and shooting. He had a good voice, and it is said of him, as descriptive of character, that he danced after his elder daughters had grown up. He was a captain in the Middlesex Volunteers, and already a man of fifty-five.

George Christopher appears to have been the founder of Christopher's, a firm of wine-merchants which still flourishes in Jermyn Street, Piccadilly. *The Family of Christopher* (a book of amateur merit, valuable, however, for the nineteenth century,) does not refer to this association with trade. But it notes the connection with Great Ormond Street (which is confirmed by testamentary evidence), and the London directories show that between 1816 and 1824 at least, George Christopher and Son, and later William Thomas Christopher (William Thomas was the name of the eldest son) carried on business as wine and brandy merchants in Great Coram Street nearby, moving to 41, Great Ormond Street by 1827, but retaining premises in Great Coram Street for many years. Ultimate confirmation is afforded by the census returns for 1851, where George Christopher describes himself as 'retired wine-merchant.' The family's links with the firm had evidently been broken before he died ten years later. All its records were burned during an air-raid in the Second World War. It is believed that the Christopher interest passed to members of the Tatham family.

Morton House stands not far from the parish church, which terminates a delightful row of eighteenth and nineteenth century riverside dwellings, immediately overlooking Chiswick Eyot. During our period one of these was designated by Thackeray as Miss Pinkerton's academy for young ladies, in *Vanity Fair* the scene of Becky Sharp's articled pupilage. At Morton House, the pleasantly panelled rooms, painted white, with their bolection mouldings around the fireplaces, and their air of commodious well-being, have more recently been the abode of Eric Kennington the sculptor. The house fronts directly on to Chiswick Mall, but behind it lies a sizeable garden. Of the Christopher children, four brothers, ranging from thirty-two to twelve, survived, with seven sisters between thirty-four and eleven years of age, two of whom were married. William and Arthur, probably, and Leonard certainly, were still living at home. George had entered the East India Company's service. Of the girls Margaret, the eldest, was married to Major John Bell of the 1st Regiment of Foot. Caroline's husband was Nelson Robinson; with their children, who eventually numbered nine, they migrated to Canada. Isabella, Emma, Selina, Louisa, and Matilda were still unmarried.

Into a family which he had hardly known, Alfred was now received, preparatory to entering a school of some sixty boys at Bexley, Kent, in July 1834. Two paternal uncles, John and Thomas, the latter his future father-in-law, had been at Eton. But even if expense had not militated against a public school education, good private schools such as Mr. John Barton kept at Hall Place, Bexley, were much favoured at this time by upper class parents.

Hall Place is a fine building, noticeably akin to a college, consisting of two quadrangles, of which the older was erected about 1540 by Sir John Champneys, whose descendant William Champneys was at this time curate-in-charge of St. Ebbe's, Oxford, and subsequently became an evangelical leader well known to Christopher, preaching for him at St. Aldate's in 1868. The later part of the house, towards the river Cray, was added about 1650. It passed out of the Champneys family and in 1796 became a boarding school for young gentlemen. Five years later Julius Jeffreys, inventor of the first respirator for warming the inhaled air, was born there, a son of the headmaster. After changing hands once or twice early in the century, Hadarezer Stone acquired an interest in the school which he retained until 1835. When Christopher first joined it, therefore, he was under Stone; but John James Barton, who had matriculated as a fellow-commoner of

Peterhouse, Cambridge, in 1834, was already in process of taking over.

Under Barton, according to a prospectus of 1843, " The internal arrangements of the School " were " in a great measure modelled on those of the Schools of Prussia, which were visited by the PRINCIPAL during the summer of 1834." In spite of this somewhat forbidding statement, the curriculum, both as regards subjects and time-table, shows a remarkably liberal approach to education as then understood. Classics and mathematics were superintended by the Revd. J. G. Handford, a graduate of Corpus Christi College, Cambridge;[1] French and German by the Revd. G. Ott, who had taken his degree at Strasbourg. Boys were prepared for the universities and many went into the service of the East India Company. On Sundays they attended Bexley parish church, the scene in the previous century of the ministry of the Wesleys' friend Henry Piers. In 1849 Barton moved his pupils to Brighton, where as Portland School they occupied a building vacated by Brighton College, and remained until 1855. For a time another school took possession of Hall Place. Later it reverted to private use, and until 1943 was the home of a dowager Countess of Limerick, from whom the ownership passed to Bexley Corporation, who now employ it to house a school for girls.

At Hall Place, in spite of having received little formal education, Alfred Christopher's mathematics gradually took him to the top of the school. It was here too that he developed his love of cricket. The origin of the skill which won him a place in the Cambridge eleven of 1843 he attributed to being taken with a party of boys to Chislehurst, where he watched for the first time a 'round-arm' bowler in the person of Alfred Mynn, at a match between Kent and All England. He also saw the impressive batting of Fuller Pilch. On this occasion the Hall Place boys met others from a Blackheath school, whose master sometimes played (under a suitable pseudonym) for England. Not unnaturally his eleven habitually beat all the private schools in the neighbourhood. They challenged Christopher's school and expected to win. But Christopher set to work to practise 'round-arm' bowling. It was then not lawful to raise the elbow above the shoulder, and novices frequently bowled wide. Nevertheless, when the day of the match came, Christopher

[1]Afterwards Rector of Shereford, Norfolk.

9. HALL PLACE, BEXLEY, KENT, 1806

A. M. W. Christopher, at Hall Place School 1834–39

10. HALL PLACE, BEXLEY, 1964

began to bowl well. He soon took one wicket, which gave him confidence, and then another. He proceeded to take three wickets with three successive balls, and clean bowled seven batsmen in the first innings. As he himself put it, " It is as true as anything I ever wrote in my life, but it will require unbounded confidence in my truthfulness to believe it, that this redoubtable, trained, scientific Eleven only got one run off the bat in the first innings and the Hall Place boys won the match."

The school which the opposing side represented was that of Nicholas Wanostrocht, whose great-uncle, Nicolas Wanostrocht, had been French tutor in Earl Bathurst's family, and had subsequently founded the Alfred House Academy near Camberwell Green. After Wanostrocht's death, first his nephew Vincent Wanostrocht, and then Vincent's son Nicholas, carried on the school. The latter's " devotion to cricket is said to have been somewhat detrimental to the more strictly academic portion of the curriculum." When he played for England he appeared as 'N. Felix', and became well known as the author of *Felix on the Bat,* one of the classics of cricket, lately republished. In 1830 he moved his school to Blackheath, " where he was long a familiar figure from the zeal with which he instructed his pupils in the rudiments of the national game."

Young Christopher was also good at drawing, but at this he never attained more than second place in the school, for he remained below Louis Desanges, who spent six years at Hall Place, and was the only schoolfellow whom Christopher could recall as afterwards achieving fame. Desanges, the great-grandson of a French nobleman, and the son of émigré parents, became a well-known artist and portrait painter, who illustrated in a series of pictures the deeds of those who had won the Victoria Cross. That harshness of punishment in schools, and its unhelpful association with religion, was declining throughout the Victorian era, is suggested by another of Christopher's comments on his early days. " When I went to school, the favourite severe punishment of one of the Masters, not an unkind man, was to require a boy to write out the 119th Psalm. Who would give such a task now?"

Meanwhile true spiritual influence was at work upon young Alfred through the example of his sister Isabella, " a living evidence of Christianity to me as a boy and a young man." Sixteen years older than he, she devotedly nursed their mother during a long illness. Her elder sister had married in 1829, so to her as the next eldest daughter fell the lead in household affairs. Mrs. Christopher was an invalid for two years, and upon her death in 1836 — she was the first of the family to be buried in the Christopher vault in Chiswick churchyard — Isabella nevertheless believed she had not done all she might for her, and fell into a state of morbid despair. " She was the most holy one of the family," Alfred wrote in after years, " in the eyes of her brothers and sisters, yet she thought she could not be saved. I was her young brother of 16 years of age, who knew but little of the Bible.[1] I had only one qualification for helping her, which was this: I felt certain that if anything could help her, it must be in the Bible, for she would care for no book of less authority. So I began to search the Scriptures. I thought there was a great probability of finding something that would help to comfort and encourage her in 'the Book of the Prophet Isaiah.' So I began to read the first Chapter of that Book. When I came to the 18th verse, 'Come now, and let us reason together, saith the Lord: though your sins be as scarlet, they shall be as white as snow; though they be red like crimson they shall be as wool,' I started up and ran upstairs to my dear sister's bedside. I felt that was a text suited for a great sinner, which was what my dear sister thought herself to be, though all her family knew her to be a great saint. I repeated this one verse over and over again. My most effective sermon was all text & *nothing in addition* to it. In her 95th year I asked her 'What was the text which restored you, through the Spirit Who used it, to peace, health and usefulness?' She repeated Isaiah I. 18. She said 'That text was *thumped* into my heart all night as I lay awake.' I had forgotten the text, but I think I never can forget my sister's answer to my question."

Here we see the uninhibited action of a boy brought up in an atmosphere where the Bible's authority was taken for granted, whose characteristic sympathy for his sister was deeply aroused. We are reminded of what a leading journal said on the occasion of the one hundred and fiftieth anniversary of the Bible Society, about " the status which the Bible had among English evangelicals at the beginning of the nineteenth century. To them it was not merely a

[1]Another account by Christopher reads "baptised, confirmed, but unconverted"

necessary part of the apparatus of the religious life, but a fount of salvation, a book which had the power to guide men to their true destiny. To possess it was to own an incomparable treasure, to have virtually at one's daily command an infallible authority in all that was necessary to peace of mind . . ."

But Alfred Christopher was not yet a Christian. Nor did he have a spectacular conversion. Rather was it after various Christian influences had touched him over a considerable period of years that he finally acknowledged the claims of Christ and yielded himself to Him. The first of these influences came from his sister. After her mother's death, she proved equally solicitous for her father. She had a strong aversion to boats and trains; but in spite of her nervousness, she faithfully accompanied George Christopher on all his travels. Young Alfred was able to trace all her devotion to their parents, and all her unselfish love for her brothers and sisters, to her Christian principles, and this biassed him in favour of those evangelical doctrines which he knew were at the root of the holiness of her character and the usefulness of her life.

The second link in the chain was the Revd. Charles Goodhart, incumbent of St. Marys' Chapel, an evangelical outpost in Castle Street, Reading, at this time a man of thirty-five. Isabella Christopher contrived for her brother to spend three months with Goodhart before going up to Cambridge. Like many clergymen of those days, Goodhart took a number of resident pupils, which is doubtless one reason why he did not live in the adjoining chapel house. Goodhart in fact resided at 11, Castle Street, now numbered 63, and known as Holybrook House. Like many of the homes with which Christopher was connected during the first half of his life, Holybrook House is an attractive and indeed remarkable building, which has been described as "an especially fine mid-eighteenth century mansion." Goodhart's ministry was of a deeply spiritual and thoroughly Biblical character. "A rich blessing attended [it], and his Sermons were the means of leading many to Christ." Among the latter were members of the Sutton family, already well known as seed merchants, of whom Martin Hope became a life-long friend of Christopher (they were approximately the same age) and liberally aided his work at St. Aldate's. Christopher himself listened attentively to the sermons at St. Marys' Chapel, and "often felt unhappy in the knowledge that he was not converted." Goodhart impressed Christopher for life with the conviction that evangelical principles were at once scriptural and truly representative of the Church of England. This was an abiding influence; but it was not conversion. Several years were to pass before Alfred Christopher became, in the evangelical sense, and in his own estimation, a Christian.

Charles Joseph Goodhart had taken his degree from Trinity College, Cambridge, as twenty-second wrangler, in 1826, and with a second class in the classical tripos. Among his curates at St. Marys' Chapel was Charles Hole, church historian, who became Lecturer in Ecclesiastical History at King's College, London, and whose *Life* of Archdeacon Phelps doubtless originated in their mutual connection with Reading. A man of strong character, in later days Goodhart was Minister of the Park Chapel, Chelsea, a benevolently autocratic Secretary of the Church Missions to Jews, and finally Rector of Wetherden, Suffolk. During Christopher's early years at Oxford, he was an honoured annual speaker at gatherings for undergraduates, and a welcome preacher at St. Aldate's.[1] Of Goodhart, Christopher wrote: "He adorned the doctrine of God his Saviour in all things; and his life was a living argument in favour of the Gospel he so faithfully preached. I valued his preaching, his expositions at family prayer, his conversations, his character, and yet remained alas unconverted, of which fact I am grievously certain. Let no one be discouraged about himself. God's love is so great that his forbearance is wonderful ... I remember hearing him [Goodhart] say that he never had so much as a doubt that the Bible is really the Word of God, inspired from beginning to end by the Holy Spirit. This fact is all the more interesting because Mr. Goodhart was a man of intellect and scholarship, who took double honours at Cambridge, a man of an enquiring mind and of the greatest truthfulness of character. The prophecies concerning the Premillenial Advent of our Lord," he added, "and the future of the Jews were subjects of the greatest interest to him. I have observed through life that the people who have seemed to me to have the strongest faith of all have been those who have most diligently studied the prophecies in the Old

[1]A. M. Goodhart, who succeeded A. C. Benson as an Eton housemaster and died at Oxford in 1941, and H. C. Goodhart, second classic at Cambridge in 1881, Fellow of Trinity and Professor of Humanity at Edinburgh, were his grandsons.

11. HOLYBROOK HOUSE, READING, 1962
A. M. W. Christopher, here a pupil of
C. J. Goodhart, 1839

12. CHARLES JOSEPH GOODHART
1804–1892
Minister of St. Marys' Chapel, Reading, 1836–52

Testament with minds established in the belief of the New Testament. Mr. Goodhart was one of these." Dr. William Marsh, among the most saintly clergymen of the nineteenth century, considered Goodhart, " whom he loved with the heartiest sympathy and regard, . . . one of the noblest of the witnesses for God and His Truth in our country."[1]

The influence of Isabella Christopher on her younger brother may be compared with that exercised about the same time by her namesake Isabella Fox on her brother Henry Fox, the Indian missionary, while he was at Rugby and Wadham. It is a coincidence that the Fox family also came from county Durham. It was however another sister whose devotion made it possible for Alfred Christopher to go to the university. At school a Cambridge examiner suggested that he should be sent to Cambridge, and Mr. Barton, his headmaster, himself strongly recommended such a course. But it was felt impossible for his father to afford the expense, having so many children to provide for. Margaret was three years older than Isabella, and the eldest of the family. After being married for seven years to Major Bell, in 1836, the year of her mother's death, she was left a childless widow. Receiving a pension sufficient for her own needs, she resolved to earn what she could and contribute substantially to her brother's expenses at Cambridge. Intelligent and accomplished, she became governess to the twin daughters of the Revd. Mr. Le Bas, Principal of the East India Company's college at Haileybury.

Though of Huguenot extraction, and the author of lives of Cranmer and Jewel, Le Bas was a high churchman of the school of Hugh James Rose; but as a former Fellow of Trinity College, Cambridge, he was sympathetic towards Mrs. Bell's aim. She lived in the Principal's household, and was thus able to devote the whole of her salary for four years — at the end of which Le Bas resigned the principalship — to the object she had in view. Alfred's eldest brother William, stimulated by her example, added something more; and their father was able to make up the difference. According to J. and J. A. Venn's *Alumni Cantabrigienses,* Alfred Christopher had

[1]It is of interest that Goodhart was the first clergyman in Reading (and, it is said, in the Oxford diocese,) to introduce an early morning administration of Holy Communion, "some years before it obtained in any other Church" in the town.

himself been a pupil at the East India College; but there is nothing among Christopher's own reminiscences to suggest this; and his name does not appear in the list of students 1806-57 included in *Memorials of Old Haileybury College*. It was Margaret Bell too who helped their youngest brother Leonard to have a satisfactory start in life. He had gone out to India to take up an appointment there, but was most unhappy. His sister read extracts from his letters to Mr. and Mrs. Le Bas, with the result that the former exerted his influence with one of the directors, and obtained a cadetship for him in the East India Company's army.

Thus mentally and spiritually, Alfred Christopher owed much to his two sisters. Humanly speaking, he would not have gone up to the university at all if he had not called forth the self-sacrifice of his sister Margaret; and he would never have known Goodhart, had it not been for the influence of his sister Isabella. If he had not come within the orbit of Goodhart's teaching, he might not have been so ready, when a freshman at Cambridge, to attend the ministrations of William Carus, who was carrying on at Holy Trinity church and elsewhere the work of Charles Simeon.

Chapter II

Cambridge and After

1839 - 1844

CHRISTOPHER was admitted a sizar of St. John's College, Cambridge, on 13 May 1839. He was eighteen years old. His choice of college was determined by the fact that the new Master of St. John's, Dr. Ralph Tatham (elected shortly before: he had been a Fellow since 1802), was his father's second cousin. St. John's also had a notable evangelical connection, though that is unlikely to have been in the minds of his family and advisers. Here, nevertheless, Wilberforce and Clarkson had been educated. Here Henry Martyn had become senior wrangler and Fellow. Further back, Rowland Hill, younger brother of Sir Richard Hill, both important figures in the eighteenth century revival, had been a marked undergraduate witness to his faith, despised by most save the college boot-black. The Hon. Henry Ryder, the first evangelical bishop, was a member of the college. Early in the nineteenth century the fellows had included Archdeacon Hoare, Chancellor Raikes, Cunningham of Harrow, and William Jowett, the first Cambridge missionary of the Church Missionary Society. A little later came Francis Close of Cheltenham, Henry Melvill of St. Paul's, Henry Law of Gloucester. Near contemporary with Christopher was Thomas Boultbee, also elected to a fellowship, and appointed subsequently first Principal of St. John's Hall, Highbury. Thirty years later he preached for Christopher at St. Aldate's. Rupert Rowton, afterwards an Oxford neighbour as Vicar of

Eynsham, was a year senior. When Christopher went up as a freshman " his smiling face talking to a friend in St. John's was one of the first I observed."

Charles Simeon, the great evangelical leader, had been dead for over two years, and his successor both as Vicar of Holy Trinity and as chief pastor among similarly minded undergraduates, was the saintly William Carus, Fellow and Senior Dean of Trinity. He was also at this time Evening Lecturer at Great St. Mary's, the university church. On Sunday evenings, too, Carus sponsored a meeting for the young men. This was held at first in the college rooms — made famous by Sir Isaac Newton having occupied them when he was a Fellow — where Carus lived, over the great gate of Trinity. To these gatherings Christopher was soon introduced by a fellow freshman. The first half-hour was taken up with tea and talk; then Carus gave an address. When Christopher originally attended only twenty or thirty assembled. But the numbers increased very rapidly — to between one and two hundred before Christopher ceased to frequent the meetings — and the college allowed Carus to build a large room for the purpose behind the chapel. Sometimes a visitor, one of Carus's friends, such as Bishop McIlvaine of Ohio, or a missionary, would speak. Describing these occasions in 1891, Christopher recalled that " The Dean gave us an interesting and very profitable Christian address, the reverse of anything dry and tedious." This cannot be too retrospective a judgement, as Christopher was in the habit of attending Holy Trinity on Sunday mornings, where he usually heard Carus preach, and Great St. Mary's in the evenings, where he again heard Carus. Carus preached to large congregations and perhaps was reminded of them when he occupied the St. Aldates' pulpit from time to time during Christopher's early years at Oxford. Certainly he became a liberal contributor to the fund for purchasing the advowson of St. Aldate's, which led to the appointment of Christopher. At the very end of Carus's life, as " one of his oldest friends ", Christopher could write in connection with St. Matthew's, Oxford, " I was struck by the liberality and affection with which he more than once helped me during the present year to finish Grandpont Church without debt."

These were leisurely days at Cambridge. The university had roused itself to a considerable extent from eighteenth century torpor;

13. ST. JOHN'S COLLEGE, CAMBRIDGE, 1962

A. M. W. Christopher's rooms 1839–40, first floor, windows fourth and fifth from right

but academic calm still prevailed and nineteenth century reformers had not yet laid their hands on ancient statutes. Undergraduates were not expected to exert themselves unduly, and were indeed left very much to their own devices. Trinity and St. John's were then beyond comparison the two principal and rival colleges. The college was a more important factor in life at Cambridge than the university. Men of the same college formed a much more distinct social entity than later on, and college loyalty was axiomatic. At St. John's, where Christopher had rooms (E.4) in the third court, up one flight of stairs, overlooking the river and 'Bridge of Sighs' — his status as sizar indicates that he received financial assistance from the college — he was brought into touch with evangelical activity in the university by some fellow undergraduates. This influence largely ceased when, at the end of his first year, he migrated to Jesus College.

Christopher was discouraged by the results of the second college examination at St. John's. His classics were by no means as strong as his mathematics — in the event he did not enter for the classical tripos — and he was dissatisfied with his place as fifteenth in a large first class. An intimate acquaintance, John Adams, the senior wrangler of 1843, and afterwards an eminent Cambridge astronomer, was first. (Christopher met him in a train fifty years later, and was delighted to find him still a humble believer in Christ.) But while mathematics were better taught than classics in the smaller colleges, from 1839 onwards St. John's was superior in this respect even to Trinity. At Jesus certainly, there was much less competition. Twenty years previously, members of Jesus were "the most numerous of the lesser colleges"; but there had been a steady decline.

Christopher read with William Hopkins, senior Esquire Bedell, justly considered, as Christopher recalled, the best private tutor in the university. For Hopkins was known as the 'senior wrangler maker,' who by 1849 could claim that he had had nearly two hundred wranglers among his pupils, including seventeen seniors. Hopkins, who had himself been seventh wrangler in 1827, was also a geologist of note, and in 1853 served as President of the British Association. It is perhaps not surprising therefore that in 1841 Christopher gained a scholarship at the first examination held at Jesus College since his admission in 1840.[1] Nevertheless, Christopher in after

[1]The rooms which he occupied cannot now, it is said, be identified.

life regretted his migration — then a recognised and not altogether uncommon practice — considering that he had lost much both in the way of preparation for the mathematical tripos, and also in personal associations. He generally recommended undergraduates to keep to the college they first joined.

Christopher's removal from St. John's seems to have involved giving up attendance at Carus's Sunday evening gatherings. On this he had some characteristic reflections: "I have reason to humble myself before God on account of my undergraduate life at Cambridge. How much happier and how much more useful I might have been if I had yielded myself to God at the beginning of my course, and had kept stedfastly to the use of those means of grace to which I was introduced in my first term." These words remind us that Christopher, though favourably inclined towards Christianity, had not yet accepted that faith for himself. He was wont to recall the differing experience of one whom he knew well as a brother clergyman in Richmond, Walter Dumergue, afterwards Vicar of Fareham, who preached for him at St. Aldate's in 1860. On his first Sunday morning in Cambridge, Dumergue was about to go for a walk, but allowed himself to be persuaded to attend St. Michael's church, where the Regius Professor of Greek, James Scholefield, one of Simeon's associates, was Vicar. Impressed at seeing there one of the cleverest men of his college — Ragland, later Fellow of Corpus, and afterwards known to Christopher as a missionary in India — he accepted an invitation to attend a college Bible reading, to which he subsequently went regularly. "We who attended that Bible reading," he told Christopher, "were like a wall to each other from the temptations of the University."

Three of Christopher's sisters took husbands while he was an undergraduate. First, in 1840, Emma, seven years older than himself, married Captain George Cautley, afterwards major-general, and in 1841 Christopher's first nephew by this alliance, Christopher Cautley, was born. His next sister, Selina, was married in the following year — 1841 — to Captain William Thomson, who also became a major-general; but the wedding took place in India. In the long vacation of 1842, Louisa, less than a year older than her brother, was married to their second cousin Montagu Tatham, a London solicitor.[1] The wedding was conducted by the Master of St. John's — the Revd. Dr. Ralph Tatham — second cousin once removed of both bride and groom. Of this union a daughter was born in the following year. Two Robinson nephews, sons of Christopher's sister Caroline, were also born during this period. The first break in his own generation came in 1842, when Christopher's brother George Eumenes, a surgeon in the Bengal Light Cavalry, who had been invalided home, died at Wiesbaden in Switzerland at the age of thirty-six.

Jesus College in Christopher's time was a small society with only sixty undergraduates. Nevertheless in 1842 the Jesus boat went ' head of the river.' But all the eight took their degrees that year, and Christopher was one of the unfortunate crew who had to take their places. He used to tell with grim glee of the inevitable result, how they were bumped in every race.[2] Cricket, however, was a more individual matter. The Jesus ground adjoined the college. Christopher afterwards felt that he had taken too much advantage of its proximity, especially during his third year; and "...often I played cricket in my head, when books of mathematics were before my eyes." But Christopher always insisted that a man's reading need not suffer through games, granted a resolute will — citing Denman, afterwards a high court judge, then stroke of Trinity First Boat and presently senior classic.[3] In those days, cricket matches began after breakfast — eaten by Jesus men in a tent set up near the ground. Christopher at least achieved a 'blue'. He was chosen to play for the university against Oxford in 1843. Two other university-side matches are recorded for that year, in both of which Christopher took part. In May, Cambridge defeated the Marylebone Cricket Club on Parker's Piece. Christopher went in second, made fourteen (the third highest score) and was run out. A week later at the same place the university drew with the town, the game being unfinished owing to heavy rain. Christopher

[1]Another second cousin, Julia Tatham, had married in 1831 George Richmond, the portrait painter.

[2]In the Lent term, 1843. Christopher rowed number two. In the May races the crew held their place at seventh each day.

[3]It may be doubted whether Christopher was aware that as the son of a peer Denman was allowed to enter for the classical tripos without competing for mathematical honours.

succumbed to the bowling of Fenner, whose name is preserved in that of the existing cricket ground at Cambridge.

The university match followed a fortnight later. That year it was decided to hold it at Oxford instead of at Lord's. Christopher, though still in residence, had taken his degree some months before; but the Oxford men generously allowed him to play. There was as yet no railway between Cambridge and Oxford — only a stage coach once a day. By that the team travelled. "We were hospitably received," Christopher wrote, "the first night at a supper party at Wadham College." The Cowley Marsh ground was wet, and the match was played on Bullingdon Hill, by Shotover, on the high ground beyond Headington, some three miles out of the city — where it was so windy that the bails could hardly be kept on. Christopher, having the reputation of a steady bat, was sent in first, with G. J. Boudier, Fellow of King's and afterwards Rector of Ewhurst, Sussex, whose "lively cricket was much admired". One of the Oxford bowlers, Moberly (probably Henry Moberly, Fellow of New College, later a master at Winchester), was very formidable and fast, and the Cambridge pair was obliged to play extremely cautiously. Only fifty runs were made in the first hour, to which Christopher contributed eighteen; but one of his leg hits was into a distant turnip field, and he scored six for a lost ball. Christopher would frankly say that a rapid scorer could easily laugh at him as a great 'muff' for having remained in for an hour and only scoring eighteen. But, he added with a smile, "Such a player never had to face Moberly!" And after all that first hour, at the end of which Christopher's wicket fell, had something to do with the winning of the match, for it seemed to take the confidence out of the Oxford bowling. As *The Oxford Magazine* said after Christopher's death, "...he claimed only to have kept his wicket by steady blocking; he was far too much of a gentleman of the old school to speak of 'stone-walling'." In any case, Christopher's score was the third largest for his side, and none of the Oxford batsmen made more than twenty-one. Cambridge won by over fifty runs.

Christopher was wont to remark on how at the time he little expected to be forty-six years rector of a church in Oxford. But in spite of his long residence in his adopted university, he remained a Cambridge man at heart. The victories of his old university, in the cricket field or on the river, always delighted him; while those of Oxford had a precisely opposite effect. Dr. Griffith Thomas recalled the Canon's momentarily solemn face many years later whenever as his curate he entered his study with news of an Oxford success in the Boat Race. Whether Christopher played cricket after going down is not recorded. He himself has left no further reference to active participation in the game. It seems likely that he would have played until his ordination. Probably he followed the example of Henry Venn the elder, who having played for Surrey in a match against All England the week before he was ordained, laid down his bat for ever. In the Lent term of 1840, Christopher joined the Union Debating Society, and in 1842 became what was then called an honorary member, implying membership for life. The records are too scanty to show whether he took an active part in debates. But his life membership served him decidedly well during fifty-four years in Oxford, where it carried the privilege of using the rooms of the sister society.

Christopher had not devoted all his time to cricket and rowing. In January 1843 (the same month as his cousin, Dr. Tatham, entertained the Queen and Prince Albert at Cambridge), he was nineteenth wrangler (his name appearing about the middle of the list, above most of those who had been above him at St. John's in 1840), which in that year is said to have been equivalent to a 'first', and which, considering his early educational handicaps, was no insignificant achievement. During the two terms after taking his degree, he took private pupils, and formed a reading party of undergraduates to go to Beaumaris in Anglesey for three months during the long vacation. Pupils were comparatively few, however, and how Christopher employed his time during the following months is not known; but much of his attention must have been given to his cousin Maria Christopher, to whom he became engaged during the first half of 1844.

This was not the only attachment of its kind in Christopher's immediate family. His eldest brother William married their cousin Harriett Christopher and his sister Louisa had married her cousin Montagu Tatham. Though Maria was four years his senior, there was talk of a five years' engagement, for Christopher had no prospect of being able to provide for a wife. To him five months seemed too long; and he was greatly relieved when it was suggested to him that he might like to become principal of La Martinière, a school for Anglo-Indian boys in Calcutta. Sir Edward Ryan, formerly Chief Justice of Bengal, and associated in legal work with Sir Henry Seton, one of the puisne judges, who was Maria's uncle, had come home in 1843 and was entrusted with the choice. The fact that he knew Sir Henry (an *ex officio* governor, as Sir Edward had been, of La Martinière), however, though fortunate, was incidental. Sir Edward was visiting the East India Company's college at Haileybury, and enquired of Professor Heaviside, who taught mathematics there, whether he could tell him of a suitable man. Heaviside had been one of Christopher's examiners at Cambridge and also knew how his sister, Margaret Bell, had worked for her brother's sake. He suggested his name, with the proviso that he might not know enough classics.

Christopher was invited to Haileybury and given a paper of mathematical problems. One of these he was able to work out in an original way which delighted Heaviside. The latter's recommendation and Christopher's testimonials almost decided Sir Edward Ryan, who in later years became Vice-Chancellor of the university of London. But there was still no proof that Christopher knew enough Latin and Greek. Sir Edward proposed that in a week's time, Christopher should visit the Revd. Dr. William Mill, formerly Principal of Bishop's College, Calcutta, then Christian Advocate at Cambridge, to be examined in classics. Christopher declared that he had never worked so hard any week of his life as he did at a Greek play, the *Andromache* of Euripides, and the *Odes* of Horace (books which he had thoroughly prepared for his 'little-go'), which he proposed to offer for examination, though he had not looked at them for two years. " I had a Bride-Elect whom I loved intensely — and whom I had really loved ever since I was six years of age when she was nearly ten years old". The result was that Christopher knew his books thoroughly and after a good dinner at Brasted Rectory, Kent, where Dr. Mill was incumbent, he did not feel nervous when he went into the study. The examination lasted for the remainder of the evening, and Dr. Mill was perfectly satisfied. Fortunately, Christopher felt, he was not called upon to do any Latin composition or answer any general questions of grammar. He believed that Dr. Mill was a merciful examiner who did not think it needful to ask him very hard questions. Christopher retired to bed extremely happy, and the result was an appointment before he was twenty-four to take charge of an important educational institution.

Mrs. Philip Harden, Maria's mother — her father had died when she was two years old and in 1830 his widow had married Lieutenant Philip Harden, R.N., son of Nathaniel Harden of Hadley House — and, it is said, her aunt (presumably Caroline Millard: neither survived to see daughter and son-in-law or nephew and niece return to England) not unnaturally thought that Christopher ought to go out alone and try the appointment for a year, his bride to follow if he found it satisfactory. But at this the young lady spoke out with a decision which astonished those who had known her as a gentle, submissive, and unselfish daughter. "If I go out at all I must go with him as I cannot follow him not knowing whether I shall find him alive when I land." This settled the matter. The quiet daughter and niece had after all a mind of her own, and Christopher was ever grateful to her for this determination. Doubtless, too, she acted wisely, for Christopher would have been at a decided disadvantage beginning the difficult work at La Martinière without the help of a wife. Christopher himself wrote in 1907: "My four complete years in India would, I believe, not have been as successful and useful as they were if she had not been with me during the important first year."

A relation who had been in India married to a civilian tried to pour cold water on the scheme by saying the promised income was insufficient and that not a rupee could be saved. Christopher smiled and perhaps expressed a little confidence in what an economical wife could do; and in the event, though not without wifely care, he saved a considerable sum each month. Another difficulty was lack of ready money. The governors of La Martinière allowed a sum for passage and outfit; but that would only cover the passage for two. He therefore borrowed two hundred pounds from his father, and his aunt lent him two hundred more, so that he might not land in India without adequate resources. In spite of a heavy life insurance premium, he was able to send home all he owed during the first fifteen months at La Martinière, out of an income from which he had been told he could not save 'one rupee'. Including rent-free quarters, it was worth, after four years' hard work, nearly £1000 *per annum*. Christopher went on saving and the result stood him in good stead during his early days at Oxford.

All difficulties having been removed, the wedding took place in the old Georgian parish church of Chiswick (since rebuilt,) on 15 June 1844. The service was conducted by the Revd. Edmund Harden, Vicar of All Saints, Upper Norwood, probably a brother of Maria's step-father. Even then there could not but be misgivings. The bride's elder sister had married, and had gone with her husband to the West Indies, where she died. Her eldest brother, an ensign in the Bombay Grenadiers, had died soon after joining his regiment. Christopher's elder brother George had died of an illness brought home with him from India; while a cousin, whose sister was at the wedding, died a young officer in a native regiment in India. No one in the two families was more generally beloved than the bride, and it was impossible not to be fearful for her. Yet bride and bridegroom lived together for nearly sixty years.

The 'wedding tour' was spent first in the Lake District, and then with Dr. Stenson at Bourton-on-the-Water. William Stenson, Christopher's erstwhile playmate, had recently bought a very tall hunter, but had not discovered that it had a trick when galloping of catching one hoof in another and coming down. Christopher mounted this horse, and was galloping across some smooth grass, when the creature's hooves became entangled, bringing it to the ground, and sending its rider far away over its head. Much soiled by his fall, Christopher was unhurt. But with characteristic respect for God's providence, he was wont to express his thankfulness for having been preserved on that occasion. Instead of enjoying a long married life, he might have been killed on his honeymoon.

Chapter III

India

1844 - 1849

ALFRED AND MARIA Christopher joined the *Monarch*, a first-rate passenger ship, at Spithead on 2 August 1844. Three days later she sailed from Torbay. They were accompanied by Alfred's younger brother, Lieutenant Leonard Christopher, who was returning to India after sick-leave. Another passenger was a seventeen-year-old cavalry cadet named Loch, son of James Loch the economist. Henry Loch became Governor of Cape Colony and a baron. Alfred Christopher renewed his acquaintance when Loch was Governor of the Isle of Man; and it was through Loch that Christopher's elder son, Henry Seton Christopher, found his vocation as bursar of King William's College on that island. The voyage to India, round the Cape of Good Hope, took three months, during which it is said that the vessel did not come in sight of land. Three months was in those days unusually speedy; and it was rare not to put in at St. Helena, Madagascar, or Mauritius, if only to replenish supplies. Especially was this so since the passengers included, besides a number of returning civilians, a hundred or more recruits of the 39th Regiment. Nevertheless, three months at sea doubtless seemed long enough, though perhaps not to Leonard Christopher, as he fell in love with a fellow passenger, Miss Ann Brae, who was travelling in the company of her parents and sisters. In due course, the ship reached the low sandbanks of the mouth of the Hooghly, and took on board the pilot for the remaining seventy miles to Calcutta.

There the Christopher party was met by the carriage and native servants of Sir Henry Seton, Maria Christopher's uncle. Sir Henry was not the first of her relations to serve in India, for her great-uncle David Seton had died Lieutenant-Governor of Surat in 1803, and a great-great-uncle, Andrew Ramsay Karr, had been Governor of Bombay.

La Martinière was a remarkable institution. Claude Martin, the founder, was a Frenchman, born at Lyons in 1735. He arrived in South India as a private in the French army; but after a time he joined the English forces, and rose to the rank of major-general. In 1775 he was seconded to the service of the Nawab of Oudh to be Superintendent of the arsenal at Lucknow. He held office till his death twenty-five years later, having been exempted from further military duty in 1779 on grounds of ill-health, with permission to remain at Lucknow. In this lucrative post, but mainly through various successful business ventures, he amassed a large fortune.

By birth Martin was a Roman Catholic, but, Canon Josiah Bateman has written, "he knew and cared little about religion: and, in reality, had none. His last Will gave sad evidence of unforsaken sin, and utter ignorance of 'the things that accompany salvation'. But it showed he had a conscience." Bateman, who had served as bishop's chaplain in Calcutta, was doubtless somewhat prejudiced on moral grounds. General Martin's biographer, S. C. Hill, writing from a less didactic if secular standpoint fifty years later, is inclined to be more tolerant towards one whom Warren Hastings described as "a brave and experienced officer and a man of honour." For it cannot be denied that his contribution to education in India was considerable. By his will already referred to he bequeathed the greater part of his property to found schools at Lyons, his birthplace, Lucknow, and Calcutta, of whatever kind seemed most necessary. The investment of the money, in the case of Calcutta, and the scheme of education, were left entirely to the discretion of the Indian government and the Supreme Court. General Martin died in 1800, but his bequest lay dormant for over thirty years, partly owing to relations who contested its validity.

By 1832 the capital had trebled itself with interest and the Supreme Court of Calcutta issued a decree establishing a school, to be called, by the terms of the will, 'La Martinière'. At first it was proposed to connect this school entirely with the Church of England, the testator having appointed a protestant government to carry out his will and directed that the pupils should attend, at least for an annual sermon on the anniversary of the founder's death, "the Church" in Calcutta — at a time when only an anglican one existed. The Bishop of Calcutta, Dr. Daniel Wilson, went so far as to write home to secure a clerical headmaster. But an educational controversy which arose in England was reproduced in India. At the second election of the four governors nominated annually, who, with Governor-General, Bishop, Judges, Advocate-General and Council members *ex officio,* formed the governing body, Dr. James Charles, the senior Chaplain of the Church of Scotland, and Dr. St. Leger, the Roman Catholic Vicar-Apostolic, were elected. After much negotiation it was eventually agreed that education in the school should be based upon "the general principles of Christianity, guarded by all the ancient creeds and confessions, as held in common by the English, Scotch, Roman, Armenian and Greek Churches." The school was not to be placed under any particular denomination of Christians, and no points in dispute between the churches concerned were to be touched upon in the course of public instruction.

It fell to the Bishop, the Vicar-Apostolic, and the presbyterian Dr. Charles, to frame a plan of religious instruction and to compose a catechism and form of worship for use in the school. They proposed that the religious teaching should be divided into two parts: the one general, the other particular; the one embracing those truths of Christianity which are held in common by five main divisions of Christendom; the second relating to discipline, church government, the sacraments, and other matters on which differences more or less important exist. The first part was to be taught daily and publicly by the headmaster of the school; the second privately and on particular days by the ministers and teachers whom the parents of the respective children might, with the approbation of the governors, select. Agreement was reached that the following were held in common: "1. The Being of God; His unity and perfections. 2. The holy Scriptures of the Old and New Testament, a Revelation inspired by the Holy Ghost. 3. The mystery of the adorable Trinity. 4. The Deity, Incarnation, Atonement, and

Intercession of our Lord and Saviour, Jesus Christ. 5. The fall and corruption of man, his accountableness and guilt. 6. Salvation through grace by the meritorious sacrifice and redemption of Christ. 7. The Personality and Deity of the Holy Spirit, and His operations and grace in the santification of man. 8. The indispensable obligation of repentance towards God, faith in Christ, and continual prayer for the grace of the Holy Spirit. 9. The moral duties which every Christian is bound to perform towards God, his neighbour, and himself, as they are summed up in the Ten Commandments, and enlarged upon in other parts of holy Scriptures; all based on the doctrines above specified, and enforced as their proper fruits."

The proceedings were inevitably lengthy, each one feeling that considerable responsibility rested on himself, and especially when the committee turned its attention to preparing a form of worship. The Vicar-Apostolic had never read the English liturgy. Neither the Bishop nor Dr. Charles was familiar with the Roman missal. In due time a catechism and form of family prayer were worked out, amid an atmosphere of openness and candour. But these œcumenical labours, so far in advance of their day, proved singularly thankless. The Vicar-Apostolic was recalled by the General of the Jesuit order, to which he belonged, to be charged with having conceded fundamental principles, and improperly indulged in social intercourse with the Bishop. The presbyterian Chaplain, Dr. Charles, was called to account by the Church of Scotland. And the Bishop, in Bateman's words, "met praise which he did not desire, and censure which he did not deserve." At home in 1839 a government proposal for a scheme of education for all parties cited the case of La Martinière, and commended Bishop Wilson. A subsequent debate in the House of Lords showed that the Bishop's motives, as an evangelical churchman, had been neither appreciated nor understood.

Notwithstanding the unsatisfactory results of compromise, Christopher entered wholeheartedly into the scheme — which is the main reason for describing it at some length — and insisted to the end of his days that such a method was the best solution of the problem of religious education in England. The Martinière plan showed, he considered, "the wisdom of doing the best that is practicable under the circumstances," and as late as 1906 he advocated it in a pamphlet. By his large-heartedness and his intense desire for Christian unity, he anticipated a method of religious instruction which has been widely adopted in the twentieth century.

The school was opened, in spite of misgivings, in 1836, and "a succession of admirable masters" presided over it. Christopher was the first from an English university. Indeed his one predecessor, W. Masters, appears to have held office only during the earliest, formative years, a fact which is emphasized by his being known as Headmaster rather than Principal. A fine building, designed by an amateur, Judge Robert Rattray, based on the plan of University College, London, and for long regarded as one of the best in Calcutta, had been erected at the corner of Lower Circular Road and Loudon Street at a cost of £17,000. The dome and portico unhappily became casualties of an earthquake in 1897, and were not rebuilt. At first the structure was used (strictly partitioned) for girls as well as boys; but about 1843 'La Martinière for Girls' was housed separately, at a further cost of £10,000. There still remained £157,000, which yielded an annual income of £6,280 for the support of the two schools. A few European children attended. The majority were Anglo-Indian — there were no native pupils — and nearly half were paying scholars. Not all came from Calcutta; a considerable number were from the then North-West Provinces, Burma, and the Straits Settlements. Under Christopher there were latterly some two hundred boys. Those on the foundation were mostly children whose fathers had died, and who would but for that have received a good education. Roman Catholics were forbidden to have anything to do with the school. Nevertheless only one Roman Catholic mother withdrew her son in Christopher's time. She wished to re-marry, and on no other terms would the priest perform the rite. But she sent her boy back to the school the following month. Christopher was amused to think that "She must have learnt something from the Jesuits."

As he wrote in 1862, "The Principal [took] a position in the best Society of Calcutta." The school, where in those days the Principal and his family occupied the east end of the main building, stood amid the large houses of leading citizens, judges, merchants, and others. Among these Sir Henry Seton, who from the first acted as a second father to his niece Maria — he himself was a bachelor

— already occupied an established place, not least with his legal brethren as the author of *Forms of Decrees in Equity,* which reached a seventh edition in 1912. Christopher's heart, however, was in his work rather than in social life, and on arrival in Calcutta — then a " somewhat sleepy, stately, palatial city with its wide park-like maidan, broad streets, huge white houses and enervating atmosphere " — on 11 November 1844, he took immediate charge of the school.

Latin, Greek, and mathematics were taught as in England. One foundationer who left, at the age of sixteen, in 1850, after nine years at La Martinière, had read, for example, Xenophon's *Anabasis,* the tenth book of Homer's *Iliad,* and St. John's *Gospel,* in the original Greek. Three of Christopher's pupils, on examination for assistantships with the Trigonometrical Survey of India, were said by the deputy Surveyor-General, Captain Henry Thuillier, brother-in-law of W. S. Landor, and afterwards a notable Surveyor-General, to have had " no one in sight of them." A. W. W. Steel rose to be head boy under Christopher, and under Christopher's successor, Henry Woodrow, a Fellow of Caius, his uncle was persuaded to send him to Cambridge, where he was bracketed second wrangler and was himself elected a Fellow of Caius. He became known as a leader of Christian work in the university, served for some years as Vicar of the Round Church, St. Sepulchre's, and assisted in the founding of Ridley Hall. Thus Christopher lived to see him the friend of many men in numerous generations of undergraduates, mainly during the 'sixties and 'seventies, and engaged in a parallel ministry to that which he himself was to exercise at Oxford. Another of Christopher's pupils who like Steel gained the school's gold medal and who afterwards became well known was Sir Charles Paul, Advocate-General of Bengal, who entered Trinity College, Cambridge in 1849.[1]

Meanwhile there were many difficulties facing the new Principal. It took two years to solve the disciplinary problems with which Christopher found himself confronted. The foundationer referred to above, afterwards, as the Revd. A. Stark, a missionary of the Church Missionary Society in Bengal, latterly at Holy Trinity,

[1]He spent a short time at King's College, London, before going up to the university. This accounts for there being no reference (under previous place of education) to his much longer period at La Martinière in J. and J. A. Venn's *Alumni Cantabrigienses.*

14. LA MARTINIERE for Boys, CALCUTTA, before 1897
A. M. W. Christopher, Principal 1844–49

15. ST. ANDREW'S, MOGRA HAT, BENGAL, 1849
from a drawing by A. M. W. Christopher

Calcutta, mentioned them in reminiscences he contributed to the centenary number of *La Martinière Chronicle,* published in 1900 in commemoration of General Martin's death. " I regret to say," Stark wrote, " that in those olden times the tone of the School was not what it might have been . . There was a visible change when the Principal arrived."

This was the period of his life to which Christopher ascribed his conversion. In after years it was a favourite and frequent topic with him, that in trying to do his best for his boys, he was brought to feel his own spiritual limitations. He found that although he could give his pupils knowledge, he could not make them Christians. He could ensure that they knew what was right and wrong, but to do what was right and to resist and overcome the temptation to do what was wrong necessitated divine power. Nothing, he used to say, did so much to bring him to Christ, as the feeling that without God's grace he could not prevent the boys from being overcome by temptation to evil. In the words of one of his undergraduate friends at Oxford, " It was while he was in India that he made the great discovery of the power of God's grace. He would say that it was by endeavouring to turn unconverted young men into good ones that he proved that without God's grace it could not be done and that he himself learned to trust no longer in his own power, but in a Crucified Saviour." He came to see — which was unusual in those days — that boys could be " lovingly made to understand what Jesus Christ would do for them, if they would trust Him and give themselves to Him, and that when this was done it might be that more would learn to live for Him." Christopher, of course, is not the only schoolmaster who has emphasized the need of grace in the case of boys. He himself used to cite as another example Canon Lyttleton's experience as Headmaster of Eton.

Looking back after many years, in 1899, Christopher wrote: " There is a really important lesson to be drawn from the undoubted fact that I was not converted when I went to India, which lesson is that even when Scriptural Evangelical teaching by no means results at the time when it was received in Conversion of heart, God does not in all cases allow it to be useless. I thank God that I knew enough truth to make me unhappy when I was not a Christian. When I did not love the Lord Jesus Christ, I could not forget those who did . . . And I never cared for any different teaching. But with all my mercies, I was not a real Christian, or *anything like one*. But the early teaching of the truth was not to be in vain. If I have been at all useful during the last sixty years, it just proves the marvellous perseverance of God's love. Let no one try it as I did." Thus the influence of his sister Isabella, of Charles Goodhart, of William Carus, and, we may conclude, of the Bishop of Calcutta (whose palace stood only a few hundred yards from La Martinière, close to the cathedral site,) and his circle, bore fruit in the heart and mind of one who was to influence many.

An event which doubtless served to provoke serious thoughts occurred early in 1845, when Sarah Harden, Maria Christopher's mother, and sister of Sir Henry Seton, died at the age of fifty-eight. Only one parent now remained either to husband or wife, though neither had reached thirty. Six months later Caroline Millard, who had been a second mother to Alfred Christopher, and was aunt both to him and to Maria, also died. She was, however, ten years older than her sister-in-law.

There can be no doubt too that in India the uncertainty of human life, especially in those days, was brought home constantly to those Europeans who had eyes to see. " I had a call at this time," wrote Christopher, " from Major-General Valliant, a gallant soldier. He handled his brigade ably and gallantly at the battle of Maharajpore. My early love of the army and the habitual exercise of my imagination in picturing and acting in all the battles of which I read in the newspapers or in books of history, made conversation with this brave General, who had so recently gained a victory for his country, most interesting and animated. General Valliant left me to take his ride. He was seized with cholera that night and died in the morning, and was buried in the evening after his call upon me." In another reminiscence of those days, Christopher recorded: " The cemetery for my part of Calcutta was near La Martinière and I sometimes walked in it. There are always several graves kept ready bricked and plastered, for in that climate if a man dies in the morning he must be buried in the evening. If he die in the evening he must be buried in the early morning. It is impossible to look at those prepared graves in the Calcutta Cemetery without the thought 'Is one of those for me?'."

The Indian climate had other perils. In 1846 Christopher became deaf. Recovering from an attack of fever, he dosed himself frequently with the customary quinine, which is liable to cause deafness. Another factor was the cylindrical shape of the great hall of the school, a round room the whole height of the building, beneath the central dome. Subsequently bisected when a new hall was built in 1915, this had an echo which made it difficult for him to hear the boys construe even before deafness came on, and he believed the strain had begun to induce the defect. The affliction remained with him all his life. His ear-trumpet was one of the most familiar sights at religious meetings. Far from being daunted by the trying limitations involved, he seemed to be spurred on to undertake tasks and to face difficulties which might have daunted others. Amidst noise, as when travelling in a train, his hearing improved, and he would say, "Now, mind, no secrets, now." At other times he could remark " It is a blessing to be deaf; you cannot hear the disagreeable things people say about you." By way of illustration he would add: "If a beggar goes away without getting what he wants, he murmurs out something. I put my hand to my ear and say to him, 'What did you say?' But he never says it again."

In the following year Bishop Wilson, who was in many ways a remarkable and outstanding man, consummated his great cathedral project. After long preparation, he was able to consecrate the building on 8 October 1847. Christopher was present. Eight years had elapsed since the first stone was laid. The fabric, built of brick, covered with chunam, a kind of plaster, in the manner of the early Gothic revival, and necessarily adapted both to the needs of the climate and of protestant worship, was far from unattractive architecturally. "And now the Consecration Day has dawned. The whole . . . crowded, every seat occupied, every aisle filled. For the first time the voice of praise and prayer ascends. Then all is hushed, and the venerable Bishop's voice is heard repeating as his text the sublime words of inspiration:—'Will God in very deed dwell with men on the earth? Behold the heaven and the heaven of heavens cannot contain Thee, how much less this house which I have built' (2 Chron. vi. 18). The discourse founded on these words lasted for an hour . . . The service, which had commenced at half-past ten, was not ended till half-past three.

Then followed the assembling at the Palace, and all the kind congratulations and addresses incidental to such occasions." It is hardly surprising to learn that after this, Dr. Wilson, who had already served longer than his three immediate predecessors together, was laid aside for several days. From 1862, the cathedral choir was — and still is — provided by La Martinière boys.

The author of the history of the Christopher family, Alfred Christopher's younger son, states that his uncle, as Lieutenant Leonard Christopher, married his seventeen-year-old bride, Ann Brae, whom he had met on the voyage out in August of the previous year, in Calcutta Cathedral on 25 October 1845. This will refer to St. John's church, which was then still in use as the cathedral, and where those Martinière boys who were members of the Church of England had attended on Sunday mornings. There also they supplied the choir. An alabaster model of St. Paul's Cathedral, Calcutta, presented by Bishop Wilson in recognition of generous financial assistance on the part of his university, must have been familiar to Christopher in his Oxford days when he visited the picture-gallery of the Bodleian. It has since been given away, and has disappeared.

Meanwhile, Christopher had other interests. In 1846 he examined in mathematics and natural philosophy the senior scholarship candidates from all the government colleges of North India. "The way in which he fulfilled these duties," we are told, "brought him to the front in Indian scholastic circles." In 1847 he gave a course of experimental lectures in electricity, throwing them open freely to senior students of the native colleges in Calcutta. Many attended, and Christopher was encouraged by the presence from time to time of Bishop Wilson, himself one of the leading luminaries of the intellectual renaissance at Oxford earlier in the century, of J. H. Pratt, then Wilson's chaplain, afterwards Archdeacon of Calcutta, third wrangler of his year at Cambridge, and of Drinkwater Bethune, a member of the legislative council, who had been fourth wrangler in his day.

The nineteen able and penetrating pages of the Principal's report, included in that of the institution as a whole, for the period March to September 1847, show the quality of Christopher's capabilities as a schoolmaster. A copy preserved in the India Office Library contains a few corrections apparently in his handwriting. Extracts from reports since 1845, printed at the back, reflect consistent improvement, not least on the part of the pupils in telling the truth. We also see how demanding was the curriculum, and that, with nearly two hundred boys on the books, the numbers in the school had reached a record. In his final report, Christopher was able to write: "Some of the senior boys, impressed with a sense of their duty towards their schoolfellows, and a desire for their welfare, have quietly exerted themselves to effect good in a degree which I have not known in previous years." Stark refers to the healthy influence of one or two boys he remembered who went up to the third floor morning and evening for prayer and Bible reading. He implies that lack of organised 'manly' games was an adverse factor, cricket alone being played. Christopher's own prowess at this would have given him a great advantage in gaining the boys' respect, and it may well have contributed to their readiness, during his last two years, to attend in large numbers a voluntary Bible class he then felt able to hold on Sunday afternoons. This was in addition to the morning service at church or cathedral, and an evening one in school, of an interdenominational character, at which the Principal was required to read a sermon. The latter was held in the hall under the dome, where the masters, with the Principal enthroned in their midst, sat facing the boys, ranged round in rows, and a lectern was the only ecclesiastical furnishing. At this time and for many years afterwards the school, run on English public school lines, had few rivals, and was recognised as "primus in Indis."

A visiting governor reported in 1847: "I must not omit to add that I was most struck with the happy understanding which obtains between Mr. Christopher and the boys composing his class. He has complete authority over them, and yet it is entirely of a moral character and is most mildly exercised." In the same year the secretary of the committee of acting governors transmitted to Christopher a resolution of 6 July: "The Committee have commissioned me to express to you their high approbation of your zeal and talents in directing the educational course of 'La Martinière', and although the very success of your pupils cannot fail to yield you a well deserved satisfaction, they deem nevertheless this to be a fit opportunity for publicly recording their thanks for success which they feel convinced, is entirely due to your own ability and exertion. Nor is it only to ability and zeal, however eminent, well directed, and successful, that they desire to extend their commendation, but they have remarked with equal satisfaction, the affectionate care which you have extended to the sick and suffering children; especially on the late occasion of the Cholera; and the deep interest with which you always watch over their moral, as well as their intellectual advancement."

In May 1848 Sir Henry Seton caught cold in one of his eyes. This set up inflammation, destroyed the sight of the eye, and appeared to be breaking up his health. Christopher borrowed a steamboat from the Government, and took Sir Henry down to the mouth of the Hooghly for the sake of better air. It came on to blow hard, and as the steamer was flat-bottomed, the captain was afraid she might turn over if exposed to a heavy sea. He therefore steered into the Sunderbunds, a region supposed to be as unhealthy as any in Lower Bengal. Between the great streams by which the water of the Ganges is poured into the bay, there were numerous mud banks, covered with trees and undergrowth. As the boat rounded a corner, a magnificent tiger showed itself. Almost immediately Sir Henry exclaimed "See, see! Another tiger." All looked eagerly, but could see nothing. Presently the chief bearer said with respectful gravity, "Cat, Sahib." A cat was walking along the gunwhale of the steamer. Sir Henry's one eye had not yet learnt to do the duty of two.

The trip did not improve Sir Henry's health, and he was ordered home. It was felt that Maria Christopher must accompany her uncle and nurse him. In any case she herself had had several attacks of illness, particularly of cholera, and more than once had seemed unlikely to survive; a child — a "fine boy" — had been born dead in September 1847, at Sir Henry's house, nearly two miles away at Garden Reach, and their doctor had warned her husband that her health would not last permanently in the climate of India. Christopher, however, whose thoughts had turned to the ministry, was sure that his own duty was to remain at his post until a successor could be found. This decision, as he often remarked, affected all his subsequent life. Otherwise he would not have seen Christian mission work. As long as his wife was in India, he could not think of leaving her to go up-country, in case she was taken seriously ill. But when she had left he was able to gratify a long harboured desire and use his remaining vacations in visiting mission stations.

Maria Christopher sailed with Sir Henry Seton in June, and nursed him day and night until he died in her arms off Mauritius on 26 July. Anxious that her uncle's body should not be buried at sea but preserved for interment at St. Helena, she asked for a coffin to be made. The ship's carpenter had deserted, but the third mate sawed off the thick end of a spare mast and scooped it out so that it was capable of holding the spirit necessary for the preservation of the body. There was some doubt as to whether enough spirit could be spared; but the rough, scratch crew were ready to deny themselves for a lady, and asked to be put on half rations for a time, to ensure a sufficient supply. The ship should have reached St. Helena three weeks after leaving Mauritius; but owing to strong gales and a heavy cargo took seven.

This had a remarkable sequel. The vessel had not anchored more than a quarter of an hour before Maria Christopher heard guns firing a salute to the flag on shore. Enquiry revealed that the new arrival was the *Vernon,* a fifty-gun frigate from Bombay, on which Maria Christopher's brother, Thomas Borradaile Christopher, was first lieutenant. This seemed the more extraordinary as Maria Christopher knew that the vessel had two more years to serve on the India station. While her brother was superintending the furling of the sails after anchoring, he was surprised by a message brought from the merchantman. "Your sister is on board that ship with the body of her uncle." He came across as soon as he was free from duty, and found her so weak that he could not hear what she said. Yet she had arranged to attend her uncle's funeral by herself, and attend she did, with her brother and the Governor, Sir Patrick Ross, who had in the previous year lost his wife. Lady Ross had become a Christian during the last months of her life, through the faithful witness of Henry Elliott of St. Mary's Chapel, Brighton, who was in the following year to guide Alfred Christopher during the first weeks of his ministry.

No ship stopped more than twenty-four hours at St. Helena, to take on water, and it is not difficult to understand how easily brother and sister might have missed each other. The *Vernon's* bottom had been found to be defective, and the Admiral had ordered her home. Yet it is clear to the eye of faith that the coincidence was providential. Christopher frequently referred to it as an instance of the loving kindness of God, — one sparrow "shall not fall on the ground without your Father." The captain of the *Vernon* offered a passage to Mrs. Christopher but she felt she could not forsake the merchantman (*Earl of Dalhousie*) and Captain Ord, to whose care she had been committed, and who had done everything in his power to palliate the discomforts of her voyage. The ship was caught in gales which drove her towards America, and Maria Christopher actually sighted Newfoundland on her way from St. Helena to England.

On arrival at Plymouth, Maria Christopher learned from the newspapers that her beloved brother Wilmot, whom her brother Tom had lately met in India after a separation of twenty years, had been killed in action. He had married, while his sister and brother-in-law had been in India, Caroline, elder daughter of Judge William Simpson of the Indian Civil Service, and there was one son, from whom the present representative of the Christophers of Hadley descends. Another brother of Maria's, James Christopher, had married in 1847 a daughter of the Revd. John Hardy, Vicar of The Lee, Herefordshire. This lady, Martha Jane, was through life an almost exact contemporary of Alfred Christopher, having been born in 1822 and dying in 1915. Alfred's younger sister, Matilda, had also married, at Chiswick, in 1847, William Sealy, eldest son of Lieutenant-General W. D. Sealy. William and Matilda Sealy migrated to New Zealand, where they brought up a family of four sons and two daughters.

Another item of family news which reached England about this time was the death of Caroline Robinson, Alfred's elder sister, which occurred in 1848, in Canada, at the age of forty. She left nine children. Many of the family events, however, since Alfred and Maria Christopher's departure for India had been happy ones. No less than nine nephews and nieces were born during the four years. Apart from Wilmot Christopher's son, all were sons or daughters of Alfred's brothers and sisters. The rise of the next generation no doubt to some extent offset the loss of Alfred's sister and Maria's brother. From her uncle Sir Henry Seton, Maria inherited five thousand pounds. It says much for her economy (and, in days before the Married Women's Property Act, for her husband's too) that at her death over fifty years later this capital was still at her disposal, and when the life interest she left her partner in wedlock expired ten years later still, her sons were able to divide it between them. It is probably not a coincidence that Sir Henry's death immediately preceded the opening by Christopher, before he returned home, of an account at Messrs. Coutts, who remained his bankers throughout life. Their ledgers show that considerably more money was paid in annually than Christopher had personally at his disposal, and this is believed to be due to his acting for relations, especially when they were abroad.

Maria Christopher having sailed from India in June 1848, her husband used the following September vacation to visit the station of the Church Missionary Society at Benares. During the Christmas vacation he travelled round the missions of the Krishnagur district. The missionary John Weitbrecht and his wife had been among the Christophers' greatest friends in Calcutta. No doubt this association had helped to stimulate Christopher's interest in missions. In July 1848 he again examined, this time in history, for the government scholarships, and the papers for correction arrived in time for the steamer trip up the Ganges to Benares, where Leupolt, a veteran missionary who survived from the days when German candidates were admitted in default of English, was labouring. Christopher had a note of introduction to the Chaplain at Dinapore, nine miles beyond Patna, where he had grieved to see the great opium warehouses tolerated by government. This was Henry Martyn's station, where he had seemed to witness almost in vain. The Chaplain, Harington,[1] soon asked whether his guest had a brother in the Indian Navy. Christopher replied that, having married his cousin, he had a brother-in-law of the same name who was a captain in the service. Harington then handed Christopher a newspaper which showed that Wilmot Christopher had died of a wound received at the siege of Multan.

Christopher's grief was tempered by the knowledge that Wilmot had become a Christian as a young officer on the *Benares,* through the

[1]Probably H. H. Harington of Magdalen Hall, Oxford, an East India Company chaplain who died in 1862.

faithful witness of a midshipman named Campbell, who was directly or indirectly the means of the conversion of all the midshipmen and officers, including, finally, the captain. Many years later Christopher met Campbell, a white-haired old captain, as a result of his enquiry after Wilmot's only son. He ascribed all his success to his mother's prayers for his conversion. Wilmot Christopher became an earnest follower of Christ, and sought to start a mission in the Maldive Islands. He had been able to supply food to Dr. Krapf, a well-known East African missionary, when in extreme need. Montagu Burrows, who had served in the Indian Navy before becoming Chichele Professor of Modern History at Oxford, told Christopher in later years that he had met Wilmot Christopher at Trincomalee and had received spiritual help from him. He had preserved a long letter from Commander Christopher among his papers.

When hostilities broke out between the native Governor of Multan and the East India Company, Wilmot was appointed second-in-command of a flotilla and sent up the river to assist at the siege of the city. Two young subalterns, Edwardes and Lake, had with great spirit and energy raised an irregular native force and kept the Governor's army in check. One, as Sir Herbert Edwardes, was afterwards well known at the time of the Mutiny, and to supporters of the Church Missionary Society as joint-founder of the Peshawar mission, in which capacity he was among the speakers at Christopher's Oxford missionary meetings in later years. The other, as Major-General Lake, became lay secretary of the society. Wilmot Christopher was guiding a column which was to attempt an escalade. Fearing that the ladders were too short, he pressed forward to make sure, and was shot in the ankle. His foot was amputated, and he wrote home in cheerful spirits to ask for an artificial foot by return of post. But a second amputation proved necessary, and he died after the operation.

On landing at Benares, Alfred Christopher made the acquaintance of Leupolt, who was half-way through his forty years' service in India: one of the best missionaries of the church that he knew, Christopher used to say, although one of the least apparently successful. He accompanied him to several preaching chapels in the city. A catechist read the Bible aloud to a gathering crowd, and after a time Leupolt preached. When he saw that he had a number of sufficiently interested hearers, he went into the chapel, which was soon crowded with an attentive audience. On one occasion after the service, a fine sepoy struck his staff on the ground and said "What the Sahib says is true, and they are fools who deny it." What interested Christopher most among the results of mission work at Benares was a class of young men who were being trained by Leupolt to be catechists. They knew English, and thus Christopher was able to examine them. He found they had a good knowledge of the Bible, and seemed to treat the book and its message with deep reverence. Indeed, "He has since said," we are told, "that they knew it better than he did himself at the time." Whilst at Benares, he went up to Chunar, a hill-fort a few miles higher up the river, the first station to which Daniel Corrie, afterwards Bishop of Madras, was appointed when he went out to India as a chaplain.

Christopher used to say that he could never forget the village of Segra, just outside Benares. It was a village of apparently happy Christian families. Every father and every mother in that place had been saved from starvation during a famine by missionaries and civilians and others who had sent them to Leupolt. "God be praised," wrote Christopher, "for Christian civilians and Christian officers. Not only for their gifts and painstaking efforts, but also for their prayers and the answers to these which the 'God of all grace' has so evidently given." On his way home to Calcutta, Christopher called at Serampore, formerly a Danish settlement, where the baptist missionaries Carey, Ward, and Marshman, worked when missionaries were not allowed in the territory controlled by the East India Company. Dr. Carey's study seemed to Christopher one of the most sacred places in which he had ever stood, for he felt it was sanctified by much prayer and labour in translating the Word of God into the chief languages of North India.

Christopher returned to his work at La Martinière for another term. In Calcutta itself he had that year been much impressed by the activity of the fine Scottish missionary Duff, who also had a school there. "In the year 1848 . . . I had listened to [Dr. Duff] as he was examining the three hundred senior students of his great missionary school and college of a thousand native boys and young men . . . He first examined them in various branches of knowledge, and his powerful mind and the brightness of the students he had himself helped to train, made the questions and answers an intellectual treat. He then examined them in the Word of God: and the extent and accuracy of their acquaintance with the most interesting of all books to many educated natives, even before they are really converted, surprised me greatly. It was the most wonderful of all the missionary colleges I ever saw or heard of, and Dr. Duff began it with an attendance of only five students on the day when he opened it," — this is spite of secession, and beginning again, in 1843. Christopher also visited other nonconformist mission stations.

Christopher's successor was to arrive in January 1849. At that time the Revd. William Keane, a Cambridge acquaintance, afterwards Rector of Whitby, was learning Bengali in a native settlement at Krishnagur, about sixty miles north of Calcutta, and he invited Christopher to spend a fortnight of his Christmas vacation in going round the Church Missionary stations of the locality. This enabled Christopher to see something of missionary work in a country district. He called first at Agapara, a riverside mission station about six miles above Calcutta. On Christmas Eve 1848, he arrived at Krishnagur, and was welcomed by a seasoned missionary, the Revd. C. H. Blumhardt. The native congregation on Christmas morning was large and devout, joining heartily in the responses and singing. Christopher was the first layman, with the exception of civilians appointed to the district, who had ever taken the trouble to visit these missions. But for his friend 'Paddy' Keane, he would hardly have done so himself.

The next station they visited was Chupra, where a German missionary named Krückeberg attracted people from neighbouring villages by his reputation as a doctor, and preached the gospel to every sick person who came to him. From Chupra, Christopher and Keane rode on to Kapasdanga, a prospering mission station with a pretty village of four hundred Christians, made up of neat cottages shaded by plantations, and supplied with excellent schools for boys and girls. Here the missionary was a Mr. Krauss, whose only means of obtaining a good missionary wife had been to send his picture to England by the hand of his friend Weitbrecht, who found a missionary-minded governess in the household of Captain Trotter at Dyrham Park near Barnet, and prevailed on her to go out to India to marry his friend. A most happy marriage resulted.

Christopher next visited Retnapur, where the missionary Lipp had obtained much influence by acting as mediator between landlord and tenants, and as a peacemaker in general. This he used to promote the gospel. At the next station, Solo, there was a remarkable German missionary, a bachelor named Bomwetsch, with a prosperous girls' school. Here Christopher was present at the wedding of a Mrs. Alexander, widow of one missionary, who was now marrying another. At the wedding breakfast, Bomwetsch spoke against missionaries marrying. He thought that bachelor missionaries were less distracted from their work. But not long after, he married one of the native girls whom he himself had educated.

As a result of spending his vacations in this manner, Christopher felt he could justly meet the criticisms of missionary effort so often made by those not familiar with it. At Krishnagur, the judge's family, although at that time including grown-up daughters, living within five hundred yards of the Church Missionary school, and invited there twice a year to a public examination carried out in the English tongue, never once took the trouble to cross the threshold. It has often been supposed that impressions of missionary work on the part of those who have been abroad must be reliable. To Christopher this example served as a test-case. He also visited two missions of the Society for the Propagation of the Gospel nearer Calcutta, at Barripûr and Mogra Hât. He always felt thankful for this opportunity and wrote an account of his visit, which was printed in the following October in one of the society's *Quarterly Papers*.

Christopher reached Barripûr, some six miles south of Calcutta, on Saturday 27 January. The next morning, with two missionaries, he set out for Mogra Hât, about twelve miles further south. " There is no road, so we had to ride for about eight or ten miles across the country, — rice-fields, varied here and there with patches of jungle, generally veiling native villages; and a rough ride it was. The time was nearly mid-day, and the sun was intensely hot, though this was the cold weather. I was glad to find shelter at the end of our ride under the mat covering of a *salti*[1]." About a hundred and forty native Christians assembled for worship, and the sacrament

[1]Long, narrow canoe, made from a single tree trunk.

was administered to ninety-two. " My little sketch of the church at Mogra Hât[1] was taken from the opposite bank of the canal. Two flourishing tamarind trees shade the east window. Some of the neatly thatched huts of the Christian village are seen in the background. A native is punting a *salti* along the canal."

Christopher had to hasten back to Calcutta to receive his successor. Henry Woodrow had been a pupil of Dr. Arnold at Rugby, where he was in the sixth form with T. V. French, afterwards a great missionary, who became Bishop of Lahore. French arrived in India a few years later. Many incidents in Woodrow's career are incorporated in *Tom Brown's Schooldays*. The governors of La Martinière — among whom none had supported Christopher more consistently than Archdeacon Dealtry, subsequently Bishop of Madras — besides sending him a handsome written testimonial, further testified their approbation of his services by paying his passage home. He left Calcutta in February by Peninsula and Oriental steamer. At Madras he spent a night at the house of T. G. Ragland, Fellow of Corpus Christi College, Cambridge, who acted as Church Missionary secretary there, living on his fellowship like John Tucker of Corpus Christi College, Oxford, before him. The venerable Bishop of Calcutta, who was making his fourth visitation of his diocese, and the future Archdeacon Pratt, were also staying with Ragland. After family prayer the next morning, the Bishop went round the little company, laid his hands on each of their heads and gave them his blessing. Dr. Wilson had already given Christopher a letter of recommendation for holy orders addressed to the Bishop of London, Dr. Blomfield. Under date 3 November 1848 he wrote " I . . . only wish I could give him a Title in my own Diocese;" and to Sir Edward Ryan expressed the opinion that Christopher had "raised the Martinière to the highest pitch of reputation and conciliated all the Governors in a remarkable manner." Daniel Wilson was not a man to bestow praise lightly. Christopher, he considered, was a " learned, amiable, pious person, particularly attaching in his disposition and conduct," as well as being " a thorough churchman in principle." Wilson was a strong churchman himself. His testimony to Christopher's churchmanship even as a layman is therefore of weight.

[1]Plate 15.

Shortly afterwards, Christopher was delighted to find himself on board the *Ripon,* which was commanded by a definite Christian, Captain Moresby, the officer who had been in command of the *Benares,* and who had held out longest against the Christian movement promoted by the midshipman Campbell. It was known that Christopher was returning home with the purpose of offering himself for ordination, so he was asked to conduct divine service on the first Sunday. After reading prayers, he read a sermon of Dr. Chalmers, the eminent Scottish preacher, whose works were in the saloon library. On the second Sunday, within twenty-four hours of Suez, Christopher again officiated. The first lesson was the chapter which describes the drowning of Pharoah and his host. A lady afterwards remarked on the coincidence of this portion happening to be the lesson for the day, when they were passing near the probable scene of the disaster. But Christopher had chosen the lesson himself. In March they arrived at Southampton, and the joy and thankfulness of husband and wife being together again can be better imagined than described. Forty-eight years later Christopher recalled: "I used to think how good God would be if He allowed me to rejoin my wife . . . and live for six months only afterwards." Such was the effect of India on a mind now attuned to grace.

Chapter IV

Richmond

1849 - 1855

THE BISHOP OF CALCUTTA had also given Christopher a letter of introduction to the Bishop of Winchester, Dr. Charles Sumner, one of the most prominent evangelical churchmen of the day and brother of the Archbishop of Canterbury. Dr. Sumner recommended him to apply for a curacy to the Revd. John Hales, Perpetual Curate of St. John's, Richmond, which served some four thousand souls. Richmond, though not far from London, was, until 1877, in the diocese of Winchester, which included all Surrey, reaching as far as Southwark. Hales, calling on his prospective curate, " being a very prudent man," Christopher wrote, "asked to see my wife." He added, " I believe that interview inclined him the more towards me." Hales still proceeded with circumspection, however, and during a few days spent at St. Johns' Parsonage, Christopher proposed that he might write out answers to written questions, lest his host " should be disappointed afterwards." But that was not likely, and Christopher for his part came to consider that he could not have served under a better man, or in a more interesting sphere of work. He was accordingly ordained by Bishop Sumner at Trinity 1849, on Sunday 8 July in the chapel at Farnham Castle. He had proceeded M.A. at Cambridge earlier that year. The subscription book at Winchester, confirmed by a copy of the Bishop's licence to officiate preserved at County Hall, Westminster, in the Surrey archdeaconry deposit, shows that Christopher's stipend

16. BISHOP'S CHAPEL, FARNHAM CASTLE, HAMPSHIRE, 1962
where A. M. W. Christopher was ordained, 1849, 1850

17. CHARLES RICHARD SUMNER, D.D., 1852
Bishop of Winchester 1827–69
Who ordained A. M. W. Christopher

was £100 *per annum*, though his bank account does not appear to record payment; he may have served, as was then not infrequent, gratuitously, for the sake of the title and training he received.

The Revd. John Dixon Hales, formerly scholar of Trinity College,[1] Cambridge, afterwards Canon Hales, and Rural Dean of Kingston-on-Thames, had been incumbent of St. John's, Richmond, for twelve years. The erection of the church was begun in 1829, as a chapel-of-ease in the old parish of Richmond. A parochial district, or 'district chapelry', was formed in 1838, but not until 1856, the year after Christopher's departure, did St. John's become a separate parish. The church of St. John the Divine remains, with the exception of the east end, to which a chancel was added about 1900, and the loss of the north and south galleries, much as Christopher must have known it. The now grey brick building, with stone ornamentation, was not large, though it seated twelve hundred. Its external appearance is described to advantage in the words of a contemporary print of which a copy hangs in the vestry. "It is in the Gothic style of the beginning of the fourteenth century . . . At the west front there is a handsome entrance in the centre, with a decorated window, on each side of which is a gothic niche. Above are flying buttresses and an enriched gable, the whole being surmounted by a light and elegant bell turret, which terminates in a small spire. The general effect is singularly pleasing, and combines in the happiest manner the graceful lightness of gothic architecture, with that character of venerable stability so desirable in a building dedicated to the most sacred purposes and connected with the most awful and endearing interests of future generations."

The interior is similarly in the manner of the early gothic revival, with an unusual gallery, the front of which, until recently, was V-shaped. This last, perhaps, is accounted for on learning that the architect was Lewis Vulliamy — son and grandson of famous clock and watchmakers in Pall Mall. His better-known work included the contemporary Christ Church, Woburn Square, and the parish churches of Highgate and Sydenham. About the same time, he 'gothicised' Ashburnham Place, Sussex. It is said that "As a gothic architect his early churches prove him to have been far in advance of his contemporaries . . ."

[1]Contemporary there with C. J. Goodhart.

Funds were voted for the building of a parsonage for St. John's in 1843, but the house, in the Kew Road, then doubtless surrounded by fields, did not prove big enough, and Hales subsequently enlarged it. Alfred and Maria Christopher themselves lived there from 1851 to 1855. With a later addition still, it continues to serve as the Vicarage — a tall, pleasant, grey brick house, in the late Georgian manner, with a good garden behind. Hales, who was made an honorary canon of Rochester in 1877, remained Vicar until his death in 1879. When Christopher became his curate he was a man of forty-nine. Unhappily the episcopal visitation returns for this period are neither among papers remaining at Winchester, nor at County Hall, Westminster, and with the modicum of light they might have thrown on Christopher's curacy, seem to have disappeared.

In 1879 a drastic change took place at St. John's, which Christopher, as well as the parishioners, must have felt acutely. The patronage was vested in the Vicar of Richmond for the time being, and the reigning incumbent, though a Fellow of King's College, Cambridge, was a tractarian. He decided that there ought to be one church in the neighbourhood where the prevailing version of extreme anglo-catholicism should be practised, and he deliberately appointed a clergyman who would introduce it. The innovations of this gentleman led to a revolt among the congregation and the formation of a secessionist body which eventually built Christ Church, Richmond, in memory of Canon Hales. It is not surprising, therefore, that a more adequate setting for the performance of the mass was felt to be needed than that provided by the communion furnishings of a neo-gothic chapel-of-ease and thus a spacious chancel, in a somewhat incongruous version of gothic, was added early in the twentieth century. A comparatively recent incumbent, Canon V. A. Demant, has become Regius Professor of Moral and Pastoral Theology at Oxford.

When Christopher arrived to take up his duties, he and his wife settled into a house in Park Shot, a street not far from the church, where they lived for nearly two years. A comparison of rate books suggests that they in fact occupied number 6, at one end of "a very attractive terrace of three Georgian houses." At number 7 resided the Hon. C. P. Villiers, Member of Parliament for Wolverhampton, and latterly 'Father' of the House of Commons. Apartments at

18. ST. JOHN'S, RICHMOND, SURREY, 1844
A. M. W. Christopher, curate 1849–55

19. ST. JOHN'S, RICHMOND, interior, 1831
Pulpit on right; reading desk and clerk's pew, left

20. JOHN DIXON HALES
1800–1879
Incumbent of St. John's, Richmond, 1837–79
A. M. W. Christopher, his curate 1849–55

number 8 were occupied, from 1855 to 1859, while the Christophers were still living in Richmond, by Mary Ann Cross, otherwise George Eliot, the novelist, who wrote there her *Scenes of Clerical Life*. But these two houses have been replaced. Hales was away on holiday, and the Parsonage was inhabited by the Revd. Henry Venn Elliott, incumbent of St. Mary's Chapel, Brighton, a former Fellow of Trinity College, Cambridge. Elliott, who was taking his annual rest, was one of the most distinguished evangelicals of his time. During Hales's absence, he was to be responsible for the preaching, and Christopher for the visiting. Elliott accompanied the new curate on his first pastoral visit, and gave him the benefit of his experience. He read a few verses of Scripture, applied them to the occupant of the sick bed, and then prayed aloud.

Some years later Elliott told Christopher a story, which the latter often used as an illustration of how God sometimes employs things of trifling importance to bring about his purposes. " I went to my present position in Brighton " — which was peculiarly influential — " entirely because the door of the Dean of Christ Church at Oxford was painted red! " Dean Gaisford's dislike of the hunting men attending chapel wearing pink under their college surplices (open in front) was well known, and he eventually issued an order forbidding the practice. The next morning the Dean found that his front door had been painted a bright vermillion. The offence was traced to the two sons of the Duke of Wellington, the Marquess of Douro and Lord Charles Wellesley. The Duke showed his disapproval of the severe punishment imposed (rustication for two terms while translating the whole of Thucydides) — after he had obliged his sons to accept it — by transferring them to Trinity College, Cambridge. Their private tutor in the interval was the Revd. H. M. Wagner, afterwards Vicar of Brighton, who accompanied them to Cambridge and thus was introduced to Elliott, the 'Father' of the college, a capacity in which he examined candidates for admission. When Wagner became Vicar of Brighton, he prevailed on Elliott's father, who was a parishioner, to acquire the patronage of St. Mary's Chapel and to appoint his son as Minister.

Bishop Sumner examined his deacons not only by written examination, but by requiring them to send him three sermons which they had preached on three specified Sundays. After looking through these, he chose one of the authors to preach one of his sermons at the evening service in the chapel of Farnham Castle — his episcopal residence — on the day of the ordination. Christopher was selected for this office at Trinity 1850, when the ceremony was held on 7 July. On that occasion he met, as one of the Bishop's examining chaplains, Dr. Richard Trench, afterwards Archbishop of Dublin, whose niece became the wife of Christopher's second son. Less than a year later, Bishop Wilson wrote to Dr. Sumner, asking him to try to persuade Christopher to accept the post of rector of St. Paul's School, Calcutta, an anglican grammar school for European and Anglo-Indian boys. Christopher was invited to Farnham to discuss the proposition; but he had no hesitation in declining the offer, on the ground that he could not again expose his wife to the Indian climate. Nor did he desire to resume the work of a school-master when he could devote himself directly to the work of the gospel.

Those who were familiar with Christopher in later years would have seen in his Vicar, had they known him, in some measure at least a human model which Christopher had used in the formation of his own character. " Canon Hales," commented *The Richmond and Twickenham Times* reporting his death in 1879, " was a man who was esteemed by all parties, whatever their opinions, and however widely his views might differ from their's, for there was something about the gentleness and kindness of his disposition which at once disarmed opposition, even should any be felt, and commanded respect from men of all shades of opinion. It is not a little remarkable in these days of heated religious controversy that a clergyman carrying out so consistently in practice the opinions which he held should still be so highly and universally respected, and indeed beloved . . . The secret of the respect in which Canon Hales was . . . held, lay not in intellectual brilliance, pulpit eloquence or rare originality of thought, but in things of even greater worth than these — loving earnestness in the cause of his Master, goodness and thorough consistency of conduct." All these words might equally have been written of Christopher in his maturity. As Dr. Anthony Thorold, Bishop of Rochester, said in his funeral sermon, Hales's people " loved him because of the truth which he taught, of the duty which he faithfully discharged, and of his exceeding goodness

— his greatest talent, because he was an epistle read and known of all men, an epistle of Christ."

After two years, the failure of the second Mrs. Hales's health obliged her husband to arrange with the Bishop for Christopher to take charge of the parish and to live in the Parsonage, where he and Maria Christopher remained rather more than three years. A junior curate was provided to work with him. From May 1850 to June 1851, the Revd. Thomas Bisset, afterwards Vicar of Pontefract, had served as second curate.[1] He was not in fact replaced until September 1852, when the Revd. Theodore Wilks, later Vicar of Woking, began duty which he continued until November 1854. His successor was the Revd. Joseph Hall. The parish registers[2] reveal that the practice of private baptism was by no means unusual at St. John's. Burials still took place in the old churchyard of Richmond. In addition to his parochial duties, Christopher held Bible classes at several private schools for girls, and a weekly service at the Police Station.

While he was in charge of St. John's, the parish was visited by cholera, and he remembered that Edward Hoare of Ramsgate, afterwards Canon Hoare of Tunbridge Wells, and himself a former curate of Richmond parish church, when telling him of his experience of the disease, was particularly insistent that it was washing the clothes of those who had died of it which spread the infection. Christopher entreated the mother of a young woman who had died of cholera in Richmond to burn her clothes and bedding, even promising to pay her the value of what was destroyed. When he got home, it occurred to him that he might have to pay for the clothes, and yet they might not be burnt. So he took a thick walking stick, and returned to the stricken house, where he found the mother preparing to wash her daughter's clothes. He made a fire in the garden, held the clothes over it with his stick, and burned them all. There was no more cholera in that part of Richmond.

In 1851, instead of taking an ordinary holiday, Christopher went on a fortnight's tour on behalf of the Church Missionary

[1]For three months at the end of 1856, Bisset acted as curate of St. Aldate's, Oxford, to Christopher's predecessor, the Revd. T. C. L. Layton.

[2]No other ecclesiastical records of this period appear to survive either locally or, of consequence, with those archives of the parish of Richmond (then including St. John's), now deposited in the Record Office at Kingston-on-Thames.

Society, preaching sermons and addressing meetings. One of the parishes he visited was Madeley in Shropshire, the scene, in the early days of the evangelical revival, of the shining labours of John Fletcher. When any visiting preacher arrived, Fletcher used to summon his flock by ringing a hand-bell. Christopher had cause to remember this when at one village he found only three women and a few children present to hear Captain George Greenway, R.N., for many years Association Secretary for the Church Missionary Society in Wales, and himself, speak about the society's work. The local clergyman seemed to have made little effort to gather his people; so Christopher borrowed a bell and a boy and went round the rows of colliers' houses, the boy ringing the bell. Not unnaturally a woman rushed out and said " Oh! You will wake the baby! " But Christopher managed to calm her. He then started going into every cottage, informing the people that he had been in India, and had come to tell them about the missionary work which he had seen. One woman was peeling potatoes. "My good woman, you have peeled as many potatoes as your children ought to eat in one day! Pray come to the Missionary Meeting." The woman must have been of the same opinion as Christopher, for she at once wiped her knife on her apron and came. Another woman was making a frock for her daughter, and replied to an earnest invitation: " I want to finish this black frock tonight." Her husband came to Christopher's assistance and said " O Molly, you can get up an hour earlier tomorrow morning." So Molly came down with her husband and their daughter. At another house a man asked " Will there be anything there to drink?" Christopher spoke kindly to him and when he had finished his round with the bell, overtook the man going down to the meeting, and taking him by the arm, spoke to him of " so great salvation " and entreated him to neglect it no longer. The deputation returned to the schoolroom in less than an hour and found it full. Thus early in his ministry, Christopher's winning manners stood him in good stead.

Christopher's children were born at Richmond. Henry Seton, baptised at St. John's by Mr. Hales, came first, in 1850, followed the next year by Caroline Eliza, baptised by her father. Alfred Wilmot was born in 1853, but he died nine months afterwards, and was buried in the family vault at Chiswick. The youngest child, Alfred Charles, was not born until March 1856, when his parents were living in their third home in Richmond, Tudor Place, opposite the Green. Seven more nephews and nieces were born during Christopher's curate days, three of them children of Leonard Christopher. In 1855, Maria Christopher's brother Thomas, of the Indian Navy, married Selina Harpur, daughter of Major W. C. Harpur of the 80th Regiment.

Christopher's time was already fully occupied, but presently he felt obliged to add to his labours by preparing for the press a *Memoir* of his friend Weitbrecht, 'The Missionary of Burdwan'. The widow returned to England in 1853, and with encouragement from Henry Venn, Honorary Secretary of the Church Missionary Society, set about collecting materials for a life of her late husband. Family records, letters, journals, and official reports were drawn on. But, as Venn said in his preface, "it still remained to reduce these documents into the compass of one volume, and to exercise that discriminating judgement in the selection, which could be better performed by a friend, than by one so nearly connected with the subject of the Memoir." Mrs. Weitbrecht approached Christopher. "Your Mother," he told her son long afterwards, "brought me a large pile of manuscript in her fine neat handwriting and told me what she wanted. I replied that my parish work was too heavy for me to do it but that I would look for someone else." Several people, better fitted for the task, as Christopher considered, and with more leisure, declined to undertake it. Rather than leave his friend without the help she required, Christopher took the work in hand. Considering that the published volume runs to over six hundred closely printed pages, it may be imagined why Christopher was reluctant. Nevertheless, the revised manuscript was ready for the printers early in 1854, and Christopher wrote a spirited introduction of fifteen pages, which incidentally affords early evidence of his love of tracts, several being recommended in footnotes.

There can be no doubt that he himself delighted in this record of a career remarkable, even in days of great missionary sacrifice, for its spirituality and faithfulness. "I believe", he wrote, "that no one who is 'looking unto Jesus,' no one who is praying for the gift of the Holy Ghost, can read this Memoir without being drawn, thereby, nearer to the Saviour; without being lifted nearer to heaven." Nor could the parallel with the Crimean War, then moving towards its climax, be neglected. ". . . sergeants and corporals are requesting that they may be reduced to the ranks, that they may volunteer for the terrible war in the East; old sailors are trying to disguise their years, that they may be allowed to stand to their gun again, before the heavy batteries of Russia; and shall it be, that the young Christian men of England, hear in vain of the need, which He who bought them with His own blood, has of their devoted service . . .?" Before the year was out, the book, published, like many evangelical works during the middle of the century, by Nisbet, had gone into a second edition. It is known to have continued to influence the work of missionaries in the field for many years.

This was Christopher's only considerable venture in literary activity; and the extent of his initial success leaves some desire that further efforts on a comparable scale had come from his pen. But he was primarily a man of action, and remained true to character. It was, however, during this period that he produced his first tract. *Look and Live: being Thoughts on John I.29* was published in 1854. It included an appeal for the work of the Society for Promoting Female Education in the East, a small agency designed to evangelize women in Palestine, Egypt, India, Ceylon, and China, which had been founded in 1834 by the Hon. and Revd. Baptist Noel, and was one of the precursors of the Zenana Bible and Medical Mission. Most of the twenty-three pages of this tract consist of a well-constructed sermon. "May the Holy Spirit enable us, dear Reader, to behold Christ as 'the Lamb of God, that taketh away the sin of the world . . .' 'Behold!' and *with what eye* shall we behold Him? Shall it not be with the eye of faith? with this eye alone can the guilty behold a freely offered pardon held down to him as he lies in the depths of conviction of sin . . . the sins of a guilty world were laid on His head, and He bare them in His own body on the tree."

In the summer of 1854, the Crimean War was sadly if indirectly brought home to Alfred Christopher and his wife. Maria Christopher's brother Thomas was in command of a man-of-war steam tender at Calais, engaged in embarking French soldiers in English ships to take part in an expedition against Russian ports in the Baltic. His brother Charles was staying as Tom's guest aboard the

21. 6, PARKSHOT, RICHMOND, SURREY, 1962
Home of A. M. W. Christopher 1849–51

22. ST. JOHNS' VICARAGE, RICHMOND, rear view, 1962
Home of A. M. W. Christopher 1851–55

23. ST. JOHN'S, RICHMOND, 1962
A. M. W. Christopher, curate 1849–55

tender, and employing some of his leisure in sketching the Frenchmen on deck. The vessels were too closely docked, and it was difficult to manœuvre. One day the tender was coming alongside the battleship *Algiers,* and Tom Christopher noticed a rope hanging in a loop from the main yard of the vessel. He thought the mast of the tender would clear it, but it did not, for the loop caught the mast and in a moment the mast snapped and fell on to the deck. Seeing a sailor pointing, he looked more closely. His brother was lying on the deck, his head struck by the falling mast. He never spoke again.

Alfred Christopher had come down from the pulpit one Thursday evening, and moving towards the vestry, he saw his brother-in-law, Tom, standing in the doorway. Realising at once that he brought bad news, he asked, " What is it, do tell me?" " Poor Charlie's gone, killed at my very feet," was the reply. Alfred Christopher's duty was first to go up Richmond Hill to break the news to the dead man's wife, and then to tell his own wife, Charlie's sister. It was one of the saddest days of his life. Shortly afterwards he himself became seriously ill — one of the contributory causes was undoubtedly the extra work involved in editing Weitbrecht's *Memoir* — and in April 1855, his sister Louisa Tatham died, leaving three children. She was only ten months older than himself. Yet these sorrows were to be crowned by one greater still.

In August 1854, Christopher took his wife and children to Sandgate for their annual holiday. Two cousins were also staying there, and with two ladies lodging in the next house, they all went by boat to see Dover Castle. On the way Christopher read aloud a brief life of Charles Simeon of Cambridge. The weather was very hot, but feeling cold as the evening drew on, he took an oar, first from one boatman, then from another, and plied it vigorously. Of that little party, two, if not three, died of cholera within two days,[1] and Christopher believed that if he had not rowed all the way he might have been attacked. Alfred and Maria Christopher hastened home with their babes, and sought advice from their doctor, Frederick Julius, father of Churchill Julius, one of Christopher's

[1]One was probably Mary Henley Christopher, a grand-daughter of John Christopher of Crook Hall, and therefore a first cousin once removed, who died at the age of twenty-two on 2 September 1854; another may have been Christopher's own son Alfred Wilmot, who died nine months old in the same September, the registered cause of death being 'fever'.

undergraduate friends at Oxford who afterwards became Archbishop of New Zealand. Dr. Julius lived on Richmond Green. Christopher at once resumed his pastoral work, but when he came home from visiting the afternoon after his return, he felt ill and went upstairs to bed. He did not come down again for several months. Every day he became worse, and appeared to be on his death-bed. "I was dying of 'gastric fever,' which I suppose is much the same as . . . 'typhoid fever'." Being one of the local secretaries of the British and Foreign Bible Society, Christopher was well known to the nonconformist ministers of Richmond, and in every dissenting chapel as well as in the parish church and St. John's, public prayer was made for his recovery. Christopher rejoiced to speak of this as a testimony to the uniting influence of the Bible Society.

Nevertheless he grew worse, and Dr. Julius called in an eminent London consultant. On leaving St. Johns' Parsonage, the great man said "He can't live." Dr. Julius did not mention this to anyone, but went home and told his wife, who was Maria Christopher's dearest friend in Richmond, "Nothing but prayer can save him. Medicine takes no effect whatever upon him. Go round and gather another prayer meeting." That night the schoolroom was thronged with praying Christians, and although it was a Saturday evening, the Vicar of Teddington, the Revd. Alfred Wilkinson, came over to lead the supplications. By this time the sick man had made "many friends by his genial kindness and earnest persuasive preaching." Working men were there in their working clothes, some deeply stirred, such was Christopher's influence. When Dr. Julius called at eleven o'clock that night for his fourth visit, he found that the change he had longed for had taken place. Thereafter his patient never looked back, though six weeks afterwards he was still so weak that he had to be lifted by his wife and nurse from bed to couch. All through his long life — he never had another serious illness, though fears were expressed at this time as to the possible effect on his heart — he thanked God for those united prayers. And it is remarkable that shortly before, his Vicar, Mr. Hales, had also been raised up from what seemed likely to be his death-bed, and was able to continue his work at St. John's for many more years.

The pulpit[1] at St. John's was the place where Christopher learnt to preach extempore, from notes. After he had been in charge of the parish for some little time, he commenced the practice on a week-day evening. In those days sermons were far more frequently, and, it may be added, effectively, read than they are now. But Christopher was convinced that a clergyman would lose many opportunities of usefulness in the course of his ministry, if he could not, after careful preparation, speak with facility from notes. When he had made his first attempt, an intelligent Christian lady, the headmistress of a girls' school at which he held a monthly Bible class, said to him in the kindest possible way: "Dear Mr. Christopher, please never try to preach extempore again! You know, dear Mr. Christopher, some clergymen have gifts!" Preaching was never Christopher's strongest point and he entirely acquiesced in her judgement. He therefore smiled and expressed agreement with her unfavourable opinion of his sermon. Nevertheless, in spite of what he called that "sisterly discouragement", he continued to preach from notes every Thursday evening. He was conscious of being slow to improve, but in time he acquired confidence. When he had difficulty, he regarded it as a sign that he had not given sufficient time to preparation. Eloquence, Christopher was wont to remark, is a rare thing, though it is less rare for a young man to imagine he possesses the gift. It is possible to be interesting and instructive without it. In after years, Christopher used to tell the story of the headmistress against himself, because he thought it might encourage "some of the young soldiers who are coming on to replace the old soldiers, who are very soon going off."

Christopher believed that, apart from its effect on his later life, if he had not persevered in overcoming his difficulty in speaking, he would not have been asked to undertake deputation work for the Church Missionary Society. In the event, no sooner had he recovered from his illness than Henry Venn, who had heard from an experienced association secretary of a rousing address which Christopher had given, invited him, in the spring of 1855, to become Association Secretary for their 'western district' of England. The idea appealed strongly to Christopher, and he gladly closed with the offer.

[1]Seen on the right in Plate 19.

Chapter V

Association Secretary

1855 - 1859

A COMMITTEE of the Church Missionary Society had been appointed in September 1854 to look for an association secretary to replace the Revd. G. T. Johnston. This subcommittee included some well-known names, in particular Captain the Hon. F. Maude, R.N., for many years treasurer of the society, and the Revd. Edward Auriol, Rector of St. Dunstan's-in-the-West, Fleet Street, a man highly regarded in the evangelical world as possessing much spiritual wisdom and practical sagacity, who five years later was partly instrumental in nominating Christopher to St. Aldate's, Oxford, and became an occasional preacher there as a result. After six months, the committee, with the Revd. Henry Venn as secretary, recommended the appointment of Christopher. The General Committee approved their choice on 12 March 1855; and Christopher's letter of acceptance, dated from Richmond on 19 March, is preserved in the archives of the society. Otherwise, a few brief business letters written by Christopher during the period 1855-9 alone survive at Salisbury Square. The association secretaries' reports for these years have unhappily perished.

". . . the official representatives," wrote Dr. Eugene Stock, historian of the Church Missionary Society, ". . . have been the Association Secretaries. The title is not a good one, as it confuses them with the Secretaries of Associations, who are locally appointed . . . For the Association Secretary does not conduct the affairs of the local Associations, nor does he collect funds. He is in fact a permanent 'Deputation' for a given district, seeking to influence the clergy and others, preaching and speaking constantly, guiding the missionaries and others sent to his district from time to time as 'deputations', and reporting the progress of his district to headquarters. Most of these officers are clergymen giving their whole time to the work and receiving a stipend . . ."

The personnel at this date included several men who afterwards became well known in more exalted positions. Shortly before Christopher, W. Pakenham Walsh, ultimately Bishop of Ossory, had served; and shortly afterwards came Robert Billing, subsequently Bishop of Bedford. In 1858, the Revd. George Knox, father of Edmund Knox, seven years later an undergraduate follower of Christopher and later still Bishop of Manchester, became a colleague. Apart from addressing meetings themselves, it was the duty of association secretaries to provide deputation speakers for missionary meetings in their areas. Christopher took over the large Western District, which included Oxfordshire, Berkshire, part of Buckinghamshire, Hampshire, the Channel Islands, Dorset, Wiltshire, and Gloucestershire. The population of these counties was well over a million and a half, served by more than two thousand churches. The difficulty of providing efficient deputations for the whole of six counties, the Channel Islands and a quarter of a further county, was increased by the natural preference of most parsons for an address by someone with personal knowledge of missionary work. But several leading evangelical clergy in the area, notably Charles Oakley of Wick in Gloucestershire, — one of the men who were offered St. Aldate's before Christopher, — Carr Glynn, Rector of Witchampton, and Charles Bingham, Rector of Bingham's Melcombe, a former Fellow of New College, Oxford, both in Dorset and themselves both previously, and subsequently, honorary association secretaries of the society, rendered invaluable help in their respective localities.

During Christopher's first year, one hundred and twenty-six sermons with meetings are recorded for the Western District, together with a hundred and ninety-one sermons only and seventy meetings. Of these, Christopher himself preached ninety-two sermons and spoke at one hundred and thirty-four meetings. Eighteen new pulpits were included and five new associations formed, making a total of sixty. The annual revenue from the district amounted to over £11,000. In the following year, 1856, there were one hundred and sixty-two sermons with meetings, two hundred and thirty sermons only, and seventy-eight meetings only. Thirteen new associations were formed, but three others lapsed. Christopher secured thirty-one new pulpits, himself preached one hundred and two sermons, and addressed one hundred and fifty-three meetings. The total revenue, however, despite these exertions, rose only slightly. Christopher's own salary amounted to £300 *per annum,* and travelling expenses averaging £100 annually were also allowed. During these years the Christophers lived at Tudor Place, Richmond, a solid, Queen Anne house on the Green, with a later front, now number 45, adjoining Old Palace Terrace, next to the celebrated Maid-of-Honour Row, with the old Palace of Richmond beyond. Here on 20 March 1856, their youngest child, Alfred Charles, afterwards the chronicler of the Christopher family, was born. Two months later the infant was baptised at St. John's by Mr. Hales. In 1855 and 1856 the latter's son John played cricket for Cambridge, and it seems likely that their mutual interest made a bond with his father's curate while the younger Hales was a schoolboy at Rugby.

In the first year of his new work, Christopher and the Revd. J. T. Tucker of Tinnevelly formed the deputation to Weymouth, then known as Melcombe Regis, where Charles Bridges, a celebrated biblical expositor, and nephew of Dr. Nathaniel Bridges, one of the evangelical leaders at Oxford during the latter part of the eighteenth century, was Vicar. After the evening meeting, the visitors supped with the local treasurer of the Church Missionary Society, William Eliot, a banker, father of Dr. Philip Eliot, subsequently Dean of Windsor.[1] Grace was said by Bridges in a form which thereafter Christopher himself adopted. Guests at St. Aldates' Rectory soon became familiar with " We thank Thee, O Lord, for these and all Thy *undeserved* mercies, through Jesus Christ." Bridges was best known for his commentary on *Psalm CXIX*, and the Rector of Swanage, the Revd. R. D. Travers, told Christopher that on one occasion his parish clerk gave notice that the sermons on the following Sunday would be preached by "the Revd. Charles Bridges, author of the CXIX Psalm" !

[1]Thus grandfather of the Rt. Revd. P. H. Eliot, remembered in the Oxford diocese as Bishop of Buckingham 1921-44.

24. TUDOR PLACE, RICHMOND GREEN, SURREY, 1962
Home of A. M. W. Christopher 1855–59

"It is a wonderful privilege," wrote Christopher in an article for *The Record* published in 1899, "to be an Association Secretary of the C.M.S. I thank God that the revered Henry Venn asked me to become one in 1855 . . . I used to compare myself to a fly swimming about in the cream of the clergy. It was a very small portion of the cream with which I came in contact — a mere teaspoonful; but it was real cream. The chief great fault which I perceived in a few of them was that they did not labour to get up missionary information. They did not read, mark, and fix in their memories interesting facts from the C.M.S. Reports. It is something very like a sin not to do this . . . How difficult it was in those days to find a sufficient number of Deputations who were masters of their subject!" The article was an appreciation of General Sir Arthur Cotton, who had lately died. "How delightful it was to obtain from Sir Arthur Cotton his consent to attend with me a round of C.M.S. Village Meetings! He was not a man who reserved himself for important town Meetings; he was just as willing to attend a village Meeting as a Meeting in Oxford. It is a delightful thing" — and this was his point — "to be in contact daily — morning, noon, and evening — with a man of real grace and love of the Lord's missionary work. A C.M.S. Association Secretary is a man to be envied — especially if he can secure as a co-deputation such a brother as Sir Arthur Cotton!"

Sir Arthur's company was no less congenial because of his association with India. He it was who as a young engineer had persuaded the government of Madras, much against their will, (described by Christopher as "the commonsense people,") to allow him to construct a vast net-work of canals and dams in order to guard against the failure of rain for the crops and to provide a cheap means of transporting them. By his example the plan was adopted elsewhere in India. Sir Arthur was recognised as the greatest engineering genius that India had ever known. As Christopher himself said: "He worked for the good of his fellow-creatures, and to make manifest to the heathen, by benefits which they could understand, the benevolent character of Christianity . . . What a mercy it is when a genius is a true-hearted believer in the Lord Jesus Christ, constrained by our Redeemer's great love to devote life to His richly rewarded service!" At this date, Sir Arthur's brother, the Revd. Dr. Richard Cotton, also a devout evangelical — but as short as Sir Arthur was tall — was Vice-Chancellor of the university of Oxford, and remained Provost of Worcester College on Christopher's arrival there four years later.

When Christopher went to Marlborough for the first time, there was so little interest in the work of the society that only two clergy were present at the afternoon meeting, and they had driven more than eleven miles. The entire attendance was miserably small. A zealous tradesman provided dinner for the deputation, the two clergymen, and some others, after which Christopher told the story of the village where he went round with a bell. He then proposed to divide Marlborough between those present, and as far as possible to call from house to house, asking the people to attend the evening meeting. He himself took the College, of which the Revd. George Cotton (first cousin once removed of Sir Arthur), in 1858 the successor of Daniel Wilson as Bishop of Calcutta, was at that time the Master. Christopher called on him, and asked leave to go to the boys on the cricket field and invite them to the meeting. The desired permission was readily given, and Christopher went, telling the boys that he had visited missionary stations in India, and wished to let them know what he had seen. It seems not improbable that he made some reference to his having been in the Cambridge Eleven of 1843. In the event, nearly a hundred came to the meeting, as did Cotton, though as a master at Rugby he had become a disciple of Dr. Arnold. When the other member of the deputation had finished his address, the boys got up to go to chapel. Christopher asked Cotton to allow them to remain, and at once a master was sent to bring them back. But there were four hundred boys in the school, and although Christopher longed to speak to the other three hundred, he felt he must take care not to go too far. As he was silently praying that he might approach Cotton in the best way with this further request, the latter passed him a piece of paper, on which was written: "When can you come down and address the boys in the College Hall?"

Another school which Christopher visited was Cheam. Of seventeenth century origin, under the successive rule of Dr. Charles Mayo and the Revd. Henry Shepheard, both fellows of their colleges at Oxford, the school had assumed a pronounced evangelical tone during the first half of the nineteenth century, and had produced such outstanding men as the Hon. Samuel Waldegrave, whom Christopher was shortly to meet, and who became Bishop of Carlisle. Under the Revd. R. S. Tabor, the age of the boys was first confined to being preparatory for the public schools then entering the beginning of their meridian of popularity. Tabor held annually a Church Missionary meeting in the school garden for the boys (who at this time included Lord Randolph Churchill — father of Sir Winston — whose father, the seventh Duke of Marlborough, was a convinced evangelical), and supporters in the neighbourhood. Christopher is said to have attended every year from 1856 to 1861. There he first met his friend Arthur Kinnaird, afterwards eleventh Baron Kinnaird, who was then nine years old and preparing to enter Eton. The room which Christopher occupied in the school was quite close to Kinnaird's, and they soon made friends, more especially as the boy's parents were already friends of Christopher, who used to stay with them at their London house in Pall Mall East. "After that," Lord Kinnaird wrote many years later, in reference to his school days at Cheam, "as the Canon and my father and mother were interested in the same kind of work, I continually came across him."

On his first visit to Salisbury in 1855, Christopher was struck by the fact that several of the most considerable tradesmen were decided evangelical Christians, zealous supporters of the Church Missionary Society and of the Church Pastoral-Aid Society, though living in a predominantly high church city. He found that this was the result of a Bible class for young tradesmen conducted nearly twenty years before by the Revd. S. R. Capel, then Evening Preacher at St. Thomas's, Salisbury, and afterwards Rector of Wareham, Dorset. The influence of Dr. Hugh Pearson, Dean of Salisbury from 1823 to 1846, may have also been a source of encouragement to them. Both Capel and Pearson were Oxford evangelicals of an earlier day.

Christopher stayed with the Hon. Samuel Waldegrave, who had resigned an All Souls' fellowship on becoming Rector of Barford St. Martin, a few miles out of Salisbury, in 1844. He had been Bampton Lecturer in 1854. Christopher never forgot the family prayers after breakfast. Waldegrave encouraged his poor parishioners who were unable to go to work through infirmity or age, to come and join them. The stone floor of the kitchen was covered with a thick corded matting. Thus the neighbours were made welcome and comfortable. Waldegrave, while himself a double first-classman, had the gift of expounding the Scriptures lucidly so that their meaning was made clear to all those present at that "happy and profitable half-hour."

Dr. Walter Hamilton, the Bishop of Salisbury, a high churchman who in Oxford days had been an evangelical, could appreciate an address such as Waldegrave gave at the Church Missionary meeting in Salisbury when Christopher was one of the deputation. At the end of the proceedings, Dr. Hamilton said "This meeting has come up to what I think a Missionary meeting ought to be." Not long afterwards, a residentiary canonry became vacant at Salisbury, by the appointment of another evangelical, Robert Bickersteth, to be Bishop of Ripon. The tradesmen alluded to above, and others, united in prayer that the Rector of Barford St. Martin might be appointed to it. Christopher was walking in Salisbury one morning when it was announced in *The Times* that Waldegrave was to be the new canon. Seeing one of the tradesmen on the other side of the street, he crossed over and said, "Well, what do you say to Mr. Waldegrave's appointment to the Canonry?" "O Sir," was the reply, "we feel as if we could ask the Lord for anything now." When Waldegrave was Bishop of Carlisle (while bishop he preached for Christopher at St. Aldate's more than once before his premature death in 1869) he ordained that man, who became the useful incumbent of a populous London parish.

Another Christian home which greatly impressed Christopher during his first year of travelling for the Church Missionary Society was that of Henry Moule, Vicar of Fordington, by Dorchester, where happiness was the dominant note. It is fully and delightfully described in *Memories of a Vicarage* by Bishop Handley Moule. The Vicar and his wife were two of the most remarkable of the many Christians with whom Christopher became acquainted on his travels. Moule, a former Fellow of Christopher's first college of St. John's, Cambridge, and himself of no mean ability, was the father of a distinguished family of brothers, then growing up, among whom Handley became Bishop of Durham, Charles, President of Corpus Christi College, Cambridge, George, Bishop of Mid-China, and

Arthur, Archdeacon of Shanghai, three of whom came to Oxford for Christopher in after years. The two latter preached at St. Aldate's in the 'sixties. Dr. Handley Moule — who spoke at a 'missionary breakfast' at Oxford in 1886 — was converted through the ministry of one of his father's converts, Captain Handley, an army officer who had taken orders. Thus, as Christopher used to say, Moule was his own son's spiritual grandfather.

In 1856 Christopher was one of a deputation to the Channel Islands. He took his wife, his daughter Caroline, then a child of four, and his infant son Alfred, and settled them in lodgings at Ryde. Caroline was not well, but did not seem positively ill. Christopher therefore went to Southampton, and crossed to Guernsey to fulfil his first series of engagements. After preaching on the Sunday and addressing meetings on the Monday and Tuesday, he learnt that his daughter had become dangerously ill. He hastened back to the Isle of Wight as soon as possible, and found the little girl insensible, with no likelihood of a return to consciousness. He then had to make one of the most difficult decisions of his life. Not only was he engaged to preach twice on the following Sunday, but his fellow deputation speaker was obliged to leave Jersey on the Monday morning, and the friends of the society were depending wholly upon Christopher for two meetings at St. Helier's that day. It was grievous to desert his wife at such a time of trouble, even though her sister Caroline was also staying in the house; but it seemed clear that he ought not to leave the two meetings in Jersey without anyone to give information, and he felt he must return.

He did so, and on the Tuesday morning went back to Ryde. But Caroline had "fallen asleep" soon after he left. On reflection, he believed he had done right. As God's work was concerned, and he went for that, he had been confident that God would take care of his wife. But the decision to leave her was the most painful he ever had to make, and few, perhaps, would have had the courage or the sense of duty to do it. Some days later they buried the child in the burial ground of St. Thomas's Chapel, Ryde, the young curate of Holy Trinity, J. S. Barrow, afterwards Prebendary of Chichester, officiating. All through their lives, to Alfred and Maria Christopher the loss of their one daughter was a very sad memory. Nor was it the only tragedy which touched them closely during this period.

The deaths of their infant son, followed by those of Maria Christopher's brother Charles in 1854, and Alfred's sister Louisa in 1855, have already been recorded. A month after Caroline's death, Alfred's brother Arthur Ainsley Christopher, a city merchant and agent, died, unmarried, at the age of thirty-nine. In 1858, Alfred's eldest brother, William Thomas Christopher, who had been in partnership with his father in the wine trade, died at Brighton at the age of fifty-five. He had married as his second wife his cousin Harriett, but there was no issue. After these and other recent gaps in their family circle, the death of Herbert Sealy, Alfred's nephew, in the following month, in distant New Zealand, must have seemed comparatively remote.

One of the best friends of the Church Missionary Society in Gloucestershire was Alan Cornwall, Rector of Newington Bagpath near Wotton-under-Edge, who with John Emeris of St. James's, Gloucester, had been instrumental in founding the first regional evangelical fellowship, the West of England Clerical and Lay Association. Cornwall told Christopher of the smallest Church Missionary meeting he had ever attended. He and another clergyman had driven in an open carriage a long distance through rain, only to find that their audience consisted of the village schoolmistress and three little girls. The Rector of the parish had gone away without making any arrangements. The two clergymen, however, took great pains to interest the little girls. Afterwards a young man came up to them and said: "I have long been thinking of offering myself for Missionary work. I was in the dark room behind you when you were speaking. The door was a little ajar, so I could hear all that was said. What I heard has decided me to offer myself to the Church Missionary Society for any one of their Missions." He did, was accepted, and became a useful missionary. The story appealed to Christopher as showing the unpredictable value of even the most unpromising audience.

At Bristol, Christopher was on ground somewhat familiar from his boyhood days at Downend. Charles Pinney, the mayor who had escaped through the roof of the Mansion House during the riots of 1831, still lived as "a warm friend" of the society. A member of a well-known local family, he entertained Christopher during his visits to the city, at Camp House, Clifton. In later life, Christopher was in the habit of emphasising that it was by personal effort that much of the society's income is raised. He remembered a lady at Clifton who had but small means herself, and her acquaintances were people of small means. She began collecting for the Church Missionary Society when she was a girl at school, and when he knew her she was not a young lady, but she had in her life collected in small sums three thousand pounds for the work.

A visit to one veteran clergyman, a member of a Wiltshire county family, whose name has not been recorded, was a reminder that the evangelicals were much stronger than they had been. He told Christopher that in the early days of his ministry there were only two evangelical clergymen within a long distance of him, Dr. John Williams of Stroud, the editor of Hawker's *Works,* and the Revd. Thomas Methuen of All Cannings, brother of the first Lord Methuen. Another stalwart with whom Christopher stayed was the Revd. John Tucker, Vicar of West Hendred in Berkshire. An undergraduate friend of the Kebles and of Thomas Arnold, he had passed from a fellowship at Corpus Christi College, Oxford, to the secretaryship of the Church Missionary Society at Madras, where as incumbent of the church attached to the mission, he had met Christopher's brother-in-law Wilmot. It was with his successor, T. G. Ragland, that Christopher had stayed on his way home from India.

As Oxford was in the Western District which Christopher was working for the society, he had had some contact with the city before he came to live there. In 1856 he moved a resolution at the annual meeting. In February 1857, he was one of the deputation. He was already exerting personal influence. J. E. Matthews, a gifted mathematician who came up to Pembroke in the following year, was reading for his scholarship examination, as a private pupil, at Litton's Hall, in Holywell, the first permanent private hall to be opened in the university, under its Master, the Revd. E. A. Litton, a former Fellow of Oriel, the Bampton Lecturer of the previous year, and a notable evangelical theologian. "Canon Christopher", wrote Matthews in later years, "was the first person to speak to me about my soul and its salvation; and therefore I owe him an esteem and reverence and affection beyond any other human being . . . I walked up to Headington School-room with the Rev. E. A. Litton and Mr. Christopher; and heard the latter speak at the village missionary meeting on 'Motives, Methods, Men'—an address full of the fire of love . . . That visit is well remembered by me . . . for I had been brought up in the belief that as a baptised man I was necessarily a Christian in the full sense of the word, and that 'conversion' was to be preached to such poor benighted creatures only as the natives of Africa!" It seems clear that Christopher was the means of Matthews's own conversion. The latter always believed that this visit to Oxford had something to do with the offer of the rectory of St. Aldate's to Christopher two years later; but there is no evidence to support such a view.

Another undergraduate, G. A. Allan of St. Alban Hall, who matriculated in 1861, also had a previous acquaintance with Christopher, who had first visited his father's parish of St. Mary's, Cricklade in Wiltshire in 1857. "It was Mr. Christopher's custom," he recalled, "to go round the place during the day, calling on many and buttonholing others in his efforts to induce them to attend the Meeting in the evening. Needless to say, the Meetings on these occasions were crowded beyond the capacity of the room itself, and many stood outside to listen. As a boy I was allowed the privilege of being Mr. Christopher's companion in the above rounds. At the Meeting he urged the people to besiege the Rectory next day for Collecting Boxes, and said he was 'sure Mr. Allan would not mind if they pulled down his bell.' (My Father, however, was not so sure about that.)"

In the same year, Christopher was asked by Carr Glyn of Witchampton whether he would like to become Secretary of the British and Foreign Bible Society. He had in fact been sounded when the vacancy first occurred, and now replied "I feel that I have been Providentially prepared for the work of the C.M.S., and called of God to it . . ." In declining, he proposed the appointment of a colleague, the Revd. John Mee, Association Secretary of the Church Missionary Society for its 'eastern district', who was in due course selected, and who in 1861 became Dean of Grahamstown. In 1858, Christopher was requested by the committee of the Church Missionary Society to take charge of their 'London district', twelve miles round St. Paul's, with an office at Salisbury Square, and there again he worked with all his immense energy. Some idea of the extent of his labours and their development may be gained from the fact that on his resignation in 1859 the area had to be divided into three. Christopher did not altogether desert his old district. On 2 August 1859, three weeks before his new association with Oxford was due to begin, he was preaching at Whippingham, in the Isle of Wight. Osborne House was in the parish, and the following day Christopher noted " The Queen & Prince Albert &c &c were present on Sunday morning."

The English edition of *Living for Christ: A Memoir of Virginia Hale Hoffman* by the Revd. Dr. Cummins, Rector of St. Peter's, Baltimore, carried a preface of twelve pages by Christopher dated February 1859, but without any indication of Christopher's connection with the author or his exemplar, who had been the wife of an American episcopalian missionary in West Africa, and who died in her twenty-fourth year in 1856. "We should lose much," Christopher wrote, "if we were left in ignorance of our brethren and sisters who have gone forth from the United States to live for Christ among the heathen. This Memoir introduces us to a group of true-hearted missionaries in a mission which will probably be a new field to most English readers." The missionary spirit had sunk deep into Christopher's soul. "The miserable condition and awful prospects of the heathen, as blind and in darkness and under 'the power of Satan', 'without Christ — having no hope, and without God in the world,' are well understood by a large number of intelligent, well-educated, Christian young men. Yet the Church Missionary Society and other Societies appeal most earnestly to qualified young clergymen and laymen to offer themselves for the highest work to which a man can be called, and to nearly all they appeal in vain. The Saviour by His last commandment speaks to the consciences of those for whom He shed His blood; and the reply is, 'I pray thee have me excused'."

The offer of the living of St. Aldate's, Oxford, prompted by the recommendation of an unnamed clergyman, a graduate of Pembroke College, Oxford, who had heard him speak at a missionary meeting held in a barn at Shanklin in the Isle of Wight, reached Christopher during the summer of 1859, in circumstances which can hardly have seemed, from an earthly point of view, in any way propitious. The benefice had been vacant for some months. Several Oxford men had been approached, and all had declined it.

Nor was Christopher surprised that they should have done so. On going to inspect the parish, he found it much decayed, with schools and parsonage house almost derelict. The basic stipend was extremely small. Yet the possibilities of the place could be seen by a man of vision. Christopher consulted Henry Venn, a former Fellow of Queen's College, Cambridge, who curiously had also been, like Christopher, nineteenth wrangler. He was much attached to Venn, and Venn advised him to go there. Thus at the age of thirty-nine, Christopher was led to the scene of his life-work.

Chapter VI

Background at Oxford

1735 – 1859

IT HAS SOMETIMES been supposed that Alfred Christopher was a pioneer in the evangelical field at Oxford. This is certainly the impression, for example, given by Dr. W. F. Scott in the Oxford chapter of *Christ and the Colleges,* edited by the present Archbishop of York, Dr. Coggan, in 1934. But it is now established that Oxford had already been, for many years, the seat of a flourishing evangelical school. Though in that respect overshadowed by the reputation of Cambridge men, Oxford evangelicals had in fact played a highly important part in extending the work of the whole movement. On the other hand, tractarianism was of more recent growth in the university, and that in turn had been followed by a liberal movement in religion, accompanied in some quarters by an evacuation of belief which opponents did not hesitate to describe as rationalistic. In order to appreciate, therefore, the background against which Christopher started work in 1859, we shall require to make a brief survey of several aspects of the preceding period.

The evangelical movement in Oxford had had its beginnings, as it happened, close to St. Aldate's church. George Whitefield the evangelist had his experience of conversion while an undergraduate at Pembroke College, in the year 1735. When John Ryle, afterwards Bishop of Liverpool, who had himself been converted as an undergraduate of Christ Church, came to Oxford to preach for Christopher in 1865, he was mildly disgusted to find that the college porter could not answer his enquiries as to which rooms Whitefield had occupied. The south aisle of St. Aldate's served as Pembroke College chapel until 1732, and thus Whitefield narrowly missed worshipping there daily as Samuel Johnson had done a few years previously, and Sir Thomas Browne, author of the *Religio Medici*, in the previous century. Whitefield did not remain at Oxford after taking his degree, but he preached at St. Aldate's to a crowded congregation on the afternoon of his second ordination, which took place in the cathedral on 14 January 1738/9. Four months later, Vice-Chancellor Leigh threatened to arrest him if he ever officiated again in Oxford. The Wesley brothers, converted in May 1738, had also ceased to reside, though both were fellows of their colleges; but they came up at regular intervals to preach, in their turns, the message of the revival from the university pulpit. Both, however, were silenced after a forthright sermon from John Wesley on St. Bartholomew's Day 1744. Thus from the first, the evangelical doctrines met with opposition at Oxford no less, but no more, than elsewhere.

The earliest parochial centre of evangelicalism in Oxford was St. Mary Magdalene. The benefice was held from 1748 to 1763 by the Revd. Joseph Jane, also a Student of Christ Church, to whose support the evangelical movement at Oxford owed its first pulpit. Jane himself was a less prominent figure than his curate, the celebrated Thomas Haweis, whose stormy five years' ministry at St. Mary Magdalene was terminated in 1762 by the action of the Bishop of Oxford. Both town and gown had flocked to hear Haweis preach. After him, James Stillingfleet, Fellow of Merton, took the lead among the small band of evangelicals in the university. But he left Oxford in 1767; and almost immediately the smouldering hostility to evangelical religion broke out afresh. In the following year, six undergraduates were sent down from St. Edmund Hall on account of their evangelical opinions and practices. Yet it was at St. Edmund Hall that the evangelicals were to gain their first real foothold in the university. Soon afterwards, Edward Spencer, already in orders, matriculated there, and as an older man was able to give some lead. His place was in due course taken by Nathaniel Bridges, Fellow of Magdalen — whose nephew, Charles Bridges, Christopher had encountered at Weymouth. Not till 1783, however, with the appointment of Isaac Crouch, one of Spencer's pupils at his rectory of Wingfield, Wiltshire, as Vice-Principal of St. Edmund Hall, did the movement begin to attain academic recognition, although during these years some of the most honoured leaders of the third generation passed through the university as undergraduates.

With the advent of Isaac Crouch, evangelicalism became 'the religion of Teddy Hall.' But Crouch's retiring yet engaging character slowly won the regard of the university authorities; and even at this time the majority of future evangelical leaders from Oxford were to be found scattered, as undergraduates, throughout the colleges. Towards the turn of the century, the situation improved still further. Thomas Fry, George Faber, and William Yeadon, all Fellows of Lincoln, came to stand with Crouch in the university. This opened the way for a renewal of evangelical representation among the parishes of Oxford. For twenty years, from 1802 to 1822, William Yeadon was curate-in-charge of All Saints. Intellectually, too, the evangelicals at Oxford were playing their part in the revival of learning. Crouch was succeeded at St. Edmund Hall by the scarcely less well-informed and decidedly more conspicuous Daniel Wilson, who as Bishop of Calcutta befriended Christopher. St. John's became a noticeably evangelical centre; several of the fellows imbibed the doctrines of the spiritual revival, and one, John Natt, became Vicar of St. Giles' in 1809. He exercised a faithful ministry, not without opposition, for almost twenty years. The evangelical succession at St. Edmund Hall was secured by an arrangement whereby John Hill became Vice-Principal on Wilson's resignation in 1812. Hill remained at his post for nearly forty years. He was made first secretary of the Oxford association of the Church Missionary Society in 1825, a position in which Christopher in due course succeeded him.

Dr. John Macbride, an evangelical layman who began a successful tenure of the principalship of Magdalen Hall in 1813, was still in office when Christopher arrived at Oxford in 1859. After a very short interval, Christopher took over from him, at his request, the work of senior honorary secretary of the local auxiliary of the Bible Society. Under him, Magdalen Hall — now Hertford College — produced a number of notable men, evangelicals included. At the same time St. Ebbe's started on its long career as a principal stronghold of parochial evangelicalism in Oxford, when Robert

Francis Walker, Chaplain at New College, served as curate there from 1813 to 1815. Some years later, Dr. William Wilson, Fellow of Queen's, and afterwards Canon of Winchester, became the first in the regular evangelical succession at the church as curate-in-charge. The Rector of St. Ebbe's, the Revd. William Hanbury, was already housed in a lunatic asylum. Though not more than mildly deranged, he was never able to return to his duties, which, it being impossible in law to deprive him, continued to be performed by proxy until his death in 1868. This state of affairs was well known in Oxford and when Christopher began to suffer from serious insomnia shortly after his appointment to St. Aldate's, he anxiously debated whether he ought not to resign while he was able to execute a deed of resignation. Wilson's successor, Henry Bulteel, a former Fellow of Exeter, seceded from the Church of England in 1831; but under William Champneys, Fellow of Brasenose and afterwards Dean of Lichfield, the reputation of the church was more than restored.

At the same time Wadham College under a vigorous new warden, Dr. Benjamin Symons, who reigned for forty years, became an evangelical stronghold. Henry Linton, who was Rector of St. Peter-le-Bailey throughout Christopher's earlier years in Oxford, was a young Fellow of Magdalen from 1831 to 1835. In the latter year, Edward Litton, no mean theologian, whom Christopher found Rector of St. Clement's, was elected a Fellow of Oriel College, just as the tractarian movement was developing in its shadow, and, with Henry Shepheard, afterwards Headmaster of Cheam School, he remained a member of its senior common-room throughout the fateful years that followed. Worcester College under Richard Cotton, Pusey's brother-in-law, Provost from 1839 to 1880, and Pembroke College under Francis Jeune, Master from 1843 to 1864, assumed an evangelical aspect. It was through Dr. Jeune's influence that the advowson of St. Aldate's was sold by the college to evangelical patrons in 1859. When Christopher was instituted to the living, Jeune was Vice-Chancellor. St. Martin's, Carfax, then the city church, where Crouch and Symons had been Lecturers, had an evangelical ministry during the incumbencies of Hayward Cox, Vice-Principal of St. Mary Hall, and Richard Hales, from 1830 to 1860, when W. S. Bricknell, Vicar of Eynsham — a radical evangelical influence — and

Robert Gandell, Tutor of Magdalen Hall — less militant but no less definite — were among the last Lecturers on an Elizabethan foundation.

In the late 'thirties, St. Ebbe's had been full to overflowing; and the evangelicals had planned Holy Trinity church as a chapel-of-ease. The Hon. Samuel Waldegrave, Fellow of All Souls, afterwards Bishop of Carlisle, and Charles Baring, later Bishop of Durham, were in charge of St. Ebbe's, and under Waldegrave's leadership, Holy Trinity became the first 'Peel District' in the country. The Prime Minister was so pleased with Waldegrave's prompt application of his measure (which facilitated the formation of new ecclesiastical districts, hitherto only possible by separate acts of Parliament) that he allowed Waldegrave to nominate Joseph West, Chaplain of Magdalen and New College, as first Minister. Twelve years later, Christopher made Waldegrave's acquaintance, as we have seen, at Barford St. Martin Rectory. West remained Vicar of Trinity parish during Christopher's first ten years at St. Aldate's. Only with difficulty can lovers of Oxford be reconciled to the extinction of this church. Yet the fine early gothic revival structure itself has met a melancholy, not to say shameful end, little more than a hundred years after devoted labour brought it into being. It is not altogether unfitting, however, that the parish, though originally taken out of St. Ebbe's, has been united with St. Aldate's.

Thus Christopher came to a city where evangelical religion was far from non-existent in its own right; but more recent movements tended to overshadow it. Tractarianism had troubled Oxford during the 'thirties and 'forties. Liberalism had reasserted itself in the 'fifties. Theological debate at Oxford was still carried on against a largely anglican background. The gates of the university were closed to dissenters, whether protestant or Roman, until 1854[1], when they were opened slightly. Not until 1871 were nonconformists given full academic status. Thus dissent, at the time of which we are thinking, was restricted to a few chapels in the city.

In England there had long existed a distinctively 'high church' party, though it was mainly confined to clergy and squirearchy: unlike puritanism and evangelicalism, it never developed the dimensions

[1]But from 1828 to 1831 Sir Henry Moncrieff, as Minister of East Kilbride one of the leading founders of the Free Church of Scotland, was an undergraduate of New College, taking a degree and serving as president of the Union.

of a widespread religious movement. It had been liable to assume a semi-political hue; but by the early nineteenth century it had become 'high and dry'. As a school of thought it remained faithfully protestant. Thus the old high church party were no better pleased with the tractarians than were the evangelicals. A movement which appeared to have as a rather ill-concealed aim the undoing of the Reformation settlement was likely to meet with opposition from anyone representative of the Church of England at that time. It is not easy for the modern anglican to realise how thoroughly protestant in appearance church interiors remained until long after 1833, the year which has been generally accepted as marking the beginning of the tractarian movement.

The idea that the Thirty-Nine Articles could be interpreted other than in the light of the traditional protestantism of existing schools of thought had yet to make its way. 'The errors of Rome' were still a conscious danger. Any conception of the church as primarily 'anglo-catholic,' a body which at the Reformation had been purged of certain later mediaeval accretions, but remained substantially sacerdotalist in doctrine, seemed incredible to all recognised church leaders. The Church of England, it was true, was undoubtedly that 'one, holy, catholic, and apostolic Church of Christ established in this realm.' But it was also 'that pure and reformed' branch of the universal church which had existed in England long before the grave errors and superstitions of mediaeval dogma — culminating in the blasphemy of the mass — had overlaid the truth of the gospel as revealed in the Scriptures. At the Reformation a glorious light had shone in the spiritual darkness and the divine terms of salvation were seen to be based on grounds quite other than had been inculcated for many centuries. The services of the English church had been altered accordingly. The changes were formulated in the Articles and expounded in the Homilies.

As long as this outlook was generally accepted — and it has recently received a lengthy and learned confirmation — few difficulties arose. But it turned out that the reformers had not been over precise in their attempts at definition; and it became a tenable point of view that they had in practice gone beyond the limits of necessity at a time when feelings ran high, and that many features of the pre-reformation church might be said to be dormant in the Church of

England, rather than extinguished. The leaders of the new school of thought were Oxford dons. John Newman was Vicar of St. Mary's, the university church, a living to which he had succeeded as a Fellow of Oriel. John Keble, an older man, was also an Oriel Fellow,[1] and Professor of Poetry. Edward Pusey, who alone of these remained in Oxford when Christopher arrived there, had been a member of the Oriel senior common-room before becoming, at the age of twenty-nine, a Canon of Christ Church and Regius Professor of Hebrew. They began by propagating their views in a series of lengthy tracts, from which their usual soubriquet is derived. Before long, bishops of various schools began to denounce them. The Bishop of Oxford, the Hon. Dr. Richard Bagot, himself a high churchman, was eventually driven insane by the distressing circumstances surrounding the rise of tractarianism in his diocese. But in spite of their professed reverence for bishops, the tractarians held on their way.

Opposition was aroused in the university. The Provost of Oriel, the Principal of Brasenose, scented danger. A plan to erect by public subscription a memorial to the protestant martyrs who had been burned opposite Balliol College was carried through by Dr. Cotton, Provost of Worcester. Designed by Sir Gilbert Scott, it stands to this day at the top of St. Giles's, close to St. Mary Magdalene, "in grateful commemoration of . . . Thomas Cranmer, Nicholas Ridley, Hugh Latimer Prelates of the Church of England who near this spot yielded their bodies to be burned bearing witness to the sacred truth which they had affirmed and maintained against the errors of the church of Rome and rejoicing that to them it was given not only to believe in Christ but also to suffer for His sake . . ." The project was oversubscribed, and the remainder of the fund was used to rebuild the north aisle of St. Mary Magdalene. The memorial itself was felt to be most appropriate to the situation. The historic protestantism of the church and university was affirmed and commemorated. As regards the tractarians, the memorial stood, in Dean Church's words, " a decisive though unofficial sign of the judgement of the University against them."

The strength of this feeling was put to the test in the following year when Keble's term as Professor of Poetry came to an end. The most promising candidate was Isaac Williams, a Fellow of Trinity.

[1]Until 1835, when he accepted the living of Hursley, but remained professor.

But he was an acknowledged tractarian, the author of a particularly distasteful tract. James Garbett, Fellow of Brasenose, a polished classical scholar and " a representative evangelical," was put up as an opposition candidate. It was Garbett who became Professor of Poetry. His Bampton Lectures of that year, entitled *Christ as Prophet, Priest, and King: being a Vindication of the Church of England from Theological Novelties,* were widely acclaimed.

When Pusey was condemned for teaching heresy in 1843, and suspended from preaching in the university for two years, the Warden of Wadham was among the six doctors who passed judgement. (At an earlier stage in Newman's career, before the tractarian movement began, when he was still nominally an evangelical, Symons had 'ploughed' him in the schools.) It is not altogether surprising, therefore that Dr. Symons's nomination as Vice-Chancellor in 1844 was contested by the tractarians. But this was an act of exasperation. Symons was elected by an overwhelming majority of convocation. Just then, W. G. Ward, a Fellow of Balliol, one of the most extreme tractarians, published his *Ideal of a Christian Church.* Ward claimed to hold every Roman Catholic doctrine as a member of the Church of England. This was too much, and Dr. Symons presided as Vice-Chancellor over the convocation at which Ward was deprived of his degrees, which had been given on conditions Ward was held to have broken. The offender presently became a Roman Catholic. Not long afterwards Newman followed him. The tractarian movement seemed to have been suppressed. In the university for the time being it was; but it persisted there and elsewhere, and during the next thirty years was fighting hard for recognition.

At Oxford a reaction set in. Arthur Stanley, Fellow of University College, later Dean of Westminster, and two Fellows of Balliol, Benjamin Jowett, afterwards the well-known Master of the college, and Frederick Temple, who ended his days as Archbishop of Canterbury, were the leaders in a movement which began to regard traditional orthodoxy as no longer tenable in the light of modern knowledge. Once again the natural tendency of man to exalt his reason was taking hold on the church. Once again, but in a different manner, the gospel of the Reformation was assaulted. The doctrine of the righteousness of Christ imputed to the believer was denounced as immoral. The reality of hell was questioned. Doubt was cast on the importance of the Old Testament. Miracles were explained away. Bodily resurrection was repudiated. When Jowett in 1855 published his lengthy *Epistles of St. Paul to the Thessalonians, Galatians, Romans* and almost simultaneously was appointed Regius Professor of Greek, Dr. Macbride, the Principal of Magdalen Hall, delated him to the Vice-Chancellor, under an ancient statute, for having "denied the catholic faith." Vice-Chancellor Cotton, however, though sharing Dr. Macbride's evangelical views, was hardly the man to deal effectively with a situation additionally distressing in that Jowett was a member of a well-known evangelical family. Cotton required him to subscribe the Articles afresh; but he declined, not unnaturally, to be admonished. Convocation showed general disapproval by refusing to augment the new professor's salary. In spite of its distinguished adherents, liberalism never exercised as wide an influence as tractarianism.

The practical counterpart of this liberal movement in theology was university reform. For generations the colleges had existed on a system of closed scholarships, limited to candidates from certain schools or areas, and on closed fellowships, confined to members of the society, and carrying no obligation to teach or to reside, provided the holder remained a bachelor and after a few years took holy orders. In some ways this plan worked better than has been commonly allowed. But it did not suit the reformers of the mid-nineteenth century. More open to question was the dictatorship of the university exercised by the Heads of Houses as almost the only members of the hebdomadal board. In spite of his share in this privileged régime, Francis Jeune, Master of Pembroke, led the campaign in the university. He was the only college head on the government commission appointed in 1850, and he largely influenced its decisions. Warden Symons, his wife's uncle, was not a little offended. John Conington, Corpus Professor of Latin, before his conversion to evangelical opinions had devoted most of his time to advocating the changes proposed. But the evangelicals, unlike the tractarians, who feared the break-up of the ecclesiastical organisation of the university, were divided outside as well as inside Oxford. Sir Robert Inglis, the senior Burgess for the university, and a staunch evangelical, protested loudly in parliament. Lord Harrowby, a particularly distinguished evangelical layman, like Inglis a member of

Christ Church, consented to act as a member of the commission. In the result, the majority of fellowships were in due course thrown open, and the hebdomadal board was reconstituted. But it took another commission in 1872 to complete the transformation of the old Oxford into the new.

The evangelicals may have been in two minds as to the value of university reform. In regard to the advent of tractarianism and liberalism there could be no such uncertainty. Both were plainly satanic. Tractarianism was a thinly disguised revival of Romanism. Liberalism was a denial of revealed truth. After Newman's secession, evangelical parents thought more seriously of sending their sons to Cambridge. But for one reason or another, many young men of evangelical views continued to come to Oxford, and the importance of protecting them from the dangers of the new religious influences did not escape the attention of those of the Oxford evangelicals who had grown up, for the most part, in a calmer, less complicated atmosphere. The first thing to do was to pray. The Oxford Prayer Union (in due course Christopher became a member of its committee) was founded in 1850. Older stalwarts of Oxford evangelicalism like Bishop Daniel Wilson, who in a university sermon of 1846 had denounced tractarianism as 'semi-popery', joined at once. Recent and older graduates were linked together after they ceased to reside at Oxford.

Prayer led to action. A small but memorable gathering of Oxford evangelicals, called by Edward Hathaway of Queen's, a barrister of Lincoln's Inn, was held early in 1853, at 9, Lincoln's Inn Fields, the office of the Lawrence Asylum.[1] William Champneys, formerly Fellow of Brasenose and curate-in-charge of St. Ebbe's, now Rector of Whitechapel and a residentiary Canon of St. Paul's; Edward Auriol of Christ Church, Rector of St. Dunstan's-in-the-West and a Prebendary of St. Paul's, the Nestor of the evangelicals; Anthony Thorold of Queen's, then curate of Whittington, Lancashire, afterwards Bishop of Winchester,[2] were among those who met to consider the situation, which they

[1]Founded in 1849 "for the orphan and other children of European soldiers serving or having served in India," and called after Sir Henry Lawrence.

[2]These names are given on the authority of Christopher's own recollection. But as he dated this meeting 1856, there may be room for doubt whether Thorold, a young curate in the north of England, was brought into consultation at this early stage. Between 1854 and 1857 he was certainly in London as

regarded as grave indeed. "The state of things in the University at that date," wrote Hathaway, "was painful in the extreme. Of those in subordinate authority there, very many promulgated a fully developed sacramental system — other minds, having laid aside the onerous practices of an effete Tractarianism, the spirit of which they had never caught, had betaken themselves to a universal disbelief; while, in other quarters again, Rationalism was gaining ground with a very marked progress." The conference concluded that "a wise and faithful preaching of the Gospel from the parochial pulpits offered the best remedy for the evils deplored". The determination was reached "to watch and pray for opportunities of securing an Evangelical ministry, of sufficient attractiveness and power, in one or more of the Oxford parishes."

In their general reading of undergraduate needs, Hathaway and his friends, while early in the field, were not alone. Writing on the religious life of Oxford thirty years later, the Revd. G. W. Gent, Principal of St. Mark's College, Chelsea, and a former Tutor of Keble College, could say, "It is, however, to the Parish Churches that we must turn if we wish to see the religious undergraduate in his spontaneous development. For the religious undergraduate has usually been the religious schoolboy, and the religious schoolboy draws as much of his inspiration from the Parish Church of his home as he does from his school chapel. Again, it is just at the age when men come up to the Universities that religion begins to have a full meaning for those who are earnest and singlehearted; it is no longer simple conformity to rules imposed from above; it is the dominating impulse which not merely transforms their own lives, but cannot rest unless it is, at least in a degree, doing something for the souls of others. The mere Academic religion is felt to be too narrow and formal; men want to be in closer touch with the poor and downtrodden, and to have some share in the ministrations of the clergy, whose vocation it is to follow thus closely in the steps of their Divine Master. And again, the Parish Churches have an advantage which the College Chapels can never possess. *They are not closed in the*

curate of Holy Trinity, Marylebone, and after that as Rector of St. Giles-in-the-Fields. On the other hand, Hathaway and Thorold had been contemporaries and friends at Oxford. Unhappily most of Bishop Thorold's papers were destroyed after his death. Nor do those of Dean Champneys survive in his family.

vacations. They have all that swing and movement, all that energetic life and fullness of reality, which can only result from the regular and uninterrupted discharge by an institution of its appointed functions . . ."

In 1853 it was feasible enough to purchase the right of nomination to many livings. But the colleges owned the patronage of the majority in Oxford. Normally the fellows of the college concerned presented one of their own number on a vacancy occurring. Such a man might of course be "one who loved Evangelical truth," as when Edmund Knox became Vicar of St. John's[1] in 1874, and as was apparently the situation at St. Aldate's during the short incumbency of Christopher's predecessor; but "the small value of the living made it certain that he would be a young man, whereas the exigencies of the case called for Christian teachers full of years and experience." The sixteen city churches then yielded an aggregate income of under £1,700 a year. All but five were in the hands of colleges. Attention was therefore directed to those in the gift of the Lord Chancellor. It was felt that if, on one of these becoming vacant, the appointment could be obtained for "a man of God — advanced in the Divine life, faithful, wise, affectionate, and anxious to lay himself out for the spiritual good of members of the University — the liberality of Christian friends might be relied upon for providing an income adequate to his position." Augmentation to at least £500 a year was contemplated. Auriol, Champneys, and another Canon of St. Paul's, the Hon. Montagu Villiers, Rector of St. George's, Bloomsbury, shortly afterwards appointed Bishop of Carlisle, became trustees of a fund to make such provision.

The first opportunity occurred earlier than had been anticipated. St. Clement's, where Newman had been curate to John Gutch, Registrar of the university and antiquarian, fell vacant in 1855. An immediate application to Lord Chancellor Cranworth was successful, and the Revd. J. N. Moody of Oriel was appointed. His attractive character and ministry drew crowded congregations. The spirit in which he worked is shown by a letter to Hathaway dated 2 September 1856: ". . . the Income being so scanty. I feel it to be, however, an unspeakable privilege to be there in

[1]Merton College chapel being the parish church.

the position in which from this circumstance no temptation of gold and silver comes across my path to continue in it, but the love of souls and the care of Young Men in the University." But ill health which had brought him back from a missionary station in India led to his death in 1858. "Members of the University of all grades were in the habit of attending his ministry, though at great inconvenience, his church standing in a distant suburb of the city; and several, both graduates and undergraduates, mourned him at his death as their most valued spiritual instructor." Contrary to all probability, however, Edward Litton, a 'double-first' who had formerly been a Fellow of Oriel and was Bampton Lecturer in 1856, and who had served as Moody's curate, was appointed to succeed. But he resigned in 1861, and the next appointment did not go to an evangelical. Both Moody and Litton were comparatively young.

More lasting success by this method was obtained in the case of St. Peter-le-Bailey. In view of the relatively central position of the church — then at the corner of New Inn Hall Street and New Road — the promoters of the fund had recognised from the first the importance of trying to secure it when it became vacant. The incumbent, the Revd. John Penson, had been in office at least since 1800.[1] He was also Vicar of Brize Norton, where he lived as early as 1808, and where four and five years later, he was still resident. In 1825, however, he had a house in St. Thomas's, Oxford, but after 1833 he apparently became permanently non-resident as far as St. Peter's was concerned. His deputy at Oxford for ten years was Stephen Reay, a sub-librarian at the Bodleian Library, who in 1840 was appointed Laudian Professor of Arabic. There followed a period of tractarianism, under W. B. Heathcote, afterwards Warden of Radley, and W. H. Chepmell, whose curacies were assisted by J. H. Pollen,[2] the latter, from 1847 to 1852 incumbent of Pusey's church, St. Saviour's, at Leeds, afterwards a

[1]He became curate of St. Peter's about September 1793, and signed the marriage register from January 1794 as 'Rector'. The diocesan archives (and Mrs. McClatchey in her *Oxfordshire Clergy 1799–1869*) suggest (the visitation return of 1854, however, conflicting) that he was not instituted until 1800. Penson may have been instituted twice, as in the contemporary case of Rector Hanbury of St. Ebbe's.

[2]It is apparent that Pollen was not himself curate of St. Peter's, as his biographer and the author of an article in the *Dictionary of National Biography* state, nor were Heathcote and "the Rev. Mr. C—— of Jesus College" (*i.e.* Chepmell) his rectors.

prominent Roman Catholic layman, artist, and author, who at this early stage in his career decorated the ceiling of St. Peter's as well as that of the chapel at Merton, his own college. Penson evidently became alarmed, for an abrupt transition ensued. In 1846, S. M. Barkworth, subsequently first Vicar of Greyfriars, an evangelical stronghold at Reading, was put in as curate, to be followed after a few months by Dr. Peter Maurice, Chaplain of New College, well known to the university of his day as a protestant controversialist, having been as early as 1833 the author of *Popery in Oxford*. Their successor in 1847 was another evangelical, R. C. Hales, who remained curate for nine years, although he became Rector of St. Martin's, Carfax, in 1852. The aged incumbent of St. Peter's resigned in 1856, a victim perhaps of the reforming zeal of Bishop Wilberforce, though he was still Vicar of Brize Norton when he died in 1858.

"Many providential indications" suggested to the organisers of the 'Oxford Fund' that the Revd. Henry Linton, Vicar of Diddington, Huntingdonshire, and a former Fellow of Magdalen, would make an excellent rector. For the primary concept, in days of more scriptural respect for age, had been "to plant in Oxford a father in Israel, rather than a younger man." Lord Chancellor Cranworth agreed to nominate Linton, the committee undertaking to augment generously a stipend which amounted to less than £100 a year. Nevertheless, acceptance involved Linton in a loss of income, as well as separation from the neighbourhood of family estates to which, however, he did not succeed, as it turned out, until 1877.

The appointment of Linton "more than realised, in many important particulars, the original design . . . His years and experience, and large practical wisdom secured for him an amount of influence with senior members of the University, which parochial clergymen of less mature age could not have reached; while his courtesy, suavity of manner, great simplicity of character, and holy self-forgetfulness readily won the confidence of younger gownsmen." He made a point of being acquainted with the latter; but his intercourse with undergraduates was never as extensive as Christopher's. In 1858 between thirty and forty university men were attending his evening service. At first his work suffered from the disadvantage of his not being able to find a house — there was no rectory — nearer than Rose Hill, though by the early 'sixties he was established at

25. EDWARD PENROSE HATHAWAY
1818–1897
Barrister-at-Law
Rector of St. Ebbe's, Oxford, 1868–73

26. HENRY LINTON
1804–1887
Fellow of Magdalen College 1831–35
Rector of St. Peter-le-Bailey, Oxford, 1856–77

Northbourne in the Woodstock Road. It also suffered from the fact that the majority of the parishioners had petitioned the Crown to appoint the Revd. Dr. Peter Maurice, their former curate. Linton alluded to this disappointment "in a very touching manner" in his first sermon, which, according to Stephen Quelch, a life-long inhabitant of Oxford, who was present, not more than twenty people attended. Linton and his family, however, soon gained the confidence and respect of the parish generally, and the families of several Heads of Houses attached themselves to his ministry.

Two years after Linton's appointment an unexpected opportunity arose, of even more importance on account of the permanence offered by it. Edward Hathaway learnt that Pembroke College might be willing to sell the advowson of St. Aldate's. The suggestion originated from the Master himself. Sitting one day in the rooms of the Union Society, Dr. Jeune remarked to William de Quetteville, a young Fellow of Pembroke, who was like himself a Jerseyman and decidedly inclined to evangelical opinions — "You should get your evangelical friends to buy St. Ald's," adding that he thought the college would sell. De Quetteville immediately wrote to Hathaway. There was no time to be lost. Six hundred pounds was forthwith subscribed by four sympathisers, the Revd. Henry Linton, the Revd. C. P. Golightly of Oxford, Canon Carus, formerly of Cambridge, Rector of St. Maurice's, Winchester, as well as a residentiary of the cathedral, and R. C. L. Bevan, the banker, a member of Oriel College. An urgent appeal was addressed to others. It was at this stage proposed to vest the right of presentation in three trustees, Edward Auriol, William Champneys, and William Carus. (Carus had given as much towards the purchase money as all the other subscribers together). In the event, another friend, the Revd. Edmund Hollond, a Suffolk squarson, supplied the entire five hundred pounds which were still needed, and a stipulation was introduced that the advowson should be conveyed to Simeon's Trustees,[1] a body of evangelicals who administered the patronage of the livings which Charles Simeon of Cambridge had acquired before his death in 1836, and to which others had from time to time been added in like manner. Hollond,

[1]Among these were Carus, Auriol, and Hollond, whose grandson, Dr. H. A. Hollond, was Rouse Ball Professor of English Law at Cambridge from 1943 to 1950. The senior trustee was the Revd. Dr. W. Marsh of St. Edmund Hall.

who was in deacon's orders, and who had been an undergraduate follower of Simeon, by prudent administration of his estate, was able to give large sums for this purpose.

The story is told that as Hathaway was descending the stairs of the Master's Lodgings at Pembroke, having concluded his business satisfactorily, he encountered the Bishop of Oxford. News had reached Samuel Wilberforce at Cuddesdon that there was a danger of St. Aldate's falling into the hands of the evangelicals. He at once ordered his horse, having resolved to offer Dr. Jeune two hundred pounds more than Hathaway and his friends. But it was too late. The transaction had been completed. The living of St. Aldate's was a royal gift, presented to the college by King Charles I. The story went round that Pembroke College had sold a church to build a dining hall. It is true that the society was in need of money to pay off some building debts. But the purchase price, one thousand pounds, did not, according to the college historian, go towards discharging them. It appears that the real reason why the fellows were so willing to part with this piece of their property lay in the fact that "Its emolument was scarcely £100 per annum; the rectory house was all but a ruin, as was the parish school house. The College thus found itself burdened with a living, the charge of which no member of the body was willing to accept." This time Hathaway and his friends decided that on the first vacancy — which occurred in the same year — "it would be advantageously supplied by the nomination of a clergyman, who, in point of age, might stand to undergraduates in the relation of an elder brother." It will be seen that the motive underlying the acquisition of the St. Aldates' advowson was in fact the same as that which Canon Smyth recognises in the case of Charles Simeon's patronage trust earlier in the century. In his fifth Birkbeck Lecture of 1937-8, Smyth concedes that this was "love to immortal souls," with a view to establishing a settled ministry and "fixing the gospel there in perpetuity." St. Clement's passed into broad church hands in 1861, after having had an evangelical ministry since 1855, and it was not finally regained until 1878. St. Ebbe's, after nearly fifty years of evangelical oversight, had a tractarian curate-in-charge from 1860 to 1868. It was not only desirable to provide evangelical ministries; it was necessary to ensure continuity of teaching.

The incumbent of St. Aldate's, the Revd. T. C. L. Layton, a former Fellow of Pembroke, was a man of only thirty-six, but he had obligingly expressed some intention of resigning and he ceded the living early in March 1859. He had been Rector of St. Aldate's for three years, and apparently held evangelical views himself, having been curate to John Hatchard at Plymouth. At this point unlooked-for difficulty arose. Various Oxford men were approached, but in spite of their evangelical sentiments, and the promise of financial assistance, none of them felt in a much better position to accept the living than had the fellows of Pembroke. Charles Oakley (author of the hymn "Hills of the North, rejoice") who as a Pembroke first-classman[1] and a known favourite with Dr. Jeune, seemed particularly suitable, and whose social status was underlined by his being a brother-in-law of the Earl of Ducie, unfortunately kept the patrons waiting for two months before declining. (Nevertheless he preached twice at St. Aldate's early in Christopher's time, but died a few years later.) The idea of appointing a Cambridge man had never entered the heads of Auriol or Hathaway, who were chiefly concerned in the search. But time was passing. The period of six months allowed to patrons for making a nomination was rapidly running out. The Bishop of Oxford would soon enjoy the right to appoint without having had to pay for it.

Then the Pembroke graduate, whose name has not been preserved, having heard Christopher speak at a missionary meeting at Shanklin, wrote recommending him both to Auriol, who had seen him several times a week at the headquarters of the Church Missionary Society, and to Hathaway, who had heard him address a meeting at Harrow where he himself lived. By the same post, without waiting for consultation, Auriol and Hathaway were independently offering the living to Christopher. "Long, anxious, and prayerful" had been the enquiry for one qualified for the work, and willing to accept it. Christopher himself had no intention of leaving a position for which he felt specially adapted. But he went up to Oxford to see the church and parish. He was present on the occasion of the monthly communion. It was not an encouraging experience. There were only

[1]An examiner in 1859-60 for the new honour school of law and history, he is said to have refused an Australian bishopric.

a dozen communicants, including the wife of the curate-in-charge. Christopher, with characteristic faith in one he considered better able to judge than himself, put the decision in the hands of Henry Venn. That honoured man said: "I think it is your duty to go to Oxford." In accepting the living, Christopher told Hathaway[1] that if he and his associates found they had made a mistake, they should say so at once, and he would resign as soon as a suitable man could be discovered. "For," said he, "I am sure the Committee of the C.M.S. will take me back as an Association Secretary." But as Hathaway wrote, "It soon became manifest not only that the appointment was of God, but that it was a conspicuous token of the large favour and blessing He had in store for Oxford."

The parish of St. Aldate's in 1859 consisted mainly of a part of the east side and most of the west side of the important street which forms the principal thoroughfare leading southwards out of Oxford from Carfax to Folly Bridge. Very few dwellings, apart from Grandpont House, existed then in the Berkshire portion of the parish beyond the river. The majority of those in St. Aldate's proper consisted of somewhat squalid courts behind the main street, several of which were cleared when the Christ Church War Memorial Garden was laid out, and the men's non-collegiate building, now Linacre House, erected, with the Police Station beyond. Some of the houses fronting the high road, and a few in Pembroke Street, were of sixteenth and seventeenth century date, or earlier, including the one called the Old Palace (of Robert King, last Abbot of Oseney and first Bishop of Oxford,[2]) and 83 St. Aldate's, part of a fifteenth century dwelling, which became in Christopher's time the original of 'Alice's shop'. Wolsey's almshouses, now the Master of Pembroke's Lodgings, adjoined the church. Pembroke College was mainly within the parish boundary, though as part of the 'Parish of the Colleges and Halls of the University of Oxford'

[1]The deed of presentation in the diocesan archives shows that Christopher was in fact presented to St. Aldate's by Samuel Hanson of Epsom, a partner in a city firm of fruit importers, and already a subscriber to the fund for supplementing the income of St. Peter-le-Bailey and St. Clement's. This was prepresumably a convenient legal arrangement. The deed was witnessed by Hathaway's clerk, on 15 August. The Master and Fellows of Pembroke had conveyed the advowson on 3 February to Hanson and a London solicitor, Robert Sweeting, whose firm had been negotiating with them since the previous October, and were also subscribers to the augmentation fund. In the following February (1860), Hanson conveyed the advowson to Simeon's Trustees.

[2]There is no evidence that it was ever Bishop King's palace.

27. ST. ALDATE'S, OXFORD, *c.* 1844, with CHRIST CHURCH beyond

28. ST. ALDATES' RECTORY, OXFORD, before 1877

it was free from parochial jurisdiction. To the west lay St. Ebbes' and Holy Trinity parishes; to the north and east, St. Martins', Carfax; to the south, the Hinkseys. The total population in 1859 amounted to less than 1,200 and consisted mainly of 'poor'. The parish officers were normally supplied from among a minority of local tradesmen. The schools were in bad condition. The old Rectory, in Pembroke Street, was not considered habitable. But the church, standing opposite Christ Church, and close to many of the colleges, was excellently situated from the point of view of influencing university men.

In spite of the drastic reconstruction involved in Christopher's plan of enlargement, St. Aldate's retains a number of interesting features from earlier days. Christopher himself, or his architect, preserved five small Norman arches from the chancel. But a church had probably stood on the site even earlier. St. Aldate *may* have been a Saxon saint, St. Eldad. It has often been suggested that the name was a corruption of 'saint at the old gate', for the south gate of Oxford stood between Wolsey's almshouses and Christ Church; but there was in mediaeval times another church there, St. Michael's-at-Southgate, destroyed when Wolsey's great quadrangle was planned. In the course of the centuries several versions were used: St. Toll's, St. Oolde's, and even St. Olave's; and every true Oxonian knows that 'St. Aldate's' is always referred to as 'St. Ald's', pronounced 'St. Old's'. It is probable that the present chancel arch marks the position of the original Norman one, although the dimensions of the church have been extended everywhere else. The south aisle was originally built in 1336 by John de Docklyngton, fishmonger and five times Mayor of Oxford. The north aisle was erected by Philip Polton — who was probably not, as is often stated, a Fellow of All Souls, but was certainly Archdeacon of Gloucester, — in the middle of the following century. In the reign of Queen Elizabeth I, an attractive upper storey was added to Docklyngton's aisle, the chamber thus created being used first as a lecture room, and afterwards as a library, by Pembroke College. This had been taken down before Christopher became rector.

A rich fifteenth century font was adorned in Queen Anne's time with a handsome wooden cover, the crossing of the Red Sea being painted on its panels. The fine alabaster tomb of John Noble, who in 1522 died Principal of Broadgates Hall — the predecessor of Pembroke College — was also preserved in Christopher's reconstruction. At the west end of the church are two small wall-brasses of late sixteenth and early seventeenth century date, commemorating younger members of Christ Church and Broadgates Hall in their academic robes — fitting ornaments in a church which was to be so particularly concerned with the spiritual welfare of undergraduates. The building held about four hundred and fifty people. Only thirty-five seats, however, were available for the poor of the parish. The pews were ranged north and south, with some east and west, so that as many worshippers as possible could see the preacher in the pulpit in the middle of the south wall of Docklyngton's aisle. This pulpit was of early Georgian design with a sounding board. But the seating dated only from 1832, though it followed a previous arrangement. A singing gallery, with an organ, was placed in the lower portion of a small west tower, which, with its spire, was of the early fourteenth century. The font stood beneath the gallery. Christopher moved it to its present more prominent position in 1860.[1]

It may be supposed that some notable clergymen had served as rectors of St. Aldate's. Many of the presentations made by Pembroke, however, had fallen — probably owing to the small value of the living — to rather undistinguished fellows of the college, few of whom retained it for longer than a few years. Indeed, since the Reformation scarcely more than half a dozen of Christopher's predecessors had been men of mark. Nicholas Pullen, instituted in 1565, became Principal of St. Edmund Hall. Richard Cluett, Rector from 1614 to 1617, was made Archdeacon of Middlesex. His successor, John Wall, who held the living until 1637, became a Canon of Christ Church, and continued to hold his canonry throughout the Commonwealth and Protectorate, in spite of some doubts as to whether his protestantism was sufficiently pronounced. Several of his sermons — including *Evangelical Spices* (1627) — were published while he was Rector of St. Aldate's, "where he gained some fame as a preacher." He was also a benefactor of the city. Archbishop Williams described him as "the best read in the fathers that he ever knew."

[1]After the rebuilding of 1862, it was resited near the south door, where it remained till 1925, when it was restored to the place to which Christopher had moved it in 1860.

William Stampe, the first nominee of Pembroke, and naturally (as the King had presented the advowson to the college) a staunch royalist, held the living from 1637 to 1641, but was imprisoned after sequestration by the Westminster Assembly, and died an exile at the Hague. William Hawkins, a descendant of Sir John Hawkins, a theologian of some note and Professor of Poetry 1751-6, held the living at the end of his life, from 1796 to 1801. One of the earliest Bampton Lecturers, his attitude towards evangelicalism may readily be guessed from the fact that not long after the expulsion of the 'Six Students' from St. Edmund Hall in 1768, he preached and published two university sermons entitled *The Pretences of Enthusiasts considered, and confuted*. Two successive Masters of Pembroke must not be overlooked. William Sergrove was Rector 1774-89, and John Smyth from 1789 to 1796. A more recent incumbency, though only of six months' duration, had been that of Henry Polehampton, instituted in 1849, whose subsequent association with India would have been of particular interest to Christopher. In 1855 he accepted an East India chaplaincy, reached Calcutta in 1856, and was appointed chaplain to the Lucknow garrison. Early in the siege of 1857 he was wounded by a stray shot, dying a fortnight later while the first great attack was being made on the Residency. Havelock afterwards attested the value of his influence.

All these names, however, are overshadowed by two others: Thomas James, first Bodley's Librarian, and John Hall, Bishop of Bristol. James, a man as well known for his strong protestantism as for his remarkable scholarship, became Rector of St. Aldate's in 1602, the year that he was appointed Librarian, and held the living for twelve years.[1] John Hall was a divine in many ways after Christopher's own heart. "A puritan by birth and education," as a popular young Fellow of Pembroke he was elected Master of the college in 1664, and was instituted to St. Aldate's in the same year. To his church he attracted, by his "edifying way of preaching," large congregations of what Anthony Wood, the antiquary, a high churchman, called "the precise people, and scholars of Oxon." In 1676, Hall became Lady Margaret Professor of Divinity, and after

[1]Bodley himself had sat under Calvin as a youthful exile, and remained a convinced protestant.

he had preached " sharply and bitterly against the papists " at St. Mary's on 5 November 1678, during the first excitement of the Popish Plot, Wood could only speak of him as a " malepert presbyterian." He was in fact a doctrinal calvinist.

In 1691 Hall was nominated Bishop of Bristol. But the endowments of that see being notoriously poor, he continued to hold his mastership of Pembroke and the rectory of St. Aldate's, *in commendam,* till the end of his life. Indeed, he lived chiefly at Oxford, in the new Lodgings which he had built at Pembroke, and was " known more in than out of Oxford," it was said, " as a good man laughed at by the wits, but esteemed for his godliness by pious people." In spite of strong disapproval of his views, the antiquary Hearne acknowledged him to have been " a learned Divine, a good Preacher and his lectures . . . excellent . . ." According to Calamy, the only favourable contemporary so far quoted, he knew how to bring "all the theology of the Westminster assembly out of the church catechism." " To some extent a representative man," says Dr. Abbey, he was " the only bishop upon the Bench of a school of thought which once numbered so many distinguished names in the English hierarchy." Nevertheless in 1695 he was considered by many a fit person to succeed Tillotson as Archbishop of Canterbury. In his life-time a considerable benefactor of the college, dying in 1709/10, he bequeated his books to Pembroke library, which was then transferred from the upper chamber of St. Aldates' south aisle and brought within the college walls. A tablet high above the south door of the church, recently restored, recalls his benefactions to the parish. His epitaph at Bromsgrove — he had been born at the Vicarage there — records the zeal with which he had driven back "ingruentes Romae et Socini errores".

The parish clergymen of Oxford when Christopher was appointed were hardly of this stamp. But it is a fact that there were no less than six parishes with evangelical ministries in 1859 — St. Martin's, St. Clement's, St. Ebbe's, St. Peter-le-Bailey, Holy Trinity, and St. Aldate's itself. In most of the other churches of Oxford, a moderate churchmanship prevailed. The only ones where 'ritualistic' practices had been brought in on an elaborate scale were the rather remote St. Thomas's, where T. Chamberlain, Senior Student of Christ Church, had been incumbent long before his introduction of vestments about 1854, and St. Paul's, Walton Street, a daughter church of St. Thomas's. St. Mary's, the university church, was no longer a centre of tractarian influence. Newman, it is true, had been succeeded after an interval, by Charles Marriott, but in 1859 Percy Chase, Principal of St. Mary Hall, was Vicar, to be followed, in 1863, by John Burgon, champion of the older orthodoxy.

As regards evangelical representation in the university, Dr. Symons remained Warden of Wadham until 1871. Dr. Cotton's reign at Worcester had over twenty years to run, until his death in 1880. Dr. Macbride, Principal of Magdalen Hall, held office until 1868. But already by 1859, these worthies were all comparatively elderly. Macbride was eighty; Symons was seventy-four; even Cotton was sixty-five. Dr. Jeune, a vigorous Vice-Chancellor from 1858 to 1862, became Bishop of Peterborough in 1864. Charles Heurtley, Lady Margaret Professor of Divinity since 1853, and an authority on the creeds, continued to hold his chair until 1895. Robert Walker, who had been Professor of Experimental Philosophy since 1839, and a noted evangelical preacher, died in 1865. John Conington, Corpus Professor of Latin since his conversion in 1854, lived only until 1869. Robert Payne Smith, Headmaster of Kensington Proprietary School, had accepted a sub-librarianship at the Bodleian Library in 1857, partly in order to facilitate his literary researches.

Robert Gandell, Tutor of Magdalen Hall, and secretary of the Oxford auxiliary of the Church Pastoral-Aid Society from 1854 to 1866, became Laudian Professor of Arabic in 1861, holding the chair — from 1880 with a canonry at Wells — until his death in 1887. The Pembroke fellowship of William de Quetteville, who had been to some extent instrumental in acquiring the St. Aldates' advowson but who took a country living in 1861, lapsed in the following year. William Knight of Worcester and Alfred Peel of All Souls were Fellows of their respective colleges until 1863. Peel, however, had a living in Ireland. Knight certainly did not reside, for since 1851 he had served as an assistant secretary to Henry Venn at the London headquarters of the Church Missionary Society, in which capacity the new Rector of St. Aldate's was already familiar to him. William Willson, in much later years an ally of Christopher's when an Oxfordshire incumbent, was from 1859 to 1864 a non-resident Fellow of St. John's, preaching at St. Aldate's in 1860.

Thus Christopher came to a city and university in which evangelical religion had flourished and was flourishing. He came to the diocese of Oxford at a time when there was considerable feeling, not confined to evangelicals, that this part of the province of Canterbury had developed symptoms of an "alarming state". In particular, the diocesan college founded five years earlier at Cuddesdon, had put on an advanced high church complexion, and clerical mistrust had been voiced, if hardly allayed, by public discussion in a series of pamphlets. Early in 1859, C. P. Golightly, once Newman's curate, but for many years a non-party man, had published *Facts and Documents,* a general indictment of nascent anglo-catholicism in the diocese. In April, E. A. Litton, Rector of St. Clement's, Oxford, addressed the Bishop, Dr. S. Wilberforce, in an open letter signed by seventy-five diocesan clergy. A month after, W. R. Fremantle, subsequently Dean of Ripon, wrote his *Reasons for Signing.* (This did not prevent his acting within a few years as secretary of the early diocesan conferences.) Later on in May, John Tucker, now one of the surviving veterans from the Corpus of Arnold and the Kebles, as recently at 1848 its Vice-President, but with missionary experience in India, wrote a *Rejoinder* to the Bishop's official reply to Litton.

Already in February, though not as a direct result of Golightly's agitation, which had been going on since 1857, the Vice-Principal of the college at Cuddesdon, H. P. Liddon, by whom Christopher was called to the defensive on a notable occasion twenty years later, had resigned. He was appointed, however, Vice-Principal of St. Edmund Hall, whence for the next three years, and thereafter from Christ Church, he exerted a considerable influence on undergraduates. His principal at the Hall, the Revd. Dr. John Barrow, had terminated the vice-principalship of E. A. Litton in 1854, thereby ending an evangelical tradition which had existed without intermission since 1783. While Liddon was Vice-Principal, Barrow himself resigned his office, and in 1867 became a Jesuit. Such trends seemed even more disturbing to those who remembered the Church of England in far different shape, than they did to later generations, who had known them as a major influence all their lives. At a period of crisis, what Christopher did bring to Oxford was a unique personal quality, and it is this which constitutes one of his principal claims to a full record of life and work.

Chapter VII

Beginning at St. Aldate's

1859 - 1862

CHRISTOPHER was instituted — privately, no doubt, but by Dr. Wilberforce in person — on 27 August 1859; and thus began an incumbency which was to make a Cambridge man a veritable part of Oxford. On the following day he read himself in. "Read the 39 Articles & declared unfeigned assent and consent thereto." The invaluable series of preachers' books of St. Aldate's, amounting to comprehensive service registers, initiated by Henry Swabey on his institution in 1851, and unusual at so early a period, show that Christopher did not subsequently officiate until 16 October. The Revd. Francis Hannan, an Irish clergyman, continued to take the services as he had done previously. Christopher retained his assistance until Christmas 1859. The delay in moving to Oxford was no doubt partly caused by the problem of where to live. Probably it seemed unwise at this early stage to spend money on the old Rectory. The new Rector could not tell how long he might remain. There were other objects — the schools, for instance — for which it would be necessary to find considerable sums. Christopher was a good 'beggar'; but it was not in his nature to start first on improving his own parsonage by such means. His personal resources were strictly limited. But the nearest house — and it was emphasized that it was not considered a big one (certainly its garden is small) — both available and suitable, was in Park Town, a formally developed private 'estate', dating from the same decade, then on the outskirts of north Oxford[1] and over a mile from St. Aldate's. The Christophers called it 'Richmond Lodge'. They had lived at Richmond for ten years, and in spite of some grievous associations, it was endeared to them.

The evidence of the available Oxford directories of the period as to which was the house occupied by Christopher is seriously confusing, and there are no rate books of this date. But examination of title deeds has shown that Richmond Lodge was 1, Park Town, which however did not pass into Christopher's own possession until 1862. For many years this property has been known as 68, Banbury Road. Until recently an upstairs study was lined with dark built-in book-cases similar to those installed by Christopher at St. Aldates' Rectory when he rebuilt it. Nearby, at 5, Park Crescent,[2] lived a congenial if elderly neighbour, the Revd. Thomas Tyndale, who had been an undergraduate friend of Bishop Daniel Wilson of Calcutta, and had retired from the living of Holton, near Wheatley, to spend his last years in Oxford, where he died in 1865. In the later 'sixties Christopher had among his neighbours in Park Town the Revd. Edwin Hatch, Vice-Principal of St. Mary Hall, historian of the early church and author of the hymn "Breathe on me, Breath of God" (who had become a member of the Church of England through the ministry of a friend of Christopher, Dr. J. C. Miller, Rector of Birmingham), the Revd. Dr. Joseph Bosworth, Rawlinson Professor of Anglo-Saxon, and Rector of Water Shelford, Buckinghamshire, another survivor from the eighteenth century, the Revd. W. D. Macray, chronicler of Magdalen men, author of *Annals of the Bodleian Library,* and a young curate of St. Mary Magdalene, C. J. H. Fletcher, well-known in later years as a broad church Rector of Carfax. It cannot be said that when Christopher came to Oxford he received a very hearty welcome. He was a Cambridge man (as indeed was Bosworth), and he did not possess the distinctive manner or the distinctive culture of the Oxford of that day. In any case he belonged to an unfashionable school of thought; and he was at first treated with coldness. It was only with the passage of time that opinion changed, and men of all shades of belief came to

[1]There were no houses at this time between the Parks and Park Town.
[2]Now 22, Park Town.

honour him for his sincerity, his whole-heartedness, and his transparency of character.

Every day, Christopher went into the parish. Certain words of the puritan John Eliot, the first missionary to the North American Indians (Eliot was also a member of Jesus College, Cambridge), which Christopher was never tired of quoting, must have seemed particularly apposite at this time: "Prayer and pains through faith in Jesus Christ will accomplish all that it is God's will for us to do." Christopher had two primary obligations: towards his parishioners, and towards the undergraduate members of the university. To some extent they intermingled. It was not likely that Christopher would make much impact on the learned world of Oxford; but that was not his appointed task. Although a wrangler, he was not an intellectual, much less a scholar. "Divagations of a literary character," recalled Edmund Knox, afterwards Bishop of Manchester, a scholar of Corpus in the mid-'sixties, "caused his ear-trumpet to drop lower and lower or even to be laid aside." There were others in Oxford far better equipped to bear witness to the truths of evangelicalism in the senior common-rooms. Yet there was an undoubted weakness here, as far as influencing the keenest undergraduate minds was concerned. Christopher, however, was accustomed to remind his university friends that a man who took his stand as an evangelical must not be content with mediocrity in the schools. "No one," wrote John Matthews of Pembroke, afterwards Vicar of St. Peter's, Derby, who took a first class in mathematics in 1861, "could have shewn a greater interest in our studies or rejoiced more heartily at any success we gained in 'The Schools'. I seem to feel still his warm grip of the hand, to see his face lighted up with gladness, and to hear his cheery 'Oh, I'm so glad; thank God'."

To the majority of university men, however, it was probably of more significance that Christopher had played — albeit on the wrong side — in university cricket. Generally speaking, he was intellectually competent; and his organising ability was important both for his parochial and university work. His deafness, though, at least in theory, was a grave disadvantage. Yet his character was such that to know him was to love him. Arthur Downer, a Brasenose undergraduate of the later 'sixties — afterwards Vicar of St. Cuthbert's, Bedford, and author of *A Century of Evangelical Religion in Oxford*

— tells us: " It was an inspiration to be in his company. Can anyone who ever met him in the streets of Oxford forget his greeting? When still ten yards away, his features lighted up with pleasure as he recognised a friend. 'Ah, *brother,*' he would say with a fervour that was irresistible, and he would grasp one's hand with such cordiality that hard indeed must have been your heart if it did not glow with a responsive thrill . . ." The parish was not allowed to suffer in favour of the university men who soon began to attend his church. The same writer observed that " In his parish work among a poor population he was earnest and diligent." " We often met him," wrote Matthews of Pembroke, " coming out of the dingy courts in his Parish, on our way to or from Folly Bridge (for the River and the Boats)."

From the first, Christopher 'laid himself out' for the good of town and gown alike. To him, as Bishop Knox has said, "Professors, Christ Church undergraduates, College servants, shop-keepers, labourers, were all . . . beings with immortal souls, either saved or lost." "He felt," wrote George Butler of University College, afterwards Rector of Broad Mayne, Dorset, who was in his second year in 1859, and had been Secretary of the Union the term before Christopher's arrival, " that each of the thousand men[1] at Oxford passing through his course there would be going out into a wider sphere of action either positive for good, or negative, or positive for evil; and he was anxious to do all that in him lay to bring each one under gospel motives, that so the unsaved might be won to Christ while yet young, and that those who were already inclined to God's ways might be strengthened for an active service in after life." Christopher was certainly not the man to suffer from any misgivings as to whether the spiritual welfare of undergraduates could be exclusively the concern of the college tutors and chaplains. In any case in those days college chaplains were more inclined to think of their duties in terms of taking services. In order to bring himself into line with his academic surroundings, Christopher took an *ad eundem* degree in 1860 and always wore an Oxford master's hood. In order to make sure that as far as possible parish and university alike received the attention which was their due, he took a curate.

[1]In 1860 there were in fact some 1,400 undergraduates. Even this figure, however, is not appreciably greater than the probable number of junior members of the university at the beginning of the thirteenth century.

He himself has recorded the way he was led to the man who was to assist him in the pastoral work of St. Aldate's for most of his first eight years. " I was one day walking in the Parks praying for a good curate. I can almost remember the tree I was passing when it flashed across my memory that Mrs. Symons, the wife of the late Warden of Wadham . . . had remarked to me that 'if Moody, of St. Clement's, had lived he would have had Nash, of Worcester, as his curate.' I instantly went to the Porter's Lodge of Worcester College to inquire where Mr. Nash lodged. I found him in St. John's [*sic*] Street. After talking with him I felt convinced God had guided me to the right man." Tom Nash was still an undergraduate, but older than usual, having been in business, and known to his friends as 'Father Nash'. He had been superintendent of the St. Clements' boys' Sunday School. He took his degree in 1860, and was thirty when ordained at the end of the year.

It appears that Christopher also considered an offer from Robert Girdlestone of Christ Church, afterwards first Principal of Wycliffe Hall. Girdlestone, however, was deemed to be unsound on baptism! Meanwhile Christopher engaged the Revd. George Collins to act as his assistant, until the man of his choice was ready. Collins had been a lieutenant in the 4th (King's Own) Royal Regiment in India. He had then gone up to Cambridge to take a degree, and Bishop Sumner of Winchester ordained him in 1857. On leaving St. Aldate's he became incumbent of St. Mary's, Bradford. In May 1860 Christopher commenced a Thursday evening service. On the afternoons of the first Sunday in the month, he introduced a service of Evening Prayer for children, when attendance soon averaged 170, which approximately corresponded to the number of children in the Sunday School. Evening Prayer for adults was apparently already held at 7 p.m. In October, Christopher introduced a new hymn book — "Kemble's",[1] which was now widely used in evangelical churches.

At Advent, Thomas Augustus Nash was ordained on the title of St. Aldate's, and remained with Christopher until 1868. Christopher loved and respected his curates, and they in turn revered him.

[1]*The Church Psalmody* of Charles Kemble, a Wadham man, for many years Rector of Bath. A third, enlarged and adapted, edition, containing hymns and psalms, appeared in this year.

" I worked with dear Mr. Christopher," wrote Nash, " in the closest bonds of love and affection for nearly eight years, and never saw or heard an inconsistency in his life." Those were the early days of the total abstinence movement. The older evangelicals had taken their daily glass of wine as a matter of course. But force of example was beginning to be considered by many as one of the best ways to reduce the bad drinking habits of working men and women. Christopher himself was never an abstainer. A bottle of Marsala was usually in evidence in the dining room at the Rectory in later years. But Nash soon gave up drinking alcohol altogether, and found that his temperance work helped his parochial activities. *The Fourth Annual Report of the St. Aldate's Christian Temperance Society*, with Nash as president, shows that by 1866 premises had been acquired at 62, St. Aldate's, results were encouraging, and weekly meetings were being held in the boys' school. As might be expected, Christopher himself was not an officer, but " his unvaried kindness upon all occasions " is acknowledged. Not content with a curate, Christopher installed a Scripture reader, Mr. W. Pledge, in the old Rectory.

Even before Christopher was fairly settled at Oxford, and perhaps to some extent because of his advent, changes were taking place among the other incumbents and dons who represented evangelicalism in city and university. In 1860 George Cameron, after thirteen years, gave up his curacy-in-charge of St. Ebbe's. In the following year he became Vicar of Heckington, Lincolnshire, where it happened that one branch of the Christophers survived into the nineteenth century, and where it may well be that the family as a whole originated in the fourteenth. Cameron's successor at St. Ebbe's was a tractarian, the Revd. S. Y. N. Griffith, afterwards Vicar of Cumnor, who remained in charge until the death of the unfortunate Rector in 1868. Richard Hales resigned Carfax in the same year that Cameron left St. Ebbe's. In 1861 Edward Litton ceded St. Clement's. Thus three Oxford parish churches ceased to have an evangelical ministry soon after Christopher's arrival, though two were ultimately regained. In the university, however, Monier Williams, a devout evangelical, was elected Boden Professor of Sanskrit at this time, holding his chair until 1897; Robert Gandell of Magdalen Hall, who was Senior Proctor in 1860, became Laudian Professor of Arabic in 1861; and W. H. Ranken, afterwards Vicar of

29. A. M. W. CHRISTOPHER, *c.* 1862

30. ALFRED CHARLES CHRISTOPHER
and HENRY SETON CHRISTOPHER, *c.* 1862
Sons of A. M. W. Christopher

31. MARIA FRANCES CHRISTOPHER, *c.* 1862
1816–1903
Wife of A. M. W. Christopher

Christ Church, Surbiton, was a Fellow of Corpus Christi College from 1862 until 1869.

Before we pass on to a description of Christopher's early activities in Oxford, some reference must be made to Mrs. Christopher, "one of the most amiable and gracious ladies," Downer has recorded, "whom I have been privileged to know"; "one whose influence," George Butler wrote, "lay in using it without asserting it." An undergraduate contemporary of Downer, though two or three years his junior, Francis Aglionby of Queen's, afterwards Vicar of Christ Church, Westminster,[1] has left a more elaborate tribute. "Her's was a character of rare gentleness and sweetness, a character in which were blended many of the higher Christian graces. A more devoted wife and mother never lived, and her influence was a sweet savour of Christ, wherever it was shed abroad. Many of the younger members of the University whose privilege it was to enjoy the hospitality of Richmond Lodge . . . will carry with them through life, fragrant memories of the gentle lady who dispensed it." "Great must have been the strain upon her," continues Butler, "that this invasion of the home would involve; but whether we made our visits one or two of us at a time, or a hundred at a time by invitation, the same placid spirit, and kindly smile, and warm welcome were never wanting."

Of their five children, two alone remained to her and her husband when they came to Oxford, Henry, aged nine, and Alfred, aged three. Maria Christopher's sister Caroline was apparently living at Richmond Lodge in 1860; but Miss Eliza Seton, sister of Sir Henry, who had resided with her niece and nephew by marriage for some years, died soon after their arrival. She was buried in St. Sepulchre's Cemetery, Walton Street. Thus early in Christopher's Oxford life it was necessary to provide a family burial place locally. No further interment, however, was called for until that of Maria Christopher forty years later. Here eventually, in a vault the existence of which he had known of during all but the earliest months of his ministry at St. Aldate's, Christopher's own remains were to be laid. His father, George Christopher, was still living at Morton House, Chiswick, in 1859; but he too died, in April 1861, having reached his eighty-second year. He left Alfred a reversionary interest in half his estate (approximately £4,000) on the death of his daughter Isabella, who

[1]Father of the Rt. Revd. J. O. Aglionby, Bishop of Accra 1924–51.

lived until 1898, when her brother was in his seventy-ninth year. By codicil, however, Alfred received £100 outright. With numerous relations, Christopher's life was punctuated at fairly regular intervals by family events, deaths, marriages, and births, of more or less intimacy. Two years after his father died, in January 1863, he lost his sister Matilda, followed a fortnight later by his brother-in-law General Thomson. In 1864 his elder son, Henry, was commissioned as a midshipman in the Navy; but he continued only three years in the service. Shortly after young Henry went to sea, Christopher's sister Margaret, who had made possible his Cambridge education, died at Chiswick. A note in the preachers' book of St. Aldate's suggests that the Rector received a telegram of summons as he was conducting divine service.

Christopher's influence soon made itself felt. " It was a great delight to some of us," recalled John Matthews, then a scholar of Pembroke, " when in 1859 the poor living of St. Aldate's was sold by Pembroke College . . . to learn that Mr. Christopher had accepted the post." Matthews, as we have seen, had met Christopher at Oxford in 1857. He was the first undergraduate to call at Richmond Lodge. Another second year man who quickly became intimate with the new Rector of St. Aldate's was John Sharp, also of Pembroke, afterwards for many years Secretary of the Bible Society. Sharp acted as librarian of the Church Missionary Collectors' Association, whose library Christopher allowed to be kept in the upper room at the Rectory which was used for parochial purposes. " In common with other undergraduates," wrote Sharp, " I could not but feel the earnestness and sincerity of his endeavours to help us spiritually, and especially to deepen our interest in missionary work." Sharp went down in 1860, but he remained a friend for fifty-three years.

A similar friendship existed between Christopher and George Butler of University, who was introduced to the new Rector of St. Aldate's by his friend Thomas Cawley of Wadham, afterwards Rector of Bittadon, Devon, during Christopher's first week in Oxford. Meeting in High Street, opposite the Turl, " He received us in that hearty friendly way in which he ever received everyone, as becomes one who feels himself a debtor to all men . . ." George Tonge of Magdalen Hall and Worcester, from 1864 to 1867 curate to Henry Linton at St. Peter-le-Bailey, when he saw "a good deal" of Christopher, was another who "was half through my undergraduate course, and at once I joined myself to those who rallied round him . . . Alongside of the depth of conviction and intense spiritual earnestness of our dear friend there was a refreshing frankness and naïvete which, if it sometimes provoked a smile, made one feel how genuinely human he was." Nevertheless Tonge did not attend St. Aldate's regularly as he had a Bible class in St. Clement's, though he frequented Christopher's Saturday evening prayer meeting. It seems likely that J. F. Kitto of St. Alban Hall, a contemporary of Sharp and afterwards a leading London evangelical, latterly as Vicar of St. Martin's-in-the-Fields from 1886 to 1903, and Prebendary of St. Paul's, was yet another who was drawn to St. Aldate's in 1859; as also perhaps was Henry Wace of Brasenose, who had taken a first in mathematical moderations in 1858. Wace became Bampton Lecturer in 1879, and a prominent evangelical; he was Dean of Canterbury from 1903 to 1924, in 1909 writing a preface for Christopher's *Quousque*. "My earliest recollections of Canon Christopher," wrote Dr. Allan Smith, Dean of St. David's, in 1915, "go back to 1860, when I first went up to read in Oxford before entering the University. From that time till his death he was a warm and generous friend . . ." For some years, we are told, the name 'Kittites' was used to describe Christopher's followers, as in Charles Simeon's days at Cambridge, men spoke of 'Sims'.

Christopher did not wait for undergraduates to call on him. He at once set about visiting them. Francis Pilcher of Oriel, afterwards for many years Rector of St. Clement's, Oxford, and father of Dr. C. V. Pilcher, co-adjutor Bishop of Sydney from 1936 to 1956, was one of the first recipients of such a visit. Pilcher had lately arrived from Australia, and a few days before the Michaelmas term of 1859 he came to lodge at 8, Merton Street. He had not been there many hours before Christopher called upon him. Before many minutes had passed he had knelt down with him in prayer. Cases of sickness — always an unpleasant experience in college — were as promptly visited. At least one undergraduate, George Allan of St. Alban Hall, never forgot Christopher's thoughtfulness in this connection. "I think it was not later than the second day of my illness that Mr. Christopher sent his Curate (Mr.

Nash) to see me. I never understood how he had so quickly heard of my indisposition . . . " With the same kind of influence at work in the parish as well, it was not surprising that St. Aldate's gradually filled. By 1860, average attendance at ordinary services was 300. Communicants, of whom a list was kept, numbered approximately 48 at festivals and 23 at the monthly administration. It is fair to say that this, in some measure, represented a return to the state of affairs in the second year at least of the previous ministry. At the episcopal visitation of 1857, Rector Layton returned 70 communicants at great festivals, 40 at the monthly sacrament, and an attendance, which was increasing, of between 300 and 400 at Morning and Evening Prayer. In 1854 the numbers had been even better. Swabey — who had two curates and lived at the Rectory — reported 80 and 50 communicants, with 400 to 500 as the average number of his congregation. By 1861 the church was overflowing. In term time seventy or eighty undergraduates were present at morning or evening service on Sundays.

From the first, Christopher had proved attractive to young men, in church as well as in personal intercourse. The Revd. Charles Smith, latterly Rector of Didsbury, wrote in 1913: "It was in the autumn of 1860 when I was, for a time, living near Oxford, that I went one evening to his church and heard him preach. His text was 'Almost thou persuadest me to be a Christian.' He began his sermon with these words, 'Of all the souls in this congregation who will be lost for ever, none will so bitterly regret it as those, who will have to admit that they once were 'almost' Christians.'" Such a style of preaching may sound indiscreet to modern ears, but it bore fruit. "As I heard the words," continues Smith, "I said to myself, — 'That is exactly my case.' I had been religiously brought up by the best of parents and had fully intended to give my heart to God, but I knew quite well, as I sat there, that I was but an 'almost' Christian. After the service I went back to my home, straight to my room, and on my bended knee told God exactly what my state was, and asked Him, with all earnestness, to make me altogether a Christian. The prayer without doubt was heard and answered. The great change took place then, though I had afterwards many ups and downs, yet it was the turning-point in my life. I was soon after exposed to the strong temptations which assail a young man, and I have no doubt that the Lord, to whom I had just given myself, was my Protector and Deliverer from the snares by which I was surrounded. Some years after that, when I saw dear Canon Christopher,[1] I told him the facts of the case and it was, of course, a great joy to him to know that he had been the means of leading me to God."

Christopher, although an able platform speaker, was not a remarkable preacher, a fact of which he was well aware. Yet he was competent enough to guide others. "Dear Nash," he wrote, "did not at once become the excellent preacher he was for so many years. Like many other humble-minded men, he at first preached in a low and somewhat monotonous tone of voice. I said to him, 'If you would only preach your sermons as if you felt they were worth hearing, they would, I think, do more good.' He replied, 'But I don't think they are worth hearing.' However, in time he got over the early tameness of manner, and became an awakening Mission Preacher, as well as a preacher valued by Bible-reading Christians who desired to be built up, strengthened and taught."

In the pulpit, Christopher was inclined to repeat himself, a fault which was not without its advantages, as one of his undergraduate hearers of those days, Allan of St. Alban Hall, afterwards Rector of Puckington, Somerset, has recorded. Allan's father, as Rector of St. Mary's, Cricklade, had been, as we have noticed, one of Christopher's supporters in the association work of the Church Missionary Society. Naturally his son attended St. Aldate's when he came up to Oxford in 1861. "I had been brought up under strong Evangelical teaching," wrote Allan, "but I am indebted to Mr. Christopher's clear and reiterated exposition of some cardinal truths for a more intelligent and defined understanding of them than I ever had before. It is true that there *was* iteration in his preaching, and I remember a friend . . . assigning this as a reason for not accompanying me to St. Aldate's one Sunday evening. I suggested that there was some comfort in knowing *what* you *were* going to hear! . . . It may be recalled that one of his first congregation said to Dr. Fairbairn,[2] 'We like your preaching, because we aye ken what ye'll say afore ye've said it'."

[1]Smith came up to Wadham in 1863.
[2]Perhaps A. M. Fairbairn, first Principal of Mansfield College.

Conscious of his own shortcomings in this respect, Christopher was doubtless all the more anxious to procure well-known evangelical preachers to address his congregation. Some of the most celebrated clergymen in the evangelical world responded to his invitation. The opportunity which it offered was not to be neglected. Thus we hear of Canon Hugh Stowell, of St. Edmund Hall, leader of the evangelicals at Manchester; of Hugh McNeile, afterwards Dean of Ripon, whose influence dominated Liverpool; of John Miller, Rector of Birmingham, a former scholar of Lincoln (who had preached at St. Aldate's for Christopher's predecessor in 1857); of William Carus, still a residentiary Canon of Winchester, but now Vicar of Christ Church in that city, under whom Christopher himself had sat as an undergraduate in Cambridge; of Thomas French, "the most distinguished of all C.M.S. missionaries," who had been a Fellow of University College, and became Bishop of Lahore; of John Richardson of Bury St. Edmund's, afterwards Archdeacon of Southwark. These gentlemen had not travelled long distances for nothing! French preached for over an hour. Stowell was longer still. Christopher himself had to stand up near the pulpit in order to benefit at all. "Now, brother," he would say, when a strange preacher came to St. Aldate's, "you must make the deaf hear."

An examination of the preachers' books of St. Aldate's affords some notable additions to the above, not mentioned elsewhere, for the first six years of Christopher's incumbency. During the earlier 'sixties came Vincent Ryan of Magdalen Hall, Bishop of Mauritius; George Smith, also of Magdalen Hall, Bishop of Victoria, Hong Kong; Charles Perry, Bishop of Melbourne; David Anderson of Exeter College, Vicar of Clifton, formerly Bishop of Rupertsland; Samuel Crowther, Bishop of the Niger, the first African bishop in modern times; John Utterton of Oriel, Archdeacon of Surrey, afterwards first suffragan Bishop of Guildford; and two former Fellows of Wadham, Stephen Langston of Southborough, Kent, and Thomas Vores of St. Mary's-in-the-Castle, Hastings. These were all "men of renown" among the evangelicals. It would not have seemed right to Christopher to invite into his pulpit a clergyman who preached in any other strain.

Christopher's own deficiencies in preaching made him the more sympathetic toward diffident ordinands. Most young clergymen, he maintained, could acquire the power of preaching from notes with facility and usefulness, and he often recommended undergraduates to learn to speak in this way. He went so far as to prescribe a formula, which he wrote down in later years. "Take one, or perhaps two portions of Bishop Ryle's 'Expository Thoughts on the Gospels'.[1] Fix the clear divisions in your memory, or if you cannot trust your memory at first, have these divisions written on a sheet of note paper with a few of the leading thoughts under each division. Read over all that Bishop Ryle says on that portion three or four times. Then go and read the portion of the Gospel, and give your expository thoughts as best you can, without your sheet of note paper before you, at a cottage lecture to half a dozen elderly women and others, taking care that there is not among them such an intelligent Christian as I had as a hearer at my first 'extempore' Thursday evening lecture! I do not believe that there is one young Clergyman in ten who could not, if he will only persevere in this plan, acquire the power of extempore speaking and preaching with sufficient facility. I do not recommend him to give up writing sermons. If he have to preach twice on one Sunday I should recommend him to write the morning sermon."

Visiting preachers at St. Aldate's were also commissioned to give a Bible reading on the previous Saturday evening in the old Rectory. It was not a large house, and the only room in which undergraduates could be assembled was severely cramped. The ceiling was so low that it was possible for anyone standing to touch it with his hand. The 'Upper Room', as Christopher called it, was apt to be somewhat crowded. Christopher himself normally gave a Bible reading and led the extempore prayer which followed. He never tired of expounding *Romans* V and VIII. But, adds Allan, "I feel that *not once too often* did I listen to Canon Christopher in 'a course on Romans'." "Many times," wrote Downer, "have I sat listening with intense feeling to his simple fervent words." Again Aglionby elaborates: "His insistence upon the doctrines of grace, his appeals to us to believe in the love of a living, personal Saviour and to trust Him fully, his urgent exhortations to seek out those about us and bring them to the knowledge of Christ — all these were indelibly engraved on our hearts . . . " This sentence,

[1]First published in the 'fifties and 'sixties.

it deserves to be remembered, was written by a man whose name stood alone in the first class of the honour school of theology in 1873. These meetings, begun in Hilary term 1860, were held by Christopher for forty-five years.

In the middle 'sixties three contemporaries who were to be influential in the first part of the twentieth century, Edmund Knox, Francis Chavasse, both of Corpus, and John Diggle of Merton, subsequently Bishops of Manchester, Liverpool and Carlisle respectively, regularly sat under Christopher in the 'Upper Room', together with Diggle's brother — like the three bishops a first-classman — who became chairman of the London School Board, and Churchill Julius of Worcester, son of Christopher's doctor at Richmond, afterwards first Archbishop of New Zealand. Christopher, Bishop Ingham tells us, was a great introducer. "You two ought to know each other," he would say; and thus generation after generation of evangelical undergraduates from different colleges made acquaintance through St. Aldate's. The first generation, which Allan of St. Alban Hall met in this way, included William Hooper of Wadham, a first-classman of 1859, afterwards well known as the most learned missionary of the Church Missionary Society in India, the Wathens, of the same college and vocation, Edward Moore of Worcester, later one of the first clerical supporters of the Keswick movement, and the Bardsleys of Queen's, sons of Canon Bardsley of Manchester, that great progenitor of clergymen who had been guided to ordination under the ministry of an Oxford evangelical of an earlier generation, George Grundy of Hey.

Christopher began a course of sermons on *The Epistle to the Romans* early in his Oxford life. He felt that such an important part of the Bible ought to be familiar to his young friends, especially those training for the ministry; and he took immense trouble over these discourses. In the second term of their delivery, he was much startled and pained by a letter from two of the trustees of the living begging him seriously to consider whether his style of sermon, and especially 'a course of sermons', was likely to attract the undergraduate world. The complaint — that the sermons were dry — had been forwarded by a Pembroke undergraduate, described by one of his contemporaries as " a weak, fidgetty, fussy man." Christopher

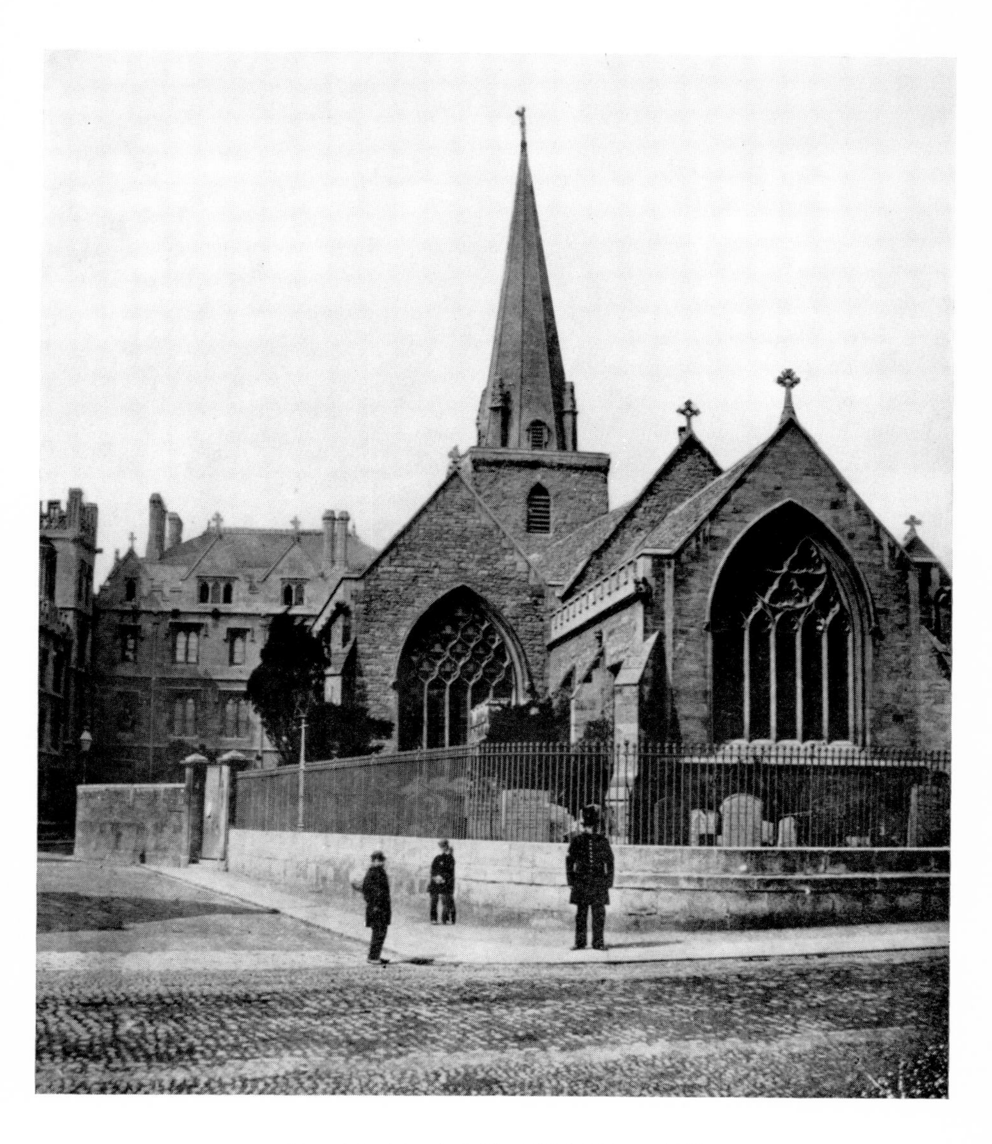

32. ST. ALDATE'S, OXFORD, *c.* 1861
Before A. M. W. Christopher's reconstruction

33. 68, BANBURY ROAD, OXFORD, 1963
formerly RICHMOND LODGE, PARK TOWN
Home of A. M. W. Christopher 1859–71

34. 68, BANBURY ROAD, OXFORD, 1963
Garden entrance to former drawing-room

was greatly upset, and having previously received some warm thanks from two or three other undergraduates for the clear and full statements of truth these sermons contained, he asked them to write a few words of grateful acknowledgement which he could send to Edward Hathaway, and to Henry Venn, who had strongly recommended his appointment. "Before these letters were forwarded by us," wrote John Matthews of Pembroke, "he withdrew his request; telling us, with a humility that drew us to him more closely than ever, that it was far better for him to submit with patience to the rebuke his Heavenly Father had graciously allowed him to receive." "My forty-six years' Ministry," wrote George Allan, "owes indeed much to what I learned from this revered Teacher of my younger days."

It was in fact in personal relationships that the secret of Christopher's influence lay. Downer has recorded that "It was Mr. Christopher's practice in term time to remain at home during the day[1] to receive visits from undergraduates, to each of whom he addressed words of warm sympathy and counsel, frequently inviting them to join with him in prayer; and he used to furnish them with tracts and books of an Evangelical character." "His geniality of manner," wrote Aglionby, "and cordial welcome won the heart of every new comer. There was none of the reserve which too often chills and constrains intercourse between older and younger men. If you found him alone, or with others when you called, he gave himself fully to you, entering into your interests, giving cheer and sympathy out of a full heart, and as a rule committing you in earnest prayer to God's keeping when you left him."

Nearly fifty years later, Bishop Chavasse of Liverpool recalled, at the dedication of a new, stained glass east window at St. Aldate's, how it was in October 1865 that as a freshman he went with a letter of introduction from his vicar in the country to call on Christopher at Richmond Lodge. At that time, he said, the Rector's figure was strong and upright, his step firm and elastic, his hair black, his smile the same attractive one which made every generation feel at home with him at once. His voice too, as George Butler has noted, was distinctive . . . "though perfectly natural, and free from parsonic intonation, [it] was yet peculiarly his own, of a rich timbre, with

[1]Between 3 and 4 p.m., according to an invitation printed on the last page of *A Few Thoughts,* a paper by Christopher published in 1868.

an emphatic pressure upon each syllable, and then a lengthening of the tone before the next syllable followed. It was a voice that was easily so imitated as to be recognisable as intended to represent his." Bishop Chavasse remarked that he remembered well going back to his college after his interview with Christopher feeling he had met with one who was a true father in God, and one to whom he could look for strength and counsel in the vicissitudes of university life. Of an interview in similar circumstances five years later, Ernest Ingham of St. Mary Hall, afterwards Bishop of Sierra Leone, wrote: "The loving sympathy, and 'the word of prayer' at the end of the visit, 'commending my University course to the Lord' — it was a revelation to me. It came most naturally to him, but to me it was almost a shock to kneel down in some place other than a church in such a familiar way. And from that moment I was one of Christopher's disciples."

"It must not be supposed," wrote Aglionby, "that he could never unbend. He had a delightful sense of humour, and no one could enjoy a good story more heartily or tell one with more charm. His stories and anecdotes did not suffer in the least from repetition. It was a treat when you could start him upon reminiscences of his earlier life. He loved to tell how he first came as a Cambridge undergraduate to play the Oxford Eleven . . . It was all but impossible for one who was continually making fresh acquaintances amongst young men to know each one whom he met. This made no difference to Canon Christopher. He would greet a young man with much warmth, converse with him for some time and if he had not meanwhile recalled his name, he would say most naïvely 'Dear brother, what is your name?' ! "

Nor was it only in undergraduate days that Christopher watched over the interests of his university friends. Charles Waller of University College — a nephew of George Cameron of St. Ebbe's, and a descendant of the poet Edmund Waller — took his degree with some distinction in 1863. After serving a brief curacy with William Pennefather at St. Jude's, Mildmay Park, he proposed going out to India, as his fiancée had been asked to take charge of a school for Anglo-Indians there, and young Waller was assured of work in the same place if they went out married. Waller wrote to Christopher to ask him for a recommendation. Christopher replied that he was "not going to set a razor to cut a hedge stake" — nor would he send him to India for the sake of it — but that he had just heard of something which would exactly suit Waller, namely the position of tutor at St. John's Hall, Highbury, under its Principal, the Revd. T. P. Boultbee. This theological college had only been founded — by Alfred Peache, a rich Wadham man, who was Vicar of Mangotsfield, and his sister — the year before, and Boultbee had been managing it alone. Now, however, the Principal had written to Christopher — a contemporary at St. John's, Cambridge — to ask him to recommend a tutor. Waller's letter arrived about the same time, so Boultbee was told that God had offered Waller to him, and that he would refuse him at his peril! Poor Waller was exceedingly shy,[1] and said so little for himself at the ensuing interview that Boultbee nearly rejected him. Yet in due course Christopher's judgement was more than justified, for Dr. Waller — who was elected first Denyer and Johnson scholar at the second award in 1866 — succeeded Dr. Boultbee as Principal.

The distribution of helpful books and tracts was a ministry which Christopher seemed to have made peculiarly his own, and many references occur to the practice from beginning to end of his Oxford life. "It was Mr. Christopher's delight," wrote Matthews of Pembroke, "to fill our bookshelves with the choice works of sound Divines." Almost every undergraduate who came to his study went away loaded with books and pamphlets. Sometimes he lent larger books, Dean Goode's *Divine Rule of Faith and Practice,* E. A. Litton's *Church of Christ,* or *The Book of Common Prayer: its History and Interpretation* by Canon R. P. Blakeney, one of the founders of the Church Association, who came to preach at St. Aldate's in 1867. A copy of the latter, with an inscription recording Christopher's gift of it to a Pembroke undergraduate, W. E. Malaher, in 1866, is now in the library of Tyndale House, Cambridge. He also gave away missionary books — to G. W. Butler, the biographies of Thomas Ragland and Henry Fox, both of India. Through reading the life of Ragland, Butler was led to offer himself for Christian work abroad, and was accepted; but family circumstances made it impossible for him to

[1]This seems surprising in view of the fact that in 1862 Waller had been Secretary of the Union.

go. Arthur Downer, when he paid his first call on Christopher, also in 1866, was presented with Mason's *Christian Communicant*. Sometimes Christian authors would send him a supply of books they had written, and the sermons of Canon Clayton, Vicar of Holy Trinity, Cambridge, were thus liberally distributed at Oxford.

One of Christopher's great favourites was *Christ Our Example* by Caroline Fry. He had been requested to open a discussion, at a clerical and lay conference, on the question "Is the Example of Our Lord brought forward in a sufficiently systematic manner by Ministers of the Gospel?" Christopher asked three friends, Charles Goodhart, Dr. Miller, Rector of Birmingham, and the Revd. S. R. Capel, Rector of Wareham, which they considered to be the best book on the example of Jesus Christ. Each one, without knowing that the others had been consulted, named Miss Fry's work *Christ Our Example*. Christopher mentioned this at the conference, and a clergyman, "known for his sound Scriptural writings," rose and said that when he had been an undergraduate at Oxford thirty years before — the tractarian movement was then at its height — he had fallen under the influence of 'mistaken teachers', but the reading of *Christ Our Example* was used of God to deliver him from the erroneous views which he had adopted. Christopher's recommendation of the book produced an increased circulation, and by 1872 the eighth edition was exhausted. Christopher then took upon himself the risk of publishing a ninth edition at one-third the previous price, in order to secure wider reading of it. To this edition, published by Hatchard, still at that time the leading evangelical publisher, he wrote a preface and broadcast leaflets recommending its usefulness. Christopher felt that the special merit of the book was that it was written with a clear understanding of the gospel of divine grace, without a belief in which no one would ever be able to follow the example of our Lord.

Another favourite was *God's Way of Peace* by Horatius Bonar. This he first used in 1862 on the recommendation of Canon Garratt of Ipswich that it was "the best uninspired book for the anxious ever written." Christopher highly esteemed Garratt, and he was not disappointed. Only a week after reading it, he sent one to a friend "of mature age, highly cultivated mind, and long-established Christian character, loved and honoured by many who knew his great value

I had seen him for some time wasting away in health, though continuing a very important work, requiring the full force of his clear mind and sound judgement; but I never discovered the cause of his worn look until...he wrote me—'Dear friend, pray for me that I may not doubt my acceptance with God in Christ.' I felt at once that *God's Way of Peace* was the very book for him, and sent it to him by return of post, thanking God that in his providence He had just led me to read it. About a month afterwards I received the following letter from my friend: 'My dear friend and beloved brother in Christ Jesus our Lord, — I shall have reason to adore and praise our reconciled, and loving, and gracious Father and God throughout eternity, that it pleased Him to put into your heart to send me *God's Way of Peace;* and still more, that He put it into the author's mind so to write, and yet more, that it pleased Him in his own infinite wisdom, grace, and pity, that such wondrous news should be true. It has pleased the God of all grace, within the last fortnight, not only to lead my soul from darkness into light, but to translate me into the kingdom of his dear Son, snatching me a brand (as it seemed already consuming with the unquenchable fire) from the burning. Some day, if I live, I will tell you all. Now, dear brother, pray for me (Col. i. 9–12); and that I may be kept from ever doubting the word, the grace, or the love of our God, or the efficacy of the blood of my Saviour and Lord; and that I may be emptied of self, and kept very low before the cross, looking ever on Him who hung there for me'."

About the same date, Christopher sent a copy of *God's Way of Peace* to his brother Leonard in India. General Christopher afterwards told him that this book showed him the gospel for the first time in his life. Furthermore, that copy was immediately used of God to help someone else. A brother officer who had led his regiment bravely at the Battle of Cawnpore was mortally ill in Leonard Christopher's house. Passages from Bonar's book were read to him and the dying man at once laid hold by faith on Jesus Christ, and died praising God for revealing Himself at the eleventh hour. Christopher was still using *God's Way of Peace* at the end of his ministry at St. Aldate's. In November 1904, Bishop Paget of Oxford wrote to acknowledge with touching humility a copy which Christopher had sent to him.

A sequel to *God's Way of Peace* was *God's Way of Holiness,* which Christopher was instrumental in persuading Dr. Bonar to write. While being shown round Holyrood Palace, stopping on the landing where Rizzio's body was thrown after assassination, Christopher took the opportunity to urge Bonar to add two or three chapters on holiness to *God's Way of Peace,* to make it more complete as a gift. Bonar replied "No! I prefer to keep the unity of the subject." "Then," rejoined Christopher, "you *must* write another book on holiness." "Well," said Bonar, "what shall the title be?" Christopher thought for a moment and then replied "God's Way of Holiness," and Bonar was allowed no rest until the sequel was actually written. Christopher followed up his request with a letter in which he again suggested adding to *God's Way of Peace,* or, as an alternative, the writing of a new book. When *God's Way of Holiness* appeared in 1864, Christopher with huge delight wrote a long letter for insertion in *The Record* which the editor (Edward Garbett of Christ Church, Surbiton, the Bampton Lecturer of 1867 — when he was secured to preach at St. Aldate's) printed instead of the review he had intended to include. Christopher answered incidentally some criticisms which had been made by reviewers of *God's Way of Peace.* When published independently as a pamphlet, the letter ran to twenty printed pages. "Dr. Bonar," Christopher wrote, "has now given to the Church a work far more valuable than the single chapter could have been for which I asked."

Christopher was also a consistent distributor of tracts. Bishop Chavasse of Liverpool, recalling his own undergraduate days in the 'sixties, remarked that "He had seen him on a beautiful summer's night, as crowds of well-dressed people were streaming up from the river, giving out tracts — tracts as courteously received as they were given. But what it cost him to stand there, for he was a high-principled and sensitive man, was only known to those who were closest and dearest to him. He deemed it to be his duty, however, and if his heart might shrink within him, he did it because he thought it to be right. Whether men agreed with him or not, they were deeply impressed . . ."

Writing for one of the first numbers of *The Fireside News* in January 1884, Christopher himself described his feelings when giving away tracts on board ship on Lake Superior in 1871. "Before starting for Canada I had taken care to supply myself, as I hope most Christian travellers do, with a large stock of interesting little books full of the Gospel. God who blesses uninspired sermons can use uninspired tracts. I have heard a clergyman speak against the practice of giving tracts, but he had had no experience of the blessing which attends it. He had missed many opportunities of being made a channel of blessing to others, and of receiving in return an increase to his own faith. One of the great interests of tract giving is that the gift of a tract often leads to an interesting conversation. I had given small Gospel books to most of my fellow-passengers on the Lake Superior steamer: but from some cause I was, for a time, afraid to offer one to a certain gentleman. Fears in the Lord's work are often follies, the unwholesome fruits of distrust. I have often felt afraid in the good work of tract giving, but I never prayed for courage without receiving it. I did so on this occasion, and I thought to myself: — 'I shall never meet this man again until the judgment day. If I miss the present opportunity of seeking his good I may never have another.' He was about to land at the next little port; soon he would be getting together his luggage. I lost no more time and offered him a Gospel book suited for an intelligent man; the result was one of the most interesting conversations I ever had . . ."

Walking one day with his two sons from Menai Bridge to Beaumaris, Christopher was giving away tracts to people they encountered. A young woman to whom he offered a tract said "I have met you before, Sir, I believe." "Where?" he enquired. "In a railway carriage near Perth. You gave me a tract then." She went on to speak with thankfulness of that tract and the talk they had when Christopher was on his way to take part in an annual conference organised by Colonel Macdonald Macdonald.

Christopher was on intimate terms with the Revd. Henry Barne, Vicar of Faringdon, a remarkable man who as an undergraduate at Trinity in the 'thirties had been active as a member of the Union and a tractarian. He subsequently adopted strong evangelical opinions. Barne often came into Oxford to see and to help Christopher in the early days at St. Aldate's, no less because Christopher once rebuked him rather severely for not having adequately prepared an address. He was not without a sense of humour. At Richmond

Lodge undergraduates were frequently entertained to meals; and Barne, who greatly esteemed Christopher, had more than one story in this connection. "Dear [Christopher] is a true 'lover of hospitality'. His wife on one occasion appealed to me at their breakfast table: 'did I not think it a little hard upon her, that much as she enjoyed the society of his friends, and delighted to welcome them, he should constantly forget to apprise her of their coming, and in consequence subject her to the greatest inconvenience in making suitable preparation for them?' My dear friend, at the bottom of the table, finding out by this time that we were discussing him, asked an explanation, and with not a little *malice prepense* I repeated our conversation. He was just commencing a gentle remonstrance, 'Oh, no, my dear, now you know it is not so,' when the servant opened the door and ushered in three gentlemen, each closely following the other. 'Oh! my dear!' said my self-convicted friend, surprised out of his former assertion, 'I quite forgot to tell you before! I invited them all to breakfast!'"

A similar occurrence took place on another of Barne's visits. At half-past ten at night Christopher and his party returned from a religious meeting, at which the former had been speaking. "My dear," said he, "I have just invited seven gentlemen to breakfast to-morrow; but we must have it punctually at half past seven, owing to three of their number being engaged early." "Oh, how could you!" exclaimed Mrs. Christopher, "I have nothing to give them but a bare beef bone, and the milkman never comes until eight o'clock." "Oh, I will provide a breakfast," said the incorrigible husband, and he kept his word. "A few minutes after six o'clock the next morning he sallied forth into the streets, a basket in one hand, a huge milk jug in the other. After visiting five pork butchers in succession, to find their premises still unopened, he contrived to purchase some three dozen sausages, and overtaking a milkman on his return home, he triumphantly secured two quarts of milk." It is said that the breakfast was a complete success. Everyone laughed at the sausages,[1] and Henry Barne's humorous account concerning them served as a relish. Christopher was in any case an early riser. He often referred to this, not to commend himself but to recommend the habit to others. "It cannot be doubted," wrote

[1]Then a novelty.

G. W. Butler, "that it was by saving time in the early morning he was able to get through the great amount of work that the addition of the care of young Oxford to the pressure of a populous town parish necessarily involved."

Shortly after Christopher began his work at St. Aldate's, he became a victim of sleeplessness. This might well have terminated his Oxford career at its very beginning, for his doctors could not cure him. When the trouble was at its worst, a trying incident occurred which illustrates Christopher's loving faithfulness. Six or seven undergraduates had come up to the university from Christian homes, and were themselves men of prayer, though reading philosophy for the final classical school had seriously shaken their faith. In their distress they formed themselves into a little society called 'Lovers of Truth', and met every week with the object of considering the best answers they could find to their difficulties. They began their meetings with prayer, for they had not given up hope in God. They sought for deliverance from their doubts and their prayers were answered. Those of them he knew were among the best men Christopher met during his first months at Oxford. One of them — probably W. H. Hooper of Wadham — had obtained a first class in *literae humaniores,* and was accepted by the Church Missionary Society as a candidate. But a clergyman with whom he happened to stay wrote to Henry Venn, describing him as a member of a secret society called 'Seekers of Truth'.

Venn wrote quite severely to Christopher, saying that a missionary was a man who had found the truth and went to tell the heathen of it. Christopher felt sure that there had been a misunderstanding, and although at the time very unwell through continued sleeplessness, and ordered not to do anything, he went to the man's lodgings, asked him a number of questions, wrote down his replies and sent them to Venn. That letter removed all doubts and hesitations, and the young man lived to be recognised as one of the most learned and useful missionaries of the Church Missionary Society. Thus Christopher acted not only as a bulwark against rationalism, but also as a real friend to those who felt its attraction. His sympathy was a great link with university men. "In our undergraduate days," wrote Matthews of Pembroke, "no one entered more lovingly into our sorrows than this very true and dear friend. It was so evident that he had our highest welfare at heart. Well do I remember how he covered his face with his hand for a moment of ejaculatory prayer when on a Sunday evening three of us waylaid him after Service with some request. The Heavenly guidance had been sought — not in vain; for he replied 'Yes, it has to do with the Lord's work; tell me all about it'." Downer has emphasised in his *Century of Evangelical Religion in Oxford* that "Amongst the qualities which render a man of spiritual character acceptable to young men, none is more needful than warm and even effusive sympathy. Canon Christopher had it[1] and that was what made his influence greater than that of other men no less able and devoted than himself."

It was at this time that a brother clergyman in Oxford, knowing that the Rector of St. Ebbe's had been for many years in a lunatic asylum,[2] and fearing the worst results of Christopher's insomnia, suggested that perhaps he ought to resign the living while he could legally do so. With characteristic energy and promptitude, Christopher at once went up to London to consult Edward Hathaway as to his duty. That shrewd man smiled at the idea and encouraged Christopher to trust God for deliverance. But something had to be done for the sleeplessness. Medical advice urged a long sea voyage, and the result was a trip round the Mediterranean in a vessel calling at Gibraltar, Malta, Constantinople, Smyrna, Syria, and Alexandria.[3] Sleep did not come between Liverpool and Gibraltar, for five days and five nights, but there was then a gradual recovery, and before reaching Constantinople, Christopher had begun to visit the sailors in the forecastle, using his opportunities, as he usually did, so well, by telling them of instances of conversion and by reading the Bible and praying with them. A big seaman who was captain of the forecastle said: "We shall be glad to see you, Sir, as often as ever you can come." During a week spent at Constantinople, the Ambassador's Chaplain, the Revd. Charles Gribble (like his visitor a member of St. John's College, Cambridge), invited Christopher to

[1]In common, Downer goes on to say, with F. J. Chavasse, and H. C. G. Moule of Cambridge, afterwards Bishop of Durham.

[2]Being housed in 'the Warneford', however, as late as 1857 he attended services in his own church, where he sat among the congregation.

[3]A fly-leaf inscription in the copy of one of the series of Ryle's *Home Truths* which Christopher gave to Captain J. R. Bell, in remembrance of seven weeks aboard his ship during the spring of 1860, which happily fell into the hands of a friend of the author, preserves the actual date of this trip, confirmed by the relevant preachers' book at St. Aldate's.

preach on Good Friday in the Embassy chapel. Gribble, Christopher used to relate, as a missionary in the backwoods of Canada, had been instrumental in the conversion of a vigorous young Englishman named Bowen, who, after working at his own charges as a missionary in Palestine, became Bishop of Sierra Leone.

When at Constantinople, Christopher visited Dr. Pfander, a missionary of the Church Missionary Society, who was the able fellow-labourer of Bishop French among Mohammedans in India, and a cousin of Weitbrecht. While Christopher was calling on Pfander, four Turks came in to see him. One was a Christian man, the others were enquirers. Christopher often said that he never saw any man look as happy as that Christian Turk, though he had given up more than most men for Christ's sake. As the nephew of one of the richest pashas in Constantinople, he had lived to the age of forty in his uncle's palace on the shores of the Bosphorus as his heir. But a Bible came into his hands, and he read it until he became convinced that Jesus was indeed the promised Messiah, the Son of God, the only Saviour of sinners. He felt he must confess his new faith at all costs, although he knew that if he were baptised his uncle would cast him off, "not with a shilling but without it". Yet he had given up all, and appeared to be the happiest of men, though when Christopher saw him he was wearing a threadbare garment. On Easter morning, Christopher preached in the consular chapel at Smyrna. Most of the sailors who could get leave came to church. In the afternoon he preached on the deck of the steamer, about three-quarters of a mile from shore, and some residents came aboard to attend, including a Roman Catholic lady who besought him to join 'the True Church'. After calling at Alexandria, the vessel turned homewards towards Liverpool, bringing Christopher quite recovered, " with heart and soul full of the CXIII Psalm."

Chapter VIII

Building

1862 - 1865

CHRISTOPHER was a man who took bricks and mortar in his stride. To him they were a means to an end, and his capacity for detail was of particular service to him in all the building projects he was called upon to undertake. The parish schools of St. Aldate's, though little more than twenty years old, were in a deplorable state. The boys (of whom there were 65 on the books in 1860, with 75 girls) had only cold flagstones beneath their feet. The walls of the girls' school were made of lath and plaster. Boys threw stones at them and made holes through which wind and rain entered. Better buildings were clearly needed. But the parish chiefly consisting of courts on either side of a main street, it was difficult to find an adequate site on the city side of Folly Bridge. In November 1861, however, eight cottages adjoining the old school yard on the east side of St. Aldate's were put up for sale by auction, and Christopher bought them for £610, using his Indian savings to do so. This meant that the whole yard could now be devoted to the school; but there the matter had to rest for the time being. The estimate for new buildings was £1,400; and a more urgent requirement still was to enlarge the parish church in which there were only thirty-five seats allotted to the poor of the parish. The remaining four hundred and twenty were insufficient in term time in view of the increasing number of undergraduates attending Sunday services, especially in the evening. For many years the churchwardens had paid the expenses of divine worship — organist, clerk and sexton's salaries, heating, lighting, and cleaning — from the rent of the church houses. But in the autumn of 1861 the Charity Commissioners prohibited this use of parish funds, and at a full vestry on 18 October, it was found necessary to levy on the parishioners a voluntary church rate of fourpence in the pound. This was unfortunate in view of the need to raise money for major developments.

Nevertheless, early in 1862, Christopher began to tackle seriously the rebuilding of the church. No doubt it was an ancient structure. But Christopher aimed to double its seating capacity, and antiquarian considerations could not come first where immortal souls were concerned. In any case the diocesan surveyor, G. E. Street, who was to achieve a national reputation, had already carried out alterations a few years before.[1] Testimonials were solicited from influential evangelicals by Edward Hathaway and formed into a twelve-page booklet for insertion with the appeal, which embraced schools as well as church. It was useless to expect much response from the parish itself, in view of the poverty which prevailed. The bulk of the money had to be found outside. Dr. Cotton, Provost of Worcester, wrote a characteristic letter deploring the discouragements to the church attendance of the poor. The Warden of Wadham, Dr. Symons, opining that "Mr. Christopher's energy has already thrown a new appearance over the parish," points out that "The influence which the ministry of this church does already, and is likely, for the future, to exercise in Oxford, renders the accomplishment of Mr. Christopher's plans a matter of great importance. I am convinced that all, who feel an interest in the object for which the Rectory of St. Aldate's has been secured, would promote it very essentially in enabling Mr. Christopher to execute the purposes for which he is labouring . . ."

[1]Further back, in 1843, it had been necessary to enlarge by extending the north-east part of the church. Both this and more expensive work still in 1832 were carried out under the eye of H. J. Underwood, the architect of St. Paul's, Walton Street (1836), and the now demolished Summertown (1833) and Holy Trinity (1843) churches. By contrast to Underwood, Street's name does not occur in the churchwardens' accounts, but he may have been employed on the chancel, for which the Rector was financially liable. Thus Street was perhaps responsible for the battlements seen in Plate 32, which do not appear in somewhat earlier pictures of the church. Vestry minutes are not extant before 1865.

Hugh McNeile, Hugh Stowell, Thomas French, and John Miller alike testified from personal experience of having recently preached there, that the church was too small. When Stowell ministered, the standing-room in the aisles was filled. Miller spoke of the "make-shift" schools, and with reference to Christopher, "He deserves every sympathy and help from those who can appreciate the untiring labour of a simple-hearted, loving servant of Christ, in a post of incalculable importance." T. R. Birks, presently Professor of Moral Philosophy at Cambridge and incumbent of Holy Trinity, added with regard to the schools that "It is most unseemly that such a parish, under the shadow of one of the largest and richest Colleges, should be so ill provided with this important means of parochial instruction." Henry Linton's local knowledge enabled him to say "He does not meet with the full response here to which his labours of love entitle him . . ." James Bardsley of Manchester could represent feelingly "that I have three sons who teach in his schools and attend his various meetings." John Venn of St. Peter's, Hereford, Henry Venn's cousin, strikes a familiar note when he says "The sum which is required for the purpose is a large sum to raise in these days, when almost every Society and Institution are sending forth their urgent appeals for money." William Knight, Fellow of Worcester since 1845, and one of the secretaries at Salisbury Square when Christopher worked for the Church Missionary Society, recorded that "I have watched with deep thankfulness his course at Oxford . . . He has succeeded, as far as anyone who has been there within my recollection, in gaining the affections of the undergraduates." Knight had preached at St. Aldate's in 1860.

William Fremantle, Rector of the Claydons, in Buckinghamshire, afterwards Dean of Ripon, who had been a contemporary Fellow of Magdalen with Henry Linton, could only echo the chorus of praise. "I feel that the Lord has greatly prospered Mr. Christopher's work in the University." Alexander Dallas, Rector of Wonston, Hampshire, and founder of the Irish Church Missions to Roman Catholics, who had known the benefit of John Natt's ministry at St. Giles', when an undergraduate at Worcester College, referred to Christopher's "Christian boldness" in putting forward his plan. Canon Carus wrote "Surely there are many Oxford men in the country who will feel it a privilege to help him to complete the good work, which he has so energetically commenced. Such was the case when Trinity Church, Cambridge (Mr. Simeon's), required rearrangement and enlargement, at a cost of 3,000*l*. The appeal then made to friends in various parts was met with an immediate and generous response. Now, is not St. Aldate's quite as important as Trinity? and will not Oxford act as heartily and liberally as Cambridge?"

The testimony which Christopher valued most was that spontaneously provided by his undergraduate friends. The moving spirit was John Matthews of Pembroke. He and a few others drew up, without Christopher's knowledge, a letter expressing their appreciation of his efforts on their behalf. It was signed by over eighty junior members of the university, though "none were pressed to sign." Moreover "all who have signed it are in the habit of attending the prayer-meeting at St. Aldate's Rectory, or at Wadham College[1], and . . . the majority attend the services at St. Aldate's Church on Sunday morning or evening." Some interesting names appear, including those of William Dawkins, afterward Professor of Geology at Manchester, Charles Pearson, subsequently Lord Advocate of Scotland, and Oswald Reichel, who became Vice-Principal of Cuddesdon College in 1865, and, among certainly continuing evangelicals, William Myres, who married a daughter of Henry Linton and whose son, Sir John Myres, became Wykeham Professor of Ancient History, Francis Pilcher, afterwards Rector of St. Clement's, Oxford, and William Hay Aitken, subsequently founder of the Parochial Missions Society and Canon of Norwich.

The appeal itself — two copies are preserved in the diocesan archives, and the only others known to survive are also in the Bodleian Library — in which Christopher asked for £2,600 for the church and £1,400 for the schools, was put out in February 1862. There were 457 adult sittings. At least 250 more free seats were required. Christopher proposed to add 274, making 731 in all, which with 70 for children made a total of 801. In the schools there were some 85 boys and 70 girls. Christopher wished to rebuild the two existing rooms and add an infants' school. Believing that the parish could not reasonably be expected to support both church and school projects, he asked parishioners to help with the schools and took the whole

[1]In Mrs. Symons's drawing room.

responsibility for the church himself. But as he pointed out, "My own means are very limited, and the expenses of the Parish to me exceed the amount I receive from the living. If I were not assisted by Christian friends, it would be altogether out of my power to retain the incumbency." A letter from the Bishop of Oxford, Dr. Wilberforce, commending Christopher's plans, was printed as part of the appeal, with a promise of £15 on the day the church was reopened. A large building committee had been formed, but most of the work was done by a small sub-committee. Two notes in Christopher's hand, relating to the business, dated 1 and 5 April 1862, are preserved in the diocesan archives. A preliminary list of subscribers included the Dean and Canons of Christ Church severally, most Heads of Houses, W. E. Gladstone (university Burgess and Chancellor of the Exchequer), and the seventh Duke of Marlborough, who shared Christopher's spiritual outlook.

On 15 June the last services were held in the old church. For nearly a year the congregation of St. Aldate's worshipped elsewhere — on the following Sunday morning at Holy Trinity, with "most of the congregation present." Trinity church, with its gallery, held seven or eight hundred people, and the St. Aldates' parishioners continued to attend there in the mornings, though once or twice they went to St. Martin's, then still standing at Carfax. In the evenings they had their own service at St. Mary Magdalene. Among those who preached for Christopher here was the well-known Canon Edward Hoare, Vicar of Holy Trinity, Tunbridge Wells, on whose advice Christopher had dealt firmly with the clothes of the cholera victim at Richmond. For those who could not get to St. Mary Magdalene, a service was held in the St. Aldates' schoolroom. Weekday activities went on as usual. Among these were weekly lectures in the school, prayer meetings, and Bible classes for young men at the Rectory, as well as those held monthly for young men, and for young women, and a devotional meeting for communicants.

St. Aldate's church, with the exception of the tower and spire, (deferred for lack of funds, these were reconstructed in 1873, at a cost of a further £2,000) was practically rebuilt, and so enlarged as to accommodate nearly twice the number of parishioners and others who might wish to attend. The south aisle, which had hitherto been of three bays, was extended as far as possible at both ends, and the north aisle (to the west end of which a vestry was added) at its eastern end, shortening the chancel externally and making the church almost rectangular. The classical south porch and West family chapel on the south side of the chancel consequently disappeared. The top part of the tracery of the existing east window of the south aisle was left in position. The old seating arrangements were abandoned, and the new pews faced east. This, though Christopher would hardly have allowed it, was in fact a concession to the prevailing tractarian ideas about church architecture. Some small Norman arches in the chancel (relatively little of this arcade was original) were preserved by transferring them to the east wall of the north aisle, and John Noble's tomb was moved to its present site. Otherwise, apart from the outside wall and windows of the north aisle, the font, and a large assortment of mural tablets, little remained of the old St. Aldate's by the time John Christopher, Christopher's cousin and architect,[1] had finished his work. Heating pipes were installed (two stoves had been the only means of warming the old building) and the church was lighted by *coronae* of gas jets. C. Curtis of Pembroke Street was the contractor. This name has disappeared from among Oxford builders, but that of his clerk of works, Mr. Loxley, is still familiar.

The roofs were extensively renewed, and the pink granite pillars[2] which support those of nave and aisles were the object of Alfred Christopher's special concern. He desired that as few people as possible should be prevented from seeing the reader and preacher or *vice versa,* and he obtained from his friend Lord Haddo, a devoted young Christian, a gift of granite from the Aberdeen quarries of his father, Lord Aberdeen, so that the pillars might be more slender than if they had been made of stone.[3] Lord Haddo died a few years later, after succeeding to the earldom, and Christopher was wont to say that he wished he had asked such a man for a more spiritual gift.

[1]Better known as the designer of Monico's, Piccadilly Circus, lately demolished.

[2]Recently painted over.

[3]It is noticeable that the pillars of St. Philip's and St. James's, a new church in St. Giles's parish built mainly in 1860-61, are of the same material. Here also, though for a different reason, it was desired that the view should be unimpeded, and it may be that Christopher borrowed the idea of using granite from this local example.

The enlargement of the church involved the removal of some coffins from surrounding vaults and graves. The proceedings of the workmen were viewed with displeasure from a house overlooking the churchyard, and one of the sons of the house, meeting his Rector in the Cornmarket, took occasion to 'cut' him very markedly. Christopher was not insensitive to this kind of behaviour — though it could scarcely have been the first time he had met it — but he bore it well. In the following year the same spirit manifested itself in a printed bill which was the work of Henry Holder, a former guardian and overseer of the poor, and himself by trade a printer. Headed *St. Aldate's Parish Vestry, Holy Thursday. To the Non-Nobs,* Holder's bills declared that "As the ostensible object of the Rector in having the church enlarged was for the better accommodation of the parishioners and as only a select few (80 'Nobs') have had seats appropriated to them, it is desirable that the Non-Nobs should assemble and meet together at the aforesaid Vestry, in protest against such an unchristian — uncharitable distribution in the Parish House of Prayer! The whole culpability rests on the head of the Rector. He avowed the object for which he wished the Church to be enlarged — he has had his own will and his way in everything.[1] The sanctity of the grave has been violated . . . The Non-Nobs . . . snubbed and treated with contumely . . ."

Meanwhile Christopher had other things to think about. India was never far from his mind, and at this time he was concerned to find a new principal for La Martinière, since Lucas Ewbank, a Fellow of Clare College, Cambridge, intended to resign early in 1863. The appointment had been entrusted by the governors to Christopher and a retired Bengal civilian, Mr. E. Currie, who had been an acting governor for many years. Accordingly, in July 1862, Christopher printed a circular giving information about the school, its constitution and its organisation. Only laymen were eligible, but "To a man of real piety and energy, the Principalship of La Martinière would prove, under God's blessing, a position of very great usefulness." The school had clearly flourished since Christopher's days, under three distinguished principals, two of whom

[1]The condition of the church was in fact giving cause for local concern prior to Christopher's arrival. Not long before June 1859 the churchwardens paid the then considerable sum of £5 7s. for a builder's report on the state of the fabric, including tower and spire.

had been fellows of Cambridge colleges. In the event C. W. Hatten, a graduate of Caius College, Cambridge, was appointed. He had been a university pupil of Christopher's Martinière pupil, A. W. W. Steel. Like Christopher, Hatten came home to be ordained, in 1866, and was subsequently Rector of Bodle Street Green, Sussex. An account of Christopher in the centenary number of *La Martinière Chronicle* records that "for many years he was actively interested in the School, and was frequently asked by the Governors to select the masters who came out to join the staff." Christopher was also interested in the Calcutta Normal School, founded in 1851 to train women teachers. He acted as secretary of the London auxiliary committee, of which Mr. and Mrs. Arthur Kinnaird, parents of his young friend at Cheam, and afterwards Lord and Lady Kinnaird, were the moving spirits. In 1861 it had developed into the India Female Normal School and Instruction Society. From this work sprang the zenana missions.

Another event of 1862 was Christopher's first visit to the conference at Barnet, organised by the Revd. William Pennefather, Vicar of Christ Church, Barnet. The Barnet Conferences, for the deepening of the spiritual life (held later at Mildmay Park, when Pennefather was Vicar of St. Jude's), were in some measure the predecessors of the Keswick Convention. Christopher did not know Pennefather, who, however, had invited him by letter to attend the gatherings that June; and he was greatly interested by the confidence in the simple gospel of God's grace which he found there. He was especially struck by two "very attractive Christian young men," Stevenson Blackwood[1] and Lord Radstock,[2] and he listened with appreciation to some simple expositions of the Bible given by Captain Trotter, an officer of the Life Guards who was the owner of Dyrham Park nearby, where Weitbrecht had found a wife for the missionary Krauss. Trotter had been sent by his family as a worldly young man to Paris to bring to her senses a sister of his who had been converted. The result, however, had been his own conversion. Details of this formed one of Christopher's favourite stories. Another was that of the Christian washerwoman who washed hard so that she could take one day off in the year to attend the conference, only

[1]Afterwards Secretary of the Post Office.

[2]Granville, third Baron Radstock.

to find on arrival that there was no room in the schools where the meetings were held. This came to the knowledge of the organisers and was thus indirectly the means, under God, of a room four times as large being built.

Christopher's deafness greatly hindered him from enjoying such occasions to the full. "I sat with my ear trumpet on a step of the platform, and Sir George Pollock, the hero of Cabul,[1] who was also very deaf, sat with his ear trumpet opposite to me." Twenty-four years later these stations of the deaf still prevailed. When Eugene Stock of the Church Missionary Society took Miss Constance Gordon-Cumming, a well-known lady traveller, at her request, to the Mildmay Conference of 1886, " She particularly objected to the two good men (Canon Christopher was one) who sat at either side of the speaker with ear-trumpets lifted up to hear his address. 'They might be very good men,' she wrote to [Stock], 'but they had no business to exhalt their horns in the congregation'![2] It reminded her, she said, ' of the elephants raising their trunks to do homage to Buddha'!" But Miss Gordon-Cumming did not appreciate other and more important aspects of the conference, and as Christopher said in reference to himself and Sir George Pollock in the 'sixties, " How little we cared about making ourselves 'objects' to those who had good hearing, if we could catch some of the good simple Scriptural words which dropped with grace from the mouth of the speaker. I always hope that the sight of my battered tin trumpet makes some of those who have good hearing, grateful for it." Christopher was himself a speaker at the Mildmay Conference of 1872.[3] Pennefather — who had preached at St. Aldate's in 1868 — died the following year. It was not only at conferences and in church that Christopher's ear-trumpet was in evidence. Bishop Ingham, referring to the year 1873, wrote " I had been teaching for a few terms in St. Aldate's Sunday School. We had a short gathering of teachers for prayer after the young people left. I ventured to offer a short prayer. Christopher noted the fact and at once drew near and placed his trumpet under my mouth! It was a terrible moment never to be forgotten! "

[1]Captured during an Indian campaign of 1842. General Pollock was gazetted Field-Marshal in 1870, at the age of eighty-four.

[2]This may refer to a period in Christopher's life when he had a pair of trumpets, curved like rams' horns, fixed to his head.

[3]When D. L. Moody, the American evangelist, was also present on the platform, during his first extended visit to England.

St. Aldate's church was reopened on Thursday 23 April 1863. The Bishop of Oxford had been advertised as preacher, but on Dr. Acland's advice, Dr. Wilberforce was obliged to remain at home. He nominated the Warden of All Souls, Dr. Francis Leighton, to preach in his stead.[1] After Morning Prayer and sermon, a luncheon was held in the Corn Exchange at which one hundred and eighty principal parishioners sat down, together with the Dean of Christ Church, Dr. Liddell, the Warden of All Souls, the Archdeacon of Oxford, Dr. Clerke, and the Mayor. It was a great occasion. After the meal, the healths of the Queen and of the Prince and Princess of Wales were first drunk. In proposing Christopher's health, Dr. Leighton remarked that he was ". . . not surprised to hear the name of their Rector received with so much applause . . ." The Dean of Christ Church referred to Christopher's "merits and service" as being "so well known to all persons in this city." *The Oxford Chronicle,* devoting two long columns to the 'Restoration of St. Aldate's Church' in its issue of the following Saturday, opined that "It may now be regarded as one of the most beautiful, as well as convenient and commodious parochial churches in the city."

On the following Sunday Christopher read prayers and Dr. Miller of Birmingham preached morning and evening. The sacrament was administered to eighty-four persons. Unhappily, however, the building was not free from debt. Much less were the schools provided for. The latter were not built till 1865, although at the luncheon Henry Linton confessed his surprise at hearing Christopher already speaking of a start on the schools before the present debt was paid off. Nevertheless, Linton offered £100 towards the church if six others would give the same. In spite of this, in March 1864, a "considerable" portion of the expense of what Bishop Wilberforce called "restoring your Church" still rested on Christopher.[2] Doubtless the situation was not improved by the fact that the curate and churchwardens of St. Ebbe's were also

[1]Dr. Leighton was also Rector of Lockinge, Berkshire.

[2]Payment for seats to be reserved was introduced in May 1864, and this practice, which produced an appreciable income, continued throughout Christopher's incumbency and the two following ones, until 1922. The needs of the fabric may also have prompted the first occasional collections at ordinary services, in 1862, though these were doubtless necessitated partly by the prohibition on the use of parish charity funds for the maintenance of public worship. For many years after, collections were not taken every Sunday.

appealing for financial help to 'restore' their church. St. Ebbe's had been virtually rebuilt fifty years before. But at that time a thoroughly protestant treatment had been accorded to the interior, and Griffith, the tractarian curate-in-charge, was naturally dissatisfied. The parish church, he says, in an appeal embracing £2,000, "is a square building, with plain deal pews, unusually high and narrow, half of which look eastward and half westward, the pulpit being in the centre of the south wall," and thus occupying the same position as the one in the unrestored St. Aldate's, a position which, curiously enough, is still frequent in Roman Catholic churches on the continent, as well as in reformed churches in other countries. Twelve hundred pounds had been collected for St. Ebbe's since 1861. Six hundred more were needed to enable the architect, G. E. Street, "to divide the present area of the Church into a chancel, nave, and north aisle, — to add a new aisle to the south side — with open sittings throughout for five hundred persons." The existing church held seven hundred people; but Griffith was not popular, and his aims were not those of Christopher. The Bishop of Oxford, however, wrote: "I know scarcely one [church] in the Diocese which seems to me more urgently to need such a work."

Bishop Wilberforce, who had held the see of Oxford since 1845, did not take after his father, William Wilberforce, the philanthropist, but was a high churchman — though not a tractarian — of the newer school. He preached only twice at St. Aldate's during the ten years of Christopher's incumbency which passed before his translation to Winchester to succeed Bishop Sumner. In 1854 he had founded the theological college at Cuddesdon which had already caused grave disquiet in the diocese on account of its anglo-catholic tendencies; and although he had championed traditional orthodoxy before a British Association meeting at Oxford in 1860, his own theological presuppositions were open to suspicion. An organiser, however, rather than a theologian — though not, as Burgon labelled him, 'the re-modeller of the episcopate', an honour which belongs to John Sumner as Bishop of Chester — he had early introduced, long before it became statutory, a diocesan conference. It was managed in a secretarial capacity by an evangelical, the Revd. William Fremantle, Rector of the Claydons, who had been cox of the Oxford crew in the first university boat race in 1829, and was afterwards Dean of Ripon. But this did not prevent the Bishop from causing concern to the Rector of St. Aldate's, who wrote in some distress to Edward Hathaway after a conference held in 1864.

"I felt the Bishop's Address on Inspiration to be unsatisfactory & told Fremantle my opinion immediately after the Meeting. He said that he quite agreed with me. When Dr. Lee[1] & Canon Wordsworth[2] had finished their addresses the time was exhausted & the Meeting broke up without any discussion.

"The next day the Bishop explained himself to mean that whilst he did not believe that any error whatever had been *proved* to exist in the Bible, yet if there was ever proved to be an error on a matter not referring to any doctrine, this would not shake his faith in Divine Revelation. For example if it could be proved that St. Paul instead of having left his cloke at Troas as he thought he had (2 Tim. IV. 13) really left it elsewhere, this would not shake his faith. However the Bishop's words on the first day seemed to go beyond this.

"Your note has led me to write to the Bishop asking him to write me briefly his opinion as he intended to express it, with liberty to send it to the Standard or any other paper in correction of the Report." Christopher whole-heartedly favoured the policy of the so-called 'neo-evangelicals' — Ryle, E. Hoare, and E. Garbett — in taking part in such gatherings. "I am more than ever in favour," he continues, "of Fremantle's standing by the Conference and bringing *into* it all the truth he can.

"If he had not had the arrangement of the Conference, we should not have had two Evangelical men Cadman[3] & T. T. Perowne[4] to open the subject 'Zeal for God' on the 2nd day, & perhaps not Archdeacon Lee on the first day.

"Moreover I was astonished at the small amount of power of speaking amongst the high Church Clergy present. If we had more faith & went to the Conferences after much prayer & study of God's Word in connection with the subjects we might be enabled to bear a testimony to the truth which God would bless."

[1]Probably William Lee, Professor of Ecclesiastical History at Trinity College, Dublin, who in this year became Archdeacon of Dublin.

[2]Christopher Wordsworth, Vicar of Stanford-in-the-Vale, Berkshire, and Canon of Westminster, a nephew of the poet; afterwards Bishop of Lincoln.

[3]W. Cadman, Rector of St. George's, Southwark, later Canon of Canterbury.

[4]Fellow of Corpus Christi College, Cambridge, afterwards Archdeacon of Norfolk.

These sentiments are typical of Christopher's large-hearted evangelical churchmanship combined with awareness of the opportunity offered for evangelicals to bear witness to their distinctive tenets. Thirty years later, commenting on the state of affairs which had since arisen, Hathaway wrote: " How sadly things have retrograded since then. Imagine two Evangelical speakers at your Diocesan Conference: strangers brought from a distance! " Christopher's letter also shows how firmly at that date — before destructive higher criticism had gained its hold on the church, though Bishop Colenso (who was inhibited from preaching in St. Martin's, Oxford, by Wilberforce's successor) had already given cause for alarm — the evangelicals adhered to the traditional doctrine of the inspiration of Scripture as the vehicle of revealed truth. One of Christopher's qualities which deeply impressed Dr. Griffith Thomas many years later was " his simple and strong faith in the power of the very words of Scripture. He would quote texts in sermons, write them in letters, print them in booklets, and even almost 'drag them in' at meetings, with the evident conviction that 'the Word of God is living and powerful' and 'would not return to Him void'."

Hathaway was not content with acquiring the advowson of St. Aldate's. He and his friends had envisaged a wider influence at Oxford. St. Peter-le-Bailey was in good hands while Linton remained incumbent; but when E. A. Litton, Moody's successor at St. Clement's, retired to a country living in 1861, a pronounced broad churchman was appointed. At St. Ebbe's a tractarian had succeeded Cameron as curate-in-charge in 1860. Four years later, opportunity, by then the subject of prayer since 1853, presented itself in the shape of an Augmentation Act, designed to improve poor livings in the gift of the Lord Chancellor, whereby money received in exchange for advowsons would be added to the endowment of the benefices concerned by the Ecclesiastical Commissioners. Under Hathaway's superintendence, Henry Linton acquired the patronage of St. Peter-le-Bailey, Lord Shaftesbury[1] became temporary patron of St. Ebbe's, and Dr. Symons, the Warden of Wadham, obtained St. Clement's. This time there was no indirect inducement to associate these churches with Simeon's Trust, and in April 1864

[1]A brief note from Shaftesbury to Christopher, dated 4 April 1866, preserved in the Bodleian Library, shows that they were not unacquainted.

they passed into the hands of five trustees of their own: Auriol and Hathaway, H. Linton and W. W. Champneys, Canon of St. Paul's, (both former fellows of their colleges), and John Campbell Colquhoun, a Scottish landowner who had been one of the first presidents of the Union Society. As Hathaway wrote, "It was important that all the Trustees should be Oxford men." This time, too, Christopher, as well as Linton, having begun to show what in practice could be done in such parishes, Hathaway's appeal was oversubscribed. It was felt appropriate to use the surplus to augment the endowment of St. Aldate's. By an ironical coincidence, Pusey wrote of Oxford a few months later "The Evangelicals somehow never took root here," words apparently echoed in 1894 by Dr. J. H. Overton in his *English Church in the Nineteenth Century,* with reference to an earlier period he supposed to be largely inimical to evangelicalism at Oxford.

At this time the ritualistic controversy was one of the major problems in the minds of churchmen. Christopher adopted two positive ways of meeting the situation. On a national scale, in 1865, he helped to found the Church Association, a body set for the defence of the reformed protestant faith of the Church of England, against the romanising and mediaevalising policy of the adherents of the English Church Union founded in 1859. In its early days, Christopher was associated with many distinguished men in Church Association work. Both Henry Linton and William Champneys, neither of them militantly evangelical, were at their side. Even when later on some evangelicals felt they could not support its ruthless exposures, Christopher remained a loyal adherent. This does not mean that he approved of everything the Church Association did, for it is known that he did not; but he never allowed any such difference of opinion to lead to severing his connection. On the contrary, he usually presided at Church Association meetings in Oxford, as chairman of the Oxford branch, and in time became a Vice-President of the parent body, as Dr. Macbride of Magdalen Hall was from its foundation until his death a few years later.

Christopher was convinced that the principles of the Reformation were endangered, and he was not one to withhold his help or his influence on the score of fear or loss of standing. In mid-career at Oxford he was to become involved on this very ground in a sharp encounter with Henry Liddon, who took up his rapier on behalf of the aged Dr. Pusey. It was a poignant tribute, many years later, that Sir John Conroy, President of the English Church Union, paid at a meeting of the Oxford diocesan conference: "When I was at Oxford, no one but Canon Christopher ever spoke to me about my soul." Conroy had been an undergraduate at Christ Church in the middle 'sixties. Christopher was wont to say: "What God has done in one heart He can do in another. How many of the best and most useful of our Reformers were at one time priests of the Church of Rome. Never let us despair of Roman Catholics or of Ritualists. God is able to work in them mightily by His Spirit, and to open their understandings, and to show them the contrast between the system of the Romish Church and the Gospel of the grace of God!" Presently a caricature of Christopher appeared in a series called 'Great Guns of Oxford'. It showed the Rector of St. Aldate's, attired as a monk, standing in front of a holy table ornamented in a fashion then peculiar to anglo-catholic churches. Some years previously *The Ecclesiologist* had commented unfavourably on the small candlesticks on the communion table at St. Aldate's. This was before Christopher's time, and a bigger pair had been presented; but after a while "changes took place", and they were returned to the donor, probably by Christopher or his predecessor, eventually finding a home at St. Philip's and St. James's, where they are still in occasional use.

Christopher's other method of countering anglo-catholicism was more personal. Stimulated by the appearance of Newman's *Apologia Pro Vita Sua,* published in 1865, he secured the widespread circulation in the university of Scott's *Force of Truth.* In the previous year, Charles Kingsley had seemed to implicate Newman in an accusation of intellectual dishonesty. Newman had remonstrated privately and by pamphlet. Kingsley held on his way, and the result was the *Apologia.* From it Christopher learnt of the early influence on Newman of Thomas Scott the evangelical commentator, to whom, Newman declared "(humanly speaking) I almost owe my soul . . . I so admired and delighted in his writings, that, when I was an undergraduate, I thought of making a visit to his Parsonage[1], in order to see a man I so deeply revered. I hardly think I could have given up the idea of this expedition, even after I had

[1]At Aston Sandford, near Thame.

taken my degree; for the news of his death in 1821 came upon me as a disappointment as well as a sorrow. I hung upon the lips of Daniel Wilson, afterwards Bishop of Calcutta, as in two sermons at St. John's Chapel[1] he gave the history of Scott's life and death. I had been possessed of his 'Force of Truth' and Essays from a boy; his Commentary I bought when I was an under-graduate. What, I suppose, will strike any reader of Scott's history and writings, is his bold unworldliness and vigorous independence of mind. He followed truth wherever it led him, beginning with Unitarianism, and ending in a zealous faith in the Holy Trinity. It was he who first planted deep in my mind that fundamental truth of religion . . . Besides his unworldliness, what I also admired in Scott was his resolute opposition to Antinomianism, and the minutely practical character of his writings. They show him to be a true Englishman, and I deeply felt his influence; and for years I used almost as proverbs what I considered to be the scope and issue of his doctrine, 'Holiness rather than peace,' and 'Growth the only evidence of life.'"

Christopher thought that the time was a favourable one, especially in view of that other tide of error which was flowing as fast as anglo-catholicism, the rationalism which prevailed widely among the junior members of senior common-rooms, and through them was liable to reach their pupils, to bring before undergraduates *The Force of Truth,* Scott's remarkable narrative of the way in which God had led him from a unitarian belief to a saving knowledge of the Christian gospel and a life of untold usefulness. He wrote to the committee of the Religious Tract Society, who had the work in print, saying that seventy-five undergraduates had accepted an invitation to come to his house to hear Canon Carus, and asking the society to give a hundred and fifty copies of Scott's book for presentation, one for each undergraduate and one for a friend. His plan went no further; but as a result of his letter, copies numbering over three thousand were sent by the society to every undergraduate at Oxford and Cambridge. Christopher carefully corrected the latest university calendar, and his old pupil Steel, a Fellow of Caius, arranged for a completely up-to-date list of Cambridge undergraduates to be available, and the Religious Tract Society distributed the books by post.

[1] Bedford Row, London.

A sequel occurred seven years later, when Christopher was addressing a meeting of young men at Montreal and was urging them to use every opportunity open to them for Christ and His gospel, however small it might seem to be, not only because it is a great duty to do little duties, but also because the doing of the little duty may, in God's providence, lead on to some greater and more useful effort of which they had not thought. He gave as an illustration the gift of the hundred and fifty copies of Scott's *Force of Truth* having led to the distribution of over three thousand. A clergyman in the meeting came on to the platform and said " I was an undergraduate at Oriel College when that distribution was made. I read Scott's book with great profit to myself, and I have lent it to my friends, who have received profit from it. I lend it one after another to my more intelligent parishioners and it is doing duty at this time in a house in my parish ten miles from Montreal."

Chapter IX

Widening Influence

1865 - 1874

CHRISTOPHER'S concern for the townspeople of Oxford was manifested in 1865 by his activity in connection with Sunday closing of public houses. He was the first person asked to sign a requisition to the Mayor to convene a meeting about the matter; and afterwards he was requested to move the first resolution at the intended meeting. In these circumstances he wrote to three Oxford newspapers a letter which was presently printed in tract form by the Oxford committee of the National Sunday Closing Association as an *Address to the Citizens of Oxford, and especially to Working Men, on the propriety of closing Public Houses and Beer Shops on the Lord's Day.* The title-page informs us that Christopher was at this time president of the Oxford auxiliary of the national Association.

Like most evangelicals of his century, but in common with many other churchmen, Christopher was a strong advocate of Sunday observance. It is natural, therefore, to find him writing " Let working men be assured that their best Friend is God. All that they have of rest on the Lord's Day they owe to God. The command of God to keep holy one day in seven is the working man's protection from being made to work every day of the week. We know that most working men are in the power of their employers. Employment is eagerly desired. To be out of work is rightly dreaded. The children are craving for bread. The father's wages are the only supply. If there were no Divinely appointed day of rest, no Sabbath 'made for *man*', and not for the Jew only, what would prevent the covetousness of some employers from denying the working man his necessary rest, from prematurely wearing out his body with unbroken toil, and withering his soul by keeping him away from spiritual food? Let working men be faithful to their best Friend. Let them honour 'The Lord of the Sabbath' by honouring His day; and let them be encouraged by the promise (I Samuel ii. 30) 'Them that honour Me, I will honour, and they that despise Me, shall be lightly esteemed.'" He produced some cogent arguments in favour of the particular prohibition in question. He reprinted a letter to *The Times* from forty-seven publicans in support of Sunday closing. He drew attention to the fact that in 1854-5 — when Victorian respect for religion was near an optimum — "Evidence was placed before the Parliamentary Committee . . . showing that in the Parish of St. Mary-le-bone, London, there were more people in the drink shops on Sunday Evening than in all the churches and chapels."

Most telling was the conversation between the Revd. Dr. White of Liverpool[1] and a working man he met casually in the street. "Well, Tom, what do you think about closing the public houses on Sundays?" "Think, sir," said Tom, "it's the whole talk among us, and we all wish it was done. It would be a grand thing for us." "Do you mean to say you do not go to the beershop ever on Sundays, or that those who go would not be angry at us for closing them up?" "No, sir," said Tom; "here's the way of it. I go out without any notion of going into a public house, but I meet an acquaintance. We begin to talk about the times. We go in just to have one glass, he treats me, and I treat him, and then we go on till we both spend our money; and if we have money enough, may be, get drunk. Then we go home and fight with the wife and children. It's the men who suffer most and spend the most money in the public house on Sundays who would be the most pleased to see them shut up." "Well, but the gentlemen all say it is the working man and his beer that make them not willing to see these places shut up on Sundays." "I know that, sir," he replied, "they say that, but if they will come amongst us, and let us tell our own story they will find that the

[1]Probably the Revd. Dr. V. M. White, a presbyterian minister in that city.

working people, with few exceptions, want them shut up altogether on Sundays. I'm not a teetotaller; I take a drop, and sometimes more than I should; but the opening of these places on Sundays is a sore curse to the poor man and his family. They are just tempting us to do wrong, and then punishing us if we do . . ."

In Scotland crime had diminished since the passing of a bill closing public houses on Sunday in that country. Having read the evidence, Christopher wrote "My compassion for those working men who are drawn off on the Sunday from God and His Gospel, and so from pardon, peace, holiness, and happiness, by the open public house, has been deepened, and I have confidence in them that, however much a few of them may be for a time misled on this question, even these will in the end be found shrewd enough to distinguish between those who really love them and their families, and those who love their wages. They know very well that the ministers of Christ, and a multitude of Christian laymen, desire them to have out of their own hard-earned wages, more comfortable homes, more warmth, more meat, better clothing for themselves and for their helpless wives and children, so dependent upon their unselfish care and self-denial. They know that we wish them to be happy with their families in their own homes on the happiest day of the week, and to go with joy to God's house of prayer; to be happy in time, and happy through the full and free salvation of our Lord Jesus Christ in eternity."

To Christopher, no narratives were more interesting than ones which illustrate the grace of God towards individuals. He loved to recount those which became known to him in the course of his work at Oxford. A high favourite concerned John Ryle, afterwards Bishop of Liverpool.[1] During the twenty-eight years which followed the day on which Ryle took his bachelor's degree after a 'first' in 'greats', he had not set foot in Oxford. He did not proceed M.A. until 1871. In 1865 Christopher invited him to preach at St. Aldate's and to stay at Richmond Lodge. His host never forgot the story of his conversion to God. Ryle had been a prominent member of the undergraduate world, treasurer of university cricket as well as a Craven scholar. Ryle's scout told Arthur Downer that as an undergraduate

[1]Father of Dr. H. E. Ryle, Bishop of Winchester, and grandfather of Professors G. and J. A. Ryle of Oxford.

he was full of fun and mischief, but never did anything to be ashamed of. He was not, however, a Christian. One evening he had wandered into a parish church in Oxford, possibly St. Ebbe's (he could not remember), and during the slow, measured reading of the second lesson, from the second chapter of *The Epistle to the Ephesians,* as the eighth verse was reached, "For by grace are ye saved . . . through faith; . . . and that not of yourselves: . . . it is the gift of God . . .", Ryle was converted.

When he was first ordained, he modelled his style of preaching on Canon Melvill of St. Paul's — whose eloquence Christopher remembered from listening to him at Great St. Mary's, Cambridge. Ryle told Christopher that he had preserved these sermons in the style of Melvill written in a very neat, small hand, on which Christopher's comment was "What will those say to this who have had the privilege of receiving letters from Bishop Ryle?" It was unfairly alleged that only one compositor was able to read Ryle's handwriting. His terse and clear style did not subsequently resemble Melvill's at all. Dr. Hawtrey, Provost of Eton, whose pupil he had been, was reported to have said "None but an Eton boy could write that English." But Ryle had changed his style deliberately, during his curate days, from a strong sense of duty, when he found that farm labourers did not understand his more polished sermons. He remarked to Christopher "I crucified my style for the sake of the villagers in Hampshire."

In the same spirit, Ryle for years wore shabby clothes, Canon Bardsley told Christopher, while paying off some of the small depositors of his father's bank, which had failed. Christopher would say characteristically, "When Bishop Ryle and I have both fallen asleep some of the self-denying good works of a great preacher of Justification by Faith without the works of the Law, will become known, for which some of the opponents of the great truth of Justification by Faith declared in the Eleventh Article of our Church, do not perhaps give him credit now." The remainder of Ryle's story has become familiar enough — how he worked as a country parson until over sixty, studying and writing his instructive tracts and books, still so widely read, and spending the last twenty years of his life as Bishop of Liverpool. It was on the occasion of his first visit to St. Aldate's that he sought George Whitefield's rooms at Pembroke, only to find that the servitor's garret of the great evangelist was forgotten, though that of Dr. Johnson, his contemporary, was not.

Another, if less distinguished, son of Pembroke, Robert Payne Smith,[1] became Regius Professor of Divinity in 1865. Thus for the remainder of the decade, two of the divinity chairs — Charles Heurtley being Lady Margaret Professor — were held by evangelicals. Payne Smith preached occasionally for Christopher at St. Aldate's, but his personal influence was not as strong as, for example, in the next decade, that of another canon of Christ Church, Edward King, afterwards Bishop of Lincoln. Hector McNeile, a son of Christopher's friend Dean McNeile, became a Fellow of St. John's in the same year. The Bampton Lecturers of the day included Thomas Bernard, Vicar of Walcot, in 1864, according to Stock the "most spiritual of Bampton Lecturers," (who preached at St. Aldate's at this time,) Edward Garbett, of Christ Church, Surbiton, editor of *The Record,* subsequently a founder of Wycliffe Hall, in 1867, and in 1869 the Regius Professor himself.

Among other notable preachers for Christopher during the period covered by this chapter were Bishops Alford of Victoria, Hong Kong, and Gell of Madras; Sir Emilius Bayley, Vicar of St. John's, Paddington; and Daniel Wilson the younger, Vicar of Islington, son of the Bishop of Calcutta of the same name whom Christopher had known in India. By 1866 the average congregation at St. Aldate's was 700. The number of communicants had risen to 80 at festivals and New Year's Day, and 70 at the monthly communion, approximately three times as many at the latter as in 1860, bringing the total up to what it had been in 1851. The names on the Sunday School roll too, had risen, to 264, a hundred more children than six years previously. Litany and sermon were held now on Wednesdays. Some had ceased to attend church for fear the spire would fall. Declared a dangerous structure, it was taken down (for £26) in 1865 and not rebuilt till 1873. Christopher himself was recognised, by 1867, — when he is so described in an appeal for the organ put out by the churchwardens — as "our greatly-beloved Rector".

The poorly constructed school buildings were demolished in July 1865, and the children were temporarily taught — boys on one side

[1]Father of W. H. Payne Smith, Vice-Principal of Wycliffe Hall 1880-83, and Student of Christ Church 1875-1943.

and girls on the other — in the university boat-house, Isis Street. The new schools were ready by the following January. These — of 'white' brick faced with Bath stone — designed by J. T. Christopher, the Rector's cousin, who was always employed on such occasions — erected by C. Selby of St. Aldate's, who later built a new rectory — continued to serve the parish until 1946. Pulled down in 1961, their site, on the east side of the main road, towards Folly Bridge, is at present occupied by a car park.

The opening on Tuesday 22 January 1866 was a public occasion not far short in importance of the reopening of the church in 1863. This time the Bishop of Oxford, Dr. Samuel Wilberforce, was able to be present. Divine service was held in church at 3 p.m. in the presence of a crowded congregation. The Bishop, Archdeacon Clerke, Christopher, and Nash, took part, a sermon being preached by Dr. Wilberforce from *Romans* 12.7, and a collection amounting to over £100. Afterwards Christopher entertained about two hundred persons at tea in the schools, where Mrs. Christopher presided at a sale of work at one end. The Bishop, the Vice-Chancellor, — Dr. J. P. Lightfoot, Rector of Exeter College, — the Provost of Oriel, Dr. Hawkins (who had been elected in preference to Keble nearly forty years before), the Master of University College, Dr. F. C. Plumptre, the Principal of St. Mary Hall, Dr. D. P. Chase, Canon Payne Smith, Regius Professor of Divinity, Canon Shirley, Regius Professor of Ecclesiastical History (who died later in the year at the age of thirty-eight), J. W. Burgon, Vicar of the university church, H. Linton of St. Peter-le-Bailey, S. Y. N. Griffith of St. Ebbe's, J. D. Hales of St. John's, Richmond, Christopher's old vicar, E. P. Hathaway, then curate of St. Giles-in-the-Fields, London, and the Mayor, J. C. Cavell, were among those present. The tea, produced by Mr. Boffin, was pronounced very satisfactory. The Bishop, whose zeal for all forms of church extension was well known in the diocese and beyond, expressed his sympathy with the work and his "esteem for their worthy Rector." He noted with particular pleasure the goodwill evident from all quarters, and made a powerful appeal for financial support. The Vice-Chancellor congratulated the Rector on behalf of the university, which had contributed £100. Like many other academic clergy of the day, Dr. Lightfoot, being also Vicar of Kidlington, had knowledgeable sympathy with the parochial life

35. BELL-COTE, ST. ALDATES' SCHOOLS, 1960
Built 1865; demolished 1961

36. PULPIT, ST. ALDATE'S, OXFORD, 1964
Erected 1863

37. RECTORY ROOM, ST. ALDATE'S, OXFORD, 1964
Built 1869, at rear of Rectory rebuilt 1878

38. RECTORY ROOM, interior, 1964

of the church. Christopher returned thanks for both speeches, commenting on the Bishop's part in promoting the reconstructions of the past few years, — his presence now being a compensation for his enforced absence from the opening of St. Aldate's, — and remarking that the three hundred free seats there were well filled with working people. Provost Hawkins said a few words, and Dr. Payne Smith (a substantial contributor) recalled the mean buildings screening the church in his undergraduate days at Pembroke, compared with its present attractive appearance. Alderman Randall of Grandpont House, J. T. Christopher and C. Selby, architect and builder respectively, Messrs. Linton, Hathaway (whom Christopher introduced as the primary agent in his coming to St. Aldate's), Hales, and Nash, all had their say. The building cost some £1600, and much of this had still to be raised.

In 1866 there were 98 boys and 71 girls, in addition to 95 infants, in the schools. Log books of the boys' school covering the years 1868 to 1900, and of the girls' from 1863 to closure in 1910, show that Christopher for many years, and his curates always, visited and taught several times a week. Two minute books of managers' meetings — 1866 to 1903; 1903–28, 1930 to final closure in 1946 — likewise bear witness to the constant attention paid by Christopher (as by many other parish clergy of the period), to the *minutiae* of education in the locality where he was minister.

Christopher was not content with church services as a means of evangelization. He took the Town Hall and secured the ministry of well-known evangelists. These meetings were not at first successful. But in 1867, at Christopher's request, Henry Bazely, a young resident graduate, sent to Hathaway, who was now in holy orders, and shortly to become rector of St. Ebbe's, a letter which incidentally bears its own testimony to what Christopher was achieving. "At the close of last Term Mr. Christopher suggested to me that you would be glad to have some account of the efforts which have been lately made in Oxford for bringing a saving knowledge of the Gospel home to unawakened souls in the city and the University . . . We have indeed very great reason to thank God for the measure of success which he bestowed upon the undertaking, far beyond that which we, in our weak faith, ventured to expect. Two years ago, when a series of services somewhat similar in character was held in the

Town-hall, the attendance was very poor, and no fruits, as far as we know, have ever appeared. This result, I doubt not, was due — in God's providence — to the coldness and indifference which many of us showed towards the work. This year, thank God, the contrast is very great — large numbers have come together to hear the Gospel, and already we have been permitted to witness the power of the Gospel manifested in the conversion of sinners. Ten public meetings were held in the Town-hall, and one in the Music-hall.[1] Six were conducted by Lord Radstock, two by Mr. Haslam,[2] while the remaining three were taken respectively by Mr. Blackwood, Colonel Rowlandson, and Captn. Fishbourne. At all of these the attendance was very good — at some the room was crowded to excess. The people were always very attentive, and a deep tone of solemnity pervaded the meetings, while there was not a trace of unwholesome excitement, nor an approach to disorder. Numbers used to stay for the prayer meeting which was held after the address was concluded, and thus opportunities were found for speaking privately to individuals, the results of which in some instances were very encouraging . . . The full results of the Word preached are known to God only; but we are aware of several cases of conversion, effected by the instrumentality of the recent services. These are exclusively among the townspeople, who always formed a very considerable majority at the meetings. It is satisfactory to hear from Mr. Nash that all these converts are standing steadfast in the faith which they have professed. A public prayer meeting, open to the whole city, was commenced at the end of June — it is held in St. Aldate's Old Rectory, and begins daily at noon. Though the numbers naturally are rather fluctuating at first, it is on the whole well attended, and has been found to be a means of drawing together those who are earnest in working for God, and of softening denominational prejudices. At the same time it affords a ready method of keeping up some intercourse with the new converts. The members of the University did not attend the meetings in such numbers as we desired and expected. This was partly due, no doubt, to the time of year . . . I must not forget to mention two very interesting occasions on which a number of University men met together

[1]This perhaps refers to the Holywell Music Room.

[2]W. Haslam, a well-known evangelist, Rector of Buckenham, Norfolk, later of of Curzon Chapel, Mayfair, who preached at St. Aldate's in May 1867.

— once in Mr. Christopher's house, when seventy of his undergraduate friends were present, and listened to two short addresses from Lord Radstock and Lord Adelbert Cecil[1] — the other occasion, a breakfast to which forty-eight came by special invitation from Mr. Christopher to meet Mr. Haslam . . . One undergraduate — a scholar of his College, an able and influential man — was led through conversation with Lord Radstock to experience the joy and peace of believing, and to come out boldly and take his stand decidedly on the Lord's side. The effect of the services with regard to the University has been chiefly to stir up those who were growing cold and sluggish in work for the Lord . . . A prayer meeting for the Junior Members of the University, which used to be held twice a week, and was attended by only six or eight on an average, has developed into one which is held every evening, at which double the number are usually present. We cannot be sufficiently grateful to Mr. Christopher, for the interest and trouble which he took in the services and the arrangements for them — without his valuable help, advice, and encouragement, such an effort — if ever it had been made — would have, humanly speaking, been in vain, or would have fallen far short of the success which has actually attended it. Only those who reside there can be fully conscious of the blessing which Mr. Christopher has been and is to the young men of Oxford."

It was thus that the Daily Prayer Meeting, to which Bazely appears to allude, and held for many years at St. Aldates' Rectory, came into being. Arthur Downer, a devoted son of Oxford, then an undergraduate at Brasenose, must be permitted to give his account of its origin. " While this work was at its height and was creating no little stir among us, one morning in the Summer Term, 1867, I was walking with C. H. C. Ward, of Exeter College, near the Schools, between Brasenose and Broad Street, while he, in his enthusiastic way, was expatiating on the need for constant prayer for so important an enterprise. I offered my room in what was then No. 10 in the Back Quad of B.N.C., for a prayer-meeting every evening, and though the Eights were in full course, we had twelve or fourteen men daily with a great spirit of prayer. The next term F. J. Chavasse of Corpus proposed that this meeting should be held, with Mr. Christopher's permission, in St. Aldate's Old Rectory, 40

[1] Brother of the third Marquess of Exeter.

Pembroke Street, and this was done. In this way originated the Oxford University Daily Prayer Meeting . . ." Downer also mentions other speakers at the Town Hall, including the Earl of Cavan and Joseph Samme, 'the Costermonger.'

Before proceeding further, some description must be given, on account of Christopher's great love for him, of the author of the above letter, Henry Bazely, who graduated in 1865 and remained in Oxford until his death in 1883. Christopher's esteem for Bazely was such that he desired that they should be buried as closely as possible to each other, and their remains lie in nearby graves in Jericho cemetery, Walton Street. Henry Casson Barnes Bazely was the son of the Revd. Thomas Bazely, sometime Fellow of Brasenose. While a schoolboy at Radley, he reacted against the sacerdotalism of the Warden, William Sewell, and became strongly evangelical, with a decided tendency towards ecclesiastical puritanism. He was a classical scholar at Brasenose from 1861, and being subsequently appointed to a Hulme exhibition was obliged to continue residence after taking his degree. He maintained himself as a theological coach, for which his fine, clear, sound mind admirably suited him. Bazely was to become a powerful spiritual force in the university city. He it was who began open air preaching at the Martyrs' Memorial in 1870. For the present he was an enthusiastic follower of Christopher, though he did not feel able to accept his curacy in 1868.[1] He in fact became fascinated by Scottish presbyterianism, and founded a presbyterian chapel in Alfred Street,[2] St. Giles's. Then he had second thoughts, was made deacon, and for nearly a year, in 1876, served as curate of St. Aldate's. But he soon felt that he had taken a false step, and withdrew, shortly afterwards renewing his presbyterian ministry, in Nelson Street. Bazely's was in truth a somewhat awe-inspiring character, with a strong streak of calvinistic piety; but he was a most devoted Christian, beloved by many of Oxford's poor.

As might be expected, one of Christopher's main objects in all his work at Oxford was to arouse interest in foreign missions. From 1861 till 1907, and possibly later, he served as a secretary of the Oxford association of the Church Missionary Society. Minute books do not seem to have survived for these years; but a

[1] In this year, rather than subscribe the Articles, he took a B.C.L.

[2] Now Pusey Street.

number of annual reports are preserved in the Bodleian Library. From the latter it appears that at least until 1876 the senior secretary was E. A. Litton, a former Fellow of Oriel, Rector of St. Clement's till 1861, thereafter Rector of Naunton, Gloucestershire; and until 1881, Prebendary Gandell, Professor of Arabic, who in 1880 became in addition a Canon of Wells. From 1863, however, Christopher was described as 'Resident Secretary'; but the custom of having two or three other clerical secretaries still obtained. Among the most memorable of his activities were his 'missionary breakfasts'. It was by these that he was widely known in later years among men of all schools of thought in Oxford. But during his first decade or two, pressing the claims of the foreign mission field was exceedingly hard work. Bishop Gore, preaching in St. Aldate's after Christopher's death, referred to this as one of the most striking of his achievements. "He supposed," he was reported as saying, "that by this time it might be said it had come about that it was a mere sign of stupidity not to take an interest in missions . . . but in the days of which he was speaking, forty years ago, things were very different; undoubtedly the missionary cause was very unpopular, it stood very much where it was represented as standing in the pages of writings of men like Thackeray and Dickens. It was a matter of ridicule, and all sorts of silly jests could still be made by reasonable people about it. The minds of most Englishmen were possessed with the idea that there was enough to be done at home. It was in that atmosphere Canon Christopher had again the courage of his convictions, and in a way which in this city and in the University, and throughout the world, helped to play no insignificant part in producing the great change in public opinions and in the minds of Churchmen which they had witnessed. He insisted from the beginning in keeping the cause of the evangelisation of the world to the fore, not from any motive of political or imperial or universal expediency, but solely and simply from the one common motive that this was the command of Christ, and that there was no other name whereby men might be saved except the name of Christ."

An illustration from the 'sixties, once often quoted, now forgotten, suggests more than one point besides. At that time the Society for the Propagation of the Gospel supported evangelicals, — missionaries and bishops, — in the field, and even though he would not subscribe to a society which maintained agents who propagated advanced tractarianism, Christopher usually attended the annual meetings in Oxford, and was always thankful if he could stir up his high church brethren to be more zealous for their society. Thus he went to a meeting presided over by Bishop Wilberforce and addressed by Bishop Selwyn, the missionary-hearted bishop from New Zealand. He was again present six years later when Dr. Selwyn was again the speaker, and when that bishop expressed his surprise that there had not been a meeting of the society in Oxford since his previous visit, in 1860. Once Christopher went so far as to speak himself.

One method by which Christopher sought to stir the existing apathy was by inviting leading missionary advocates to address meetings of undergraduates at his house. These gatherings, at least between 1861 and 1864, were held once or twice a term. They were, according to G. A. Allan, "memorable occasions . . . The three reception-rooms were filled with men, chiefly Undergraduates — even in those far-back days — and the hall and staircase were crowded." Here Allan heard Thomas of Tinnevelly, Bishop Russell of China, and Dr. Miller of Birmingham. When the house was full, the front door was locked that the speaker might not be interrupted; but late comers were let in at the side garden door[1] and the staircase was used as a safety-valve. Those already seated on the stairs were requested to go higher and higher to make room on the lower steps for the latest comers. The speaker addressed his scattered audience from the bottom of the staircase.

When John Thomas spoke there were a hundred and ten undergraduates present. He had had a very remarkable conversion, and Christopher used to say that the facts could be vouched for because the clergyman who was instrumental in bringing it about, the Revd. J. B. Byers, a Pembrokeshire incumbent, was a relation of his by marriage. When Thomas first went to Tinnevelly, there were few baptized converts, scarcely any native communicants, only one girl at school and very few boys. When he addressed the undergraduates at Richmond Lodge, there were in his district ten thousand baptized native Christians, three thousand native communicants, twelve hundred girls at school, and sixteen hundred boys.

[1]Plate 34.

A meeting was usually held at Christopher's house before a 'missionary breakfast'. Downer recalled Sir Bartle Frere, then Governor of Bombay — who was given an honorary D.C.L. in 1867 — speaking on one such occasion in the later 'sixties. Another speaker was Sir Herbert Edwardes of the Punjab, already mentioned in connection with the siege of Multan, also an honorary Doctor of Civil Law. Among those who spoke for Christopher at the turn of the decade, Bishop Ingham heard Bishop Barker of Sydney and Captain Nevile Sherbrooke, who matriculated from St. Alban Hall a few years later and became incumbent of the Portman Chapel, London. Aglionby remembered hearing both Frere and Edwardes at the first at-home he attended at Richmond Lodge.

Exactly when the missionary breakfasts — held annually in one of the principal hotels — first began, is not altogether clear. Christopher used to speak of their having started in 1877[1]. But it seems almost certain that he intended to refer only to those financed by the Dowager Lady Buxton. There are references on the part of one-time undergraduate friends to missionary breakfasts ten and fifteen years earlier. We hear that this work was begun in a very small and quiet way. We learn, too, of a breakfast party of undergraduates at the Clarendon Hotel to listen to Dr. Moffat of the London Missionary Society, after a life-work in South Africa. The young men were delighted with "one of God's own nobility," as Christopher called him, "a Nonconformist ornament of the one Church of Christ, 'the blessed company of all faithful people'."

The plan was in any case similar. Christopher invited a first class speaker recently returned from the mission field to address a breakfast party of upwards of a hundred men of every school of thought, dons as well as undergraduates. All were supplied with packets of missionary literature to take away. One of the envelopes for 1889 is preserved in the Bodleian Library. Printed on it is a word to the recipient. "Dear Friend, Kindly place this packet in your pocket DURING the Breakfast. It would grieve me if in the hurry of going out at 9.50 you left it behind. I entreat you to read the enclosed. Sincerely yours, A. M. W. Christopher." "How well I remember," wrote Bishop Ingham, who matriculated in 1868, "the

[1]In 1879 "the usual annual Church Missionary Breakfast" is referred to for the first time in the annual report of the Oxford association.

first Missionary breakfast I attended at the 'Clarendon' in the Cornmarket! How careful Christopher was to assure us that we should get away in time for our ten o'clock lectures! Who can measure the influence of opportunities like these?" Christopher issued personal invitations. " Those of us," wrote G. W. Butler, " who remember seeing him writing letters, by the score, heap upon heap at the Union, especially when some special matter was on hand, well know how hard he worked as a correspondent. Special arrangements had to be made, I believe, so that the Union letter-carriage might not be over-burdened by the great increase of letters thus occasioned."

Perhaps the most memorable missionary meeting during the period under consideration was the one held (partly under Christopher's auspices) in 1869 in the dining hall of Brasenose College as a farewell to Thomas French, a former Fellow of University College, and John Knott, an erstwhile Fellow of Brasenose, Junior Proctor in 1853 and originally curate of St. Paul's, Oxford, who had abandoned tractarianism in favour of evangelical beliefs. Both men were going to India. French, it was remarked, was leaving behind a wife and eight children; Knott a benefice worth £800 a year. Edward Hathaway, then living at Oxford, wrote that " An event precisely similar had never before occurred in the history of the University." The meeting drew most of the principal men in Oxford. More effective still, perhaps, was Christopher's personal, carefully but unselfconsciously balanced influence on individuals. Equally, as Arthur Downer has recorded, " he put before us the ideals of service in missionary work abroad and in the great parishes of our large towns."

Christopher was clearly no less sympathetic towards other evangelical societies. He served on the local committee of the Church Pastoral-Aid Society from 1860 for at least twenty years, being a vice-president of the Oxford association from 1899 to 1908 and probably longer. Again, between 1881 and 1904, if not earlier and later, he was a member of the committee of the Oxford and Oxfordshire Auxiliary Society for the Promotion of Christianity amongst the Jews, later known as Church Missions to Jews, of which in the 'sixties his friend Goodhart was Secretary at headquarters.

Christopher's influence was not only felt in Oxford. In 1868 he read a topical paper, which was subsequently printed, at Derby, during the annual conference of the Clerical and Lay Association for the Maintenance of Evangelical Principles in the Midlands, entitled *A Few Thoughts on the Best Means of Fortifying the Minds of Educated Young Men against Infidelity and Popery.* The pages of this little work do not display profound thought; but they typify the character of the man. Christopher was bent on bringing to the attention of his brethren from ordinary parishes some practical considerations in regard to undergraduate Christianity. He maintained that the best Christians are those who come up as freshmen well grounded already in the faith. He went on to remind his hearers that during half the year, undergraduates are presumably amenable, during vacations, to parochial influence.

"You will greatly help those who are working for Christ in the universities, if you will send up truly converted men, well instructed in the Word of God. Encourage wealthy Christians to use their talent in sending up decided young men who have been already tried and proved to be Christians taught of God, but who cannot themselves afford a university education. One clergyman known to me, has been the instrument in helping to holy orders fourteen young men from out of his own congregation. Some valuable young men I have known at Oxford were converted to God when engaged in business . . . If we bear in mind that undergraduates are only half the year resident in their university, and that the other half of the year some of them are within the reach of some of you; and if we also remember that those who have been brought out of Tractarian errors, have generally been able to trace their deliverance to conversation with some well-instructed, faithful, loving friend, who has led them to search the Scriptures honestly; I think we shall see that one of the most blessed results of this Conference might be for the Lord to stir up *every one* of His faithful servants now present to use more courageously, more hopefully, more perseveringly, *personal efforts* to bring the truth of the Gospel, direct from the Word of God, before such young men as are known to them, and to apply this truth faithfully and in true Christian love to their consciences. It was in this way two young men, known to me, were brought to God *before* they came up to Oxford. Their influence was felt even when they were freshmen; and they have never wavered, but have steadily promoted the daily undergraduates' prayer meeting held in my Rectory, and other Christian efforts, and have used personal endeavours to bring God's truth before other undergraduates . . .

"One of the principal reasons why many young men fall so easily under the influence of earnest but mistaken teachers, is, that they have never been well instructed in the doctrines of the Gospel, and so have never been drawn to Christ as a living personal Saviour. Not a few are even unable to distinguish clearly between justification and sanctification. We cannot be too clear in fixing in the minds of young men the passages of Scripture which establish a doctrine. Earnest and affectionate exhortation is necessary, but if this, and not *Scriptural instruction,* be the characteristic of our teaching, we shall leave our young friends to be unsettled by Baptists, drawn away by Plymouth Brethren, or to become the subject of a Tractarian reaction, or even of a Neologian overthrow."

As usual Christopher advised giving to such men suitable books and pamphlets. It may here be observed that in common with all true evangelicals, he had no hesitation in repudiating, in love, false religious systems, whether heathen, pagan, or Christian. After all, the New Testament as well as the Old abounded, not least in the recorded sayings of Jesus, in allusions to the snare of wrong belief, propagated by the misguided teaching of those to whom Christopher always charitably referred as 'mistaken men'. "May He use whom He will, to make known to many of our university men those glad tidings which, when they are through the Spirit received into the heart, fill it with joy, and hold it for ever with power from the Lord, against the intrusion of deadly religious error."

At the annual clerical meeting held at Southport in the following year, Christopher read another typical paper, on *How may the Clergy further the Supply of suitable Candidates for the Ministry?*, which was also printed in pamphlet form. Already the prayers he had asked for the previous year at Derby seemed to have been answered. "The fact which fills me with most thankfulness is one not connected with those who are working for Christ in Oxford, but more with you and others who seek the souls of young men before they go to the University. It is this — that of late more truly converted young men have come up to Oxford as freshmen. These men are steadfast and most helpful to us. They have not merely evangelical opinions, but they have *life in Christ* . . . Certainly God is giving a spirit of prayer to an increasing number of undergraduates in our Universities. I have good reason to hope that more men really pray in their College Chapels than formerly." Prayer therefore formed his main theme. He appealed too for greater Christian devotedness.

Christopher also spoke of the need for more discretion among the parish clergy as to suitable candidates for the ministry, quoting his friend Boultbee of St. John's, Highbury: "We want three things. 1st.—Sincere devoted piety. 2nd.—Real brightness and intelligence. 3rd.—Industry in its form of perseverance. We do not want merely a good, dull young man, who has a notion that he would like to be a clergyman. But how to get our dear brethren to discriminate, to discourage the one, and to suggest to the other, is a difficult thing indeed. But our young men certainly want guidance." Christopher had taken some trouble to inquire into the possibilities of the newly introduced 'unattached students' system at Oxford, whereby men might take university degrees without being at the expense of joining a college —the 'scholares non ascripti'. The Revd. G. W. Kitchin, one of the delegates, afterwards Dean of Durham, informed him that for a total of £166.10s. a man could read for a degree, clothes, travelling, and books being additional expenses. Christopher, on Kitchin's recommendation, appealed for scholarships of £25 a year "to be given to those who pass the best examination in the contents of the *English* Bible."

Finally he cited the example of the Bardsley and Moule families, where the sons of evangelical clergymen had mainly, without the slightest parental pressure, entered the ministry which their fathers' good example had set before them as the most desirable form of Christian service. Henry Moule of Fordington, father of Handley Moule, Bishop of Durham, had written to him "Imperfectly as I have done it myself, I would say that if the Clergy would further the bringing forward of fit men for the ministry, they must give themselves far more than is commonly done to *prayer in the spirit of our Liturgy;* they must live more to God, delighting in Him and in His service; they must separate their families from worldly pleasures, *and from such reading as does not tend to strengthen, elevate, and improve the mind.* Lastly — I believe that if the Clergy would exert the influence they ought to exert for good, they must prepare themselves to cease very much from *Public Schools,* and be for their own families, and very much for their parishioners, more complete *instructors*." It is perhaps pertinent to add that this attitude towards the public schools, fairly common among evangelicals of the day, was not shared, for example, by Christopher's friend Ryle.

Christopher's influence was felt as much in the home as outside or in intercourse with visitors of an hour or two. In May 1868, Thomas Raine, a rather serious young man of eighteen, member of a Durham family, came to stay at Richmond Lodge in the company of his cousin, Caroline Smith, who was a cousin at one remove of Alfred and Maria Christopher, being grand-daughter of John Christopher of Crook Hall, elder brother of Alfred's father. It was his first visit to Oxford, for Raine was an undergraduate of St. Andrew's; later in life he was ordained, and became Rector of South Witham, Lincolnshire. For the present, Raine felt, the approach to Oxford from the railway station " might very well be taken for the entrance to a third rate manufacturing town." Nor, in spite of favourable spring weather and luxuriating foliage, did the remainder of the drive to Richmond Lodge please him much better. As soon as he began exploring, however, he was charmed, indeed bewildered, " by the number and the beauty of the Colleges," and began to " think rather disparagingly of my little Alma Mater." An impression at least as happy was made by his host and hostess.

" Mr. Christopher," Raine noted in his diary, " is a most delightful man: so pious, good, and amiable. He affords a striking proof that Religion can be made a pleasant as well as an edifying and proper topic of conversation. Mrs. Christopher is also very kind and good." These comments were entered on the day of arrival, 11 May. The following day "Mr. Christopher expounded at prayer time very beautifully the tenth Romans." 13 May was Raine's nineteenth birthday. He did not write in his diary till three days later, after he had left Oxford. Looking back he could say: " It seems to me that I have in the last few days taken a fresh shoot, so to speak, in the knowledge of God, in yearning after Christ, in realising more fully the power of prayer. And this I am sure is the result, through God's grace, of my meeting Mr. Christopher, whose piety and zeal make me ashamed of my own pride and coldness of heart."

In the Oxford parishes changes were again taking place. The most important of these was at St. Ebbe's. At last, in 1868, the insane and now aged Rector died, and it was not unsuitable that the choice of the trustees fell upon one of their own number, Edward Hathaway, who had done so much for the cause of evangelicalism in Oxford and who had been ordained in 1864, to a curacy with his old college friend Anthony Thorold, afterwards Bishop of Winchester. A sketch of Hathaway's life in *Home Words* for 1897 informs us that he had consulted Christopher in his chambers at Lincoln's Inn as to the advisability of ordination at the age of forty-six. Hathaway had a good legal practice, but it was not the sacrifice involved which caused him to hesitate. Christopher told him: " If you only live to preach Christ six months, it is worth your being ordained." Christopher had warmly advocated his appointment to St. Ebbe's, and had called on undergraduate friends to pray for it, so strongly did he feel that it would make for the extension of spiritual influence in Oxford. The new Rector found the reconstruction of the church unfinished, and was also obliged to add to the small Rectory[1] designed by Street and erected by Cameron. Hathaway held Greek Testament classes for undergraduates, but he never took as prominent a part in the university work as Christopher. Nevertheless, the latter greatly welcomed the residence in Oxford of one whom he respected so much. His church gradually filled to overflowing. When the church schools of Oxford were threatened, Hathaway led a successful campaign against the introduction of a school board. In 1869 Joseph West was followed at Holy Trinity by Robert Guinness of Queen's, and in 1870 by Sydney Linton of Wadham, a son of Henry Linton of St. Peter-le-Bailey, and, like Christopher, a cricket 'blue', who afterwards became Bishop of Riverina. In the university, Edmund Knox was elected a Fellow of Merton in 1868.

At St. Aldate's, when Thomas Nash was appointed by Bishop Pelham of Norwich to be minister of a new district, St. Philip's, in Heigham,[2] in 1868, Christopher worked the parish alone for several months. Nash preached his farewell sermons on 19 July. Bazely declined to succeed; but he agreed to become a " regular

[1]Employing as architect J. T. Christopher.
[2]Starting with no church, hall, or parsonage, in due course he became Vicar.

lay helper" in the parish, and served in that capacity from October 1868 to December 1869. This, declared his biographer, the Revd. E. L. Hicks, then a Fellow of Corpus, subsequently Bishop of Lincoln, "was of the greatest advantage to him," for "Every kind of agency that could be devised in a populous city parish, worked on the Evangelical plan, was here in operation." Christopher eventually appointed as curate a friend of Bazely's, Henry Charles Sturdy, a non-graduate, who worked for his degree, as a member of Christ Church, while serving his curacy. Sturdy, who officiated for the first time on 2 May, was as much attached to Christopher as his predecessor had been. "From the year 1869 to 1873 [*sic*] it was my great privilege to be his curate . . . I shall never cease to thank God for the six years during which I worked so happily with one who was the very embodiment of Christian love. This will be acknowledged by all who knew him as his chief characteristic." By 1869 communicants numbered over 100 at festivals and approximately 120 each month. The rise in the latter was partly due to the introduction of an additional communion service, an early administration taking place on the second Sunday in the month at 8.30 a.m. Three years later, with the further introduction of an evening communion (the order of addition and the proportionate increases are interesting), the average monthly figure was 200. No doubt the larger numbers of communicants was the reason for Christopher's gift of communion plate. He presented to the parish a large silver paten of 1868 and a sizeable goblet-shaped cup of 1863, both by Barnard, and inscribed "Ecclesiae Sancti Aldati dono dedit Aluredus Gulielmus Christopher A. M. Anno Domini 1872." Sunday School attendance in 1869 totalled over 300 children every week.

It was at this time that the press at St. Aldates' Rectory for the undergraduates' Bible readings had become so great that better accommodation was essential. One Saturday evening in Trinity term 1869, Charles Goodhart was present to give the address. The crowd of university men in the upper room overflowed on to the staircase outside. After the meeting Christopher pointed out to Goodhart how greatly a larger room was needed, one which might also be used for parochial gatherings and other religious objects as well. Goodhart could not but concede the point. Christopher immediately said " I want you to give me this large room ," to which Goodhart replied " I wish I could afford to do so." Christopher remarked that this was a small matter, and as he did not intend to go begging all over the country for the cost of the room, he suggested that if Goodhart would write about it to six friends, whose names Christopher supplied, they would give the entire cost. Goodhart willingly undertook to do this, and the six friends — of whom the first was Martin Hope Sutton, the seed merchant, a pillar of the newly erected church and parish of Greyfriars, Reading, who owed his conversion to Goodhart's ministry at St. Marys', Castle Street — subscribed the whole of the six hundred and forty pounds needed to build in the garden behind the house the well-known Rectory Room, holding from the first two hundred and fifty people. *The Oxford Chronicle* of 16 October 1869 records that " The Rector of St. Aldate's is building . . . a large meeting house for his parishioners . . . from the designs of Mr. John T. Christopher." Constructed of grey brick (originally "white") with stone dressings and a slate roof, it is not a beautiful erection, and it fills most of the Rectory garden; but it is hardly possible to exaggerate what has been its usefulness, not only to the parish, and in university ministrations, but also for the annual gatherings of evangelical societies. Christopher delighted to recall meetings held in that room, and to comment that where cabbages had grown, now souls grew. He would refer to his curates holding evangelistic assemblies and Bible classes in it, and to the many men well known in after life who attended the undergraduates' Bible readings. Here too he had shelves fitted and established a missionary library. On one wall hung a large card bearing the significant inscription EFFORT AND PRAYER. In his zeal Christopher was sometimes apt to forget how time was running on, and to add " one thing more " when his young hearers were feeling that they ought to be elsewhere. Some of them therefore presented a large-faced clock for the Rectory Room — it has only within recent years been replaced — as a help to bringing the proceedings to an end at the proper moment.

Among the first of those who often knelt there together on the coconut-matting were A. W. Poole of Worcester, afterwards Christopher's curate, and first Bishop of Japan, E. N. Hodges of Queen's, who became Bishop of Travancore, E. G. Ingham of St. Mary Hall,

M

later Bishop of Sierra Leone, H. Evington of Pembroke, subsequently Bishop of Kyushu, H. G. Grey of Wadham, Indian missionary, afterwards Principal of Wycliffe Hall, and R. H. A. Schofield of Lincoln, soon to be one of the earliest medical missionaries, most remarkably qualified, of the China Inland Mission, who, while reading physics — he took a first class in natural science in 1873 — won the Hall-Houghton Greek Testament prize. After Schofield's death in China in 1884, Christopher wrote: " Of the great number of undergraduates who, during the last quarter of a century, have attended habitually throughout their Oxford course the meeting for prayer and the exposition of the Word of God held at St. Aldate's Rectory every Saturday evening, I can remember no one who appeared to me to be more truly spiritual than dear Robert Harold A. Schofield, scholar of Lincoln College. For four years I had ever before me at that meeting the healthy, pure, and kindly countenance of the future medical missionary . . . attracted to the meeting by its spiritual character and scriptural teaching . . . That which God did in one heart He can do in another. What wonderful possibilities lie open to the union of prayers of faith for the outpouring of the Holy Spirit on our Universities! The Holy Spirit is able to make hundreds of undergraduates as willing to go anywhere and to do anything for Christ as dear Schofield was . . . what an amazing effect would be produced by an outpouring of the Holy Spirit upon Oxford, Cambridge and Dublin Universities! " Reading Schofield's life was to inspire a disciple of Christopher to volunteer for the China Inland Mission fifty years later.

"Dear Sturdy" was musical, and usually played the first hymn at the Saturday night meetings, as well as opening in prayer. Sturdy had previously been curate of St. Stephen's, Spitalfields. While there he 'discovered' George Wheelhouse, whom he was the means of transplanting to Oxford. Wheelhouse had been a private in the army, and in his early days both he and his bad-tempered wife were addicted to alcohol. When he went to India with his regiment, he did not write to her for several years. But on his return he found her converted, good-tempered, and lovable. The result was that, deeply impressed, he himself was converted. After leaving the army, he worked in an iron foundry in east London, and used his spare

39. A. M. W. CHRISTOPHER, *c.* 1870

40. MRS. CHRISTOPHER with her son HENRY, *c.* 1870

time to engage in evangelistic work. Thus Sturdy encountered him, and brought him to Oxford, where he laboured as a Scripture reader for many years. Preaching Sunday by Sunday at the Martyrs' Memorial, he became a well-known character in Oxford. At St. Giles's Fair he was an earnest helper of Bazely. We are told that "when Christopher held meetings for working men . . . his testimony was mightily used of God."

Sturdy and Christopher and Bazely were associated in Town Hall meetings for working people. Unknown to Christopher, a dying undergraduate asked his father to send the Rector of St. Aldate's fifty pounds to promote the simple preaching of the gospel among them. Sturdy has left an interesting account of what resulted. Before he came to St. Aldate's, he met Bazely at a prayer meeting in Arthur Downer's rooms at Brasenose. When he had moved to Oxford, this led "to my joining him in all kinds of Evangelistic work, such as the distribution of Handbills. These were scattered all over the poorer parts of Oxford, and brought crowded audiences, chiefly of working people, to the old Town Hall, to hear the Gospel preached by men like William Taylor, formerly a Navvy, who were supplied from week to week by the Evangelization Society . . . I attended those meetings and can testify to the remarkable power and beautiful simplicity, with which the five 'Rs' which the Evangelization Society required their agents to proclaim (Ruin, Redemption, Regeneration, Righteousness, Responsibility) were set forth. Never shall I forget one of William Taylor's addresses on 'The Great day of His wrath is come; and who shall be able to stand?' (Rev. vi. 17). I used to look out at the after meetings for 'wounded birds' . . . I think it was after an address by 'Charles Smith,' a working man, that I espied a young fellow whose sad face impressed me with the thought that he was anxious about his soul's salvation. I went to him, and asked whether it was so. On hearing his reply in the affirmative, I took him to a private room in the Town Hall, which was used by us as a kind of vestry, as there was necessarily a certain amount of disturbance in the large Hall, occasioned by the people leaving, and the conversations which others were holding with those who had been impressed. We prayed together. Young Ll. Lloyd gave his heart there and then to God. I asked him to join us in our St. Aldate's Sunday Schools, as a Teacher. He did so. He also attended H. Goodier's

Bible Class (afterwards Canon Goodier[1]), and there the missionary spirit was kindled in his breast, which led to his entering the C.M.S. college at Islington, and to his becoming the honoured and faithful Missionary at Fuh-chow."

Meanwhile at Richmond, Mr. Hales — who had preached at St. Aldate's in 1866 — probably foreseeing that his successor would not be an evangelical, had built Holy Trinity church, and had secured to it a parish carved out of his own. Its first incumbent, the Revd. Evan Henry Hopkins — a rising young engineer who had been ordained after his conversion some years before — had been curate at Portman Chapel, London, and it is recorded that his appointment to the new church at Richmond in 1870 was made partly on the recommendation of Canon Reeve, Minister of the Portman Chapel, and partly on that of Christopher. Hopkins had preached at St. Aldate's in November 1869. Thus Christopher exercised a guiding influence in a ministry which was to be potent in Richmond and to reach many thousands through the Keswick Convention and the journal which Evan Hopkins founded to promote his views on 'the higher Christian life,' a newspaper — *The Life of Faith* — which still flourishes.

On the night of Tuesday 28 June 1870 a rapid and fatal fire broke out in Collis's shop, 96 St. Aldate's, almost next to the church. Henry Collis escaped through a first-floor window; but his sister-in-law, Miss Mary Jackson, and a maidservant, Fanny Clifton, perished because the parish fire-escape had been removed to a yard nearly half a mile distant, and no ladder was at hand. The house was destroyed. Fanny Clifton had been only a few weeks in the parish. Mary Jackson had been for years well known to the Rector as a sincere Christian, " of an exemplary spirit and conduct, an habitual Communicant, and a constant attendant at the various Bible Classes and Prayer Meetings, held at St. Aldate's Rectory." She was also a member of Mrs. Hathaway's Bible class at St. Ebbe's, and, Hathaway wrote, " one of the brightest Christians belonging to it." " It is remarkable," he added, " how the Spirit of Jesus ripens His fruit ere He plucks it . . ." Little did Hathaway think that three years later his wife would likewise die suddenly in tragic

[1]J. H. Goodier of B.N.C., curate of St. Peter-le-Bailey 1870-72, later Vicar of Holy Trinity, Ripon, and honorary canon.

circumstances, and that he himself, in the fullness of years, would not recover from fatal burns. The classes and meetings at St. Aldate's to which reference is made above were the Women's Bible Class held at the Rectory every Monday evening at 8 p.m., with an attendance of 30 to 40 (one for men was held on Thursdays at 8.45 p.m., when between 20 and 25 came); and prayer meetings at the Rectory after the Sunday and Wednesday evening services, and at 3 p.m. on Sunday afternoons. Christopher officiated at Mary Jackson's largely-attended funeral in South Hinksey churchyard, and preached a memorial sermon on the Sunday morning following, 3 July, in St. Aldate's church, which was printed *verbatim* in *The Oxford Times*.

Speaking from *St. Luke* 12. 37, "Blessed are those servants, whom the Lord when He cometh shall find watching," Christopher enlarged on the uncertainty of life and the fact that the true Christian is ready for death at any moment. Mary Jackson had received the sacrament on the previous Sunday. "I cannot have a doubt that last Sunday morning she not only eat the bread (1 Corinthians xi, 26, 27, 28) given her 'in remembrance that Christ died for her', but also fed on Christ in her '*heart, by faith with thanksgiving*'. And so taking to herself the Lord's Atonement, not *only* in the solemn ordinance of the Lord's Supper, but also day by day in the exercise of a living faith, she was and is partaker of the benefit of Christ's death as the divine *Substitute for sinners*. What a wonderful transition was her's! The last moment of her consciousness on earth was amidst the terror of devouring flames, within a very few feet of this church; the next moment of consciousness she found herself 'absent from the body, present with the Lord.' Preserved in Jesus, no flames could ever reach her saved soul. Washed in His precious blood, no thought of the sins of earth can ever grieve her. She has found Him more gracious than her faith could have conceived, and the joy of His presence beyond anything for which she hoped. He who enabled her, by the faith He gave her, to wash her robes and make them white in the blood of the Lamb, has wiped away all tears from her eyes. She regrets not the tribulation of her last few minutes on earth, for she knows that she has done with sorrow for ever. There are no more weary days before her, for she has thus early been taken by the gracious Author of her salvation to the rest which remaineth for the people of God

. . . She walked by faith in the Son of God, who loved her and gave Himself for her. When on her last Sabbath she was asked by a Christian friend how she was, she replied, 'Happy, joyously happy'. During her last evening on earth, a few hours before the fire, she said to another friend, '*I have never felt so near to Jesus as now*' . . . let me entreat each one present to ask himself 'Am I *watching* for my Lord's return, and am I ready for that, or for the call of sudden death that at any time may exchange my preparation and watching on earth for meeting my Lord?' As you love your souls, as you desire eternal happiness, be faithful with yourselves this day, and make out by honest self-examination, whether you are watching, or *not* watching for the return of the Lord Jesus; whether you are living for Him, or *not* living for Him; whether you are believing on Him, or *not* believing on Him, so as to love Him, and live for Him, and work for Him; whether you are converted, or unconverted; whether you are saved through faith in Christ's blood, or whether you are still in a lost state . . ."

Christopher did not neglect his opportunities! Yet it is a curious fact that many years later, in 1931, a correspondent of the same newspaper in which this sermon was first published, could say that Christopher was so overcome by what had happened that he was unable to preach at the funeral, and that his place had been taken by "the Rev. – Nash, the curate, afterwards Dean [*sic*] of Norwich." The initials 'H.C.' appended to this letter suggest the name of Henry Chaundy, who as a lad had known St. Ebbe's under Hathaway, and survived till after the Second World War. The sermon which Christopher himself preached was afterwards printed in pamphlet form and sold by Harper, newsagent, at 31, St. Aldate's, " one dozen copies for sixpence ".

About this time, while Henry Elliott Fox, son of Henry Watson Fox of Wadham, the Indian missionary who may be regarded as the Henry Martyn of Oxford, was curate to Edward Hathaway (Fox being also a barrister) at St. Ebbe's, Christopher was in " the greatest difficulty I ever had in Oxford." Its nature is not revealed; but " I was in great trouble: I could do nothing more. I had done all I could." Shortly before, Christopher had attended a breakfast party for undergraduates held in Fox's lodgings in Cornmarket Street; Lord Radstock had also been present, and after the meal

41. ST. ALDATE'S, OXFORD, and Pembroke Street, between 1865, when spire dismantled, and 1870, when building on right destroyed by fire

Low CHURCH MINSTRELS entertaining
an enthuastic audience at the
Puritan School "Penny Readings"

42. "LOW CHURCH MINSTRELS", Oxford, *c.* 1870

H. LINTON	A. M. W. CHRISTOPHER	?	E. P. HATHAWAY	W. W. MERRY
St. Peter-le-Bailey	St. Aldate's		St. Ebbe's	All Saints

he drew the company's attention to *II Chronicles* 20. 12: "We know not what to do; but our eyes are upon Thee." It was a great help to Christopher. Soon afterwards, in a manner quite unexpected, the difficulty was removed. Remarking that "I have not a very good memory," but reminded by the presence of Lord Radstock, Christopher told this story at the anniversary meeting of the China Inland Mission at Mildmay Park in 1880. "Now that text has been a blessing ever since, and I do feel it is just the text to have in mind when we think of China's 400,000,000 . . . We are so entirely helpless that we are necessarily cast upon the Lord. Ever since that text was brought to my mind I have been thankful for the great difficulties of my life. When I am thoroughly helpless, thoroughly unable to meet the difficulties, and to overcome them, then I fall back upon that precious text . . . And again and again the Lord has helped me, and so He will help the China Inland Mission."

In the same year as the fire in St. Aldate's — 1870 — Christopher's sister Emma, wife of General Cautley, died. One of her sons, the Revd. Proby Cautley, had married Frances Hutton, whose father, the Revd. Henry Hutton, Rector of St. Paul's, Covent Garden, was a noted evangelical leader. Thus Christopher's family, though in the main unsympathetic to his views, was not without other clerical supporters of evangelical truth. In 1872 Maria Christopher lost her brother Commander Thomas Borradaile Christopher, a naval hero of earlier days, whom we last encountered at Richmond in 1854, and who in 1866 had married as his second wife Elizabeth, daughter of their first cousin John Danby Christopher. But in 1873 their sister Caroline — Christopher's cousin — made a belated, and unfortunate, marriage to the Revd. John Nagle-Gillman, who shortly became Vicar of Hennock, Devon. This union, however, was not so important to Alfred and Maria Christopher as a wedding which took place in 1871, when their elder son, Henry Christopher, had married, at the age of twenty-one, Julia Lucena, daughter of the Revd. Lorenzo Lucena, Reader in Spanish in the university, and, with his wife, a regular worshipper at St. Aldate's. Both Mr. and Mrs. Lucena were Spaniards.

As a young ordinand, Lucena had taken first classes in philosophy and theology at the university of Seville, and obtained a fellowship at his college of San Pelagio, Cordova. He was ordained into the Roman Catholic priesthood; but after eight years as Professor of Theology at San Pelagio, he severed his connection with the Church of Rome and became a member of the protestant episcopal church at Gibraltar, where he met his wife. He then came to London and was licenced to officiate in the Church of England. The Society for the Promotion of Christian Knowledge engaged him to carry through the press an edition of a Spanish version of the New Testament. For twelve years he was in charge of a Spanish congregation at Gibraltar and in 1842 was made an honorary canon of the cathedral there. In 1858 Lucena was appointed the first Reader in Spanish at Oxford. In seven years he performed unaided the colossal task of revising the text of the Spanish Bible published by the Christian Knowledge Society. For these labours he was created in 1877 an honorary M.A. of Oxford, which seems rather scant recognition. Mrs. Henry Christopher was descended maternally from the Barons de Aquila and the Dukes of Terranova. Christopher's first grandchild, Ada, was born to Henry and Julia Christopher in 1872, followed in the next year by Eleanor, later a well-known Principal of St. Hild's College, Durham. Another grand-daughter, Selina, died in infancy.

The wedding of Henry Christopher and Julia Lucena was solemnized in New York, and in the following year the Rector of St. Aldate's took a longer holiday than usual, during the long vacation, in order to visit his son and daughter-in-law in Canada, where they were engaged in farming.[1] A characteristic incident occurred on the journey. Bishop Ingham recalled: "I met him once at Lime Street Station, Liverpool. He was en route to Canada. He had a Times Newspaper in his hand. 'I don't often buy a Times,' he said, 'but I bought one today and I will tell you why. There was a Roman Priest in the train, and I longed to give him a little booklet I had with me but I did not dare. So it occurred to me that I would buy a Times. I did so and read it for some little time. I then passed it over to the Priest who happily was very glad to see it and seemed to enjoy it. And when at Crewe the Priest left the train I asked him if he would mind taking with him a little booklet I had written. It was a complete success, and who can tell what may happen?'

[1]According to one account this farm had been purchased by Alfred Christopher.

. . . Did anyone ever more industriously advertise good books, or seek to win, by constant sowing?"

After experiencing " great kindness " in Liverpool from the family of an undergraduate, Christopher sailed in the *Prussian,* of which, he was pleased to find, the captain was a Christian, who prayed and sang hymns with his men. In time prayer meetings were held by a number of passengers each afternoon and evening, and at these the captain played his harmonium. Some Christian Swedes, although they spoke no English, nevertheless attended. Off Newfoundland big ice-bergs were seen. Passing Labrador the ship was for a long while in sight of land before, on a Sunday morning, she reached Quebec. That evening Christopher preached in the protestant cathedral. The next day, having visited Montmorency Falls, he passed on, still by ship, to Montreal, one thousand inland miles after entering the gulf of St. Lawrence, and thence to Ottawa, where he admired the "noble" parliament buildings, then only ten years old. Some distance from Ottawa, Christopher visited his brother-in-law, Nelson Robinson — widower of his sister Caroline since 1848 — whom he had not seen for many years. Christopher then took a smaller steamer to Prescott, where he boarded a train for Toronto. From the latter he went in another train to reach his son's farm, where he was much pleased with the wild country and enjoyed a happy reunion.

Another of Christopher's favourite stories of conversion was linked with the ensuing stage in his journey. Next, he has recorded, " I went on board a steamer at Collingwood which is the head of the Georgian Bay, the north-east part of Lake Huron. My object was to pass up the rapids of St. Mary, and then by the ship canal into the strait of St. Mary, which connects the waters of Lake Superior and Lake Huron, and so into and round that great inland sea, 420 miles long by 180 broad, with a circuit of 1,750 miles." Almost the first passenger he noted was a tall, venerable, one-armed man, who turned out to be a minister of the gospel who had lost his arm in the American war of 1812–3. He had been a naval officer, but after conversion through reading the Bible, he had retired and became a missionary to Red Indians. Later he had been appointed agent of the Bible Society in Canada.

Christopher next visited London, Ontario, where his host was the Bishop of Huron, who, as Archdeacon Hellmuth, had, with Bishop Cronyn, his predecessor, stayed with Christopher, and preached at St. Aldate's, a few years previously. Like a very different character likewise known to Christopher, Stern of Abbyssinia, Bishop Hellmuth was a converted Jew. Of Stern, Christopher used to say: "I never forget hearing him relate in Oxford how Jews in Arabia crowded his tent until midnight, and shed tears when they heard how their forefathers had persecuted and crucified the promised Messiah." At the Bishop's request, Christopher preached in London Cathedral, afterwards addressing clergy alone. There can be little doubt that Christopher's bracing approach, bringing, too, up-to-date news of Christian developments in Oxford and England, would be particularly appreciated by those working, often in comparative isolation, far from the mother country.

This visit was followed by a trip to Niagara Falls — "very magnificent" — a part of the Niagara River which for a few miles symbolises the wholly unguarded boundary between Canada and the United States. A little later Christopher went back to his son's home to say goodbye. Returning to Toronto, he preached to two big congregations in the cathedral, addressed a Sunday school, and next day spoke about Oxford to a large gathering of ladies and gentlemen. At various times during this part of his tour, Christopher visited three of Miss Macpherson's distributing homes (which he had been determined to see) — one near London, one at Belleville, one near Montreal — for children with unsatisfactory backgrounds in London and other large English towns, from one of which eight hundred children had already been planted out in as many farmhouses. At another, Christopher saw a happy, healthy boy, whose father had been in the habit of holding him by the ankles, head downwards, and flogging him. Christopher did not readily forget this. Eleven years later he referred to it in an assize sermon at Oxford.

Christopher now crossed the border into the United States, and went to Chicago, where he was impressed by the huge, new buildings. Then he travelled to Rock Island, where he took a boat down the Mississippi to St. Louis. Only eight years had passed since the end of the American Civil War, and here Christopher was in the atmosphere of the south, surrounded everywhere by survivors and signs of the recent conflict. While his primary concern would have been for the anti-slavery aspect, it seems possible that this part of his journey was prompted in some measure by his interest in the military side. He travelled by way of Harper's Ferry, associated immediately before the outbreak of war with John Brown, "one of the first martyrs in the cause of anti-slavery". After a short stay at Washington, seeing places of interest, Christopher passed on to New York, through Baltimore and Philadelphia. At New York he preached twice. Twenty-five years later Dean Barlow when Vicar of Islington rationed those who wished to speak from the floor at the Islington Clerical Conference to three minutes each. "One minute more," cried Christopher, "than was allowed me at a meeting in New York to speak on the progress of the Gospel in Europe." Amid the finest country he had ever seen, Christopher went by steamer up the Hudson River — its cliff-like Pallisades often compared with the Rhine valley — to Albany. From here, amid constant reminders of the much earlier French and Indian wars, he proceeded by train to Montreal, passing through Saratoga and Fort William Henry.

At Montreal, Christopher preached in two churches. Next day, from breakfast onwards he spent a joyful morning with Bishop Ashton Oxenden, Metropolitan of Canada, an Oxford man from before Christopher's time, well known in England as well as in Canada for his strong evangelical witness and simplified theological writings. Either on this occasion or during his previous visit to Montreal, Christopher spoke at a meeting of young men, and had the encouraging experience, already described, in connection with Scott's *Force of Truth*. Having taken a steamer back to Quebec, a happy voyage home ended for life Christopher's travels abroad. At Oxford in October two hundred parishioners and friends expressed their respect and esteem for their "worthy Rector" by gathering to greet him in the Rectory Room, which was decorated with mottos — "Welcome Home Again" — "In Everything Give Thanks".

Before he left, Christopher had been busy trying to secure a satisfactory appointment of schoolmaster in his parochial schools, where numbers remained fairly constant, with approximately 225 children in all. One application he had particularly liked — from a Mr. C. C. Cole, who described himself as an evangelical. Christopher wrote advising him how to address the managers, " Include . . . all you have said to me, *excepting* the word '*Evangelical*'. I am thoroughly Evangelical, though I hope more in the spiritual than in the party sense. But it will be well to avoid any *party* terms in addressing the Managers." There was no house, but Christopher offered to pay the rent of one out of his own pocket, as he was "so anxious to have a true-hearted, spiritually minded Christian master." He urged privacy — " not however from your own Clergyman, your natural adviser." Christopher had been a schoolmaster himself and knew well the value of securing a good man to teach the children of St. Aldate's. He was prepared to take infinite trouble in the matter. Cole was duly appointed, and worked in the parish for over twenty years.

At last in 1873, after eight years without the familiar spire, it was possible to complete the rebuilding of St. Aldate's church. The old tower was demolished and replaced by a new tower and spire of similar proportions and design, with facings of Gibraltar stone. For this the architect responsible was, as before, J. T. Christopher, the cost was some £2,000, and the contractor Mr. Symm of St. Giles's.[1] The work took the best part of a year.

The tragic death of the first Mrs. Hathaway in 1873 was a great shock to her husband. She was found drowned in the river. She had been reading on the bank and had evidently fallen into the water. When Arthur Downer, in temporary charge of St. Clement's, called to offer his sympathy, Hathaway told him that he and his wife had been praying for complete sanctification. "God, he said, had answered their prayer, but in one way for her and another for him." Not long afterwards Hathaway resigned St. Ebbe's, and William Barlow, subsequently Vicar of Islington, and Dean of Peterborough, was appointed to succeed him.

By 1873 Christopher's edition of Weitbrecht's *Memoir* was out of print. Christopher himself had had difficulty in reducing the original to six hundred pages. Mrs. Weitbrecht was now compelled to abridge the work still further, in order to ensure republication. Christopher wrote a review of it which was printed in pamphlet form. "Let me, as one who knew Weitbrecht in India, and as one who lives

[1]The same firm effected the additions at the base of the tower in 1960-61.

43. 68, BANBURY ROAD, OXFORD, 1963
formerly RICHMOND LODGE, PARK TOWN
Home of A. M. W. Christopher 1859–71
Rear view, former drawing-room below; study, first floor

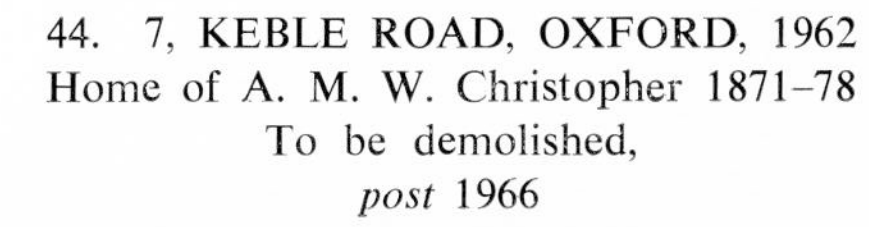

44. 7, KEBLE ROAD, OXFORD, 1962
Home of A. M. W. Christopher 1871–78
To be demolished,
post 1966

45. ST. ALDATE'S, OXFORD, and PEMBROKE COLLEGE, *c.* 1875

among educated young men, and as one who prays for more true missionaries, entreat those who read this paper to exert themselves to place this memoir, with much prayer, in the hands of Christian young men. They may thus be used of God to lead some to consecrate their lives to the highest work to which a young man can be called, — that of preaching Christ crucified to the miserable heathen. It may also stir up some to encourage the sale of this memoir to know that they may thereby help the widow of one of Christ's missionaries."

Another change which took place towards the close of the period covered by this chapter was Christopher's removal from Richmond Lodge to 7 "Keable Road", a new terrace of houses opposite the site where Keble College was rising. The move occurred in 1871. The house[1] was no larger than that in Park Town. But it was considerably nearer St. Aldate's. In the 'eighties it was the residence of Archer Thompson Gurney, a well-known divine and author. Here Christopher remained until he rebuilt the Rectory in 1878. Soon after moving to Keble Terrace, Christopher incorporated as a member of Trinity College. In 1872 his uncle Millard's bequest to that college became operative, and no doubt the Fellows were ready to show gratitude for the endowment of a lectureship, chemistry scholarships, and chemical and physical laboratories by opening their gates to their benefactor's nephew. Thomas Millard died at Downend in December 1871, leaving Christopher ("my friend and connection") his residuary legatee and executor. To the President and Fellows of Trinity he bequeathed eight thousand pounds "to advance Mathematical and General Science". It was the largest single benefaction, apart from their founder's endowment, that they had ever received. Christopher himself may have inherited about the same amount. Ivy Bower, in which his uncle held only a life interest, passed to a Millard cousin. The suffix "of Downend", therefore, sometimes applied to Christopher — for example, in Burke's *Landed Gentry* — is hardly justified.

In Michaelmas term 1872 a raw young Welshman, John Owen, came up from a strict nonconformist home to Jesus College as a

[1]The property was on a long lease — St. John's College being the ground landlords — and Christopher paid £816 for this, in May 1871, to the Revd. R. W. Greaves, an Oxford evangelical who had been Rector of Tooting. The voters' lists give Christopher as still at Richmond Lodge in October 1871.

scholar. On his first Sunday he happened to attend St. Aldate's, and was immediately drawn to Christopher. Though not confirmed till 1879, he was soon a teacher in the Sunday School, and for the next four years St. Aldate's was his spiritual home in Oxford. After teaching at Lampeter and Llandovery, he became Dean of St. Asaph at the age of thirty-four, and Principal of St. David's College, Lampeter, in 1892. Five years later he was nominated Bishop of St. David's, occupying the see until his death in 1926. Of the various influences under which he came at the university, his biographer says "perhaps Canon Christopher of St. Aldate's ranks foremost; he was a great steadying force in John Owen's life at Oxford, as he was saintly, and wise and kind. He was a living witness to him of the reality of the gospel truths which stood firm when men's opinions fluctuated, and the young man never forgot their talk together when they went to say goodbye; and how in his simple natural way Canon Christopher had gone down on his knees to pray for him before he left him." Writing in the Welsh church newspaper *Y Llan,* Bishop Owen himself said in after years: "I used to go frequently to the devotional meetings which he had for students, and to the annual breakfast which he gave for the purpose of meeting foreign missionaries. It was there that I had the privilege of meeting Moffat and Livingstone. The Canon's Sunday devoted to foreign missions had a great influence on me." Bishop Owen's theological views broadened considerably as the years went by, but, his daughter and biographer wrote in 1962, "he never ceased to be evangelical in sympathy."

It seems likely that another Welsh bishop, a more pronounced evangelical than Owen, Joshua Pritchard Hughes, who held the see of Llandaff from 1905 to 1931, had come within Christopher's orbit at Oxford. Hughes, the son of Joshua Hughes, a strongly protestant Bishop of St. Asaph, went up to Balliol in 1867, but of his Oxford days no account appears to survive. Another Balliol man, William Macdonald Sinclair, two years junior to Hughes, son of an evangelical clergyman (both father and son were presidents of the Union), may be similarly classified. The younger Sinclair, a friend of F. J. Chavasse, became Archdeacon of London in 1889.

Two other testimonies to the importance of Christopher's work for undergraduates have survived from the later years of this period. Dr. Aglionby, afterwards Vicar of Christ Church, Westminster, and biographer of Edward Bickersteth, Bishop of Exeter,[1] who came up to Queen's in 1868, tells us: "I was an utter stranger, my earlier life, till the preceding year, having been spent in Virginia. I had no school friends at the University and knew only one or two persons to whom I had been given letters of introduction in Oxford. The saintly Bishop of Carlisle, Dr. Samuel Waldegrave,[2] who knew me, wrote to each of the triumvirate of Evangelical clergy who had parishes in the town, the Revd. A. M. W. Christopher, Rector of St. Aldate's, the Revd. Henry Linton, Rector of St. Peter-le-Bailey . . . and the Revd. Edward Penrose Hathaway, Rector of St. Ebbe's, and asked them to call upon me. They were unknown to me even by name, and when an invitation came from Canon Christopher to an at-home in his house, Richmond Lodge, I was at a loss to make out the name of my correspondent, as those who remember his hand-writing will readily understand . . . He was as 'the shadow of a great rock in a weary land' to a youth whose heart God had touched and who felt utterly alone, without religious fellowship or friendship. Many and most varied were the friends, not a few of them lifelong, for whom I was indebted to his introduction or acquaintance. For years I went regularly to his meetings for undergraduates on Saturday evenings, where he would pray and expound the Scriptures, chiefly Romans V and VIII . . .

"It is wonderful and inspiring to look back upon the patient, aye the enthusiastic efforts of this devoted servant of Christ to reach and help the successive generations of young men with whom he came into personal touch . . . as they passed through the University. He was known and beloved by many hundreds of them and many more received books and tractates, some of which at any rate would acquaint them with subjects that would otherwise never have been brought to their notice. Many who in later years became high Churchmen, or broadened out from the position which they occupied in their undergraduate days, have thankfully owned their obligations to him for a grasp of Evangelical truth which they never afterwards lost. His love unfeigned to all of whatsoever school of religious thought who loved our Lord Jesus Christ in sincerity, his childlike simplicity, his godly sincerity, the upwardness of

[1]His father-in-law.

[2]In whose diocese the Aglionby family were landowners.

his whole character and demeanour, adorned the holy doctrines which he taught and commended them to all within the range of his influence. It will only be known at the last how such lives and labours as his and in such places as he occupied, will have affected for good the Church of England. Many will rise up and call him blessed . . . Any recollections of our dear friend would be sadly incomplete without some reference to Mrs. Christopher . . . All who knew her and her beloved husband, will give a most fervent response to the words, 'Sint animae nostrae cum illis'."

As with Aglionby, so it was with another stranger in England two years later. Ernest Ingham of St. Mary Hall, afterwards Bishop of Sierra Leone, says "I came to Oxford straight from Bishop's College School, Lennoxville, Canada, in 1870. It was a very cold plunge! After a term or two a clergyman in the South of England gave me a letter of introduction to Canon Christopher. It required some little courage to call. Shuttleworth[1] represented the strong Tractarian attitude, and Hannington[2] the worldly section at St. Mary Hall . . . And Christopher was voted *impossible*! That call was one of the turning points in my life . . . It is impossible to express in any adequate language all that Canon Christopher was to me . . . The outstanding impression was not what Christopher *said* but *the life he lived*. He used to tell us that men would not read books of evidence that we might place in their hands, but they would diligently study our own lives. *He* had nothing to fear in this respect. He impressed me profoundly . . .

"A Mission that Canon Aitken conducted at St. Aldate's stands out in my memory as the time of my full awakening . . . Perhaps I specially liked the ordinary Saturday nights in the Large Room behind the Pembroke St. Old Rectory when the Epistle to the Romans would be in evidence. It was not very long before I found myself attending the daily prayer meeting in the Upper Room for half an hour after 'Hall' with its cocoanut matting . . . If we joined the early Saturday dinner at 7 Keble Terrace we heard many a Missionary incident hitherto strange to us . . . Canon Christopher remained a close friend to the end. He guided me to the curacy

[1]Edward Starkie Shuttleworth, curate of St. Barnabas's, Oxford, 1877-9, afterwards Vicar of Egloshayle, Cornwall.

[2]James Hannington, martyr, first Bishop of Eastern Equatorial Africa, who was converted after his ordination.

of St. Matthew's, Rugby, from which I got more spiritual help than anywhere else in my ministry, and where I met my wife and also met C.M.S. work shortly after . . . Few men of the present generation who inherit Oxford Pastorates, a Wycliffe Hall, and many other helps, realise that Christopher was to us *all these things rolled into one* in those now far back days when he interpreted the Gospel to us by his own loving, genial life, kindly spiritual influence, and sterling work."

Chapter X

A New Doctrine

1874 - 1878

CHRISTOPHER'S middle and later life unfolds with an unwavering if colourful consistency; so that it is easier to select historical limits for different periods of his ministry than it is to discover turning-points. Nevertheless it certainly appears that the year 1874 marked an important development in Christopher's experience, which could not fail to be reflected in his influence on others. Hitherto he had regarded the new 'holiness movement' with that suspicion which it aroused in many of the evangelical leaders. Brought from the United States in 1872, the teaching of its advocates, at least as commonly reported, seemed to verge on semi-perfectionism. For they asserted that the Christian life, far from being, for the individual, a constant battle with not infrequent defeats, was intended to be lived on an altogether higher plane of continuous victory over sin, and a continual, overflowing sense of God's peace.

Few evangelical notables were inclined to favour the doctrines which, chiefly by means of the Keswick Conventions, were ultimately to permeate the evangelical world as a whole, and in 1877 Christopher's friend Ryle went so far as to publish a book on holiness, in which the traditional evangelical view was set out and the new beliefs humbly exposed to critical comparison. It will at first, therefore, seem a matter for surprise that Christopher should have adopted them. Yet for him to do so was much in character with his loving spirit and uncalculating earnestness. It is perhaps not without significance that one of the earliest clergy to give the movement his support was Evan Hopkins, whose appointment as Vicar of Holy Trinity, Richmond, had been made, as we have seen, partly on Christopher's recommendation.

Meetings were held in various places, including Cambridge, and notably at Broadlands, near Romsey, where William Cowper-Temple, afterwards Lord Mount-Temple, had assembled at his country seat, with its memories of Palmerston, a remarkable conference embracing all schools of thought, from quakers to extreme high churchmen, in July 1874. There it was felt that the meetings must be repeated on a larger scale. The difficulty was, however, to think of anywhere which could accommodate the numbers envisaged. It was Stevenson Blackwood, later Secretary of the Post Office, who (though a Cambridge man) said "Why not at Oxford?"

The general response was in favour of this proposition. But it was known that several suggestions for holding 'conversational meetings' with undergraduates at Oxford, such as had been held at Cambridge, had been declined, and there was a commendable unwillingness to influence the young men "in any way not fully approved by their friend, the Rev. A. M. W. Christopher." The Rector of St. Aldate's felt an honest anxiety lest in fact the current of teaching should not be fully scriptural. The proposed conference, however, would be held in the vacation. For then undergraduate lodgings would be available in addition to whatever accommodation the hotels of the city might be able to offer. Robert Pearsall Smith, an American quaker, went up to Oxford after the Broadlands conference and called on Christopher, who was on the point of leaving for his annual holiday. We have Christopher's own account of what followed. "I did then," he afterwards recorded, "what I hope I do always, I asked the Lord to guide me, and trusted Him to do so. After prayer I felt certain that it would not please the Lord Jesus for me to refuse to help a believing effort to promote in His people, by the use of His holy Word with prayer, holiness and devotion to His service . . . Mr. P. Smith's visit was a brief one. There was no time to consult brethren, so I acted upon the conviction given me, and did what I could to promote the

Conference. My mind was at once guided to two Christians to do the necessary work . . ." Charles Badcock acted as honorary secretary and Henry Collis arranged all matters connected with lodgings for visitors. Both were capable tradesmen.

The programme of meetings was planned during early August at Langley Park, Norfolk, the seat of Sir Thomas Beauchamp, father of the Revd. Sir Montagu Proctor-Beauchamp, one of the well-known Cambridge missionary 'seven' of ten years later. From Langley Park invitations went out to attend a " Union Meeting for the Promotion of Scriptural Holiness. To be held at Oxford, August 29th to September 7th, 1874 . . . Oxford has been selected, as between one and two thousand persons can be accommodated . . . A number of prominent ministers from France, Germany, and Switzerland are to be present". The promoters had secured the name of the Dean of Canterbury to head the list of those inviting attendance. This was certainly remarkable in view of the general attitude of evangelical leaders, for Dr. Payne Smith had but lately resigned the regius professorship of divinity at Oxford. It is true that he was primarily a Syriac scholar, but he had played a principal part in establishing the new honour school of theology.

For other distinguished names the promoters had had to rely on laymen. The Earl of Chichester, President of the Church Missionary Society, Lord Farnham, Sir Thomas Beauchamp, Stevenson Blackwood, and three Members of Parliament — William Cowper-Temple, Samuel Morley, virtual founder of a well-known hosiery firm and of a noble house, and Arthur Kinnaird — were prominent enough. Clerical supporters included Hay Aitken, the young evangelist, William Haslam, the converted tractarian, and E. W. Moore of the Brunswick Chapel, Marylebone, one of the earliest and for many years one of the few clergymen to advocate the new doctrines. Haslam was already a friend of Christopher's, who, as we have seen, had invited him, from time to time, to preach at St. Aldate's. Aitken and Moore had been undergraduates at Wadham in the early 'sixties. Kinnaird was a friend of even longer standing. Christopher himself signed, and his former curate, Thomas Nash. Theodore Monod represented the reformed churches abroad; and even Edward Hathaway, though no longer rector of St. Ebbe's, was prevailed on to lend his countenance to the invitation.

The response was gratifying. More than a thousand people were willing to "wait upon God for the attainment of a higher measure of 'Scriptural holiness'." This historic gathering has not received the attention it deserves, and a comparatively full account is called for. Prayer meetings were held at 7 a.m. in the Corn Exchange. "The streets of Oxford formed truly a striking scene; from eight hundred up to a thousand persons passing through them at this early hour, with the quiet earnestness of their purpose depicted in their countenances . . ." A simple countryman, questioned at the door of the Corn Exchange, said, "Don't you know? It's all the Christian folk in the world . . . " The convention in fact represented "to a great extent a meeting of Christians who, while walking in full unvarying assurance of the forgiveness of sins, were yet feeling a painful deficiency in their own personal experience as to maintained communion with God, and uniform victory over sin."

The first meeting was held on Saturday 29 August at 11 a.m., in St. Aldates' Rectory Room. Christopher opened the proceedings with prayer and read *Psalm 113*. Pearsall Smith and others addressed the company, which was as yet far from complete. After an early prayer meeting and a 9.30 a.m. meeting on the following Sunday morning, Christopher preached in St. Aldate's from *St. Matthew* 1. 21: "Thou shalt call His name JESUS: for He shall save His people from their sins."

The activities of these two days were, however, only preparatory to the week of meetings which was to follow. A seven o'clock prayer meeting lasted each day until 8.30 a.m.; from 9.30 a.m. to 11.30 a.m. the conference broke up into groups for 'conversational meetings' (held in smaller rooms in the Town Hall), conducted by men already prominent in the movement, the Revd. W. E. Boardman, Theodore Monod, Dr. Asa Mahan of Oberlin College, Ohio, Evan Hopkins, and Lord Radstock. From 11.45 a.m. to 1.30 p.m. there was a general meeting; from 3 p.m. to 4 p.m. prayer meetings, and Bible readings for ladies in the Corn Exchange conducted by Mrs. Pearsall Smith, who in later years lived at Iffley, in order to be near her son Logan, by then a well-known writer; and these were immediately followed by another general meeting lasting until 5.30 p.m. From 6 p.m. to 7.30 p.m. a ministerial conference, open to all, was conducted; and from 7.45 p.m. to 9.15 p.m. a fourth general meeting. The intervals allowed for meals grew steadily shorter as the day progressed; and it is difficult to imagine those who dispersed to lodgings being ready in time for the next session. But while there was no excuse for shirking, it may be assumed that there was no obligation to attend each one.

At the first ministerial conference, "the Rev. Mr. NASH, of Norwich," Christopher's former curate, witnessed to the value of the new teaching. He described "most feelingly how, after many years of earnest service, he had attended a consecration meeting at Sir Thomas Beauchamp's the previous year, and there had learned what it was to lay aside the last weight, and to trust fully for everything to Christ . . ." On the following Monday the Revd. J. Turner testified to the immediate results of the new emphasis in his parish of Deddington in north Oxfordshire. Christopher himself remained to the fore. He was soon using a familiar method. On the morning of Wednesday 2 September, at his invitation, about a hundred and fifty people breakfasted together in the Clarendon Hotel. All the incumbents of Oxford churches were invited, with their curates. But "some were not in Oxford on that day." Nevertheless "High Churchmen and Low Churchmen sat side by side . . ." to hear Pearsall Smith, supported by Christopher and Nash.

On the following day, Thursday, between one and two hundred persons rose to signify, by singing, blessing received during the conference thus far. One of these was Canon Harford-Battersby, Vicar of St. John's, Keswick, who, in his undergraduate days at Balliol, and for some years after, had been a decided tractarian. On the 4th a breakfast for foreign pastors was held at the Randolph Hotel, and the Revd. E. W. Moore gave his testimony. Christopher opened the early prayer meeting the next day, when, later, representatives from abroad included the German Baron Julius de Gemmingen, converted the year before, and two Dutch noblemen.

A meeting for children was held on the Sunday. Monday 7 September was the tenth day. Letters from Miss F. R. Havergal, the hymn-writer, who was in Switzerland, were read at the ladies' meeting. The following morning the conference ended with a prayer meeting devoted to praise and thanksgiving, led by Harford-Battersby. But meetings continued to be held in the Corn Exchange throughout the week, at which Lord Radstock was a prominent figure; at 7 a.m. and

3 p.m. for Christians and in the evenings for the unconverted. The latter had in any case not been neglected. Lord Radstock had preached in the streets of Oxford during the conference proper, and particularly during St. Giles's Fair, when he and Admiral Fishbourne had taken their stand near the Martyrs' Memorial. It may be surmised that Bazely, who had started open-air preaching on that site a few years earlier, and was always present at St. Giles's Fair, as a decided calvinist viewed the proceedings with misgiving. Certainly his views on the new doctrine as set out in his own words and printed in the eighth chapter of his biography make instructive reading.

Numbers of letters were received acknowledging blessing obtained during the ten days. Their writers ranged from "a High Church lady" to the congregational minister at Oxford. The Vicar of Bicester, the Revd. J. W. Watts, a senior man who had held his living since 1843, was among the local clergymen who expressed their appreciation. Christopher himself wrote " My heart has been full of praise during and since the Oxford Conference, because God so graciously led me to help in this good work . . . A short time ago, I could not have believed that I should see my way to promoting such a Conference, and I never had faith to expect such a manifestation of God's power as there has been."

The following year a similar convention was arranged at Brighton, and a month or two later Canon Harford-Battersby planned a smaller gathering for his friends in the north. His parish of Keswick made a natural meeting place, amid lakeland scenery. In spite of some initial difficulty, the promoters carried on as best they could. They managed so successfully that the Keswick Convention has been an annual event in the evangelical world, attracting thousands of people yearly, as it does to this day.

It has not appeared whether Christopher attended the conventions when they were held in the north. Nor is it quite clear how permanent an effect 'the Oxford Conference' had upon him. But it is obvious that he thoroughly approved most of what was said and done there, at a time when others were holding back. With Harford-Battersby, he was called on to defend the new teaching in the religious press, but, we are told, " they failed to satisfy their critics." Christopher, however, was too much of an individualist to become distinctively stamped with the marks of any movement with which he was associated, and at the age of fifty-four he was less likely to be stampeded into regarding most of his previous life and ministry as a comparative failure. Yet there can be little doubt that what became known as 'Keswick teaching' remained embedded in his own teaching and thinking. Certainly, according to the recollection of Canon Cox of Cheltenham, his curate in the 'eighties, among the literature which he so freely distributed were " many of the devotional writings of the Oxford, Mildmay, and later the Keswick Convention . . ." Moreover in 1875 Christopher introduced at St. Aldate's, in addition to Kemble's hymn book, *Songs of Grace and Glory*, a useful compilation made by the Revd. G. B. Snepp, Vicar of Perry Barr, Birmingham, a prominent supporter of the holiness conventions. It does not seem, however, that these 'Hymnal Treasures of the Church of Christ, from the Sixth to the Nineteenth Century', were particularly biassed in their selection. Evan Hopkins and H. W. Webb-Peploe became regular occasional preachers at St. Aldate's. Christopher could not know that this doctrine, as it spread through the evangelical world, was destined to make considerable alterations in the character of evangelical witness in the years ahead.

In modern times, evangelical influence in England was probably at its height during the 'fifties of the nineteenth century. That of the tractarians was not then widely spread. Both Archbishops, a number of distinguished bishops, and other dignitaries of the church, were staunch evangelicals, supported in both houses of parliament and throughout the country by able and prominent laymen. During the 'sixties, however, evangelicals themselves noticed a spiritual decline in their work — reflected in their missionary endeavour — which a revivalist movement already begun in 1859 had failed to avert. The new teaching about holiness seemed to some to be an answer to prayer. Christopher, as we have seen, though cautious at first, welcomed it thankfully. He could not forsee that even in his own life-time, and during his incumbency of St. Aldate's, the pietism of the Keswick movement would be a contributory factor in changes which would affect the evangelical position intellectually and, in the Church of England, as regards churchmanship. Protestant convictions came to be less firmly held. Christopher himself, with his respect for scholarship, his decided churchmanship, and faithful protestant witness, was not lacking on any one of these counts. Moreover such developments were still thirty years ahead. Meanwhile, Christopher's personal unconcern with scholarly matters, except in so far as they bore directly on the work of the ministry, naturally inclined him to take his stand with those whose keenness for Christ was so intense, and towards whom he was also drawn by the very catholicity of his own attitude to nonconformity, based as it was on a great love of the church as "the blessed company of all faithful people." It may be doubted, as has been implied already, whether even before 1874 his intellectual lead was as strong as the needs of his more thoughtful undergraduate friends demanded. Nevertheless he had under his immediate influence, during the later 'sixties, three young men — Edmund Knox, Francis Chavasse and John Diggle — who as diocesan bishops during the first quarter of the twentieth century were a potent force in the English church. After 1874 such names hardly occur. Doubtless this was partly due to other causes; but it remains to some extent significant of the importance which must be attached to Christopher's sympathy with a new influence in evangelical doctrinal teaching.

In the following year Christopher was a speaker at a very different type of gathering. The Church Congress had started unofficially in 1861. The promoters tried to be fair in their invitations to speakers, but for various reasons the evangelicals were inclined to hold aloof. Three trusted men, Ryle, E. Hoare, and E. Garbett, led the way towards a bolder attitude, and in spite of opposition from the ultra-militant section of their party, after 1869 evangelical attendance improved. At Stoke-upon-Trent in October 1875, Christopher contributed a paper. Another Oxford incumbent, the Revd. T. V. French, Rector of St. Ebbe's, afterwards Bishop of Lahore, had read the first paper the previous day on 'Missions and Missionary Bishoprics'. After Canon Curteis, Principal of Lichfield Theological College, the Bampton Lecturer of 1871, had spoken on 'The Supply of Clergy', Christopher addressed himself to the same subject.

"The great reason," he pointed out, among other wise and practical observations, "of the too scanty supply of clergy for real missionary work at home and abroad is, that many of our Christian young men are wanting in *two* things. These are the very things which we elders also most need, and nothing will unite our hearts more today than the deep feeling and humble acknowledgement of our common need, and our loving trust in the Lord Jesus to supply that need. If we elders had these two things in a higher degree, God would make us to be much more efficient in promoting the supply of clergy. These two things which our Christian young men most need are, *first,* entire unreserved devotion of themselves to the Lord Jesus to do His will and His work, at any cost, in any position, in any parish, in any climate, to which He may draw them by showing them the spiritual destitution of sinners for whom He died. The *second* thing needed is, the means to the above end, namely, simple, thorough, unhesitating faith in the Lord Jesus Christ for grace sufficient to enable them to do any work to which He may call them; and grace sufficient to enable them to yield to Him that entire devotion of themselves to His service which he requires of His redeemed people. We must have a greater number of young *laymen* entirely consecrated to the Lord for His work, before we shall have a sufficient supply of clergy."

Speaking " As one who has known hundreds of undergraduates at Oxford and Cambridge during the last sixteen years, and who never knew so many true-hearted Christian young men anywhere else," he yet was not inclined to underestimate the usefulness of non-graduate clergy, or of men ordained later in life. He realised too, on the other hand, that a gloomy view of the secularising results of university reform — a further stage had been reached in 1872 — was taken in some quarters. But, he said, " I am altogether opposed to the adoption of a faint-hearted, desponding tone with respect to our universities, as if these great seats of learning and nurseries of the clergy were to be abandoned to unbelievers." On this he enlarged while speaking at an interesting session on 'Recent Legislation and Religious Instruction in our Universities'; and for another thirty years he laboured in this spirit at Oxford.

As time went by the Rector invited fewer well-known preachers to occupy the pulpit at St. Aldate's. It may be that Christopher himself felt more confident; it may be that he came to feel — perhaps partly unconsciously — that a local ministry consistently exercised, even if of less ability than might be obtained from afar, was of greater usefulness to his flock. Distinguished preachers, however, often with missionary experience and less often of outstanding intellectual power, continued to be heard from the St. Aldates' pulpit. Of these the only regular visitor had not been a missionary and had a first class academic record. Until 1880, when he became first Bishop of Liverpool, J. C. Ryle invariably preached, during the 'seventies, at least once a year for Christopher. That there was a special affinity between them, in spite of pronounced differences in character, may easily be deduced from a comparison of the Bishop's published sentiments with those of the Rector of St. Aldate's. Nor was the affinity altogether theological, for both were cricket blues. Had Christopher been a few years older they would probably have met first, though on opposing sides, in a university match. During this decade other preachers whose names were household words of those days were Sholto Douglas, afterwards Lord Blythswood; Charles Clayton, Rector of Stanhope, former Fellow of Caius College, and Vicar of Holy Trinity, Cambridge; Bishop Ryan, no longer of Mauritius, who was Vicar of Bradford and Archdeacon of Cleveland; and, again, most notable of these, the veteran Charles Perry, in Christopher's Cambridge days a Fellow of Trinity, now retired from being first Bishop of Melbourne. The Bishop of Oxford, Dr. Mackarness, who had succeeded Wilberforce in 1870, preached once (confirmations apart) during the nineteen years of his episcopate. But he was a consistent supporter of the local association of the Church Missionary Society.

Meanwhile Harry Sturdy, after six years as curate to Christopher, during which he had taken second class honours in the theology school as a member of Christ Church, had accepted in 1875 the living of St. Mark's, Dewsbury.[1] His successor was Arthur William Poole, a man of some parts, the only one of Christopher's curates to find a place in the *Dictionary of National Biography*. An Old Salopian, he had come up to Worcester College in 1868 to read classics, but neither in moderations nor in 'greats' did he achieve more than a comparatively undistinguished class. He had gone down in 1873, and after spending a short time as a schoolmaster, he thought of making medicine his profession. He had entertained a leaning towards the Plymouth Brethren, but during the course of a

[1]In the following year he married Florence, a sister of Wilson Carlile, who took orders a few years later and became well known for his work as founder of the Church Army, of which Christopher was an early advocate.

year or two his scruples were overcome and he was made deacon as curate of St. Aldate's in 1876.

Henry Bazely had to surmount even stronger scruples than Poole's before he, minister of a Church of Scotland chapel in Alfred Street, Oxford, and hitherto, from personal conviction, a strong presbyterian, could become Christopher's curate. Bazely had begun to feel that in the south as a Scottish presbyterian (he was not a member of the Presbyterian Church of England) his usefulness was limited. Was it really impossible to enter the established ministry? In many of his works of mercy he was associated with dear friends who were in English orders. For example he had been the moving spirit in founding an Oxford College Servants' Society, designed to make better spiritual and material provision for 'scouts'; but he remained in the background, and the first president, elected in 1872, was Christopher. When the headquarters was moved out of St. Aldates' parish in 1876, Christopher resigned. Bazely was pressed to succeed him, but he felt it would be an advantage if the president were a fellow of a college, and Edmund Knox of Merton was chosen. Christopher remained a vice-president till his death. The society itself does not appear to have survived the First World War.

One consideration which hastened Bazely's decision was the approaching mission which was to take place in all Oxford parishes in January 1876. " He had never ceased to respect the Church of England, but when he saw her bestirring herself for evangelising effort, he yearned to go back again to his spiritual mother." He closed the Alfred Street chapel and started to work once more as a layman in St. Aldate's parish, which he knew so well. His diary for January and February 1876 " testifies to unceasing labour; there is repeated mention of endeavours to bring into the refuge fallen women whom he had found in the street; of Sunday afternoon services at the gasworks; of services on Sunday nights at the lodging-house in St. Thomas'." On 12 March he was made deacon at Banbury by Dr. Mackarness. His friends were thankful; but he was soon put to the test. In April an old acquaintance, the Revd. F. J. Jayne, afterwards Bishop of Chester, invited him to preach at the newly-founded Keble College, an offer which he felt impelled to decline firmly, as acceptance would seem to show sympathy with "an institution which is popularly — and, I suppose, not unjustly — regarded as intended

46. ARTHUR WILLIAM POOLE, D.D., *c.* 1884
Curate of St. Aldate's, Oxford, 1875-76
The first Bishop of Japan, 1883-85

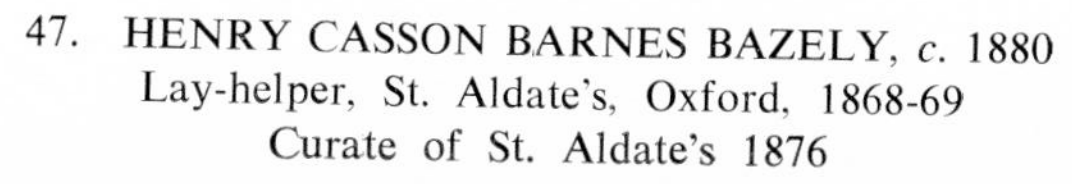

47. HENRY CASSON BARNES BAZELY, *c.* 1880
Lay-helper, St. Aldate's, Oxford, 1868-69
Curate of St. Aldate's 1876

48. M. H. NOEL
Vicar of St. Barnabas's, Oxford

A. M. W. CHRISTOPHER
Rector of St. Aldate's, Oxford

to promote the views of those members of the Church of England who, as I cannot but think, are (albeit unconsciously) preparing the way for a return to the errors of Rome, and hindering union between the Church of England and the sister Churches of the Reformation." He was able to add, however, "that, as regards yourself, if you were as a parish minister to ask me to officiate for you, I should rejoice to show my hearty sympathy with your work by doing so."

Bazely's own parochial activities gradually revived his old scruples. "He realised, as perhaps only a parish clergyman can, the deep significance of the formularies and ritual of the Church, and what are the principles involved in the use of the prayer-book. Those principles he felt to be opposed to his innermost convictions. He could minimise no longer; he felt compelled to draw back, as from a false step." On 10 September he preached for the last time in St. Aldate's. "If he had not followed his conscientious convictions," wrote Christopher, "his mental health, I think, might not have stood the strain. I never felt so strongly as when I saw the painful conflict in Bazely's mind, that we must not think hardly of every brother who leaves the Church of England."

While he was curate of St. Aldate's, it was convenient for Bazely to continue living at 2, Folly Bridge; and during a difficult period of his life he found it possible to move to his lodgings a pupil who was in the last stages of consumption. Though not poor, the young man had no parents or home in England, and he was a sceptic in religion. On 13 October, Bazely entered in his diary "G. frater in Xto obdormivit in Jesu 1.30." "That he died a believer," says Bazely's biographer, Bishop E. L. Hicks, a Fellow of Corpus in the early 'seventies, "was greatly due, under the blessing of the Holy Spirit, to the convincing argument of Bazely's Christian love and self-sacrifice." According to Bazely it was chiefly owing to reading the recently published biography of the saintly Dr. William Marsh, who had been a contemporary of Bishop Daniel Wilson at St. Edmund Hall.

Bazely had already sent his resignation to the Bishop of Oxford, which Dr. Mackarness refused to accept until he had complied with the requirements of the Clerical Disabilities Removal Act of 1870. "It seems," Bazely wrote at the time, "that until I relinquish the rights and privileges of the office of deacon in accordance with the provisions of that Act, I am liable to be prosecuted by the Bishop, if I officiate in England elsewhere than in the Established Church . . ." In 1877 he was again ordained in the Scottish church, and presently built a chapel in Nelson Street, Jericho, one of the poorest parts of Oxford, where he ministered until his death four years later.

Other clerical changes in Oxford, which affected Christopher, were occurring at this time. Henry Linton[1] succeeded to his family estates in Huntingdonshire and Lincolnshire in 1877 and resigned St. Peter-le-Bailey. His place was taken by Francis Chavasse who had worked in Preston and Holloway since graduating from Corpus in 1869. Chavasse had obtained a first class in the school of law and modern history. Although his biographer has used the word 'venerable' to describe Christopher at this period, the latter was only fifty-seven; but the fact remains that Chavasse was a much younger man, still in his thirties, and, in spite of his retarded stature, an attractive person who preached well. The new St. Peter's, built specially large three years before in order to accommodate undergraduates, began to fill up with university men.

During the next ten years the influence of St. Peter-le-Bailey, under Chavasse's guidance, grew considerably. Christopher himself described it in a letter to *The Oxford Times*. "An Anonymous Ritualistic writer . . . who signs himself 'Oxonian', tries to make your readers believe that what he calls 'Success', as respects large congregations and a large proportion of communicants in them, is only to be found in Ritualistic Churches, and not in those which are Protestant and Evangelical . . . 'Oxonian' ignores the success given to St. Peter-le-Bailey Church, Oxford, the Rector of which (Rev. F. J. Chavasse) is as truly Protestant and Evangelical as any member of the Church Association can be . . . Every Sunday evening 150 chairs have to be placed in the aisles of St. Peter-le-Bailey Church to increase the number of filled seats from 600 to 750. More than 500 members of Mr. Chavasse's congregation partook of the Holy Communion last Easter Day. My own Communicants on Easter Day were only two hundred and sixty. But even

[1]He had been made an honorary canon of Christ Church in 1871, a measure of diocesan recognition accorded to two (himself and Christopher), and offered to a third (French of St. Ebbe's), of those brought to Oxford livings by the evangelicals in the second half of the nineteenth century. It was also given to the first Principal of Wycliffe Hall, R. B. Girdlestone, in 1882.

these were six times as many as those on the first Easter Day after I became Rector of St. Aldate's."

"Take care, dear brother, you do not enlarge your church," Christopher would say to Chavasse, " or I shall have no congregation left. God bless you! " Chavasse cited this remark many years later as an example of one of Christopher's most prominent characteristics, " his self-effacement. He saw God and forgot himself . . . He never dreamt of his own interest, gain, self-advancement, and the praise of men . . . It must have been a sore trial for one of his years, and for one who had toiled as he had in that parish and University, to see his congregations dwindling and growing less and less. Yet he never spoke a resentful word, and never showed the slightest sign of jealousy . . . A man who could show such a spirit was a man who lived in the presence of God."

Christopher made the same remark to the new Vicar of Holy Trinity and to the new Rector of St. Ebbe's and probably to the new Rector of St. Clement's. For in the same year the saintly Harry Grey of Wadham, grandson of Earl Grey of the Reform Bill — likewise first cousin of that Lord Halifax who was president of the English Church Union, and, more distantly, a cousin of Lord Grey of Falloden, Chancellor of the university from 1928 to 1933, — later Principal of Wycliffe Hall, was instituted to Trinity parish, and he too attracted undergraduates to help him in the work of a poor and difficult neighbourhood. Moreover, Thomas French, Rector of St. Ebbe's since 1875, had been consecrated Bishop of Lahore, and Alfred Pearson of Lincoln College, another of the younger generation, afterwards Bishop of Burnley, had succeeded. Chavasse, his contemporary as an undergraduate, wrote in 1878 that he was " a capital fellow. He is filling his church . . ." In that year Francis Pilcher, for whom Lord Nuffield made his first bicycle, was appointed Rector of St. Clement's on virtually the first vacancy[1] occurring since the advowson was acquired for the Oxford Evangelical Trust in 1864. Lord Nuffield's biographers record that Pilcher not only "took an interest" in the young William Morris but gave him his first production order. Pilcher was a big man, and he needed an exceptionally large bicycle. Used every day it was a mobile advertisement, and other orders followed. (Forty-four years later, reverting to Lord

[1]His immediate predecessor lived only a few months after institution.

Nuffield, the machine was still in good condition). Pilcher also had been one of Christopher's young men. The heart of the Rector of St. Aldate's doubtless rejoiced as he witnessed those whom he had guided taking up important and responsible positions in the parish life of the university city.

Whether he was as delighted about Robert Girdlestone's appointment as first Principal of Wycliffe Hall, since unsound views on baptism were said to have disqualified him for the curacy of St. Aldate's in 1859, is perhaps less certain. But Christopher "took lovingly" Girdlestone's refusal to join the Church Association in Oxford. A similar refusal on Chavasse's part, Christopher regarded as perfectly right. The Church Association had entered on a highly litigious stage in its career, and many evangelical churchmen were withholding their support. Christopher never used the slightest influence to persuade his curates to join it. "It does not matter with an old fellow like me," he said to young Griffith Thomas ten years later; in Chavasse's case, "it would have halved his influence in the University."

Wycliffe Hall was founded in 1877 as an evangelical theological college in Oxford. The sister foundation at Cambridge, Ridley Hall, did not come into existence until two years later. The two colleges owed their inception to a group of senior clergy and laymen, who were impressed with the need of providing theological training for graduate ordinands, hitherto thought scarcely necessary. The two halls had trustees and a committee in common but separate councils. Christopher's name occurs in the earliest list of committee members, in 1881, together with that of his former curate, T. A. Nash. In the same year Christopher was elected, as was almost inevitable in view of his position and influence in Oxford, a member of the council of Wycliffe Hall. Thus is does not appear that he took any part in founding the Hall, though John English, who became Christopher's curate in 1878, speaks of him as assisting "in establishing Wycliffe Hall." It may be that at first he was not altogether convinced of the necessity for it. The church had after all managed to maintain its ministry for many hundreds of years without such institutions. That Christopher did not harbour any but the best feelings towards Girdlestone is evident from the latter's own testimony. "He was kindness itself when I returned to Oxford in '77

. . . When I was at death's door with Typhoid in '79 he used to come up to the house[1] and pray with anyone he could find (sometimes with the cook in the kitchen)." In common with other resident evangelicals, Girdlestone[2] preached regularly at St. Aldate's.

Changes of a different nature were also taking place in Oxford. Gladstone's first period as Prime Minister saw the appointment of more than one advanced churchman to positions of influence which they would not have been given previously. Among them was Edward King, Principal of Cuddesdon College, and afterwards Bishop of Lincoln. In 1873 he had become, amidst protests, Regius Professor of Pastoral Theology. His gracious, loving character was in many ways akin to Christopher's; and from Christopher it might be thought he borrowed the idea of a garden room for undergraduate meetings. At first his private gatherings for university men were held in his Lodgings; but in 1876 it became necessary to adapt a wash-house and equip it with the inevitable coconut-matting, chairs, and, in this case, a harmonium, which seemed to him "very simple but very lovely" — "a little 'Bethel'." Like Christopher he had, as his biographer says, a "genius for sympathy," and some men looked forward to Friday evenings at Canon King's as others did to Saturdays at St. Aldates' Rectory. Here was an influence of a different kind to that of Chavasse and other younger evangelicals, to counteract the attractions of what Christopher had to offer, one which would tend to draw away those on the fringe of his flock. Not till 1885 did it cease, with King's preferment to Lincoln. Chavasse's biographer, Canon Lancelot, and others, have drawn attention to King's personal magnetism in comparison with Canons Heurtley and Payne Smith, but while the former was certainly of a retiring nature, the latter had become Dean of Canterbury two years before King came to Christ Church. Dean Goulburn, moreover, speaks of Heurtley as, with Christopher and Linton, among men to whom, between 1863 and 1876, "the young life of Oxford in those days was indebted."

"Dear A. W. Poole," as Christopher said, ". . . laboured in faith and love amongst us for two years." Poole went out as a missionary

[1]The original 'Wycliffe Lodge', on the corner of Banbury Road and Norham Gardens, previously 'Laleham,' where one of Arnold of Rugby's sons had taken pupils.

[2]A first cousin of Col. G. H. Morrell of Headington Hill Hall, Oxford.

to India in 1878. While at St. Aldate's he started language study with a view to work abroad. His friend of undergraduate days, Edward Hodges, afterwards Bishop of Travancore, came to Oxford at the beginning of 1877 for a few months' special reading, at the same time assisting the veteran missionary T. V. French at St. Ebbe's. Poole and Hodges made a beginning at Sanskrit together. "The only available time," wrote Bishop Hodges, "was after all parochial engagements were over." French, with his great experience and oriental learning — he is said to have founded, about 1875, the Oxford Missionary Association of Graduates, of which Christopher was a member from its inception — would come and help them. Poole's address at a Church Missionary Society annual meeting a few years later so impressed the Archbishop of Canterbury, Dr. Tait, that he was offered the missionary see of Japan, which he held for only two years until his death in 1885. Writing to his old Rector from India in 1880 he remarked ". . . nothing has struck me so much since I left [Oxford] as the number of men I have heard of since, whom one would have thought most unlikely who are now converted and living and working as earnest men of God. I mentioned this to Watson[1] once as an encouragement to College Prayer Meetings where their ungodly companions are lovingly prayed for, and since then I have heard of more instances . . . Please give messages of affection to all with whom I was associated in Christian work in St. Aldate's. I often think of my short but happy time there . . "

After Poole, as Christopher was wont to relate when reciting, as he delighted to do on any occasion which offered, the tale of his curates, "the faithful, diligent and gentle John English came to us, and was much valued, especially by the sick and afflicted . . ." English had been trained, on Christopher's recommendation, by Boultbee and Waller at St. John's Hall, Highbury, and he had already served two years as curate of St. Paul's, Poole. "From morning till night," English wrote, with reference to Christopher at this time, "he was busily engaged in his Master's work, whether in his study engrossed in correspondence, or in the parish, sympathising with those in need or sorrow."

[1]Another Worcester man, afterwards, as the Revd. J. G. Watson, Rector of St. Ebbe's 1909-13.

English has recorded how, attracted originally by Bazely, (and initially to Oxford by Christopher's reputation and welcome,) a twenty-nine year old matriculation candidate named Tucker called upon him, as curate of St. Aldate's, to ask for baptism, and that after instruction at his hands, he was duly baptised by Christopher, in the presence of Bazely and himself. He was a regular attendant, Archdeacon Shepherd has recorded in his biography, at Christopher's Saturday evening meetings and a helper in the open-air services on Sunday evenings at the Martyrs' Memorial. Before long he had a district in St. Aldates' parish, which he visited in his spare time. In due course the young man was confirmed by the Bishop of Oxford. He was Alfred Tucker, presently of Christ Church, artist and athlete, afterwards well known as a statesmanlike Bishop of Uganda, and latterly a Canon of Durham. While an undergraduate he had a picture hung at the Royal Academy. In 1882 he was ordained to a curacy with Edward Hathaway at St. Andrew-the-Less, Clifton. Hathaway was "then and for many years afterwards . . . his confidant and adviser in all his deepest concerns." Archbishop Davidson of Canterbury wrote in a preface to the biography: "the story of his life, in all respects notable, is in some respects unique. There has been no other instance in English history of a prominent artist, whose pictures are to be seen in the Royal Academy and elsewhere, having a sudden call to Holy Orders and responding to it with enthusiasm."[1] In the Archbishop's opinion, he was "a constructive statesman of the first order," a view which will be readily endorsed by those who are familiar with the history of Uganda.

In view of the influence of his younger brethren at Oxford it was perhaps particularly fortunate that Christopher should have decided shortly before 1877 to rebuild St. Aldates' Rectory, which had been declared by an architect to be incapable of further repair. Residence in Pembroke Street, close to his church, would make him decidedly more accessible than he was in Keble Terrace. In any case he would no longer have to use up so much energy in walking backwards and forwards from and to his parish, a consideration of some importance,

[1]This statement overlooks the case of the Revd. M. W. Peters, R.A., (1742-1814), who took orders in 1783 after he had attained "a considerable position as an artist", and had exhibited regularly at the Royal Academy from its first exhibition.

presumably, to a man of his age, however energetic. It seems now remarkable that for the first eighteen years of his ministry at St. Aldate's, Christopher lived upwards of a mile from the scene of his parochial activities.

In March 1877 Christopher was making an appeal for funds. A copy of his circular preserved in the Bodleian Library shows that already subscribers included the Earl of Aberdeen[1], the Bishop of Durham, Dr. Charles Baring,[2] the Dean of Canterbury, Dr. Payne-Smith, Sir Henry Peek, Member of Parliament for Mid-Surrey, the Vice-Chancellor, Dr. J. E. Sewell, Warden of New College, the Dean of Christ Church, Dr. H. G. Liddell, and eleven other Heads of Houses. Christopher mentioned his earlier building activities in the parish — church, schools, Rectory Room — and pointed out that he had left till last the rebuilding of the Rectory. He desired to erect "a simple but commodious Parsonage."

Edward Hathaway again lent his assistance. As in 1862, he collected personal testimonies to Christopher's work and printed them in the form of a booklet for circulation with the appeal. Men who remembered Christopher's arrival in Oxford vied with those who had lately gone down in speaking of the worth of the Rector of St. Aldate's and of the need to support him in rebuilding his rectory house. There were not wanting those whose letters were tinged with pain. The Revd. David Pitcairn of Magdalen, curate of Chipping Campden, afterwards Vicar of Monkton Combe, wrote "Hearing that Mr. Christopher's Rectory in Pembroke Street will soon be a ruin, I cannot but feel for it the regret one would for an old friend. It is associated with many hallowed scenes, and with many brothers in Christ . . . "

The state of the Rectory needed little emphasis. "I can quite imagine," wrote Francis Aglionby, "its condition by this time to be almost dangerous for human habitation . . . In the chilling and deadening atmosphere of scholastic life in the University, many of us turned to 40 Pembroke Street, and our loving friend there, at the Saturday evening gatherings especially, as to a little sanctuary from which we never failed to derive refreshment and comfort in the spiritual life." J. A. Faithfull of University College, curate of St.

[1]The seventh Earl, younger brother of the sixth, who, as Lord Haddo, had procured granite for the pillars when St. Aldate's was rebuilt.

[2]A former president of the Union and curate of St. Ebbe's.

Margaret's, Brighton, presently Vicar of Holy Trinity, Leicester, who had lately gone down (before which however he had been one of those undergraduates who even in those days worshipped at St. Ebbe's), and whose name had stood alone in the first class of the honour school of theology in 1876, as Aglionby's had done in 1873, wrote "I am convinced his ministry has been the means of the conversion of many, and of the spiritual development of many more . . . I can imagine nothing more unfair than that he should have to rebuild his Rectory . . ."

Francis Chavasse, not yet arrived from Upper Holloway, declared to Hathaway: "I look back with growing thankfulness to God upon the benefits I received from my intercourse with him, Canon Linton and yourself, during my Oxford life. It helped to crystallize good impressions already made, and to keep me steadfast in 'the old paths'." His contemporary and friend, Edmund Knox, since 1868 a Fellow of Merton, could say, with reference to the patrons' appointment[1] in 1859, "I need not tell you how amply the wisdom of their choice has been justified by the success of Mr. Christopher's labours here. His well-known zeal, fervent love, and devoted piety must have made him, by God's blessing, valuable anywhere. The position of St. Aldate's Church has undoubtedly enabled him to utilise his talents in a rare degree for the benefit of members of this University." He mentioned also the "very serious hindrance to his usefulness that he was formerly obliged to live at *a great distance* from his work; and even now, he and his successors must lose a most important position for University influence, as long as the present tumbledown building is allowed to stand on the site of St. Aldate's Rectory."

There seems to have been a suggestion that the new parsonage house should be erected in some sense as a mark of esteem. One of Christopher's earliest friends at Oxford, the Revd. George Butler, incumbent of St. Thomas's, Edinburgh, began his letter by saying: "I am delighted to hear that so practical, so permanent, and so well merited a testimonial to our very dear friend, the Rev. A. M. W. Christopher, is proposed . . ." "I do not doubt," concluded Edmund Knox, "that, especially from Oxford men, who understand the importance of the object . . . you will find hearty co-operation in the

[1]Knox was evidently unaware that Christopher's presentation was not in fact made by Simeon's Trustees.

effort." Of the ten contributors to the booklet, as many as seven had taken first classes in the schools, a point which Hathaway was at pains to emphasise in view of the frequent disparagement of the scholarship and abilities of "undergraduates who hold distinctive Evangelical opinions." It was no less a tribute to Christopher. An early undergraduate friend, George Tonge, heard Bishop Waldegrave of Carlisle (a 'double-first' of 1839) tell his ordination candidates that a man who took his stand on the doctrines of grace must be prepared to bid farewell to any reputation for learning.

One hundred and fifty men, chiefly undergraduates, subscribed £100, a gift which they accompanied by a warm appreciation of Christopher's work on their behalf. Some of the names appended to the document became well known in their day, notably Sir W. F. A. Archibald, Fellow of St. John's 1869-73, afterwards a Master of the Supreme Court and father of R. T. Archibald of the Children's Special Service Mission in India, Sir George King, a Master in Chancery, Archdeacon Buckland, Dr. Wells, Warden of Wadham, and, interestingly, two nonconformists, both then recent graduates from New College,[1] Nathaniel Micklem, Q.C., father of Dr. Nathaniel Micklem, sometime Principal of Mansfield College, and his friend R. F. Horton, subsequently a distinguished congregationalist divine.

The Rectory built in consequence of this appeal still remains in use. Tall and large, its heavy mid-Victorian exterior of brick, originally 'white', with stone quoins, Christopher was determined that it should be big enough for a man with a numerous family, such as his successor might well be. He could not forsee that within fifty years of his death, small families and no staff would be the order of the day. In any case it was necessary to think of the undergraduates. The study on the first floor was designed as one arm of the drawing-room, with folding doors which could be opened when a large gathering was expected. The Rectory Room, however, as holding a much greater number, remained behind the new house. The latter was finished by October 1878, but Christopher did not part with his lease of Keble Terrace until December of that year,[2] when he was able to sell it for £400 more than he had given. J. T. Christopher, the

[1]And presidents of the Union.

[2]The voters' lists show him as still there in October.

49. ST. ALDATES' RECTORY, OXFORD, 1962
Home of A. M. W. Christopher 1878-1905

Rector's cousin, was architect of the new parsonage, and its builder was C. Selby of Bear Lane. The cost amounted to over £4,000.

Canon Cox of Cheltenham has left a graphic description of the Rectory and its environs as he remembered them in the 'eighties, ". . . crammed in as it is in a very narrow, ancient and cobbled Oxford street, strangely dark, not to say gloomy, without a vestige of anything naturally green or refreshing. It suggests a house described by Charles Dickens, which had somehow got into a crowd of smaller buildings and was quite too big ever to get out again. After thirty and more years one hears still the incessant rumble of the drays and carts conveying beer, in those days, and all sorts of commodities, along a street where there is insufficient room for two vehicles to pass one another without difficulty, where newsboys and vendors of all sorts were perpetually making the air unpleasantly resonant, and the clatter on the pavement was only interchanged by the hilarious noises emanating from many windows along the funnel-like street of undergraduates' lodgings. Amidst all that rather forbidding environment, though only a few paces from the glorious antiquities of Oxford's architecture, inside a door approached by stone steps and a dark chocolate coloured porch resided our well-beloved rector . . ."

In spite of some unattractive features, the workmanship of the new house was good, and the building has worn well. Very soon its associations were no less hallowed than those of the old Rectory. One clergyman, who preferred to sign himself 'Laus Deo', afterwards wrote: " I went up to Oxford as a Freshman, October 1878. Though I was a Public School boy, I had been a Home-Boarder and so I felt lonely in the midst of a new, strange world. My first Saturday night I went to St. Aldate's Prayer Meeting for Varsity men. As I entered, the hymn was being sung, 'How sweet the name of Jesus sounds in a believer's ear', and I felt I had found *home*. From that day the sympathy, the advice, the hospitality, the prayers and the life of Canon Christopher helped me more than I could or ever can say."

Chapter XI

"Speaking the Truth in Love"

1878 - 1882

CHRISTOPHER was always on the watch to maintain the historic protestantism of the Church of England. He had been delighted with the authority which J. B. Mozley's works *On The Primitive Doctrine of Baptismal Regeneration* (1856), and *Review of the Baptismal Controversy* (1862), lent to the interpretation of the doctrine of infant baptism followed by many evangelicals. Mozley, a leading tractarian appointed by Gladstone to be Regius Professor of Divinity in 1871, had in fact changed his views as a result of examining the whole question after the Gorham judgement of 1850. Before Mozley's death in 1877, Christopher obtained permission to publish extracts from his books in the form of a pamphlet entitled *Baptismal Regeneration,* which he circulated widely and was several times reprinted by him and afterwards by Canon Hay Aitken. He felt strongly that misunderstanding of this doctrine lay at the root of all the errors connected with 'ritualism'. Nor did he hesitate, as we have seen, to write to the secular newspapers about such matters, then, however, a more common practice.

A serious charge of antinomianism having been made against the teaching of Martin Luther, a lengthy letter from Christopher had appeared in *The Oxford Times* for 4 August 1877. It reflects clearly his spirit in controversy. "Avoiding all the bitterness which too often has hindered the usefulness of Christian controversy, in Christian kindness, let me shew what Luther's doctrine really was with regard to faith and good works, and compare it with that of the Church of England. I will trust that those who have misunderstood, and therefore have misrepresented Luther, will be glad to read the following extracts from his great work on St. Paul's Epistle to the Galatians. When he has so clearly expressed his meaning with regard to the relation between faith and works, it would not be fair and just by means of other quotations separated from the context, to try and make out that his meaning is something else . . . My object is not to wound those with whom I contend, but to win them to God's truth. I will, therefore, not write any severe words of those who have been misled with respect to Luther's doctrine and so have misrepresented it, but I will ask them, with the charity and calmness of those who desire only to know the truth concerning this and other matters, to consider Luther's doctrine as contained in the extracts I have given above . . . May the God of truth lead all His children to discourage in all sections of the Church that mode of controversy which consists in picking out sentences from a Christian writer which may tend to disparage him, and at the same time omitting to quote any of the other passages which would explain his real meaning. Is it quite impossible for some of us who differ strongly in doctrine, to combine to introduce the startling novelty of fairness in religious controversy?"

It may be a matter for some surprise that the editor of *The Oxford Times* should be prepared to devote a long, closely printed column to such a letter. But it is important to remember that in those days many Oxford citizens were in some degree instructed protestants, and the stand which Christopher was accustomed to take by no means marked him out as eccentric or even out of step with the majority in the Church of England. In the following month the World's Evangelical Alliance — an interdenominational body founded in 1846 — held its annual conference at Oxford, and Christopher took a prominent part in the proceedings. On the first day he was invited to give the opening address, welcoming the visitors to Oxford, when the Dean of Canterbury, Dr. Payne Smith, former Regius Professor of Divinity, responded on behalf of those attending. That week the leading article in *The Oxford Times* was headed 'Visit of the Evangelical Alliance'. There was no attempt to adopt an impartial attitude — any more than in politics the newspaper concealed its "aggressive Conservatism". It would be unlikely that the writer was merely speaking for himself when he wrote: "It is fortunate, we think, in view of the sham Romanism so prevalent in Oxford at the present time, that this city should have been selected for the annual conference of that brave and true body of Christians — the Evangelical Alliance. The presence here this week of so many earnest and honest men from many parts of the world . . . has . . . purified the atmosphere, and we feel Oxford is once more the site where the Bishops suffered martyrdom, where the candle was lighted by good old Latimer, which by God's grace shall never be put out in this realm of England, and not a propaganda where fledgling curates, who delight in calling themselves priests, parade the streets in Romish garments . . . as for the clergy of the Christopher and Bazely type, men of fidelity to Protestant principles, they are in a miserable minority."

About the time when he at last resided at 40, Pembroke Street, Christopher became involved in a controversy with Canon Liddon. Henry Liddon had been brought up as an evangelical, but for many years he had been a devoted follower of Dr. Pusey. That eminent leader of the tractarians was still Regius Professor of Hebrew, as he had been forty years before, and he still lived in the canon's Lodgings in the angle of Tom Quad nearly opposite St. Aldate's church. Liddon, a much younger man, had by then become a colleague, as Dean Ireland's Professor of the Exegesis of Holy Scripture, while retaining his Christ Church studentship. A Church Association lecturer, the Revd. T. H. Gill, afterwards Vicar of Tonbridge, was advertised to speak in the Town Hall, with Christopher as president of the Oxford branch in the chair. Dr. Pusey had recently recommended to the English clergy the Abbé Gaume's *Manual for Confessors,* which he himself had 'adapted' for anglican use. It was not surprising that Gill should choose to speak about this manual. But Liddon viewed the matter in the light of a personal insult to his aged friend.

A correspondence of some length ensued between Liddon and Christopher. Liddon's original protest has not survived, but it is clear that he besought Christopher not to preside at the meeting. A small part of the correspondence is reproduced in Pusey's *Life.*

The interest of the remainder is sufficient to justify its inclusion as an appendix to the present volume, especially as no trace of it appears to survive among the Liddon papers at Keble College. Some extracts will show its general character: Christopher writing with unfailing courtesy, yet never yielding to an opponent whose replies are increasingly tinged with acerbity.

"It is a great grief to me," Christopher wrote on 27 November 1878, "that the Abbé Gaume's Romish book, the teaching of which I believe to be utterly subversive of the Gospel of Christ, should have been published by Dr. Pusey as adapted by him to the use of the English Church. I respect Dr. Pusey for his age, his learning, and specially for his great and valuable work on the Book of Daniel; and generally for his opposition to Scepticism, but if the dearest friend I have on earth were to publish a book subversive of the Gospel, and teaching 'Another Gospel which is not another', it would be my plain duty in faithfulness to Christ, and in love to the souls of my fellow men to do what I could to help to expose this pernicious perversion of the Gospel . . ."

Such strength of language will be distasteful to many professing evangelicals. Yet the essentially loving spirit of the writer cannot be called in question. Moreover, he had lately had a visit from Pastor Chiniquy, who stayed with him either in this year or in 1876. Chiniquy had been a Roman Catholic priest, first in Canada, then in the United States. His life-long love of Bible teaching eventually caused his bishop to withdraw his authority, and he and his flock left the Church of Rome. Such a living example of the incompatibility of Roman Catholic beliefs and scriptural Christianity could only add to Christopher's already decided convictions. In any case reference to the work of which he is speaking goes a long way to explain his feelings.

On the subject of penance, Dr. Pusey had thrown the mantle of his approval over such statements as: "Penance should not only be medicinal and protective to the new life, but also vindicative in expiation of past sin." "He [the penitent] is to come to you, and then you will give him some further penance in acquittal of his debt to God." Even advocates of sacramentalism might be surprised to be told that one 'Our Father' "would be a very light penance for repeated adulteries or other impurities," or that "No penance is more useful than frequenting the Sacraments."

Gill made bold to suggest that "The whole system . . . substitutes the life of sight for the life of faith, and shuts out the Mediatorial work of the Son of God." If the latter seems to go too far, what, in the light of the doctrine of justification by faith alone, expressed in Articles XI and XII, could be made of "These good works . . . have a greater efficacy for the expiation of sin"? Moreover, the Abbé Gaume, in insisting that the confessor acts as judge, alleges that, as far as the penitent is concerned, "it is not man, but GOD whom he obeys." After this a quotation from St. Philip Neri to the effect that "he who obeyed his Confessor was sure not to be called to account for his actions by God" follows naturally enough.

Unhappily, as it would seem, Dr. Pusey, who had eliminated certain passages altogether — thereby more deliberately countenancing those he retained — and had translated others very freely, had allowed some paragraphs to stand, towards the end of the manual, which sound extraordinarily damaging to his own position. "Be assured that this is one of the gravest faults of our day in the administration of the Sacrament [*i.e.* penance], that it is the road by which a number of Christians go down to hell . . . Poor murdered souls! . . . Perhaps out of fourscore persons plunged into habitual sin, more than threescore and ten have been lost through these ignorant and luke-warm confessors. This dialogue may seem a fable. Would to God it were not founded on constant and mournful experience!"

"The Lecture itself," wrote Christopher, "will be sufficient justification of all who have promoted it. Dr. Pusey's book is the fullest justification of their conduct. The Lecture was listened to by a large audience which crowded the Town Hall on Monday night with the deepest attention." With regard to the choice of subject, he had already stated: "I did not in any way suggest the subject of the Lecture, nor did the Church Association or anyone connected with it, but when it was proposed to me, as I had already seen the book, and had formed a very strong opinion of the utterly unscriptural character of its teaching, I could not, without unfaithfulness to Christ, reject the subject, or refuse to preside at the Lecture."

Dr. Liddon replied the same day. "Nothing, I fear, would be gained, if I were to enter on the subject of the Lecture, at which you thought it well to preside . . . What I venture to urge is this. If controversy be a duty, it ought, if possible, to keep clear of personalities. Your Lecturer was not obliged to select Dr. Pusey's book as the text of his lecture. To do so in Oxford was to offer a public insult to the most distinguished professor of Divinity in the place . . . It was the fact that *Dr. Pusey,* well known in Oxford, and living in the same street, had written the book, which gave zest to the subject, and commanded the attention of your audience, on Monday, at the Town Hall. I have known Dr. Pusey intimately for 32 years; and I do not affect to be indifferent to such a discreditable proceeding as that of Monday evening. I regret with all my heart that so good a man as yourself should be associated with it, upon whatever grounds; and I think it sincere to say to you what I have said, and shall say, to others." In a postscript he adds: " Dr. Pusey has no idea that I have written to you. I do not suppose that he has heard of the Lecture."

To this Christopher rejoined: " In the exercise of the like cordial frankness as you have so kindly claimed in your notes to me, you must suffer me to point out that it is exactly that long and intimate affection for Dr. Pusey, to which you refer that disqualifies you for sitting as judge upon my conduct . . . You evidently forgot in the moment of writing that Dr. Pusey has, within the last three months, publicly invited criticism by two overt acts absolutely unparalled in the history of our Church since the Reformation. He has adapted and published for use in our Protestant Communion a Roman Catholic 'Manual for Confessors'. And when one hundred Protestant Bishops, in conference assembled, have solemnly and unanimously condemned the practice of habitual confession, Dr. Pusey has publicly challenged the correctness of their decision or else the justice of their censure." This refers to a resolution of the Lambeth Conference of 1878. In September, Pusey had published a letter to Dr. Tait, " our Presbyterianizing Archbishop of Canterbury," which he entitled 'Habitual Confession not discouraged by the Resolution accepted by the Lambeth Conference', and wherein he exercised a characteristic ingenuity in refusing to accept the plain meaning of the bishops' affirmation.

" You seem to deprecate public criticism of Dr. Pusey's recent volume here in Oxford," Christopher continued, " on the ground partly of his distinguished position amongst us, and partly of his being resident here. Can it be your calm opinion that we who are pledged most solemnly, the Lord being our helper, to 'banish and drive away all erroneous and strange doctrines contrary to God's Word,' are freed from any such obligation if the teacher of such doctrines is a distinguished professor of Divinity in the place where we live?" Was St. Paul guilty of a 'discreditable proceeding', he goes on to inquire, and did he "offer a public insult" to one still more distinguished than Dr. Pusey, when he withstood St. Peter to the face? "It has escaped your notice," Christopher pointed out, "that when you wrote about the 'indulgence of party passions,' you were borrowing wholly from conjecture, and in no degree from fact. And no less so when you volunteer the remark that the large attendance at the recent lecture was due to zest which personalities lent to the subject. The attendance at prior lectures of the Church Association in Oxford has been just as large. And I have known the lecturer as a valued private friend for many years, and I can say honestly that he is not actuated by religious partisanship, does not deal in 'sharp' or 'exasperating' sayings at another's expense, and has no pleasure in those who do. If not in this life, assuredly dear Dr. Liddon in another, it will be made clear to you that to speak earnestly and valiantly for Divine truth, even if in doing so the speaker has to blame to the face and by name one revered for his years and position, is entirely compatible with Christian love and the bond of peace."

In a further letter Liddon, writing now from London, having gone into residence at St. Paul's, where he held a canonry, complained that "One who was present at the lecture said that 'Dr. Pusey was *well* groaned at'." On this point Christopher was not in a good position to speak with certainty, but he consulted three friends who were able to reassure him that there was no groaning at Dr. Pusey. "If in a different part of the Town Hall your informant heard anything not sufficiently marked to be heard or remembered by my three friends, it was probably due to the indiscreet proposal publicly made by some friend of Dr. Pusey's that three cheers should be given for him . . ." Liddon declined to withdraw the epithet 'discreditable', for "It represents, in my opinion, the least they [the proceedings in question] deserve in the way of censure: and I must once more say how pained I am that a man like yourself, — whom I have always hitherto associated with the devotional and Christian rather than the fierce and merely controversialist section of the Low Church party, — should have been in any way mixed up with them."

"I must needs try to obey God rather than man, and to be true to His Commission and to my ordination vow," Christopher rejoined, "remembering that in the same sentence in which He says to me ἔλεγξον He prepares me by His word ἀκαίρως to expect that many will regard my obedience as unseasonable (II. Tim. IV.2)." The upshot of Liddon's attitude appeared to Christopher to amount "to this — that no Oxford clergyman may, while Dr. Pusey lives, call in question from his pulpit any one of the Professor's doctrinal statements in connection with his name. By reason of the respect due to his age and position — which I ex animo concede to him — he is to have, in your judgement, such absolute dominion over the faith and practice of his brethren in the ministry, that their congregations are to find them dumb whenever Dr. Pusey has spoken."

"Indeed, you mistake my claim on behalf of Dr. Pusey . . ." wrote Liddon. "But while I am, also, as far as possible from deprecating criticism of what he writes, I submit that it should be addressed to knowledge and reason, and not to passion . . . the University Pulpit is much more at the command of those who dissent from Dr. Pusey than of those who agree with him; and, if his opponents can say anything that is theologically entitled to serious consideration, they are very sure to carry with them a very large number of minds." The next day Christopher wrote his final disclaimer to Liddon, who replied in a lengthy letter, the kernel of which is contained in the sentence: "My conclusion is not disturbed by the fact which you mention, and which I *unreservedly* believe, that many of the persons concerned in managing the Church Association are in their private capacity, very estimable indeed." "How much I wish" he concluded, "that in view of our immense dangers, from the Church of Rome on one side, and from sheer unbelief on the other, we of the Church of England could learn to tolerate each other, and to trust to God the Holy Spirit to teach us what is right, or to unteach, what is wrong, in our faith! . . . Dear Mr. Christopher, in view of another world, there are better things to be done here on earth, than presiding at lectures against Dr. Pusey in the Oxford Town Hall."

The above was written on 17 December. Shortly afterwards Christopher referred to Gill's assertions in a letter to *The Oxford Times*. This drew a response, very different in tone to Liddon's comments, from Pusey himself. "I am distressed to see," he wrote on Christmas Eve, "that . . . you have endorsed Mr. Gill's accusation against me of subverting some of the very fundamental doctrines of Christianity: and first of the Atonement." On the question of expiation, he remarked surprisingly "I had no idea that any would identify it with our Lord's Expiation on the Cross. Those for whom I edited the book would not." In a postscript he added "Since writing the above, I have determined to cancel all the pages in which the word 'expiate' occurs,[1] although Bp. Taylor uses the word 'expiatory' of repentance." "It certainly was an oversight" he admitted, "that I overlooked the word 'extraordinary supererogation' . . . I have now cancelled the page, though I fear that Mr. Gill would dislike the change, since he will have a stone the less to throw at me. And now, in the time when the Angels first sung at the Blessed Nativity of our Dear Lord, 'Peace on earth, goodwill towards men', do let us try to understand each other as well as we can. It has always been a joy to me to recognise the truths, which your friends hold, . . . and to feel how much we had in common. It is a hard battle which we, who love our Lord, have to fight with those who deny Him. At least let us pray Him, for one another."

Christopher's reply has not survived, but on New Year's Day 1879, Pusey wrote again: "I thank you much for your kind wishes and kind present, which I shall value as a testimony of your Christian charity. But pray do not write to me, as 'eminent' or yourself, as 'inferior'. It pains me so, who knows myself to be nothing . . . You write to me, as if I were a Ritualist. I never was. But I think them the objects of an unjust persecution founded on an unjust judgement . . . I have been thinking what I would ask you to accept as a New Year gift from me; but I mistrust anything of my own. So will you accept a volume of one, whose belief I shared in all things, but whose humble loving soul escaped rubbing people up, as I did somehow Mr. Gill. With every good wish for this and all your coming years . . ."

[1]It does not seem that this intention was carried out. The second printing appears to be identical with the first.

It is recorded in Pusey's *Life* that Christopher had sent to Pusey a copy of Bonar's *God's Way of Holiness*. In return Pusey gave Christopher some *Lenten Sermons* by Keble. Christopher also despatched as a New Year's gift to Liddon, Mozley's *Review of the Baptismal Controversy*. Pusey lived for another three years. Just before the end of his life the Secretary of the Church Association publicly asserted that Pusey had challenged a legal prosecution which he knew was technically impossible, and Pusey repudiated the suggestion in a letter to *The Times* on 24 January 1881. Liddon also wrote to the editor of that journal, and as a result there was a slight echo of the debate between him and Christopher in a further exchange of letters.

The correspondence between Liddon and Christopher may now seem incongruous and its tenor out-moded. But it is redolent of the atmosphere of a time when feelings ran high. Moreover, it is worthy of remembrance that Pusey, Liddon, and Christopher alike accepted the traditional view of the inspiration of Scripture. It was when Liddon discovered that in choosing Gore as the first head of the Pusey House (founded in 1884) he had selected a man who was not faithful to this belief that he began to break up in spirits and in health. Both Pusey and Christopher — and indeed the Oxford clergy as a whole — had fully approved the action of Bishop Mackarness when in 1874 he inhibited Bishop Colenso, who had denied the doctrine of verbal inspiration, from preaching at Carfax church. Naturally, therefore, the biblical teaching on false doctrine, and the proper attitude towards purveyors of it, made the issues between high church and low church seem much more than a question of emphasis. It was a matter of life or death. Nor was this veiled by an appeal thus early to the common ground between them. Moreover, the changes which Pusey and his friends had brought about in parts of the establishment were quite without historical precedent in the reformed English church — as Dr. Darwell Stone and other later anglo-catholics have admitted — and in 1878 they seemed far more revolutionary than they do now, on the one side calling for justification and on the other for condemnation.

Liddon's reference to the university pulpit might seem to imply that the evangelicals would be hard pressed to defend protestant opinions at that level. But he may have had in mind that the

Bampton Lecturer of 1878 had been the Revd. C. H. H. Wright, a protestant controversialist, and that in 1879 Dr. Wright was to be followed in that office by another staunch upholder of the Reformation, Henry Wace, afterwards Dean of Canterbury. One of the select preachers, too, at this period, was Canon J. C. Ryle, shortly to become the first Bishop of Liverpool. Another was Canon A. W. Thorold, who had been associated with Hathaway in the early days of the plan to provide evangelical ministries in Oxford, and who was appointed Bishop of Rochester in 1877.[1] Francis Paget, later Bishop of Oxford, believed that Liddon was too prone to controversy. Certainly it was he and not Christopher who began this one; but it cannot be said that either were loath to defend their point of view.

With regard to the previous Church Association meetings in Oxford to which Christopher refers, it is interesting to note that one of these, on 27 November 1877, was the occasion for his friend Ryle to deliver as a lecture his 'James the Second and the Seven Bishops', afterwards incorporated as a chapter in *Facts and Men*, published in 1882. Some months earlier, when the speaker, the Revd. Joseph Bardsley, Rector of Stepney, who was thought worthy of a Lambeth D.D. in 1881, maintained that "Modern Ritualism necessitates the re-assertion of the great Protestant Principles of the Reformed Church of England," the chair was taken by a layman, James Bateman, a Fellow of the Royal Society from the age of twenty-eight, and who, although it was forty years since he had gone down, was described, properly, as "of Magdalen College". His son Rowland, an undergraduate in the 'sixties, was at this time earning a distinctive reputation with the Church Missionary Society in India, and had doubtless been known to Christopher.[2] There was a large attendance and "a good deal of uproar." Other lectures had been given by the Revd. Dr. S. Wainwright on 'Confession: Not Auricular', and by the Revd. A. A. Isaacs on 'Sacerdotalism—Its Influence on the Home, the Church, and the Nation'. In 1881 James Inskip, father of Lord Chancellor Caldecote, spoke on 'Altars, Priests, and Sacrifices'. In the following year the Revd. Dr. Concanon took as his subject 'The Burning of Bishop Latimer in Broad Street, Oxford, and what led to it', followed soon afterwards by Dr. Wain-

[1]This succession of select preachers was maintained in the 'eighties by Prebendary Wace, Canon R. B. Girdlestone, Canon T. D. Bernard and F. J. Chavasse.

[2]He certainly spoke to university men in St. Aldates' Rectory Room in 1884.

50. A. M. W. CHRISTOPHER, *c.* 1880

wright on 'Reformation or Deformation'. In 1883 Canon Taylor, later Archdeacon of Liverpool, sought to answer the question 'Are the Ministers of Christ's Gospel Sacrificing Priests?' After a stormy meeting, F. C. T. Jansen, a non-collegian, later for over fifty years Vicar of Newton Solney, Derbyshire, recalled — the speaker's "closely reasoned and trenchant utterances" on the 'Power of the Keys' had found their mark — "it was amusing to both sides present to hear Canon Christopher thank his opponents for their courteous behaviour," putting everyone in good humour to go home.

"The Church Association lectures in Oxford" Jansen considered, looking back, "were from every point of view a great success." In this assessment W. G. D. Fletcher, during the mid-'seventies of St. Edmund Hall, and a seat-holder at St. Aldate's, afterwards widely known as an antiquarian, concurred in 1920, when Vicar of Oxon, Shrewsbury. "The best work the C.A. did was its lectures, which were very largely attended by Undergraduates." From 1878 to 1882 Fletcher was curate to Harry Grey, later Principal of Wycliffe Hall, at Holy Trinity, Oxford, publishing *The Blackfriars at Oxford* in the latter year. Fletcher in fact, as "a hot-headed young protestant lawyer", was "largely responsible" for the founding of an Oxford branch of the Church Association. "I thought we ought to have a *local* branch of the C.A. in order to oppose the strong *local* branch of the E.C.U.,[1] & possibly prosecute the Rev. H. M. [*sic*] Noel[2] in the Law Courts! . . . it is only fair to say . . . that *Mr. Christopher was most strongly opposed to the formation of any Oxford branch*; and when it was formed would not hear of any prosecution . . . Mr. C. said he would stand by it, though he deprecated its formation." In view of Christopher's unhesitating riposte to Liddon's first and every succeeding thrust, this is a particularly interesting side-light. It is also interesting that one of the leading laymen of the Oxford branch was Walter Walsh, author of *The Secret History of the Oxford Movement.* All the public meetings took place in the Town Hall and at almost all of them Christopher was advertised to preside. It is a somewhat surprising example, therefore, of literary unreliability, that Bishop Knox — writing, it is true, in his eighty-seventh year — states in his autobiography, with reference to evangelical life at Oxford during the

[1]English Church Union. [2]Vicar of St. Barnabas's', Oxford.

years 1865 to 1880,[1] " I cannot recall a single meeting of the Church Association held there." In 1886, the Revd. C. H. Wainwright spoke on 'The Church of England Scriptural in her Teachings and therefore Protestant'. In 1888 Isaacs was again the lecturer on 'The Dangers and Difficulties which beset the Church of England'. Wainwright's lecture, as reported in *The Oxford Times* for 6 March was reprinted by Christopher for distribution in tract form. Isaacs's second lecture was also reprinted as a tract.

The lectures created much interest and led to considerable 'heckling' from undergraduates. After Inskip had spoken, the Rector of St. Clement's, Francis Pilcher, in proposing a vote of thanks, became involved in an interchange with some members of the audience. He answered their questions with so much brilliance, force, and good nature, that he completely captured the assembled company. His answers, needless to say, were subsequently published in tract form. It was at this meeting that C. J. Casher, a scholar of St. John's, and afterwards a first-classman in theology, who had come up to Oxford inclined to high church views, was led to see the strength of the evangelical position. He became honorary curate of St. Aldate's when he was ordained, working in that capacity during the remainder of Christopher's incumbency. Another lifelong upholder of the Reformation, Dr. Henry Gee, had been a scholar of Exeter during the late 'seventies, and it seems probable that he likewise would have supported Christopher at these and other meetings. From 1880 to 1900, Gee served on the staff of St. John's Hall, Highbury, for three years under Christopher's friend Boultbee, in 1896 editing with W. J. Hardy their well-known *Documents Illustrative of English Church History*. Subsequently Master of University College, Durham, Gee was Dean of Gloucester from 1917 to 1938. His papers are not at present available to throw possible light on his undergraduate days.

It is not to be supposed that Christopher enjoyed controversy. Frank Webster, a devoted undergraduate admirer who became curate of St. Aldate's in 1882, left on record that " It was the transparency of his character that endeared him so to us all. If he was tried and anxious about anything he made no effort to conceal it.

[1]He was a resident Fellow of Merton 1868-85.

I specially remember how he shrank from taking the chair at controversial Meetings. It was a task which he disliked immensely, for he was a thorough man of peace and love, but he did it as a duty, and for days before we felt how he was bracing himself for it. If he was encouraged, and he nearly always was, then his joy and thankfulness were infectious, and his eyes glistened as he said, 'I think, dear friends, we ought to read the 103rd Psalm'." The tone of Christopher's controversial work may be judged by the following extract from a brief address given in St. Aldate's church a few days before a lecture by Dr. McCarthy of Dublin in 1882.

"If we are grateful to God for His Gospel, we shall desire to obey the words which His Holy Spirit taught St. Jude to write for our learning. See the 3rd verse of his Epistle. 'Beloved when I gave all diligence to write unto you of the common salvation, it was needful for me to write unto you & exhort you that *ye should earnestly contend for the faith which was once delivered unto the saints*.' In love to God & to our fellow men around us we should endeavour to correct with Bible Truth corruptions of the Gospel. Every clergyman of the Church of England at his ordination was asked by the Bishop this question 'Will you be ready with all faithful diligence, to banish and drive away *all erroneous & strange doctrines contrary to God's Word*?' And he replied solemnly 'I will, the Lord being my Helper.' That which divides the Church is religious error — that which tends to *unite* Christians to each other is Gospel Truth . . . There is no need for bitterness in controversy. The truth may be spoken in love. Controversy is simply the correction of religious error with God's truth . . . *Without controversy* the Church of England wd. never have been reformed — without controversy it can never be *kept reformed*. Cranmer, Latimer & Ridley thought it worth while to die a cruel death to maintain the truths which are the subject of next Friday evening's Lecture in our Church. Surely it is worth sharing a little reproach to help to preserve their good work from being undone."

For some years the diocesan theological college founded by Bishop Wilberforce under the shadow of his palace at Cuddesdon had given rise to grave misgivings among protestants in the three archdeaconries of Oxfordshire, Berkshire, and Buckinghamshire. Quite early in its history Henry Liddon had been obliged to resign the vice-principalship on account of the anglo-catholic tone which he was promoting there. By 1878, that is in twenty-four years, twenty former Cuddesdon students had gone over to Rome, and it was decided to move in the diocesan conference "that this Conference desires . . . to express its opinion . . . that the teaching in the said College does not deserve the confidence of members of the Church of England." Behind this protest was the Revd. Charles Golightly, like Bishop Mackarness an old Etonian, who had been financially disqualified for an Oriel fellowship in the 'thirties, but who became a life-long resident in Oxford. Edmund Knox, now Dean of Merton, and afterwards Bishop of Manchester, was asked to propose the resolution. The Revd. G. N. Freeling, Vicar of St. Cross, and, like Knox, a Fellow of Merton, but well known as an advanced high churchman, wrote to his colleague and to Christopher to try to avert action which might be painful to the Bishop. Knox was much exercised, but felt it his duty to proceed. Christopher explained to Freeling that "It was the recent deep lamentations of one of the most respected high church country Incumbents in the Diocese to Mr. Golightly concerning the influence of Cuddesdon College on the Diocese which led the latter to act as he has done . . . It will be at a very great sacrifice of feeling, that anyone stands by the young brother who feels it to be his duty to Christ to speak out . . . Now that persecution has ceased I think that one of the greatest trials to which Christ's servants are exposed is to be required by faithfulness to oppose publicly an extreme party, towards some of whom, like yourself, one feels a sincere regard . . ."

Christopher was as usual in constant touch with Edward Hathaway, then living at Clifton. On 7 October Hathaway wrote: "It looks as if God, in answer to His children's prayers, were bringing all who favour the truth at Oxford to one mind. I am very thankful that Sir H.V[erney]. sees his way to act so resolutely . . . Under the circumstances I suppose that *you* must second Knox. I detect how you itch to do so. And *rather* than not speak at all, you had better do so . . ." No such opportunity as Hathaway envisaged in fact came Christopher's way, as the conference, after a strong denunciation of the motion by Archdeacon Purey-Cust, on the advice of Sir Robert Phillimore, a leading ecclesiastical lawyer, who had been chancellor of the diocese and who raised points which Hathaway, also a barrister, had already anticipated ("the case as it now stands differs *very materially* from that made by G[olightly]'s pamphlet"), resolved that it should not be entertained. Golightly, however, was ready for this, and copies of the speech Knox intended to deliver were extensively distributed at the doors of the Sheldonian Theatre.

Subsequently it was decided to memorialise Bishop Mackarness and a copy of the memorial lay for signature at St. Aldates' Rectory. Many weeks passed after the public advertisement of it in connection with the name of the Bishop of Oxford and eventually Dr. Mackarness wrote to Christopher, in view of "considerable inconvenience, and some misrepresentation," asking that if it was in fact intended to present the memorial it might be done at once. Fearing, perhaps, Christopher's tendency to write to the press at all times, the Bishop added a postscript. "This letter is *not* intended for the newspapers." Two days later the address, signed by twelve peers, one hundred and fifty-five lay magistrates, five hundred and fifty-two churchwardens, and one hundred and twenty-two other lay members of the conference, was presented to the Bishop. The incident has been somewhat lightly passed over by Dr. Owen Chadwick in his *Founding of Cuddesdon*. The reference to a small part of it in Mr. Evelyn Waugh's *Life of the Right Reverend Ronald Knox* can only be described as lacking context. Also Mr. Waugh makes the departure of Edmund Knox (his hero's father) from Oxford in 1885 dependant on the appointment of F. J. Chavasse to Wycliffe Hall, — which was not made until 1889, — and rashly speaks of Knox as then "the only effective champion of evangelicalism in Oxford," although Chavasse had already been at St. Peter-le-Bailey for eight years, and neither, as we have seen, were alone in the distinctive religious impact of their work in the city and university.

While defence of the protestant heritage of the national church was a constant duty, there was no lack of direct spiritual effort on the part of evangelicals in Oxford, and of Christopher in particular. This might perhaps seem doubtful in view of such judgement as that of Dr. Elliott-Binns in his *Religion in the Victorian Era*. Referring to Oxford in the 'seventies, he says "The Evangelicals were also weak. Their leader was Canon Christopher at St. Aldate's . . ." In spite of admitting some improvement when Wycliffe Hall was founded and F. J. Chavasse came to St. Peter-le-Bailey, both in 1877,

Elliott-Binns was not enthusiastic about this period in the history of Oxford evangelicalism. It is therefore as relevant as it happens to be refreshing to have the view of a contemporary observer, unlikely to have been favourably biassed. In 1878 appeared *Oxford: Its Social and Intellectual Life,* by a young bachelor of arts, A. M. M. Stedman, which in its revised form of nine years later, *Oxford: Its Life and Schools,* has already been quoted. The original publication was decidedly disapproved by the college authorities at Wadham, where Stedman had lately been an undergraduate, and where he was subsequently a notable benefactor; but as he became in 1889 the founder of a well-known publishing firm (which soon included Kipling's early works in its list), changing his name to Methuen in 1899, his contemporary impressions are of considerable interest now. " In Oxford," he wrote, " the advocates of Evangelicalism are numerous and active, and are as fully alive as their opponents to the necessity of impressing young men in their favour. Their churches are not perhaps so numerous and attractive as those in which Ritualism is practised, but their ministers exert a great influence, and draw large numbers to their services."

The autumn of 1879 was the occasion of a major positive work for God in the form of a parochial and university mission centreing on what a later Bishop of Oxford, William Stubbs, was wont to call 'the quadrilateral' — St. Aldate's, St. Ebbe's, St. Peter-le-Bailey and Holy Trinity — and St. Clement's. It was conducted, like so many of those days, by Hay Aitken, whom D. L. Moody spoke of as "the Prince of mission preachers". The mission apparently owed its origin to H. E. Campbell of Exeter, afterwards Archdeacon of Furness. To him, therefore, as he had since left Oxford to be ordained, Christopher wrote at length describing the results. His letter, an example of the many which poured constantly from Christopher's pen, gives so vivid a picture of the whole occasion, and is so revealing of its writer's character, that it seems justifiable to quote it in full.

St. Aldate's Rectory, Oxford.
November 24, 1879

My dear Campbell,

The Mission conducted by Mr. Aitken in Oxford closed this morning with an administration of the Holy Communion in St.

Peter-le-Bailey Church at 7 a.m. Many undergraduates and others who are full of thankfulness for the Mission attended. The congregation last night in St. Aldate's was crowded to the doors. Chairs and benches were placed in the Chancel and aisles in every available space. Yet many stood. The Church seats eight hundred, but I think twelve hundred must have listened to Mr. Aitken's last awakening striking sermon. A body of zealous undergraduates gave tracts to this great congregation as they left the Church. At half past eight o'clock in the evening of Sunday November 9th, one of the results of the zealous efforts of earnest Oxford undergraduates was seen in Mr. Chavasse's Church. More than five hundred undergraduates nearly filled St. Peter-le-Bailey after the usual parochial congregation had left it. Every week day evening of that week about a hundred undergraduates were present during Mr. Aitken's course of sermons. More could not be expected as the examinations were at hand, and are now in full progress. At half past eight on Sunday evening, November 16th, about four hundred undergraduates heard Mr. Aitken preach. On that day the galleries of the University Church had been twice filled with undergraduates and many had heard Canon Ryle preach in my Church in the evening as well as his afternoon sermon before the University. We were not, therefore, surprised that not more than four hundred undergraduates came to Mr. Chavasse's church, after such a full Sunday. Mr. Aitken preached in Mr. Chavasse's Church (Nov. 10-14), a course of five afternoon sermons on 'Some of the Intellectual Difficulties common at the present time'. Last week he preached in St. Aldate's on the weekday afternoons, on 'Some of the Spiritual Difficulties common in the present day'. These afternoon sermons were well attended by general congregations. Every week day evening last week, excepting Saturday, St. Aldate's has been filled with an earnestly attentive congregation. Some nights we have been crowded and obliged to use chairs in the Chancel and aisles. Notwithstanding the snow on Friday night the Church was full. There was a good gathering of undergraduates on Saturday night to hear a sermon from Mr. Aitken specially addressed to them. The Sunday afternoon sermons to *men only* were largely attended. It is a most striking sight; a large Church full of men only. The working men as well as others came in great numbers. An invitation was left at every house in our parishes each week day. I sent for eight thousand one page tracts from Drummond's Tract Depository, Stirling, and printed an invitation on the back. A different tract was used each day. The district visitors and others left them daily with kind and earnest words. Mr. Aitken's evening sermons have been specially striking and awakening. He has preached Christ most faithfully. Early in the Mission some good people criticised the earnest manner of the Mission preacher; and a few, who have not, like myself, known his reality and true devotion to God and God's work when he was an undergraduate in Oxford, and during the subsequent fifteen years of his zealous, laborious ministry, called his actions 'theatrical'. But towards the close of the Mission criticism was hushed and objectors began to see the folly of missing the benefit they might derive from weighty matter in the sermons through occupying themselves with finding fault with the preacher's manner. The truth is, there are many people who can look on with perfect calmness, and without any 'excitement', (as great earnestness of manner is usually called) on the crowded road of which our Lord said: 'Broad is the road which leadeth to destruction and many there be that go in thereat'. They can contemplate, without any of the intense sorrow and earnestness which some, more lukewarm than he, call 'excitement' in a Mission preacher, the drunkard who is ruining his health, prospects, and breaking the heart of his wife, or the greater number who are simply neglecting Christ and His great salvation, and so are cutting off their own escape from the Wrath to come.

"They do not enter into the intense love of souls felt by the zealous preacher, or into his earnestness in seeking, as God's servant, by any means to save some. They do not, at the beginning of a Mission, consider what reason to praise God there is, that in a day of much unbelief, such a multitude of persons should be drawn together to hear of the Lord Jesus Christ and His great salvation. It takes some days for those to whom the preacher is a stranger, to enter into his intense love of the people before him, especially of those who are in danger of losing for ever the glorious opportunities of a zealous, useful Christian life, and the peace, joy, happiness, and eternal glory of those who live by faith in the Son of God Who loved them and gave Himself for them. Can the preacher be blamed for being in earnest to win these to Christ, and so thereby to a present and an everlasting happiness by the declaration of an immediate and eternal salvation, which is free without money and without price to all who truly accept the Lord Jesus Christ by faith? When a brave man places a ladder to the window of a house in flames, and mounts it with energy in his effort to save one who might without him perish, even the calmest spectators who are the most free from any undue 'excitement' when their fellow creatures are in danger whilst they themselves are in safety, do not find fault with the action of the man's arms, but fix their attention rather on the great object he has in view, in seeking to save the life of a fellow creature. He may even shout to cold unfeeling spectators, and call out to them to help to save life, and no one thinks he speaks too loud. Why then should the earnestness of a preacher's manner when his mind is possessed with the apostle's question: '*How shall we escape if we neglect so great salvation?*' lead people to undervalue the weighty matter which he brings out from God's Word for the eternal benefit of all who will receive it into their minds and hearts? Yet those who like calm, logical argument will hear abundance of this if they attend a course of Mr. Aitken's sermons.

"Some graduate fellows of Colleges, as well as undergraduates, have appreciated the force of Mr. Aitken's reasoning. Like yourself, he obtained a good place in an Oxford Class list, and is probably a better preacher than he would have been if he had not been successful in the Oxford Schools. It has been interesting to observe how many of the undergraduates who have attended Mr. Aitken's sermons have worn Scholars' gowns.

"I am sure many Christians in the Isle of Man are asking God's blessing on Mr. Aitken's forthcoming Mission in St. Thomas', Douglas. The one essential thing to success is that 'the Hand of the Lord' should be with the Mission preacher that a great number may believe and turn unto the Lord. (See Acts XI). Among the things which have, under God's blessing, promoted the success of the recent Mission, I place first, the prayerfulness and zeal of undergraduates, and secondly, the thorough union in heart and effort of the Incumbents of five poor parishes in the City of Oxford, Messrs. Chavasse, Pearson, Pilcher, Grey and myself. My church happened to be the largest, so most of Mr. Aitken's sermons to a general congregation in the heart of Oxford were preached in my church, but my brethren in the three adjoining parishes worked as zealously to promote the attendance of their people at St. Aldate's as if the Mission had been altogether in their own churches. The Mission during the first week was conducted in St. Clement's, Mr. Pilcher's Church, at another end of Oxford. That first week was of great importance in arousing attention as well as being useful in that parish.

As there is often a prejudice against what are called 'After Meetings,' I will just say that, as conducted by Mr. Aitken in my Church, after his sermons, they were made most useful. It would have been simply cruel to have deprived awakened and anxious people of the great help and comfort of Mr. Aitken's addresses and conversations during the 'After Meetings.'

You will have reason to praise God through life, dear Campbell, that He put it into your heart to originate this Mission and to take all the pains you have taken to arrange and prepare for it. We do not know how much in future years of zealous work for God, in and from Oxford, may be in some way or other connected with Mr. Aitken's Mission. May you have grace to live and work for God as usefully as the domestic chaplain of the faithful Bishop of Sodor and Man[1] as you have done as an Oxford undergraduate. I earnestly hope that Mr. Aitken's Mission at St. Thomas' will be made use of to many in the Island I know and love so well. I am sure that many of the fifty undergraduates who have had private conversations with Mr. Aitken, as well as a larger number among the other hundreds who have heard him preach, will pray with all their hearts for God's abundant blessing on his preaching in the Isle of Man. We still make it a special object of prayer at the usual Saturday evening meeting of undergraduates in my Rectory Room, which you used to attend, and I am sure Aitken will ask the prayers of Christians in the Isle of Man for the University and city in which he has so recently laboured.

Ever sincerely yours,
Alfred M. W. Christopher

Revd. H. E. Campbell

The year 1879 was also that in which the Oxford Inter-Collegiate Christian Union — an association of evangelical undergraduates — was founded, and Campbell had been its first president. To what

[1]Dr. Rowley Hill.

extent Christopher was connected with the infancy of a society which exists today in unabated vigour, is not recorded. But all its early presidents, including George King of Corpus, later Master in Chancery, Frederick Baylis of Christ Church, subsequently Vice-Principal of Wycliffe Hall, and the Hon. W. Talbot Rice, also of Christ Church, afterwards Rector of St. Peter-le-Bailey, were among his undergraduate friends; and two of them, Frank Webster and Alfred Cox, became his curates.

Webster had drawn King into a group which worked in the Oxford slums with Henry Bazely. "All Bazely's colleagues," wrote Archdeacon Buckland in King's biography, "were, like Bazely himself, loyal supporters of A. M. W. Christopher." It may be wondered whether, in view of Bazely's ecclesiastical position, he was altogether a satisfactory influence on undergraduates. "I can truly say," wrote Webster, "that on no single occasion did Mr. Bazely attempt to dissuade me from taking Orders in the Church of England . . . Indeed, it is to him that I owe very largely that appreciation of the value of order and discipline, that love of unity and hatred of schism, which are the elements of good churchmanship. I have often said that Mr. Bazely was the first to make me a churchman."

Referring to the presence of Bazely and his undergraduate friends at Christopher's Saturday evening meeting, Buckland added, "Men of distinction often came to speak at it; but attendance sometimes had its trials. The Canon would call upon one undergraduate or another to offer prayer. The man singled out may have been seated some way down the room, and Christopher was always unwilling to miss a word of prayer. It was his custom, therefore, at such times, to leave the platform and make his way to the row in front of the man about to pray. He then extended a large ear-trumpet in the direction, and as near as possible to the lips, of the speaker, with results which were embarrassing not only to him but to those over whose legs the Canon had stumbled on the way. King suffered in turn, but like the rest, would have done anything for the great-hearted old man who brought us together." Another firm supporter in the early 'eighties was Charles Oman of New College, who was elected to an All Souls fellowship in 1883 (he was convinced that his churchmanship hindered his election at his own college), and later became Chichele Professor of Modern History and Member of Parliament for the university. "I was a staunch Low Churchman," he tells us in *Memories of Victorian Oxford,* "and not infrequently took my seat in old Dr. [*sic*] Christopher's Saturday evening prayer meetings at St. Aldate's." It seems likely that a Merton postmaster of this date, John Wright, pupil of Edmund Knox, then Fellow of the college, would have been another who found his way more than occasionally to Christopher's meetings. Very little information is forthcoming about his Oxford days, but from 1909 to 1933 he was an evangelical Archbishop of Sydney.

Christopher was certainly called upon two years later to help an undergraduate move to found a university branch of the Church Association in Cambridge, in order to counteract the activities of the English Church Union. Evangelical opinion in Cambridge was divided over the matter. Nevertheless Christopher attended a meeting called there, and a branch was formed. The young men who hoped that Christopher's advocacy as a Cambridge man would contribute towards that end were not disappointed, though the branch does not seem to have long survived. Christopher also took a deep interest in the Oxford Prayer Union — founded, as we have noticed, in 1850, and still at this time in full vigour — and always accompanied those graduates and undergraduates who enjoyed the hospitality of Middle Claydon Rectory, Buckinghamshire, at the annual gatherings there[1] during the later years of the incumbency of W. R. Fremantle, who in 1876 became Dean of Ripon: Claydon being likewise the ancestral home of Fremantle's brother-in-law Sir Harry Verney, a prominent supporter of the Church Missionary Society as well as one of the protestant leaders in the Oxford diocesan conference and elsewhere.

In spite of his strong evangelical convictions, Christopher was on excellent terms with the high church incumbents in Oxford. A popular story declared that at the baptism of Chavasse's twin sons,[2] whereat they received the names of Christopher and Noel, the Rector of St. Aldate's and the Revd. M. H. Noel, Vicar of St. Barnabas's, a new church in St. Thomas's parish, had stood together as sponsors. This was apocryphal, but it typified the relationship, at least on Christopher's side. Several years previously, Bishop Ingham

[1]Previously held at Islip, when the rector was the Revd. Francis Trench, elder brother of Archbishop Trench.

[2]One afterwards rector of St. Aldate's, and bishop of Rochester.

recalled, "I remember my surprise on coming upon Christopher once arm in arm with Noel . . . There was no resisting the love of the man!" "Who that saw it," wrote Francis Jansen, "can ever forget the hearty handshake and beaming smile with which . . . Mr. Noel . . . was greeted at the Missionary breakfast?"

A closer friend, however, was the Revd. W. B. Duggan, Vicar of St. Paul's, whose likeness may be seen on his memorial in that church. For Christopher he "entertained so genuine an esteem" that speaking on one occasion at a clergy dinner, he cited the Rector of St. Aldate's as an example of integrity. "Where will you find a sincerer spirit, with a will more resolutely fixed upon one purpose, more anxious to win souls to his own most honestly entertained views of truth, more constant in season and out of season to speak of his Redeemer, than the Rev. Alfred Christopher?" In January 1881 a friendly interchange took place between them. Duggan wrote: "Having occasion to comment on some current topics in the local number of the Dawn of Day I found myself irresistably led to deprecate the inconsistency — (as it presents itself to my mind) of some of the leaders of the Church Association. I have stripped my reference of names and as much as possible of personalities but still it is there, and therefore although it says nothing that has not been better said by others before, I feel morally bound to send you a copy."

Duggan had written: "This leads me to pass to a matter which at this time must be much on all our minds, I mean the sad divisions in the Church. When we look around on the sin and misery of the world, and feel that the times demand the union of all who love their Saviour and their brothers if the earth is to be freed from its burden of pain, — when we study the minds of people, and hear on various sides of cultured men and women who cannot bring themselves to recognise the presence in the universe of a Creative Will, and of an Almighty love, it is heart-breaking to see Christian ministers driven to prison or deprived of their sphere of work, because they cannot accept a most doubtful interpretation of directions about some details of their service. A future generation, looking at these things in a truer proportion than we can, will be amazed that good men who are every day themselves violating the plainest rubrics should invoke the force of the State against others who have large legal authority for their own interpretation. For example, there is a most excellent clergyman in Oxford who always takes the chair at meetings against Ritualists; and yet what do we find at his own church? No daily office, though the Prayer Book says, 'all priests and deacons are to say daily the morning and evening prayer, either privately or openly, not being let by sickness or some other urgent cause.' No celebration of Holy Communion on Saints' Days, although the Prayer Book expressly provides a Collect, Epistle, and Gospel for those occasions. Frequent violations of the rubrics, as by only saying the words of administration once in the administration of the consecrated elements, although the explicit direction is 'when he delivereth the Cup to *any one*, he shall say . . .' I do not quote these things to stir up bitter feelings against one whom I respect and love, but only to illustrate the cruel inconsistencies of which a minister may be guilty when he allows his Christian temper to be warped by his party prejudice."

Christopher replied: "Last week I was visiting sick and other afflicted relatives at a distance from Oxford and much occupation since my return on Saturday last has delayed my reply to your letter. Let me first thank you for your courtesy in sending me a copy of your publication. The Church Association is a body of men faithful to the Scriptural doctrines of the Reformation and to the Articles of our Church which denounce 'the sacrifices of Masses' as 'blasphemous fables and dangerous deceits'. They believe that it is their duty to God and man to contend earnestly for those Scriptural doctrines and for the Articles which express them as the doctrines of the Church of Christ. They are willing to bear any amount of reproach in performing that duty, which often costs them a pain for which they get no credit. The Church Association has charged itself with the onerous task of ascertaining the law Ecclesiastical and in a very few flagrant cases in trying to enforce it, but only where and because the illegal practices in Church ritual or ceremonial of which it sought formal condemnation, were vehicles of or accessories to false doctrine. If my omissions were intended by me to propagate, or as adjuncts to, erroneous or unscriptural doctrines, then I could recognise the relevancy of your charge of inconsistency. You are well aware that the omissions particularized by you are known to and sanctioned by every Bishop on the Bench, while the ritual additions which the Church Association is seeking to repress have been publicly denounced by the whole English Episcopate."

Christopher enclosed a copy of a sermon preached in St. Aldate's by the Revd. T. K. Cheyne, Fellow of Balliol, and subsequently Dean Ireland's Professor. Cheyne is usually thought of as a pioneer of Biblical criticisim who grew increasingly liberal and ended in doubtful attachment to Christianity. But he had a short evangelical phase, having apparently adopted evangelical views in 1880. Christopher had great hopes at the time that he would become more conservative theologically, but in fact, after a while, the reverse was the case.

Of inconsistencies on both sides it is needless now to speak at length. Christopher's appeal to episcopal authority was only of contemporary weight. Duggan's reference to the saints' day collects, epistles, and gospels overlooks the fact that these occur in the ante-communion service. On another occasion Duggan wrote to Christopher, who, desiring the best possible reply, sent the letter to Edward Hathaway, whom he was accustomed to consult on almost every matter of importance. Hathaway wrote an answer which Christopher thought so admirable that he simply copied it out and forwarded the result to Duggan! Twenty-three years later, Christopher visited Duggan on his death-bed and was cordially welcomed by him.

At the diocesan conference in October 1882 a motion was proposed: "That it appears to this Conference desirable, in the interest of the Church, to promote the dissolution of the two Societies known as the Church Association and the English Church Union". Christopher moved an amendment: "That it is the duty of all who value the Reformation to oppose, at any sacrifice of feeling, the attempts now being made to assimilate the services of our Church to those of the Church of Rome; and that the Church Association, being the only organisation that exists for the express purpose of resisting systematic efforts to undo the Reformation Settlement, cannot yet be dispensed with."

The speech with which Christopher supported this amendment showed his skill as a protagonist. After explaining the origin of the Church Association as a direct result of the founding of the Church

Union, he went on to cite well-known authorities, from the Archbishop of Canterbury downwards, in support of his contention that serious efforts were being made to pervert the teaching of the Church, from which it followed that a Church Association was necessary. He quoted (in a manner to which Hathaway took exception) Archbishops Longley and Tait, Dr. Harold Browne of Winchester, Dr. Christopher Wordsworth of Lincoln, and Dean Burgon. He quoted Cardinal Manning to show that the ritualists were advancing Romanism in England. He quoted a book for which Pusey had written a preface, in which it was stated "We are teaching men to believe that God is to be worshipped under the form of Bread . . ." He entreated all 'Protestant Churchmen' to strengthen the hands of a society which "had done a great and good work for the Church of England."

Chapter XII

Middle Years at Oxford

1882 - 1890

ONCE MORE the action changes from controversy to evangelism. For 1882 was the year of Moody and Sankey's mission at Oxford, which culminated in a meeting at the Corn Exchange attended by a thousand undergraduates, over a third of the total number in the university. Moody, however, is said to have been less successful in Oxford than in Cambridge, where he had lately been. Christopher was chairman of the committee of all denominations of protestant ministers and laymen who promoted the mission, which opened on 13 November, little more than a month after the diocesan conference referred to above. As at Cambridge, there was some disturbance by rowdy undergraduates, but as the week progressed Moody secured increasing attention. A correspondent of *The Christian* wrote: "We have seen a good many of Mr. Moody's and other evangelistic meetings, but if we can trust our memory we have never seen any like this." Nor was that purely evangelical opinion. At the Church Congress in the following year, Dr. Ince, Regius Professor of Divinity, referred to the response on this occasion as "a very signal thing". A considerable number of men had professed conversion, and Christopher was overjoyed.

One whose heart also lay very close to the spirit of Moody, Frank Webster, became Christopher's curate about this time. For nearly twelve months Christopher worked the parish single-handed, until Webster had attained, by Advent 1882, the canonical age of twenty-three. John English had left St. Aldate's in the previous year. In response to a special enquiry from Bishop Gell of Madras — who had preached at St. Aldate's in 1871, and whose name had appeared in the same tripos list as Christopher's — the latter had strongly recommended him for a government chaplaincy in India. Francis Scott Webster had been a scholar of Pembroke, had taken a 'double-first' in mathematics, and is probably the only man who has ever combined the functions of secretary of the Union Debating Society and Salvation Army preacher. Webster, as may be imagined, was, like his rector, not altogether conventional. He had come up to Oxford as a member of Evan Hopkins's congregation at Holy Trinity, Richmond — where the Carlile family also worshipped and one of the parishes where the Church Army originated. He attended Christopher's Bible reading on his first Saturday evening as a freshman, in Michaelmas term 1878, and had been an enthusiastic and devoted supporter of all Christopher's works throughout his undergraduate days.

"I never missed those Saturday Meetings, and have a vivid impression still of the kindly and affectionate way in which he expounded the Scriptures. The addresses were real expositions. One of his favourite books was I Thessalonians. He never attempted an elaborate analysis, but brought home to us the real gist of the teaching, and he enforced it by numerous stories and incidents culled from his wide experience." Webster was one of the faithful few ("sometimes the very faithful and the very few," A. P. Cox, his successor, noted) who attended Christopher's daily prayer meeting in the Rectory at 7.30 a.m. He had to obtain special leave from his college to go outside the gates before 8 a.m. But, he recalled, when Rector of All Souls, Langham Place, and a Prebendary of St. Paul's Cathedral, "the warmth and fervour of those little gatherings, with hymn and exposition and extemporary prayer (we usually numbered about 7 or 8) helped to carry me through the somewhat cold and mechanical Chapel Service of the College at 8 a.m."

In the small Rectory Room, which can be entered both from the Rectory hall and from the passage beside the house which leads to the Rectory Room itself, "throughout the year" — Cox continues — "Sundays and week days, Christopher was to be found every morning at half past seven . . . never yielding . . . When there was an early Communion Service at the Church this Prayer Meeting was not omitted. Only a few seemed to know about it: but in its spirit and idea it may well recall Charles Simeon and the roof of King's Chapel[1] at Cambridge." The early prayer meeting had become an institution even when Christopher lived in North Oxford. The Revd. James Legge, a retired missionary of the London Missionary Society, came to live in Keble Terrace in 1875, as the first Professor of Chinese in the university. Speaking on the occasion of Christopher's golden wedding anniversary in 1894, Professor Legge remarked that after arrival in Oxford he had been struck by seeing his neighbour going out every morning at seven o'clock.[2] When he heard that it was to attend his early prayer meeting he found out the secret of Christopher's successful work.

Webster had also been a regular visitor at Christopher's Saturday luncheon, where in term three or four undergraduates were always amongst the guests. The fare, according to Webster, was invariable — always roast ribs of beef and simple plum pudding, "of which our genial host generally took two helpings, for the encouragement of the young men. The stories with which Mr. Christopher enriched the conversation will never be forgotten. The tactful way in which the opening for them was secured, the manifest delight of the narrator, and the spiritual influence resting upon the testimony, for they were nearly all stories of remarkable conversions and definite answers to prayer, made a deep impression, and it seemed quite natural and right when prayer was proposed at the close . . . and we all knelt around the table when the Rector poured out his heart in prayer."

Among Webster's friends was another supporter of St. Aldate's, also a Pembroke man, Joseph Mullins, afterwards, as the Revd. Dr. J. D. Mullins, a well-known Secretary of the Colonial and Continental (now the Commonwealth and Continental) Church Society. Yet another member of his circle was David Stather Hunt of Merton, subsequently, as Canon Stather Hunt, Vicar of Holy Trinity, Tunbridge Wells.[3]

[1]In fact the reference should be, not to the chapel roof, but to that of the Fellows' Building, when Simeon had his rooms on the top floor and was wont to pray walking unseen in the centre gulley.

[2]Legge himself, it is said, started his studies daily at 4 a.m.

[3]Father of the present Vicar of St. Mathew's, Grandpont, Canon D. K. Stather Hunt.

Webster had been taught and helped and influenced by Henry Bazely, and Bazely was anxious that he should become curate to Christopher. During the interval — a course at a theological college not being then regarded as usually desirable for graduates — he was to do what he could, as Bazely had done, in a lay capacity in St. Aldate's parish. Knowing that he had given much help to the Salvation Army in Greyfriars, Christopher suggested that he might use that experience in trying to win for Christ some of the hundreds of working men and women in St. Aldate's. So Webster was, in Christopher's words, " let loose in the Parish," where the Rector gave him a completely free hand. The result was 'The St. Aldate's Church Salvation Army,' a name which reflected its leader's admiration for the work of William Booth.

During the vacations Webster had been a member of Evan Hopkins's 'Church Gospel Army' at Richmond. Two or three other parishes had independently given birth to similar efforts to reach working men, and of these Wilson Carlile's in Westminster was headed by the young business man lately ordained whose life work began with the 'federation' of the small, separate 'armies' into 'The Church Army'. Thus St. Aldate's is one of the parishes which fathered this movement, in its early days often looked at askance on account of its unconventional methods. According to Webster himself, " the whole Parish was turned upside down with Marches and Open-Air Services four or five nights a week. With such a warm-hearted Rector it was easy indeed to attach to the Church those who had been won by the Gospel. There were six adult working-folk at the first Confirmation. The Rector prepared them, and I remember the gleeful way in which he described how he commenced proceedings. 'I wanted them to feel at home, so I said, "All who believe that their sins are forgiven for Christ's sake put up one hand".' How far he took them in the Church Catechism I don't know, but they all became regular communicants, and ran well."

At Oxford, while still a lay worker, Webster started by holding services in the Victoria Theatre, but shortly transferred them to St. Aldates' Rectory Room, " where he formed a mission band of earnest young laymen, which eventually became one of the first Church Army corps. The work soon attracted favourable notice, and Bishop Mackarness, interviewing him shortly before ordination, urged that

51. FRANCIS SCOTT WEBSTER, *c.* 1884
Lay-helper, St. Aldate's, Oxford, 1881-82
Curate of St. Aldate's 1882-85
As first Principal, Church Army Training Home, Oxford, 1883-85

52. TRINITY COLLEGE GROVE, *c.* 1883

Top row: I. WILLIAMS, former Fellow of Trinity; C. GORE, Fellow of Trinity (afterwards Bishop of Oxford). *Middle row:* Cardinal J. H. NEWMAN, honorary Fellow of Trinity; A. M. W. CHRISTOPHER, Rector of St. Aldate's; H. G. WOODS, Fellow of Trinity. *Bottom row:* W. STUBBS, Regius Professor of Modern History (afterwards Bishop of Oxford); S. W. WAYTE, former President of Trinity; R. ELLIS, Fellow of Trinity

it should continue." The need for systematic training of evangelists caused Webster and Carlile to plan a training home, which was set up in St. Aldates' parish with Webster as honorary warden.[1] "Before the home had been open many months the Bishop, whose interest in the movement was keen, called and informally examined the men in training, expressing himself thoroughly satisfied with their progress, and with all the arrangements. He consented to become a patron of the Church Army, and was the first bishop to give this official sanction."

One of those trained at Oxford under Webster, Capt. P. Prior, who was afterwards ordained, tells us that "The Principal of the Training Home . . . was a real go-ahead, earnest man of God. He used to come in each morning and give us lessons in getting up addresses, lectures on the Prayer Book, Church history, etc., and occasionally took us out for open-air work in the afternoon. One afternoon we went to the fair for an open-air meeting. The Principal's coat was torn, our tunics were soon in pieces, and our caps were treated like footballs. They spat in our faces, bad eggs were thrown and all kinds of refuse hurled at us, but by God's grace we were enabled to told on; and here I learnt that I must have courage, endurance, and grit. It did us much good, and we enjoyed evensong at the Cathedral so much better that evening (we used to attend daily)." One of Webster's methods on such occasions met with unexpected success. "I have often walked backwards," he himself wrote, "through the Pleasure Fairs at Oxford, and invariably find that it disarms all serious opposition." Under Webster's "enthusiastic guidance," the Training Home made steady progress. But for various reasons Oxford was not considered altogether suitable as a situation and in 1885 the Home was moved to London, Webster going with it. Until that date the Church Army work was associated with that of the Church Parochial Missions Society, founded by Hay Aitken, another of Christopher's former undergraduate friends.

Church Army meetings, with their short testimonies and brief prayers, were not adapted to a deaf person; but Christopher loved to attend the prayer meetings. He could watch the lips to see who were taking part and though frequently by the time he had got his ear-

[1]Webster himself lived at Littlegate House, subsequently Holy Trinity Vicarage.

trumpet in position, the prayer or testimony was over, he moved on, bright and encouraged, so thankful that men and women were drawing near to God. The only time Christopher interfered in his young friend's activities was when, after a few days' practice, he tried to play the violin at one of the street services. Even Christopher's deafness was not sufficient to prevent him insisting on his being content with his concertina! Speaking in 1889, Christopher could say "Some of the working men converted to God in this and the following years are among our most useful Christian workers in the parish now." Once ordained Webster continued to preach in the streets and in the Rectory Room. "I specially observed with thankfulness," said Christopher, "his patient diligence and earnestness in seeking to apply the Word of God to individuals at the 'after meetings' with much prayer with one at a time."

The Church Army owed much to Christopher's appreciation of its work during those early days, when support was especially needed. To *The Church Army: Its Doings in 1885,* he contributed an earnest commendation. "We always hear from those intimately acquainted with Missionary work among the Heathen, of the importance of 'Native Agency'. The Evangelization of the vast population of India and China is simply impossible without the extensive employment of native agency. In England, truly converted and truly zealous working men, organised in every parish in a company of the Church Army, appear to me to be the native agency we require to keep the Gospel living, and bring personal experience of its power in working man vernacular, upon the vast mass of working men who are utterly neglecting God and all that concerns the true happiness of themselves and their families for time and for eternity . . . At the daily 7.30 a.m. prayer-meeting yesterday morning and at the Church Army meeting in my rectory room after the evening service in church, three converted Oxford cabmen were present, whose honest, manly faces beamed with Christian happiness. Their open testimony to the change wrought in them by the grace of God and to the happiness they have found in Christ, is most encouraging to those who wish to know of a Saviour Who can and will save them from their sins and their miserable consequences. God is able to use these men to bring in other cabmen, a class not very accessible to clergymen. We need workers for God among every class of working men, and we may find them by means of the Church Army. Some of our Church Army working men have been made very useful in villages which can be reached from Oxford. They have visited them by the invitation of the parochial clergy, and have helped and encouraged the local workers. After four years experience of the Church Army, I am thankful to God that He inclined me to allow my late valued curate, the Rev. F. S. Webster . . . to establish and work a company of the Church Army in my parish. I feel quite sure that it has been a blessing to my parish ever since. I believe God has opened this door for our church to the increasing population of England. Let none try to shut it."

At every possible opportunity Christopher engaged in his work of distributing tracts. "He prayed over it, he laboured at it, he rejoiced in it," wrote Webster. "Often have I seen him just before midnight carrying to the General Post-office in St. Aldate's a large waste-paper basket full of tracts addressed to Members of the University. Even social functions he made use of, and would go to a garden-party with tracts filling his pockets." On one occasion the younger generation of his family thought they had prevented such untimely and embarrassing activity — as they conceived it — at a Governor's garden party in the Isle of Man. All his pockets had been quietly emptied, and those in the secret set out with a light heart. They were presently disillusioned by the sight of Christopher offering tracts. More alert than they had supposed, he had taken the precaution of stuffing a few packets into his elastic-sided boots.

"It was very seldom," adds Webster, "that a tract offered by Mr. Christopher was refused. His warm-hearted love and genuine sympathy were so manifest that they disarmed all criticism and opposition." "His tract giving in the public thoroughfares on festal occasions, such as boatraces," wrote A. P. Cox, "first with Henry Bazely, afterwards with generations of undergraduates, was wonderfully well received. The last time I ever saw him give a tract in the street was to the head of an Oxford College. He knew him perfectly well as a friend and neighbour. I remember witnessing the kindly greeting, the polite acceptance, the enthusiastic conversation which followed." Books as well as tracts were still given away, especially to undergraduates. F. C. T. Jansen, who matriculated in 1884, remarked "The writer can take down from his shelves some half-dozen volumes, each bearing the name of Christopher, followed by an affectionate inscription and a text of Scripture. There must be very many who could do the same."

Christopher was much interested in what was known as the Miles Platting Case. Under the Public Worship Regulation Act of 1871, diocesan bishops' acquiescence was required before any clergyman could be prosecuted at law for ritualistic practices. As a result, several bishops, chiefly on grounds of conscience, had vetoed proceedings against anglo-catholic incumbents. Bishop Fraser of Manchester, however, allowed the law to take its course in the case of the Revd. S. F. Green of St. John's, Miles Platting, who was consequently imprisoned for neglecting to obey a court injunction to adhere to the liturgy of 1662 contained in the authorised Prayer Book. As in other similar cases, the matter caused very great indignation in certain quarters, and charges of persecution were freely made. Protestant churchmen, on the other hand, were grateful to the Bishop for his firm stand. The living was declared vacant: whereupon the lay patron nominated Green's curate, who refused to give an undertaking to desist from the practices to which objection had been taken. The Bishop declined to institute and an action was brought against him. From all over the country resolutions of appreciation and sympathy flowed on to the episcopal letter tray, among them one from the Oxford branch of the Church Association. The Bishop — who was not an evangelical but a high churchman of the older school — sent Christopher a graceful acknowledgement.

Christopher's friend Ryle, now Bishop of Liverpool, with whom he was frequently in correspondence, was doubtful about the value of addresses from party bodies. Whether he knew what Christopher had in mind is uncertain, but he wrote to the Rector of St. Aldate's, as trenchantly as ever, on 19 January 1883: "I should have thought common sense would have told every one that addresses to the B. of M. should certainly *not* come from 'Unions,' 'Associations,' 'Societies,' &c. direct. Of course the last thing he likes is to be treated as the representative of a 'party.' I have written letters, till I am tired, urging men to approach him in this style 'We the undersigned *Clergymen and laymen* thank you heartily for the position you have taken up about the vacant living of Miles Platting, and assure you of our sympathy.' This is what the Sheffield people have done & the Bishop is evidently pleased. Why the loyal Churchmen of the W. England Soc: could not do the same, I fail to see. As it is, they look like the men of 'Meroz'.[1] Of the London clergy I will not write what I think. The blight of helplessness & extreme caution seems upon us. I never forget the bitter language used about Bishops in the last ten years. And now, when at last a Bishop makes a bold stand men seem afraid of saying 'God bless him'." Bishop Ryle had already written to Christopher in this strain a fortnight before. "The astonishing apathy of the London Clergy & Laity creates immense difficulty at this crisis. If the heart is weak, the extremities move slowly . . . If the Clerical & Lay Evang. Unions all over England do not take up the question & come forward actively to support the Bp. of Manchester they are useless institutions, & will soon find there is nothing left worth fighting for, in consequence of their timidity and supineness."

The subject came before the Oxford diocesan conference. Christopher pleaded, on an amendment of the Revd. John Arkell, since 1880 Rector of St. Ebbe's, that, as Christians, it was essential to vote calmly and in the light of the facts. He quoted *The Standard*: "Mr. Green is, in reality, no sufferer for conscience sake . . . He is asked either to obey the law, or to place himself in a position in which the law will have no claim upon his obedience. This is not persecution"; *The Guardian,* on the ritualists: "There is an intolerance in opinion of all who cannot go with them, an insulting defiance of Episcopal authority, and an exaggeration of grievances felt and of questions at issue, which are of evil omen to the peace of the Church and to the honour of Christianity in the eyes of the world"; the Lord Chancellor:[2] "That the first duty of every subject of the realm was to yield obedience to the law"; and the Archbishop of York:[3] "I do not think that the attempt has been wholly vain; for it has proved to me that the cell from which we should be glad to lead him forth is locked on the inside." While the action against the Bishop was pending, Goodhart wrote to Christopher: "Most heartily do I enter into the anxiety of yourself & others as to *the present crisis*

[1]"Curse ye Meroz, said the angel of the LORD, curse ye bitterly the inhabitants thereof; because they came not to the help of the LORD, to the help of the LORD against the mighty". (*Judges* 5.23, from the Song of Deborah.).
[2]Lord Selborne.
[3]Dr. Thomson.

. . . I am half afraid whether the Evangelical body has not the full quota in Gideon's army of the fearful & afraid & indifferent & temporising. But the Lord can and will give the victory to the 300 faithful ones; only let them be 'valiant for the truth,' & not be cowed by the ill-natured reproaches which false friends join in hurling at them."

Dr. Henry Law, Dean of Gloucester, wrote from Bournemouth: "I cannot . . . but feel that every effort should be made to assure the Bishop of Manchester that he may rely on all support of purse & lip & pen from thousands of sound Protestants in our land. I should be thankful if the Church Association would address him, & call upon its auxiliaries to do likewise." The Revd. J. B. Whiting[1] of St. Luke's, Ramsgate, summed up the situation: "I tried last Monday in London to stir up men to move. One said he thought it had better rest, from another . . . came the excuse that he was a Rural Dean, others also seemed to doubt the expediency. I thereupon wrote direct to the Record and the Times making the suggestion that apart from all Associations and Unions signatures should be sent at once . . . I am very tired of the difficulties raised by so many to any decisive action in this and many other matters. My own view is (I may be wrong) that the time is come for Evangelical men to make themselves felt. This Ritual business has been so conducted as to lead the world to suppose that we are fighting about trifles. Why not boldly state that it is not Ritual, but Ritual as a symbol of false doctrine, that we dread . . . ?" This was in effect the opinion of the court, for judgement was given in favour of the Bishop.

Towards the end of 1882, Henry Bazely's health began to give his friends cause for serious anxiety. Exhausted physically and mentally by years of incessant labour, he had broken down in May of that year. A prolonged holiday effected no permanent good, and in January 1883 Bright's disease set in, accompanied by great suffering. By the last week in February his end was manifestly near. Christopher was with him about eleven o'clock on the morning of 1 March. Shortly before noon he had to leave in order to preside at a large prayer meeting in the Corn Exchange. He opened with a prayer for Bazely's release from agony. Christopher returned[2] to find

[1]A former colleague of Christopher as an association secretary of the Church Missionary Society 1856–61.

[2]To 32, New Inn Hall Street, where Bazely had lived for some years, a few doors from F. J. Chavasse, Rector of St. Peter-le-Bailey.

his dear friend "absent from the body and... present with the Lord." As he was praying for Bazely in the Corn Exchange that faithful spirit had gently passed away.

"Nothing I have seen in man," wrote Christopher, "has so humbled me as the effects of the grace of God in this dear brother. The indwelling of the Holy Spirit hallowed his life, illumined his character, and humbled his friends . . . Never during my quarter of a century in Oxford have I seen such a spontaneous demonstration of respect and regard as took place at dear Bazely's funeral. The working people streamed out of the poor parishes . . . I saw some of the best and some of the worst people of my own parish in the mixed multitude . . . Dear Bazely's grave is scarcely a yard from the one which is intended to be my own . . . It is not unsuitable that the earthly remains of those who were so united by Christian love in life should, after a while, be so near to each other in death . . ." With this tribute by Christopher, Bishop Hicks (who was not an Evangelical) concluded the last chapter of Bazely's biography.

Nor were Christopher and Hicks alone in their estimate of Bazely. A few years later the Revd. G. W. Gent, a high churchman, wrote in *Oxford: Its Life and Schools*: "Those who wish to gain some insight into a side of Oxford religious life which does not come prominently forward, should read Mr. Hicks' life of Henry Bazely. All of us who were 'up' in the 'Seventies', can remember the tall spare figure standing, Bible in hand, at the Martyrs' Memorial, and preaching the Gospel to all who were willing to stand and hear. But until this book came out few beyond the circle of Bazely's personal friends understood or appreciated the entire self-devotion and deep religious enthusiasm of the man. . . . He seems to have had in a marked degree the gift characteristic of the saint — an actual and dominating sense of the constant presence of God . . . It must be admitted at least that to him and to men like him, is to be attributed much of the increased hold which the 'Evangelical party' have, of late years, obtained upon a certain section of undergraduates. We must not forget indeed," Gent adds, "the abiding and whole-hearted service which has been rendered to that party for so many years by its Oxford Nestor, the Rev. A. W. M. [*sic*] Christopher."

A few months later Christopher received an invitation to preach in the university church. The Vice-Chancellor — none other than

Benjamin Jowett, celebrated both as Master of Balliol and as broad churchman, whose family, however, had been evangelical in outlook — called upon him to deliver the assize sermon at St. Mary's on 6 July 1883[1]. This was a seasonable recognition and an opportunity. Christopher preached on *The Heart of the Lord Jesus Christ towards the Lost,* from *St. Luke* 19.10, "The Son of man is come to seek and to save that which was lost." He spoke of the love of Jesus towards all lost sinners. He cited interesting examples of God's love extended through others towards men and women, mentioning the Edinburgh Ragged School of Dr. Guthrie, the children's homes of Miss Macpherson, some of which he had visited in Canada in 1872, the Salvation Army and the Church Army, then both in their infancy in Oxford. "Let us . . . have a hearty sympathy with all who are earnestly seeking to save 'the lost' by teaching them the free and precious Gospel of the Grace of God. If we cannot have unity in all respects let us be united in seeking to have and to exercise the heart of the Lord Jesus towards the lost. And let us remember that the lost include not only the criminal class and those likely to fall into crime, but all who are not saved by faith in Christ."

In October 1883 Christopher again found himself addressing an auditory which included notable and learned men. The Church Congress, at which he had read a paper when it assembled at Stoke-upon-Trent in 1875, was meeting at Reading. One subject on the programme was 'The Church in the Universities.' Christopher had spoken in 1875 to a similar topic. But it was not inappropriate that he should once more speak during the discussion which was stimulated by the papers of the Revd. R. Appleton, Fellow of Trinity College, Cambridge, afterwards Master of Selwyn College, and Canon J. Wordsworth, Oriel Professor of the Interpretation of Holy Scripture at Oxford, subsequently Bishop of Salisbury. Their papers were followed by addresses on the part of Dr. Edward King, Professor of Pastoral Theology at Oxford, afterwards Bishop of Lincoln, and the Revd. J. E. C. Welldon, then Master of Dulwich College, later Dean of Manchester. Interesting views were recorded in the light of the final passing of the old clerical order at Oxford and Cambridge which was coming about since the second and third

[1]It was exactly half a century since Keble, on an occasion which came to be considered as the start of the tractarian movement, had performed the same office.

university commissions of 1872 and 1877, and of the serious degree of unbelief which had been prevalent at least at Oxford for twenty years and more. The Master of Selwyn College, Cambridge, the Hon. and Revd. A. J. Lyttleton, spoke when the meeting was thrown open for discussion, followed by the Regius Professor of Divinity at Oxford, Dr. Ince; Archdeacon Denison, the veteran tractarian leader; Christopher; the Warden of Keble, the Revd. E. S. Talbot, afterwards Bishop of Winchester; and Sir John Conroy, President of the English Church Union.

"I venture to speak," Christopher began," as a Cambridge man who has worked at Oxford for the last twenty-five years, and has in that time known many of several successive generations of undergraduates . . . I cannot take a desponding view of the present state of Oxford; there is, of course, a dark side, but there is also a bright side. I believe that the influence of spiritual religion is on the increase both at Oxford and Cambridge . . ." He proceeded to refer to the sad condition of affairs at Oxford in the previous century, reflected in the expulsion of the 'Six Students' and Whitefield's letter to the Vice-Chancellor. "What a contrast in the state of things now! Meetings in the rooms of undergraduates at Oxford and Cambridge, for the reading of the Holy Scriptures, and prayer, are a common thing. I rejoiced to hear," Christopher added in passing, "the Regius Professor of Divinity allude so kindly to the mission at Oxford last November of Messrs. Moody and Sankey . . ." Consequently, Christopher declared, in the spirit of his speech of 1875, "If the difficulties in Oxford had been tenfold what they are, and the number of unbelievers had been ten times greater, it would still have been our duty to say in faith to our Father, as did an ancient King of Judah, 'O our God, we have no might against this great company that cometh against us, neither know we what to do; but our eyes are upon Thee.' Not that I regard sceptics in Oxford as enemies, but rather as mistaken friends . . ." Again in passing, he could not resist recommending Dr. Andrew Murray's *Abide in Christ* for undergraduate reading. But he went on to speak of the value of Christian evidences. "It is of great importance to promote among young men the study of Christian Evidences. The last book an ordinary young man would read, without special encouragement, would be a book on Christian Evidences. Might not some of those

Christians to whom God has given the talent of wealth, found scholarships in colleges at Oxford and Cambridge, to be given to those who pass the best examination in Christian Evidences? . . . It is too often the case that young men come up to the Universities knowing little of the Holy Scriptures, and nothing at all of Christian Evidences. Can we be surprised that they take up with unbelief with which they are sure, in some way or another, to come in contact, either at the University or somewhere else? After all, the great preservative of a young man from error, is the prayerful study of the Word of God."

Less than a year after his assize sermon, Christopher was himself compelled to appeal to the law by bringing an action for libel. The circumstances were unfortunate in the extreme. An unhappy relationship had developed between his wife's sister Caroline and her husband only a short time after their marriage in 1873. The Revd. John Nagle-Gillman was then unbeneficed, but in 1875 he was appointed, by a lay patron, Vicar of Hennock, in Devonshire. Presumably Dr. Frederick Temple, then Bishop of Exeter, and afterwards Archbishop of Canterbury, knew of no reason to decline to institute. Nevertheless, by cruelty and ill-treatment, which went so far as refusing her the sacrament, Nagle-Gillman sought to gain possession of his wife's means, and was foolish enough to bring a suit in the Chancery court against her co-trustees, Alfred Christopher and another clergyman, Canon Dixon[1]. The Master of the Rolls pronounced against Nagle-Gillman in severe terms, and in 1876 Mrs. Nagle-Gillman felt obliged to commence divorce proceedings. In the event a separation deed was agreed to, by which Nagle-Gillman, in return for financial consideration, undertook to have no communication with his wife, and that she might live anywhere in the land. Meanwhile Caroline Nagle-Gillman had come to live at St. Aldates' Rectory, and for some years there was silence.

But during the later 'seventies, Nagle-Gillman became a sick man, and his mind preyed on the fact that, as he believed, Christopher and his wife had persuaded Mrs. Nagle-Gillman to leave him, and thereby ruined his domestic life. As he brooded, he came to look on Christopher with malicious hatred; and in December

[1]Probably Dr. R. Dixon, Vicar of St. Matthew's, Rugby, a former Principal of King William's College, Isle of Man.

1882 he took the extraordinary step of travelling to Oxford, armed with a quantity of printed bills denouncing the Rector of St. Aldate's. He managed in the dusk to trick the official bill-poster, and his man (who in any case could scarcely read), into fixing a number of these on recognised public notice-boards. The bills alleged immorality between Christopher and his sister-in-law, and went so far as to assert that this relationship was of very long standing, inasmuch as Christopher had originally courted Caroline Christopher, but as she was thought too young to marry, he turned to her elder sister. Caroline was in fact only two years younger than Maria — and therefore two years older than Christopher — and had been twenty-six in 1844 when Christopher married her sister. Fortunately the bill-poster got an early inkling of the scandalous nature of the bills and the same evening tore one down and took it to Christopher, having despatched his assistant to cover up all the others. Christopher immediately sent it to the Archdeacon for transmission to the Bishop. He was recommended by them not prosecute. But two years later, on 1 March 1884, Nagle-Gillman again came to Oxford and distributed similar bills in the Union and elsewhere — in the course of which he was arrested — as well as sending copies through the post to leading residents of all kinds. This time the Bishop advised that Christopher had no alternative but to enter an action, and the unhappy story was aired in the city court at Oxford on 7 March. Great interest was inevitably shown, and many local clergy, including Archdeacon Palmer, the Master of Pembroke, Dr. Evans, and the Revd. G. N. Freeling, Rural Dean of Oxford, were present. The libel, beginning " It is right, and time at length, that this BAD MAN should be exposed . . ." was printed in full in *The Oxford Chronicle* the following day. The defendant was committed for trial at Reading assizes. Bail was allowed in £500, but no one could be found to advance this sum, Nagle-Gillman was kept in prison.

The trial did not come on until 24 April. Meanwhile the position in which Christopher found himself called forth remarkable expressions of sympathy and support. An address of confidence was circulated in the university — of which part of the original is preserved in the Bodleian Library, and is reproduced as Plate 53 — and on 10 March it appeared in printed form. It bore the signatures of the Archdeacon of Oxford and all the leading academic figures of the day, the Vice-Chancellor, Dr. Jowett, Dean Liddell and the Canons of Christ Church severally, all the Heads of Houses, the Registrar, the Senior Proctor, many professors, fellows of colleges and Oxford clergy, beside a host of masters, bachelors and undergraduates. Three of the most telling were those of Christopher's adversary Dr. Liddon, the President of the Church Union, Sir John Conroy, and the Jesuit in charge of the new Roman Catholic chapel in St. Giles's, called St. Aloysius'. All alike joined in this expression of sympathy, "Sincerely and affectionately," — " each year you have lived or ministered amongst us has increased our esteem for you." Many of the signatories had been strongly opposed to Christopher in his teaching and work; but they testified unreservedly to the unquestioned blamelessness and purity of his life.

Liddon wrote to Christopher the same day: " Certainly I cannot recollect any more cruel or shocking wrong of this description than that which has been done you. If I may judge by my own feelings, it will draw towards you the warm sympathies — and the earnest prayers — of your brother-clergy and of many other Christians; and in this way, I trust, it will result in a blessing both on yourself and on your work, such as you would most desire." The Bishop of Oxford had written three days before: " I do grieve heartily that this necessity is laid upon you, but plainly you had no choice. We shall all — I am sure — be ready to give any testimony you may need in the course of the proceedings. It is a painful prospect for you, but we must not doubt that all will be ordered aright. Certainly there can be *no doubt* as to your course now." Both these letters were published in *The Oxford Chronicle* on 15 March, together with one from a Christ Church undergraduate, F. W. G. Walker, who said: "I venture through the medium of your columns, as an undergraduate, and in the name of other undergraduates, to express my very deep sympathy with Mr. Christopher on the outrageous libel and scandalous defamation of character which has been imputed to him, a man of unsullied reputation, and universally respected. I think that I am fairly representing public opinion when I say that there exists not in Oxford anyone, either of his parishioners or of us undergraduates, who gives the slightest credence to any part whatever, of a story so diabolical as that promulgated by Mr. Gillman."

An address of sympathy from the congregation and parishioners of

St. Aldate's carried 633 signatures. In the opinion of Prebendary Allan Smith, then Vicar of Swansea, and later Dean of St. David's, the university address was "one of the most remarkable letters ever published in Oxford." This view, written down in after years, was generally taken at the time. "Such an expression of sympathy," *The Oxford Chronicle* remarked, "is absolutely unique, and without a parallel in the history of the University." Certainly no greater testimony to the real worth of the man could have been called forth. But some precedent has come to light in the form of a printed address to the Proctors, one of them R. W. Church, later well known as a tractarian leader, after the affair of Tract 90, in 1845. Though the signatories were numerous, however, it is noticeable, for example, that no Heads of Houses signed, and it is evident, both from the signatures and from the known circumstances, that the document, by contrast with the later memorial, represented a section of university opinion rather than the university as a whole. With regard to Christopher himself, Canon Girdlestone, then Principal of Wycliffe Hall, tells us that "He was specially brave when the libel was launched again him."

On arrival at Oxford station to go down to Reading for the trial, the Rector of St. Aldate's found the Vicar of St. Paul's waiting to accompany him, to bear witness to his character. Christopher was deeply touched. "I had not asked him to do this, but I thought it a very brotherly act." Duggan travelled with him to Reading. Public interest was as great as ever, and the court, presided over by Mr. Justice Lopes, was crowded. Duggan was not the only clergyman present to support Christopher. The Master of Pembroke again attended, together with the Vicar of St. Giles' (the Revd. L. L. Sharpe), who gave evidence, the Revd. E. A. Knox, Fellow of Merton College, afterwards Bishop of Manchester, the Rector of St. Ebbe's, the Revd. J. Arkell, Mr. Archer, churchwarden of St. Aldate's, and others. The prisoner pleaded guilty, and threw himself on the mercy of the court. He was represented by Queen's Counsel, who stated that he and his colleague could tender no other advice to the Vicar of Hennock. Referring to Christopher, Nagle-Gillman's counsel said ". . . no one, I venture to think, stands more highly in the City of Oxford, and in the University of Oxford, than Mr. Christopher . . ." The best that could be done for Nagle-

Gillman was to bring witnesses to show that he was normally of a kindly disposition. The judge deferred sentence to the next day, when he stated that the offence was so serious that in spite of any pleas of extenuation, and Christopher's own recommendation to mercy, the defendant's actions had been deliberate, and were calculated to do grievous harm, and that therefore he could not do less than sentence him to three months imprisonment. As his own counsel had said, Christopher would probably emerge from the ordeal with his reputation not only unsullied but enhanced, and this, though scant consolation, certainly proved to be so. It is surprising to learn that Nagle-Gillman retained his living until his death in 1900. Temple left the Exeter diocese the year after the case, and it may be that Edward Bickersteth, Bishop from 1885 until he also died in 1900, was persuaded by Christopher to take no further steps against the Vicar of Hennock. Unfortunately, however, the trouble did not end with the trial, for scurrilous post-cards came at intervals for years afterwards, indeed up to the time their author died. When the trial was over, and counsel were together in the barristers' room, Christopher suggested thanksgiving to God for the issue, and at once went down on his knees, followed by the members of the legal profession. One who was present remarked to Griffith Thomas that it was probably somewhat unusual in their experience.

Christopher had now completed twenty-five years as Rector of St. Aldate's. This was the occasion of another address, dated 1 January 1885, from parishioners and undergraduate friends, accompanying a cheque for one hundred and ten guineas and a fine bracket clock. Griffith Thomas refers, not to a clock, as recorded in contemporary local newspapers, but to an oil portrait. This portrait, he says, hung in the Rectory dining room, and showed later generations that the white-haired Rector had had coal-black hair when at the height of his influence in Oxford. In fact, Christopher's hair was by now greying. The late Miss Eleanor Christopher, who lived at the Rectory for two years in the 'nineties, did not recall such a picture, and no trace of it appears to exist.[1] It would have seemed appropriate if Christopher had sat to George Richmond, who painted many ecclesiastical figures, whose wife Julia, a Tatham, was Christopher's second cousin, and who was even classed by G. W. E. Russell as

[1]It may have perished in a fire at Bishops' Repository in 1919, when many of Captain Seton-Christopher's belongings were burned.

54. A. M. W. CHRISTOPHER, *c.* 1885

55. MRS. CHRISTOPHER, *c.* 1885

an evangelical. Writing of the period of this presentation after Christopher's death, Francis Jansen commented: "How well one remembers not the figure photographed in the Record, but the more vigorous and energetic personality of those days, standing at the steps that led to the Rectory Room ready with a hearty handshake and beaming smile, the trumpet at once to the ear to catch the name of the new-comer, and then a warm invitation to breakfast or lunch during the ensuing week . . . It is not easy to remember all one could wish of four years of crowded Oxford life so far back as 1884–1888, but through them all the figure of Canon Christopher is plainly seen — alert, keen, sympathetic, enthusiastic, and the avowed leader of the Evangelical clergy and laity, and of all things Evangelical in the University and City of Oxford." Contemporary opinion confirms this impression. A brief account of Christopher in *Home Words* for 1884 remarks that "Mr. Christopher's labours at Oxford have been greatly blessed . . . His influence in the University can hardly be overestimated. Hundreds of young men preparing for the ministry have been deeply indebted to him for the devoted interest he has taken in their spiritual welfare."

Some months later, Henry Drummond of Edinburgh author of *The Natural Law in the Spiritual World,* held a mission in the university, urged by a consensus of invitations, including one from Christopher. Though Drummond had worked with Moody twelve years previously, his theological position had undergone certain changes in a liberal direction, and he did not wish to be identified with any party or traditional methods of evangelism. On his arrival, in October 1885, he found Christopher waiting for him. The Rector of St. Aldate's had proposed to hold a meeting for Drummond. Hundreds of circulars had been printed, only to be held back on receipt of a telegram. In person, Christopher was not to be denied. "What could I do?" wrote Drummond, "I had really no excuse for refusing, so the thing must go on, though I fear he will find he has caught a tartar. After all, if anything is to be done in Oxford, this party [The Evangelical] must be carried along with it. They will supply great and essential elements."

No doubt Christopher was present at the meeting in Wycliffe Hall when Drummond explained his theological views and methods of attack to "all the Low Church workers . . . they seemed much surprised at the former, *i.e.* our *views,* but did not instantly burn me at the stake, as I feared. On the contrary, they asked many questions, and, on the whole, I think this meeting was useful. I had no idea it would be part of my work here to run a tilt at the evangelism current in the place, but nothing is really more needed." After dining with Vice-Chancellor Jowett alone (there were the usual silences) and meeting Dean Liddell ("I thought him very appalling"), Drummond's discouragement was complete. "I said they wanted leaders here, but really they are almost hopeless." This tone is one which has not been unknown on the part of other well-meaning strangers to Oxford.

Frank Webster presently preached his last sermon as curate of St. Aldate's from the pulpit (then on the south side of the chancel arch) in which he was one day to preach Christopher's funeral sermon. He was called in 1885 to become Principal of the Church Army Training Home in London and Lecturer of Brunswick Chapel. Within a few years he was appointed Vicar of St. Thomas's, Birmingham, a parish of ten thousand souls. In July 1885 the death occurred of Arthur Poole, since 1883 the first Bishop in Japan, who had been curate of St. Aldate's 1876-7. He was only thirty-three. To take Webster's place at St. Aldate's came Alfred Peachey Cox, a non-collegiate graduate, afterwards Canon Cox, Vicar of Christ Church, Cheltenham. His most conspicuous contribution to the work of the parish was not made until 1888, when he was the means of establishing the St. Aldates' parish magazine. Like Webster, Cox had known Christopher as a personal friend ever since he came up as a freshman in 1880, when a former school-fellow had effected an introduction "through the medium of probably the best known ear-trumpet in Christendom, into which every curate had to preach his first and every other sermon . . . My name, or rather someone else's name, with quite a different sound, I saw duly registered in his C.M.S. pocket book, as indispensable an adjunct as the ear-trumpet, for luncheon at the Rectory on the following Saturday. From that moment I shared . . . in his kindliness, his hospitality, his spiritual fatherliness. In that relationship I knew him for more than twenty-five years: and only those, and they were very many in the course of his Oxford life . . . who were in close touch with him, can quite appreciate the charm and the quaintness of that wonderfully good and kind and in the truest sense of the term, 'gentle-man'."

Cox had a sense of humour and appreciated Christopher's. He also appreciated the amusement of which Christopher was sometimes the cause. "Withal there was a delightful undervein of humour. Few men I have known laughed more heartily when there was something really amusing, than Canon Christopher, and I should think few men have laughed more heartily and innocently than when recalling together something intensely funny in which the dear old man was the cause of their merriment: no one who really knew him could laugh 'at' him, except a silly unappreciative cynic with a very limited outlook on life. But no one could be very long with him under ordinary circumstances without some little joke lighting up matters of deepest moment. Shall I ever forget — when I was his curate — to recall one of many incidents — rushing to the railway station to meet at 8.15 p.m. a learned doctor of divinity? He happened to be a Church Pastoral-Aid 'deputation' for the following Sunday in Oxford.[1] He was being utilized to address Undergraduates on Saturday night at 8 p.m. The meeting had been assembled half an hour before I could push him up in a hansom cab from the station to the meeting. As we two entered the door rather breathless, said the Canon from the high platform at the other end of the room, with Bible and waving ear-trumpet, 'Ah: Ah: here he is at last! Come along brother!' and without a pause to hear one word from the new arrival, whom he showered with voluminous greeting, 'Now I will ask dear Dr. So and So to give us his address on the Philosophical Aspect of . . .' and then followed a very high-sounding title to the 'Lecture'. We might all have been in for 'Greats'! 'What? what?' interjected the visitor, 'What is all this?' and leisurely drawing out his spectacles and looking with cautious interest at the invitation card, gazed silently at the title of the lecture, then at the Canon, then at us: and quietly remarked, 'This is the first moment I have been made aware of the subject of my lecture to you.' The next moment was critical: but the humour of it all saved the situation. The conversation that then and there went on out loud between the chairman and the lecturer was about the best

[1]Probably Dr. John Hart-Burges, Rector of Devizes, in November 1887.

thing we had ever been entertained with. The learned doctor had been travelling about the country and had received none of the Canon's later correspondence. In the end he gave us a number of racy stories connected with pastoral visitation in a great sea-port town, and the occasion was closed by a most solemnizing and earnest prayer from Canon Christopher enough to make us all wish to be Pastoral-Aid curates on the spot."

Those of different theological outlook could likewise write appreciatively of these gatherings at this period. In 1887 the Revd. G. W. Gent, Principal of St. Mark's College, Chelsea, and a former Tutor of Keble College, whose estimate of Henry Bazely has already been given, contributed a chapter on 'The Religious Life' of the university to the composite work entitled *Oxford: Its Life and Schools.* "High and Broad," he tells us, "as well as Low Churchmen, have all, at times, found themselves in the large Room at S. Aldate's Rectory, and have gazed with interest at attentive rows of undergraduates, whose faces would indeed have been strange at churches of a different school, but whose numbers and enthusiasm impressed one with a sense of strength . . ."

"Of course," Cox goes on to explain, "it was the charm of his personality which drew out the love of his young friends and his curates towards him . . . The power of his life was Love and Prayer and God's Word. He was in his way quite unique, exceedingly deaf, shuffling along in later years, dressed in a long heavy frock coat, generally in a tall hat, the tip of his ear-trumpet sticking out of a pocket behind, the radiant genial welcome of a drawn out 'Ah . . . Brother' which was quite irresistible,[1] his invariable habit of praying about everything and everybody everywhere. You were on your knees before you knew where you were, amidst heaps and masses of papers, books, and tracts which perennially strewed the study floor, chairs, tables, window ledges, mantel shelf and any available inch of space. Who would have had it otherwise? Not one of us. I found it perfectly delightful."

Christopher's sleeplessness had been far from ended by his sea voyage in 1860. But in 1885 he was thankful at last to obtain a prescription which not only "under God's blessing, cured me, but also keeps me cured." Naturally this made a great difference to his

[1]As Downer had noted twenty years before.

life, especially as he grew older. In 1898 he could write: "I have never had a really sleepless night for eleven years."[1] Whereas "for many years I was liable to most grievous attacks of sleeplessness." He had consulted in vain a number of eminent London physicians. It was while on holiday in Castletown that a local doctor had supplied the remedy. "No one who has not suffered, as I have suffered, from prolonged attacks of sleeplessness can fully estimate my deep thankfulness to God for having guided me in my distress to Dr. Clague . . ." Moreover, the medicine had the merit of cheapness. "My annual bill . . . gets smaller every year," he wrote in an article published to help other sufferers. "This year," in spite of having to send to the Isle of Man, "it was only twelve shillings." Christopher's general health was good. "During these eleven years, excepting an occasional cold, I have never had anything the matter with me." A man who can say that of his sixty-seventh to seventy-eighth years, is in a better position than most to continue to prosecute his life-work with single-minded vigour.

It was not surprising therefore that in writing an introduction to *Our Father; or, The Lord's Prayer Expanded in the Words of Holy Scripture,* "compiled by A Mother for the use of her Sons", published in 1886, Christopher should say "How full of teaching and encouragement are the prayers of Scripture! I never used the prayers in the Psalms so much as I did rather more than a year ago, during a prolonged and very trying attack of sleeplessness. No words seemed to me, at that time of trial, so well suited to express the desires of my heart as those of the Psalmist. And some of these prayers have been answered to me ever since; the cure of my sleeplessness, and the means of preventing its return, forming one of God's gracious answers. Surely one way in which the Holy Spirit 'helpeth our infirmities' when 'we know not what we should pray for as we ought' (Rom. 8.26) is by bringing to our minds His own inspired words . . . I feel truly thankful that two admirable series of prayers *in the very words of Scripture,* the one for private and the other for family use, have been published in this volume." A "brother clergyman" had decided to issue the work,[2] and his initials, C.H.W., below a

[1]This may be inaccurate, as the evidence shows that it was in the summer of 1885 that the cure was found.

[2]Not included in Halkett and Laing's *Dictionary of Anonymous & Pseudonymous English Literature.*

preliminary note, perhaps identify him as the Revd. Charles Henry Waller, Principal of St. John's Hall, Highbury, an undergraduate friend of the Rector of St. Aldate's in the early 'sixties.

In 1886 the Bishop of Oxford, Dr. Mackarness, appointed Christopher an honorary canon of Christ Church. Though mainly a testimony to his indefatigable advocacy of missions, ("Half a hundred such men in the country," wrote Canon Cox, "would speedily change the whole face of the Church in regard to World Evangelization"), it did almost as much credit to the Bishop's large heartedness as it did to Christopher's earnest and faithful work. Christopher and Mackarness had not infrequently been somewhat at variance; but in the House of Lords the Bishop had cited Christopher by name as one who knew how to combine controversy with Christian love.[1] Christopher was instituted on 30 September. He told one of his parishioners that the appointment would make no difference to his views and churchmanship. It is perhaps significant that the Bishop's letter offering the stall was not among those which Christopher preserved. The honour, received with humility, was none the less welcome to him and his friends, though, in Downer's words, "a very small acknowledgement of his great services to Christ and the Church. But it was not for such things that he laboured."

One of Christopher's most strongly held beliefs was in Christian unity. The 'one-ness' of God's people was a subject very near his heart. This was among the reasons why he was so enthusiastic a supporter of the Bible Society. He regarded it as in some respects the best instrument for bringing together Christians of various denominations. There was scarcely a speech or prayer of his for the society in which he did not refer to this; and in later years he was particularly thankful for the advocacy of the society's claims by such high church bishops as Dr. Jacob of St. Albans, Dr. King of Madagascar, and Bishop Mitchinson, Master of Pembroke.

"There are some who lament 'our unhappy divisions'," Christopher declared, "who do not bear in mind that there is a state far worse than that of our present 'unhappy divisions', and that is a unity in unscriptural doctrines such as that which existed in the Church of Rome before the Reformation. How awful would be the

[1]This is a tradition authenticated by Dr. Griffith Thomas. No such reference can be found in the Bishop's parliamentary speeches; but these are only printed in summary form.

56. A. M. W. CHRISTOPHER, *c.* 1887

57. MRS. CHRISTOPHER, *c.* 1887

state of Ritualistic parishes now if there were no Protestant Nonconformists preaching Christ in them, and doing what they can to make known His unsearchable riches of grace . . . God be praised for all who are helping to make this soul-saving knowledge known where, without them, the full free everlasting Gospel would not be preached. We are Christians first, and Church of England Christians in the second place. There is amidst all the apparent divisions of Christendom only one Church of Christ, the Church of all true believers, the Church of all those who are 'born again not of corruptible seed, but incorruptible by the Word of God which liveth and abideth for ever.' Can any one who knows the truth of the Gospel, and abhors the erroneous teaching which keeps people from real union with Christ, desire that a visible unity should be produced by the sacrifice of the spiritual unity of true believers; that all the preaching of Christ by Nonconformists should be silenced and replaced by the inculcation of sacerdotal error?"

This spirit permeates a paper which Christopher read at the Ryde Conference of the World's Evangelical Alliance in 1886, his subject being *Union of heart amongst Christians essential to the Evangelisation of the World*. Only as this union could be realised, he believed, would the full blessing of God be received on missionary work. It was a characteristic address. "Surely many of the differences and controversies which exhaust the mental energies of Christians are of trifling moment when compared with the evils which might be avoided by union of heart amongst Christians." He cited examples, such as the London Missionary Society handing over work in Tinnevelly, in 1864, to the Society for the Propagation of the Gospel. He entreated those whose principles allowed them, to join the Evangelical Alliance. "I trust no considerations of policy will hold them back. Too much of so-called policy is bad policy, for it misses the Lord's blessing." He did not care for what George Whitefield called 'trimming'. "The Lord Jesus Christ is calling us to unite on the great doctrines which form the Basis of the Evangelical Alliance; shall our ears be deaf to the call of the Lord Jesus, and open only to party cries and sectional differences? Should we not rejoice in the sacred eloquence of a Chalmers, the Christian poetry of a Bonar, the expositions of a Matthew Henry, the allegory of a Bunyan? 'Haste, brethren, to the rescue; fly!' The hand of the Lord will be with us if we unitedly preach the Lord Jesus, and a great number will believe and turn unto the Lord." Christopher's views on this subject were further expressed in a sermon published in 1890 under the title *Uniting Christian Love*. "Sincere love to the brethren, as through the abundant gift of the living water of the Holy Spirit it rises higher and higher in the soul, will overflow sectarian separations and political differences, and will unite Christian heart to Christian heart. It will unite Christians in works of faith and labours of love and will gather strength as it does so. I will ask any Clergyman of our Church who has taken part as I have for many years in God's work by the British and Foreign Bible Society, the Religious Tract Society, and the London City Mission, whether he has not received an increase of faith and love by such union in Christ's work with Non-conformists? And how readily genuine love which raises us above pride and touchiness is returned by Non-conformists . . . When I am on my knees praying beside a spiritually-minded Non-conformist brother, I find that my heart is one with his. The same faith lifts it up from earth to heaven. By the same trust in the blood shedding of the Lord Jesus Christ we enter together into the holiest, with the same longing desires for more faith, more love, more holiness, more of a self-sacrificing spirit, more devotion to Christ. We draw near together to the throne of grace that we may both as fellow sinners, obtain mercy, and both, in similar weakness, find grace to help in time of need. Shall I do thus, and feel thus when on my knees, and am I afterwards to treat with coldness the brother, whose heart was as full of love as mine when engaged in prayer?" Christopher, no doubt, had in mind partly the somewhat stiff attitude taken by some evangelical churchmen towards nonconformists on the ground that they were schismatics, but mainly the far stiffer attitude towards them taken by high churchmen and anglo-catholics, some of whom regarded them as heretical. The justice of both his protests has since been generally admitted.

As early as 1885, a localised edition of the Church Army *Gazette* was in use at St. Aldate's, in common with one or two other churches, as a parish magazine. The St. Aldates' parish magazine proper was at first, when begun at the New Year 1888, a single sheet. Cox, the originator of this, was naturally appointed editor. The first number announced, in language typical of the time, over the signatures of Christopher and Cox: "The Magazine will be delivered as soon as published every month. It will be a bright and cheery friend, looking in periodically. Sure to be a favourite with the family all round. Giving a good deal of information. Telling many a good tale. Cheerful but wise. Costing very little; eating nothing, although staying a long time." Three hundred copies of the first issue were sold. This was an important step forward. Parish magazines had scarcely been thought of when Christopher first came to St. Aldate's. *Home Words*, an evangelical 'inset', started publication in 1875. It took several years for such an idea to spread through the parishes. The wording of the above suggests that some regular religious reading matter — probably *Home Words* — was bound up with the local news from the start. At once a flood of light is thrown on the innumerable parochial activities of St. Aldate's, and on those who took part in them.

One of the earliest numbers refers to the resignation of Bishop Mackarness on account of ill health, and to the appointment of his successor, William Stubbs, Bishop of Chester, formerly Regius Professor of Modern History. We learn that Canon and Mrs. Christopher spent their annual August holiday in the Isle of Man, after attending the yearly school treat held at Holton Park, near Wheatley, the home of Mr. and Mrs. W. E. Biscoe,[1] and the bank holiday parochial excursion by water to Nuneham. In October, Christopher secured the Lord Chancellor, Earl Cairns, to speak at a well attended annual meeting of the Bible Society in the Town Hall.[2] In anticipation of the New Year, Christopher agreed to Cox's suggestion that there should be two early administrations of Holy Communion each month; and in view of larger numbers at the Wednesday evening services, it was decided to revive those formerly held on Fridays.

In December, Charles James Casher of St. John's College was ordained as honorary curate of St. Aldate's. He had taken a first class in theology in 1885, — the best 'first' of those who were examined with him one examiner told his tutor, — and in 1886 was senior Denyer and Johnson scholar. But he was not strong, and

[1]Among a list of "Hearty Protestant givers, friendly to Christopher," in a private memorandum of E. P. Hathaway, is the name of W. E. Biscoe, son of the Revd. T. G. Tyndale and father of Canon Tyndale-Biscoe of Kashmir.
[2]Lord Shaftesbury had done the same in 1883.

the extent of his parish work was understood to be limited by his health. This did not prevent him from having a Bible and book stall each year at St. Giles's Fair. (George Wheelhouse used to sleep under it at night as a guard.) During the few years before Dr. Heurtley's death in 1895, he was assistant lecturer to him as Lady Margaret Professor. Casher, who took the degree of doctor of divinity in 1903, stayed with Christopher through the remainder of the Canon's time at St. Aldate's, receiving a purely nominal stipend. Like Christopher, Casher was a zealous distributor of tracts. Towards the end of his ministry at Oxford, his rector could say: "Look at my dear brother Dr. Casher! The chief joy of his holiday is in giving away tracts. He must have given out a quarter of a million in his life-time. They cannot all have been without result." Many were handed by him outside Christ Church gate — the highway being in St. Aldates' parish — to the crowds passing up from the river during Eights' Week or Torpids.

By February 1889, however, Cox was "on the wing". He had been curate for over three years, and he now quitted St. Aldate's partly in order to enlarge his experience. "We must hope that the thought was given him by God," wrote Christopher in the parish magazine, "it certainly was not given him by us." On his departure Cox was presented with the usual 'handsome clock' and the six volumes of Ryle's *Expository Thoughts on the Gospels* as handsomely bound. Christopher spoke at length on this occasion about the seven able and beloved curates who had served him. He and they had buried more than a thousand people out of St. Aldate's in the course of thirty years — "More people than the Church could hold if the aisles were filled as well as the seats . . ." It was a very solemn thought. Cox went to take the duty for a few months at Holy Trinity, Scarborough, for the Revd. J. A. Faithfull, who was obliged to rest. He afterwards became curate of Paddington, was subsequently Vicar of Wembley, and later an honorary canon of Gloucester. His successor at St. Aldate's was the "beloved Griffith Thomas."

William Henry Griffith Thomas had been in orders since 1885, as curate of St. Peter's, Clerkenwell. At King's College, London, he had been under the influence of Henry Wace, afterwards Dean of Canterbury, then Principal. He had written to Canon Christopher in July 1888, enquiring about the possibility of an Oxford curacy with which he could combine reading for the degree which owing to family circumstances he had not been able to take at the usual time. Christopher replied that he himself needed curates who would be able to give every afternoon to visiting (there were now nearly three thousand parishioners) and that in any case there was no vacancy. At the same time he already predicted a first class in the schools if Thomas came to Oxford and read theology, sending literature about the examinations. With much good sense he wrote, "If you had not been Gospeller at the Bishop of London's Trinity examination [*sic*] and obtained a first Class in the 'Preliminary', I should have said to you that life is too short for an ordained man to apply himself to pass Oxford Examinations. But as I think from your past success that you would obtain a first Class in Theology the case is different. Some position of usefulness may be opened to you as a first Class Oxford man which would not be open to you as a King's College Associate."

The correspondence continued. No curate of his, Christopher observed, had ever left him for another curacy! But he might recommend Cox for a living, though he could do nothing else to make an opening. Meanwhile, impressive letters of recommendation were reaching Christopher, notably from Canon Howell, Vicar of Wrexham, one of the ablest Welsh preachers, who especially commended Thomas's own sermons. Five months passed, during which Cox became ill and it was evident that he could not continue to work in the Oxford climate. At 5.15 a.m. on 3 January 1889, Christopher wrote: "I have already been at my desk more than an hour & must not rise from it without writing to you . . ." Christopher was now satisfied that Thomas could combine his reading with his parish work without detriment to the latter, and wrote five days later: "I require a thoroughly zealous loyal curate to do faithfully what I cannot do — tho' I desire to work hard early & late . . . Last night I posted an important letter just before midnight & did not get to sleep until about 2 a.m. & was up at 6 and I have been working all day. God may call me any day but I am not conscious of having less strength than at any other time in my 30 years Incumbency of St. Aldate's but from the double nature of my work I have never satisfied myself about my visiting. I pray Daily that I may be more filled with the Spirit and have more love of souls given me". Webster and Cox had had £140 *per annum* and he proposed, in spite of the limitations involved in reading for a degree, to give Thomas the same. In February the future principal of Wycliffe Hall was installed at 3, Isis Street.

Christopher was about to reach his seventieth year but he was supported by two able colleagues — both of whom had passed the best examination in divinity of the deacons ordained with them and had, therefore, read the Gospel at their ordination. He was to remain Rector of St. Aldate's for another fifteen years; and one of his larger achievements, the building of St. Matthew's church, and the erection of a separate ecclesiastical district of Grandpont, with a school of its own, was still only a cherished plan. Probably, however, the years of his best work now lay behind him, during the thirty years he had already been rector, though he was spared to do much else as well. His letters to Griffith Thomas show that he was still more than commonly active. On 23 May 1889 he wrote: "I was up for Grandpont at 4.20 a.m. but I could not have gone to sleep again & it is my best time. I wrote & posted 16 letters by 6.15 a.m. post & then bathed & dressed. I am not earlier out than Hanleys brewers' men.[1] I meet a cart at the same spot in Pembroke Street each morning."

On arrival at Castletown in the Isle of Man for his summer holiday he was soon writing thankfully "These are the lodgings to which I came when suffering from my last severe attack of sleeplessness two years ago. How different am I in point of health & strength now!" Throughout this holiday he was busy writing letters to collect money for his Grandpont project and as a result obtained £214. On 15 August he could say, however, "I have had one day & two afternoons up the mountain streams, so have done something besides write. I wish I caught as many souls at each effort as I do trout." 20 August was his sixty-ninth birthday. The following morning at 6 a.m. he wrote "I have overslept myself!" He sends thanks for three telegrams "of love, faith and Scriptural Prayer" from St. Aldate's. "Thank all who have prayed for me. Let them ask that I may be filled with the Spirit & that the great love of Christ may constrain me to live not for myself but for Him that died for

[1]Doubtless supplying The Red Lion, a public house then nearly opposite the Rectory.

58. ST. ALDATE'S, OXFORD, *c.* 1890

59. C. J. CASHER
Honorary curate of St. Aldate's, Oxford, 1889–1905

W. H. GRIFFITH THOMAS
Curate of St. Aldate's 1889–96

A. M. W. CHRISTOPHER
Rector; *c.* 1890

me." On 2 September he walked seven miles to Kirk Arbory church and back, preaching three times and supping with the squire, all "*without fatigue*". On the previous Saturday he had risen at 3.30 a.m. as he had to call "the boys" at 5.30 for the crossing to Liverpool. The elder 'boy', Henry, who lived on the island, was thirty-nine. Alfred, his younger brother, was about to sail for Ceylon. During the intervening two hours " I had a good write . . . for Grandpont."

Young Alfred Christopher had matriculated from Christ Church in 1875, but had gone down without taking a degree. Popular legend said that while his son was an undergraduate Christopher had failed to distinguish him in the street from his undergraduate acquaintance in general. The young man proceeded to the Royal Military Academy at Sandhurst and in course of time was promoted captain and adjutant in the Seaforth Highlanders. After service in the Afghan War of 1879-80, he became aide-de-camp to Sir Richard Temple and Sir James Fergusson while successively Governors of Bombay, and then to the Hon. Sir Arthur Gordon, afterwards Lord Stanmore, Governor of Ceylon. His elder brother Henry, who had been Secretary to the trustees of King William's College, Isle of Man, for a number of years, was in 1886 appointed Bursar of that school. In 1875 Henry's youngest daughter, Edith, was born — she kept house for her grandfather in Oxford after Maria Christopher's death, — to be followed in the next year by a son, George Seton Christopher. Eleven years later, in 1887, another son was born, Charles Mordaunt de Aquilar Christopher. Certain connections at Oxford arose through the Revd. Henry Ashington, Rector of Brauncewell, Lincolnshire, a rather senior first cousin of Canon Christopher. He had a daughter Frances who in 1880 married Charles Firth. They settled in Oxford in 1883, and from 1904 to 1925 he was Regius Professor of Modern History, being knighted in 1922. Lady Firth's sister married a Fellow of New College.

Two of Canon Christopher's brothers-in-law, General Cautley in England, and William Sealy in New Zealand, died in 1881 and 1886 respectively, the General being buried in the Christopher vault at Chiswick. Deaths were also occurring in the next generation. Three of Christopher's nephews died during this period, — Arthur Christopher, son of his brother Leonard, and, like himself, a cricketer, in 1874, shortly after leaving school at Wellington; William Sealy, son of his sister Matilda, in New Zealand in 1881; and William Cautley, son of his sister Emma, at Cairo in 1883. Christopher's nephew Leonard, son of his brother of that name, married in 1878 Florence Lane, a member of the family of Mistress Jane Lane, who saved the life of King Charles II. Another nephew, Percy Tatham, married as his second wife in 1885 Ethel Wilson, a great-niece of the Bishop whom Christopher had known in Calcutta.

Throughout the period Christopher's work for the Bible Society and the Church Missionary Society went on unceasingly. The great missionary breakfasts were held every year, and in the 'eighties the speakers included Bishop French of Lahore in 1884, the Bishop of Oxford (Dr. Mackarness) and the Principal of Ridley Hall (H. C. G. Moule, afterwards Bishop of Durham) in 1886, the Bishop of Oxford (Dr. Stubbs) and Bishop Ridley of Caledonia in 1889. French — who in 1880 had written to Christopher from India: "I rejoiced with you most unfeignedly in the remarkable and unparalleled success of your C.M.S. breakfast party" — sent a description of his own visit to Oxford for this purpose to his daughter Edith. "It was striking seven as I knocked or rang at 8 Merton Street,[1] and right glad I was, to have a quiet evening with E.[2] and E,[3] though I got an hour or two of writing. Dreams of the great gathering at the Clarendon Hotel next morning kept me awake some hours, but as a poor man about to be executed sleeps at last, they say, so I got some four hours of refreshing rest, and was helped through by God's goodness better than I feared. It was an alarming sight though, nearly 200 young men or nearly that round the breakfast tables, then others were brought in from another breakfast-room, who could only stand round the doors, poor fellows. Mr. Christopher prefaced my address, and I spoke three quarters of an hour, then Dr. Ince[4] followed with compliments. There was a lunch of great dignities in Merton Common-room after . . ."

Two years later, in the presence of the Bishop, with Principal Moule, several Heads of Houses, and a number of professors and

[1]Where, curiously enough, Christopher had first met Francis Pilcher of St. Clement's, when calling on him as an Oriel freshman in 1859.

[2]Edmund Knox, Fellow of Merton, afterwards Bishop of Manchester, his son-in-law.

[3]His daughter Ellen, Knox's first wife, mother of Monsignor Ronald Knox. She is commemorated by the lych-gate of St. Ebbe's.

[4]Regius Professor of Divinity, whose name had appeared with French's in the same first class of *literae humaniores* in 1846.

canons, Christopher remarked, towards the conclusion of the breakfast, that "They had met as believers in the Lord Jesus Christ, and their object was His Glory in the salvation of souls by the Gospel. He was able to pour out His Holy Spirit upon the University, and fill every Head of a College, every Professor, every Tutor, every Undergraduate, with the Holy Ghost — and to make it one great desire of his life to promote obedience to Our Lord's last command."

Christopher was elected a vice-president of the Church Missionary Society in 1888. In the following year, a like honour was offered by the Church Association, whose battles at Oxford he had made his own. Not for another nine years would the Bible Society offer him the same recognition. Christopher had been a member of the original council of the Church Association, and it was fitting that his labours for the protestant cause should have some acknowledgement. In accepting the council's invitation he wrote to the Secretary in terms which sum up his personal position:

"The Church Association is the only Church of England Society which has laboured during the last twenty-four years in every lawful way to counteract the efforts now being made to pervert the teaching of the Church of England on essential points of the Christian faith, and to assimilate her services to those of the Church of Rome.

"This Association has gone steadily on its faithful course, in the midst of misrepresentation and undeserved reproach, endeavouring, in dependence on the blessing of the God of Truth, to preserve the blessed results of the Reformation to the Church of England.

"I regard it as the truest charity to do all we can, in the Name of our God, to oppose efforts to undo the Reformation, and to pervert congregations from the simplicity of the Gospel. Charity should not be exclusively kept for the teachers of Romanizing errors. Some charity should be reserved for those who may become their unhappy victims.

"It is surely worth bearing all the misrepresentations and reproach poured upon the supporters of the Church Association, to help uphold the 'Doctrines, Principles, and Order of the Church of England' in every lawful way, and to preserve at least some members of our beloved Church from the Ritualistic process of gradual preparation for the terrible plunge of perversion to the Church of

Rome! It cost our Reformers something more than reproach and misrepresentation to bring about the Reformation. It cannot but cost God's faithful servants something to preserve the Reformation by His help at this crisis.

"I wish that all true-hearted Evangelical men realized the present danger of our Church. If they did, I am sure they would not be apathetic, supine, and unfaithful at such a time as this.

"The inspired writer of the thirteenth chapter of the first Epistle to the Corinthians surely knew what true charity is, but see how he wrote in the first chapter of the Epistle to the Galatians of those who preach 'another Gospel;' and see also in the second chapter of that Epistle how he 'withstood Peter to the face because he was to be blamed.' Are the Romanizing corrupters of our Church better men than St. Peter?

"I measure the value of the Church Association not so much by its success as by its Scriptural objects, and the faith and courage of its members in seeking to obtain them.

"The success of Cranmer, Latimer, and Ridley in preserving the Reformation they had so well begun, did not seem to be very great when they were being burnt alive within a quarter of a mile of this rectory. Yet we know what great results God ultimately gave to their noble self sacrifice for the cause of His Truth.

"Let us pray that God may raise up in our Church at this crisis men of the same brave, faithful spirit of our martyred Reformers, and use them to put to shame the feeble and timid Protestantism of the present day.

"Holding the opinions which I have expressed in this letter of the faithfulness of the Church Association in labouring in every lawful way for the preservation of the blessed results of the Reformation in the Church of England, I willingly accept the office of a Vice-President, to which the Council have invited me, and the reproach which is attached to it.

"I pray that the Holy Spirit may fill all the members of the Church Association with the faithful charity which He created in St. Paul. I pray also that He may move the hearts of many more of our loyal fellow-Churchmen to unite heartily with them in their difficult labours for the preservation of the faithful Church of England, which was taught of God in the riper days of the Reformation to cast out of her Prayer Book the word 'altar', and with it all the false doctrine which is now connected with that word."

It will be seen that Christopher did not distinguish, as later evangelicals have learnt to do, between the distinctively Anglo-Roman section of the anglo-catholic party and the teaching of those who would regard themselves as 'English catholics.' This, however, is likely at most to indicate unawareness of a distinction which he would hardly have thought important. That he feared for men's souls if anglo-catholicism in any form gained ground in the Church of England is abundantly clear. Not for him an eclectic disregard of what may be necessary to salvation. Here is the key to his consistent support of the activities of the Church Association. It should be realised that he did not take up as extreme a position as many in his day. He gladly recognised the merits of the older high church school. In matters of liturgical innovation — for example in regard to saying or singing the psalms — he was prepared to change his mind. But in the main he stood by the understanding of anglicanism which was generally accepted until anglo-catholicism had had time and opportunity to exercise a widespread influence — the moderate churchmanship of the three historic schools of thought, outwardly indistinguishable, in the reformed Church of England, which grew out of the Elizabethan settlement.

Chapter XIII

More Building

1890 - 1896

LONG BEFORE the turn of the century, the city of Oxford had already begun that great expansion which has so largely altered its former character. In St. Aldate's proper there was no possibility of further building. But now the large area of the parish on the farther side of the river, which had hitherto worn a rural aspect, was beginning to succumb to the need for additional housing. This was the district known as Grandpont and Cold Arbour, traversed by the main road to Abingdon, and surrounded on three sides by water. At the Grandpont end, nearer to Folly Bridge, a population of at least a thousand had grown up, so rapidly that the need for a new church there was not generally realised until it had become urgent. As late as 1889, Grandpont was in Berkshire, but in that year it was transferred to Oxfordshire, and brought within the city boundary.

A few years earlier, Christopher had not unnaturally thought that, with St. Aldate's church rebuilt, new schools, a rectory room, and finally, a rectory, provided, no more building would be needed in his time. Now, in his seventieth year, he was faced with the task of finding the money for a completely new church, with a school in addition. Another man would have sought well-deserved retirement. But Christopher, though conscious that he might not live to see the work finished, had no thought of retiring. The Principal and Fellows of Brasenose — with Christ Church the principal landowners in that

60. ST. MATTHEW'S, GRANDPONT, OXFORD
Architect's drawing, 1890

61. ST. MATTHEW'S, GRANDPONT, 1894
Built by A. M. W. Christopher, 1890–1

62. ST. ALDATE'S, OXFORD, MEN'S BIBLE CLASS, *c.* 1890
W. H. Griffith Thomas, curate, and A. P. Cox, former curate, seated in front

part of Oxford — generously gave him an excellent site. Christopher thereupon issued, in April 1889, an appeal for funds,[1] supported by the Bishop, Dr. Stubbs, and the Archdeacon of Oxford, Dr. Palmer. Money began to come in steadily. The new church was to be a chapel-of-ease to St. Aldate's. By the following April Christopher felt justified in signing the contract, in faith, so that building, by Messrs. Symm, might begin at the best season of the year. Christopher was most anxious that the church should be worthy of its evangelical provenance. It was necessary, therefore, to raise the then large sum of some six thousand five hundred pounds. By June 1890 over half of this had been subscribed, and the walls were already rising. The Bishop of Oxford laid the foundation stone on the 21st. Christopher's cousin, John Christopher, who had superintended the rebuilding of St. Aldate's thirty years before, was again employed as designer. Christopher had thought it well to bring the choice of architect before the annual vestry meeting of 1889;[2] there had been unanimous agreement, however, and the result was a church in the perpendicular style, without tower or structural chancel, capable of holding six hundred people, well finished and furnished.

To those who thought that too much money was being spent, the Canon would say that he desired members of the university and others to know that evangelicalism did not mean bareness or cheapness or slovenliness, but that everything should be as reasonably good as possible. In the event, the church, with its fittings, cost nearly eight thousand pounds. But all of it had been collected by the time the building was ready for use in the following year.

Most of the well-known evangelical leaders and many others, including those who had valued the ministry at St. Aldate's as undergraduates, besides prominent men in the university, contributed. Donations were usually comparatively small; but they were numerous. The business was complicated by the need for building a school as well, for which a further two thousand five hundred pounds was

[1]A copy is preserved in the Bodleian Library. The names of initial subscribers included eleven Heads of Houses. A bound collection of papers relating to the founding of St. Matthew's is in the possession of the parish. A second appeal was necessary in March 1891, of which a copy is in the Bodleian.

[2]The vestry minutes, though complete from 1859 to 1905, and mostly in Christopher's own hand, form a scant outline record with little information of more than administrative interest.

required, to say nothing of six hundred pounds presently for enlarging St. Aldates' schools. Brasenose College again gave a site, John Christopher was again the architect, and Grandpont was provided with its school in 1894, a 'memorial stone' having been laid by the Duke of Marlborough. All the additional money was found within two years. Both school building and scholars received gratifying approval. The diocesan inspector said that "the parishioners are to be congratulated upon having secured such excellent School premises," and when the government inspector came round in 1895, the pupils did so well that they were excused examination the following year.

To raise ten thousand pounds single-handed, between the ages of seventy and seventy-five, was in itself no small achievement, and the fact that he was able to do so constitutes a tribute to Christopher's character. His appeals, indeed, always had an almost irresistible, personal and spiritual note. "I entreat Christians, for the love of Christ, to help me in my last building effort for my parish . . . which will, I trust, long after my removal prove a channel of blessing to many souls." As soon as the church was nearly ready, Christopher appointed the Revd. Howard Colclough, a graduate of Trinity College, Dublin, and a clergyman of ten years' experience, as curate-in-charge. St. Matthew's was consecrated by Dr. Stubbs on 29 October 1891, and the church shortly acquired a large congregation. Miss E. Abigail, who until 1963 sang in the St. Aldates' choir, remembers Christopher coming to preach at St. Matthew's when she was a small girl, placing a black ear-trumpet on the ledge of the pulpit before his sermon, and using it to communicate with the curate in the reading-desk below.

By 1890 the hymnbook used at St. Aldate's had been changed to *The Hymnal Companion to the Book of Common Prayer,* an increasingly popular collection in evangelical churches, edited by E. H. Bickersteth, who in 1885 had become Bishop of Exeter, fifteen years after his hymnbook was first published. Colclough was musical, and before he accepted his Oxford curacy he obtained an assurance that the psalms would be sung, rather than said, in St. Matthew's. In those days this was a decided innovation, especially in an evangelical church. During his earlier years at Oxford Christopher had been approached by some who wished that the psalms should be sung in

63. ST. MATTHEW'S, GRANDPONT, OXFORD
Interior, *c.* 1910

64. JOHN THOMAS CHRISTOPHER, 1889
(as Master of the Salters' Company)
Architect for St. Aldate's and St. Matthew's

65. GRANDPONT SCHOOL, OXFORD, 1964
Built 1893-94; closed 1959

66. STANDARD 2, ST. ALDATE'S BOYS' SCHOOL, OXFORD, *c.* 1898
W. L. Freeman, headmaster; Miss B. F. Shrimpton, form mistress; H. E. Green, pupil-teacher. W. H. Ward, third row, fourth from left (p. 302)

St. Aldate's, but he refused, saying "You can sing them over my grave." With the abandonment of the metrical psalter earlier in the century, chanting the psalms had been introduced into some of the lesser parish churches by anglo-catholic clergy, and on that account alone the practice was open to suspicion. But there came a time when Christopher altered his point of view, and on one occasion he allowed Griffith Thomas to have the psalms sung at a week-night harvest thanksgiving. This was the first time the psalms were sung in St. Aldate's. Many people liked the change, but Griffith Thomas was surprised when the Canon deliberately, and without further influencing, announced that, for the future, the psalms would be sung at the Sunday evening service. This was resented by a few, and by more than one he was reminded of his former attitude. But whenever he had made up his mind he was not easily moved, and the psalms were sung in the evening,[1] with the aid of the Magdalen psalter, from that time forward. No one left the congregation.

It so happened that just then Edward Hathaway, who had not heard of this recent development at St. Aldate's, wrote a letter to his friend the Rector in the course of which he highly deprecated the practice. Christopher, however, felt strongly that in a town, at least, young people and others would avoid an evangelical church where the psalms were said, and perhaps go instead to a ritualistic one. "It is practically driving people away from the Gospel who most urgently need it." Yet there was more to be said on the other side than might now occur to a generation accustomed to the singing of one psalm rather than the saying of three.[2] In most other respects, it need hardly be said, the services of St. Aldate's were those of the historic anglican type. The Prayer Book liturgy, strictly followed, was read from a reading-desk facing the people. The sermon was preached in a gown. The choir was not robed. The communion service was conducted from the north end of the holy table. The worship relied on spiritual understanding rather than on external aids. For all services, Christopher himself was attired in a 'celebration surplice' of ample proportions and length, with hood and scarf. This surplice, as is still customary in college chapels, was open in

[1]At morning service they continued to be said, until the end of Christopher's time at least.

[2]With this in mind the correspondence on the subject between Christopher Hathaway is printed as a third appendix, which throws some light on an issue formerly living and now dormant rather than dead.

front, fastened at the top with a button, and with it the Canon wore no cassock. To preach, he took off his canonicals and put on an M.A. gown over his ordinary clerical dress, in general accordance with a time-honoured custom maintained for university sermons even yet, but for several centuries, like the north end position for the minister at holy communion, universal in the Church of England. It may be noted too that Christopher never wore the clerical ('Roman') collar introduced in the 'seventies and 'eighties; to the end he used, in common with many other clergy, some form of normal collar and white tie, as had been usual in his younger days.

In spite of the increasing disparity in age, Christopher still treated his curates with abundant respect and affection. Griffith Thomas himself wrote "never can I forget those seven happy years of loving fellowship. It was often most embarrassing to be referred to and pushed forward as Canon Christopher was wont to do in his large-hearted love for his curates. On one occasion I remonstrated with him on the way in which he announced me in connection with several meetings and services during the following week. 'But,' said he, 'how am I to avoid it? I want them to come and hear the Gospel.' 'Well,' I said, 'suppose you just announce me as "the preacher of this evening," instead of using my name so many times.' The next Sunday he announced that the sermon would be preached by 'the preacher of this evening,' that the Women's Bible Class would be taken by 'the preacher of this evening,' and so on for my various engagements of that week, always ending with 'the preacher of this evening.' This was of course infinitely worse and so I begged him, if he must announce me, to return to the former practice. It is well known that our beloved old friend's preaching powers were not so great in the latter days as they were at first and that congregations were not so large when he preached. One Sunday evening in the pulpit he looked over his spectacles at the congregation and said: 'I see a larger congregation than usual here this evening. You did not expect me to preach. Well, he will be preaching next Sunday, so bring all you can to hear the Gospel'."

Both in 1893 and 1896 Christopher noted some increase in attendance at the Sunday evening services, and this doubtless was partly due to Griffith Thomas. At the primary visitation of Bishop Stubbs in 1890, Christopher submitted as the 'chief hindrances' to

Christian work in the parish "Indifference, worldliness, drink; among children, bad example of elder lads and often of parents," causes which, allowing for differences of contemporary description, remain in general remarkably consistent.

Early in 1890 there was a proposal for an annual 'National Protestant Congress'. Christopher was prepared to support it and went so far as to write a letter to *The Record* which shows what his feelings were: "I have but little time to attend Conferences. Only twice in my life have I made time to attend a Church Congress; once when I had to read a paper at Stoke-on-Trent, and once at Reading in this diocese. But is not the Reformation in danger?" He went on to cite the unity among English protestants in 1688 and the change of heart which the events of that year had produced in Archbishop Sancroft, who from being a life-long opponent of nonconformity became very tender towards the protestant dissenters and instructed the bishops and clergy to be likewise. "Well said, Archbishop Sancroft! May your words be heeded now! What God has done once He can do again. He can unite true-hearted Protestants in earnest prayer and energetic persevering efforts to counteract all attempts to undo the Reformation." It does not appear, however, whether the National Protestant Congress ever materialised.

But the Church Association was as active as ever — the prosecution of Bishop King of Lincoln for questionable ceremonial practices was in progress — and at the annual meeting in the following June, Christopher moved the adoption of the report and proposed a number of gentlemen for membership of the council. It is interesting to note — in connection with the declining support of the society — that these included Lord Robert Montagu, P.C., Sir C. R. Leighton, Bt., the Hon. P. Carteret-Hill, D.C.L., Capt. the Hon. C. E. Hobart-Hampden, Sir John Coode, General Sir C. Palliser, Admiral Rodd, Col. Macdonald Macdonald, and other influential laymen, but no single clerical dignitary. "His dearest friend," Christopher remarked, during the course of his speech, "once said a thing he should never forget. He had an elder brother at Oxford who many years ago was perverted to Rome by the teachings of the late Dr. Pusey, and he remembered his dear friend saying that it was worth working as a galley slave for twenty years to save one man from being perverted to the Church of Rome.[1] He did not ask those before him to work as galley slaves, but to support the only society which for twenty-four years had been striving in every lawful way against the Ritualism so adapted to pervert people from the faithful Church of England to the Church of Rome. Think of the father who had attended regularly his parish church. In that same seat his mother used to sit, and there used to pray for her children, and there he received the Gospel of the grace of God, and there he was brought to Christ. But what happened afterwards? *Now* the father dared not take his children to the parish church for fear that they should be perverted to Rome. He would ask them to keep some of their charity for such people as these. How did St. Paul write of the teachers of error? They did not wish anyone to remain in his error, but they wished everyone who was in the wrong to change his mind and become right. It was in love that St. Paul gave the Church the warning in Gal. i.–8. What he wrote was not that they should show charity to false doctrine, but warn men not to preach it. The Church Association worked under misrepresentation of every kind, but its work was especially a work of love." Christopher's continued support of the Church Association did not mean that he was any the less a deeply consecrated Christian minister. With him there was no hardening with the approach of age.

Death was beginning to take its toll among old friends and senior contemporaries of Christopher. William Carus, formerly of Cambridge and latterly a Canon of Winchester, died in August 1891, to be followed in May 1892 by Charles Goodhart, since 1868 Rector of Wetherden, Suffolk, where Christopher conducted his burial service at the close of a fifty-five years' friendship. Canon Liddon had died in 1890. When Cardinal Newman died in 1891, a proposal was made to erect a statue to him in Broad Street, Oxford. It was felt by many, however, that to place such a memorial so near to the spot where the Reformation martyrs were burnt would be an insult to their memory, Even to Dean Hole of Rochester, a moderate high churchman, this seemed to be like "choosing the parade-ground for the place to do honour to a deserter." With the assistance of Commander A. P. Williams of North Oxford, the local secretary

[1]This remark is attributed elsewhere to E. P. Hathaway.

of the Protestant Reformation Society, Christopher worked energetically to defeat the plan. Opposition to it was headed by Dr. William Ince, Regius Professor of Divinity. Some leading ritualists attended a meeting in Christopher's study, presided over by Dr. Ince, who was supported by Professor Burrows. Correspondence ensued in the Oxford press, and a large and enthusiastic meeting of protest was held.

On the morning of 26 January 1892, Christopher was ready with hundreds of printed copies of the inscription on the Martyrs' Memorial for distribution to the inhabitants of Oxford as they entered the Town Hall, where presently he was among those who spoke, along with the Principal of Wycliffe Hall, F. J. Chavasse. The Vicar of St. Barnabas's, the Revd. M. H. Noel, who was not present, sent Christopher a note to the platform concurring in disapproval of the memorial anywhere in Oxford. The hands of over a thousand men were held up against the statue, and not more than fifteen for it, although two-thirds of the city council were in favour of the idea. Christopher felt "God blessed that meeting." Hathaway suggested an appeal to the Duke of Norfolk and other promoters "as English *gentlemen*." The city fathers offered a site other than in Broad Street; but the statue was put up in Birmingham. Old friends had been praying at a distance. J. E. Matthews, one of Christopher's earliest undergraduate adherents, wrote from St. Peters' Vicarage, Derby, when the issue was as yet uncertain: "to rejoice with you that this clever device of Rome for glorifying its eminent leader and devoted partizan in the centre of that University which he had done so much to corrupt was . . . likely to be defeated through God's great mercy."

Christopher was thankful for Dr. Ince's personal influence. "We have great reason to praise God for having raised up one whom He has prepared to resist the efforts of the Ritualists to undo the Reformation. A man was needed who would have great influence with the large body of High churchmen of the old school, who are firm supporters of the Reformation . . . ". Christopher adverted to this in proposing a vote of thanks at the annual meeting of the Church Association in June 1892. He referred, too, to the fact that the Association had been successful in maintaining the protestant character of the Church of England on no less than sixty points.

Supporters "must also show their thankfulness to God by an *Evangelistic* Protestantism, zealous for the salvation of sinners by means of the gospel of God's grace, and by *a loyal Church of England* Protestantism — never dreaming of giving up their flocks to the wolves so long as the Thirty-nine Articles and the Prayer Book remained unaltered . . . Some people were trying to be Evangelical without being distinctively Protestant, which was like trying to dance on a tight-rope, very dangerous." Another high churchman of the older school whose sympathy delighted Christopher was Sir William Odling, Professor of Chemistry at Oxford. In 1902 he allowed Christopher to publish in *The Record* a letter, part of which read: "Though I do not ticket myself as a member of the Evangelical party, I sympathize warmly with the position it now occupies as the sole champion of the Church of the Reformation and its sole defence against rampant sacerdotalism."

Another death of the early 'nineties was that of Thomas Chamberlain, the only Oxford incumbent of the period whose ministry — though vastly different in character — can be thought of as comparable, at least in terms of length, to Christopher's. Chamberlain, also a Student of Christ Church, had been Vicar of the poor parish of St. Thomas's for fourteen years when Christopher began work at St. Aldate's. He was the first clergyman in Oxford to introduce tractarian ideas and practices in his parish, and vestments in particular. But he was a cleric of an older school even so, " scholarly, dignified, and courteous in manner." Like Christopher, he was not at his best in the pulpit. Unlike Christopher, he achieved his aims without much personal attraction. He " was not a man that made many friends. His reticence and shyness, combined with an indomitable will that did not brook opposition . . . did not attract men widely to him." Moreover as early as 1869 his health began to fail, and in 1883 he preached for the last time in St. Thomas's, never entering the church again. At the Bishop's request, however, he remained incumbent. But " this retirement from the scene of his active labours . . . led to his being almost forgotten . . ." It will be seen that Chamberlain's influence was hardly of the quality or extent of Christopher's. He is chiefly remembered today as the nominal founder of St. Edward's School, Oxford, which in fact owed its survival to the efforts of Chamberlain's protégé, Algernon

Simeon, a great-nephew of Charles Simeon of Cambridge, whose opinions are quoted above.[1]

Oxford was one of the last places in England which heard D. L. Moody. In the hope of meeting a large number of undergraduates, the veteran evangelist gave the final days of his concluding visit to this country, in November 1892, to the university city. Again Christopher headed the committee formed to make the arrangements. Indeed, as *The Christian* reported, "Mr. Moody's visit has been largely brought about by Canon Christopher's influence and effort." Daily prayer meetings had been held beforehand. The main meetings — from Friday to Monday — were conducted in the Corn Exchange and the Town Hall. A large block of front seats was reserved for undergraduates in the Corn Exchange. "Several distinguished personages," including Lord Kinnaird, were present on the platform, " and of course Canon Christopher, with his horn, anxious to catch every word . . ." High churchmen, it was noted, were conspicuous by their absence. Nevertheless, " the precious fruits of Christian unity appeared throughout, led by the large-hearted Canon Christopher, by whose persistence the visit of Mr. Moody to Oxford was brought about . . . The marked difference between the rowdy reception which Mr. Moody met with ten years ago with the undergraduates and the respectful hearing which was accorded to him during the four days of his recent visit is full of cheer. It indicates that evangelical work is better understood." It was at one of these meetings that J. H. Oldham of Trinity, afterwards well known as Dr. Oldham, Secretary of the International Missionary Council, was converted.

Another 'Grand Old Man', W. E. Gladstone, had visited Oxford in the previous month. As an undergraduate at Christ Church he had worshipped regularly at St. Ebbe's, but for the greater part of his life he was a decided high churchman. He had recently become Prime Minister for the third time. On 24 October he delivered the first Romanes Lecture, taking as his subject 'Mediaeval Universities'. Sir Charles Oman, then a young Fellow of All Souls (where Gladstone had been an honorary fellow since 1858), was, as we have noticed, an undergraduate admirer of Christopher. " I had been a pretty regular attendant at Canon Christopher's Saturday evenings . . ."

[1]They may be compared with the uncritical references to Chamberlain's character in *In West Oxford,* edited by T. W. Squires (1928).

he reiterates, in *Memories of Victorian Oxford*. In another book of reminiscences, *Things I Have Seen*, published in 1933, he recalled an incident which for a short time, and in spite of Christopher's disapproval of Gladstone's Home Rule policy for Ireland, which he regarded as favouring popery, brought the veterans together.

"Mr. Gladstone spoke from a desk placed on a low dais, erected for him on the floor of the Sheldonian Theatre. In the front row of listeners was a very aged[1] and much respected Evangelical clergyman, Canon Christopher, of St. Aldate's. Christopher was almost absolutely deaf, but retained some touch on the sounds of the world by means of a very large and long ear trumpet, well known to the entire University. After straining his hearing for five minutes, and finding that he was getting no profit from the lecture, the good old canon took a most extraordinary step. Lifting up the chair on which he was sitting, a solid one, such as is prepared for magnates of the front row, he brought it forward to the very foot of Mr. Gladstone's pulpit, and mounted upon it in his gown, bringing his ear trumpet to within two feet of the lecturer's mouth. The effect was as if he was levelling a big bell-mouthed blunderbuss at Mr. Gladstone's head, so large was the instrument. And this seems to have been the effect upon the lecturer, who stepped back for a moment as if he were expecting to be fired upon. After a short anxious peering downwards, he detected what the machine really was[2] and resumed the lecture with much aplomb."

In the following year a domestic dispute arose in St. Aldate's. A parishioner wrote to the Oxford newspapers attacking the churchwardens for discontinuing an allowance of coal to the poor out of the parish charities. In fact, under a scheme made by the Charity Commissioners in 1886, gifts of coal had been abolished; but from a balance in hand, which was exhausted in 1890, the trustees were allowed to spend a portion on coal. A few weeks before Christmas 1891, the trustees applied to the Commission for leave to spend money on coal. The Commissioners took a month to reply, and when they did so stated that they could not sanction such expenditure except by amendment of the scheme. Christopher, who was chairman of the trustees, made a full statement of the facts (which

[1]Christopher was in fact only 72; Gladstone was 83.
[2]Gladstone's own power of hearing had greatly diminished with old age.

was printed for distribution) at the vestry meeting held in April 1893 and appealed to the anonymous parishioner to declare himself. No one came forward, and what had been expected to be a difficult meeting passed off smoothly enough. Shortly afterwards, however, one of the feoffees objected to the trustees' money being used to pay for church heating in St. Aldate's and St. Matthew's, and this objection was upheld by the Commissioners. An enquiry was ordered and Christopher's administration of the parish charities was generally approved by a visiting adjudicator. Thus even Christopher, though a man of transparent integrity who had been for over thirty years Rector of the parish, and was now well over seventy, was subjected to those occasional attacks from small-minded persons familiar to many incumbents in the Church of England.

It was during the 'nineties that Christopher, who had for so long been a great distributor of tracts, turned his attention to writing a number himself. From time to time he had written one before. *Salvation in the Lord Jesus, from the Dominion of Sin* and *Saved by His Life* had appeared in the 'eighties or earlier as part of an 'Envelope Series'. *An Apostolic Entreaty Earnestly Repeated* ("*Receive not the grace of God in vain*") was published by Hatchard in 1889. A year later Messrs. William Hunt — the publishers of Bishop Ryle's tracts — began to print for Christopher. By the turn of the century they had produced at least a dozen small pink booklets, usually about sixteen pages long, with such titles as *Sowing to the Flesh and its Consequences; Sowing to the Spirit and its Reward* (1890), *The Word that Judgeth* (1892), *Personal Experience* (1894), *Dead unto Sin; Alive unto God* (1896), *Thirst* (1897), and *The Love of God* (1899). This series, however, did not prove as popular as the earlier ones. By 1913 *Salvation in the Lord Jesus* had reached its ninety-fifth thousand. This and *Saved by His Life* were published throughout by Morgan and Scott. The remainder were taken over by Thynne in 1901 and two reached a third edition. Those published by Hunt were of a straight forward Biblical character, carrying the recommendation of Christopher's authorship, but not otherwise distinguishable from many contemporary products of their kind, of which Bishop Ryle's are *par excellence* the prototype. In 1894 Christopher wrote a chapter for a small work entitled *What is the Gospel?* Archdeacon Sinclair of

London, Archdeacon Howell, and Handley Moule, presently Bishop of Durham, were also contributors.

At the annual conference of the West of England Clerical and Lay Association for the Maintenance of Evangelical Principles held in 1893 at Cheltenham, a discussion on 'The Evangelical Teaching of Today; What are its Excellencies and what its Defects?' was opened by request with a paper by Canon Christopher. He had asked a number of lay and clerical friends for their opinions, and these he gave *verbatim*. Sir Arthur Blackwood, Dr. Eugene Stock,[1] M. H. Sutton of Reading, and, among the clergy, E. P. Hathaway, C. J. Casher, W. H. Griffith Thomas, with others, gave their views. There was fairly general agreement upon two points: that evangelical preaching was not sufficiently expository, and that congregations were addressed as if most present were converted whereas formerly they were treated as in the mass unconverted. On the other hand, holiness was stressed more than it had been.

Thus to invite the opinions of others and to present them to his audience was typical of Christopher's highly individual approach. To him it was neither an easy way of dealing with the subject, nor an elementary one. "It is the duty of anyone who has undertaken to open this subject at such an important Conference to endeavour to obtain evidence, from competent witnesses, with regard to the *facts* of the case on which alone a true judgement can be formed . . . I am quite sure that the very words of my correspondents will be far more interesting to you than if I used their letters simply as containing materials for a paper of my own." This was not merely due to humility. It was the way Christopher's mind worked, a mind which had remained in some ways boyish and therefore fresh. He himself felt that the central truth of appropriating the righteousness of God by faith was insufficiently proclaimed. He also emphasized the need for the minister to be filled with the Spirit, and referred to the practice of having a prayer meeting for twenty minutes before evening service at which the people could freely pray for their clergy in the latter's absence. It had lately been adopted at St. Aldate's and was held in the vestry. When printed in pamphlet form Christopher's paper made yet another booklet of this period.

[1]Editorial Secretary of the Church Missionary Society.

In the same year a new evangelical venture was started at Oxford. For some time Francis Chavasse, who in 1889 had exchanged the rectory of St. Peter-le-Bailey for the principalship of Wycliffe Hall, succeeding Canon Girdlestone, had felt that the burden of looking after the undergraduate members of their flocks fell too heavily on the shoulders of the evangelical incumbents in the city. He now proposed that a pastorate, consisting of one or two clergy acceptable to young men, should be established to meet this need. Edward Hathaway took the chair at a meeting called at the headquarters of the Church Missionary Society in Salisbury Square, and Christopher became a member of the committee. The pastorate was duly founded, and for the next few years a young ex-cavalry officer who had taken orders, Henry Gibbon, son of the revered Canon Gibbon of Ripon, worked on his own in this way. He also acted as curate of St. Peter-le-Bailey, where the Hon. William Talbot Rice became rector in the same year. After a while a second chaplain was appointed. How far the early activities of 'the Pastorate' affected Christopher's work is difficult to say. He was ever ready to welcome any new agency for promoting evangelical truth among undergraduates; but it seems improbable that he personally found that 'the Pastorate' made much difference to his labours.

Another event of 1893 was the death of Caroline Nagle-Gillman, Mrs. Christopher's sister. From time to time she had lived in Oxford, as we have seen, with her sister and brother-in-law. She died in September after a lingering illness. This was rather more than a personal grief, for Mrs. Gillman, as she was known, had taken a keen and prayerful interest in St. Aldate's, and her work for and attendance at the annual missionary sale was well known. She had returned to Oxford four years previously in charge of Ada and Elly Christopher, two of the Canon's granddaughters, to live in lodgings with them near the Oxford High School for Girls, which they were to attend. Eleanor Christopher, after two years in Germany and two in Paris, became in 1894 a 'home-student', and during her residence in the university reading modern languages, she lived with her grandparents at St. Aldates' Rectory. She recalled that her grandfather and grandmother always walked by themselves after Sunday morning service in the Broad Walk by Christ Church Meadow, an old-established place of promenade.

One day a violent thunderstorm came on after they had set out. Their return was anxiously awaited at the Rectory. Presently the elderly couple appeared, drenched with rain, but quite unperturbed.

In the year following Caroline Nagle-Gillman's death, Alfred and Maria Christopher celebrated their golden wedding. The marriage had taken place on 15 June 1844. When it became known that this fiftieth anniversary was imminent, the affection in which the Canon was held found expression in considerable activity. A committee was appointed with Griffith Thomas as chairman. A circular was issued to parishioners and members of the congregations of the two churches, and another to friends in the university and throughout the country, the latter being signed by the Regius Professor of Divinity and representative incumbents in Oxford. Nearly three hundred pounds was received in subscriptions.

The golden wedding day passed off most successfully. Many bouquets of flowers, telegrams, and presents were received at the Rectory. After Holy Communion at St. Matthew's at 7.30 a.m., the organist played "the wedding march". At a second administration in St. Aldate's at eleven o'clock, the Rector preached from *Psalm CIII*, and again at a short evening service. By seven o'clock in the evening the Rectory Room was packed with an enthusiastic audience, who rose and cheered when the Canon entered with Mrs. Christopher on his arm. Dr. Ince was in the chair and made a felicitous speech. Other speakers included Pilcher of St. Clement's, Professor Burrows, who had known Maria Christopher from girlhood, Duggan of St. Paul's, and Dr. Legge, the Professor of Chinese. Frank Burden, the Rector's warden, read an address to which were appended more than seven hundred signatures. The chairman then presented the Rector with a cheque for over two hundred and fifty pounds (further subscriptions arrived later) and expressed the hope that he would not transfer it to one of his numerous charities.

Christopher replied at considerable length, detailing a large part of the history of his married life, in a speech full of humour, which at times convulsed his audience. Finally he led those present in prayer and the chairman pronounced the benediction. A vote of thanks to Dr. Ince by Sir William Herschel, one of the secretaries of the Oxford auxiliary of the Bible Society, was dispensed with. The address, read by Burden from a copy, was later given to the

67. ALFRED and MARIA CHRISTOPHER
Golden Wedding, 1894

68. BIBLE STALL, ST. GILES'S FAIR, OXFORD, *c.* 1895
C. J. Casher, curate of St. Aldate's; Miss J. Brooks; ? Miss S. Williams

Rector in book form, with illuminated lettering and miniature photographs of Canon and Mrs. Christopher, as well as of the two churches,[1] on the title-page. The latter remains in the family. A Bible presented to Christopher on his golden wedding day by the Misses Hales, Headmistresses of Ascham School, Oxford, is in the possession of the author.

A few months later Christopher became involved in complaints brought against the conduct of a Church Association colporteur in north Oxfordshire. This man had taken part in religious services in nonconformist chapels and was alleged to have made untenable statements about the sacraments. He had also visited parishes without the consent of their incumbents. Christopher corresponded with the Secretary, who agreed that taking part in nonconformist worship was inadvisable, denied that their agent had disparaged the sacraments, and prevaricated about visiting parishes without permission.

Even Edward Hathaway, to whom Christopher sent the correspondence, could only say, in a letter addressed with delightful economy to 'Revd. Canon Christopher, Oxford', and which throws incidental light on Christopher's character, that "the Secretary's letters ...strike me as eminently foolish. As usual they deal with side issues only, and are stuffed full of considerations with which you are fully acquainted, but are really irrelevant to the matter in hand. His statement that you incur no 'responsibility' through mistaken or reprehensible conduct on the Agent's part is a fallacy. You *are*, while Chairman of the Oxford Association, compromised by it. Forgive me if I point out how that, by reason of the waves of pressing calls on your attention and time succeeding one another with such rapidity, you are often in danger of letting matters of importance drop. Now, for my part, I have a strong conviction that in every issue actually brought before our attention and conscience, it becomes our clear duty *not* to let it pass without our *securing* as far as possible, some ameliorating *results* for the future in connection with the circumstances. So here, take advantage of what has transpired, and *insist* upon regulations for the Van-driver's conduct being put *in print,* and then sent you for approval. If this is not done, or the rules are not altogether satisfactory, and such as you can, if need

[1]That of St. Matthew's is reproduced as Plate 61.

be, quote, I would resign the Oxford chairmanship . . . Do not let the occurrence drift into the past *re infecta*."

Shortly after this, on the fiftieth anniversary of his arrival in Calcutta on 11 November 1844, Christopher had published in *The Record* a lengthy account of La Martinière in relation to contemporary problems of religious instruction, at the time of a London School Board election. Archdeacon Palmer and his brother Lord Selborne were much interested by it. Edward Hathaway was less enthusiastic. He considered that Christopher had been indiscreet in broadcasting the religious arrangements of the school. Again he was the candid friend. "You habitually delight in the *press*, as much as I dislike the publicity now given to every one's affairs by it."

It may fairly be asked how Christopher's undergraduate work — now that he was in his seventy-fifth year — was faring at this period. Napier Malcolm of New College, who took a second class in classical moderations in 1892, was once the recipient of a visit from the Rector of St. Aldate's which Malcolm promptly described to his friends with merriment. Christopher, who had been put on the rather sensitive young man's track by his godly parents, called on him in college, and before conversing with him, locked the door! Nevertheless Malcolm became a Christian not long after, and within a few years was a missionary of the Church Missionary Society in Persia. Another notable missionary of the society was at Oriel about this time. E. A. L. Moore, son of Dr. Edward Moore, Principal of St. Edmund Hall, took a 'first' in classical moderations in 1891. His father was not an evangelical, and it seems likely that Christopher among others would have encouraged him. He went out to India in 1896, and was Bishop of Travancore from 1925 to 1937. George Davey, of the same college, latterly Vicar of Weston-on-the-Green, near Oxford, wrote to Christopher after he had passed on to Wycliffe Hall in 1898: " Some of the very happiest memories that dear Cope[1] and I will take from Oxford will be thoughts of the Saturday night meeting which tho' small perhaps, yet at least has been a real blessing to *two* who like to be present whenever possible."

In the middle 'nineties, however, men like Temple Gairdner, afterwards a well-known missionary in Cairo, and J. H. Oldham, whose

[1]C. E. Cope of Wadham, afterwards Vicar of Christ Church, Stone.

conversion in 1892 we have already noticed, later Secretary of the International Missionary Council, were both up at Christopher's own college, Trinity, and with them are associated names like those of W. E. S. Holland of Magdalen, who presently did notable work in India, and Paget Wilkes, a scholar of Lincoln, co-founder of the Japan Evangelistic Band. But though Gairdner and Holland, for example, were both presidents of the Oxford Inter-Collegiate Christian Union, we do not find in the biographies of Gairdner or Wilkes any mention of Christopher or St. Aldate's. It is true that the authors have not associated them with any place of worship in the city; and that Holland, and Guy Warman of Pembroke, afterwards Bishop of Manchester, are known to have helped at St. Matthew's. It is true that Christopher's Saturday meetings had a place on the terminal card of the Christian Union, and that he himself was patron of their Missionary Union. Nevertheless we are left with the impression that some of the leading evangelical undergraduates were found elsewhere on Sundays. This is confirmed by Dr. Oldham, who recalls that he and his friends went sometimes to St. Aldate's, while attending St. Peter-le-Bailey at least as frequently. But a freshman of 1894 who afterwards distinguished himself in the schools by taking 'firsts' in history and theology, who became secretary of the Inter-Collegiate Christian Union, and who was destined to succeed Christopher as rector, George Foster-Carter of Brasenose, retains vivid memories of the hospitality which was still dispensed to undergraduates by Canon and Mrs. Christopher.

"My first meal in Oxford was at St. Aldate's Rectory . . . The scenes since have become familiar, but to the boy who had just left school, and had mainly come in contact with the normal and the 'proper' clergyman, they were at once novel and arresting . . . That very dark dining room, looking out on to the narrow street, with the high-walled houses opposite, made more sombre by the most dismal of wallpapers; the thin fragile hostess, like a piece of delicate china, with the early-Victorian curls and cap, and the whispering voice coming, as it seemed, from far away; the host at the other end of the table, so absolutely the complement of her, with a face so full of sunshine that even the dusk of that dining room was forgotten; the ceaseless fund of conversation, which had perforce to be a monologue, because of a deafness almost beyond cure of the ever-ready ear trumpet; the long grace, so long that sometimes the viands got cold, yet so real that only the mere eater could easily be offended at it, the stories of Henry Venn, of Hedley Vicars,[1] of Henry Martyn, or of some 'soldier of the cross', which were the inevitable relish of the meal — all these things are clear in memory still. The talk in the study followed; it was, as always was the *tête-à-tête* with him, a triangular conversation. Another Presence was intensely real, the long prayer with which it ended was so exactly and quaintly a talk . . . with One whose friendship was such a vivid, close, personal thing that one could not but be reminded of...Moses' intercourse of old, who spoke to God 'as a man speaketh face to face with his friend'. The study itself almost asks for description: hopeless disorder, yet with a method in its madness; ingress and egress almost barred by a pile of tracts or booklets; tomes of Puritan and evangelical divinity, somewhat forbidding in their aspect, lining the well-stocked shelves. A capacious cupboard, with innumerable pigeon-holes, from each of which some tract found its way into pocket (if pockets were large enough for such a load) or into hand before the interview was concluded. It was 'sui generis', that study! . . . It must weep for the days when it was redolent of India, of Charles Simeon, and of Ryle's tracts, and dispensed its soul-medicines . . . far and wide."

One of the many other matters which claimed Christopher's attention at this time was the Grandpont school, which was opened in 1894. In May of the previous year, he had had to issue a further appeal, of which a copy is preserved in the Bodleian Library, in order to bring in the last few hundred pounds needed towards the total of over £2,000. Bishop Stubbs had written: "I think that you generally do obtain the success, and I am sure that you will have the blessing." That both followed, we have already noticed. Since Christopher had rebuilt St. Aldates' schools in 1865, not only had the number of children in the parish considerably increased, but the civil authorities had begun to take a more active and demanding part in primary education. Thus by the early 'nineties their minutes show that the managers found themselves faced with urgent requests for improvements and enlargements. They therefore decided that the only course was to add the infants' accommodation to that used

[1]A Christian officer killed at the siege of Sebastopol.

by the older boys and girls, and to transfer all infants to Grandpont. This led, in the autumn of 1895, to another domestic crisis in the parish.

The parents on the city side of Folly Bridge were soon up in arms against their small children having to walk so far. Correspondence in *The Oxford Times* tended to exculpate Christopher. 'Parent' wrote "...who is the originator of this plan? I cannot think it is the good old rector, whose kind heart always seems to speak sympathy for the weak, and especially for little children!" 'Right against Might' protested in *The Oxford Chronicle* "Canon Christopher must now know how determined the parents of St. Aldate's are not to send their infants to Grandpont...He must think, too, that he has been wrongly advised. Why does he not take the reins into his own hands once more ...?" A public meeting of protest was to be held on 15 September. "I ought not to interfere", wrote Hathaway, "in a matter, the full details of which I have not mastered. But is it altogether wise, that the Managers should all be absent from Monday's meeting? As the proposed change affects the poor and their children, may not such absence be misconstrued?". Christopher himself was the only manager present at St. Aldates' schools when the younger children were directed, through their mothers, to the new infant school.[1] Superficially this action doubtless seemed unjust, but Christopher believed it was the wisest course, and he was not to be intimidated.

Archdeacon Palmer died in October 1895 and an illustration of Christopher's spirit is to be seen in his appreciation of a man of a different school of thought. As Fellow of Balliol, Corpus Professor of Latin, and since 1878 Archdeacon of Oxford, Palmer had lived in the city for fifty years. Preaching in St. Aldate's, Christopher spoke of the "powerful intellects and the great learning of those two remarkable brothers, Lord Selborne and Archdeacon Palmer." After a warm reference to the efforts of the Archdeacon in connection with the Revised Version of the New Testament, he continued: "God be praised for the grace given him to adorn the doctrines of God his Saviour, by his humility, his unselfishness, and his usefulness, for all the readiness with which he gave time to help

[1]Separate infants' school log books remain in the possession of St. Matthews' parish, the first from 1871 to 1895, the second from 1894 to 1959, when the school was closed. These show that Christopher was a regular visitor until October 1904.

his brethren with his advice and influence. I have had reason to be grateful to him for many years for the help which he gave the Church Missionary Society at its anniversaries; for liberal contribution to the building work to be done in this parish; for accessibility whenever I needed his advice; for his entire freedom from the prejudices of party spirit; for his brotherly kindness under all circumstances. Such a life of honoured usefulness as that which closed, to the great grief of many last week, glorifies God."

In the following year Howard Colclough left St. Matthew's on appointment as incumbent of St. Thomas's, Edinburgh, an important evangelical outpost in the northern capital. When he came to St. Matthew's there were three or four church workers. He left behind nearly a hundred. In the Sunday School there were over two hundred scholars. He could feel that "God has used me, and made St. Matthew's the birthplace of souls." Christopher now desired to work the two parts of the parish together as far as possible. The Revd. G. E. Badger was appointed curate of St. Aldate's, and sermons were to be preached in rotation at the two churches by the Rector and his three curates, except that Badger would normally preach once each Sunday at Grandpont.

This marked a change in the administration of St. Matthew's. Hitherto the church had been run on independent lines, as though it were a parish church. But Christopher foresaw that this might make trouble for his successor — as indeed it did — if the church became too independent, and at a meeting in St. Matthews' vestry on Easter Tuesday 1896, he felt obliged to risk some unpopularity by instituting a church council instead of the 'vestry' which had hitherto existed. St. Matthew's, he pointed out, was a chapel-of-ease in St. Aldates' parish, and the only legal vestry was that which met in the parish church. He therefore nominated Job Gray[1] as his chapel warden, and informed the meeting that, at a later date, after time for consideration, they could elect a second warden and six sidesmen.[2] Badger preached his first sermon in St. Matthew's on 17 November. He had taken a second class in theology in 1893, as a

[1]Gray was an experienced church officer, who had been churchwarden of St. Aldate's as far back as 1868.

[2]The minutes of "Vestry Meetings" from 1897 to 1905, usually presided over by Christopher, are preserved among the parochial records of St. Matthew's. Previous minutes (1891-96), in a "small book", appear to be no longer extant.

non-collegiate man, and for the intervening two years had been curate of Holy Trinity, Bordesley, Birmingham.[1] In 1897 he returned to Birmingham as curate of Aston, and in 1900 he became Vicar of Bishop Ryder's Church, Birmingham, where he remained until 1933, becoming an honorary canon of Birmingham in 1925.

The year 1896 was to bring even bigger changes. Griffith Thomas accepted the important ministry at St. Paul's, Portman Square, London, where the congregation included many influential laity. Without his curate's knowledge, Christopher arranged for a visit from and an interview with a representative of the trustees, among whom was Lord Kinnaird, and when the offer came, urged him to accept the charge. Griffith Thomas did not wish to leave St. Aldate's, and had already declined more than one opportunity; but, he said, " If you push me out, I must go." Christopher was rightly anxious to launch his colleague — who had taken a first class in theology, as his rector had predicted, in 1895, after winning the Junior Hall-Houghton Septuagint Prize in the previous year — on a wider sphere of usefulness. No less than eight hundred people were present in the Examination Schools for a farewell gathering, and some handsome presentations were made.

One of Thomas's particular interests had been the Sunday Schools, of which he had been superintendent, and which he left with a staff of over sixty. This meant that in the parish as a whole, including St. Matthew's, there were at this time ninety Sunday School teachers, a strength which diminished only slightly during the remaining period of Christopher's incumbency. At least one of these had given even longer service to the parish than Christopher himself. Miss Ann Cutler was already a Sunday School teacher when Christopher came to St. Aldate's in 1859, and a district visitor from the first to the last day of his tenure of the rectory. When she died in 1907, Christopher wrote " I have closely observed for nearly half a century her consistent stedfast adherence to the Evangelical truths and the holy Precepts of the Bible, which she daily fed upon." With reference to her collecting for the Bible and Jews' Societies he commented, "How many hundreds of miles dear Miss Cutler must have walked for Jesus . . . She is now, we cannot doubt, 'present

[1]This was the church where, in 1879, the Vicar, the Revd. W. R. Enraght, had been condemned by the Dean of Arches for 'ritual' irregularities.

with the Lord,' (2 Cor. v.8). How dear Mrs. Williams[1] will have welcomed her, and those she led by the help of the Holy Spirit through His Word to the Lord Jesus Christ in the Girls' Sunday School, and in the homes of the poor which she visited . . ."

Henceforth, until his return to Oxford in 1905, Griffith Thomas contributed to the St. Aldates' parish magazine as 'London Correspondent'. "All through my nine and a half years in London," wrote Griffith Thomas of his old rector, "it was a privilege to have his friendship and confidence, and his visits to our house were always a great joy . . ." In January 1896 Christopher had been elected one of the few honorary members (who at that time included F. J. Chavasse and H. C. G. Moule, and later Griffith Thomas himself) of the National Club, of which the club-house was then in Whitehall Gardens. His proposer was a Trinity man, the Revd. J. E. Campbell-Colquhoun, who had been up at Oxford just before Christopher came there, and whose father, John Colquhoun, had been one of the original trustees of the Oxford Evangelical Trust. The club, of which Campbell-Colquhoun was chairman, had been founded in 1845 by the sixth Duke of Manchester to promote the protestant interest in parliament, and it was mainly supported, as it still is, by evangelicals. Christopher was re-elected each year until his death. "He was once visiting me in London," Griffith Thomas continued, "and asked the proper cab fare from Paddington to our house. He then gave the cabman something extra together with a tract, 'for' he said, 'you cannot possibly give a tract if you only pay the exact fare.' On . . . similar visits we would go to the door to greet him, but we always had to wait while he gave the cabman the fare, the tip and the tract. He would accompany his gifts with the earnest recommendation to read the tract saying 'It has done me good and it will do you good also.' This, spoken in a loud voice (due to his deafness) could be heard all around as well as by the cabman, whose face clearly showed no little embarrassment. But our beloved friend did not notice, perhaps did not think of this; enough for him to be about his Master's business."

[1]Wife of F. W. Williams, Superintendent of the Industrial School, St. Aldate's.

Chapter XIV

Later Years at Oxford

1896 - 1900

GRIFFITH THOMAS'S successor as senior curate, the Revd. George Stephen Jones, was appointed on the recommendation of the same Welsh clergyman, Archdeacon Howell, as Griffith Thomas himself had been. Jones had for four years been senior curate to D. J. Stather Hunt at St. Paul's, Stratford. "He is a fine hearty fellow" wrote Stather Hunt (who had been nominated to succeed Canon Hoare at Holy Trinity, Tunbridge Wells), in language characteristic of the day, "and distinctly spiritually minded, and very earnest . . . He is an able man all round . . ." Jones had read for orders at St. Aidan's College, Birkenhead. While at St. Aldate's he became a member of Pembroke College and studied for a degree, which he took in 1901 with a second class in theology. He was a good preacher, "full of Celtic fire and enthusiasm," and began a flourishing men's service on Sunday afternoons, which quickly numbered over a hundred.

About this time Christopher was interested in a plan to secure the former dining hall of New Inn Hall, which had been incorporated with Balliol on the death of its last principal in 1887, as a place for holding religious meetings for university men. The scheme was fostered by the Rector of St. Peter-le-Bailey, the Hon. and Revd. W. Talbot Rice, close to whose church the hall was situated. If purchased, the building, with large room above and library with caretaker's rooms below, was to be known as the Bishop Hannington

Memorial Hall, in memory of James Hannington, a St. Mary Hall man whose name as a martyr in Africa was still fresh in the public mind. The total cost would be £4,500. " I am glad you are working for Hannington Hall," Hathaway wrote to Christopher, who presently became a trustee. " To *you* mendicancy must by this time have become a second nature." " *On the understanding* that it should be the place for the Meetings of the Oxford Intercollegiate Christian Union," as Christopher wrote when a dispute arose in 1902, nonconformists worked for the hall as well as churchmen; and the Inter-Collegiate Union itself raised over a thousand pounds. The total cost having been promised, the hall was purchased, and opened by Sir John Kennaway, an old Balliol man who was President of the Church Missionary Society, in January 1897.

Christopher could not but notice that in Oxford high church support for missionary work was hardly forthcoming on a scale comparable even to that of the evangelical minority. As he himself put it: "No one will dispute that Oxford is on the whole, a thoroughly High Church place. Most of the well-to-do people in Oxford are High Church, if they are Church people at all. But it is a fact that in the years 1895–1896, three poor parishes in Oxford in charge of Evangelical Incumbents, raised more than twice as much as all the parishes in Oxford, rich and poor together, raised for the S.P.G. . . . I know enough of High Churchmen to believe that if the facts were thoroughly brought before the minds and consciences of rich High Churchmen, the S.P.G. would be enabled to send out twice as many Missionaries as it sustains at the present moment."

St. Aldates' parish had already provided, in Christopher's time, three missionaries from its senior Sunday School teachers. The Revd. J. W. Tims had gone from St. Aldate's to the Church Missionary College at Islington, where he trained for orders and became a missionary in the north-west of Canada, among Blackfoot Indians. In 1895 he was appointed by his bishop Archdeacon of Macleod, and ten years later he became a doctor of divinity of St. John's, Manitoba. The Revd. J. J. Bambridge worked in India, where he was Principal of the Church Missionary Society's school at Karachi and a Fellow of Bombay University, before returning home to a living in Canterbury. His contemporary, the Revd. Llewelyn Lloyd of China, has already been mentioned. These two likewise prepared for

69. G. E. BADGER
Curate, St. Aldate's, Oxford, 1895-97

G. S. JONES
Curate, St. Aldate's, 1896–1901

C. J. CASHER
Hon. curate, St. Aldate's, 1889–1905

A. M. W. CHRISTOPHER
Rector; *c.* 1897

70. MISSIONARY BREAKFAST, OXFORD TOWN HALL, 1899

Dowager Lady Buxton, Mrs. Christopher, A. M. W. Christopher standing,

missionary ordination at the Islington college. By the time Christopher resigned in 1905, three more St. Aldates' Sunday School teachers had gone to the mission field.

In 1896 Christopher adapted for St. Aldate's a comparatively new idea then being pressed from headquarters in connection with the 'Three Years Enterprise' of the Church Missionary Society. Eighty recruits were sailing for the foreign field that summer, and as a result of an appeal to individuals, associations, and parishes, all were provided for by a scheme for supporting 'Our Own Missionary'. One of these was Edmund Elwin, a Merton man who had been curate to the Hon. W. Talbot Rice at St. Peter-le-Bailey since his ordination in 1894, and about to proceed to Sierra Leone. He went supported to some extent by all the evangelical parishes of Oxford, but mainly by St. Peter's, though substantially by St. Aldate's. The choice was more than justified by the fact that in 1902 Elwin was made Bishop of Sierra Leone, in succession to Taylor Smith, only eight years after taking his degree. It then became necessary to appoint another 'Own Missionary', and the Revd. F. W. Hinton, formerly a classical scholar of St. John's, who had also been curate of St. Peter-le-Bailey, was selected. This time — no doubt to Christopher's personal satisfaction — India was the field of work, in which Hinton remained for many years, becoming a Canon of Lucknow.

To interest high churchmen and others in the missionary cause was one reason why Christopher invited members of all schools of thought to his missionary breakfasts, which at this period were more popular and largely attended than ever. George Pilkington, Cambridge classical scholar and missionary in Uganda, was in 1896 the first layman, and the first young man, to address those assembled. No one, Dr. Stock understood, had ever made a deeper impression than Pilkington, "just because, while manifesting intellectual ability and culture, he spoke from his heart in, and of, the power of the Holy Ghost." Griffith Thomas felt that "His simple and artless narrative of spiritual need and spiritual revival among the missionaries in Uganda, as told to the 'grave and reverend seignors' of Oxford, was something to be remembered for life." The Canon himself was particularly impressed by the way in which the seniors valued the breakfasts. A year later, at the age of thirty-three, Pilkington was killed in Africa. Other speakers since the breakfast was last mentioned had included the Archbishop of York, Dr. Thomson (1890), the Bishop of Exeter, Dr. Bickersteth (1892), Dr. Bruce of Persia (1894), and Bishop Ridley of Caledonia again (1895). Bishop Tucker of Uganda, whom Christopher had baptised as an undergraduate, was the speaker in 1902. Eugene Stock was present on this occasion, and heard the new Bishop of Oxford, Dr. Paget, move a vote of thanks. " It is well known ", Stock recounted in his *Recollections*, "what a remarkable gathering this is of leading men of all schools and parties, as well as of undergraduates." Bishop Mitchinson, Master of Pembroke, said to him on that morning, " You know, this is a sort of Noah's Ark, clean and unclean beasts!" Thomas Alvarez, secretary of the Niger Mission of the Church Missionary Society, who had been an undergraduate at Jesus College in the early 'nineties, was another relatively junior speaker in 1904. One of the last experiences of Bishop Ingham in connection with Christopher was when the Canon told him he was going to attain to " the blue ribbon of Missionary privilege " — " a thing to live for." The Bishop was to be asked to address the missionary breakfast! In fact he did so twice, as a Far Eastern tour secured him a second benefit. " It was a severe ordeal and a great privilege."

During the concluding fifteen years of Christopher's ministry at St. Aldate's the pattern of visiting preachers perceptibly altered. The service registers show that he relied more on his curates, notably Griffith Thomas, Casher, and Jones. The plan of inviting evangelical leaders to fill the pulpit, especially in term, was no longer followed. Distinguished visiting preachers were still to be heard, however, from time to time, — from the Archbishop of York, Dr. Thomson, in 1890, to the Bishop of Down and Connor, Dr. Welland, in 1902; and still an occasional missionary bishop: Peel of Mombasa, Reeve of Mackenzie River, and Ingham, formerly of Sierra Leone. Men like Canon Gibbon of Ripon also preached for the Church Missionary Society, a service performed in 1894 by Dr. Ince, Regius Professor of Divinity. In the same year came Taylor Smith, afterwards Bishop of Sierra Leone, and well known as Chaplain-General during the First World War. Evan Hopkins and Edward Moore took a series of 'convention' services, on 'Keswick lines', in 1895. Stuart Holden, destined to succeed Griffith Thomas at St. Paul's, Portman

Square, was much appreciated in 1904. One or two unexpected names occur, for example H. D. A. Major in 1905, then reading theology at Exeter College but already in orders, afterwards a leading modernist. And there was one exception to the relative absence of leading evangelical preachers. During the last ten years of Christopher's incumbency, Dr. C. H. H. Wright, the Bampton Lecturer of 1878, whom Christopher was to be responsible for securing to the work of the Protestant Reformation Society, was a regular visitor to St. Aldate's. Beginning in the period when he was Grinfield Lecturer on the Septuagint, 1893–7, from 1899 Wright sometimes preached as often as two or three times a year. In this respect he succeeded to the mantle of Bishop Ryle.

The select preachers before the university for these years continued to include evanglical names — Dr. H. C. G. Moule of Cambridge, afterwards Bishop of Durham, in 1894, Archdeacon Sinclair of London, a Balliol graduate, in 1897, Archdeacon Diggle of Westmoreland, a former lecturer at Merton, in 1899, and Dr. F. J. Chavasse, Bishop of Liverpool, a second time in 1900. Both Diggle and Chavasse had regularly sat under Christopher as undergraduates, as is likely had Sinclair.

Although Christopher, like many clergymen, was inclined to feel that he had little time to attend conferences, he did in fact — as will have been apparent in these pages already — go fairly regularly to one conference or another. At the Islington Clerical Conference of 1897, of which the high-light was an address by Prebendary Wace[1]— then Principal of King's College, London — on 'The Main Purpose and General Character of the Thirty-nine Articles' — " strongly Protestant in tone, it made a deep impression " — Christopher was ready with practical suggestions for disseminating the teaching of the papers read. After some reference to the booklets giving a full account of the conference proceedings, reprinted from a supplement to *The Record*, Bishop Ryle's tracts and books were strongly recommended. All this was in accordance with custom and character.

[1]Another speaker was Canon G. S. Streatfield, who (like Wace) had probably been in touch with Christopher when an undergraduate at Oxford, having taken a 'first' in law and history from Corpus Christi College in 1866. At this later time he was Vicar of Emmanuel, Streatham, and known outside evangelical circles as author of *Lincolnshire and the Danes.*

"People often smiled," wrote one of Christopher's curates, "at his constant and earnest recommendation of books and pamphlets and his urgent entreaties at the Islington Clerical Meeting to purchase *The Record* with the reports of those gatherings. Indeed, on occasions he himself felt it necessary to disclaim financial connection with that paper. But all these appeals were part of the Canon's intense desire to spread the truth as he conceived of it, feeling confident that 'truth is mighty and prevails.' He was sure that if people would only read, they would be instructed in truth and safeguarded against error, and it may be questioned whether, since his departure, we have had anything like the same wise and valuable counsel from those in public places. There are plenty of useful works that only need to have attention called to them to prove afresh their worth."

As far back as 1892, Edward Hathaway had written from Holbrook Rectory: "I really have not got a minute for thought outside my parish. There are so many sick to see. But, in fact, my life's work is all but done. This fierce rheumatism at the base of the brain is too masterful now." Hathaway resigned Holbrook the same year and retired, after a short interval, to Tunbridge Wells. His concern, however, for the Oxford Fund was as strong as ever, as business-like letters to Christopher about the stipend of St. Aldate's alone would show. When making official returns Christopher had to be watched. "You are not called upon," Hathaway wrote in 1894, "nor are you at liberty, in replying to the questions, to make any mention of the subsidy from the Oxford Fund. When you were good enough to think of accepting poor St. Aldate's, I explained to you in writing that the contribution was to you personally as a private present, and in no way to the benefice — and, more than that, that you were distinctly to understand that whatever you might receive from me would never be anything but a private present that might terminate anyhow, for a repetition of which even from one half year to another you must not reply or reckon upon."

Ten days later he was obliged to write again. "In your return of the income of St. Aldate's you must *not* include the dividend, or principal, of the £470 India 3½ per ann. stock. It is a private fund . . . against which your benefice has no sort of claim. It has been lately increased to £500 stock, and it is because the stock-holders have just offered it to the Ecclesl. Commrs. to be met by an augmentation from their Common Fund, that the Bishop has issued his inquiry." Perhaps going through old papers, in 1895, Hathaway found and sent to Christopher his letter of 1864 already referred to, and also Nicholas Moody's letter of 1856, quoted previously: "His *information* that St. Aldate's is 'an important but poor parish near Ch. Ch.' will amuse you. In the 40 years what hath not God wrought!" Towards the end of May 1896, Christopher received a letter marked 'Private'.

T. Wells,
May 19, 1896

Dear Brother,

In the last fortnight premonitory indications have been graciously given me that, in all probability, my Home-call is near at hand.

Brain and heart are, seemingly, both giving way, as shown by faintings in which however I have not yet lost consciousness. You will be envying me.

I mark this 'private' because I am desirous that my wife shall not be alarmed, nor receive inquiries about me that she must needs answer.

You know what I owe you — and how all these years your unbroken affection has been a chief joy and stay of my life.

My physician tells me that my heart's action is stronger than I think. But as to the brain and its symptoms, perhaps I know more than he. Anyway 'all is well'. And now to business.

The question seems urgent — who will become *working* secretary of the Oxford Fund?

Fox[1] with Barlow[2] consent to be Trustees. Their names will increase the confidence of contributors and the public. But of course neither of them has time to write even a single letter for it.

[1]Prebendary H. E. Fox, Honorary Secretary of the Church Missionary Society, Hathaway's curate at St. Ebbe's 1869-73.

[2]Dr. W. H. Barlow, Vicar of Islington, Hathaway's immediate successor as Rector of St. Ebbe's, 1873-5, and afterwards Dean of Peterborough, when he was select preacher at Oxford 1902-4.

But the Fund can only be kept up by continuous begging, month in and month out, the whole year round. Nearly half the income comes in *donations,* and these as a rule are not repeated.

Fox has suggested *Thomas* to act as the Trustees' deputy.

Is he the man? His being resident in London is in his favour — and his connection with Portman Square Chapel will give him access to the purses of well-to-do people.

Has he the sustained diligence, and business habits, and accuracy, and the beggar's genius, and savoir faire which an unabashed and steadfast mendicant requires for the special post?

Barnes-Lawrence[1] is out of the question — if only because he is one of the 2 nominal Secretaries of the *Pastorate* — and it and the Oxford *Fund* now frequently clash.

On your death, St. Aldate's must, I feel, cease to draw from the 'Fund'— though I shrink from the thought of your exodus. Who, as your successor, can find income to support the expenses of, and pay for, 2 churches?

Ever yrs. affecty,
Edw. P. Hathaway

Almost unaided, Hathaway had raised for the Oxford Fund since 1857 some £40,000. Christopher's stipend had never in fact fallen short by a penny of the additional £360 a year promised him in 1859.[2] It is hardly necessary to add that without this his work at Oxford would not have been possible. Griffith Thomas did succeed Hathaway as secretary, and for a number of years the fund continued to make up, though in declining degrees, the stipends of the Oxford evangelical livings. After Griffith Thomas's removal to Canada in 1910, the fund languished still further, in spite of a legacy of £3,000 from Mrs. Hathaway in 1909. A small sum was still paid yearly to the Rector of St. Aldate's in the 'twenties; and the fund was finally extinguished — after lying dormant for many

[1]A. E. Barnes-Lawrence of Worcester College, Vicar of St. Michael's, Blackheath.

[2]From relatively small beginnings in 1868, Hathaway had built up an endowment fund for the benefice of St. Aldate's which at his death brought in some £80 *per annum,* and attracted a substantial grant from the Ecclesiastical Commissioners in addition. Through his agency, several capital gifts had been made direct to the Commissioners for the same purpose.

years — as late as 1957, by which time the need of it in its old form had finally passed away, just over a hundred years after its inception.[1]

In August 1896, Hathaway wrote briefly to Christopher, who was spending his usual holiday in the Isle of Man: " I am in sad pain, as always now. Pray that I may be sustained, and kept patient." After his death in 1897, Christopher wrote: "No words of grateful love can adequately express what I myself owe to dear Hathaway for his unfailing, most brotherly and unselfish help in all the difficult work of St. Aldate's during the last thirty-eight years." His loss was not made the less sorrowful by the tragic circumstance that the cause of death was serious burns sustained when Hathaway's bed-hangings caught fire while he was reading in bed. But now the devoted heart, the precise mind, and the handsome person of his "dearest friend" were at rest. Greatly contrasting in their disposition — the one over-flowing with single-minded love towards his fellow-men, the other by nature reserved and critical, but both characters made new by the Holy Spirit — they had been united in a great common love for Christ and a just appreciation of each other's qualities.

It seems probable that it was Griffith Thomas's separation from Christopher in 1896 which brought into being the idea of a biography. Christopher agreed to supply notes " for the sake of accuracy, perhaps I may venture to add interest & usefulness. There are certainly some . . . which may glorify God's loving Providence." Hathaway was an obvious source of information about the evangelical cause at Oxford during the period in question; but he was already a sick man. Thomas had proposed to write to him for a detailed account. Christopher was obliged to say, in view of what Hathaway had lately written to him, " he would think me cruel if I encouraged you to write to him as you propose. If you write at all it must be your *own* doing. If you do write to him you had better not ask for 'a few pages,' but only for a few lines. I think it will shock him the idea of anything whatever being published about me even after my death. And that I should approve the idea

[1]It is remarkable that in the same year, 1957, the Rector of St. Ebbe's, the Revd. B. C. Gough, was moved to open a fund associated with Hathaway's old church, in connection with a prayer fellowship called 'The Friends of St. Ebbe's', which performs the same function as the Oxford Fund, namely, to provide a more adequate evangelical ministry among undergraduates.

and supply notes to help to carry it out will seem to him the very opposite of Christian modesty. I doubt whether you will get a line from him unless it be a rebuke to yourself and to me. Yet as he is 78 & in such poor health there is no time for delay if you do it. His intellect is as clear as ever *at present,* but he may soon get worse in body & mind & go where there is no post needed."

Christopher himself spent a small part of his visit to Castletown in 1896 recording incidents and facts. Four years later to the very day — such is the pace of literary efforts amidst parochial calls — Christopher wrote from the same place: "I only have a general idea from a memory which has been at work four score years, of what I have written to you already. I may therefore repeat. But this will not matter much, as *you* need not repeat when you come to use the notes. But *at once,* before you leave on the 29th the hospitable, genial, and spiritually-healthy Deanery of St. David's[1], write to Mrs. Hathaway[2] 10 Calverley Park Tunbridge Wells & ask her to note down for you any facts of interest connected with her beloved husband's good work for Oxford. For Example (1) *the date* of the only Committee Meeting held in his Chambers 4 Old Square Lincoln's Inn[3] which decided to try & obtain for Evangelical men some of the Incumbencies of parish Churches in Oxford & left Hathaway to do it all . . . Obtain *at once* from Chancellor Allan Smith[4] whilst you have the unique opportunity, all the facts you can, about Canon Linton's appointment to St. Peter le Bailey in 1856 & his character & work in Oxford. He may require to refer to notes at home. Do not leave him without a list of questions to be answered. You have for three days more an opportunity which may never occur again. Ascertain that each of my statements about his late father in law[5] is correct . . . Suggest at once points on which I might write."

[1]Archdeacon Howell, Griffith Thomas's original sponsor to Christopher, had become Dean of St. David's.

[2]The second Mrs. Hathaway was a daughter of Captain H. Woods, R.N., of Littlegate House, Oxford—which the Hathaways gave as a vicarage for Holy Trinity parish and now belongs to St. Aldate's.

[3]This invitation appears to have been, however, to attend a meeting at 9, Lincoln's Inn Fields. Hathaway's chambers were in fact at 5, Old Square.

[4]One of Christopher's undergraduate supporters in the 'sixties, then Chancellor, and afterwards Dean, of St. David's.

[5]Canon Linton.

Most of the questions Thomas was to ask Mrs. Hathaway, to which Christopher himself apparently did not know the answers, are resolved by reference to the papers of the Oxford Fund preserved by Hathaway and handed on to Griffith Thomas. A few queries — such as who else attended the inaugural meeting besides those already mentioned — remain unanswered. Thus sixty-nine years have elapsed since Griffith Thomas began to gather essential material for a life of his beloved rector. Some years before the Canon's death he appealed for information in the church newspapers. He repeated this request in 1913. The result is seen in the many personal reminiscences, both by Christopher himself, and of others about him, which are scattered throughout these pages.

One of the replies refers to this period of the Canon's life. The writer, Miss Lucy Harvey, alludes to his brother Leonard. " It gave me great joy to read in the 'Christian' that you are going to write a book on Canon Christopher's life. I had the privilege of living as cook housekeeper to his brother General Christopher at Ealing for over 12 years and during that time it was with great pleasure that we looked forward to the short visits of Canon Christopher and especially to the way he used to conduct the prayers morning and evening. His presence was a great help spiritually. General Christopher once asked me what I thought of him. I replied just a living epistle. On one occasion he came for just a few hours. He came into the kitchen to see others and myself and he asked if he should pray with us. We replied yes. That is over 12 years ago but that short impressive prayer lives with me to this day and I wondered if other ministers of the Gospel would work like that what a great power for good they would be . . ."

General Christopher, the Canon's favourite and younger brother, died in 1901. His wife, whom he had met on board ship with Alfred and Maria Christopher in 1844, died just before Christopher left St. Aldate's.[1] But a loss which came home to the Canon perhaps even more forcibly was that of George Seton Christopher, his elder grandson, a midshipman in the Royal Naval Reserve, who was twenty when he died at Saigon, Indo-China, in 1897. Only Charles Christopher, aged ten, remained to carry on the male line. The Canon's

[1]They have now no male descendant, and their principal representatives in the female line have no relics of Canon Christopher or his near relations.

younger son, who in 1893 took the name of Seton-Christopher, was childless. He had married, in 1892, Melesina Chenevix-Trench,[1] a niece of Francis Chenevix Trench, at whose rectory at Islip Christopher had been wont to attend in its early days the meetings of the Oxford Prayer Union. She was a niece also of Archbishop Trench of Dublin, whom the Canon had met as examining chaplain to Bishop Sumner of Winchester in 1850. Her sister Ellen was the wife of Algernon Coote, a well-known evangelical layman, who presently succeeded as premier baronet of Ireland.

Christopher lost his surviving sisters before their brother Leonard's death left him for twelve years the last member of his generation alive. Selina, widow of General Thomson, died in 1896 — only two years before her elder son — and Isabella, at the age of ninety-four, two years later. Both ended their days at Chiswick, at Bellevue, between Morton House and the parish church, where Miss Christopher's large annual gathering of nephews and neices and any friends they liked to bring to lunch and watch the Boat Race was a family occasion for several decades. The Canon never forgot her influence upon him as a boy and young man. Nelson Robinson, Christopher's brother-in-law, died in Canada in 1893. Six years later Christopher officiated at the wedding of Cosby Christopher, grandson of his wife's brother Wilmot, when he married Miss Sybil Pile, now Mrs. Cyril Davis. Their only son, Colonel Jack Christopher, is the present representative of Maria Christopher's side of the alliance, the Hadley branch of the family. The eldest branch, descended from Christopher's father's elder brother, is now represented by Mr. John Christopher, grandson of the architect of the rebuilt St. Aldate's and of St. Matthew's. There is no male descendant of the Christophers of Chiswick.

In 1898 St. John's, Liverpool, was pulled down to make way for 'city improvements'. The last incumbent was Dr. C. H. H. Wright, a well-known authority on the Reformation. Dr. Wright had been Bampton Lecturer in 1878, Grinfield Lecturer on the Septuagint, another Oxford appointment, from 1893 to 1897, and, as we have seen, a regular preacher at St. Aldate's. Christopher took an early opportunity of writing to the press urging that the services of Dr.

[1]Their portraits may be seen in Chelsea Town Hall. Alfred Seton-Christopher was Mayor of Chelsea 1925-6.

Wright be secured for the Protestant Reformation Society. As a result an invalid clergyman whom Christopher never met gave anonymously £250 *per annum* towards a suitable salary, and other friends made up the required amount. Punctually every quarter for five years a cheque arrived at St. Aldates' Rectory for Christopher to pass on. It then became necessary, owing to the death of the donor, to make a further appeal. "God can use the feeblest of His servants in His work if the effort made pleases Him", wrote Christopher. "That letter . . . from the Rector of a poor Oxford parish was made to be worth £1,250 to the merciful work of the Protestant Reformation Society . . . And now who, among those saved by grace, will take the place of the generous brother who is 'absent from the body and present with the Lord'?". This appeal appeared in *The Record,* supported by one from the Dean of Norwich, Dr. Lefroy, a former Liverpool incumbent. Dean Lefroy had originally been a broad churchman, but had become an evangelical through the preaching of D. L. Moody.

"The Church of England has been sustained, especially in the ancient University city of Oxford, by the spiritual perception, conversation, advocacy, and untiring diligence of my venerable friend, Canon Christopher. His work is as varied as it is strong and true. It may be doubted if any portion of his labour has been more fertile than that which, through his persuasive pleading in your journal, enabled the Protestant Reformation Society to secure the services of the Rev. C. H. H. Wright, D.D. . . . Shall the disciples of that ever-blessed and adorable Redeemer, Whose transforming and restoring work is shrivelled by Rationalism and stifled by Romanism, deny us £250 per annum to enable us to continue a line of defence which was never more necessary than it is today?". Another anonymous donor, whose name was not known even to Christopher, forthwith promised £250 a year, sending bank notes to the Rectory each quarter.

Christopher's devotion to the objects of the Bible Society was marked in 1898 by his election as a vice-president. In February he received a letter from Lord Harrowby, the President, who wrote from Switzerland: "I rejoice to be the Committee's mouthpiece in writing to so valued a friend of so many years." Christopher had been secretary of the Oxford auxiliary of the Bible Society since

October 1859, and the Earl's letter, expressing the committee's gratitude "for all the invaluable assistance you have given for so many years," gave the Canon much pleasure. He had already been since 1888 a vice-president of the Church Missionary Society. Griffith Thomas was wont to say that if Christopher's heart could be seen the letters 'C.M.S.' and 'B.S.' would surely be found imprinted on it. Christopher himself recorded: "At the Diocesan Conference held in December 1895 in the Sheldonian Theatre at Oxford, when the advocates of the reunion of Christendom were looking for a possible reunion with Rome, I earnestly invited them to show their desire for reunion by attending the Annual Meeting of the Bible Society in Oxford."

By this time modernist higher criticism of the Bible, after twenty years of controversy — Dean Burgon and Canon Liddon remaining to the last as determined defenders of the traditional doctrine of inspiration as any evangelical — had gained fairly wide acceptance. But, Christopher noted in 1900, while staying in the Isle of Man: "We have not waited in vain for the Providence of God to raise up in Oxford itself men qualified to meet the erroneous teaching of the day. There is only one man in Oxford whose powers and learning have been sufficient to gain for him the Ireland, the Hertford, the Craven, the Boden Sanskrit, the Pusey and Ellerton and the Kennicott Hebrew and the Theological Scholarships."[1] David Margoliouth, after taking a 'double-first' in classics and being elected a Fellow of New College in 1881, had succeeded Robert Gandell as Laudian Professor of Arabic in 1889, a chair which he held until 1937. "That man of surpassing learning," Christopher continued, "has devoted his life to the defence of the Bible against the mistaken attacks which have had the effect of lowering its authority as the Word of God in the minds of many."

Believing it would be an advantage in a work to which he felt called, Margoliouth decided to take holy orders. On the title of his fellowship he could be ordained by any bishop he chose to ask. Christopher's friend Ryle was still Bishop of Liverpool, though in the last year of his life. Ryle had long been regarded by Margoliouth with respect and confidence "for his unflinching boldness in his declaration of the Evangelical truths clearly taught by the

[1]This last appears to be a mistake. But he had also won the Derby (scholarship).

Word of God." To him, therefore, Margoliouth applied and by him was ordained in 1899. Appropriately enough, Margoliouth had married in 1896 a daughter of Robert Payne Smith, Dean of Canterbury, orientalist and evangelical controversialist, formerly Regius Professor of Divinity at Oxford, and from its inception in 1877 till his death in 1895, chairman of the council of Wycliffe Hall. In 1900 Margoliouth published *Lines of Defence of the Biblical Revelation,* and became an examining chaplain to Ryle's successor, Bishop Chavasse. Professor Gilbert Murray, writing in the *Dictionary of National Biography,* was plainly puzzled by Margoliouth's "extreme and almost paradoxical orthodoxy."

A kindred Oxford *savant,* who repeatedly attacked the 'higher critics', — "the school of sceptical theorists who have arrogated the title of 'critics' to themselves," as he described them in the preface of *Monument Facts and Higher Critical Fancies,* a book published in 1904 by the Religious Tract Society which Christopher was fond of distributing, — was the Revd. Dr. A. H. Sayce, Fellow of Queen's and Professor of Assyriology, who had helped to translate the Revised Version of the Old Testament. As early as 1894 he had written *The Higher Criticism and the Verdict of the Monuments.* A man of extensive learning, his work as "a great *vulgarisateur*" made his more popular writing of special appeal to Christopher.

For Christopher, as a parish clergyman, was well aware of the encouragement to unbelief among the less thoughtful classes indirectly given by the advance of 'critical' views. In 1898 he contributed a preface to *The Fullness of God,* addresses by Marcus Rainsford senior, who had been incumbent of the Belgrave Chapel, London, for many years. In youth, Griffith Thomas had been greatly helped by reading Rainsford's works. When asked what books Chinese ordinands should be given to read, Henry Venn the younger had replied " The very best preparation you can give them is to soak them through and through in the Word of God." "This," wrote Christopher, "was the secret of dear Marcus Rainsford's great influence as a minister of the Gospel . . . Scripture truth flowed readily from him. On this account it was a special privilege to be staying in the same house with him, as I know from having been a fellow-guest in Chillingham Castle, Northumberland, enjoying the Christian hospitality of Lord and Lady Tankerville."

General Sir Arthur Cotton, brother of Dr. Richard Cotton, Provost of Worcester College until 1880, died in August 1899 at the age of ninety-seven. A courageous soldier, Sir Arthur, as we have noticed, was, like his brother, a convinced evangelical. He had been one of the greatest engineers who had worked in India. Forty-four years before he had assisted Christopher in village and other deputation work for the Church Missionary Society. Now Christopher wrote two attractive articles about him in *The Record,* which were reprinted as a pamphlet which has already been quoted. That summer the Canon was spending his annual holiday on Boar's Hill, near Oxford, as Mrs. Christopher's heart was too weak to allow of travelling further afield. (She was four years older than her husband, and was now eighty-three.) Another Anglo-Indian congenial to Christopher came to live in Oxford during the 'nineties. Sir Charles Umpherston Aitchison, Lieutenant-Governor of the Punjab, had retired in 1888. A year or two later he moved to Oxford, where in 1895 he received an honorary M.A. He was an active member of the committee of the Church Missionary Society, and President of the Church of England Zenana Missionary Society. Lady Aitchison called her house in North Oxford 'St. Christopher's' — after the Rector of St. Aldate's.

Meanwhile changes had again been taking place in the St. Aldates' staff. At St. Matthew's G. E. Badger had been replaced in 1897 by the Revd. G. W. Crook. Badger had "by his sympathetic and diligent pastoral visitation...endeared himself" to the St. Matthews' people. He left to become senior curate to his former vicar in Birmingham. Walter Crook, who had been twenty-second wrangler in 1889 and had taken a 'first' in theology, from Emmanuel College, Cambridge, in 1891, came from St. Paul's, Stratford, where his friend, Stephen Jones, had also served. Even in advancing years, Christopher had, apparently, little difficulty in securing curates. "To work under such a Rector as Canon Christopher," Crook wrote, "is a privilege of which any one may well be proud." Crook, however, stayed only two years. After further curacies, at Holy Trinity, Bournemouth, and elsewhere, he became Rector of St. John's, Belize, British Honduras, where he died of yellow fever in 1905. At St. Aldate's he was followed, in 1899, by Herbert Barratt, a graduate from Peterhouse, Cambridge, who for the previous three years had been curate of Hanborough, a village a few miles north of Oxford, where the Revd. William Wynne Willson, formerly Fellow of St. John's College,[1] was Rector, and where Christopher for many years usually preached on Ash Wednesday. He was still curate of St. Aldate's when Christopher resigned in 1905. Stephen Jones also left the parish in 1899, on appointment as Vicar of St. Mary's, Widnes, and in his place came David Griggs, originally a baptist minister. At Southsea he had come under Archbishop Lang's influence and after attending Wycliffe Hall, served a curacy at Baildon for two years. He too remained at St. Aldate's until 1905, when he became Chaplain of Oxford prison, graduating from Exeter College in1907. Later he was a well-loved Rector of Portland. His widow, Mrs. Barnes-Griggs, happily still survives at Headington. She recalls that Christopher was wont to walk down to Grandpont about 6 a.m., sometimes before she and her husband were up, in order to have prayer with them.

Canon T. A. Nash, accounted by Christopher his first curate, whose health whilst rector of the important parish of Lowestoft had broken down through overwork, causing him to take the small living of Little Wenlock in Shropshire, died in 1898, at the relatively early age of sixty-five. He was not forgotten at Oxford, and in his magazine, Christopher, looking back, recorded at the end of a characteristic résumé of Nash's life and ministry: "The Rector of St. Aldate's feels that the gift of T. A. Nash to be his first Curate in this parish was one of the greatest of God's many mercies to him in Oxford." Latterly, even in the country, Nash had himself required the assistance of a curate — the Revd. D. H. S. Cranage, who took part in the funeral service with Christopher. Cranage, who was Dean of Norwich from 1928 to 1945, wrote in an autobiography published in 1952: "The Rector, Thomas Augustus Nash, was a saint . . . It is difficult to exaggerate the influence which Canon Nash had, not only upon the parish and myself, but on the surrounding clergy . . ." An earlier curate, both in London and at Lowestoft, had been G. C. Bowring, scholar of Hertford, to whom, while an undergraduate, Christopher had recommended Nash and who was Vicar of Holy Trinity, Oxford, from 1885 to 1905 and

[1]Father of Dr. St. J. Wynne Willson, Bishop of Bath and Wells, 1921-37.

thereafter Vicar of Thame. Nash's only son had already died, but one of his daughters served as Home Secretary of the Church of England Zenana Missionary Society.

Christopher's own influence on his parishioners and even as an old man on the younger of them is illustrated by the case of W. H. Ward, who became a chorister at St. Aldate's in 1898, and afterwards attained the rank of chief shipwright, R.N. In 1961 Mr. Ward wrote from Cowley: "I sang in the choir for some 4 to 5 years. It was during that time that I came as a boy very closely associated with that true son of God. He was to me the ideal servant of God. He knew what I've learnt since what was meant, and required, to walk and talk with God. He lived and gave out his life with his Father down here. The very atmosphere of God was always around him. His whole life he put into his desire to do his work for souls well . . . He knew the heart and soul of man, and us boys too. The words he spoke to us often, to lead us into the Kingdom of God, bore rich fruit. I was only a boy its true, but many things he said sank deep, and fitted me for what my future was to lead me into . . . his life helped me to serve my God as he'd wished it."

With the turn of the century a change was coming over the ecclesiastical complexion of Oxford. In April 1906, by which time the change was more pronounced, a remarkable article appeared in *The Guardian,* entitled 'Clerical Changes in Oxford'. It was contributed by 'An Oxford Correspondent', who from some of his remarks was clearly a fairly advanced high churchman. "There still lingers in some circles the impression that 'the Oxford Movement' was so called because it was characteristic of Oxford, and that no one could enter the University without being drawn into it. But this impression is exaggerated where not ill-founded. 'The Oxford Movement' has never been even predominant in Oxford . . . It may be asked how this may be, when there are Keble College and Pusey House, not to mention other permanent witnesses to the strength of 'The Oxford Movement', exerting their influence in the academic world. The answer is partly that movements have a tendency to exhaust themselves, and partly — what no one can read the *Life of Dr. Liddon* by Mr. G. W. E. Russell, without seeing — that the foundation of Pusey House caused a severe blow to the Pusey influence, however little that result was anticipated. From the foundation of Keble College[1] until the opening of Pusey House[2] the influence of 'the Oxford Movement' was steadily growing in Oxford and through the country, but with the foundation of Pusey House it passed its zenith, and the decay was rapid after the publication of *Lux Mundi*[3] in 1889, coincidently with the departure of its first Warden[4] from Keble, and the appointment of Mr. Chavasse to be Principal of Wycliffe Hall.

"A great deal of this popularity of the Tractarian tradition was due to its support by persons highly placed in both parties of the State, especially Mr. Gladstone and Lord Salisbury . . . Newman, Liddon, and Church dying so quickly one after another, caused a great break in the Tractarian tradition, and the departure from Oxford of Drs. Talbot and Gore left a gap which has never yet been filled. Their strong personalities have been succeeded in their respective posts by earnest and scholarly representatives of their party, while at Wycliffe Hall the reverse process has taken place, and their contemporary, Mr. Girdlestone, was succeeded first by the strong and attractive personality of the present Bishop of Liverpool[5] and then by Mr. H. G. Grey[6]. . .

"But not only was the High Church party thus weakened, its policy was so engineered as to provoke the Liberal and Evangelical opinion of Oxford into determined antagonism . . . Liberalism was provoked into aggression, and its success can be registered . . . by the disappearance of two religious practices from the life of the undergraduates. There is now no afternoon sermon preached before the University, and attendance at evening church has been practically extinguished by fixing Hall on Sundays at 7 p.m., and requiring dinner in Hall on Sundays as a condition of keeping term. Yet in the early eighties St. Mary's could be packed in the afternoon to hear Bishop Boyd Carpenter's sermons on Elisha; and how many a young man felt the most home-like part of Sunday was getting to church

[1] 1868.
[2] 1884.
[3] In which Charles Gore and other younger high churchmen accepted the modernist 'higher criticism' of the Bible.
[4] Dr. E. Talbot.
[5] Dr. Chavasse.
[6] A former Vicar of Holy Trinity, who returned to Oxford from the Indian mission field in 1900.

in the evening and hearing Mr. Merry[1], or Mr. Chavasse, or the preachers advertised at St. Barnabas's! . . .

"All the college livings in Oxford are now entirely separated from the old conditions of dignity and emolument, and it is not easy for married men to follow in their poor incumbencies bachelors who have enjoyed in addition to the strictly ecclesiastical revenues those of a Fellowship, and perhaps also of an official position in college . . ."

Although this article was written the year after Christopher's retirement and contains no reference to his work at St. Aldate's, it reflects a contemporary, knowledgeable, and perhaps accurate impression of the climate of Oxford ecclesiastical life during the later years of Christopher's incumbency. There can moreover be no doubt that the long witness which Christopher himself had borne to evangelical truth in Oxford was not without its influence in preparing the way for such developments. When the new Bishop of Liverpool, Francis Chavasse, called at St. Aldates' Rectory to say goodbye after twenty-three years as a fellow labourer in Oxford, it was thirty-five years since he had visited Richmond Lodge as an undergraduate and met Christopher for the first time. "The words which the beloved Bishop then spoke to me," the Canon wrote, "were amongst the kindest ever addressed to me." Chavasse knew well that the same loving influence which he had felt in the 'sixties was yet being exercised by Christopher, of whom it could still be said — a year or two before, in a sketch of his character and work which appeared in *The Christian Portrait Gallery* — "His gentleness attracts, and his enthusiasm rouses a like feeling in others . . . There is a certain winning sweetness about his nature which makes many friends for him." To retain these special graces as long as possible in evangelical work at Oxford was an advantage which, among others, doubtless outweighs any consideration which might have suggested the advisability of an earlier retirement.

[1] W. W. Merry, Vicar of All Saints 1862-84, subsequently Rector of Lincoln College.

Chapter XV

Ending at St. Aldate's

1900 - 1905

CHRISTOPHER'S eightieth birthday was 20 August 1900. In August 1820 he had been born; in August 1844 he had sailed for India; and in August 1859 he was instituted to St. Aldate's. Another anniversary of 1900 was the centenary of La Martinière, which had been founded, but not established, in 1800. Christopher, whose photograph[1] — the only one of a former head — was published in the centenary number of *La Martinière Chronicle,* wrote to the headmaster, W. H. Arden Wood (probably he knew Christopher when at Oxford): "God be praised for sparing me so long, and my dear wife also, who sailed with me round the Cape to Calcutta in 1844."

The Revd. F. J. Hazeldine, then of Kingham Hill, who as an undergraduate at Queen's had known and loved Christopher in the early 'nineties and as curate of St. Clement's from 1893 to 1896, felt that God had laid it upon him to commemorate the birthday fitly, and he prepared a scheme for providing funds to found exhibitions at Wycliffe Hall, Oxford, and Ridley Hall, Cambridge, to be known as the 'Christopher Exhibitions'. "The idea came to my mind because of the many times Undergraduates, who used to attend my Sunday Afternoon Bible Readings in Oxford, told me that expense alone kept them from spending a year at Wycliffe Hall . . .". Lord Kinnaird, John Deacon the banker, Sidney Gedge, M.P., and H. Smith-

[1]The same as that reproduced from another copy as Plate 54.

Bosanquet consented to act as trustees of the fund. Over £500 had been promised when a public appeal was made in November 1900. Dr. Chavasse, who had lately relinquished the principalship of Wycliffe Hall, and Dr. H. C. G. Moule, then Norrisian Professor of Divinity at Cambridge, and formerly Principal of Ridley Hall, headed the sponsors. "By his life, counsel, prayers, and gifts, he has helped many an Oxford Man on his way to the ministry . . . " wrote Dr. Chavasse. "I know only too well," said Dr. Moule, "after 19 years' experience at Ridley, how many good and promising men are precluded from residence by lack of funds, and I can think of no more appropriate way than such a foundation could offer for expressing our loving thankfulness for the noble life and work of Canon Christopher."

Other supporters included the contemporary Principals of Wycliffe and Ridley, H. G. Grey and T. W. Drury, afterwards Master of St. Catharine's College, Cambridge. The latter stated: "None who know Canon Christopher can think of him without feelings of affection as well as of esteem. Himself a Cambridge man, he has devoted his life to work at Oxford, and to know that his memory will be connected in such a way with both Universities will be to him a very welcome light at eventide." The Hon. W. Talbot Rice, Rector of St. Peter-le-Bailey, wrote: "Canon Christopher's devoted work in the cause of Christ at Oxford could not be better commemorated than by raising up men of a like mind in regard to the truths of our Holy Religion. Our dear veteran leader has a very large number of friends who will I am sure gladly respond to your appeal." Sir John Kennaway, M.P., President of the Church Missionary Society, and Francis Pilcher, Rector of St. Clement's, also paid their tributes to Christopher's friendship and work. The first contributor to the fund had been Martin Hope Sutton, who had also been the first contributor towards the cost of the Rectory Room thirty years before, and who died in 1901. "Truly he is worthy;" Sutton wrote, "his influence for good in Oxford, and throughout the world, has been most valuable . . . He and I have known each other intimately for fifty years, more or less." Colonel G. H. Morrell, M.P., of Headington Hill Hall, who had been up at Exeter College during Christopher's early days at St. Aldate's, in sending a substantial cheque said: "For some 37 years I have been owing him a debt of gratitude for his kindness;

71. ST. ALDATE'S, OXFORD, *c.* 1900

72. ST. ALDATE'S, interior; east end, *c.* 1900

73. ST. ALDATE'S STREET, OXFORD, *c.* 1900

74. LITTLEMORE COURT, ST. ALDATE'S, OXFORD, 1910

and his Sunday [*sic*] Evening gatherings in Park Town (a help to many another undergraduate of 1863 and thereabouts) will live in memory long after he has gone."

Perhaps the most striking tribute of all was paid by the Bishop of Hereford, Dr. Percival, a broad churchman, who also subscribed handsomely. Percival, who had been the first Headmaster of Clifton, and then from 1878 to 1887 President of Trinity, Christopher's Oxford college, and afterwards Headmaster of Rugby, took the chair at the annual meeting of the Bible Society at Oxford in November 1900. In the course of his speech he stated that "he desired to express the pleasure with which he noticed that it was proposed to establish a 'Christopher Fund', to which he hoped to have the privilege of contributing, not only for the sake of the very good object which it would serve, but in order to do honour to their dear friend, and in doing honour to him he felt, especially in the present needs of their Church, that none of them could do better work for the Church than in taking part in establishing such a fund as this which was proposed, and which had, he understood, for its objects the training of men for the Ministry of the Church. Might it be a place for training many such men as Mr. Christopher."

The 'Christopher Exhibitions' — since unaccountably defunct — were particularly appropriate in view of the fact that one of the ways in which Christopher helped forward the cause of Christ in Oxford was by obtaining help for men who might and probably would otherwise have been prevented from obtaining their degrees. By means of personal letters to friends and appeals in *The Times* and elsewhere he was able to render assistance to many a worthy but needy man. In December 1901, for example, he made such an appeal. One somewhat unlooked-for reply came from a bank pensioner in Devonshire. "May I be permitted to have the honor (I consider it a great honor) and pleasure of contributing the Enclosed £5. towards the Cost of Completing the Education etc. of the noble young man referred to in your letter of the 17th Inst. in to-days Times." Then with reference to the undergraduate in question, "Please ask him to pray for my Conversion."

Just before the Michaelmas term of 1902, the Wadham man for whom Christopher had appealed — afterwards a clergyman — wrote from Cumberland: "Many thanks for your letter with cheque enclosed . . . I believe it will be superfluous by this time, to express my thanks to you for all the kindnesses for which I am indebted to you. Indeed, I think words would not express my feelings sufficiently for everything I owe you. I trust that my work in the past, and also that which I shall by God's goodness to me, be able to perform in the future, will be an assurance to you that your endeavours on my behalf have not been in vain, nor your confidence has been misplaced. In reading your letter, I realise a feeling of sadness stealing over me. Somehow, I seem to imagine you are committing a farewell charge to me as though you felt you were, either done with me, or that your end was near. Some of the happiest moments of my Oxford life have been spent with you, either in your study or in the Rectory Room. I shall never forget those joyous moments; and I trust that your great influence over me may continue thro'out my life. To break then with all that has been so dear to me in connection with yourself and St. Aldate's Rectory would be a grief almost insupportable. My earnest prayer is that you may not only be spared to see me graduate, but that your life may long continue to exert such a beneficent influence on Oxford undergraduates as is being done now and as has been done in the past." This letter, though perhaps a trifle precious, and even sentimental, breathes the atmosphere of reality and is a sincere tribute to a man of eighty-two. It certainly illuminates C. H. Dant's passing comment on Christopher in an account of Archdeacon Sinclair of London (an undergraduate at Balliol in the 'sixties) — forming the second chapter of his *Distinguished Churchmen,* published in this year — "still a power".

The clerical father of another undergraduate wrote from Wales in 1904: "I cannot express to you with what joy I received your letter . . . generously offering the handsome sum of £100 towards the expenses of a 4th year for my son at Oxford. I felt ready to exclaim with the prophet of old 'Truly the good hand of my God is upon me.' It is astonishing the assistance I (a stranger in the flesh) have received through you on behalf of my son. Of course, as I have often said, I cannot express in words the gratitude I feel for all your kindnesses. I beg for your prayers on behalf of my son that the 4th year (D.V.) at Oxford will under God's blessing be the means of strengthening and making him bold and valiant for the true Gospel of our Lord and Saviour Jesus Christ. I thank God that my son was brought under your notice. Your good influence and books (which he reads carefully) have been most helpful to him in his spiritual life." Another clergyman wrote: "I have an ever grateful sense of the kind and brotherly help given to me in taking my Oxford course. I had only my salary of £120[1] to keep my home — for I was married — in Oxford and pay University expenses. He found this out in some way . . . and got me substantial help so that I got through my course without debt."

From the pen of one of his last curates — it is not altogether clear which, though Dr. Griffith Thomas associated it with Herbert Barratt — comes a glimpse of the ageing Rector, going diligently about his parish work to the end. "His visits to the sick and aged were frequently made and it need hardly be said invariably appreciated. I recall his often going late at night to see aged and dying people, and I know of a case in which, when over eighty, he went through a blizzard to pray by the sick-bed of a chronic sufferer who thought that he would have been better in bed than visiting her . . . His physical vitality was marvellous." Another reminiscence, certainly by Barratt, amplifies this sentence. "He was blessed with a buoyant temperament and, in spite of sleeplessness, had remarkably good health. He once told me that he did not know what it was to have a headache, and Mrs. Christopher used to say that he never felt the need of relaxation on Monday as did so many clergymen. He was full of abounding energy. This made an active rather than contemplative life his natural sphere."

"Owing to sleeplessness," the former writer continues, "he would rise about 4.30, even when over eighty years of age, saying that sleep after then was not worth while. Then he would go into his study and write letters, taking them out to what he called his 'favourite post,' 6.15 a.m. I have often had letters from him on the same day and sometimes by one and the same delivery, marked No. 1, 2 and 3, each of the last being an addition overlooked in the first letter. If he felt cold in the early morning, he would exercise with his dumb-bells, and, apart from a cup of tea about 7.0, after the maids were up, he would have nothing to eat until breakfast at 8.0 or 8.30 . . . I wish it were possible to give any true idea of his

[1]Presumably as curate.

immense correspondence and his unselfish use of time and trouble on behalf of the many who wrote to him for information . . . I myself am one who wrote to him as a stranger enquiring about Oxford, to whom he replied with a letter of two or three sheets full, together with abundant printed information and, of course, some booklets. His busy and fertile brain was ever at work and his pen was constantly and freely used to numerous correspondents, fathers writing on behalf of their sons, Incumbents seeking Curates, Evangelical leaders taking counsel with him, to say nothing of appeals for help, personal and financial . . . And then, too, the intense longing for a deeper, fuller spirituality was truly humbling in view of the saintliness of the man. Again and again would he refer to a letter he once received, asking him to find a Curate 'whose heart was aglow with the love of souls,' and he would pray with fervency that this might be true of him. Truly it was a privilege and yet a responsibility to be his Curate."

This was not least the case when it is remembered that "No curate of mine ever preaches a sermon from the pulpit of St. Aldate's without my eighty-two-years-old legs supporting thirteen stone all the time. And after all, even though I stand on a seat to be near the preacher, I cannot follow him fully." Miss Catherine Brown of Broad Street, Oxford, remembers as a child in a nearby pew watching Christopher in this position, further elevated on two hassocks, and wondering whether he would keep his balance throughout the discourse. "Almost every day," Dr. Griffith Thomas confirms, "he received enquiries from Evangelical Church people throughout the country making enquiries or urging action, and his replies were uniformly and most characteristically sympathetic and large hearted. It was impossible for him to fail to respond to any plea that he considered at all of personal or general interest, and the result was that he was sought after from all parts, and made the medium of much confidential information and action in connection with things Evangelical."

It must not be thought that the patriarch never got into difficulties. Sir Douglas Savory, formerly Professor of French Language and Romance Philology at Queen's University, Belfast, and Member of Parliament for that constituency, declares that as an undergraduate of St. John's at the turn of the century, he heard the Canon deliver the same address at the Saturday evening Bible reading three weeks in succession. But though this sort of thing doubtless made some of the younger men impatient, Christopher's worth was too well established for it to make any difference to the general estimate of him. Sir Harry Verney of Claydon, grandson of the baronet of the same name who had been a protestant stalwart in the diocese twenty years before, and great-nephew of the elder Dean Fremantle and of Cunningham of Harrow, went up to Balliol in 1900. Sixty-four years later he recalls that "at once I heard from Canon Christopher . . I did appreciate his kindness and care." The following letter from the Rector of Exeter College shows how greatly his services were still valued.

20 August 1902
Singleton Park,
Kendal.

My dear Canon Christopher,

Your kind letter reached me some three weeks ago and I deferred answering it until your birthday, in order that I may send from my wife and myself our heartfelt wishes and prayers for your welfare.

Your example and friendship have done a good deal under God's blessing to keep all those under your influence true to the faith of Christ — and I am deeply grateful to you for the help that you have given to all of us in Oxford to walk in the right way and to keep others in it. Oxford University life would have been very different without you, for you have helped us all to be more loving to each other and more hearty and outspoken in the service of Christ. I do sincerely and heartily desire that God may long preserve you — and that when the time comes for you to go "home", He will raise up others to carry on your work.

Believe me,
Very sincerely yours,
W. W. Jackson.

Jackson was not an evangelical. On his retirement in 1913 *The Oxford Magazine* spoke of him as "a faithful supporter of sound if moderate churchmanship." It need hardly be said that this makes his appreciation of Christopher's work — presently to be shown in a practical form — the more significant.

In the following year the Canon received a ten-page letter of appreciation from an undergraduate of Jesus College. It throws interesting light on changing conditions at Oxford.

38, Holywell. 20 June 1903.

Dear Canon Christopher,

After having attended regularly nearly 6 years, I should like to testify to the great benefit your Saturday-Evening Meetings have been to me. I have found them deeply spiritual, and at the same time exceedingly interesting and instructive. Especially helpful are the explanations of innumerable points which occur in such an epistle as that to the Romans . . . And no less stimulating are the Anecdotes, which so often illustrate the supreme importance of Christian influence. And the result of such teaching is ever-widening; for there must now be hundreds who through those who have attended the meetings, have heard of Pilkington's zeal, of Haldane's success in Geneva,[1] or Cotton's work in India . . . but perhaps only an Undergraduate fully realises the many calls upon his time, and the many-sided life which Oxford now demands and exacts. The list of College Secretaryships alone, shows the variety of the new interests and claims, which have arisen during the last 40 years . . . there seems very little spare time indeed . . . The College Debates are often held on Saturday nights; and there are now so many other meetings on other nights also, that students are aware that they must have regard to their work on some days of the week. For if Sports have developed, reading has developed hardly less . . . the contrast between the Oxford in which the railway was still comparatively undeveloped,[2] and the hurrying, occupied Oxford of today . . . And now, once more thanking God for the great work which you have carried on so long, and trusting that you may be spared for many years more of that continuous service which is so fruitful in blessing,

I am,
Yours most sincerely,
Thomas W. H. Hunt.

[1]Robert Haldane, 1764-1842, who in 1816 influenced many undergraduates in that university.

[2]A somewhat inaccurate allusion to the period 1866-9 when Lord Rosebery, whom he had mentioned in passing, was an undergraduate at Christ Church.

Forgotten Heroes by C. J. Casher, Christopher's honorary curate, was published in 1900. The book explored some bypaths of the history of the reformed churches, each chapter dealing with an Italian or Spanish martyr of the sixteenth century or some French one of the eighteenth. They had originally been delivered as lectures. Christopher had been present and was invited to write an introduction, which he did in thirteen anticipatory pages, afterwards reprinted in pamphlet form. "Not only have these Protestant heroes themselves been forgotten, but the grace of God which made them what they were has been forgotten with them. God has thus been deprived of much glory, and English-speaking Christians have been deprived of much profit, pleasure, and wholesome stimulus to a devoted Christian life by being kept in ignorance of these instances of God's miracles of grace." A second edition appeared in 1905.

A chapter contributed by Griffith Thomas perhaps led to another introduction being written by Christopher. *The Church and The Children* was published in 1902. This little book related to missions to the young. "What a blessed thing it is for anyone to speak for the Lord Jesus Christ to children! This is what the Sunday School teacher may do by His grace . . . Our Lord, out of the unsearchable riches of his grace, can make those who are by nature selfish to abound in love towards children, and to seek their highest good by prayerful painstaking . . ."

The publication of Bishop Ryle's *Christian Leaders of the Last Century,* the title of which was changed to *The Christian Leaders of England in the Eighteenth Century,* was taken over by Charles Thynne in the same year. The author having died, in 1900, Christopher was asked to write a preface. He confined himself to four pages. "For thirty years this most interesting and stimulating book has greatly increased the pleasure and the profit of my annual month of rest . . . We may look to Him with humble confidence to bless this book, which contains a faithful narrative of the results of His own grace in some of the men whom He chiefly used in the eighteenth century to raise up others in the present century to do a similar work. To bring about this happy result we believe that He will move many of His true-hearted servants to exert themselves promptly and zealously to place this attractive and stimulating volume in the hands of many young men;

and that He will lead some of these to go to the Lord Jesus Christ thirsting for living water . . . The more converted young men there are filled with the Spirit of God and the missionary zeal which He generates in the believing heart, the more faithful men will be found seeking the ministry of the Gospel, and ready to sacrifice better worldly prospects through being constrained by the great love of Christ to live not for themselves but for Him Who died for them and rose again . . . The difficulties of the present day are very great, but they are not greater than those which these eleven men had to encounter and in the strength of the Lord to overcome." The continued popularity of this inspiring book, nearly a hundred years after it was written, is a justification of Christopher's conviction that God would continue to bless it.

Not everyone, as may be supposed, was as appreciative of the popular historical writings of the first Bishop of Liverpool.[1] When in May 1902 Christopher wrote a letter to *The Record* recommending Ryle's *Light from Old Times,* Dr. Sanday, who had succeeded Canon Heurtley as Lady Margaret Professor of Divinity in 1895, could not refrain from mild expostulation. " I am so much accustomed," he wrote to the same journal, echoing an approach previously used by Dr. Liddon, " to see Canon Christopher's name associated with good causes that I regret greatly to find him advocating one that I could not at all describe in those terms. I refer to his letter in your last issue advising the broadcast distribution of the late Bishop J. C. Ryle's *Light from Old Times*. I know the book only from the copious extracts given, but those are enough to enable me to form an opinion of it that, I am afraid, differs widely from Canon Christopher's."

Sanday's main criticism was that Ryle's work made no use of the scientific methods of history (he admitted that the Bishop's generation had not had the opportunity to be trained in them: nor indeed was Ryle writing primarily as an historian) which had come into being in the second half of the nineteenth century, and that in regard to Archbishop Laud in particular, it over-emphasized some aspects of his character and principles, while making no reference at all to others. " I thought that we were at last learning how history

[1]Ryle himself was careful to explain (in the preface to his *Christian Leaders of the Last Century*) that these were only of general accuracy.

should be written, and what the equity and truths of history demand . . ." It is worth noticing that though both Ryle and Sanday had taken first classes in the classical schools, neither were more than amateur historians. Sanday sent his letter to Christopher for forwarding to the editor of *The Record* after perusal.

Christopher's reply was thus enabled to be printed below it. Apart from quoting Bishop Abbot's contemporary comments on Laud when Abbot was Vice-Chancellor and Laud President of St. John's, Christopher treated the matter theologically rather than historically. This called forth a justifiable — but as ever courteous — rejoinder to the effect that both Christopher and an editorial note had failed to meet Sanday's real complaint. Christopher replied with a letter two and a half columns long, which was supplemented by one and a half columns from George Foster-Carter — who had taken a first class in modern history as well as in theology — his successor as Rector, at that time curate to Francis Pilcher at St. Clement's.

Christopher was able to make a telling point. "I did not profess to give in my extracts Bishop Ryle's whole paper on Archbishop Laud. May I, in all Christian courtesy, suggest that before publicly condemning *Light from Old Times* and the faithful Bishop who has finished his work, it would have been more fair to him and more conducive to truth if Dr. Sanday had *read* his book instead of condemning it and its deceased author after only reading the extracts which I gave from it in a letter to you?" Christopher went on to quote Ryle's comments on aspects of Laud which Sanday had supposed he "ignored". He also showed how favourably Ryle's tone compared to that adopted by Macaulay when writing on the Archbishop! Sanday did not reply; but Christopher contributed another letter supporting Foster-Carter. The point at issue, however, was in fact theological. It was difficult for so convinced a protestant as Christopher — or Ryle — or Abbot — to recognise in Laud anything other than a harmful influence on the English church; to Sanday, a high churchman, Laud stood, in an embryonic way, for much with which he himself sympathised. It was only later that Sanday became a modernist. Christopher remained unmoved, offering a copy of *Light from Old Times* to any undergraduate who cared to call at the Rectory and was prepared to read it during the long vacation.

Mrs. Edith Lythgoe began to work for the Canon in 1902 as a young woman of twenty-six. In 1958 she wrote to the Rector of St. Aldate's: " I entered his household as parlourmaid when he was eighty-two and was there for three years until his retirement — when somewhat impoverished, he . . . was going to manage with one general servant. I have never ceased to remember him . . . his goodness, simple faith, charity, zeal for the Church . . . " After midnight service on New Year's Eve " the Canon used to climb two flights of stairs, tap at our bedroom doors and present the servants with 20/- gold pieces and his blessing; we never did any part of our duties without his blessing, he prayed for everything with the household both morning and evening even to the smallest item, if a dose of medicine had been taken he asked God to bless the means used . . . Canon Christopher was indeed a well-known figure in Oxford. He wore a clerical frock-coat, his metal ear trumpet sticking out of the left tail pocket and a large white handkerchief hanging half out of the right. He was fond of distributing tracts, but never to a tramp or other unfortunate person without giving first half-a-crown to get a meal. He said never force religion on a hungry person . . . I am eighty-two myself now, and it is about fifty-five years ago that I entered the service of the Christophers. They were a wonderful family and made a deep impression on me."

When Maria Christopher died in her eighty-eighth year, on a January afternoon in 1903, just before a glorious sunset seemed to typify the end of a beautiful life, the beginning of the final phase of her husband's long ministry at St. Aldate's came in sight. Dearly he had loved her; but he did not repine. He constantly praised God for all that she had meant to him during fifty-eight and a half years of married life. In the following year he wrote "*Tomorrow* June 15 will be the 60th Anniversary of my Wedding Day. I increase in gratitude that God gave me such a precious wife . . ." Mrs. Christopher had been failing since Christmas. She had rallied, however, and there was hope of recovery. After luncheon on 10 January, at her particular wish, though still confined to bed, she wound up the annual accounts of the parochial clothing club. But about four o'clock a heart attack came on, and half an hour later, in the presence of her husband and family, she passed away, " without," as Christopher observed, " the slightest apparent pain." After a service in St. Aldate's at which, though a bitterly cold day, five hundred people were present, she was buried, Francis Pilcher of St. Clement's officiating, at St. Sepulchre's Cemetery, Walton Street, in the vault which had been constructed for her aunt Seton some forty years before. "The late Mrs. Christopher," one local newspaper said, "was perhaps even more wonderful than her husband in her capacity for Christian work even in extreme old age . . ." Another recalled that she had "during more than forty years residence in Oxford endeared herself to every parishioner and to a very large circle outside St. Aldate's. Her sweet disposition, gentle care for the sick, unostentatious generosity, and, above all, intrepid spirit and devotion to the parish in every good work, had made her name a household word and secured for her a wealth of affection that it falls to the lot of few to possess."

Herbert Barratt wrote of her in his 'St. Matthew's Notes': "*A deep reverence* marked her character. Though none could appreciate humour more keenly, yet reverence held its dominant sway in her soul. One often heard her use the expression 'The One above', indicating her reference to Him of all matters. *Devotion to duty,* a strict carrying out of what she felt to be her duty was another noble mark of her life. Often when the frail body might well have been resting, the sense of 'something to be done' would not let her rest. All will remember her untiring work in connection with the Clothing Club. I have often noticed the extreme exhaustion after the work of a Monday afternoon's toil . . . Her sympathy, unselfish consideration, modesty and kindness were most prominent characteristics. Her heart was ever ready to understand and help others . . . Possessed, as she was, of a penetrating and clear judgement, it was always a pleasure to converse with her. She had a deep love of flowers and poetry. I have often heard her remark that flowers were to her a sign of God's goodness to us. In these rushing days of bustle and demonstration the message of what has been called 'the quietness of true religion' was beautifully exemplified in the life just called away from the earthly sphere . . ."

Short obituary paragraphs appeared in *The Times, The Daily Telegraph* and *The Guardian,* as well as longer accounts in the Oxford newspapers. Touching letters of sympathy flowed in, including ones from the Bishop of Oxford, Dr. Paget, the Bishop of

Liverpool, Dr. Chavasse, the Bishop of Reading, Dr. Randall (a former Archdeacon of Oxford), Bishop Ingham, Bishop Royston, from former curates, from countless relations and friends. With accustomed feeling, Bishop Chavasse wrote: "My Honoured Father in God, The news that dear Mrs. Christopher had passed away came upon us with a great shock and brought tears to all our eyes . . . The long happy unbroken love of seventy-six years, the cloudless married life of 58 years are not gone for ever, they are the pledge and foretaste of that eternal union and bliss which God has in store for you in His near presence." Two ladies who had known Maria Christopher as a neighbour for many years, sent delicately worded notes. Mrs. Liddell, widow of the former Dean of Christ Church, wrote from her husband's late Deanery: "My dear kind old Friend, One line to say, how truly my heart grieves for you on this separation from your beloved companion and friend and wife of so many, many years . . . Believe me, in grateful memory of many great kindnesses . . . Lorina H. Liddell." Mrs. Miller of Shotover House, to whom Captain Seton-Christopher had written, at the Canon's request, to prevent undue shock, said " I used to *love* looking into that sweet face so full of love, peace and gentleness. Those eyes of as pure a blue as the Heavens — we shall never see the like again. May we all meet above! " As Griffith Thomas pointed out in a tribute published in *The Record*, " She was one of the many wives of clergymen who do so much to make the ministries of their husbands a power of blessing by exercising their loving influence in the quiet of the home circle. In the great day they will share to the full the rewards of faithful ministry."

In spite of his grievous loss, and his own advancing years — he was now eighty-two — Christopher remained a strong spiritual influence in his parish. A note from a parishioner of St. Aldate's, written in 1904 about her choirboy son, shows how forcefully he still preached. "My son is very much troubled about his soul, thro' your Sermon on Sunday night, he wishes to give his heart to Jesus, and to feel that he is accepted by Him, he would very much like to have a little talk with you. When would it be convenient for him to see you? . . . I do pray it may be a real giving himself to God now." Miss Catherine Brown recalls the Canon visiting her as a small child when she was ill in bed. In a strong voice he sang to her a verse of a hymn, which she never forgot. Later, when he prepared her for confirmation, he evidently retained an ability to interest the young, for she and her fellows looked forward to their classes with him. Moreover for over twenty years, up to 1905, Edith Freeman, nursemaid in the Davenport household[1] at the top of Headington Hill, used regularly to walk to St. Aldate's on Sundays to worship at Christopher's church, two miles each way, although St. Clement's, with Francis Pilcher as rector, was only at the bottom of the hill. In November 1903 Christopher could write " my voice can still fill with ease the largest Hall in London, through God's goodness." A few weeks later he noted " I was up at 4 a.m. today." Not many months before, when arranging for the Bible Society centenary meeting in Oxford,[2] he had written to a correspondent " excuse my youthful eagerness."

It has been said that numbers attending church declined appreciably during Christopher's later years. That there was some truth in this would not have been surprising in view of the Rector's advanced age; but, in order to avoid exaggeration, it is worth while examining what contemporary evidence exists. The only services for which there are consistent records of attendance between 1859 and 1905 are those of Holy Communion. Taking the Easter communicants[3] triennially from episcopal visitation returns to 1890, supplementing them from the preachers' books to 1899 and annually thereafter, we find a fairly steady increase from less than 100 in the 'sixties, to 200 in the 'seventies, rather more in the 'eighties, to 250 in the mid-'nineties, declining to 220 in 1899, to 200 in 1901, to a regular 160 for the final years. Two factors require to be considered in addition. From 1892 St. Matthew's, which thenceforth provided for at least a third of the parishioners of St. Aldate's, accounted for not less than 100 more, in some (and most later) years as many as 150, making an average of 350 Easter communicants for the parish as a whole. On the other hand, the population rose from about 1200 in 1860 to 2000 in the mid-'eighties, to 3000 by 1890.

[1]T. M. Davenport was Registrar of the Oxford diocese.

[2]Two of the speakers, the Revd. G. B. Durrant and the Revd. F. A. P. Shirreff, had been among his undergraduate supporters. Both Durrant, an Oriel man who took his degree in 1871, and Shirreff, a Queens' man who had taken a 'first' in theology the following year, became missionaries in India.

[3]Who would be almost exclusively parishioners and other townspeople, as Easter often falls during the vacation.

These figures in general suggest that there was certainly a measurable falling off towards the end of Christopher's time, but that he may be said to have more than maintained relative numerical progress till the age of seventy-five, and with comparatively little diminution till he was well over eighty. Morning and Evening Prayer on Sundays were not so well attended during the last fifteen and more years of his ministry, which was due partly to a decrease in undergraduates. It could not be expected that the total of 700 worshippers Christopher returned as his regular congregation in the late 'sixties,[1] would be maintained when St. Aldate's was no longer the only evangelical church in Oxford where university men attended in considerable numbers. In 1881 Christopher thought that — although he never alluded to such matters in the pulpit — strong political feeling had lessened church attendance; but the churchwardens disagreed.

Undergraduates were still entertained at the Rectory. When Christopher and Noel Chavasse, twin sons of the Bishop of Liverpool, came up to Trinity in the Michaelmas term of 1904, they were invited to luncheon by their father's old friend, who could not forsee that one of his visitors — the other won a V.C. and bar before he was killed in 1917 — was destined to become Rector of St. Aldate's eighteen years later. Part of the procedure especially intrigued them. "A maid led us upstairs to his study", the former Bishop of Rochester wrote in 1958. " Without knocking she opened the door and blew a shrill blast upon a whistle hanging just inside — when the old gentleman sprang up at the other end of the long room to come and meet us."

Though he was thought to have mellowed with the years, — which was not surprising, — Christopher still took a decided stand when occasion seemed to call for it, and if necessary did not hesitate to differ from his evangelical friends. Of the former an example occurred when in January 1904 he refused to join a united committee of the Oxford diocese for arranging a missionary festival, since he believed that as a whole the Society for the Propagation of the Gospel could no longer be regarded as in any legitimately anglican sense 'high church'. He would never allow it to be thought that he condoned the teaching of those whom he considered to be

[1]No bishop of Oxford after Wilberforce asked for figures relating to Morning and Evening Prayer; and the preachers' books do not supply the deficiency.

unfaithful to the Church of England. The Bishop of Oxford's invitation to join the committee was accordingly declined. Dr. Paget and others urged him, as one who had " done more in the past than any other man in Oxford to bring together those interested in Mission work," to reconsider his decision.

To the Vicar of Sandford-on-Thames, the Revd. W. E. Sherwood, formerly Headmaster of Magdalen College School, who wrote to say that "A big missionary effort without Canon Christopher is a thing I am sure no one but yourself would dream of," Christopher replied " If all the Managers and Missionaries of the S.P.G. were High Churchmen of the good old historical type of the present Regius Professor of Divinity in the University of Oxford, I should have no conscientious objections . . . But you well know that this is not the case, and could only be so through an outpouring of the Holy Spirit for which let us all pray. O that God would give the old High Church Party, faithful supporters of the Reformation in the Church of England, the courage of faith and the energy of love to save the Church of England! The Evangelical body cannot do this without them . . ."

In the same year Christopher strongly opposed one of the early plans for reducing 'the quadrilateral' — the name given by Bishop Stubbs to St. Aldate's, St. Ebbe's, St. Peter-le-Bailey, and Holy Trinity — as a result of which St. Aldate's would have been joined to Holy Trinity, as fifty years later came to pass. In 1904, however, the scheme was devised mainly by three of the evangelical incumbents concerned, the Revd. P. W. G. Filleul of St. Ebbe's, a Magdalen man who had succeeded Arkell in 1901, the Revd. F. J. Dyson of Trinity, who succeeded Talbot Rice at St. Peter-le-Bailey in 1902, and the Revd. G. C. Bowring, formerly curate to Canon T. A. Nash, and Vicar of Holy Trinity since 1885, together with Bowring's predecessor at Trinity church, the Revd. H. G. Grey, the successor of Dr. Chavasse as Principal of Wycliffe Hall. Christopher was taking his annual holiday at Castletown in the Isle of Man. On his birthday he wrote to Grey a long letter which was published in *The Oxford Times* a few months after his death in 1913, when the plan was being revived. He was not concerned with his own position as incumbent of St. Aldate's, "provided that nothing be done which would be likely to hinder the great object for which dear Hathaway raised the money to purchase the advowson of the living of St. Aldate's, and for which the subscribers gave their donations."

This made him doubtful about a suitable successor. "My objection to the 'scheme' has nothing whatever to do with my own future, but it has to do with the far more important question whether the proposed amalgamation of two of the poorest parishes in Oxford will, or will not, help Simeon's Trustees, the patrons of St. Aldate's, to obtain a man altogether superior to myself in spirituality, intellect, learning, preaching power, and University honours, to be my successor as Rector of St. Aldate's. You and your co-signatories state that 'St. Aldate's, by its position, is suited to attract University men.' But the position of the Church will not attract University men unless there be a man of great preaching power, who shall preach regularly from its pulpit; particularly as the dining hour in the colleges on Sundays is now at the same time, 7 p.m., as the evening parochial services, and great preachers are preaching at 8.30 p.m. in St. Mary's in Term time on Sundays."

It was not a question of whether a good man would undertake the care of a combined parish of some six thousand souls. It was a question of whether he would be prepared and able to do university work in addition. "In order that the Rector of St. Aldate's may be really useful to University men, one thing that is essential among others is that he should have sufficient time to give to University men. Would the addition to the poor parish of St. Aldate's of the poor parish of Holy Trinity give the Rector of St. Aldate's more time for University men? The idea that curates can take off from the rector interruptions and references in all matters, and that the people of Holy Trinity would like to be left altogether to a curate and to see little or nothing of their rector, is, as it appears to me, a perfect delusion. Whatever the curate may do, the people, having had a vicar, will expect to have communications with their rector, which must take up some of his time."

The scheme claimed to bring the incomes of the combined parishes up to a level which would render clergy more willing to accept them, as well as providing by diversion an endowment for St. Matthew's, in order to make it a separate parish. It was a proposal on a parochial basis, for making good the financial gaps which had for so long been filled by Hathaway's Oxford Fund. As about this time St. Andrew's, an evangelical church for North Oxford, was being brought into being with much travail, Christopher naturally felt that "the immense importance of securing promptly the church in North Oxford (at least half the money required) makes it impossible to attempt to raise an endowment for St. Matthew's . . . until the North Oxford Church is safe."

Thus, so soon after the death of Hathaway, who had worked hard behind the scenes for over forty years to provide a regular annual addition of £360 to the endowed income of St. Aldate's alone, there were those who wished, in effect, to whittle down the legacy of the man by whose vision and labours five evangelical ministries had been secured and maintained in Oxford for half a century. "The advowson of St. Aldate's," wrote Christopher, "was purchased by the efforts of Mr. Hathaway, chiefly because it was hoped that the incumbent might, by God's blessing, have influence in the University. It is a parish on which a sum of more than twenty thousand pounds, chiefly given by Evangelical people, has been expended in enlarging St. Aldate's Church in 1862 by 300 free sittings, and restoring it; in building new schools in 1865; in building afterwards a mission room, and an excellent rectory; in building a new church, St. Matthew's, in the suburb of Grandpont, in St. Aldate's parish, in 1891; and a new and large infant school for the whole parish, in 1893.[1] Surely, then, Simeon's Trustees are too wise to run the risk of the next presentation to the incumbency of this parish, after all that has been done in it by Evangelical people, lapsing from the patrons, or else being offered to a clergyman, like myself, altogether inferior to the clergyman who should be at St. Aldate's for the sake of the parish and congregation, as well as for the sake of the University! A clergyman gifted by God with great qualifications, spiritual and intellectual, for usefulness among intelligent, highly-educated men, might be much attracted to the living of St. Aldate's by the hope of being made useful in the University, as well as in a parish with a moderate population. The amalgamation of the poor parish of Holy Trinity with the poor parish of St. Aldate's might possibly have the effect of making such a suitable man shrink from undertaking the double work. If my successor be

[1]The building was not ready for use until the autumn of 1894.

not a superior man the University will believe that no such men are to be found in the Evangelical body willing to accept such a church. If it should transpire that there is such a man to be had, but that the Evangelical body would not provide an income sufficient to free him from anxiety about money matters if he were willing to accept St. Aldate's, this would be likely to bring the Evangelical body and their principles into contempt in Oxford. Imagine, moreover, the indignation of many of the parishioners of Holy Trinity and St. Ebbe's if they heard that four evangelical clergymen in Oxford had suggested to the patrons of St. Ebbe's Church that 'St. Ebbe's Church could be used as a mission church or be removed!'[1] There are at least some people in St. Ebbe's who love their ancient church, and others, who do not attend it, would be indignant at the proposal to remove it. Then comes in the 'scheme': 'Amalgamate St. Aldate's and Holy Trinity, Holy Trinity serving as a mission church.' How would the Holy Trinity people, who many of them love their parish church in which Mr. West preached so long and so usefully, and Sydney Linton, afterwards Bishop of Riverina, and you yourself, who were more blessed therein than you have any idea of, like it to be reduced to a mission church? And, seriously, it might be asked, did Mr. Hathaway and his friends greatly enlarge and improve St. Ebbe's Rectory for it to be occupied otherwise than by a rector? Would those who secured, God helping them, the two churches for Evangelical teaching have approved of St. Ebbe's Church being 'removed', and of Holy Trinity being reduced to a mission church? Did Mr. and Mrs. Hathaway cordially give her father's house, her childhood's home, to be a vicarage for Holy Trinity with the idea that it would cease to be occupied by a vicar? This is not a time to increase needlessly the prejudice against Evangelical truth in Oxford . . . It is a new thing for me to differ from my dear brothers. I cannot recall ever having done so before."

Francis Pilcher, Rector of St. Clement's since 1877, wrote to Christopher a few weeks later: "You ask me to give my opinion of the scheme for the amalgamation of four parishes in Oxford into two. I think the plan most unadvisable. It would be a great loss of power. Four incumbents of four well-worked parishes are, and must be, more powerful for good than only two. This would be plain to

[1]This refers to a proposal to amalgamate St. Ebbe's with St. Peter-le-Bailey.

all Oxford Churchmen, if we were to imagine any two of the present four occupants of these rectories and vicarages to be withdrawn. It is not enough to say that the number of the Clergy would be the same, though the incumbents would be fewer. Curates are, from the nature of the case, more inexperienced, and naturally do not remain long in one place . . . My own remedy for the removal of the present difficulty would be this. To set on foot a movement for the better endowment of all the Oxford Evangelical livings. The importance of Oxford parishes to the Church of England would lead a multitude of church people to do a little; and in some twenty-five years each of the livings might be so greatly improved that the difficulty would have been overcome. A policy of fortifying the present position would, I think, tend far more to the good of the souls in the four parishes, and far more to the reputation of those who are charged with the appointment to these cures of souls . . ."

Mrs. Carus, widow of Canon Carus, one of the original contributors to the fund for buying the advowson, left £2,000 in 1904 to augment the stipend of St. Aldate's. In 1909 Mrs. Hathaway bequeathed £3,000 to the Oxford Fund. The plan to amalgamate St. Peter-le-Bailey with St. Ebbe's came into operation in 1913. Fourteen years later, in 1927, it was generally felt that the policy had been a failure, and the two parishes were separated again. When Christopher's successor resigned in 1914, however, it was announced, — much to the indignation of the people of St. Peter-le-Bailey and St. Ebbe's, — that the other half of the scheme, whereby the Vicar of Holy Trinity as the surviving incumbent would have become Rector of St. Aldate's, would not be operated immediately. Christopher's reasoning was proved correct in both cases. His church of St. Matthew's, however, secured a sufficient endowment for it to become a parish church in 1913.

Christopher's concern about his successor was doubtless partly prompted by the fact that he had written privately to Griffith Thomas that he desired a church-wide search to be made for the best man available to succeed him — "a man likely to be influential in the University as well as in the parish according to dear Hathaway's wishes", "a man filled with the Holy Spirit & His precious gifts." Christopher was much concerned about the whole matter. He greatly feared that man after man might at intervals turn down "the *costly* living offered him" as they had done in 1859 and that this time it might indeed lapse to a high church bishop. He knew that when a potential rector saw that the gross official income of the living was £43 short of essential outgoings (curates included) he might well be dismayed.[1] With the help in addition of the Oxford Fund and of his own small private means he had been able and content to manage. But would another man, however suitable and willing? Certainly it would not do to wait until death made the situation urgent. Action was needed now. He did not propose to resign at once, but as soon as a good man could be found. This would allow essential time to find such a man, and was the last effort he could make for the benefit of St. Aldate's.

"I am well and in no hurry," he wrote, still on paper with the thick black edges of deep mourning, on 9 June; "I long for the Lord to endue me with more grace & power & love of souls — that I may by His grace end my course here better than I should end it just now." He longed that someone would endow the church he loved. Then if "a thoroughly *decided* Evangelical man full of the Holy Ghost & able to accept the living & in every way suited for it" was found, he would at once resign. On the 16th he wrote "What is Faith? Surely not to despair & be content with 2nd rate or third rate, where *first rate* is needed so much." On 9 June he had enclosed a statement of the Rector's clerical income for 1903. "Will not God, if we cast ourselves upon Him in faith and prayer, show us what to do? This is a time to use the faith of that ancient King of Judah who prayed 2 Chronicles XX.12. God may know a clergyman with tenfold the grace, the intellect, the preparation of heart, the love of souls, the spiritual God-given power of attracting young men and with more than ten times my private income which is very moderate. I have never had more than two servants since Captain Christopher, my younger son, was out of the nursery. It will not do to wait until I die. We must pray and seek *now* for my successor. St. Aldate's is too precious a Church to be needlessly exposed to the risk of lapsing to the Bishop of Oxford."

[1]Mrs. Carus's bequest would add £54 a year and produce a paper balance of £11.

75. HERBERT OSBORN BARRATT, *c.* 1904
Curate of St. Aldate's with St. Matthew's, Oxford,
1899–1907

76. DAVID BARNES GRIGGS, *c.* 1910
Curate of St. Aldate's, Oxford, 1901–5
Chaplain of Oxford Prison, 1905–9

Castletown.
Isle of Man
August 20 1904
11.30. am

My dear Burden,
Return grateful
thanks to St Aldate's
represented by its
two Churchwardens,
for its welcome
message heartfelt
Love just I received.
"St Aldate's sends you
affectionate Greetings.
Thornton"
Burden

77. A. M. W. CHRISTOPHER to F. BURDEN,
Churchwarden of St. Aldate's, 20 August 1904

Griffith Thomas at once had an interview on the subject with Prebendary Eardley-Wilmot, the corresponding member of Simeon's Trust. 20 August was the Canon's birthday, and not only did he celebrate it by writing the very long letter to Harry Grey already quoted, but he also wrote at length to his churchwarden, Frank Burden,[1] on receipt of a telegraph message " St. Aldate's sends you affectionate Greetings — Burden, Thornton." This letter was written at 11.30 a.m., and it gives a revealing picture of the writer's activities earlier in the day. " I return grateful thanks to St. Aldate's, represented by its two Churchwardens, for its welcome message of heartfelt love just received . . . The clergy & laity are well united in St. Aldate's by Christian love. When I waked this morning I read the 103rd Psalm before I dressed, that my heart might be filled with thankfulness to God during the first hour of my 85th year. I went out at 6.30 for two hours walk before breakfast at 8.30. I did not walk fast but had my marked preaching Bible[2] in hand & sometimes stood & read a few precious verses & went on again enriched in mind. But I walked three miles or three miles & a half, which was sufficient for a man of 84 before breakfast. It was a beautiful morning and the sea breezes were most refreshing."

He went on to say " What a different birthday I might have had but for the goodness of God! " At a holiness convention a few days before he had attended the 7 a.m. prayer meeting each morning and had taken the Bible reading and first prayer at the request of the Revd. J. M. Spicer, Vicar of Kirk Malew, who also invited him to lead in prayer at the first meeting. At the close of that meeting he was coming down the stone steps from Castletown Town Hall when he missed his footing. Providentially, he could not but feel, his hand was on a neighbouring bannister which he instantly grasped, and saved himself. A man behind him rushed forward, but had Christopher fallen his weight was such that he would inevitably have gone head foremost down the remaining steps.

[1]Who had served as rector's warden since 1888, and continued in office till 1916.

[2]The Misses Burden of North Oxford, daughters of Christopher's churchwarden, remember vividly the Bible which the Canon used when preaching. It was so visibly evident from the large number of markers in passages to which he proposed to refer that he was a man whose preaching was deeply based on Scripture.

This suggested to Christopher that if the same thing happened coming down from the pulpit of St. Aldate's, nothing would prevent him ending on the floor, and he besought his churchwardens to consider "whether a knotted red worsted cord fixed at one end to the wall on the south side of the pulpit & passing over the pulpit where the glass of water to clear the thirst of the preacher usually stands, might be held by an aged preacher in descending from the pulpit. I remember that my dear wife at my age always took care to have *one hand free* to hold a bannister in coming downstairs. I have of late done the same," he added, "but not always. God be praised that I did so on the 16th inst. & hence it is that I could walk more than three miles before breakfast on my 84th birthday . . . I believe this to have been another instance of God having '*redeemed my life from destruction*' Psalm 103. v.4 . . . Pray earnestly & hopefully for me that I may be truly filled with the Holy Ghost & be more blessed in St. Aldate's through your united prayers before my successor comes for whom by my request the trustees & Thomas & others are looking out . . . I should however be very thankful to visit more effectively before I resign, but it is important that the Trustees should meanwhile search the whole Church of England for a man very superior to myself spiritually & as a preacher, that they may have several in view when I do die or resign . . . Return my grateful thanks to all who pray for me & I thank you & dear Thornton & all you represent for the affectionate good wishes expressed in the telegram." The loving, humble, buoyant spirit of the aged saint breathes through every line.

In October, after four months unhurried work by the patrons, Christopher was able to notify the Bishop of his desire and intention to resign in the spring of 1905. The announcement that the trustees had selected as his successor the Revd. George Foster-Carter of Brasenose College, who had narrowly missed an All Souls' fellowship when curate to Francis Pilcher at St. Clement's, who was domestic chaplain to the saintly Dr. Handley Moule, Bishop of Durham, and who married the eldest daughter of Bishop Chavasse of Liverpool, was not made until the New Year. Dr. Paget's reply to Christopher's letter is characteristic of the sympathy of its writer, resembling that of the recipient.

Cuddesdon,
Oxford
11 November 1904

My dear Canon Christopher,

I am sorry with all my heart for the true regret and distress with which, I well know, the thought of your resignation will come to those for whom and with whom you have laboured during the 45 years. And I can deeply enter into the sorrow and pain with which you must feel the Severance of ties which the long and manifold experience of your Ministry at St. Aldate's must have made manifold and strong.

But you have indeed a right to desire and to seek rest, if it please God. I cannot demur to your resignation: and I trust that the time of rest may be gladdened by the blessing which has gladdened the years of work.

Believe me, dear Canon Christopher,
Yours very sincerely,
F. Oxon.

On the previous day, at a meeting of the Oxford ruridecanal chapter, Canon J. R. King, Vicar of St. Peter's-in-the-East since 1867, a Fellow of Oriel, and a well-known high churchman, proposed a resolution of regret "that Canon Christopher had decided upon resigning the Rectory of St. Aldate's." Canon King said that Christopher had first come among them as an enemy in a Cambridge team which had beaten Oxford soundly. Oxford had not yet fully recovered! But forty-five years ago Christopher came among them as a friend, and they had all learnt to respect him for his many admirable characteristics. Although he had differed much from some of his brethren in the ministry, he had always carried on controversy in such a way that he made no enemies, and retained the goodwill and respect of those who differed from him. The resolution was seconded by Pilcher of St. Clement's, who recalled how Christopher had visited him as long ago as 1859 within a few hours of his arrival at Oxford as a freshman. He added that one singular characteristic which had struck him in his many years of association with Canon Christopher was the ardent longing of his heart for a spiritual revival amongst the undergraduates. He supposed he had knelt with him hundreds of times in private prayer, and he had hardly ever known him to omit to pray for an outpouring of the Holy Ghost upon members of the University. The result of these prayers, and those of others, he thought, were visible in many forms of religious activity in the university today.

Christopher — who since 1892 had been the senior incumbent in Oxford, (and the senior but one from 1877) — acknowledged the resolution by remarking: "My deafness has prevented my hearing a single sentence spoken by my kind brethren, but I have faith and trust in the heartfelt confidence both of those who have spoken and of those who have not spoken. I thank all very sincerely. I have always been treated with great kindness by my brethren during my forty-five years as Rector of St. Aldate's and I have never during that long incumbency experienced the slightest possible unkindness from any of the four Bishops under whom I have served, or from any of my numerous Oxford clerical brethren. The matter which weighs most upon my heart is that I have left so much undone that I ought to have done. May God mercifully forgive me for Christ's sake! I shall be most thankful to you if you will pray that I may yet serve God better during the short remainder of my life than I have done in the past, and that I may then peacefully fall asleep in the Lord Jesus. I have no intention of leaving Oxford. I do not wish to go far from the grave of the one, who was my devoted wife for fifty-eight and a half years. I thank God for all His undeserved mercies, and I trust in the Lord Jesus Christ for His all sufficient grace."

Christopher's congregation were not behind in their testimony to their revered Rector. In June 1905, the month of his actual retirement, (he had officiated little since the previous Christmas),[1] he was presented with a cheque "as a very slight acknowledgement of our loving appreciation of, and deep thankfulness for, your life and ministry in the Parish during the last 46 years. Your long ministry which is now drawing to a close has been honoured and valued not only by your Parishioners and Congregation, but as also we rejoice to know by generations of Undergraduates and Graduates

[1]In early April he spoke of having been ill for two months, though he had managed to preside in March at his missionary breakfast. He was not well enough to attend his last Easter vestry later in April.

78. A. M. W. CHRISTOPHER, *c.* 1904

of the University who are now scattered all over our land as well as in the Mission Field." The gift had not been the subject of an appeal beyond the confines of the St. Aldates' 'family', hence "the amount is no adequate expression of our praise to God, and our gratitude to you, for the years of earnest and devoted service you have given to the cause of Evangelical Truth in Oxford. The memory of your life and work will long be treasured among us, and our heartfelt prayer is that you may be spared . . . for some time . . . and that your pathway may be 'brighter and still brighter' even to the perfect day."

Societies whose principles Christopher had championed took the opportunity to voice their sorrow and appreciation. The executive committee of the Protestant Reformation Society, for example, referring to his resignation, wished to "express their deep regret that Canon Christopher should have felt compelled to take such a step. They desire to place on record their deep sense of the great services rendered by his consecrated life and faithful teaching to the whole Christian Church, and especially to the Protestant and Evangelical Cause."

Many personal letters were received by Christopher at this time. Arthur Downer, incumbent of Christ Church, Harrow Road, sometimes known as the Lock Chapel, who had been up at Brasenose in the 'sixties, wrote "The news of your coming retirement affects me deeply, as I cannot think of Oxford as the same without you. I have imprinted on my memory the first visit I paid you, when you gave me 'Mason's Christian Communicant' which, with many other books received from you, I still have and value. Then there were the meetings in the Upper Room of the Old Rectory on Saturday evenings, which I never missed, I think; and at which I used to feel such powerful influences of the Spirit of God, that it seemed like heaven . . . after that, the Town Hall meetings, the University Daily Prayer meeting . . . and many other happy efforts, which, though they took too much of one's time, did great good in other ways . . . Many happy hours have I spent in your hospitable house, with you and dear Mrs. Christopher; and, as you know, I have been so blessed as to have a dear boy at Wycliffe, under Chavasse, who had many of the same kindnesses from you that I had in my day . . ."

With Christopher's resignation on 24 June an epoch closed, and St. Aldate's could never be the same again to many who associated it solely with the honoured and beloved Rector of forty-six years. Christopher had given to his Oxford parish his best and his all from the age of thirty-nine to the age of eighty-four. Truly he had "fought a good fight". But the contest was not yet over. Eight years were to elapse before he "finished *his* course". Meanwhile this account of his active ministry may fittingly end with words which his successor, the Revd. George Foster-Carter,[1] deliberately wrote not long after Christopher's death, words which incidentally echo Simeon's self-composed epitaph at Holy Trinity, Cambridge. "Of him it was as literally true as perhaps of any since St. Paul that he 'determined to know nothing among men save Jesus Christ and Him crucified'."

It is probably inevitable that some comparison will be initiated between the ministries of Alfred Christopher at Oxford, from 1859 to 1905, and of Charles Simeon at Cambridge, from 1782 to 1836. Though separated completely in time, there is undoubtedly a resemblance which is more than superficial. Both men were evangelical leaders who ministered at well-placed churches in university towns for several decades — Simeon for eight years longer, though five years younger at the close. Both contended with different versions of latitudinarian and high church opposition, while standing with a minority in upholding, without regard to personal reputation, the distinguishing doctrines of reformed theology. As a single-minded pastor among undergraduates, Christopher is certainly comparable to Simeon. Both stood as 'guide, philosopher, and friend' to many generations of university men. A strong interest in missions, too, and especially those of India, was a common feature of their influence. In churchmanship they were not far apart, helping sympathetically to keep younger evangelicals faithful to the Church of England. Both were diligent letter-writers, Christopher more prolific, but less weighty. Both had business-like habits, and were capable of shrewd judgement. Both came to be consulted extensively by their fellow evangelicals, though Christopher lacked the statesmanlike quality of

[1]Brother of the Revd. Dr. C. S. Carter, also of Brasenose College, first Principal of Tyndale Hall, Bristol, 1925-32, and of Clifton Theological College 1932-46. Dr. Carter was an undergraduate 1901-4, but his recollections of Canon Christopher at this relatively late period were not unnaturally less distinct than his elder brother's.

Simeon's mind. Simeon perhaps had the harder task in the sense that he was creating a tradition, while Christopher was nuturing an established work. Yet Christopher had to defend evangelical orthodoxy against stronger forces of theological and other opposition than obtained in Simeon's day.

Simeon, however, was a great preacher, which Christopher was not; and here the parallel breaks down seriously, together with the further difference that, to a lesser degree, Simeon was a theologian, which again Christopher was not. On the other hand, Christopher was gifted with loving understanding of others more completely than Simeon; and Christopher in his pastoral work had the additional advantage of a wife, and one who was herself exceptionally devoted to the same spiritual ideals as her husband. Socially, Simeon came of rather more prominent stock; but again, allowing for the differences in the periods in which they lived, there was virtually no contrast here. Nevertheless it can scarcely be claimed that Alfred Christopher was a man fully comparable to Charles Simeon; and this is mainly due, not to inferiority of intellectual capacity or pastoral devotion, but to personal characteristics. Simeon's calibre ensured that his memory should not suffer eclipse. Christopher, partly on account of a somewhat accidental lack of a biography, but fundamentally in consequence of his stature, became little more than a name within fifty years of his death. This, however, is certainly an unequal fate. It might be thought that Christopher's ministry ranked with those of lesser-known evangelical leaders in universities, such as his friend William Carus, Simeon's successor; but if comparisons are to be made, Christopher would appear to stand somewhere between the two.

Chapter XVI

Work in Retirement

1905 - 1910

SIX DAYS AFTER Christopher's move from St. Aldates' Rectory to 4, Norham Road — the back garden being close to that of Richmond Lodge — the new Rector of St. Aldate's paid his first call. It might have been expected that having left the home of the last twenty-seven years and gone to a much smaller world with more limited surroundings, the old man would have felt depressed. But this was far from being the case. "Not a word of the work he had left; only tremendous enthusiasm as to some missionary biography he had been reading in the early hours before breakfast the last few mornings, anxiety that what had so inspired him should go the round of his friends, to create similar inspiration. Still, as ever, he was doing the *one thing.*"

Nevertheless, the removal must have entailed some regrets. It is said that during the married life of Canon and Mrs. Christopher, nothing had ever been thrown away. This, no doubt, is an exaggeration. But it appears to have been the case that, after Maria Christopher's death, St. Aldates' Rectory was full to capacity with accumulated letters and personal possessions, in such profusion that it seemed impossible to sort them, and sackfuls of papers were perforce burnt indiscriminately. Important and useful biographical material — including the Canon's diaries,[1] although it is not clear whether these were more than jottings in his engagement books —

[1]Then or in 1913.

was doubtless lost. The house in Norham Road,[1] it is true, was small, and would not hold a quarter of the contents of the Rectory. The task of effecting the removal did not, however, fall solely upon the Canon. Since 1903, when Mrs. Christopher had died, his granddaughter, Miss Edith Christopher,[2] one of the children of the Canon's elder son Henry, had kept house for him, and this she continued to do until his own death ten years later. As health declined, a nurse was engaged from the Acland Home who proved of great assistance to Miss Christopher, for her charge did not always realise the limitations of age, and the nurse, armed with the medical orders of his doctor, Mr. H. P. Symonds, was able to assert some authority.

In view of the financial circumstances of his former living, Christopher did not feel justified in making it chargeable with a pension to himself — at that time the only method of providing for retired incumbents. His friends, therefore, headed by the Rector of Exeter, Dr. Jackson, and Griffith Thomas, who, to the Canon's joy, almost at once became a near neighbour as Principal of Wycliffe Hall[3], made themselves responsible for a modest annual payment of £130. They in fact appealed, in June 1905, for £150 *per annum.* A letter for circulation in Oxford itself was signed by three theological professors, Ince, Sanday, and Lock, Warden of Keble, as well as Jackson, who acted as local treasurer, and others. A year later £133 had been collected, including £60 from outside Oxford. From this, it appears, the rent of 4, Norham Road was paid, as a further appeal states that "The house that has been provided for him, though as simple and inexpensive as possible, is suitable and comfortable in every respect." The list of contributors, headed by the Vice-Chancellor — Dr. W. W. Merry, Rector of Lincoln, himself an Oxford parish clergyman of low church sympathies as Vicar of All Saints in Christopher's earlier years at St. Aldate's — included nine other Heads of Houses.

[1]Subsequently from 1924 to 1937 the residence of Miss Ann Moberly, first Principal of St. Hugh's College, whose psychic 'adventure' in the gardens of the Petit Trianion remains her chief claim to fame outside Oxford. The house has lately been demolished to make way, not altogether inappropriately, for a Maison Française. In Christopher's time it was leasehold, under a sub-tenancy, from St. John's College.

[2]Believed to have been the author of a novel entitled *To The Rescue,* published in 1924, a year before the appearance of *Life's Little Laughs,* short essays by her aunt, Melesina Seton-Christopher, the Canon's daughter-in-law.

[3]He proceeded D.D. in 1906; in which year Christopher, no longer able to attend meetings, resigned from the Hall council.

When Griffith Thomas left England in 1910, Prebendary Webster became responsible for " the pension " fund as a whole. By 1912 a number of Oxford supporters had died, but the full amount had been raised, though not without difficulty, and there were still eight college heads subscribing. The money thus received, together with his own small private income,[1] supplemented by a life interest in Mrs. Christopher's slightly larger means, was just sufficient to enable Christopher to live quietly for the rest of his days.

Christopher remained honorary canon of Christ Church till his death, and in October 1905 he was licenced as a general preacher in the diocese of Oxford, though he was not able to make much use, if any, of this permission. The resignation of St. Aldate's, however, did not mean a cessation of work, even though Christopher was in his eighty-sixth year. But it brought a relief from parochial responsibility and set him free for other things. As Mr. Foster-Carter remarked: "The change of 'locale' made no change in character or in aim. The parish, indeed, to which he had ministered so lovingly for forty-six years, and to which he had given an outward equipment in buildings second to none, for never was there such a captivating or such a successful beggar, almost disappeared from his life. He did not, indeed, forget it — neither did he worry or hamper his successor, nor trouble because some inevitable changes, which he could never have sanctioned, came. Only, with the humility which was so constant and charming a characteristic, would he breathe, as often as one visited him, that impossible prayer 'that all the many things he had left undone might be performed through the new ministry.'" On the other hand, the memory never dimmed of the helpmeet of so many years. In 1907 Christopher wrote to Griffith Thomas: "Of course every day I think of my beloved wife. But not *chiefly* on the temporary separation, but upon God's wonderful mercy in giving her to me at all."

Notwithstanding a natural slowing down of his physical powers, mentally Christopher was as alert as ever. One of the great preoccupations of this period of his life was the circulation of books which he thought worthy of attention. In each he wrote a characteristic inscription, usually including several texts of Scripture.

[1]It seems clear that by the time of his death he had been obliged since 1872 to use all the capital he had inherited from his uncle Thomas Millard, leaving him at the last with little over £2,000.

79. 4, NORHAM ROAD, OXFORD, 1961
Home of A. M. W. Christopher 1905–13
His living room, ground floor
Demolished 1963

Trafalgar Day

4, NORHAM ROAD,
OXFORD.

21 Oct. 1905

My dear Challis,

You have quite cheered up your old friend in his 86th year the 47th as an Oxford clergyman.

80. A. M. W. CHRISTOPHER to F. W. CHALLIS of Oriel College, 20 October 1905

The Principal of Brasenose, Dr. C. B. Heberden, for example, had occasion in May 1907 to acknowledge a gift of Griffith Thomas's outlines from *The Acts of the Apostles,* — dedicated "To a Beloved Rector, Canon Christopher, From an ever-grateful Curate", — and wrote "to thank you most heartily," concluding with "renewed thanks to you for your constant kindness to me." As with many Heads of Houses at this time, having matriculated in the 'sixties, Christopher had been a familiar figure since Heberden's undergraduate days. When a *History of the Evangelical Party in the Church of England* was published in 1908 by the Revd. G. R. Balleine of the Queen's College, Christopher hastened to distribute copies of a work which, while short and attractively written, filled a gap in contemporary reading. About this time, too, *The Year of Our Lord,* sermons for the Sundays of the church's calendar, by Frederick Harper, another old Queens' man whom Christopher had known as an undergraduate, and who had become Rector of Hinton Waldrist, near Faringdon, was a favourite gift. The most topical, however, of these volumes was Dr. James Orr's *Problem of the Old Testament.* Christopher begged a comparatively large sum in order to distribute the book among members of the university. His idea of its importance, in times when lower views of the inspiration of the Bible were becoming increasingly popular, may be gathered from the tone of a letter which he addressed to the editor of *The Record*: "Sir, — When God has provided an efficacious antidote to the unproved theories of the extreme 'Higher Critics,' His faithful servants should make use of it for the benefit of their fellow-creatures . . ."

Christopher was still circulating widely Professor Sayce's small but trenchant work *Monument Facts and Higher Critical Fancies.* A. R. Buckland, Secretary of the Religious Tract Society, editor of *The Record,* and afterwards Archdeacon of Norfolk, who had been up in the 'eighties, wrote in 1907: "I have your kind letter suggesting a wide distribution of Sayce's 'Monument Facts'. You may be sure that I shall bear your suggestion in mind . . . It would interest you to see what a group of your former undergraduate friends now sit at the R.T.S. table." Christopher was keenly alive to the dangers of liberal higher criticism, not least in its distressing effect on some of the younger evangelicals. His own belief in and love for the Bible as the Word of God prompted him to do all he could to counteract what he regarded as subversive of the divine authority and inspiration of the Holy Scriptures. A passage in Sir James Stephen's account of "The 'Evangelical' Succession" in his *Essays in Ecclesiastical Biography* is no less relevant to Christopher than to Thomas Scott 'the Commentator,' whose *Force of Truth* the former had caused to be so effectively distributed in the early days at St. Aldate's. ". . . his advocates will plead that the Bible, as expounded by the all-believing Thomas Scott, left on his heart and life a more vivid image of Him who is the alpha and the omega of those sacred writings than was ever impressed on any half-believing, half-rejecting, interpreter . . . and that no ordinary presumption arises in favour of the superiority of that spiritual culture which has thus yielded fruits of so much greater excellence."

The course of the old man's spiritual life indeed flowed deeply. "Beloved brother," he wrote to Griffith Thomas on 6 August 1906, ". . . I was touched today by what I read in '*The Christian*' . . . that Rowland Hill[1] in his old age often repeated the words of Gambold[2] 'And when I'm to die, Receive me, I'll cry, For Jesus hath loved me, *I cannot tell why*. But this do I find, We two are so joined, That He'll not live in glory, and leave me behind.' I was alone and the second line, 'For Jesus hath loved me *I cannot tell why*,' so exactly expressed my own feeling that, for once in a way, I burst into tears. How many reasons could I give why Jesus should *not* have loved me! I have dwelt much upon His *undeserved mercies* during this illness. The gift of such a precious Christian wife for more than 59 years, June 15 1844 to January 10 1903 — is almost always in my mind. She must have thought me much more of a Christian than I was, or she could not have sailed happily to India with me on August 2 1844. God be praised that she did & doubtless I owe very much to her prayers for me. But when I think of His mercy to me in this respect & in many others I am grieved to the heart by my ingratitude in not having served Him more devotedly. Can He yet use me? He is 'able to do exceeding abundantly above all that I ask or think.' Although you have served Him so much better than I, yet I think

[1]Of Christopher's first college of St. John's, Cambridge, and for many years Minister of the Surrey Chapel, Southwark, until his death in 1833.

[2]One of the 'Oxford Methodists' from 1730 to 1733. A more exact text of the hymn quoted is printed in Gambold's *Works* (1789).

you will feel that 2nd line, 'For Jesus hath loved me, *I cannot tell why*'."

Life was not without encouragements. Some months before, Christopher had received a letter from an entire stranger, the Revd. J. W. Tapper, Rector of Stonham Parva in Suffolk. A few weeks earlier, Tapper recalled, "I drove to Needham-Market (our nearest Town) to have my Hair cut and took an opportunity of speaking spiritually to the Hair-dresser. He astonished and delighted me by saying he had good reason for believing that he was a Christian, that he owed it under God to his poor invalid wife who became a true Believer under yr Teaching at Oxford. The poor woman has been confined to her room for years but Jesus is with her and she has evidently led her Husband to Christ so dear Canon there are two souls given you of whom probably you are unaware . . ."

Norham Road was in the parish of St. Philip's and St. James's, of which the Vicar at this time was a generously minded high churchman, the Revd. Dr. Davey Biggs, who had braved the wrath of his fellow high churchmen by agreeing to the formation out of part of his parish of a parochial district with a church, St. Andrew's, which would meet the needs of evangelicals in North Oxford. From him Christopher was well content to receive the sacrament. ("There was nothing that the Vicar did to which I could at all object.") But the return to Oxford of the beloved Griffith Thomas made Christopher desire that the Principal of Wycliffe Hall might sometimes be allowed to administer to him this sacred memorial. Without saying anything to anyone he wrote to ask Dr. Biggs, as a favour, whether he would permit it — and at the the same time whether permission might also be extended to cover Francis Pilcher of St. Clement's and other friends in Oxford, including a recent one, the Revd. A. C. Macnutt, the new Vicar of Holy Trinity, who was a member of Christopher's college of Jesus, Cambridge, and had been curate to Francis Webster at All Souls, Langham Place. To Christopher's great pleasure, Dr. Biggs returned a warmly favourable reply. The Vicar's aged parishioner at once wrote to Griffith Thomas "to arrange with my brethren to administer the Lord's Supper to me once a week so long as I am not allowed to go to Church." His granddaughter and hospital nurse would communicate with him. "My two ordinary servants prefer to partake of the Holy Communion in Church." Though his views were different, Christopher was not behind his high church friends in the value he set on this sacrament "ordained of Christ."

Christopher continued to write in a small way as well as to distribute the writings of others. When in 1906 church schools — 'The Education Question' — were a subject of political debate, he harked back once again to his Indian days, and published *An Example from India,* a lengthy pamphlet (which reached a fourth thousand) recommending the system of Christian instruction adopted for La Martinière. Like most evangelically minded people, Christopher attached greater importance to obtaining general Bible teaching in all schools than to insisting on denominational instruction in schools maintained by the rates. He adduced the names of several leading and representative men in support of the Martinière plan; but in spite of letters to *The Record* and *The Times,* the Canon's suggestions bore no fruit in his life-time beyond the cordial approval of some of his correspondents. The Education Act of 1944 may not have been indebted directly or indirectly to this advocacy; but the principle which, in this respect, it embodied would not have been new to Christopher.

Two years later Christopher's concern for the Church of England, which in spite of the Ritual Commission and its recommendations was, as he believed, steadily succumbing to incongruous liturgical innovation, moved him to publish — in conjunction with an old school-fellow, John Sharpe of Gosling's Bank, whom he had not met since boyhood but with whom he was in frequent correspondence — 'A Selection of Extracts from the Pastoral Letters, Charges, and Addresses of Leading Bishops and Clergy of the Church of England during the last Half Century, forming a strong Testimony to — and an Earnest Warning against — the Serious Danger of Disruption to which the National Church is drifting, in Consequence of the Sad Disloyalty of a Reactionary Party within the Church . . . whose main Purpose is to denounce the Principles of the English Reformation — the Supreme Blessing bestowed by God on this Church and Nation in the Restoration of Primitive Truth!' This *catena* was entitled *Quousque? Whereunto are we drifting?*[1] Published by Parker of Oxford, it ran to a hundred and fifty pages. It was in some

[1]The title *Quousque* was perhaps taken from that of an anti-ritualistic pamphlet by W. E. Jelf, formerly Student and Tutor of Christ Church, Bampton Lecturer of 1857, and a high churchman of the older school, published at the time of Bishop King's appointment as Professor of Pastoral Theology in 1873.

ways reminiscent of a much larger book which Sharpe had edited and Parker published in 1877. Entitled *Anglo-Catholic Principles Vindicated,* this contained 'A Series of Original Treatises, and Selected Portions of Published Works, with special Reviews and Notes, contributed by Eminent Prelates and Clergy of the Anglican Church: forming a chain of Testimony to the Scriptural Authority of her Doctrine and Ritual; in defence of Anglo-Catholic Principles from perversion by the revival of Mediaeval Tradition and Practices, and Romish corruptions of the Truth, — removed by our Church at the Reformation.' Of this work a third edition appeared in 1898. With a preface by the Dean of Canterbury, Dr. Henry Wace, a second edition of *Quousque* was published in 1909; and a third edition was issued on the eve of the Lambeth Conference in 1920. The series of extracts form a remarkable testimony, particularly on the part of high church prelates such as Archbishops Longley and Maclagan, Bishops Wilberforce of Oxford, Jackson of London, Wordsworth of Lincoln, and Durnford of Chichester, to the growing dangers of the Church of England from those who sought to alter or deny her protestant character.

"A disloyal, Romeward, and aggressive party," wrote Christopher in the introduction, "have gained a firm position in our Church, owing to the misplaced trust and generous forbearance of their brethren, who have too long been misled by their assumed identity with the 'old historic High Church' school, from the traditional principles of which they have widely diverged. By the powerful agency of secret societies, 'confraternities' and numerous guilds, this 'ultra-Ritualistic' party are reviving rites and practices which have a direct tendency to the most serious errors of the Church of Rome, and in the undue exaltation of Mediaeval traditions and customs to an equal authority with the Word of God, they 'teach for doctrines the commandments of men.' Thus by the gradual, though sure process of making unauthorized changes 'with a doctrinal significance' in the Church's ritual (however regarded by many with indifference, or as merely giving more life to our services), her whole system of faith and teaching is being undermined; and unless the insidious evil is firmly resisted, and by God's mercy averted, it must eventually end in inevitable loss to us as a Church of those Catholic principles of the Primitive Faith, which it has been the high privilege and glory of Protestant England to maintain before Christendom during the last three centuries . . ." Sharpe, Christopher's collaborator, was all his days an 'old-fashioned' high churchman, while a strong protestant and sad at heart at the encouragement given to 'ritualism'. Both were united in the conviction that true catholicism consisted in beliefs very different to those which actuated the promoters of the 'catholic revival'. This position Christopher also sought to maintain in further letters to *The Record* and *The Times*.

In February 1907, Christopher received a letter from an old undergraduate acquaintance, with whom he had been out of touch for for a long time. Frederic Grensted had been up at University College twenty-five years before. Now he was diocesan inspector of religious education in Liverpool (under Bishop Ryle for five years and then under Bishop Chavasse) and had a son — Dr. L. W. Grensted, Nolloth Professor of the Philosophy of Religion at Oxford from 1930 to 1950 — a scholar at his old college.[1] The elder Grensted was anxious to obtain copies of Christopher's pamphlet containing extracts from Mozley *On the Primitive Doctrine of Baptismal Regeneration.* The reprint was needed in connection with an article in *The Hibbert Journal* which Grensted had contributed. "I have very grateful memories," he wrote, "of your Oxford work in the years 1876–80."[2] Christopher's reply consisted of thirteen pages. It survives as a valued possession of the Bishop of Stepney, the Rt. Revd. F. E. Lunt, a former Rector of St. Aldate's, having been passed on to him by Dr. Grensted. "I was quite refreshed by reading your note . . . Mozley's book is unanswerable & those who are opposed to the Scriptural doctrine contained therein have at least shown themselves *very* wise in not attempting to answer it . . . No one has ever *dared* even to *try* to answer my little tract with only ten pages of extracts from Mozley. They are wise not to *draw attention* to it . . ." A lengthy discussion of the Gorham judgement followed, and a further three pages was added the next day. "Your letter," it is scarcely surprising that Grensted remarked, "was amazing . . . Of course you had forgotten me[3]

[1]Dr. Grensted clearly remembered (1957) calling on Christopher at this time.
[2]He had taken a first class in natural science in 1879.
[3]Christopher had not said so.

but there must be thousands scattered all over England, nay — the world — who in this life will never forget you . . . To write to you after a quarter of a century & get such an answer as you have sent me — is *delightful.*"

Christopher throughout his ministry laid great stress on misinterpretation of the doctrine of baptismal regeneration as the basis of all errors connected with anglo-catholicism. When he read Eugene Stock's *Recollections* in 1910, he at once wrote to point out the omission of any reference to Mozley's change of view, to which Stock replied: "I entirely agree with you. I *ought* to have mentioned Mozley's recantation, a most important event . . . my space was strictly limited! However when I have to prepare for a new edition I will sacrifice something in order to make room for the Mozley incident." Eugene Stock, the historian of the Church Missionary Society, was a moderate man, not given to polemics.

Those who received letters from the Canon were often as pleasingly invigorated as those who called to see him. Bishop Ingham, retired from Sierra Leone, had become Home Secretary of the Church Missionary Society. In November 1907 he wrote: "Your letter re 'Reports' and 'list of V.P.'s[1]' is being attended to at once. I am so glad that you feel it is a really good Report with a story worth reading! So indeed it is! How I thank God for your splendid vigour and enthusing brightness! It flows into our Executive here from your letter and makes me for one feel more braced up! Few quotations from the Holy Book are more frequently in my memory than one you used so often to make in my presence 'God is able to make all Grace abound toward you that ye[2] &c. &c. &c.' How true it is! I often tell people how you told me I should be 'like a fly swimming about in cream' . . . With love, and thankfulness for your bright beautiful letter . . ." On Christmas Eve 1908 Ingham concluded another reply: "I thank God for your Ministry to me 1870-73 in Oxford! For it was under you that the old old story got into my heart & life! "

In the summer of that year Christopher had a visit from the Revd. George Quick, Rector of Douglas, co. Cork. Quick had been up at St. Mary Hall in the late 'sixties, shortly before Bishop Ingham

[1]Vice-Presidents, of whom Christopher was one.
[2]*II Corinthians* 9. 8.

arrived there from Canada. Towards Christmas he wrote: "It was such a joy to see you in the summer & to remember all your kindness & your spiritual help. None can measure the good you have done." Another visitor from those far-off days was his former curate, the Revd. Harry Sturdy, Vicar of Holy Trinity, Anerley, who had been at St. Aldate's from 1869 to 1875. "It was a lesson to me," he wrote to Griffith Thomas, "when I last visited him, at 4 Norham Rd., Oxford, to find him still the same courteous, loving, happy old man, as eager as ever to join in prayer with everyone who visited him, & to send us away loaded with Christian literature, warmed with the genial influence of his saintly spirit, & impressed with new desires to follow him as he so closely followed his Lord & Master."

Another friend, the Revd. R. W. G. Hunter, a Wesleyan minister, who remembered him since 1869, wrote: "On returning to live in Oxford in 1908, it was not long before I called upon him. Since then I periodically visited him, and never did I leave his study without the feeling that I had been in a holy place. . . . When I called he always prayed for me and the members of my family, distinguishing them each as mentioned to him, and bringing into his prayers the various points in our conversation. I always found him at work, writing, in the chintz-covered high-backed chair which I knew so well. When preparing for the annual C.M.S. breakfast he would be up and at his desk by 4.30 a.m. Yet, however busy he was, he was always gracious, never in a hurry. In the drawers in his study and upstairs what stores of books and tracts there were, and few visitors were sent empty away. One small shelf in my own study is sacred to these mementos of his kindness."

Christopher's concern for the spiritual needs of the junior members of the university never waned. At Easter 1908 he wrote to the Revd. R. C. Burr, author of *Do You Believe? or, Aids to Faith*: "I hope to send this booklet as my Easter gift (1908) to 800 Oxford men, whom I invited to the annual Missionary breakfast in the Oxford Town Hall. I hope the taste I have given of this helpful booklet will lead many to write for a handful of this good seed . . ." In January 1908 he had posted numbers of printed cards recommending *The Glories of Jesus*, a small book of daily readings by an old Queens' man he had known, — "Sent, in his 88th year, by Canon A. M. W. Christopher, Oxford; a lover of undergraduates."

This kind of activity, however, was not altogether satisfying. The idea of a Sunday afternoon meeting came to mind. Some of his friends were secretly afraid that it would prove too much for his strength; and Christopher began to think that there was a well-meant conspiracy to prevent him from taking action. How he circumvented his guardians is best told in the racy prose of Mr. Foster-Carter. "His University Calendar is more marked than ever with names of undergraduates he knows or has been told of. He has begged a large sum of money for two churches in different parts of the land which his old curates are engaged in building. The letters to the *Record,* to the C.M.S., go on apace. To others it seemed, for a man of eighty-nine,[1] a very full life. But, as one calls again, there is a pathos in the conversation monologue. He feels his life is useless. He is not getting into personal touch with men. He is not proclaiming — and, surely, who else could proclaim it with such a wealth of love and experience — the Gospel of the Grace of God. The obstacles, it is true, seem insuperable. So weak is thought to be the state of his heart, his doctor has forbidden more than one person to visit him at a time. But he harks back to the days of the old Saturday evening undergraduate meeting, at which, at one time, the present Bishops of Manchester, Liverpool and Carlisle[2] — he is fond of telling it — were attendants together. And he longs, and wonders — and prays.

"The sequel is quickly told. In the quaintness of its methods, as in its successful conclusion, it is worth telling — it is 'the Canon' to the life. His grand-daughter and nurse (kindest and most watchful of guardians) exercise some censorship of his letters, and carry out, as strictly as he will let them, the doctor's orders.

"But the University Calendar is taken down. The list of men with qualifying marks attached is scanned. The ever-ready pen is in his hand. Some fifty letters of invitation to a meeting are the result. An unsuspecting visitor will see to the posting, and the watchful guardians shall not know. Another letter to a local firm is included. And the first intimation which these guardians have of what is now a 'fait accompli', is the arrival of a large consignment of chairs from the local firm on Saturday evening, to be ready against the next afternoon, when the meeting is to take place. The invitations have

[1]He was eighty-seven.

[2]These words were written in 1913.

been sent. Some men at least will come (about twenty did). What more can guardians, however watchful, do, except send back such chairs as the little room refuses to hold, and wait, with anxious hearts, the issue?

"And that issue is not so terrible after all. The heart is perhaps stronger than the doctor's fears. At any rate, the Sunday afternoon meeting, thus begun, goes on for four or five more years regularly — and a new zest in life comes to the heart of the veteran, who feels that he has still the power of proclaiming those Divine words which to him are Spirit and Life." At one of these meetings in 1909 the Canon said: "What an interesting volume may perhaps be written in the years to come of the way God worked with those in this room, though they are but few!"

Among them were five brothers from North Oxford, of whom the most widely known was T. E. Lawrence of Jesus, later Fellow of All Souls and author of *The Seven Pillars of Wisdom.* From his early years, as is recorded in *T. E. Lawrence by his Friends,* first published in 1937, 'T.E.' attended St. Aldate's, where "he had the great privilege of Canon A. M. W. Christopher's gospel teaching," and himself taught in the Sunday School twice every Sunday. *The Home Letters of T. E. Lawrence and His Brothers,* published in 1954, include some affectionate references to 'the Canon'. The brothers attended these meetings regularly with great delight and sometimes all five were there together. The eldest, M. R. Lawrence, dates his conversion to his preparation by the Canon for confirmation in 1903; an undergraduate of St. John's at this later time, he became a medical missionary of the China Inland Mission.

Christopher was still as anxious as ever to be in touch with new generations of undergraduates. "Be specially earnest," he wrote to him at the beginning of the Michaelmas term 1910, "in striving to bring some hopeful freshmen to this shabby little house at 3.30 next Sunday. You may bring one whom the Lord may make to be your loving brother to all eternity." In the following summer Christopher was concerned to speak to him about "the getting of men of the right sort who are *not* members of the University to come to our meetings at 3.30 on Sundays during the Long Vacations although we may not have room for them during Term. It seems a pity not to have the Room full during 'The Long'." Admiral

Sir Charles Noel and Major W. H. Rowden were among those who came. The Canon's expository thoughts were recorded from 1908 to 1912 in note books which still survive.

An exhibitioner of Hertford wrote in 1910 "to thank you, not only for the last booklet you sent me, but also for all the past literature which I have received from time to time. I have found in 'Christianity is Christ' a most luminous apologetic for the Christian Religion. I have 'doubted' the fundamentals of religion ever since the days when I did Science in School; and going on negative rather than on positive lines, I have not yet come to a satisfactory conclusion and have not accepted any system as my creed. I find my position all the more difficult because I feel *and always have felt*, that I am called to the Ministry of Christ. Possibly you, with a lifelong experience of a personal God and a splendid record of work done, could help me out of my difficulties. For such a blessing I could do no more than tender you my sincere thanks and hope for a full life of good works." W. T. Evans was duly ordained after a course at Wycliffe Hall, and became incumbent of St. Mark's, Layton, a north country living in evangelical patronage.

The son of a clergyman, the Revd. C. Townson, wrote from Lancashire in 1911: "I will read all your enclosures through very carefully and will do as you suggested in your first letter to me — communicate the help I receive from the book to the various people I meet during this long vacation. Thanking you again for your kindness to me — a stranger . . ." On the same day Arthur Frogley, a non-collegiate man, who signed himself "Your affectionate son in the Lord," wrote from Essex: "It quite gave me joy to get a letter from you yesterday." Frogley became Vicar of St. George's, East Ham. A scholar of Jesus College, Ivor Williams, had written the previous day from North Wales: "I shall be glad to show your booklet to friends of mine at the University College of North Wales here . . . I shall certainly send for the book you recommend:[1] no word of recommendation is necessary when the facts speak for themselves. This book also I shall show to my friends. Many of us will join in praying that you may be spared for us for a few more years, to give more Oxford freshmen valuable spiritual help at the age when one's mind is clouded over with doubts. My friends and I

[1] *God's Way of Peace.*

can never be sufficiently grateful to you for the fatherly interest you have taken in us."

"I shall never be able," one graduate of 1909 wrote to Griffith Thomas a few years later, "to say how much I owe to him . . . It was always almost my greatest pleasure to see and hear him speak and I believe that his memory will grow brighter and brighter as the days go on . . ."

An anonymous clergyman who had himself been under Christopher's influence thirty years before — his testimony has already been quoted — wrote in addition: "In 1910 my son joined Pembroke College and I gave him an introduction to the dear Canon . . . My son used from time to time to attend Canon Christopher's Sunday afternoon meeting for undergraduates, and he learned to reverence the [degree] of holiness in the old man's life. I was then a Vicar in Devon, but I had previously had a living within reach of Oxford, and my son and I had called on the old man together, and received his benediction in prayer. I need hardly say that every visit my son or I paid to the Canon meant the gift of books, sometimes almost too heavy to tie on to our bicycle handle-bars, and the books were written in and signed by the Canon, so they will remain heirlooms of a saintly life, a Christlike man, and a soul-winner of Varsity men."

A non-collegiate undergraduate of this period, William Carter, who was afterwards ordained, looking back on Oxford, wrote to Griffith Thomas: "What a lot I owe to him materially & spiritually. I hope one day to meet him and thank him, if I can get near enough to the grand old saint in 'the life that is life indeed'. His life was a marvellous inspiration to me. It is true as some Oxford wag put it that he used to take a text and go everywhere preaching the Gospel, nevertheless in those spiritual rambles we were led into some exquisite country. The landscape of the old man's spiritual experience was one of transcendant loveliness, & I at least always left his presence illuminated & uplifted. Life was a different thing after coming into touch with the brightness of his. The very radiance of the sweet beautiful old face was in itself a joyful inspiration. To look upon him & to hear his voice was a sermon. I always think of him with a halo about his head. His hoary head was indeed a crown of glory. I cannot contribute much in the way of incident but I remember a few words spoken to me one day illustrative of the beautiful simplicity of his spiritual life & the deep reality of his relationship to the spiritual world. I had for some reason or other omitted to pay him my usual visits. I had neither seen him during the week nor on the Sunday for a couple of weeks & I am glad to say the old man missed me. He playfully reprimanded me for neglecting him so long and as I was going away he said — 'Now dear Carter don't neglect to come & see me so long again. You know that one day you might come & knock at my door and when the maid opened it you would ask to see me and she would say "Oh don't you know, he went home the day before yesterday." And you would be very sorry you had not called in to say goodbye. I'm getting very old you know and the Lord may call for me any day.' This was said with that delightful old laugh of his. Truly death had no terrors for him."

Amidst this record of activity, it is necessary to remind ourselves that on 20 August 1910, the Canon celebrated his ninetieth birthday. His intellect was as clear as ever; but he had ceased to leave the confines of his small establishment.[1] "It is more than a year," he wrote in May 1911, "since I went outside my garden into the road! I consider a *drive* to be a waste of precious time. I would rather spend the time in walking round and round my 70 yards of path in my narrow strip of garden." Congratulations were showered upon him from many quarters and the dear old man was much gratified by the interest shown in this notable event. "May I," wrote the Revd. Charles Williams, Rector of Wolves Newton, near Chepstow, "as one who was privileged and had the honour of knowing you at Oxford in the early 'sixties[2] offer you my humble congratulations. As a young man I derived great benefit from your advice which I have endeavoured to carry out through life . . ." John Deacon, the banker, wrote from Switzerland: "I must join with those who have already offered you their warm congratulations on the 90th anniversary of your birthday. We thank God that your valuable life is spared and trust that we may have you long with us to help and guide us in our work for God's glory . . . Your kind and most practical sympathy with regard to Wycliffe Hall has been most helpful and has been greatly appreciated by me . . ." This is a

[1]A little earlier he had been wheeled round the Parks in a bath chair, taking the opportunity to distribute tracts to all the dons and others he encountered.
[2]He had graduated from Jesus College in 1867.

reference to Christopher's efforts to obtain increased financial support for the Hall. In the previous April he had received £500 from one lady for this purpose. After speaking of "your well known handwriting which has lost none of its firmness since I first knew it in 1870", Bishop Ingham went on "I do want to join in the chorus of those who thank God for your creation & preservation & for the blessings of this life & of that which is continuous with this — wh: thank God are so real to you . . . Few have more reason to thank God for you than Your affectionate somewhat younger brother . . ."

To an address sent by his former parishioners of St. Aldate's, Christopher replied appreciatively: "Dear kind Friends, It is with heartfelt thanksgiving to God for His undeserved mercy in continuing my life during ninety years that I write to thank you most gratefully for your too kind letter, 'in token of your congratulation, affection and prayers,' for me at such a time.

"Of late I have begun the morning of each day at a very early hour by praying the 51st and 103rd psalms. The 51st Psalm expresses what God knows to be my heartfelt repentance for not having used my great and prolonged opportunities of service more faithfully and zealously. And the 103rd Psalm expresses my grateful thanksgiving to the 'God of all Grace' for his marvellous forbearing, undeserved mercy, and loving kindness in retaining me in life so long.

"Notwithstanding all that I have sinfully left undone which I ought to have done, I praise Him for enabling me during the 46 years of my incumbency to preach the Lord Jesus Christ, and Him crucified to you and others."

One of the present congregation of St. Aldate's, Miss S. Bridge, values a copy of *God's Way of Peace* given to her great-aunt Miss Ann Harvey, who was then ninety-two, on 23 October 1910, "with the best wishes of A. M. W. Christopher — a 90 years old brother . . . " Some were able to call in person to express their gratitude to the Canon. When the Revd. William Carter, a recent graduate and pupil of Griffith Thomas at Wycliffe Hall, subsequently Literature Secretary of the Church Missions to Jews, and latterly Rector of Horsington, Somerset, whose testimony has already been quoted, found difficulty in September 1910 in making himself understood, he wrote down what he had intended to speak: "I have

81. A. M. W. CHRISTOPHER, 1910
in his ninetieth year

only just dropped in to say good-bye to you. . . . I want to thank you from my heart for all your very great kindness to me. What I am now spiritually I owe under God to your very practical help & to the inspiration which your wonderful faith & love have been to me . . . Do not ever for a moment allow the thought to cross your mind that because you are confined to your house that God is not still using you widely & perhaps more extensively than He has ever done before. My own experience is not solitary: numbers of other men tell me of a greatly enriched spiritual experience resulting from the influence of your life & faith. I am sure you know me sufficiently well to understand that I am not saying this merely with the desire to please but because I feel that it may sometimes be that you imagine that, shut off as you are of necessity from contact with the outer world, your sphere of influence is circumscribed, and your life-work being contracted. It is not so I feel certain . . ." Mr. Carter happily still survives to confirm his opinions of fifty-four years ago. In 1963 he wrote of Christopher "his very personality was a benediction, and his simple and radiant faith an inspiration."

Stimulated perhaps by the ninetieth birthday, but also no doubt by his impending departure from England, Griffith Thomas was busy collecting more material for the Canon's life. The response of Dr. Francis Aglionby, Vicar of Christ Church, Westminster, who wrote on 6 September 1910, — in 1891 he had succeeded to the Cumberland estates of his ancient family, which in the seventeenth century had given a principal to St. Edmund Hall, — was typical of the welcome awaiting the proposed biography. "His very large circle of friends and others who owe so much under God to his devoted labours, will feel deeply indebted to you for undertaking such a work. I will most gladly endeavour to send you some recollections of the years during which it was my privilege by God's mercy, to see a good deal of him and to be the recipient of numberless kindnesses at his hands." Griffith Thomas had already been accumulating material for a biography for fourteen years. He could not foresee that never again would he live in England. In spite of the valuable reminiscences and memoranda he took with him, the difficulties of writing Christopher's life from the other side of the Atlantic must have weighed heavily against eventual publication and certainly precluded much essential research.

Chapter XVII

Faithful to the Last

1910 - 1913

THE ANNUAL MISSIONARY breakfasts continued to the end. Even when, during the years towards the close of his life, he was unable to attend them, the Canon went on himself, as in the past, making all the arrangements, as far as possible, and sending out the very numerous invitations. In 1911 he explained ". . . in order to obtain 400 University seniors and juniors I am always obliged to invite more than twice as many as can be seated at Breakfast in the Town Hall. If I had asked fewer all evident successes would have [been] non-existent — and every C.M.S. Breakfast would have been, more or less, a miserable failure in appearance at least. So many of the men I invite are at that time in training for the 'Torpid' Boat Races, and *must* by a rule which allows no exception breakfast with their respective crews. Others are absolutely obliged to attend nine o'clock lectures in college. Others have appointments for a private hour with their college tutors. Others have their own private engagements — so that I have to invite about 900 carefully selected undergraduates . . . I can only know a small minority personally . . . I never invite anyone to the C.M.S. Breakfast except on the recommendation of some friend I can trust who does know him. . . . There were 380 guests in the Town Hall C.M.S. Breakfast in 1909 and exactly the same number (380) at the C.M.S. Breakfast in Feb. 1910 and 425 was the number in Feb. 1911. If 'the God of all grace' spares Bishop Tucker to fulfil the promise he wrote to me the day before he sailed for Africa to say farewell to his thousands of native Christians in Uganda in Central Africa, there may be more guests than can be seated in the Town Hall. So I have engaged the Assembly Room in addition to the Town Hall and the Corporation of Oxford refuse to make any additional charge for the use of this noble room. They have never made anything more than a mere nominal charge for the use of the Town Hall, that is a guinea for the use of the Kitchen. I have never paid more than this one guinea to the Oxford Municipal Authorities for the use of the Town Hall for the C.M.S. Breakfast. This is very much to their credit."

From 1878 the Dowager Lady Buxton, mother-in-law of Henry Pelham, President of Trinity until his death in 1907,[1] had met all expenses connected with the breakfasts. "Ever since, that beloved Christian lady," Christopher wrote, "has paid every pound of the cost of each annual C.M.S. Breakfast, i.e. she has paid *entirely* the whole cost of each annual C.M.S. Breakfast, including postage of all the invitations, an extra pound for extra waiters, *over* and *above* the number the Contractor thought necessary." Lady Buxton was now, however, in her ninety-eighth year. Sir John Kennaway, President of the Church Missionary Society,[2] wrote to her after being present at the breakfast of 1911: ". . . It was my great privilege & pleasure to be a partaker of your hospitality, when under the Presidency of the Vice-Chancellor[3] and in the presence of 5 Heads of Houses, a missionary address was given by Bishop Ingham, which I have rarely heard equalled for power and persuasiveness, to an audience who could be reached in no other way. I pray God that you may be spared to again invite us — and that you may be upheld all the days by the Angel of the Presence and the joy of the Holy Ghost." But Lady Buxton died in August; and it was only then that the Canon told publicly the story of her association with the breakfasts. When one of her daughters had written in 1909 to express her mother's appreciation of Christopher's part in the work, he wrote across the letter "All by the grace of God." The speaker that year

[1]Pelham was the eldest son of the Hon. Dr. J. T. Pelham, an evangelical Bishop of Norwich who had presented T. A. Nash, Christopher's first curate, to his first living and subsequently to Lowestoft.

[2]Who had been up at Balliol when Christopher first came to St. Aldate's. In 1860 he took a first class in *literae humaniores*.

[3]Dr. Heberden, Principal of Brasenose.

had been Sir William Mackworth Young, a former Fellow of King's College, Cambridge, a retired Lieutenant-Governor of the Punjab, and chairman of the India committee of the Church Missionary Society. Dr. Jackson, Rector of Exeter, had presided in the absence from Oxford of the Vice-Chancellor, Dr. T. H. Warren, President of Magdalen, who however had already taken the chair on one occasion.

Lady Buxton's family continued to send a cheque for the cost of the breakfast, and in March 1912, Christopher acknowledged receipt to another of Lady Buxton's daughters, Mrs. Pelham. " Surely it is *all* of *God* from the beginning to the end that the last Breakfast should have no less than 600 men as guests; that the Vice-Chancellor[1] of the University should be the Chairman; and that the *High Church* Bishop of Oxford (Dr. Gore) should say, when expressing to Bishop Tucker most cordially the thanks of the whole company for his most interesting and God-glorifying Address ' that so far as he knew there was not in their modern history anything as thrilling as the history . . . of the Church in Uganda ' . . . Surely dear Mrs. Pelham among the many things for which your beloved mother will throughout Eternity praise ' the God of all grace,' will be the Annual C.M.S. Breakfast during nearly 40 years in Oxford." It was fitting that two distinguished colonial bishops, both of whom had benefited as undergraduates from the Canon's ministry at St. Aldate's, should address two of the three breakfasts at the end of his life, the last which he was able to organise himself.

In February 1913, Prebendary H. E. Fox was a particularly appropriate choice as the final speaker of all. Fox's connection with India, where he was born — the son of a well-remembered Oxford missionary, H. W. Fox — his links with Cambridge as his university and with Oxford and Edward Hathaway as curate of St. Ebbe's, his connection with the speaker of the previous year, Bishop Tucker, who had been his curate at Durham after a first curacy with Hathaway at Clifton, as one of the patrons of the living of St. Aldate's, and of the other evangelical churches in Oxford, as a constant friend of Christopher's for at least forty years, above all as Secretary of the Church Missionary Society from 1895 to 1910, and finally as a future founder of the Bible Churchmen's Missionary Society, all alike mark him out as well

[1]Dr. Heberden.

fitted to stand at the end of the long line of speakers invited by the Canon. He had in fact spoken once before. In 1913 the Vice-Chancellor, Dr. Heberden, again presided, and while the numbers had returned to four hundred, some of those present were decidedly notable figures. Among the Heads of Houses, Dr. Spooner, Warden of New College, Sir John Rhys, Principal of Jesus, Dr. Jackson, Rector of Exeter, Bishop Mitchinson, Master of Pembroke, and Dr. James, President of St. John's, attended. The Archdeacon of Oxford, Dr. Archer-Houblon, and, with one exception, all the other canons of Christ Church — S. R. Driver, Regius Professor of Hebrew, W. Sanday, Lady Margaret Professor of Divinity, H. Scott Holland, Regius Professor of Divinity, R. L. Ottley, Regius Professor of Pastoral Theology — were there in force. Younger graduates included men later advanced in dignity — E. A. Burroughs, Fellow of Hertford, afterwards Bishop of Ripon, C. S. Woodward, Chaplain of Wadham, latterly Bishop of Bristol, G. B. Allen, Fellow of Pembroke, presently Principal of St. Edmund Hall and latterly Bishop of Dorchester, A. E. J. Rawlinson, later Student of Christ Church, finally Bishop of Derby, G. B. Cronshaw, Fellow of Queen's, afterwards Principal of St. Edmund Hall, and W. D. Ross, Fellow and subsequently Provost of Oriel.

The Vice-Chancellor introducing the speaker, Prebendary Fox himself, and the Master of Pembroke in proposing a vote of thanks, all made kindly references to Christopher, in whose name the invitations had gone out. There was no man in Oxford, Dr. Heberden said, who had done as much as Canon Christopher to keep up and to stimulate interest in missions. This breakfast in itself, he went on, was a most remarkable institution which Oxford owed to Canon Christopher. They could not tell what a great influence for good these missionary breakfasts might have been . . . During later years the continuation of the breakfast was much in Christopher's mind, and he was naturally, at that date, desirous that it should remain in association with his beloved Church Missionary Society. Indeed he contemplated taking steps to ensure this, but nothing was actually done. After his death the breakfast was held in 1914, under the guidance of the Revd. H. G. Grey, Principal of Wycliffe Hall. The lengthy record of this annual event was brought to a close by the First World War. In April 1913 *The Oxford Magazine* spoke of the breakfasts as "a triumph of organisation, and probably no long series of meetings has ever been marked by such a high level of speaking . . ."

There were other missionary interests as well. In 1911 a missionary conference was held in Oxford to continue and deepen the impression of the Edinburgh Conference of 1910. The chief speaker was the Secretary of the Wesleyan Missionary Society, the Revd. W. H. Findlay. Christopher particularly desired that the Bishop of Oxford, Dr. Paget, should preside at this conference. But the Bishop's ecclesiastical sympathies made it impossible. "The matter . . . is indeed of deep interest for us all. But my own relation to it is attended by difficulties to which I am bound to give careful heed." Dr. Jackson, the Rector of Exeter, was more ready. "Mr. Findlay's address," he wrote afterwards, "was very effective, the more likely to do good because of his omission of any reference to controversial topics, and his successful effort to convey to his audience something of the spirit which prevailed at the Edinburgh Conference. I am grateful to you for the opportunity you gave me of going to the Conference and making Mr. Findlay's acquaintance." Findlay himself was also appreciative. He wrote to the Canon the same day: "I am most grateful to you for the help you have so readily & so effectively given . . . and I should like to say too what inspiration I found in your faith and enthusiasm. I shall long remember, for my example and cheer, those two visits I had the privilege of paying you on Saturday; and I shall pray that you may still long be spared to bless many not only by your pen but by your presence and prayers." After having an opportunity to read this letter, Dr. Jackson concluded: "The sentiments, which he expresses to you, are as you must feel shared by very many, and by none more heartily than by . . . W. W. Jackson."

All the while the reading, book distributing, and letter writing went on. Christopher rejoiced especially in the work of his former curate, Griffith Thomas, whose *Christianity is Christ* he circulated widely in the university. Dr. G. A. Cooke, Oriel Professor of the Interpretation of Holy Scripture, for example, wrote to acknowledge a copy at Easter 1910. But a few months later Dr. Griffith Thomas resigned the principalship of Wycliffe Hall and went to live in Canada as Professor of Exegesis at Wycliffe College, Toronto. "I thank you with all my heart," Christopher wrote, "for all you

82. WILLIAM HENRY GRIFFITH THOMAS, D.D., *c.* 1912
1861–1924
Curate of St. Aldate's, Oxford, 1889–96
Principal of Wycliffe Hall, Oxford, 1905–10

have done *with* me and *for* me. My life would have been far less happy & useful if you had not been associated with me." Four days later, on 14 September, he remarked in the course of a letter: "Be sure to obtain *before you start* from London to read on the voyage '*The Mysteries of God*' by the present Bishop of London[1] . . . It is quite clear from this book that the Holy Spirit of God does vouchsafe to speak by a Bishop who is still hampered by holding the *false* sacerdotal system . . . if the Bp. of London were delivered from the sacerdotal error & *all it brings with it,* he might be used of God to save the Church of England from disruption."

The departure of Griffith Thomas involved a sad separation; but it was gladly borne for the sake of the wider influence which his former curate would exercise in Canada. The faithful Harry Grey took up again the work at Wycliffe Hall which he had laid down in 1905 to return to India. In 1912 Griffith Thomas revisited England. He found his old rector noticeably aged, but keenly interested in his commentary on *The Epistle to the Romans*. The Canon showed him the three volumes, which Griffith Thomas had given him, marked and scored deeply on almost every page. He was particularly concerned about one passage which he thought was misinterpreted, and urged his old friend to make an alteration when possible.

Amongst the last books in which Christopher showed a special interest was *The Shadow and the Substance* by Sir Arthur Blackwood — whom he had known well as president of the Mildmay Conference — which he considered particularly clear and emphatic in connection with the atonement. Another was *The Gospel according to Hosea and the Master's Gospel* by the Revd. P. C. Purves.[2] One of the last letters of thanks Christopher received was from Canon Ottley of Christ Church, Regius Professor of Pastoral Theology and a former Principal of Pusey House, who had written appreciatively on 2 January 1912, signing himself "Yours ever affectionately & gratefully . . . " Christopher had sent him as a New Year gift a "beautiful little book" on *Psalm XXIII*. "Let me wish you most heartily," Ottley added, "every divine blessing during the coming year. May you enjoy an ever-increasing measure of Light, Joy and Peace as the days pass, and the release draws near."

[1]Dr. A. F. Winnington-Ingram.

[2]Chairman of the Drummond Tract Society.

In 1911 Christopher had found great delight in re-reading yet again Paley's well-known *Evidences of Christianity*. Since 1903 he had read the entire volume three times, and now he took up the copy which he had had since undergraduate days. Sometimes before five o'clock in the morning he would pull aside the window curtains and then sleep would be improbable for some hours. Usually he began by reading *Psalm LI* and *Psalm CIII*. Then he wondered what he should read after his Bible. He felt a great interest in history, but he felt also, as he said, that he was just "on the wing" for eternity, and however innocent and useful history might be, he did not feel disposed to turn to that. ("Contemporary History" he looked at in a penny newspaper. He had given up *The Times*, after taking it for a short while. " I found it too *interesting*.") He thought of Paley's *Evidences*. In May he wrote a seven page letter to Griffith Thomas, filled chiefly with what he considered valuable and timely extracts. " 'The God of all grace' in His most undeserved mercy has spared me in life to be within nine days of the last quarter of my 91st year! If I were to die tonight, in full possession of my mental faculties, how thankful I should be for God's wonderful forbearing mercy in not bringing my life to its awful end in one of the many well remembered days when, if I had *then* died — my soul would *certainly* have been *eternally lost*! I have just said to my beloved granddaughter, Edith, 'Kindly give me Thomas's book.' What book is this? I have this morning told my Hospital nurse . . . and now my granddaughter . . . that *you* are to have the book after my death. It is the copy of Paley's 'Evidences of Christianity' which I used when preparing to pass my 'Little Go' examination[1] in Cambridge in 1840."

In August, acknowledging a birthday letter, Christopher cautioned Mrs. Griffith Thomas: " Be very careful not to overstrain your strength. Carry on your work quietly. You will do more good by working long & moderately, than by overstraining & 'breaking down'." But there was a vein of humour and even of boyishness still running through Christopher's mind. A few months previously he told Griffith Thomas: " Miss Hales's niece called a few days ago to inquire after me. I inclined my hand towards my very efficient Hospital nurse, Miss Potter, and I said to Miss Hales Junior '*There*

[1]It was customary in the nineteenth century to take this after matriculation.

is the cause of *all* the pain I suffer.' Miss Hales gave an absolute *shudder* and looked with unutterable horror at my excellent and efficient Hospital nurse. I then added quietly — 'and *all* the pain *she* gives me is when she shaves me!' Miss Hales turned away as if she had been tricked and I saw her no more. My nurse uses for shaving one of those miniatures of the machines with which, in these modern times, a lawn is shaved or mown without the use of a scythe. Of course the first time she goes over the chin there is a little trifling pain — but such as it is — it is the worst pain from which I suffer. God be praised for His goodness."

In the same month Christopher's heart was rejoiced by the unexpected gift from the Drummond Tract Depot at Stirling (founded by Henry Drummond's father) of a thousand copies of Bishop Ryle's tract *Are you Forgiven?* These came to him in envelopes already stamped, and he soon set to work to send them to senior and junior members of the university, accompanied in each case — differently worded for seniors — by a short note. "I have to guard against the Title 'Are you Forgiven?' almost affronting a poor unhumbled sinner." The passion for souls possessed him to the end, as did his gift of prayer. "Who will ever forget his prayers?" wrote Herbert Barratt, his last curate at St. Matthew's. "To a visitor from a country parish during the last two years of his life those . . . intercessory prayers were always 'heartening'. May his constant prayers for the Church of England and the world be abundantly answered."

Towards the end of 1911 Christopher was called upon to endure two grievous losses. His elder son Henry had been in ill health for some time. Christopher himself had come to be a more familiar figure in the Isle of Man, owing to his son's long residence there, than anywhere outside Oxford. By spending many of his holidays in the island, he had lived on it altogether for at least two years. A connection in fact existed earlier, as Captain T. B. Christopher, Mrs. Christopher's brother, had lived there, and it was through going to stay with him that Henry Christopher had originally been attracted to the place forty years before. In 1905 the latter had edited a useful register of former pupils of King William's College. In May 1910 he wrote to Griffith Thomas ". . . I want . . . to thank you for all you have done in connection with my dear Father. You do not know what a comfort it has been to me to feel that you were at hand for Edith to speak to when any difficuly arose . . . I want you to know how thoroughly I appreciate your kindness. It seems unlikely that I shall be able to thank you in person, as, though wonderfully well all things considered, for which I endeavour to be sufficiently thankful, I am not in a condition to travel." It was a shock, therefore, when the news came that his son had died. Henry Christopher was sixty-one. The Bishop of Oxford, Dr. Paget, himself on the verges of death, wrote a moving letter of condolence. "With all my heart I am grieved for the sudden, heavy loss which has come upon you . . ." Not long afterwards the widow, Julia Christopher, died as the result of falling off a step-ladder. As these were the parents of Miss Edith Christopher, who was keeping house for the Canon, the double tragedy was doubly brought home. A tablet in the chancel of St. Aldate's, bearing the Christopher arms, impaling Lucena,[1] commemorates Henry and Julia Christopher and their elder son George, whose death in 1897 has already been noticed.

Christopher kept in touch with many friends of former days. But as the years passed even those who, like his son and daughter-in-law, were much younger than himself, ended their earthly course before him. George Tonge, one of the earliest of his undergraduate supporters at Oxford, died in 1911. Christopher wrote characteristically and with delicate sympathy to Mrs. Tonge ". . . as one who knew and greatly valued your beloved husband (now blessedly 'present with the Lord' Who saved him by His grace), for more than half a century, I cannot but write a few words of appreciation of him, and of sympathy with you. I came to Oxford in 1859, when your dear husband was nearly at the end of his Undergraduate course . . . In the deep sorrow of your bereavement it will be part of your consolation to praise God for the goodness and mercy which followed him from his boyhood in a godly home all the days of his life. What a rich blessing was given to him during his 22 years of strenuous Christian work at Sparkbrook, Birmingham, and during his invaluable service of 19 years as Secretary of the Church of England Zenana Missionary Society! Now you will praise God for a time in the words of St. Peter, 1st Epistle, 1st Chap. 3—9, with a glorious

[1] This coat, intended to represent the Canon, has lately been painted on a shield at the north-east end of the nave roof.

prospect of a blissful eternity with him in the Kingdom of Heaven. In my 91st year I praise God for giving me for 59 years a precious Christian wife whom I loved since 1826 when I was six years old . . . How I desire to praise God for giving her to me, and you will ever praise God for giving you such a husband, and the separation is *not for ever* . . . In sympathy and hope . . ."

When Bishop Paget died a few months later Christopher wrote to the Archdeacon of Oxford a letter which incidentally illustrates his correct churchmanship. "I heard this morning with sincere regret of the death of the Bishop of Oxford, and feel very deep sympathy with his Lordship's family in their great afflicting bereavement." After explaining that age and health prevented his leaving home (owing to the weakness of his heart he was no longer allowed to go upstairs) he remarked: "I need hardly say that under these circumstances I shall not be able to testify my respect and regard for my late Bishop by attending his funeral. All I can do is to express, through you, as the chief Representative of the Parochial Clergy of the Diocese, my grief at the death of an ever kind and considerate Bishop, and my heartfelt sympathy with his mourning family in their most painful bereavement."

Even Francis Pilcher, friend and associate of fifty-three years, first as an Oriel freshman in 1859, and since 1878 as Rector of St. Clement's, Oxford, died a month before Christopher, in February 1913. "Who would have thought," wrote 'F.J.'[1] in *The Record,* referring to Pilcher's support of Christopher at Church Association lectures in the Town Hall during the 'eighties, "comparing the two, that the then grey-haired Canon would have been spared to survive his seemingly stronger and more stalwart henchman?" Like Tonge, Pilcher was nearly twenty years younger.

Two letters from the Bishop of Manchester, Edmund Knox, about this time, recalled bygone days. "Pray accept my very grateful thanks for your letter and the enclosure. To see your handwriting again makes me feel quite young, for I was barely 18 when I first saw it, and quite old for those first letters reached me very long ago . . ." "I wish I had time to answer your delightful letter. I could see your face & hear your voice in every line of it . . . You say that your heart has never ceased to beat. We know that for its very pulse is

[1]Probably Francis Jansen, Vicar of Newton Solney, Derbyshire.

love. Our wonder is that it has not suffered from enlargement, so Catholic and sincere has been the range of its affection."

During February 1912 Christopher had written to Griffith Thomas that he was able to work on as if mind and body were quite well, and that when in bed he had not the slightest pain. He added that he felt a little pain if he walked ten times round his garden, seventy yards each round. What must be one of the last letters Christopher wrote is preserved by the Revd. R. J. Benson, Rector of Pulverbatch, Shropshire, an undergraduate at Pembroke when in February 1912 he received from the veteran a rousing call to prayer. Referring to St. Paul's prayer in *Ephesians* 3. 14—21, he said ". . . what a wonderful work *Oxford* might be able to do if every believer in it from *the very weakest believer* to the strongest were to persevere in that prayer . . . If you found even ten thus to pray, & each of these persuades ten others to do so & so on, how soon a volume of prayer might go up from Oxford in the Name of the Lord Jesus! . . . The Holy Spirit can produce now humble boldness in Oxford in those who are habitually clothed with humility."

In March a fall confined the Canon to his bedroom and led to his remaining in bed. Griffith Thomas came to England on furlough that spring, and while he found Christopher's mental vigour unabated, he could not but be struck by the change in him. When the time came to say good-bye in September, on his return to Canada, he felt that it was impossible for them to meet again on earth. But as William Carter wrote of Christopher: "Truly death had no terrors for him. It might be said of his attitude to it that it was to pass not through 'the valley of the shadow' but 'the vale of the light.' He enjoyed this life to the full but he looked to the next with a joyful anticipation undarkened by the sadness of regret. He made the best of both worlds. To him death was but the consummation of life, the gateway to a richer & more exuberant experience."

By December 1912, Miss Edith Christopher was writing to Mrs. Griffith Thomas "I did say I would let you know how my patient got on . . . He has been up and down, not any more heart attacks . . . was very glad to get Dr. Thomas's last letter. It came just as he was on the look out for a letter from him. Sometimes he is so clear in his mind & ready for anything — & sometimes

4 Norham Road Oxford
24th Feb 1912

Dear Mr. Benson,

At the close of your interesting note you write ... "If only it (St Paul's prayer in Ephesians iii 14-21) were fulfilled in each of us, what a wonderful work we might be able to do!"

83. A. M. W. CHRISTOPHER to R. J. BENSON
of Pembroke College, 24 February 1912

Turn over

And what a
wonderful work
Oxford might be
able to do if every
believer in it from
the very weakest
believer to the strongest,
were to persevere in
that prayer

Continued from previous page

I have to keep a letter a few days before giving it to him . . ."

At the beginning of March 1913 Christopher — now in his ninety-third year — contracted a cold, and this developed into illness which brought on the end. In delirium his predominant thought was that a company of undergraduates were waiting in the garden for him to speak to them, and later with real passion, strong in death, he spoke to an invisible audience on the Lord Jesus Christ. Departure took place shortly before nine o'clock in the evening on Monday 10 March, in "absolute peace and triumphant quietness."

In the year he came to Oxford, Christopher had constructed a vault in St. Sepulchre's Cemetery, Walton Street, near which, since 1883, was the grave of Henry Bazely. There Mrs. Christopher had already been buried. The funeral took place on Friday the 14th.[1] On Thursday the coffin was taken to St. Aldate's, where it was met by the Rector, the Revd. G. Foster-Carter, who conducted a short thanksgiving. The body rested in church that night, and in the morning the first part of the burial service was held there. The Christopher family, headed by Captain Seton-Christopher, the Canon's surviving son,[2] was strongly represented. The three granddaughters, and one grandson, Mordaunt Christopher[3] (with the death in action of his surviving son in the Second World War, Canon Christopher's issue in the male line became extinct), his nephew Major-General Christopher, and Freville Christopher, representing the Christophers of Crook Hall and Goring-on-Thames, were among the relations present. The church was all but full.

The Warden of Wadham, the Revd. Dr. Wright-Henderson, and the Rector of Exeter, the Revd. Dr. Jackson, attended in their canonicals and Dr. Jackson read the lesson. Other robed clergy, beside the Rector of St. Aldate's, included several of Christopher's former curates: the Revd. Stephen Jones of Widnes, who read the opening sentences; the Revd. A. P. Cox of Cheltenham, Dr. C. J. Casher of Leamington and the Revd. D. B. Griggs of Portland. The Revd. H. O. Barratt of Cherington was also present. It was a particular grief to Dr. Griffith Thomas that he could not attend. A congregation of seven hundred included the Dean of Christ

[1]Copies of a black-edged card announcing the burial arrangements, and of the order of service, are preserved in the Bodleian Library.
[2]Who had been a gold-staff officer at the coronation of King George V two years previously.
[3]Who had graduated from Pembroke College, Cambridge, in 1910.

Church, the Revd. Dr. T. B. Strong, later Bishop of Oxford, representing the Vice-Chancellor, the Presidents of Trinity (Revd. Dr. H. E. D. Blakiston) and St. John's (Revd. Dr. H. A. James), the Provosts of Oriel (C. L. Shadwell) and Worcester (Revd. Dr. C. H. O. Daniel), the Warden of New College (Revd. Dr. W. A. Spooner), the Master of Balliol (J. L. Strachan-Davidson), the Warden of Keble (Revd. Dr. W. Lock), the Master of Marcon's Hall (Revd. C. A. Marcon), Canon Ottley, Regius Professor of Pastoral Theology, the Archdeacon of Oxford, the Senior Proctor, and the Principals of Wycliffe Hall (Revd. H. G. Grey) and Pusey House (Revd. Dr. Darwell Stone).

Local clergy, headed by the Rural Dean, the Revd. H. L. Wild, Vicar of St. Giles',[1] and the Rector of St. Martin's and All Saints, the city church, Dr. A. J. Carlyle, evangelical clergy, civic dignitaries, and parishioners filled the rest of the church; in particular large numbers of elderly St. Aldates' folk made their appearance, " many of whom were visibly affected." The Vice-Chancellor, — Dr. Heberden, — Sir Henry Seton Ker, Bishop Ingham, Lord Radstock, and Major Danby Christopher, were among those unable to be present.

Mendelsohn's *Funeral March* thundered while the coffin was borne from the church on its way to Jericho, where under a simple but impressively solid tomb,[2] Christopher's remains were to await the resurrection morning, in a cemetery where many Oxford notables of those days, including Benjamin Jowett, already lay. As the correspondent of *The Record* remarked, " the occasion afforded a striking testimony to the love and affection felt for the revered Canon by men and women representing all departments of Oxford life." The presence of ten Heads of Houses, out of twenty-three, after full term, was certainly a mark of recognition, perhaps unequalled at the funeral of any other Oxford parish clergyman, at least in modern times. No more had attended Simeon's Cambridge obsequies.

There was a large crowd outside the church as the coffin was placed on Frank Burden's horse-drawn hearse.[3] Many more people

[1] A former Vice-Principal of St. Edmund Hall, afterwards Bishop of Newcastle.

[2] Close to the cemetery chapel, on the south side.

[3] Photographs in *Jackson's Oxford Journal Illustrated* for 19 March 1913 show various scenes connected with the funeral, including the arrival of the Pro-Vice-Chancellor, Dr. Strong, of the Warden of Wadham, Dr. Wright-Henderson, and the departure of the hearse, with the churchwardens at its head, as it left St. Aldates'.

were waiting along the route, as the procession of carriages, headed by the hearse — preceded by the churchwardens and sidesmen of St. Aldate's on foot, and followed by a multitude of sympathisers — moved slowly up St. Aldate's, along Cornmarket, St. Giles's and St. John's Road,[1] amidst "many signs of silent grief and respect." At the cemetery gates there was another crowd, of humble folk, and as soon as the procession had passed in, as many as possible were allowed to enter to pay their last tribute of respect. The prayers at the grave-side were read by the Rector of St. Aldate's, Mr. Foster-Carter; and after the singing of "Rock of Ages," Canon Christopher's successor pronounced the benediction.

Two days later, on Sunday morning, a memorial service was held in St. Aldate's. The east end of the church and the pulpit were draped in black. The Rector officiated; and the service was attended by the Mayor[2] and Corporation, who walked in robed procession from the Town Hall. The Revd. F. S. Webster, Rector of All Souls, Langham Place, and Prebendary of St. Paul's, who had been Christopher's curate thirty years before, preached from *Romans* 1. 16, — "I am not ashamed of the Gospel of Christ." He began by referring to the glad undertone of triumph which prevailed. "Your natural sorrow at your loss of so faithful a friend and pastor has been greatly mitigated by the long interval of enforced retirement from active service. One thought only is uppermost in all our hearts today and that is to magnify the grace of God which made Canon Christopher what he was, and we rejoice to think of him at rest, and with Christ, from all weariness and pain and waiting in expectation of that glory which shall be revealed at the not far distant return of our Blessed Saviour. I count it a very high honour to have been asked to preach this sermon this morning. I did not have an opportunity of consulting the dear Canon as to what I should say this morning, but if I had I think I know what he would have said: 'Say what you like about me, dear brother, but whatever you do, preach Christ.' And I want to do both this morning . . . What then was Canon Christopher? He was, first of all, a thorough English gentleman, a Cambridge wrangler, a Cambridge blue, a man of many great gifts and powers; but he was pre-eminently and essentially a man of God, a sinner saved

[1]Now St. Bernard's Road.

[2]Councillor Hutchins, who had been a regular attendant at St. Aldate's in Christopher's time and who had built the Grandpont school in 1894.

by grace. I think we will all agree that the most prominent feature in his character and the chief factor in the make-up of his personality was pure and genuine benevolence. Believe me that whatever services may be rendered to the Faith by those able to argue clearly and cogently in its defence, the most effective champions of God's truth are those who conspicuously and manifestly live under its power. Any arguments which might be brought forward, however weighty and well put, can easily be parried by the keen intellects of Oxford men intent upon upholding the latest phase of unbelief; but the genuine piety, the love of Christ, the simple unselfconscious humble faith of Canon Christopher were arguments which no mere words could overthrow . . ."

For Christopher was a "man of prayer and such a happy Christian! Deaf people are sometimes liable to be gloomy and depressed. Though up to the last shut off from intercourse with his fellow men, he was conspicuous for his contagious joy, and literally obeyed the apostolic mandate 'Rejoice in the Lord always . . . ' He often had serious difficulties to encounter, but he always looked on the bright side. He was a confirmed optimist. His courage never failed him, his faith never wavered, and he prayed his way through all his difficulties, rejoicing always . . . He was essentially a man of peace, and he hated controversy, but he was a true soldier of the cross and never shrank from duty because it was unpopular or distasteful; so when fitting opportunity arose he did not hesitate to expound with considerable skill the Thirty-nine Articles, and bring out their clear, distinct and dignified renunciation of those serious errors and superstitions which necessitated and justified the English Reformation. A man of less steadfast faith might have wavered in his convictions and modified his principles to suit the spirit of Oxford. A man of less lively faith might have become despondent and apathetic; one less firmly rooted in love, the love of Christ and the love of men, might have become narrow and bitter; but Canon Christopher was so steadfast in faith, joyful through hope and rooted in love that he passed through the troublesome waves of Oxford life so hidden in Christ that though he had many theological opponents he had never an enemy, for his conspicuous love made all men love him. Many a man placed as he was would have decided that in view of the mediaeval spirit then so strong in Oxford,

84. FRANCIS SCOTT WEBSTER, *c.* 1913
Curate of St. Aldate's, Oxford, 1882–85
Rector of All Souls, Langham Place, Marylebone, London, 1898–1920
Preacher, memorial sermon for A. M. W. CHRISTOPHER, St. Aldate's, March 1913

some modification of the plain doctrine of the cross was necessary and justifiable. But Canon Christopher stood firm never dreaming for one instant of modifying the Gospel of God. To him the saving truth of the Gospel, what our fore-fathers called the doctrines of grace, the supremacy and complete sufficiency of Holy Scripture, the complete sinfulness of man so that he is totally unable to help himself; the complete redemption of man through the finished work of Jesus Christ, through the once-offered sacrifice of Jesus on the cross, the real spiritual regeneration of all who believe, prophesied and pledged in the sacrament of baptism but not really known and enjoyed until the miracle of conversion is wrought in the heart; the sovereignty of the Holy Spirit whose quickening and sanctifying operations do not normally or necessarily synchronise with the administration of the sacraments however much the worthy reception of the sacraments may help the believer to receive them — all these divine truths were to your beloved Rector as certain and fixed and immovable as those fundamental propositions of Euclid, concerning any contradiction of which we say, Quod est absurdum . . . To the man in the street and especially to the philosopher in the lecture room, the cross has always been a stumbling block. Christians are always tempted, especially in University circles, to put the cross in the background and adopt various modern notions more in accord with the current fancies of the day. Canon Christopher never yielded to that temptation and for nearly fifty years he preached the simple gospel of a naked cross, a cross unadorned by any flowers of rhetoric or philosophy. He lived a consistent life; he died a peaceful and triumphant death, trusting only in the cross of Christ. I come to you as it were from that little room in 4 Norham Road, where for twelve months and three days, borne without the least impatience or lack of cheerfulness, dear Canon Christopher lay patiently waiting for the call of God . . ."

Prebendary Webster concluded with just such an appeal as would have delighted the Canon. "I come to you as we think of the splendid testimony of service of that true man of God, and I ask you lovingly but plainly, — 'What is Jesus Christ to you? What is the cross of Christ to you? What is the Gospel of Jesus Christ to you? Do you know what it is to have the burden of your sin removed? Will you be baptised for the dead this morning?' " Being himself a double first classman, Webster could declare with some authority that " The culture, the intellectualism, the aestheticism, and the mediaevalism of Oxford cannot cleanse the human heart from sin. They may easily allure and attract you into promising bypaths where the evil of sin is ignored and men try to believe that the one burden which is really intolerable is no burden at all. But there is only one way which gives real peace and true happiness — the narrow way which brings us face to face with the cross of Jesus Christ and tells us that our only hope of salvation is by believing in the Lamb of God which taketh away the sins of the world. It is because that was so real to Canon Christopher that he was the man he was. These are days when men of steadfast faith, lively hope and prevailing love are sorely needed. Will *you,* as you remember all that dear Canon Christopher was to Oxford, yield *yourself* to the same Holy Spirit Who can work in you as mightily as He worked in him, and resolve, God helping *you,* to live for Christ as earnestly and as faithfully as he did?"

The Bishop of Oxford, Dr. Charles Gore — like Christopher an adopted son of Trinity College — preached at St. Aldate's in the evening. He was very thankful, he remarked, that it had been arranged that he should come that night because it gave him the opportunity of joining them sympathetically in what they were feeling about their late Rector. The Bishop went on to say that he had known Oxford for over forty years. When he first came there Canon Christopher was already a distinctive and distinguished figure in the life of the place . . . while he was a man of very distinctive convictions, and, as such a man must be where occasion required, militant, so that he was not the kind of person whom people think of as a no party man, yet he did not think that anything Christopher ever said or did stirred up any feeling of bitterness. He managed, in a way that even very many years ago excited his warm admiration, to be of unhesitating convictions and strenuous in the insisting upon them, ready always to do battle for them, without anyone ever mistaking what he said or did for bitterness, without saying anything which could break the extraordinary impression of goodness and loving-kindness which he left on the minds of everyone. In his diocesan magazine Bishop Gore wrote: "Canon Christopher has been, ever since we can remember Oxford, even those of us who are old men, such a prominent and characteristic figure that, though of late years he has not been visible among us, his passing away leaves a great gap in our community . . ."

Canon Driver, Pusey's successor as Regius Professor of Hebrew, preaching in the cathedral on the Sunday morning after the funeral, said: "I cannot close today without saying a few words in commemoration of one who, for many years a familiar figure in Oxford, passed away last week at the ripe age of 92 . . . for nearly half a century he was the immediate neighbour of Christ Church; since 1886, also, he was Honorary Canon of this Cathedral. Canon Christopher's was a striking personality, and his character was one of singular sweetness. His deep spirituality, his devotion to his Lord and Master, his ardent love of souls, his affectionate sympathy, his transparent sincerity, impressed all who knew him, and secured him the respect and regard of all shades of opinion. As has been said, 'His simple faith and unaffected piety were beautiful to witness, and he had a heart which literally overflowed with love to all.'"

The Vicar of St. Mary's, the university church — the Revd. C. A. Whittuck, formerly Vice-Principal of Brasenose — also referred to Christopher. "I would but add . . . on your behalf, as well as on my own, an acknowledgement of the debt which we all owe as Christians, as Oxford Churchpeople, and as Oxford citizens, to the late Canon Christopher. Christopher was emphatically a man who looked for no other reward but the answer of a good conscience and the knowledge of Him Whom he served. Yet there have been few prominent clergymen among us who have been more loved and honoured than he was — a convincing proof, if one was needed, of the attraction exercised on all classes of the community by steadfastness of purpose and sincerity of aim. But indeed, apart from this consideration, the man himself was entirely lovable, nay, one whom it was impossible not to love. This is not the most appropriate church, though no church in this place would be inappropriate, for recording his services, which, in Oxford at any rate, are not likely to be soon forgotten . . ."

At the city church, St. Martin's and All Saints, the Revd. W. E. Sherwood, a former Headmaster of Magdalen College School, in the absence of the Rector, Dr. Carlyle, made reference to Canon Christopher and remarked: ". . . there is no one, but feels that not only Oxford, but the Church all over the world, is the poorer through his loss. Full of energy, full of zeal, a man of very decided convictions, he yet had the wonderful faculty, not only of attracting the love and esteem of men of all parties, but also of bringing men of all parties together . . . Whence all this power and this success, for God blessed his work abundantly? Was it his zeal? Was it energy? No, for many have these. It may be said of him that he worked upon his knees, and that the source of his influence and the cause of his success was the power of prayer. He not only prayed himself, but he made all pray with whom he came in contact. He was one who most truly received the kingdom of God as a little child, and all Oxford, and all who knew him, were the better for his deep and simple faith and prayerful influence."

Mr. Foster-Carter paid his tribute at the St. Aldates' men's service on the Sunday afternoon, by prefacing it with a few short remarks. Only the previous evening, he said, had he heard for the first time how, when in his late seventies, Canon Christopher had gone out in a blizzard in order to visit a sick parishioner. And such intances of his faithfulness could be multiplied. They all told the same story. Prebendary Webster preached at St. Matthew's, Grandpont, in the evening. Christopher, he said, "never spared himself pains, thinking nothing not worth doing if he could bring home to people the love of God. He was one of the cheeriest men the speaker ever met, and doubt and gloom seemed to vanish at his presence. He was a broad Christian and a man of genuine humility, and the speaker had never known another man with such a low estimate of his own worth. Many a time when walking from the rectory in Pembroke Street he had got outside the Canon in order to give him the most honourable place inside. But always he would feel a gentle push on his arm, and they would cross the road, thus placing the Canon in the more humble position, which seemed to thoroughly content him . . . They were not to sorrow for him as those who had no hope, but as having a 'sure and certain hope' of the resurrection. They believed that Christ died and rose again, and just as surely Canon Christopher would rise again . . ."

The same evening Dr. Casher preached a memorial sermon at Christ Church, Leamington, where he had been Minister since 1906, after ceasing to be Christopher's honorary curate the year before.

His text was taken from *St. John* 9. 4, "I must work the works of Him that sent me, while it is day: the night cometh, when no man can work." After expounding this and giving an outline of Christopher's life and activities, he referred to some of the Canon's sayings by which he was deeply impressed. "Faith is trust in Christ for everything you need at every moment." "Repentance is that change of mind which leads at once to faith in Christ." "What God has done in one heart He can do in another." "The prayers of the Apostles for their converts, being inspired prayers, reveal the heart of God." "Spiritual life is often strongest when death is nearest, it often seems animated by the near prospect of a grander development."

Appreciations by Mr. Foster-Carter and Harry Grey, Principal of Wycliffe Hall, were also published in *The Oxford Chronicle*. The former repeated another characteristic story he had lately heard. "I loved him," said one man, "because, in his first visit to me in my office, though the door was open, and people might have at any time been coming in, he doffed his hat and offered prayer . . ." Grey wrote: "The zeal which in the earlier days of his pastorate at Oxford may sometimes have provoked a little amused criticism won him—though he cared nothing for popularity — during his latter years the unbounded respect of all parties and classes."

Obituary notices of varying accuracy appeared in many newspapers, including *The Times* and *The Guardian*, and in *The Eagle*, the magazine of St. John's College, Cambridge. *The Record* spoke of Christopher as "one of the best known and most widely honoured of Evangelical clergy," and *The Christian* went so far as to say that "In several important respects, Canon Christopher was one of the best-known men of our time." In these judgements the author of an obituary in *The Oxford Magazine* concurred. ". . . it would be no exaggeration to say that the man whose life in some ways seemed so uneventful was one of the best known clergymen in the Church of England." His name, admits this certainly impartial writer, was a household word in thousands of homes. "He was not a great preacher, though in old days his sermons were always worth hearing . . . yet he influenced hundreds of lives, and even where he had no direct influence, he was respected and admired." Perhaps the most impressive tribute of all was the leading article in *The Oxford Times*, which however did not fail to emphasize that "... he was a shrewd, capable man of business ..." "One of the really good men of the earth," it began, "has passed away in the person of Canon Christopher ... Englishmen pride themselves on concealing their emotions, and are so successful that they too often end in having none to conceal. Canon Christopher's faith was so real, and his love so warm, that it was impossible for him to speak on religious subjects without betraying his emotion by his voice, and sometimes by his tears ... What did mark off Canon Christopher from all other men we have ever known was that capacity for faith and love which can only be described as apostolic. St. John and St. Paul must have been like that; they had the present vision of the unseen, and so at all times and in all company had Canon Christopher ..."

The committees of those societies with which Christopher had been intimately connected hastened to pass resolutions of gratitude for his work and of sympathy with his family. The Church Missionary Society, for example, recorded a minute in which they recalled "with thankful admiration his devotion to the supreme cause of the evangelisation of the world, both by the living voice of the missionary and by the word of the Scriptures ... The Annual Missionary Breakfast was only one of the agencies, though perhaps the most conspicuous, by which he sought to interest in the great enterprise Oxford men of all grades, from the Vice-Chancellor to the youngest undergraduate."

A year later the east window of St. Aldate's church — by 1905 almost covered with creeper — was filled with stained glass in memory of Christopher.[1] An appeal was issued in May 1913, signed by the Vice-Chancellor, the Mayor, the Archdeacon, the Rector of Exeter, the Master of Pembroke, and Alderman Salter. "Canon Christopher belonged to the University and City of Oxford quite as much as to the parish," so they had confidence in asking "those who hold Oxford dear ... to aid us in preserving for the Oxford of the future the memory of one who was for so long a 'prophet amongst us,' whom Oxford must never forget." As a result two hundred and eighty pounds was raised by the people of St. Aldate's and

[1]An alabaster memorial tablet was erected in the chancel of St. Matthew's, Grandpont by the parishioners.

the Canon's friends. In October 1913, a supplementary appeal, signed by the Rector and churchwardens, was made. The window — designed by Mr. Foster-Carter — illustrates the church's duty to preach the gospel to every creature. Five figures occupy the large lights. In the centre is Christ the King. On either side are St. Paul and St. Philip the Deacon. On the outsides are James Hannington, the martyred Bishop of Eastern Equatorial Africa, representing Oxford, and Henry Martyn, the Indian missionary, representing Cambridge. An inscription below reads: "This window is dedicated to the Glory of God and in gratitude for the faithful ministry in this place of Alfred Millard William Christopher, M.A., Honorary Canon of Christ Church, Rector 1859-1905". The glass was the work of Messrs. Burlison and Grylls of Great Ormond Street, London, directed by H. S. Rogers, then and in later years as Alderman Rogers, a well-known Oxford architect, and sometime mayor of the city.

A large congregation, including Captain Seton-Christopher and the Mayor of Oxford (Alderman the Revd. W. E. Sherwood), attended to hear Bishop Chavasse of Liverpool perform the dedication.[1] Mr. Foster-Carter (the Bishop's son-in-law) had resigned the living, but was present to read one of the lessons, the other being read by Dr. Jackson, now retired from Exeter College. The service, on 5 February 1914, was conducted by the Revd. W. A. Williamson, "Rector-in-charge".[2] In his address Dr. Chavasse said that he had hesitated to accept the invitation to speak, in preference to one of Canon Christopher's curates. "But when he remembered how much he owed to him, he felt that it would be ungracious to the living and ungrateful to the dead if he held back." He went on to recall knowing the Canon when he himself was one of Christopher's undergraduate followers. He remarked that "It was not the wisdom of his word that attracted them; it was not the depth of his thoughts which he put before them, but it was the atmosphere of prayer. It was the feeling of the presence of God, and the sincere and lovable character of the man himself. Today there were scattered throughout the towns and villages of the country and in many parts of the world men who looked back with thankfulness on those all-too-short hours, spent

[1]A copy of the order of proceedings is preserved in the Bodleian Library.
[2]Vicar of St. Matthew's, Oxford, 1914-26. He had been a student at St. John's Hall, Highbury, under Christopher's friend Prebendary Boultbee.

week by week with him in prayer, and who thanked God that when at Oxford they had the unspeakable advantage of his friendship and help." Going on to refer to aspects of his character, he mentioned among other things the Canon's courage. "He saw God and was fearless. He came from a race of soldiers, and he used to tell his friends that there was a time when his highest ambition was to be a soldier himself. He brought the courage of the soldier into the work of the church. He was fearless as a church builder. He had no great means, and could expect little help from the city, yet he felt that it was God's work. He felt that it had to be done, and with tremendous courage he took it in hand . . . His courage also showed itself in his defence of what he felt to be the truth. He was never ashamed of his own convictions. They were not popular, but unpopularity never daunted him. He had seen indignant letters written to him by men of high position on account of the line he took, but he replied as he always did, with the utmost courtesy, and went on doing what he felt to be his duty . . . Now his voice and his loving heart were still . . . Today they thanked God for him . . ."

A few months later, the Bishop of Oxford, Dr. Gore, publicly instituted the Revd. T. W. Ketchlee of Exeter College as Rector of St. Aldate's. In the course of an address the Bishop said that "In St. Aldate's they could look back upon a memorable past associated as it was with the ministry of Canon Christopher. They all knew how he stood in that place, valiantly, with overwhelming self-sacrifice, and with a complete indifference to himself for all that he believed to be true . . . They knew what a wonderful blessing, a sort of halo of blessing attended his ministry . . ." These words may be taken in conjunction with the concluding sentence of a tribute by the Revd. H. C. Sturdy, curate of St. Aldate's from 1869 to 1875, which appeared in *The Record* shortly after Christopher's death. ". . . the half can never be told of the blessing God has given to the ministry of my dear old Rector . . ."

In 1916 further memorials were placed in St. Aldate's — a tablet and a pair of communion rails (of a type based on the houseling bench), the gift of the Canon's family. The north rail commemorated the Canon; the other Mrs. Christopher. The modest alabaster tablet is fixed to the chancel arch, and carries a short inscription recording the association with the church of Christopher and his wife. On this occasion the dedication was performed by the Master of Pembroke, Bishop Mitchinson, who from a long and intimate knowledge of Christopher (he had been a Fellow when the college decided to sell the advowson of St. Aldate's) could speak of him as "a consistent Evangelical Church of England man with nothing narrow about him," and as "a great peace-maker and unifier in Oxford, for he had done a great deal to make Oxford men understand each other better in regard to spiritual attitude."

In 1911 a senior clergyman, who had first heard the gospel at Christopher's lips, and who had followed his ministry at St. Aldate's from the first year to the last, the Revd. J. E. Matthews, then Vicar of Southwick, Northamptonshire, had concluded some reminiscences with the opinion that "in Canon Christopher God gave our Alma Mater, —*Cambridge* man though he was — one of His very choicest gifts." As late as 1946, a tutor of Hertford College could write: "There are many in the country today, and not a few in high office in Church and State, who owe to Canon Christopher the enrichment of a simple faith." Looking back in 1938, Dr. Downer, with his undergraduate memories of Christopher's work in the 'sixties, and his subsequent knowledge of him, went so far as to state: "We can safely affirm that no more sacred name, no more innocent or simple character, no more loving heart, or more faithful minister of Christ, is to be found in the roll of saints, who have adorned the University and City of Oxford."

One who had known Christopher during three periods of residence in Oxford since 1869, the Revd. R. W. G. Hunter, a nonconformist minister, wrote to *The Guardian* after the Canon's death in words which form a fitting epilogue to more formal tributes. "From him there radiated an influence always beneficent and beautiful, always attractive and attracting. It shone in his face, it was heard in the sympathy of his voice. Never on this earth was there a more dedicated spirit. His life was apostolic; I might use a stronger word and say of him, as of Stephen, it was angelic. Of all who knew him whilst he was among us, happy are they who could catch the light of his face, and who could enter into the spirit of the best man I ever knew."

Appendices I — VII

AA

Appendix I

CANON A. M. W. CHRISTOPHER: PLACE OF BIRTH AND BAPTISM

The birthplace of A. M. W. Christopher has been variously given.[1] He himself was presumably responsible for the entry under that heading in the (fuller) census returns for 1851. There it is 'London',[2] which at first suggests the City, and agrees with the entry in *Alumni Cantabrigienses*.[3] But the author of Christopher's obituary in *The Eagle*, the magazine of St. John's College, Cambridge, states unequivocally that Christopher was born "at Ealing, Middlesex"[4]. This is decidedly unlikely. Christopher was not baptised at Ealing; and there is no evidence of his parents being domiciled there.[5] *Alumni Oxonienses* notices Christopher's father as "George, of Enfield, Middlesex, arm."[6] This is demonstrably inaccurate as regards his private residence in 1860, the year of his son's incorporation at Oxford. George Christopher had by then for more than thirty years been living at Chiswick,[7] and continued to do so till his death a year later.[8] Some investigation of the possibility that it affords a clue to Christopher's birthplace[9] has yielded no evidence of any Christopher association with Enfield. Birth at Enfield would indeed have been at variance with Christopher's own statement, and his baptism did not take place there. On the contrary, it is conclusive, from the pointer of the London directories,[10] confirmed by rate books of Holborn,[11] that for several years before and after 1820, the normal residence of his parents was 14, Great Coram Street, Bloomsbury. Thus in 1851, Christopher might more naturally have entered his birthplace as 'Bloomsbury'; but the less precise designation 'London' may be presumed at this date not to exclude the metropolitan boroughs, while the possibility of his having been born away from home must not be entirely disregarded.

There is no reference to place of birth or baptism in *The Family of Christopher*, compiled by Christopher's son, or in Burke's *Landed Gentry*.[12] Dr. Griffith Thomas made no note of either. The present generation of the Christopher family had no information on the subject. No light is to be obtained from the archives of St. John's or Jesus Colleges, Cambridge.[13] There is no baptismal certificate retained, in connection with Christopher's ordination, in the custody of the Registrar of the diocese of Winchester.[14] Christopher's baptism is, however, noted in the genealogy deposited at the College of Arms

[1] His date of birth, on the other hand, is frequently and consistently cited, both by himself and others, as 20 August 1820.

[2] Census Return, 1851, *re* Park Shot, Richmond (Public Record Office, H.O. 1605, vol. 16 (23), p.9.)

[3] *Alumni Cantabrigienses*, ed. J. & J. A. Venn, pt. ii, vol. ii (1944), p. 35.

[4] *The Eagle*, vol. xxxv (1914), p. 215. The notice contains several inaccuracies.

[5] Information from Dr. F. A. Toufar, Reference Librarian, Central Library, Ealing, letter dated 27.7.1961, p. 1.

[6] *Alumni Oxonienses*, compiled J. Foster, 1715-1886, vol. i (1887), p. 251. In *Oxford Men & Their Colleges* (1893), 455, Foster went so far as to state that Christopher was "born at Enfield, Middlesex, 1821" *(sic)*.

[7] *The Family of Christopher and Some Others*, anon. (by A. C. Seton-Christopher), (1933), pp. 33, 35.

[8] Will, Geo. Christopher, proved London 13.5.1861. (Prin. Registry, 1867–277.)

[9] When Christopher's second son matriculated at Oxford in 1875, his father was entered as "of Richmond, Surrey, cler."—his residence at the time of his son's birth. (*Alumni Oxonienses, ibid.*)

[10] Critchett & Woods' *Post office London Directory*, 1816, p. 65, 1822, p. 70; *The Royal Blue Book* 1824, p. 89 & sig. C 4 v.

[11] Rate Books, Holborn, 1816-24. (Holborn Central Library.)

[12] Burke's *Landed Gentry*, 1952, p. 444.

[13] Letters from the Librarian of St. John's Coll., dated 19.7.1961, p.1; and from Mr. A. L. Percival, Bursar of Jesus Coll., 19.7.1961, p.1.

[14] Letter from Mr. G. H. Gardner, Registrar, Winchester diocese, dated 1.2.1961, p.1.

at the time of a grant of arms to George Christopher in 1824. In common with his younger brother and sisters, Alfred Christopher is said to have been baptised (no date being given) at St. George's, Bloomsbury,[1]—the parish church of the inhabitants of Great Coram Street. The parish register, however, while duly recording the baptism of his sister Selina on 13 July 1815, and of his next sister Louisa (born 1818) together with his brother Leonard (born 1822) on 23 April 1823, nowhere refers to the baptism of Alfred Christopher.[2] By April 1823, he would have been living at Downend, Gloucestershire; but he was not baptised at Mangotsfield, in which parish Downend was then included.[3]

A late nineteenth century draft pedigree, covering only two generations of the Christopher family, apparently in the hand of F. A. Crisp, who published many volumes of pedigrees, but which in this case does not seem to have been printed by him, is preserved in the library of the Society of Genealogists. It also assigns St. George's, Bloomsbury, as Christopher's place of baptism, but gives the date 19 November 1828.[4] Again no such entry is to be found in the St. Georges' register. But the records of St. George-the-Martyr, Queen Square, Holborn, where Christopher's father became a parishioner on moving to Great Ormond Street between 1824 and 1827, have yielded the information that Christopher was in fact baptised there,—four years at least after the alleged baptism at St. George's, Bloomsbury, recorded in the registered pedigree at the College of Arms,—on the date given above,[5] being then eight years old.[6] He was christened Alfred Millard William. One of his sponsors is known to have been either his uncle or his aunt Millard.[7] No hint is forthcoming as to why the baptism had been so long delayed. (That of Louisa Christopher, however, five years after birth, suggests that the parents were inclined to be deliberate in such matters.) But it is not inappropriate, in view of his 'war-like' bent, that Christopher should have been baptised by a minister who was a member of the family to which Sir Francis Drake apparently belonged. The Revd. Charles Digby Mackworth Drake, son of Francis Drake of Yardbury, Devonshire, sometime Envoy Extraordinary and Minister Plenipotentiary at the court of Munich, had lately been a Fellow-Commoner of St. John's College, Cambridge.[8] From 1826[9] to 1829[10] he was curate of Fenny Compton, Warwickshire.[11] (Why he officiated in London on this occasion does not appear.) In 1834, after a short incumbency in East Anglia, he was appointed, by his cousin Lord Clinton, to be Rector of Huntshaw, Devon, and held the living till his death forty years later.[12]

[1] Information from (and checked by) Sir Anthony Wagner, Garter King of Arms, letter dated 27.1.1961, p. 1.

[2] Baptism Register, St. George's, Bloomsbury. (Greater London Record Office, County Hall, S.E.1.)

[3] Evidently his uncle and aunt Millard did not feel themselves responsible for this step; or, they may not have known of its omission.

[4] D.MSS., Christopher, Soc. of Genealogists' Library, London.

[5] Baptism Register, St. George-the-Martyr, Queen Square, W.C., 19.11.1828.

[6] His date of birth, 20 August 1820, is also entered, as it is in the Heralds' pedigree (1824).

[7] *The Family of Christopher,* as cited, p. 36.

[8] *Alumni Cantabrigienses,* ed. J. & J. A. Venn, pt. ii, vol. ii (1944), p. 334.

[9] Episcopal Register, Lichfield & Coventry, 1.1.1826, cited by Mr. M. B. S. Exham, Registrar, Lichfield diocese, letter dated 19.10.1966, p. 1; confirmed by Baptism Register of Fenny Compton, March 1826 f.

[10] Baptism & Burial Registers of Fenny Compton, at Warwick Record Office, 1826–Nov. 1829; letter from the Revd. R. F. Cyster, Rector of Fenny Compton, dated 9.3.1967, p. 1.

[11] Testimonial annexed to presentation deed, C. D. M. Drake, to rectory of Dalham, Suffolk, 1830, cited by Miss J. M. Kennedy, City & County Archivist, Norwich, letter dated 5.9.1966, p. 1.

[12] *The County Families of the United Kingdom* by E. Walford (1874), p. 298; *Notes and Gleanings,* ed. W. Cotton and J. Dallas, vol. v (1892), p. 117; *The Visitations of the County of Devon,* ed. J. L. Vivian, n.d., pp. 298, 299.

Appendix II

CORRESPONDENCE OF THE REVD. A. M. W. CHRISTOPHER WITH THE REVD. DR. H. P. LIDDON & WITH THE REVD. DR. E. B. PUSEY, 1878-79

Christopher's letters are those numbered 33-37 in the Letter List (Appendix VI). Christopher and Liddon both used 'f' where a second 's' was necessary, and this usage has been altered, to comply with modern custom. Otherwise the transcriptions are as far as possible exact. Liddon's first letter is missing.

ST. ALDATES RECTORY. OXFORD

27 Nov 1878

Dear Dr. Liddon,

It is a great grief to me that the Abbé Gaume's Romish book the teaching of which I believe to be utterly subversive of the Gospel of Christ should have been published by Dr. Pusey as adapted by him to the use of the English Church.

I respect Dr. Pusey for his age, his learning, and specially for his great and valuable work on the Book of Daniel; and generally for his opposition to Scepticism, but if the dearest friend I have on earth were to publish a book subversive of the Gospel, and teaching "Another Gospel which is not another", it would be my plain duty in faithfulness to Christ, & in love to the souls of my fellow men to do what I could to help to expose this pernicious perversion of the Gospel. Mr. Gill's lecture, of which you shall have a copy next week, will prove to the Church that my description of the Romish book adapted to the use of the English Church by Dr. Pusey is a true one.

I did not in any way suggest the subject of the Lecture, nor did the Church Association or any one connected with it, but when it was proposed to me, as I had already seen the book, and had formed a very strong opinion of the utterly unscriptural character of its teaching, I could not, without unfaithfulness to Christ, reject the Subject, or refuse to preside at the Lecture.

The Lecture itself will be sufficient justification of all who have promoted it. Dr. Pusey's book is the fullest justification of their conduct. The Lecture was listened to by a large audience which crowded the Town Hall on Monday night with the deepest attention. It set forth that Gospel truth which alone can effectually correct pernicious Romish perversions of the Gospel.

It is a pain to me to give you pain dear Dr. Liddon who have shewn a kind feeling in subscribing, as you remind me, to the Schools of the very poor parish which half surrounds Ch: Ch:; and in other ways. But with the strong conviction which I have of the dishonour to the Gospel of Christ which the Romish teaching of the Abbé Gaume's Manual does, I have no choice but, at any cost, to take part in exposing this evil book. A dear friend of mine, a learned theologian of this University who has a great respect and regard for Dr. Pusey and a high esteem of his great work on the Book of the prophet Daniel, & his other efforts against Scepticism, was entirely opposed to such a lecture as Mr. Gill's being delivered, *until he had read the lecture;* when he had done this, his view was entirely changed, and he felt that duty to God demanded that it should be delivered at once, and printed for the information of the Church. I shall be greatly grieved dear Dr. Liddon if my having acted on a sense of duty to God lessens your friendship towards me.

Sincerely yours

Alfred M W Christopher

CHRIST CHURCH,
OXFORD. Nov. 27. 1878

Dear Mr Christopher,

Nothing, I fear, would be gained, if I were to enter on the subject of the Lecture, at which you thought it well to preside; or, on the very important question, as to how far Dr Pusey does "subvert" either 'the Gospel' as taught by St. Paul and St. John,—*or*—what you conceive to be 'the Gospel'.

What I venture to urge is this. If controversy be a duty, it ought, if possible, to keep clear of personalities. Your Lecturer was not obliged to select Dr Pusey's book as the text of his lecture. To do so in Oxford was to offer a public insult to the most distinguished professor of Divinity in the place.

If Dr Pusey had been an eminent Low Churchman, and had written a book to shew that Baptismal Regeneration was a "lie of Satan"; and, if, thereupon, Mr Noel or some other clergyman had presided at a meeting at which a Lecturer had exposed the *dishonesty* of Dr Pusey's book, by shewing, that as a minister of the Church, he was bound to say over every baptized child, without any qualification, "This child is regenerate"—you would, I think have thought Mr Noel's proceeding unjustifiable. The lecturer might have quoted Mr Spurgeon as agreeing with him; and might have said a great many sharp, and exasperating, and withal true things at Dr Pusey's expense. But, in the opinion of all good men, who care for higher things than the indulgence of party passions, the proceeding would have been deplorable. It would have been felt that the question whether Baptismal Regeneration is a 'lie of Satan' or an integral portion of the Gospel of Jesus Christ could have been better discussed, if the personal element were left out of sight.

But it is the *personal* element in controversy which attracts the many men who do not care very much about the solemn question of Truth or Falsehood. It was the fact that *Dr Pusey*, well known in Oxford, and living in the same street, had written the book, which gave zest to the subject, & commanded the attention of your audience, on Monday, at the Town Hall.

I have known Dr Pusey intimately for 32 years; and I do not affect to be indifferent to such a discreditable proceeding as that of Monday evening. I regret with all my heart that so good a man as yourself should be associated with it, upon whatever grounds; and I think it sincere to say to you what I have said, and shall say, to others.

I am,
Dear Mr Christopher,
Yours truly,
H P Liddon.

P.S. Dr Pusey has no idea that I have written to you. I do not suppose that he has heard of the Lecture.

ST. ALDATE'S RECTORY. OXFORD Monday Dec 2. 1878.

Dear Dr. Liddon,

A necessary visit to London & the services of the day of Intercession for Missions & of yesterday have delayed my reply to your second letter.

In the exercise of the like cordial frankness as you have so kindly claimed in your notes to me, you must suffer me to point out that it is exactly that long & intimate affection for Dr. Pusey, to which you refer that disqualifies you for sitting as judge upon my conduct. Had your relations to Dr. Pusey not been what they are, private feeling would not have usurped the place of a calm & just judgment; and you would never have suffered your pen to charge me with taking part (necessarily the principal part) in a "discreditable proceeding," and (as an accomplice) with "offering a public insult" to your friend.

You evidently forgot in the moment of writing that Dr. Pusey has within the last three months publicly invited criticism by two overt acts absolutely unparalleled in the history of our Church since the Reformation. He has adapted and published for use in our Protestant Communion a Roman Catholic "Manual for Confessors." And when one hundred Protestant Bishops, in conference assembled, have solemnly & unanimously condemned the practice of habitual confession, Dr. Pusey has publicly challenged the correctness of their decision or else the justice of their censure.

How at such a crisis a Protestant lecturer on the evils & unlawfulness of a stated practice of confession could (as you suggest) select any other book as the text book of his lecture, I am utterly unable to conceive. How under such circumstances, Dr. Pusey's friends can either suppose or wish that his recent volume should escape public criticism is equally unintelligible to me. And if so, is it really true that what would be natural and proper in any & every other town of England, becomes improper & "a public insult" in Oxford? You seem to deprecate public criticism of Dr. Pusey's recent volume here in Oxford, on the ground partly of his distinguished position amongst us, and partly of his being resident here.

Can it be your calm opinion that we who are pledged most solemnly, the Lord being our helper, to "banish & drive away all erroneous and strange doctrines contrary to God's Word," are freed from any such obligation if the teacher of such doctrines is a distinguished professor of Divinity in the place where we live? Taught by the Holy Ghost, an Apostle surely laid down another rule, when he wrote "though an Angel from heaven preach any other gospel unto you, let him be accursed." And because his fellow Apostle was in the same city at the time, was St. Paul guilty of a "discreditable proceeding" and did he "offer a public insult" to one still more distinguished than Dr. Pusey, because then and there he *withstood him to the face?* If your position is consistent with the claims of conscience, and with loyalty to truth, then no one occupying the University pulpit, or preaching in a parish Church in Oxford may animadvert upon Dr. Pusey's adapted Manual for Confessors without committing an insult! Surely dear Dr. Liddon those who hold such language are not Dr. Pusey's wisest or best friends.

You offer me an hypothesis, which is not only violently improbable but absolutely impossible. I can however accept what you really mean with the fullest fearlessness, and unhesitatingly reply that if any eminent Low Churchman, really taught by the Spirit of God, having just put forth a book on which the eyes of the whole Church were fastened, were charged with having written, contrary to Scripture, or to the formularies of the Church of England, the desire of his heart & the language of his lips would be, especially if he resided in a University City — "Here, where I live & have laboured & am known, let those who controvert my teaching, & charge me with unfaithfulness to the truth, come & make good their positions." With infinite sorrow, I can well conceive, would he deprecate as treason against truth the mistaken affection of a friend, who would try to keep from the place a conscientious opponent by the suggestion that to be "personal" in controversy is necessarily identical with being "insulting"!

It has escaped your notice that when you write about "the indulgence of party passions" you are borrowing wholly from conjecture, & in no degree from fact. And no less so when you volunteer the remark that the large attendance at the recent lecture was due to zest which expected personalities lent to the subject. The attendance at prior lectures of the Church Association in Oxford has been just as large. And I have known the lecturer as a valued private friend for many years, and can say honestly that he is not actuated by religious partisanship, does not deal in 'sharp' or 'exasperating' sayings at another's expense, and has no pleasure in those who do.

If not in this life, assuredly dear Dr. Liddon in another, it will be made clear to you that to speak earnestly and valiantly for Divine truth, even if in doing so the speaker has to blame to the face & by name one revered for his years & position, is entirely compatible with Christian love and the bond of peace.

Believe me Dear Dr. Liddon
faithfully & sincerely yours
A M W Christopher

3 Amen Court
St. Pauls EC
Dec. 3. 1878.

Dear Mr Christopher,

When I termed your proceedings in the Oxford Town Hall "discreditable", I was using the language of a highly educated man, who has no sort of sympathy either with High Church or Low Church principles, but who thinks that respect is due to age, & learning, and sanctity, such as Dr Pusey's.

Dr Pusey *himself* would be the last person in the world to shrink from criticism. He has challenged those who may think it their duty to do so, to prosecute him at law. The Church Association, apparently, thinks it *safer* to hold him up to odium before a popular and necessarily semi-educated audience.

You will, of course, take your own line. If you think that the spirit of such lectures as that at which you presided is consistent with 1. Cor. xiii, and is not rather calculated to produce in very many souls at least *four* out of those *seventeen* works of the flesh which are condemned in Gal. V. 19-21; all that I can say is that we read our New Testaments with very different eyes indeed.

One who was present at the lecture said that "Dr Pusey was *well* groaned at."

With sincere regret, but without further hesitation, I must ask you no longer to consider me a supporter of your schools, or of any other works in your parish.

Yours sincerely
H P Liddon

The Rev A M W Christopher.

St. Aldate's Rectory Oxford.

Dec 6 1878

Dear Dr. Liddon,

Your last letter has disappointed me in more respects than one. I had hoped that my statement would at once draw from you a frank admission that you had been mistaken, & a frank withdrawal of the words which stigmatized my conduct as "discreditable." It is true you tell me that that term was not originally applied to me by yourself; but you make it too clear that you have adopted it ex animo.

Would it be difficult for me to meet with more than one "highly educated man having no sort of sympathy either with High Church or Low Church principles" who would both think and say that your withdrawal of your annual subscription from the parochial schools of St. Aldate's is on your part to take a poor revenge for an imaginary wrong done by me to your friend? Would you accept his verdict? Would you deem it generous or just in me to adopt it?

I have referred to more grounds of disappointment than one, and this your mode, I will not say of retaliation but of protest causes me more sorrow than that to which I have already alluded. I had supposed always that your kind subscription was a gift to our Master, & to His poor; and have never imagined that it was personal to myself, or to be accepted by me as a stamp of your approval of my theological views, or of my conduct as a clergyman in Oxford. This entirely new view of your liberality forces me to consider how far I can consistently with self-respect, or with that freedom to act according to the dictates of conscience which I am persuaded you value as highly as do I, retain your Donation to the fund for supplying my parish with a parsonage. That house while I continue Rector of St. Aldate's will be personally enjoyed by myself. — And if it is now irksome to you to have helped in maintaining the schools for the poor of St. Aldate's, it must be tenfold more painful to you to have had part in providing a home for its incumbent of whom, to my sorrow, you now think and write so ill. It is therefore surely my duty at once to place the enclosed cheque for five guineas the amount of your donation in your hands.

I am grieved that you should have been misinformed with respect to what took place at the lecture by Mr. Gill. Distrusting my own hearing powers I have taken pains to enquire of three friends & they assure me that there was no groaning at Dr. Pusey. If in a different part of the Town Hall your informant heard anything not sufficiently marked to be heard or remembered by my three friends, it was probably due to the indiscreet proposal publicly made by some friend of Dr. Pusey that three cheers should be given for him. But in spite of the challenge thus thrown down, it is certain that neither I nor my three friends observed any groaning at Dr. Pusey.

And now in conclusion, dear Dr. Liddon, may I treat you with the freedom of a Christian brother, & honestly express my regret that you should have levelled so gratuitous a sarcasm at the Council of the Church Association. To use your own words — Is it consistent with I Cor. XIII ?

For the last twenty years it has been widely known that Dr. Pusey is absolutely safe from legal prosecution. He is not within the jurisdiction of any Bishop — & as holding a post under letters patent he is not amenable to the law ecclesiastical. Now in my judgment it would be just as generous, just as fair, & righteous, and just as charitable for me to assert that Dr. Pusey *knowing this* challenges prosecution in insincere bravado, as for you to charge the Council of the Church Association with holding him up to popular odium and resorting to that as a "safer" course than appealing to the law to coerce him. As a fact the Church Association had nothing whatever to do with the choice of the subject of Mr. Gill's lecture.

I am Dear Dr. Liddon
sincerely yours
Alfred M W Christopher

3 Amen Court EC.
7. Dec. 1878.

Dear Mr Christopher,

Your letter obliges me to ask your permission to make two explanations. In referring to the Church Association, I stated what I honestly supposed to be the fact. The handbills led me to connect the Church Association with the Lecture. And I never before heard that Dr Pusey's position protects him against an action in the Church Courts. Dr Pusey, I am very confident, has no suspicion that this is the case. Had he believed his position to be legally unassailable, it would, in my opinion, have been cowardly of him to challenge other people to prosecute him, if they thought fit. If the Church Association has been advised by competent lawyers, that the case is as you say, I unreservedly admit that my language was undeserved, and I beg to retract it. But the fact ought to be generally known.

If it were possible to continue my subscription to your schools without doing more than making an offering to Christ and His poor, I would thankfully do so. As it is, I shall transfer the subscription to a neighbouring parish. But such a subscription is inevitably a mark of sympathy, almost a vote of confidence. So long as I could think of you only as a self-denying worker among the poor, I gave it gladly; even though 'the Gospel', as taught by the Low Church party seems to me a very inadequate reproduction of the Gospel as taught in the New Testament. But when you take the Chair at such a meeting as that which was held the other day, you use your position as the Parish Minister of St Aldate's, for a purpose which my conscience tells me is very wrong. You oblige me to ask myself, how far I am right in continuing in any way to strengthen your hands.

But I hope you will allow me to return you your cheque. My feeling is in no sense retrospective; and I was bold enough to hope that my first letter might somehow have prevented your attending the meeting, & thus have saved me from all further difficulty. If I could do so, without seeming to hold out to you what you think an unworthy motive, I would say that I would gladly continue or rather increase my subscription, if I could be assured that you would not use your position for such purposes as promoting attacks on aged & holy men, who certainly have had as full opportunities of ascertaining what the Gospel really is as any of their assailants. But, I fear you would not allow me to say this: and I cannot, without insincerity, withdraw the epithet 'discreditable' as applied to the proceedings in question. It represents, in my opinion, the least that they deserve in the way of censure: and I must once more say how pained I am that a man like yourself,—whom I have always hitherto associated with the devotional and Christian rather than with the fierce and merely controversialist section of the Low Church party,—should have been in any way mixed up with them.

I am
Yours sincerely
H P Liddon

The Rev A M W Christopher

ST. ALDATES RECTORY. OXFORD

Dec 9 1878

Dear Dr. Liddon,

More than twenty years ago — before the formation of the Church Association — a small Committee of theologians and lawyers met in London to consider the duty of prosecuting Dr. Pusey in the Ecclesiastical Courts. It seemed to them that from his as the directing mind, the stream of doctrinal error, which has since risen to such a height, was invading the Church. Every one of his theological writings was carefully perused and considered, and a case was eventually laid before very eminent Ecclesiastical Counsel. The then movers were distinctly advised that, though much written by Dr. Pusey was so repugnant to the formularies of the Church of England as to ensure judicial condemnation, yet his peculiar position rendered him unassailable by any process of law.

His Canonry is only an incident of his professorship, which he holds under letters patent. The foregoing I have received from one of the lawyers concerned — but it is pretty widely known, and long has been so. The legal advisers of the Church Association & its Committee, are conversant with these facts.[1]

I am sorry indeed to seem obstinate, or to run the risk of wounding your feelings — but it will be a relief to me if you will kindly suffer my cheque enclosed to remain in your hands.

I am, I trust, above creating a sentimental grievance, or seeking to rub a blow into a sore. But humble & limited as are my position & influence compared with yours, if I forfeit my self-respect, I spontaneously throw away a force for usefulness which is Christ's gift to me. Would He have me accept, for my personal convenience & use, a gift, even from a brother, who after careful reflection persists in designating my recent conduct "discreditable"?

[1] The first two paragraphs of this letter are reproduced in *Life of Edward Bouverie Pusey* by H. P. Liddon, ed. J. O. Johnston & others, 2nd edn., vol. iv (1897), p. 318.

I am well persuaded dear Dr. Liddon, that at our earliest meeting in eternity — your first act towards me will be to express regret for having employed the term. Meanwhile I must needs try to obey God rather than man, & to be true to His Commission & to my ordination vow — remembering that in the same sentence in which He says to me ἀκαίρως He prepares me by His word ἔλεγξον to expect that many will regard my obedience as unseasonable. 2 Tim IV. 2

I will only add that you seem to me not to realize the consequence of your denunciation of me; now in reality it amounts to this — that no Oxford clergyman may, while Dr. Pusey lives, call in question from his pulpit any one of the Professor's doctrinal statements in connection with his name. By reason of the respect due to his age and position — which I ex animo concede to him — he is to have, in your judgement, such absolute dominion over the faith & practice of his brethren in the ministry, that their congregations are to find them dumb whenever Dr. Pusey has spoken.

Yours very sincerely
Alfred M W Christopher

3. Amen Court. E.C.
Dec. 10. 1878

Dear Mr Christopher,

I thank you for your interesting information on the subject of Dr Pusey's legal position. It is entirely new to me, as it will be, I think, to Dr Pusey himself.

I must, of course, accept, although reluctantly, your decision as to the cheque.

Indeed you mistake my claim on behalf of Dr Pusey. He has been criticised all his life, probably more persistently and more passionately than any other member of the Church of England. He has long learnt to do justice, and only justice, to human criticism. He would be the last person in England to complain of anything that might be said about himself. But while I am, also, as far as possible from deprecating criticism of what he writes, I submit that it should be addressed to knowledge & reason, and not to passion. If, for instance, *you* were to write a book against what Dr Pusey teaches on the subject of Confession and Absolution, it would be read by those who, (having the Bible and Prayer book in their hands) entirely disagree with you, but with the respect which is due to your character. And the University Pulpit is much more at the command of those who dissent from Dr Pusey than of those who agree with him; and, if his opponents can say anything that is theologically entitled to serious consideration, they are very sure to carry with them a very large number of minds. If I regret, I should not think of complaining of these methods of opposing Dr Pusey; but the case is very different when a strange lecturer, announced as appearing under the auspices of an extreme party organisation, addresses himself to a large number of well-meaning but half educated people on a difficult subject, — as to which it is easy to rouse their passions, but with the real bearings of which they are, necessarily, almost entirely unacquainted, — in the Town Hall. If I were an infidel, I could easily make out a much more telling case against the circulation of the Bible, than the lecturer (as reported) made out against Dr Pusey & his book, and on *exactly the same grounds;* and I should not have much difficulty in carrying a half-educated audience with me. Indeed, as I grieve to know, this has been done in London. But *our* common reply would be, partly that the warnings of the Bible against sensual sins are meant for those whom they concern, and, partly, that 'to the pure all things are pure.' Of course, I am not saying that the Bible and any human book are of the same authority: but only that they may be attacked in the same way. And thus what in your eyes is an act of loyalty to the Gospel, appears to me to be an appeal to those passions of our fallen nature which so easily shelter themselves under the sanctions of religion. Alas! the Church Association reminds me of nothing so much as of the Spanish Inquisition; and I have the same feeling of utter *moral* repugnance towards both these bodies. They work in the interest of different beliefs, and by different methods. But their animating spirit is the same.

Among the many things that I look forward to with thankful hope in another life, one is the surprise of all my Low Church brethren at finding out what the Gospel of our Divine Redeemer really is in its unmutilated grandeur, and, next, their utter wonder, that they should ever (in perfect good faith) have denounced such a servant of Christ as Dr Pusey, while on earth.

Yours very faithfully
H. P. Liddon.

Rev A M W Christopher.

3. Amen Court E.C.
Dec. 13. 1878

Dear Mr Christopher,

I am obliged to ask you to allow me to trouble you once more.

On reflection, I felt that I ought to ask Dr Pusey, whether he had ever heard of the theory that he is legally unassailable, as stated in your two last letters to me.

I enclose his reply.[1]

Will you show it to the Council of the Church Association, or anyone else who may wish to see it? I must beg you to return it to me; but you are at liberty to make a copy of it, if you think well.

Yours very sincerely
H. P. Liddon

Rev A. M. W Christopher

(*In another hand, believed to be Mrs. Christopher's*)

St. Aldate's Rectory Oxford.

Dec. 14th. 1878.

Dear Dr. Liddon

You are well aware that I am President of the Oxford Branch of the Church Association, for this was on the Bill on which you read my name, and the fact that I lately presided at a lecture connected with that Association, though the subject was not in any way suggested by it was the occasion of our correspondence, yet in your last letter to me, you write, though I feel sure that in doing so you did not intend any personal unkindness towards myself, "Alas! the Church Association reminds me of nothing so much as of the Spanish Inquisition, & I have the same feeling of utter *moral* repugnance towards both these bodies, they work in the interest of different beliefs & by different methods but their animating spirit is the same."

You began your correspondence with me by referring to St. Paul's chapter on charity (I Cor XIII) & you close it with an illustration of your own conception of Christian charity, in the Saying that "the animating spirit" of a body of faithful Brethren in Christ, deeply attached to the Church of England, & to the Scriptural principles of the Protestant Reformation is "the same as that of the Spanish Inquisition"! I *know* many of these brethren & you naturally do not. I know that their animating Spirit is that faithful love which is the fruit of Gospel truth, combined with a faithfulness to Christ which makes them abhor those deadly additions to the Gospel which gradually produced that idolatrous caricature of Christianity which we see in the Church of Rome, & which has

[1]Reproduced in Liddon, *op. cit.*, 2nd edn., vol. iv (1897), pp. 318-9.

been one of the great causes of infidelity on the Continent from which much has come to our own country.

The Christian brethren of whom you write that their "animating Spirit" is that of the Spanish Inquisition are united expressly "to uphold the Doctrines, Principles, and Order of the Church of England and to counteract the efforts now being made to pervert her teaching on essential points of the Christian faith, or assimilate her services to those of the Church of Rome, and further to encourage concerted action for the advancement and progress of Spiritual religion."

Surely these objects of the Church Association are lawful & right, and it has sought them in lawful and righteous ways.

If you knew as well as I do some members of the Council of the Church Association, such as the venerable & loveable Prebendary Auriol, I am certain dear Dr. Liddon you would yourself condemn as uncharitable your own description of their "Animating Spirit".

The Church of England is very greatly indebted to the Church Association which has proved that more than fifty of the practices by which the Ritualists have introduced disunion and strife into our Church are utterly illegal. As well might the Queen and her Judges be described as persecutors because they require the law to be obeyed, as the Church Association be described as having "the same animating spirit as the Spanish Inquisition", because it resists the Romanizing innovations which are as much out of harmony with the law of our Church as they are with the teaching of the Gospel. And those who have been proved to be law breakers by the righteous efforts of the Church Association instead of being treated as were the victims of the Spanish Inquisition, have usually had all their expenses & costs, or the greater part of them paid for them, and are glorified by their partizans.

I observe that in the whole of your correspondence with me you never attempt to justify the Romish book which Dr. Pusey has given to our Church, but you seem to make the whole question which concerns the health & usefulness of our Church for generations to come, a merely personal matter respecting your friend.

I shall praise God if at some future time you understand better the Spirit of those who act on the belief that truth is the only foundation of real unity, and if you are brought to see that it is possible in obedience to God's command to contend earnestly for the faith against Romanizing errors & practices in our Church, without any trace of the cruel "Animating Spirit" of the Spanish Inquisition.

I am dear Dr. Liddon
sincerely yours
A. M. W. Christopher

Thank you & Dr. Pusey for allowing me to see his letter received today, & for permission to forward it to the Church Association.

3. Amen Court St Pauls E.C.
Dec. 17. 1878

Dear Mr Christopher,

When I read the public hand-bills from which I gathered that you were to preside at a Meeting in which a strange lecturer was to abuse Dr Pusey publicly, my first impulse was, to say nothing about it to yourself, to say what I thought of it in the Common-Room of Christ Church or elsewhere, and, at some future time, to withdraw my subscription to your schools, without assigning any reason for doing so.

On consideration, I thought it a better course to tell you, (as in your place I should wish to have been told myself,) what a brother-clergyman thought of your proceedings. There was the hope that my remonstrance might have had some weight with you: though perhaps I ought not to have entertained it. As it is, my first impulse might have saved us both from a correspondence, which does not, I fear, help us to draw nearer to each other. To write to you at all, unless I was perfectly outspoken, would have been useless. And the result of my doing so speaks for itself.

2. You observe that I have not discussed the worth of Dr Pusey's book. There is no occasion for me to do so. If it were *proved* that Dr Pusey's book "subverted the Gospel" etc. etc. I should still hold the Meeting in the Town Hall to be discreditable, on the ground that it was combatting religious error by an appeal, not to reason & knowledge, but to uninformed & inflammable passion. There would be other ways of dealing with Dr Pusey, open to those who felt bound to combat him. There are books in which the Revealed Doctrine of Baptismal Regeneration is denied by men, who—to the astonishment of dissenters like Mr Spurgeon,—still find it morally possible to use the Baptismal Service of the Church of England. This error seems to me to be quite as dishonouring to the Work of Christ, as the Restorer of our fallen race, and quite as inconsistent with the plain meaning of Church of England language, as anything that Dr Pusey has ever written, can seem to you. Yet if a High Church clergyman were to preside at a lecture, given by some one else, in which the author of such a book was denounced, till his name was greeted with "volleys of groans" (see Rock, Nov. 29. 1878) I, for one, should think the proceedings discreditable, and I hope I should have the moral courage to tell my friends so. Nor would my judgement be less emphatic, if the writer were 78 years of age, and had done more than most men of his time for the defence and elucidation of Holy Scripture.

3. You write of "deadly additions to the Gospel" etc. etc. I would rather treat such language as the product of strong feeling than as accurate representations of thought. For I too might write about "deadly mutilations of the Gospel", and might proceed to give reasons for my strong conviction that Low Church arguments against the grace of the Sacraments have paved the way for rationalistic rejection of the Atonement, and that Low Church denials of the authority of the Primitive Church, have undermined, in many minds *known* to myself, all serious belief in the Canon of the New Testament. But this would be a large subject. I must merely say that I must not be understood to acquiesce in several expressions which I do not happen to notice.

4. Certainly I knew that you were President of the Oxford branch of the Church Association. It was with real sorrow that I heard of your connection with this body some time since. It is not easy to resign our ideals without a pang; and I was unwilling indeed to think of the hard-working friend of the poor on the platform of a Society, with *such* a spirit as this. But did not the Handbills begin with 'Church Association Lectures'? And the Rock (Nov. 29. 1878) says that the lecture was delivered "in connection with the local branch of the Church Association". I certainly therefore supposed that, whoever suggested the subject, the Church Association claimed some credit for it with its friends, and would not disclaim responsibility for it with those who think of it as I do.

I was careful to say that the religious theory which the Church Association upholds, and the methods which it is able to employ are not those of the Spanish Inquisition. The animating temper whether of the Inquisition, or the Association, can only be judged from their proceedings. My conclusion is not disturbed by the fact which you mention, and which I *unreservedly* believe, that many of the persons concerned in managing the Church Association are, in their private capacity, very estimable indeed. Yet surely also, among the Spanish Inquisitors there were gentle and conscientious men, who yet sincerely believed, that in persecuting the Spanish protestants to death, they were doing God service. They had at command gentle phrases which disguised from themselves the real character of their proceedings; and the good men of the Church Association talk, quite sincerely, I am sure, of 'zeal for the purity of the Gospel'—'ascertaining the law' & the like, while, in reality, they are filling the Church of England almost from end to end with hatred & uncharitableness which it is piteous to think of. It is a matter of notoriety that good men, when under the influence of strong party passion, or as members of a Society or corporation, will often become capable of courses of action from which, as private individuals, they would utterly shrink.

Of your estimate of the achievements of the Church Association, I will only say that it is very different from my own. And I have derived my impressions from the Record & the Rock.

How much I wish that in view of our immense dangers, from the Church of Rome on one side, & from sheer unbelief on the other, we of the Church of England could learn to tolerate each other, & to trust to God the Holy Spirit to teach us what is right, or to unteach us what is wrong, in our faith! It will, I fear, seem irony to you, if I say that Dr Pusey *is* for a great number of minds, their one great stay against the claims of Rome,—as for others, he is against the arguments of infidelity. If you *could* utterly discredit him, as a minister of the Church of England, —if you *could* "expel the unclean thing from our midst"—it would be a costly victory for the conquerors. Dear Mr Christopher, in view of another world, there are better things to be done here, on earth, than presiding at Lectures against Dr Pusey in the Oxford Town Hall.

PRAY forgive me & believe me,

Yours sincerely,
H P Liddon

Rev A M W Christopher.
Thank you much for your reference to Dr Pusey's letter to myself.

CHRIST CHURCH,
OXFORD.

My dear Sir,

I am distressed to see that in a letter to the Oxford Times[1] you have endorsed Mr Gill's accusation against me of "subverting some of the very fundamental doctrines of Christianity": and first of the Atonement.

I venture to enclose to you some prayers suggested to the dying, out of the prayer from which Mr Gill took some of his accusations. There are very many more. In his earnestness to find matters of accusation against me, Mr Gill must have overlooked them, although they are close to what he selected as ground of accusation. I send a copy of them to you, that you may think, whether he who suggested them, would "tamper with the doctrine of the Atonement"? The writer, from whom they are taken is one, whom the English love as almost one with themselves, S. François de Sales. One "who tampered with the doctrine of the Atonement" would not be such a favourite with the English people, as the author of "The Love of God", "The Devout Life", whom the English read, as if he had been one of us.

I venture also to send you a sermon, which I wrote lately as an University Sermon. With it too doubtless you would find much to disagree; but you would not say that one who wrote pp 40-42 "subverted the doctrine of the Atonement". In my University Sermons (Vol. II) there are two, written to maintain the doctrine of the Atonement against attacks, then recent. I have just been reminded, that, after my Lenten Sermon "Christ in you, the hope of glory", one, leaving the Church, said, "No one can say that he does not preach Christ." Among my adapted books one was "The Sufferings of Jesus",[2] the *one* great Portuguese book, written

[1] *The Oxford Times,* 21.12.1878, p. 8, — announcing publication of the lecture.
[2] *The Sufferings of Jesus* by T. de Jesu, ed. E. B. Pusey (1869).

by one, who suffered much for Christ, in guarding the Portuguese prisoners in Africa from apostasy.

With regard to the expression, on which Mr. Gill founded his grave charge, I had no idea that any would identify it with our Lord's Expiation on the Cross. Those for whom I edited the book would not. It did not occur to me that people would look at the book, simply, (as Mr Gill has done) to pick holes in it, or to cull out stones, to fling at me. "Expiate" (as you would see in Richardson's English Dictionary) is a word in popular use. Could I have foreseen that it would give offence to anyone, I would have substituted some other for it, and even now would cancel the pages and substitute another expression if it would do any good. In my own writings, I have taken pains, since I began writing, some 44 years ago, to use terms which would not be misunderstood, avoiding terms, which, though right and true terms, were taken in a wrong sense. Thus, I used the words "made children of God" rather than "regenerate", because people, in those days, attached the idea of *actual* conversion to regeneration. ii. In former days, I used to refer to the Homilies, for the use of the word "Sacrament" of any but the two great sacraments. My doing so gave even more offence than the use of the term itself. Yet the Homily on Swearing speaks of 'the sacrament of matrimony'. And the Homily on Common prayer and sacraments says "Although absolution hath the promise of forgiveness of sin, yet by the express word of the New Testament, it hath not this promise annexed and tied to the visible sign, which is imposition of hands. For this visible sign (I mean, laying on of hands) is not expressly commanded in the New Testament to be used in absolution as the visible sign in Baptism and the Lord's Supper are, and *therefore* absolution *is no such sacrament* as Baptism and the Communion are". It does not deny, but rather implies that it is *in some sense* a sacrament. iii. It certainly was an oversight that I overlooked the words "extraordinary supererogation", not thinking that people would think that I admitted the phrase in a sense, which would contradict the Article. I have now cancelled the page, though I fear that Mr Gill would dislike the change, since he will have a stone the less to throw at me.

And now in the time when the Angels first sung at that Blessed Nativity of our Dear Lord, "Peace on earth, goodwill towards men", do let us try to understand each other as well as we can. It has always been a joy to me to recognise the truths, which your friends hold, and to thank God for all who preached Christ, and to feel how much we have in common. It is a hard battle which we, who love our Lord, have to fight with those who deny Him. At least let us pray Him for one another.

Yours faithfully in C. J
E B Pusey

Christmas Eve 1878

Since writing the above, I have determined to cancel all the pages in which the word 'expiate' occurs, although Bp Taylor[1] uses the word 'expiatory' of repentance.

CHRIST CHURCH,
OXFORD. Jan 1 1879

My dear Mr. Christopher

I thank you much for your kind wishes and kind present, which I shall value as a testimony of your Christian charity. But pray do not write to me, as 'eminent' or yourself, as 'inferior'. It pains me so, who know myself to be nothing.

As for reading your kind present, I have just now my hands very full. I was finishing some notes on a sermon on prophecy, by which I hoped

[1] Probably Dr. Jeremy Taylor, Bishop of Down & Connor 1661-67.

to waken some out of their unbelief, and some on an old sermon on Everlasting punishment, when, on the one hand, I find myself appealed to by Dr. Farrar in his sad fierce book,[1] on the other attacked by Mr. Gill as subverting the Christian Faith. So you see, I have enough on my hands for 78.

You write to me, as if I were a Ritualist. I never was. But I think them the objects of an unjust persecution founded on an unjust judgement. For if they had been altogether wrong about the ornaments rubric, the Church of England would have misled them, by omitting 'not' in the so-called ornaments rubric.

However, this is only by the way.

I have been thinking what I would ask you to accept as a New Year's gift from me; but I mistrust any thing of my own. So will you accept a volume of one, whose belief I shared in all things, but whose humble loving soul escaped rubbing people up, as I did somehow Mr Gill.

With every good wish for this and all your coming years

Yours very faithfully
E B Pusey

3 Amen Court E.C.
Jan. 2. 1879.

Dear Mr Christopher,

I am much obliged to you for sending me a copy of Dr Mozley's 'Review of the Baptismal Controversy'. I shall value your gift; although I have been more or less familiar with the book for many years, and have talked parts of it over, with its author.

Of course it is marked by the great ability which distinguishes everything that he wrote. But the method of explaining the language of the Baptismal Service by the theory of a "charitable hypothesis", appears to me to belong to that family of theological solvents, which is apt to do more destructive work than is at all intended by the writers who employ them for a particular purpose. You would be acquainted with theories of 'accommodation' by the aid of which the great texts in the New Testament which, as we both believe, teach the doctrine of the atonement, are emptied of their natural meaning, by Socinianizing writers.

If Baptismal Regeneration is not the doctrine of the Church of England, the language of the Baptismal Service is very misleading for plain people. When administering Baptism, we are instructed to pray that "this infant, coming to thy Holy Baptism may receive remission of his sins by spiritual Regeneration"; and that God would "sanctify this water to the mystical washing away of sin"; and then, when the rite is complete, to announce that "this child is regenerate". And we teach our little children to say that in baptism each one was made "a member of Christ, a child of God, and an inheritor of the Kingdom of Heaven." It seems to me that the natural sense of this language will outlive the subtleties upon which the Gorham decision was based: and that if the Church of England had desired to leave the matter an open question,—or to deny the Revealed doctrine of baptismal grace—she would have done better to omit from her formularies passages which, to ordinary apprehensions, seem to affirm the doctrine more explicitly than does the corresponding language of the Church of Rome.

If, unhappily, I did not believe in Baptismal Regeneration, I should lose my faith in more than one Revealed Truth besides. The Rationalism which denies Sacramental Grace is the same Rationalism (only happily less consequent) as that which rejects the Atonement & the Holy Trinity: and the arguments which enable it to achieve the one result are service-

[1] *Eternal Hope* by F. W. Farrar, Canon of Westminster, afterwards Dean of Canterbury, (1878).

able enough for the other. It is a great blessing that people do not see this, in very many cases: it is better far to be illogical than unbelieving. But—truth has exigencies which are beyond control.

If, too, I rejected Baptismal Regeneration & yet consented to use the Baptismal Service of the Church of England, I should not feel at liberty to denounce Ritualists or any other persons, on the score of unfaithfulness to the *natural* sense of our formularies.

In saying this, I hope not to be thought insensible to the kind spirit which dictates, I am very sure, your New Years Gift.

I am

Dear Mr Christopher

Yours very sincerely

H P Liddon

Rev A M W Christopher

Appendix III

CORRESPONDENCE BETWEEN CANON A. M. W. CHRISTOPHER AND THE REVD. E. P. HATHAWAY

April 1891—'Singing the Psalms'

Christopher's letters survive only in draft form, the first (Letter List—Appendix VI—no. 86) in the handwriting of the Revd. Dr. W. H. Griffith Thomas, then his curate, the second (LL no. 87) in his own. Hathaway, like Christopher, used 'f' where a second 's' was necessary, and this usage has been altered here as in Appendix II. The transcriptions otherwise are again as far as possible exact.

St. Aldate's Rectory
20 April 1891

Dear brother,

Your letter has caused me grief. If I had been in the same state as I was six years ago, with a tendency to sleeplessness & without a cure at hand for it, it might have so pained my heart as to have brought on a fit of sleeplessness.

I think you hardly know how strongly you write & how painful it is to me to differ from one to whom I owe so much & to whom I have been so long affectionately attached.

Have mercy on me & consider the following facts in brotherly love.

1 I have slowly but surely come to the conclusion that it is a wrong thing in Oxford to incline young people & many others to avoid an Evangelical Church & go to [a rit]ualistic ch. near at hand, by refusing [to ha]ve the pss. sung on Sunday evg. It [is p]ractically driving people away from [t]he Gospel who most urgently need it.

2—I cannot explain away the very inspired words of God to mean the opposite of what they seem to mean.

Among these I read 1 Ch. 16. 9.[1] Ps. 105. 2.[2]

I cannot believe that my present practice *& the motive* for it are unpleasing to God. I believe that the pss. were intended to be sung.

3—I am very thankful that I adopted the practice in St. Aldate's. The eveng. congn. is steadily incrg. I wish you had seen the full ch. last night.

4—My new Curate Colclough[3] is musical & likes the singing of the psalms. Before he accd. the curacy I gave my word to him that the pss. shd. be sung in the Sunday evg. in the Grpt. Ch. as in the parish ch.

I have told Thomas[4] & others the same. I should lose their respect if I now changed against my own strong convictions of what is best for the greater number of my people—I cannot do it. Affectionately attached as we are to each other you would not sing the psalms in Holbrook[5] Church if I conjured you to do it ever so much.

5—I have to work up a congregn. for the new Church. It would be a grievous hindrance to the filling of the Ch. with people to hear the Gospel, if it were the only Evangelical Church in Oxford, or Ch. of any kind, in which the pss. are not sung on the Sunday eveng. If I were to place myself in a false position by action against my convictions, in compliance with the wish of a beloved brother the people would I feel sure, be so dissatisfied that I should be compelled to give up the attempt.

[1] "Sing unto him, sing psalms unto him, talk ye of all his wondrous works."
[2] "Sing unto him, sing psalms unto him: talk ye of all his wondrous works."
[3] H. J. Colclough, curate-in-charge of St. Matthew's, Grandpont, 1891-95.
[4] W. H. G. Thomas, curate of St. Aldate's 1889-96.
[5] Where Hathaway was rector.

6. The very few people who prefer the ps. *(sic)* to be read have them read every Sunday mg., they have their P. Bks. before them & can read the ps. *(sic)* on Sunday evgs. They wd. not inconsiderately deprive the majority of their fellow worshippers of a privilege in wh. they delight & which God has encouraged them to use.

HOLBROOK
April 22. 1891

Dear brother

By God's great goodness you are hale & well, & I have confidence that He will not let you suffer from a friend's causing you unintentional pain.

I was not aware that the Psalms were chanted in St. Aldate's. Of course with my convictions I cannot but regret it. Had I known it, I shd. have been toward & silent. But you are Captain of the ship, and are alone responsible.

The actual issues involved in the question are so far-reaching & momentous that we ought to be able to consider them without prejudice on either side, and without pain. The sole question surely must be—*Not*, does the practice *answer* numerically? But, Is God's will ascertainable in the matter? And, if so, what is it?

For 30 years past I have tried to examine these two questions from all sides, and am less & less able to escape from my deep conviction that Evangelical Clergy are more & more grieving the Holy Spirit & *driving Him* from their congregations by this unbelieving & dishonouring idea that, in order to succeed, they must compete with High Church & Ritualistic attractions to the house of God.

I wonder, dear brother, whether the thought has dawned on your mind, as it is dawning on many, that the Church of England is fast becoming too wealthy, too highly organised, too commanding, too popular—for God to be able to employ her? Ex. gr. I cannot but think that God *would have been better pleased* had your new church been less ornate & less costly.

But to return to the particular matter of chanting the Psalms.

1. You must have noticed that unregenerate persons in every church—who never think of making a response, or of speaking to God in *prayer*—do stand up & without scruple join boldly in the *singing*. It is obvious that, the more singing and chanting, the *larger* will come to be the numbers of *such* members, in every congregation. Viewed in the light of the great judgement day, would you not rather that *these* stayed away? Does not God say to them —'Who hath required this *trampling* My courts at your hand? It is iniquity, even the solemn meeting. It is an abomination with Me.' Is. i. 12, 13.

2. You do not wish me to allow that an unrythmical English prose translation of the compositions set to music by the writers of the Hebrew Psalter is something that we are commanded to sing by the texts you quote? My complaint is that the thoughtless but great tyranny of the modern usage *compels* thousands of God's dear children to *disobey* the commands of 1 Chron. xvi. 9 & Ps. cv. 2. When I was a boy, we sang every Sunday Brady & Tate.[1] Who banished those singable Psalms? Then our early Hymn books contained, in their first half or third, Psalms only. Who & what has banished these? You know well that they have disappeared before the chanting.

Last autumn we went to the chief Evangelical church in Ramsgate. The Psalms were chanted. Tho' a fully educated musician, & very fond of singing, Mrs. Hathaway could not follow, or even make out what was being sung. It made her so miserable, that she would not go a second time, but went to a dissenting chapel.

3. But I want you most to consider how the Holy Spirit is being affronted by (1) this universal concession to the demands of the world and the fleshly gratification of so many, and (2) by what amounts to an admission—so

[1]The metrical psalter of N. Tate & N. Brady, *New Version of the Psalms* (1696.)

sad in its unbelief—that a fully preached Gospel has now lost its power to attract hearers & *secure* a congregation.

Years ago poor Price[1] at St. James', Clapham, adopted the latter idea, & your argument about the young having to be kept from a ritualistic church —& that a "heartier & more ornate service" would draw them. Ripe & holy Christians—like Sir G. & Lady Pollock,[2] & not a few besides—*wrote to me* as the principal acting patron (for I had, at dear Waldegrave's[3] strong recommendation pressed Price on my colleagues) *imploring* me to interfere & hinder the changes announced, mainly the chanting the Psalms. Price would not concede the point, & the old worshippers felt forced to give up their pews. But what went away with them? just that which a minister should covet & prize most, the efficacy of the prayers of the flock for it & for himself whose prayers were the most effectual.

The catastrophe that ended everything you know of—may we not believe that it might have been averted, if 'the salt' of the congregation & their advice had not been thought lightly of?

For more than 3 years after my fever, I was shunted from place to place, each succeeding physician wishing to pass me on, because he saw the case to be incurable. So we halted at many places, but of course at no one which had not an Evangelical ministry. Being deaf, I always got seated near the pulpit, which generally turned out to be in the close neighbourhood of the choir. In *every* single case (without a single exception) the behaviour of the members of the choir was grievously irreverent, books & papers being handed down, & heads whispering about the next chant or tune, *all through the prayers*.

In proportion as the musical portion of the service is increased, will the temptation to this profaneness necessarily increase.

But what it brings with it is that the Holy Spirit is grieved, and withdraws his gracious dew from hearts & from the preached message.

The 2 points which you urge—'I must secure the young people', and 'My Curate is musical, and likes the singing the Psalms',—these, in nearly every case, cover really your argument in favour of chanting the Psalms. Because, as to be afraid of being *singular*, you will not seriously urge *that*, seeing it is just that "*whereunto we are called*."

Your words "in which they *delight*" may be true, & may constitute a very solid ground *against* the gratification. But when you close with—"& which God has encouraged them to use"—you simply beg the whole question. To my conscience it is quite mournfully terrible to hear, as perpetually, indeed everywhere I have, now one of God's own holy words torn by the human voice into 2, & even 3, quite separate & severed pieces, then half a dozen slurred over in such haste as to sound as but a single word, and then a clause in a verse absolutely inaudible, the number of syllables being so many that for very breathlessness they cannot be sounded.

You don't believe that David *so* composed his Psalms, or that the Levites *so* sung them. When our Lord stopped to say "& the Scripture cannot be broken", He was pausing over a *single* monosyllabic word of His Father's—God's! But do not Psalm-chanters virtually say with recklessness—the Scriptures *must* be broken, & shall, in obedience to the notes in front of us?

Well, dear brother, we shall soon be where not a single word of the "new song" will ever be inaudible, & where, I think, many of David's Psalms will be sung, but assuredly *not* in the guise of an English prose translation.

Yours ever affectionately
Edw. P. Hathaway

[1] A. C. Price, sometime Fellow of New College, Oxford, appointed Vicar of St. James's, Clapham, 1865.
[2] Cp. p. 132.
[3] Hon. Dr. S. Waldegrave, Bishop of Carlisle 1860-69.

Dear brother,

I must thank you for writing me so long & thoughtful a letter.

To be converted by the Gospel people must hear it, or read it. Ordinary unconverted people if they do not care to hear the Gospel will probably not care to read it. I cannot believe that the Holy Spirit is grieved if there be a larger congregation brought under the sound of the Gospel by singing the Psalms in the evening. I hope He works in more by the word than if the congregation were smaller. I hope more souls are saved by the Gospel, through the increased attendance, in the long run, & this by God's own overruling.

I don't blame you for thinking as you do. I thought the same for many years. I now believe that it would be a cruel thing to hinder people coming under the sound of the Gospel, by refusing to have the Psalms sung in the evening. The singing you describe is not that which I hear in St. Aldate's. Deaf as I am I can follow the words better than sometimes when they are read. Indeed I can follow them perfectly.

If the singing be not identical with the singing which God encouraged by the exhortations He inspired to "sing" psalms, our singing in St. Aldate's is the nearest approach we can make to obedience. It is certainly more like "singing" than saying the Psalms would be. Much depends upon *how* the thing is done. Thomas[1] who trains the Choir, will, I am sure, strive to promote reverence in the Choir & I will exhort them myself also.

In the case of the few who may not feel it easy to follow the Psalms, they have the very words of the Psalms before them in their Prayer books—so the word of God is not kept even from these.

I earnestly hope that the Holy Spirit is not grieved but is pleased to work by the preached word in more hearts than before the Psalms were sung on the Sunday evenings. Of course it grieves me that you are grieved.

It is not only the unregenerate who love to sing the Psalms, though I am thankful if the unregenerate can be brought under the sound of the Gospel, many Christian people prefer this. It does not seem right to refuse them this privilege once on the Sunday.

[1]Revd. W. H. Griffith Thomas.

ABBREVIATIONS USED IN APPENDIX IV

A.M.W.C.	— A. M. W. Christopher.
W.H.G.T.	— W. H. Griffith Thomas.
J.S.R.	— J. S. Reynolds.
Griffith Thomas	— Dr. W. H. Griffith Thomas's MS. (see p. v).
STL	— Short-Title List (Appendix V).
LL	— Letter List (Appendix VI).
O.D.P.	— Oxford Diocesan Papers (Bodleian Library).
D.N.B.	— Dictionary of National Biography.
Downer	— *A Century of Evangelical Religion in Oxford* by A. C. Downer, D.D. (1938).

Reminiscences of Canon Christopher, written 1910-17, for projected biography:

Aglionby	— Recollections, Canon F. K. Aglionby, D.D., Vicar of Christ Church, Westminster, n.d. [1910]. Pp. 5.
Allan	— Letter, Revd. G. A. Allan, Vicar of Isle Abbots, Som., to W.H.G.T., 26.6.1913. Pp. 4.
Allan Smith	— 'Reminiscences' by Very Revd. J. Allan Smith, D.D., Dean of St. David's, 22.1.1915. Pp. 3.
Butler	— 'Reminiscences of the Rev. Canon Christopher' by Revd. G. W. Butler, Rector of West Knighton with Broad Mayne, Dorset, 9.10.1910, with postscript 10.10.1910. Pp. 20 + 5.
Cox	— 'Concerning Canon A. M. W. Christopher' by Canon A. P. Cox, Vicar of Christ Church, Cheltenham, 2.1.1917. Pp. 12.
English	— Letter, Revd. J. English, Melbourne, formerly Chaplain, Indian Ecclesiastical Establishment, to W.H.G.T., 2.1.1912. Pp. 6.
Ingham	— Recollections, Rt. Revd. E. G. Ingham, D.D., Vicar of St. Jude's, Southsea, 10.5.1913. Pp. 6.
Matthews	— Letter, Revd. J. E. Matthews, Vicar of Southwick, Northants., to W.H.G.T., 19.7.1911. Pp. 8.
Sharp	— 'Canon Christopher. Memorandum by Rev. J. Sharp', Upper Norwood, formerly Secretary, British and Foreign Bible Society, 8.9.1910. Pp. 2.
Smith	— Letter, Revd. C. Dunlop Smith, Westbury, Glos., formerly Rector of Didsbury, to W.H.G.T., 15.5.1913. Pp. 4.
Sturdy	— Recollections, Revd. H. C. Sturdy, Rector of Wath, Yorks., n.d. Pp. 9.
Tonge	— Letter, Revd. G. Tonge, Highbury, formerly Secretary, Church of England Zenana Missionary Society, to W.H.G.T., 15.10.1910. Pp. 8.
Webster	— 'Reminiscences of Canon Christopher' by Preb. F. S. Webster, Rector of All Souls, Langham Place, London, n.d. Pp. 3.

Appendix IV

SOURCES

The line number is that of the end of the quotation or statement unless otherwise indicated.

CHAPTER I 1820-39

p. 1 ll. 6, 19 'A Review', by A.M.W.C., of *A Memoir of the Rev. John James Weitbrecht . . . Abridged by his Widow* (1873), p. 1. (STL no. 25).

p. 2 l. 25 *The Times,* 12.3.1913, p. 11.

l. 28-p. 3 l. 11 For references *re* place of birth and baptism, see Appendix I.

l. 29 Poor rate book, St. George's, Bloomsbury with St. Giles-in-the-Fields, 1820. (Holborn Central Library).

l. 35 *The Irish Sketch Book* by M. A. Titmarsh (W. M. Thackeray) (1843) vol. i, p. 140.

p. 3 ll. 4, 5 *The Royal Blue Book* 1829, p. 114 & sig. D2r; 1833, p. 127 & sig. D10v.

l. 11 f. *The Family of Christopher and Some Others,* anon. (by A. C. Seton-Christopher) (1933), *passim.*

l. 32 f. *Condensed History of Stockton-on-Tees,* ed. M. Heavisides (1917), pp. 39–40.

l. 36 *Notes for a Pedigree of the Tathams of Co. Durham, England, with a brief reference to the allied family of Christopher, of Norton, Co. Durham* by H. Curtis (1927), pp. v, 56, 57.

p. 4 l. 9 n. *Encyclopaedia Heraldica* by W. Berry, n.d. (Bodley cat: "c. 1830"), vol. iii (no pagination). Arms of subscribers, 17th pa.

l. 28 *The Post-office Annual Directory* 1806, p. 53.

p. 6 l. 15 f. *Our Parish: Mangotsfield, including Downend* by A. E. Jones, n.d., (preface dated 1899), pp. 169-70; illustration opposite p. 166.

Lease and conveyance, Ivy Bower, now Pendennis, Downend, Glos., to Thos. Millard, 1815; mortgages of same, 1877–1912; conveyance of same by Mrs. A. Millard, 1920. (Among title-deeds in possession of present owner, Mr. T. V. Mounstephen.)

l. 37 Griffith Thomas, p. 19.

l. 38 Will, Thos. Millard, proved Bristol 12.1.1872. (Country copy, Principal Registry, London.).

p. 7 l. 15 'In Memoriam. Maria Frances Christopher', W.H.G.T., *The Record,* 16.1.1903, p. 54.

l. 33 Letter, A.M.W.C. to W.H.G.T., 1.9.1906, pp. 6, 7. (LL no. 155.)

p. 8 ll. 9, 35 Griffith Thomas, p. 2.

p. 9 ll. 1, 16 *Ibid.,* p. 3.

p. 10 l. 4 *Ibid.,* p. 255.

l. 23 Will, Geo. Christopher, proved London 13.5.1861. (Principal Registry, 1861—277.)

l. 24	Johnstone's *Commercial Guide and London Street Directory* 1817, pp. 140, 618; *The Royal Blue Book* 1824, p. 89 (& sig. C.4, v.)
l. 29	Cp. Poor rate books, as cited, *passim*.
l. 31	Census return, 1851, *re* Morton House, Chiswick Mall. (Public Record Office, H.O./1699/f492.)
p. 11 l. 24 f.	Information from Mr. P. E. Morris, Borough Librarian, Bexley, letter dated 30.1.1961, pp. 1–2.
l. 29	Preachers' Book, St. Aldate's, Oxford, vol. ii, 9.2.1868.
p. 12 l. 6	'Hall-Place School, Bexley, Kent', prospectus (1843), p. 3. (Reference Library, Bexleyheath: HAL4:U:S:1843.)
l. 16	Information from Mr. C. W. Musgrave, Director, Public Libraries, Brighton, letter dated 31.7.1961, pp. 1–2.
p. 13 l. 8	Griffith Thomas, p. 5.
ll. 16, 21	*D.N.B.*, vol. lix (1899), pp. 290-1: art. on N. Wanostrocht by T. Seccombe.
l. 29	*Allgemeines Lexikon Der Bildenden Künstler*, ed. U. Thieme, F. Becker, & co., vol. 9 (1913), p. 103; *A Biographical . . . Dictionary of . . . Painters and Engravers* by H. Ottley (1876), pp. 51-2.
l. 35	Griffith Thomas, p. 255.
l. 38	Note, A.M.W.C., n.d., for W.H.G.T.
p. 14 l. 11 n	Letter, incomplete, A.M.W.C. to ? after death of Mrs. H. S. Christopher, 1911, p. 2. (LL no. 196.)
l. 30	Notes, A.M.W.C., n.d., p. 3.
p. 15 l. 30	Information from Mr. S. H. Horrocks, Borough Librarian, Reading, letter dated 1.2.1961, sheet attached, quoting "Mr. Sherborn's notes on 'Buildings of Architectural Interest in Reading'."
l. 32 f.	*Early History of St. Mary's, Castle Street, Reading*, by J. Consterdine, n.d., pp. 21, 23.
p. 16 l. 1	*The Christian Portrait Gallery*, n.d. (Bodley accession stamp 1890), p. 71.
l. 7 f.	*Alumni Cantabrigienses*, ed. J. & J. A. Venn, pt. ii, vol. iii (1947), p. 83.
l. 15 f.	*The History of the London Society for Promoting Christianity among the Jews* by W. T. Gidney (1908), pp. 269, 336-7, 516-7.
l. 25	Note, A.M.W.C., n.d.
p. 17 l. 2	Griffith Thomas, p. 7.
l. 6	*The Life of William Marsh, D.D.* by his Daughter (C. Marsh) (1867), p. 485.
l. 6 n	Consterdine, *op. cit.*, n.d., p. 23 & n. Cp. *An Ecclesiastical History of Reading*, ed. P. H. Ditchfield (1883), p. 39.
p. 18 l. 4	*Memorials of Old Haileybury College* by F. C. Danvers and others (1894), pp. 329-578.

CHAPTER II 1839–44

p. 19 l. 3 *Alumni Cantabrigienses,* ed. J. & J. A. Venn, pt. ii, vol. ii (1944), p. 35.
l. 22 Preachers' Book, St. Aldate's, Oxford, vol. iii, 10.12.1871.
p. 20 l. 3 Letter, A.M.W.C. to W.H.G.T., 15.8.1889, p. 4. (LL no. 76.)
l. 23 *'Speaking Years': A Memory of the Rev. William Carus* by C. Bullock, n.d. (preface dated 1891), p. 13. cp. *The History of Ridley Hall, Cambridge* by F. W. B. Bullock, vol. i (1941), p. 114.
l. 36 C. Bullock, as cited, *ibid*, pp. 12, 14.
p. 21 l. 9 *List of Past Occupants of Rooms in St. John's College, Cambridge* by G. C. M. Smith (1895), p. 39.
l. 27 *Early Victorian Cambridge* by D. A. Winstanley (1940), p. 384.
l. 37 Notes, A.M.W.C., n.d. [1900]; Griffith Thomas, p. 11.
p. 22 l. 13 *Ibid.*, p. 12.
l. 18 Preachers' Book, St. Aldate's, Oxford, vol. i, 22.7.1860.
l. 29 Griffith Thomas, p. 12.
p. 23 l. 15&n.2 *Records of the Jesus College Boat Club, Cambridge,* vol. i (1885), p. 14.
l. 19 Letter, A.M.W.C to W.H.G.T., 13.5.1911, p. 5. (LL no. 188.)
l. 25 f. *A History of the Cambridge University Cricket Club 1820-1901* by W. J. Ford (1902), pp. 186-7; Griffith Thomas, pp. 13–5.
p. 24 l. 10 *Oxford and Cambridge at the Wicket* by P. F. Warner & F. S. Ashley-Cooper (1928), p. 28.
l. 26 Griffith Thomas, p. 14.
l. 32 *The Oxford Magazine*, vol. xxxi (1913), no. 17 (24 April), p. 285.
p. 25 l. 13 *Debates, &c. of the Union Society, During the Lent Term* (1840), p. 15; *The Laws of the Cambridge Union Society, with a List of the Honorary and Contributing Members . . . corrected to October 1842* (1843), p. 15.
l. 21 *The Historical Register of the University of Cambridge,* ed. J. R. Tanner (1917), p. 502.
p. 26 l. 31 Letter, incomplete, A.M.W.C. to W.H.G.T., [1906], p. 6. (LL no. 157.)
p. 27 l. 15 Griffith Thomas, p. 17. Cf. *The Oxford Times,* 23.6.1894, letter, A.M.W.C. to Golden Wedding present contributors, 18.6.1894, p. 3.
l. 23 Griffith Thomas, ch. ix, p. 13.
p. 28 l. 7 Marriage register, Chiswick parish church, 15.6.1844.

CHAPTER III 1844-49

p. 29 l. 3 *The Calcutta Christian Herald,* vol. i, no. 20, 19.11.1844, p. 154.
l. 11 Personal recollection, Miss E. C. Christopher, 1957.
l. 13 Griffith Thomas, p. 20.
l. 16 Communication from Sir P. R. Cadell, 3.11.1957, p. 1.
l. 18 *The Calcutta Christian Herald, ibid.*

p. 30 l. 21	*The Life of the Right Rev. Daniel Wilson, D.D.* by J. Bateman (1860), vol. ii, p. 25 (–37).
l. 27	*Life of General Claud Martin* by S. C. Hill (1901), t.-p.
p. 31 l. 18	Bateman, *op. cit.,* 2nd edn. (1861), p. 285.
p. 32 l. 11	*An Example from India* by A.M.W.C. (1906), pp. 7–8. (STL no. 168.)
l. 26	Bateman, *op. cit.,* 1st edn., vol. ii, p. 37.
l. 38	Griffith Thomas, p. 52.
p. 33 l. 5	Bateman, *op. cit.,* 1st. edn., *ibid.*
l. 32	Griffith Thomas, *ibid.*
l. 34	'Information with Respect to "La Martinière," Calcutta', 1862, p. 3. (STL no. 11.)
p. 34 l. 7	*Memoirs of a Bengal Civilian* by J. Beames (1961), p. 84.
l. 17	Griffith Thomas, p. 22.
p. 35 l. 6	*La Martinière Chronicle,* Centenary Number (1900), p. 31.
ll. 23, 27	Downer, p. 28.
p. 36 l. 5	Letter, incomplete, A.M.W.C. to W.H.G.T., [1906], p. 10, postscript. (LL no. 157.)
l. 30	Griffith Thomas, p. 255.
l. 38	*Ibid.,* pp. 255-6.
p. 37 l. 15	*Ibid.,* p. 25.
l. 17	Downer, p. 30.
ll. 20, 24	Griffith Thomas, *ibid.*
p. 38 l. 2	Bateman, *op. cit.,* 1st edn., vol. ii, pp. 290-1.
l. 25	*The Christian Portrait Gallery,* n.d. (Bodley accession stamp 1890), 'Rev. Canon Christopher', p. 71. Cp. *The Christian,* 3.1.1907, 'An Evangelical Stalwart, Rev. Canon Christopher, M.A.', p. 17.
p. 39 l. 10	*La Martinière Chronicle,* Centenary Number (1900), p. 22.
l. 26	*Ibid.,* p. 25.
l. 31	*Report of La Martinière Institution, March-September 1847,* pp. 4-5.
p. 40 l. 8	*Ibid.,* p. 18.
l. 29 f.	Letter, A.M.W.C. to W.H.G.T., 24.8.1900, p. 8. (LL no. 105.)
p. 41 l. 35	*The Life of the Rev. Henry Venn Elliott* by J. Bateman, 3rd edn. (1872), pp. 180-1.
p. 42 l. 5	St. Matt. 10. 29.
p. 43 l. 12	Messrs. Coutts's, London, Register 3, p. 362; Ledgers 1848/9, p. 384, *passim.*
p. 45 l. 4	Letter, incomplete, A.M.W.C. to H. G. Grey, 30.8.1906, p. 6. (LL no. 154.)
l. 11	*The Christian Portrait Gallery,* n.d. (Bodley accession stamp 1890), p. 72.
l. 23	Letter, incomplete, A.M.W.C. to H. G. Grey, 30.8.1906, p. 14. (LL no. 154.)
p. 46 l. 8	Griffith Thomas, p. 239.
p. 47 l. 37	*Quarterly Papers,* S.P.G., No. 51 (Oct. 1849), p. 3.
p. 48 l. 5	*Ibid.,* p. 4.

ll. 28, 35 Addition (3.11.1848) to letter, Bp. D. Wilson (Calcutta) to Bp. C. J. Blomfield (London), 1.11.1848, p. 3; & letter, p. 1.
l. 31 Griffith Thomas, p. 53.
p. 49 l. 21 *Ibid.*, p. 255.

CHAPTER IV 1849-55

p. 50 ll. 12, 15 Griffith Thomas, p. 55.
l. 19 Bp. C. R. Sumner's Act Books, vol. ii, 8.7.1849. (Winchester Diocesan Registry.)
l. 21 Subscription Book, Winchester diocese, 8.7.1849. (Winchester Diocesan Registry.)
l. 22 Copy, curate's licence, A.M.W.C., 8.7.1849. (Surrey archdeaconry records, County Hall, Westminster: bundle DW/K/2/1-2304.)
p. 51 l. 6 *Alumni Cantabrigienses,* ed. J. & J. A. Venn, pt. ii, vol. iii (1947), p. 194.
l. 7 f. 'A Short History of the Church and Parish' in *St. John the Divine, Richmond: General Report of Church Work for Easter 1886 to Easter 1887* (1887), pp. 10-11. Cp. *The History and Antiquities of Richmond* by E. B. Chancellor (1894), pp. 278-9.
p. 52 l. 1 f. 'A Short History . . .', as cited, pp. 13, 16.
l. 34 Baptism register, St. John's, Richmond, Surrey, 8.12.1850 (H. S. Christopher); *Directory* for Richmond, Kew . . . compiled W. Archdeacon (1851), p. 2.
l. 36 Information from Mr. G. Turner, Borough Librarian, Richmond, letter dated 28.3.1961, p. 1. Cp. Poor rate Book, Richmond, 1850/51, p. 7. (Richmond Central Library).
p. 53 l. 19 f. Griffith Thomas, pp. 55-8.
p. 54 l. 5 Bp. C. R. Sumner's Act Books, vol. ii, 7.7.1850. (Winchester Diocesan Registry.)
l. 34 *The Richmond and Twickenham Times,* 18.1.1879, p. 6.
p. 55 l. 2 *Ibid.*
l. 6 *Mason's Court Guide and General Directory* for Brentford, Kew . . . Richmond (1853), p. 92.
l. 8 n Preachers' Book, St. Aldate's, Oxford, vol. i, 21.9-28.12.1856.
l. 12 Baptism register, St. John's, Richmond, Surrey, 1849-55.
p. 56 l. 33 Griffith Thomas, p. 60.
ll. 35, 36, 37 Baptism register, St. John's, Richmond, Surrey, 8.3.1850; 17.11.1851; 19.12.1853.
l. 38 Burial register, Chiswick parish church, 20.9.1854.
p. 57 l. 19 *Memoir of the Rev. John James Weitbrecht,* compiled by his Widow, ed. A. M. W. Christopher (2nd edn., 1854), pp. v, vi. (STL no. 4.)
l. 23 Letter, Revd. Dr. H. U. Weitbrecht to W.H.G.T., 19.5.1913, p. 1.
p. 58 ll. 1, 9 *Memoir,* as cited, pp. xxii, xx.
l. 32 *Look and Live: being Thoughts on John 1. 29* by A.M.W.C. (1854), pp. 4, 2. (STL no. 5.)

p.59 l. 14	Griffith Thomas, p. 64.
l. 35 n	Certified copy, 29.11.1963, entry, Register of Deaths, Richmond, Surrey, A. W. Christopher, 19.9.1854.
p. 60 l. 8	Letter, A.M.W.C. to F. Burden, 20.8.1904, pp. 10-11. (LL no. 141.)
ll. 17, 21	*Ibid.*, p. 10.
l. 26	*Home Words,* ed. C. Bullock, 1884, 'The Rev. A. M. W. Christopher, M.A.', p. 16.
p. 61 l. 13	Griffith Thomas, p. 70. Revised wording, M. R. Lawrence, 1962.
ll. 17, 27	*Ibid.*, pp. 71, 69.

CHAPTER V 1855-59

p. 62 ll. 12, 13	Committee Minutes, C.M.S., vol. 30 (1854-55), pp. 514 (12.3.1855), 330-31 (11.9.1854). (C.M.S. Archives, London.)
l. 15	Letter, A.M.W.C. to C.M.S. Committee, 19.3.1855 (LL no. 4); cp. Committee Minutes, C.M.S., vol. 30, p. 533 (9.4.1855).
p. 63 l. 7	*The History of the Church Missionary Society* by E. Stock (1899), vol. iii, p. 61.
l. 20	Griffith Thomas, p. 69.
l. 21	Committee Minutes, C.M.S., vol. 31 (1855-57), p. 108.
p. 64 l. 2	Abstract of Reports of Association Secretaries for 1855, Committee Minutes, C.M.S., vol. 31, pp. 108,109.
l. 10	Same for 1856, Committee Minutes, C.M.S., vol. 31, pp. 517, 516. Cp. vol. 32 (1857-59), pp. 624-5 (1858).
l. 11	*Post Office Directory of . . . Surrey* . . . 1859, p. 1291. (Here called Tudor Hs.) Cp. Letter, G. Turner to J.S.R., 28.3.1961, as cited, p. 2.
l. 16	Baptism register, St. John's, Richmond, Surrey, 16.5.1856.
ll. 32, 37	Griffith Thomas, p. 74.
p. 65 ll. 12, 23	*The Late General Sir Arthur Cotton, R.E., K.C.S.I.* by A.M.W.C. (1899), pp. 7-8. (STL no. 134.)
ll. 27, 38	*Ibid.*, pp. 8, 1.
p. 66 l. 34	Griffith Thomas, p. 75.
p. 67 l. 20	Letter, Lord Kinnaird to W.H.G.T., 10.5.1913, p. 2.
p. 68 ll. 6, 12	Griffith Thomas, p. 77.
l. 22	*Ibid.*, pp. 77-8.
p. 69 l. 24	Certified copy, 29.11.1963, entry, Register of Deaths, Isle of Wight, C. E. Christopher, 20.8.1856.
l. 36	Burial register, St. Thomas's, Ryde, I.o.W., 22.8.1856.
p. 70 l. 29	Griffith Thomas, pp. 79-80.
p. 71 l. 7	*Ibid.*, ch. vi, p. 35.
l. 26	*Thirty First Report of the Association for Oxford and Its Vicinity in Aid of the Church Missionary Society* (1856), p. 10.
p. 72 l. 6	Matthews, pp. 1, 2.
l. 24	Allan, p. 1.
l. 30	Copy of letter, A.M.W.C. to C. J. Glyn, 3.6.1857. (LL nos. 12, 98.)
l. 33	Letter, A.M.W.C. to W.H.G.T., 10.3.1896, p. 4. (LL no. 98.)

l. 37 Griffith Thomas, p. 82. Cp. letter, A.M.W.C. to W.H.G.T., 9.6.1904 (2), p. 2 (LL no. 136); and Committee Minutes, C.M.S., vol. 33 (1859-60), pp. 393-4, where abstract *re* associations "to come", but still blank.

p. 73 l. 7 Letter, A.M.W.C. to J. M. Holl, 2.8.1859, p. 2. (LL no. 18.)

ll. 19, 30 *Living for Christ: A Memoir of Virginia Hale Hoffman* by G. D. Cummins (1859), pp. xii, iii, iv.

p. 74 l. 8 Letter, A.M.W.C. to W.H.G.T., 9.6.1904 (2), p. 2. (LL no. 136.)

CHAPTER VI 1735-1859

p. 75 l. 5 *Christ and the Colleges*, ed. F. D. Coggan (1934), p. 57.

l. 7 f. Cp. *The Evangelicals at Oxford 1735-1871* by J. S. Reynolds (1953), *passim.*

p. 76 l. 1 *The Christian Leaders of the Last Century* by J. C. Ryle (1876), p. 33 n.

p. 77 l. 35 Printed notice, anniversary meeting, Oxford auxiliary, B.F.B.S., Oct. 1903 (with LL no. 122); letter, A.M.W.C. to W. P. Wakelin, 31.3.1903, p. 4. (LL no. 109.)

p. 79 l. 14 Printed statement and appeal, 'Oxford Fund', over names of E. P. Hathaway and W. H. Barlow, May 1896, pp. 3-4; cp. printed statement and appeal, 'Oxford Fund', over names of E. Auriol and E. P. Hathaway, dated London, Feb. 1864, p. 1.

p. 81 l. 14 *A History of the University of Oxford* by C. E. Mallet, vol. iii (1927), p. 268; *D.N.B.*, vol. ii (1885), art. on R. Bagot by Sir S. Lee, p. 400.

l. 34 *The Oxford Movement* by R. W. Church (1892), p. 221.

p. 82 l. 3 *D.N.B.*, vol. xx (1889), art. on J. Garbett, unsigned, p. 404.

l. 13 *Anatomy of Oxford*, compiled C. D. Lewis and C. Fenby (1938), p. 136.

p. 84 l. 23 *Oxford Union for Private Prayer*, Rules, etc. & list of present and past members (1888), pp. 3, 16; (1904), p. 3.

l. 27 Facsimile letter, to "My dear Sir", unsigned, dated 22 June [1853] from 5, Old Square, Lincoln's Inn, the address of E. P. Hathaway.

l. 27 n *First Report of Lawrence Asylum* . . . (1849), t.-p.

l. 33 n Memorandum by A.M.W.C., 24.8.1900, *re* course of evangelicalism at Oxford 1856-1900, p. 1; cp. letter, A.M.W.C. to W.H.G.T., 24.8.1900, p. 2. (LL no. 105.)

p. 85 l. 13 Statement of 1896, as cited, p. 1; cp. statement of 1864, as cited, p. 1.

p. 86 l. 4 *Oxford: Its Life and Schools*, ed. A. M. M. Stedman (1887), p. 149.

ll. 10, 15, 24 Statement of 1896, as cited, p. 1; cp. statement of 1864, as cited, p. 1.

l. 28 Cp. Letter, in facsimile handwriting of E. P. Hathaway, n.d. [1856], pp. 1-2; letter, in facsimile handwriting of E. P. Hathaway, over facsimile signatures of W. W. Champneys and E. Auriol, n.d. [1857], pp. 1, 2.

p. 87 l. 3 Letter, N. J. Moody to E. P. Hathaway, 2.9.1856, pp. 2-3.

l. 9 Statement of 1896, as cited, p. 1; cp. statement of 1864, as cited, p. 2.

ll. 22, 23 Brize Norton return, Oxford episcopal visitation, 1808. (O.D.P.d. 570 f. 54).

l. 24 Parish registers, St. Peter-le-Bailey, Oxford, 1833-56. (Now at St. Ebbe's).

l. 26 f. *Ibid.*, 1833-46.

l. 30 n2 *John Hungerford Pollen* by A. Pollen (1912), pp. 44-8, 59-60; *D.N.B.*, 2nd supp., vol. iii (1912), art. on J. H. Pollen by W. Bowen, pp. 122, 123.

p. 88 l. 4 f. Parish registers, St. Peter-le-Bailey, Oxford, 1846-56. (Now at St. Ebbe's.)

l. 6 Cp. *The Guardian*, no. 21, 16.9.1846, p. 332.

ll. 15, 20, 32 Statement of 1896, as cited, p. 1. Cp. statement of 1864, as cited, p. 2.

l. 36 Copy of letter, E. Auriol to E. P. Hathaway, 8.12.1858, in printed pamphlet *re* 'Oxford Fund' subscription due, n.d., p. 3.

p. 89 l. 7 f. *Early Recollections of Oxford, etc. . . .* by An Old Freeman (S. Quelch) (1900), p. 3.

l. 20 *The Times*, 12.3.1913, p. 11.

ll. 26, 29 Letter in facsimile handwriting of E. P. Hathaway, Oct. 1858, pp. 1, 2.

l. 31 Account book, Oxford Fund, kept by E. P. Hathaway, 1857-95: details *re* St. Aldates' advowson, pp. 8-9 from end.

l. 33 n *The Life of William Marsh, D.D.* by his Daughter (C. Marsh) (1867), pp. 443 & n.

p. 90 l. 3 Information from Prof. H. A. Hollond, letter dated 7.5.1963, pp. 1, 2.

l. 10 *The Times*, 12.3.1913, p. 11. Cp. *A History of Pembroke College, Oxford* by D. Macleane (1897), p. 467.

l. 17 Macleane, *ibid.*, pp. 433,4; *Pembroke College* by D. Macleane (1900), p. 241.

l. 23 Statement of 1896, as cited, p. 2.

l. 27 *Ibid.* Cp. statement of 1864, as cited, p. 3.

ll. 31, 33 *Simeon and Church Order* by C. H. E. Smyth (1940), pp. 203, 204.

p. 91 l. 11 Cp. copies, letters *re* advowson, from Dr. F. Jeune, 3.11.1858, and from R. Sweeting, London, 9.10.1858—inserted in account book, Oxford Fund, 1857-95.

l. 17 Preachers' Book, St. Aldate's, Oxford, vol. i, 4. 3. & 10.12.1860.

l. 29 Letter, A.M.W.C. to W.H.G.T., 9.6.1904 (2), p. 2. (LL no. 136.)

l. 31 Statement of 1896, as cited, p. 2. (Cp. that of 1864, p. 3.)

p. 92 ll. 5, 9 Griffith Thomas, ch. vi, p. 3.

l. 5 n Deed of presentation, A.M.W.C. to St. Aldate's, Oxford, 15.8.1859. (O.D.P. c. 1922.) Information from hon. secretary and solicitors to Simeon's Trustees, letters to J.S.R. dated 3.8. 1962 and 7.8.1962 respectively. Cp. Letter, A.M.W.C. to Preb.

E. A. Eardley-Wilmot, 5.9.1903, p. 3. (LL no. 118.)

l. 12 Statement of 1896, as cited, p. 2.

p. 93 l. 1 Letter, Registrar General to J.S.R., 16.5.1963, pp. 1, 2.

l. 23 Cp. *Survey of the Antiquities of the City of Oxford by Anthony Wood,* ed. A. Clark, O.H.S. vol. xvii (1890), p. 34; *St. Aldate's, Oxford, Parish Magazine,* Aug. 1897, p. 5.

l. 30 *A Biographical Register of the University of Oxford to AD 1500* by A. B. Emden, vol. iii (1959), pp. 1493-4.

p. 94 l. 9 'St. Aldate's Church and Schools, Oxford.' Appeal by A.M.W.C. (1862), p. 1. (STL no. 8.)

l. 13 f. Plan in custody of Rector of St. Aldate's (tentatively, but incorrectly dated 1832, showing addition at N.E. angle of church, 1843.)

l. 19 St. Aldates' return, Oxford diocesan visitation, 1860. (O.D.P. d. 180 f.853r.)

l. 19 n Faculty, St. Aldate's church, Oxford, 1862 (O.D.P. c. 1922); *The Chavasse Twins* by S. Gummer (1963), p. 93.

ll. 34, 36 *D.N.B.,* vol. lix (1899), art. on J. Wall by J. R. Macdonald, p. 93.

p. 95 l. 30 *Ibid.,* vol. xxiv (1890), art. on J. Hall by E. Venables, p. 73.

ll. 33, 35 *Athenae Oxonienses . . . by Anthony A'Wood,* ed. P. Bliss, vol. iv (1820), 900.

p. 96 ll. 1, 4 *The Life and Times of Anthony Wood,* ed. A. Clark, vol. ii, O.H.S. vol. xxi (1892), pp. 422, 428.

l. 10 *A Biographical History of England . . . a continuation of the Rev. J. Grainger's Work* by M. Noble (1806), vol. ii, p. 102.

l. 12 *Ecclesiastical History of England—The Church of the Revolution* by J. Stoughton (1874), p. 306.

l. 14 *Remarks and Collections of Thomas Hearne,* ed. C. E. Doble, O.H.S. vol. vii (1886), p. 343.

l. 17 *An Historical Account of My Own Life* by E. Calamy (1829), vol. i, p. 272.

l. 20 *The English Church and Its Bishops 1700-1800* by C. J. Abbey, vol. i (1887), p. 151.

l. 29 *D.N.B.,* vol. xxiv (1890), p. 73.

p. 97 l. 38 Preachers' Book, St. Aldate's, Oxford, vol. i, 25.1.1860.

p. 98 ll. 5, 11 *Facts and Documents Showing the Alarming State of the Diocese of Oxford.* By a Senior Clergyman of the Diocese (1859). cp. *The Founding of Cuddesdon* by W. O. Chadwick (1954), p. 66 f.

l. 13 *Address to the Bishop of Oxford of the Rev. E. A. Litton and Other Clergymen of the Diocese, together with His Lordship's Reply* (April 1859). n.d.

l. 15 *Reasons for Signing the Remonstrance lately addressed to the Archdeacons and Rural Deans of the Diocese of Oxford* by W. R. Fremantle (1859). This did not relate immediately to Litton's open letter.

l. 20 *A Letter to the Lord Bishop of Oxford; being a Rejoinder to his Reply to the Address of the Rev. E. A. Litton and Other Clergymen of the Diocese* by J. Tucker (1859).

CHAPTER VII 1859-62

p. 99 l. 2 Bp. S. Wilberforce's Act Book (1858-68), p. 74. Cp. Letters, A.M.W.C. to Preb. E. A. Eardley-Wilmot, 5.9.1903, p. 3, (LL no. 118); & A.M.W.C. to W.H.G.T., 22.7.1899, p. 1, (LL no. 102b.) Subscription Book (1856-62), Oxford diocese, 27.8.1859. (O.D.P. d. 104 f. 166, holograph pa. Cp. Incumbents' Declarations and Oaths 1856-66 (O.D.P. c. 871).)

l. 6 f. Preachers' Book, St. Aldate's, Oxford, vol. i, 28.8, 16.10.1859, *passim.*

p. 100 l. 7 f. *Webster's Oxford, Wallingford, Abingdon and Banbury Directory, for 1869,* p. 34; *Oxford City Directory* (1871), p. 30. cp. *Dutton, Allen & Co.'s Directory . . . of . . . Oxon., Berks. & Bucks.* (1863), p. 129; information from Mr. J. P. Wells, City Librarian, Oxford, letter dated 3.8.1962, p. 1.

l. 10 Conveyance, 1 Park Town (Richmond Lodge), now 68, Banbury Road, Oxford, to A. M. W. Christopher, 20.2.1862. (Among title-deeds in possession of present owner, Mrs. M. Graves-Morris.) Cp. MS. application to trustees of late Revd. E. Kempe for additional endowment of St. Aldates' benefice, by E. P. Hathaway on behalf of patrons, 12.12.1862, p. 1.

l. 34 *The Oxford Times,* 7.2.1914, p. 16.

p. 101 l. 8 Griffith Thomas, ch. vi, p. 4.

l. 17 *Reminiscences of an Octogenarian* by E. A. Knox, n.d. (Bodley cat: 1935), p. 109.

l. 29 Matthews, p. 7.

p. 102 ll. 7, 10 Downer, pp. 29-30.

l. 13 Matthews, p. 5.

l. 17 Knox, as cited, p. 108.

l. 21 n *The Oxford University Calendar* 1861, pp. 335-490; *An Oxford Hall in Mediaeval Times* by A. B. Emden (1927), p. 7.

l. 27 Butler, p. 16.

l. 34 *Alumni Oxonienses 1715-1886,* compiled J. Foster, vol. i (1887), p. 251; *The Oxford University Calendar* 1861, p. 331 (degree taken 14.6.1860); Downer, p. 29.

p. 103 l. 11 *In Memoriam. Thomas Augustus Nash,* ed. A.M.W.C., n.d. [1898], pp. 3-4. (STL no. 129.)

l. 13 Butler, p. 20.

l. 18 Letter, R. B. Girdlestone to W.H.G.T., 25.11.1910, pp. 1, 2.

l. 20 Preachers' Book, St. Aldate's, Oxford, vol. i, March-Dec. 1860.

l. 25 f. St. Aldates' return, Oxford episcopal visitation, 1860. (O.D.P. d. 180. f. 852v.)

p. 104 l. 3 Downer, p. 33.

l. 9 Personal recollection, Miss E. C. Christopher, 1957.

l. 11 Griffith Thomas, ch. vi, p. 11.
l. 17 *The Fourth Annual Report of the St. Aldate's Christian Temperance Society . . . 1866*, p. 5.
l. 18 Griffith Thomas, ch. vi, p. 8; cp. *Webster's Oxford, Wallingford, Abingdon and Banbury Directory, for 1869*, p. 35, & *Oxford City & Suburban Directory for 1876*, p. 54.
l. 27 *The Family of Christopher and Some Others*, anon. (by A. C. Seton-Christopher), (1933), p. 25. Cp. *Notes on St. Andrew's Church, Heckington*, compiled by H.T.S., n.d., (preface dated 1912), pp. 9-10.

p. 105 l. 6 Downer, p. 30.
l. 7 Butler, p. 12.
l. 17 Aglionby, p. 5.
l. 21 Butler, *ibid.*
l. 25 Messrs. Coutts's, London, Register 4, p. 391—Miss C. T. Christopher's account.

p. 106 l. 2 Will, Geo. Christopher, proved London 13.5.1861. (Principal Registry, 1861-277.)
l. 13 Preachers' Book, St. Aldate's, Oxford, vol. ii, 2.10.1864.
l. 18 Matthews, pp. 2-3.
l. 29 Sharp, p. 1.
l. 37 Butler, p. 1.

p. 107 l. 7 Tonge, pp. 2-3.
l. 22 Allan Smith, p. 1.
l. 24 *Christ and the Colleges*, ed. F. D. Coggan (1934), p. 57.

p. 108 l. 2 Allan, pp. 2-3.
l. 4 f. St. Aldates' returns, Oxford episcopal visitations, 1860, 1857, 1854. (O.D.P. d. 180. f. 852 v.; d. 179. f. 287 v.; d. 701. f. 285 r. & v.)
l. 17 Printed statement and appeal, 'Oxford Fund', over names of E. Auriol & E. P. Hathaway, dated London, Feb. 1864, p. 3; printed booklet, ed. E. P. Hathaway, of testimonies to A.M.W.C.'s Oxford work, March 1862, pp. 9-12.

p. 109 l. 6 Smith, pp. 1-4.
l. 18 *In Memoriam. Thomas Augustus Nash*, ed. A.M.W.C., n.d. [1898], pp. 4-5. (STL no. 129.)
l. 36 Allan, pp. 3-4.

p. 110 l. 6 f. Allan, p. 2; Matthews, p. 8; Aglionby, p. 3; Downer, p. 31.
l. 10 Preachers' Book, St. Aldate's, Oxford, vol. i, 4.2.1857.
l. 14 *The History of the Church Missionary Society* by E. Stock (1899), vol. ii, p. 65.
ll. 18, 19 Allan, p. 2.
l. 21 Griffith Thomas, p. 24.
l. 33 Preachers' Books, St. Aldate's, Oxford, vols. i (-1859-62) and ii (1863-5-).

p. 111 l. 20 Griffith Thomas, ch. v, p. 71.
l. 31 Allan, p. 4.
l. 32 Downer, p. 30.
l. 37 Aglionby, p. 2.

p. 112 l. 3 Matthews, p. 3.
l. 15 Ingham, p. 3.
l. 18 Allan, p. 2.
l. 38 Matthews, p. 4.
p. 113 l. 11 *Ibid.*, p. 2.
l. 13 Allan, p. 4.
l. 17 n *A Few Thoughts on the Best Means of Fortifying the Minds of Educated Young Men Against Infidelity and Popery* by A.M.W.C. (1868), p. 12. (STL no. 17.)
l. 20 Downer, p. 29.
l. 27 Aglionby, p. 2.
l. 35 *The Oxford Times*, 7.2.1914, p. 16; *The Oxford Chronicle*, 6.2.1914, p. 9.
p. 114 l. 4 Butler, p. 18.
l. 8 *The Oxford Times*, 7.12.1914, p. 16.
l. 15 Ingham, p. 1.
l. 28 Aglionby, p. 4.
p. 115 l. 1 f. Letter, Miss L. M. Waller (daughter of Revd. Dr. C. H. Waller) to W.H.G.T., 12.6.1913, pp. 1, 2.
l. 12 Cp. *Men for the Ministry* by G. C. B. Davies (1963), pp. 20-21; *D.N.B.*, 2nd supp., vol. iii (1912), p. 580.
l. 23 Matthews, p. 8.
l. 29 Preachers' Book, St. Aldate's, Oxford, vol. ii, 24.2.1867.
l. 32 Fly-leaf inscription, *The Book of Common Prayer, in its History and Interpretation* by R. P. Blakeney (1866). (Tyndale House Library, Cambridge: 264.031 BLA.)
p. 116 l. 5 Butler, p. 4.
ll. 10, 16 Preface by A.M.W.C. to *Christ Our Example* by C. Fry (9th edn., 1873), p. v. (STL no. 23.)
l. 35 Griffith Thomas, ch. viii, p. 24.
p. 117 l. 25 *Salvation in the Lord Jesus from the Dominion of Sin* by A.M.W.C., n.d., pp. 25-7 (STL no. 51.)
l. 38 Letter, Bp. F. Paget to A.M.W.C., 15.11.1904, p. 1.
p. 118 l. 9 Letter, A.M.W.C. to H. G. Grey, 30.8.1906, pp. 16-18. (LL no. 154.)
l. 18 Preachers' Book, St. Aldate's, Oxford, vol. ii, 12.5. & 2.6.1867.
l. 24 'A Review' by A.M.W.C. of *God's Way of Holiness* by H. Bonar (1864), p. 7. (STL no. 14.)
l. 35 *The Oxford Times*, 7.2.1914, p. 16.
p. 119 l. 22 "Canada Again", art. by A. M. W. Christopher, dated 5 Jan., in *The Fireside News*, 1884. (Cutting, preserved by W.H.G.T.)
l. 27 Griffith Thomas, ch. viii, slip attached to p. 27.
p. 120 ll. 17, 33 *Henry Barne: A Memoir* by his Widow (1887), pp. 302, 303-4.
p. 121 l. 4 Butler, p. 13.
l. 33 Griffith Thomas, ch. vi, pp. 8, 9.
p. 122 l. 6 Matthews, p. 8.
l. 11 Downer, p. 86.
l. 14 n St. Ebbes' return, Oxford episcopal visitation, 1857. (O.D.P. d. 179. f. 293r.) Cp. *The Hanbury Family* by A. A. Locke (1916), vol. ii, p. 342.

l. 22 n Copy in possession of Mr. G. E. Duffield; Preachers' Book, St. Aldate's, Oxford, vol. i, 15.1. to 4.3.1860 & 11.3 to 6.5.1860.
l. 30 Griffith Thomas, ch. vi, pp. 9-10.
p. 123 ll. 21, 31 *Ibid.*, p. 11.

CHAPTER VIII 1862-65

p. 124 l. 7 St. Aldates' return, Oxford episcopal visitation, 1860. (O.D.P. d. 180. f. 852 v.)
l. 16 Griffith Thomas, ch. vi, p. 4.
l. 21 'St. Aldate's Church and Schools, Oxford' (1862), p. 1. (STL no. 8.)
p. 125 l. 6 Printed letter, 'St. Aldate's, Oxford', issued by St. Aldates' churchwardens 28.10.1861, *re* voluntary church rate, (1861), pp. 1, 2. Cp. 'Minute Book of Rators in Vestry', St. Aldate's, Oxford (1782-1865), 18.10.1861.
l. 15 *Memoir of George Edmund Street, R.A.* by A. E. Street (1888), p. 304.
l. 15n Churchwardens' Accounts, St. Aldate's, Oxford (1815-1927), 16.5.1833; 16.5.1844. Cp. p. 130 n.
l. 31 Printed booklet, ed. E. P. Hathaway, containing letters to himself and E. Auriol, testifying to importance of A.M.W.C's Oxford work, 1862, pp. 1, 2.
p. 126 ll. 8, 13, 17, 21, 27 *Ibid.*, pp. 4, 9, 5, 5-6, 6, 7.
l. 27 In fact in 1861. Preachers' Book, St. Aldate's, Oxford, vol. i, 10.2.1861.
ll. 32, 36 Hathaway, *op. cit.*, pp. 7, 8.
p. 127 ll. 7, 17 *Ibid.*, pp. 8-9, 9-10.
p. 128 l. 5 'St. Aldate's Church and Schools, Oxford', 1862, p. 2. (STL no. 8.)
l. 19 Preachers' Book, St. Aldate's, Oxford, vol. i, 15, 22.6.1862.
ll. 28, 32 Broadsheet *re* church services during closure of St. Aldate's, dated 20.6.1862. (STL no. 10.)
p. 129 l. 16 Faculty for reconstruction of St. Aldate's, Oxford, 1862. (O.D.P. c. 1922.) Plan of alterations 1862-3 by J. T. Christopher, certified by A.M.W.C. & churchwardens. (In custody of Rector of St. Aldate's.) Cp. 'Minute Book of Rators in Vestry', St. Aldate's, Oxford (1782-1865), 13.1.1862.
l. 19 *The Oxford Chronicle*, 25.4.1863, p. 8.
l. 32 Matthews, p. 6.
p. 130 l. 8 *Ibid.*, p. 7.
l. 20 n Churchwardens' Account Book, St. Aldate's, Oxford (1815-1927), 2.6.1859. Cp. p. 125 n. and additional information p. 459.
l. 22 'St. Aldate's Parish Vestry, Holy Thursday. To the Non-Nobs . . .' by H. Holder, n.d. [1863] (Bodl. G. A. Oxon. b. 151. f. 11.)
l. 34 'Information with Respect to La Martinière, Calcutta' [by A.M.W.C.] 1862. (STL no. 11.)
p. 131 l. 2 *La Martinière Chronicle*, Centenary Number (1900), p. 24.
l. 9 *Ibid.*, p. 22.

l. 15 *The History of the Church Missionary Society* by E. Stock (1899), vol. ii, p. 162.
l. 26 Griffith Thomas, p. 244.
p. 132 l. 8 *Ibid.*, p. 256.
l. 16 n Butler, p. 10.
l. 18 *My Recollections* by E. Stock (1909), p. 270.
l. 25 Griffith Thomas, *ibid.*
l. 26 *The Mildmay Conference 1872* (1872), pp. 126-35.
l. 34 Ingham, pp. 3-4.
p. 133 ll. 13, 15, 20 *The Oxford Chronicle*, 25.4.1863, p. 8.
l. 23 Preachers' Book, St. Aldate's, Oxford, vol. ii, 26.4.1863.
l. 31 Printed letter, Bp. S. Wilberforce to A.M.W.C., March 1864, p. 1. (STL no. 13.)
l. 31 n 2 Churchwardens' Account Book, St. Aldate's, Oxford, (1815-1927), 5.5.1864. Cp. 'Minute Book of Rators in Vestry', St. Aldate's (1782-1865), 20.6.1862, 14.5.1863; Preachers' Book, St. Aldate's, vol. i, 7.7.1862, 29.5.1862.
p. 134 ll. 8,16,20 'Parish Church of St. Ebbe's, Oxford', rebuilding appeal by S. Y. N. Griffith, 1863, p. 1.
l. 26 Preachers' Books, St. Aldate's, Oxford, vols. i & ii, Aug. 1859-Nov. '69 (cp. 14.6.1863, 23.1.1866.)
p. 135 ll. 20, 33 Letter, A.M.W.C. to E. P. Hathaway, 13.8.1864, pp. 1-5. (LL no. 28.)
p. 136 l. 7 Letter, E. P. Hathaway to A.M.W.C., 11.12.1895, p. 1.
l. 19 Griffith Thomas, ch. x, p. 17.
l. 33 n Bodl. MS. Eng. lett, d. 171. f. 23.
p. 137 l. 6 Printed statement *re* advowsons of St. Clement's, St. Ebbe's, and St. Peter-le-Bailey, Oxford, over names of E. Auriol and E. P. Hathaway, London, Feb. 1865, p. 1.
l. 11 *Life of Edward Bouverie Pusey* by H. P. Liddon, ed. J. O. Johnston & others, 2nd edn., vol. iv (1897), p. 103.
l. 13 *The English Church in the Nineteenth Century* by J. H. Overton (1894), p. 86.
ll. 18, 24 *The First Annual Report of the Church Association* 1865-66, pp. 6, 4.
l. 28 Griffith Thomas, ch. vii, pp. 28, 29.
p. 138 l. 5 *Reminiscences of an Octogenarian* by E. A. Knox, n.d. (Bodley cat: 1935), p. 108.
l. 13 Griffith Thomas, p. 256.
l. 14 A copy is preserved in the Bodleian Library. (G. A. Oxon. 4to. 413 f. 222.)
l. 18 *The Ecclesiologist*, no. xcvi, June 1853, p. 218.
l. 20 *North Oxford and Its Mother Church SS. Philip and James* by H. Taunt, n.d. (Bodley cat: [1916].) No pagination. 6th leaf from t.-p.
p. 139 l. 17 *Apologia Pro Vita Sua* by J. H. Newman (edn. of 1897), p. 5.
p. 140 l. 15 Griffith Thomas, ch. vi, p. 13. Cp. *The Fireside News*, 23.11.1883, letter from A.M.W.C. dated 19.11.1883.

CHAPTER IX 1865-74

p. 142 l. 10 *Address to the Citizens of Oxford, and especially to Working Men, on the propriety of closing Public Houses and Beer Shops on the Lord's Day* by A.M.W.C. (1865), pp. 9-10. (STL no. 15.)

l. 18 *Ibid.*, p. 10.

p. 143 ll. 5, 24 *Ibid.*, pp. iv, 9.

p. 144 l. 2 Downer, pp. 99-100.

l. 8 Eph. 2. 8.

ll. 15, 20, 24 Griffith Thomas, ch. vi, p. 16.

l. 33 *Ibid.*, pp. 16-7.

p. 145 l. 14 *The History of the Church Missionary Society* by E. Stock, vol. iv (1916), p. 433.

l. 21 Preachers' Books, St. Aldate's, Oxford, vol. ii, 16.6.1867; vol. iii, 12.2.1871, 28.1.1872; vol. ii, 23.3.1870.

ll. 25, 30 St. Aldates' return, Oxford episcopal visitation, 1866. (O.D.P. c. 332 ff. 320v & 321r.)

l. 27 Preacher's Book, St. Aldate's, vol. i, 23.2.1851.

l. 34 Appeal for organ, St. Aldate's, Oxford, over churchwardens' names, 8.7.1867 (Bodl. G. A. Oxon, b. 151. f. 12).

p. 146 l. 1 Log Book, St. Aldates' Girls' School, 1863-1910, p. 23.

l. 33 *Jackson's Oxford Journal*, 27.1.1866, p. 5. Cp. *The Oxford Times*, 27.1.1866, p. 6; *Oxford Chronicle and Berks. and Bucks. Gazette*, 27.1.1866, p. 8.

p. 147 l. 15 St. Aldates' return, Oxford episcopal visitation, 1866. (O.D.P. c. 332. f. 320r.)

p. 149 l. 22 Letter, H. C. B. Bazely to E. P. Hathaway, 13.8.1867, pp. 1-4, 5-10.

p. 150 l. 2 Downer, pp. 45-6.

l. 31 Cp. *Henry Bazely the Oxford Evangelist* by E. L. Hicks (1886), *passim;* Downer, pp. 41-50.

l. 35 *Proceedings of the Church Missionary Society . . . 1860-61* (p. 138)—*1907-8* (p.170).

p. 151 l. 6 *Annual Reports*, Association for Oxford and Its Vicinity in Aid of the Church Missionary Society, 1861, p. 3, 1876, p. 3, 1880, p. 3.

l. 35 *The Oxford Chronicle*, 21.3.1913, p. 7.

p. 152 l. 11 Griffith Thomas, ch. vi, pp. 33-4.

l. 18 Allan, p. 2.

ll. 26, 37 Griffith Thomas, ch. xi, pp. 241, 244.

p. 153 l. 4 Downer, p. 32.

l. 9 Ingham, p. 2.

l. 12 Aglionby, p. 1.

l. 15 Griffith Thomas, ch. viii, pp. 11, 12. Cp. Letters, A.M.W.C. to W.H.G.T., 18.5.1911, pp. 7-9 (LL no. 189) and 24.8.1911, pp. 1-6 (LL no. 194); cp. letter, A.M.W.C. to "Sister Ruth" (1911) (LL no. 195).

l. 19 Letters, *The Record*, 28.3.1913, from "An Oxford M.A.", p. 290; 4.4.1913, from W. Pope, p. 306.

l. 23	Griffith Thomas, ch. vi, p. 31.
l. 33	Envelope, inscribed "Breakfast at the Clarendon Hotel, Sat. Feb. 9th, 1889. Speaker, the Bishop of Caledonia . . . " (Bodl. G. A. Oxon, b. 151. f. 5.).
p. 154 l. 4	Ingham, pp. 4.
l. 11	Butler, pp. 13-4.
l. 14	Aglionby, pp. 2, 3.
l. 22	Downer, p. 80; cp. *The Life and Correspondence of Thomas Valpy French* by H. Birks (1895), vol. i, p. 168.
l. 27	Downer, p. 31.
l. 32	*Annual Reports,* Oxford and Oxfordshire Auxiliary of the Church Pastoral-Aid Society, 1860 (p. 7)-61, 1863-9, 1878-80; 1899 (p. 3)-1900, 1903, 1905, 1908.
l. 35	*Annual Reports,* Oxford and Oxfordshire Auxiliary Society for Promoting Christianity among the Jews, 1881 (p. 3), 1895, 1902, 1904 (p. 3).
p. 156 l. 14	*A Few Thoughts on the Best Means of Fortifying the Minds of Educated Young Men against Infidelity and Popery* by A.M.W.C. (1868), pp. 5, 4, 7. (STL no. 17.)
l. 26	*Ibid.*, p. 11.
p. 157 l. 3	*How may the Clergy further the Supply of Suitable Candidates for the Ministry?* by A.M.W.C. (1869), p. 6. (STL no. 18.)
ll. 14, 23	*Ibid.*, pp. 18, 20.
p. 158 l. 2	*Ibid.*, p. 22.
l. 5	*Expository Thoughts on the Gospels. St. Mark,* by J. C. Ryle (1879), pp. 142-3 n.
ll. 17, 22	'Journal; kept by Thomas Surtees Raine', vol. ii (April 1868–Nov. 1869), p. 8.
l. 28	*Ibid.*, p. 9.
ll. 30, 38	*Ibid.*, p. 10.
p. 159 l. 13	*Home Words,* ed. C. Bullock, 1897, 'The Late Rev. E. Penrose Hathaway, M.A.' by C. B(ullock), p. 177; cp. Downer, pp. 38-9.
l. 17	Butler, p. 19.
l. 35	Preachers' Book, St. Aldate's, Oxford, vol. ii, 19.7.1868.
p. 160 ll. 1, 6	*Henry Bazely the Oxford Evangelist* by E. L. Hicks (1886), p. 63.
l. 16	Sturdy, pp. 1, 5.
ll. 20, 29	St. Aldates' return, Oxford episcopal visitation, 1869. (O.D.P. c. 335. f. 282v.)
l. 23	*Ibid.*, 1872. (O.D.P. c. 338. f. 297.)
l. 28	*The Church Plate of Oxfordshire* by J. T. Evans (1928), p. 122.
p. 161 l. 2	Griffith Thomas, ch. vi, p. 5.
l. 8	Letter, M. H. Sutton to F. J. Hazeldine, 30.8.1900, printed, *Scheme . . . for Founding Exhibitions at . . . Wycliffe Hall, Oxford, and Ridley Hall, Cambridge* (1900), p. 6.
l. 16	*The Oxford Chronicle,* 16.10.1869, p. 8.
l. 28	Butler, p. 4.
ll. 30, 34	Sharp, p. 1.
p. 162 l. 3	Ingham, pp. 2-3.

l. 24 *Memorials of R. Harold A. Schofield* by A. T. Schofield (1885), pp. 30, 31.

p. 163 l. 5 Letter, A.M.W.C. to W.H.G.T., 1.9.1906, pp. 8-11. (LL no. 155.)

l. 7 MS. Reminiscences by H. Chandler, n.d. [1935], p. 30. (Formerly (*c.* 1950) in the possession of the late Mrs. Chandler, now (1966) untraceable, probably destroyed.)

p. 164 l. 4 Sturdy, pp. 1-4. Cp. Letter, A.M.W.C. to W.H.G.T., 1.9.1910, pp. 1-4. (LL no. 176a.)

l. 6 Preachers' Book, St. Aldate's, Oxford, vol. ii, 24.1.1866.

l. 14 Griffith Thomas, p. 63.

l. 15 Preacher's Book, St. Aldate's, Oxford, vol. ii, 7.11.1869.

ll. 31, 34, 35 *A Sermon, preached . . on July 3rd, 1870* . . by A.M.W.C., p. 4. (STL no. 19.)

p. 165 l. 8 *Ibid.;* St. Aldates' return, Oxford episcopal visitation, 1869. (O.D.P. c. 335. f. 283r.)

l. 11 *The Oxford Times,* 9.7.1870, p. 2. Cp. *ibid.*, pp. 5, 8; 2.7.1870, p. 8; 16.7.1870, p. 5.

p. 166 l. 17 *A Sermon,* as cited, pp. 6, 8.

l. 23 *The Oxford Times,* 4.9.1931, p. 16. Cp. Bodl. MS. Top. Oxon. d. 503 f. 56.

l. 29 *A Sermon,* as cited, t.-p.

ll. 34, 36 *Extract from an Address* . . . by A.M.W.C. (1880), p. 1. (STL no. 50.)

p. 167 l. 5 *China's Millions,* ed. J. H. Taylor, July & Aug. 1880, p. 104.

l. 16 *Extract from an Address,* as cited, *ibid.*

p. 168 l. 16 *Notes of the Life and Works of the Rev. Lorenzo Lucena,* n.d. [1881], pp. 3-6.

l. 26 n *The Barrovian* (magazine of King William's Coll., I.o.M.), May 1911, p. 60.

p. 169 l. 2 Ingham, pp. 4-5.

l. 3 f. Apparently *The Oxford Times,* 21.10.1872. (Cutting, Bodl. G. A. Oxon, b. 151. f. 1, taken neither from *The Oxford Chronicle* nor *Jackson's Oxford Journal. The Oxford Times* for 21.10.1872 does not survive in the Bodleian Library, in Oxford City Library, or at the British Museum Newspaper Library, Colindale.)

l. 32 Griffith Thomas, ch. vii, p. 1.

p. 170 l. 10 *Ibid.*, p. 256.

p. 171 l. 6 Information from Dr. D. R. Porter, of Frilford Heath, Berks., 1963.

l. 13 *The Life of William Hagger Barlow, D.D.*, ed. M. Barlow (1910), p. 155.

l. 34 *The Oxford Times,* 21.10.1872. Cp. p. 169, l. 3 f. above.

p. 172 ll. 6, 8, 9 Copy of letter, A.M.W.C. to C. C. Cole, 15.7.1872, p. 1. (LL no. 31.)

l. 20 *The Oxford Chronicle,* 11.10.1873, p. 7; cp. *The Oxford Times,* 11.10.1873, p. 8.

p. 173 l. 9 *A Review* . . . by A.M.W.C. (1873), pp. 9-10. (STL no. 25.)

l. 12 *The Post Office Directory of Oxfordshire,* ed. E. R. Kelly (1877), p. 1056.

l. 14 n Assignment, 7 Keble Terrace, now 7 Keble Road, Oxford, to A.M.W.C., 27.4.1871 (among records of Oxford University Land Agent); *Voters' List, Oxford,* Oct. 1871.

l. 19 *Alumni Oxonienses 1715-1886,* ed. J. Foster, vol. i (1887), p. 251.

l. 22 *Trinity College* by H. E. D. Blakiston (1898), p. 240.

ll. 25, 27 Will, Thos. Millard, proved Bristol 12.1.1872. (Country copy, Principal Registry, London.)

l. 33 *Burke's Landed Gentry,* 1952, p. 444.

p. 174 l. 17 *The Early Life of Bishop Owen* by E. E. Owen (1958), p. 38; *D.N.B. 1922-30* (1937), p. 646.

l. 23 Letter, Miss E. E. Owen to J.S.R., 19.12.1962, pp. 4-5.

l. 26 *Ibid.,* p. 3.

p. 176 l. 9 Aglionby, pp. 1, 2, 3-4, 5.

p. 177 l. 8 Ingham, pp. 1, 2-3, 5, 6.

CHAPTER X 1874-78

p. 179 ll. 16, 22 *Account of the Union Meeting for the Promotion of Scriptural Holiness, held at Oxford . . . August* 29 *to September* 7, 1874, n.d. (Bodley cat: 1875), p. 27.

p. 180 l. 2 *Ibid.,* p. 28.

l. 14 *Ibid.,* pp. 29, 31, 32.

p. 181 ll. 3, 9, 11, 15 *Ibid.,* pp. ii, 95, v, 17.

p. 182 ll. 7, 12 *Ibid.,* p. 89.

ll. 19, 20 *Ibid.,* p. 119.

p. 183 l. 11 *Henry Bazely the Oxford Evangelist* by E. L. Hicks (1886), pp. 211-17.

l. 14 *Account of the Union Meeting . . .,* as cited, p. 362.

l. 22 *Ibid.,* p. 28.

l. 37 *The History of the Church Missionary Society* by E. Stock (1899), vol. iii, p. 30.

p. 184 l. 9 Cox, p. 6.

l. 13 St. Aldates' return, Oxford episcopal visitation, 1875. (O.D.P. c. 341. f. 316v.)

l. 17 Preachers' Books, St. Aldate's, Oxford, vol. iv, 1880, 1885; vol. v, 1887; vol. vi, 1894, 1895, 1899, 1902.

p. 185 l. 9 *Book of Common Prayer,* The Order of the Administration of the Lord's Supper, concluding alternative prayer.

p. 186 l. 18 *The Supply of Clergy* by A.M.W.C. (1875), p. 4. (STL no. 37.)

ll. 21, 29 *Ibid.,* p. 6.

l. 31 *Authorised Report of the Church Congress* (1875), pp. 353-4.

p. 187 l. 6 Preachers' Books, St. Aldate's, Oxford, vol. iii, 25.1.1874, 21.11.1875, 4.6.1876, 13.5. & 25.11.1877; vol. iv, 16.11.1879, 25.4. & 23.5.1880.

l. 20 *Ibid.,* vol. iii, 3.5.1874; 30.5.1875; 14.11.1875; 25.2.1877.

l. 22 *Ibid.,* 22.12.1872.

l. 24 Cp. *Annual Reports,* Association for Oxford and Its Vicinity in Aid of the Church Missionary Society, 1871, 1873, 1876, 1879-81, 1884-88.

p. 188 ll. 15, 16 *Henry Bazely the Oxford Evangelist* by E. L. Hicks (1886), pp. 183-4; *Oxford College Servants' Society . . . Rules . . . and Annual Report, 1876* (1876), pp. 5-6.

l. 19 *Ibid.*, 1876-1912 (1913).

ll. 25, 32 Hicks, *op. cit.*, pp. 90, 95.

p. 189 ll. 5, 8 *Ibid.*, pp. 97-8.

ll. 15, 20 *Ibid.*, pp. 101-2.

ll. 27, 30 *Ibid.*, p. 110.

p. 190 l. 2 *Ibid.*, p. 112.

l. 13 *Francis James Chavasse* by J. B. Lancelot (1929), p. 70.

p. 191 l. 2 *The Oxford Times*, 26.5.1888, p. 8.

l. 5 *Francis James Chavasse*, as cited, p. 71; revised M. R. Lawrence, 1963.

l. 14 *The Oxford Times*, 7.2.1914, p. 16.

l. 29 *Francis James Chavasse*, as cited, p. 75.

l. 34 *The Life of Lord Nuffield* by P.W.S. Andrews and E. Brunner (1955), p. 40. (Cp. illustration, p. 81.)

p. 192 l. 9 Letter, R. B. Girdlestone to W.H.G.T., 25.11.1910, p. 2.

l. 18 Griffith Thomas, ch. vii, p. 31.

l. 27 *The History of Ridley Hall, Cambridge*, by F. W. B. Bullock, vol. i (1941), p. 174.

l. 30 Minute Book, Wycliffe Hall Council (1879-1933), pp. 3, 29. Cp. Bullock, *op. cit.*, p. 193.

l. 33 English, pp. 4, 5.

p. 193 l. 3 Letter, R. B. Girdlestone to W.H.G.T., 25.11.1910, p. 2.

l. 4 Preachers' Book, St. Aldate's, Oxford, vol. iii, 7.9.1877; vol. iv, 1882 f.

ll. 18, 19 *Edward King* by G. W. E. Russell (1912), p. 59; *Edward King and Our Times* by Lord Elton (1958), p. 45.

l. 34 *John William Burgon* by E. M. Goulbourn (1892), vol. ii, p. 20.

l. 36 *St. Aldate's Church, Oxford, Parish Magazine*, March 1889, p. 2.

p. 194 l. 8 *The Life and Correspondence of Thomas Valpy French* by H. Birks (1895), vol. i, p. 322.

l. 25 Letter, A. W. Poole to A.M.W.C., 27.6.1880, pp. 6, 4.

l. 28 *St. Aldate's Church, Oxford, Parish Magazine*, March 1889, p. 2.

l. 36 English, p. 2.

p. 195 l. 5 Baptism register, St. Aldate's, Oxford (1850-89), 30.10.1878.

l. 18 *Tucker of Uganda* by A. P. Shepherd (1929), p. 29.

ll. 24, 25 *Ibid.*, p. 5.

p. 196 l. 15 'Parsonage House for St. Aldate's, Oxford.' Appeal by A.M.W.C. (1877), p. 1. (STL no. 42: Bodl. Oxon. b. 151. f. 13.)

l. 28 *Parsonage House for St. Aldate's, Oxford*, ed. E. P. Hathaway (1877), p. 11.

l. 36 *Ibid.*, pp. 12, 13.

p. 197 ll. 9, 15 *Ibid.*, pp. 15, 10.

ll. 23, 28, 35 *Ibid.*, pp. 8-9, 1.

p. 198 ll. 1, 5 *Ibid.*, pp. 9, 1.
l. 22 MS. copy of address dated 1.3.1879, 'To the Rev. A. M. W. Christopher, M.A.', pp. 7, [1909].
l. 35 n *Voters' List, Oxford,* 4.10.1878.
l. 36 Assignment, 7 Keble Terrace, Oxford, now 7 Keble Road, A.M.W.C. to J. A. Shaw, 2.12.1878. (Among records of Oxford University Land Agent.)
p. 199 l. 2 *The Oxford Times,* 12.10.1878, p. 6.
l. 21 Cox, pp. 2-3.
l. 34 Griffith Thomas, ch. x, between pp. 15, 16, inserted p. 1.

CHAPTER XI 1878-82

p. 200 l. 12 *Baptismal Regeneration,* ed. A.M.W.C., n.d. (STL no. 41.)
l. 16 Griffith Thomas, ch. vii, p. 28.
p. 201 l. 23 *The Oxford Times,* 4.8.1877, p. 8.
l. 37 *Ibid.*, 29.9.1877, pp. 4-(5).
p. 202 l. 2 *The Oxford Times,* Centenary Supplement, 7.9.1962, p. 5.
l. 16 *The Oxford Times,* 29.9.1877, p. 4.
l. 38 *Life of Edward Bouverie Pusey* by H. P. Liddon, ed. J. O. Johnston & others, 2nd edn., vol. iv (1897), pp. 318-20.
p. 203 l. 18 Copy of letter, A.M.W.C. to H. P. Liddon, 27.11.1878, pp. 1-2. (LL no. 33.)
ll. 35, 36 *Advice to Those Who Exercise the Ministry of Reconciliation Through Confession and Absolution, being the Abbé Gaume's Manual for Confessors . . . abridged, condensed and adapted . . .* by E. B. Pusey (1878), pp. 364, 355.
p. 204 ll. 1, 2 *Ibid.*, pp. 365, 358.
l. 5 *Church Association Monthly Intelligencer,* 1.3.1879, p. 84.
l. 8 Pusey (Gaume), *op. cit.*, pp. 361-2.
ll. 11, 13 *Ibid.*, pp. 177, 178.
l. 25 *Ibid.*, pp. 315-6.
ll. 30, 36 Copy of letter, A.M.W.C. to H. P. Liddon, 27.11.1878, pp. 2-3, 2. (LL no. 33.)
p. 205 ll. 14, 15 Letter, H. P. Liddon to A.M.W.C., 2.12.1878, pp. 1, 3-4.
l. 29 Copy of letter, A.M.W.C. to H. P. Liddon, 2.12.1878, p. 1. (LL no. 34.)
l. 31 Liddon, *op. cit.*, vol. iv, p. 315.
p. 206 ll. 6, 24 Copy of letter, A.M.W.C. to H. P. Liddon, 2.12.1878, pp. 2, 3-4. (LL no. 34.)
l. 28 Letter, H. P. Liddon to A.M.W.C., 3.12.1878, p. 3.
l. 35 Copy of letter, A.M.W.C. to H. P. Liddon, 6.12.1878, p. 3. (LL no. 35.)
p. 207 l. 4 Letter, H. P. Liddon to A.M.W.C., 7.12.1878, pp. 5-7.
ll. 9, 17 Copy of letter, A.M.W.C. to H. P. Liddon, 9.12.1878, pp. 3-4. (LL no. 36.)
l. 25 Letter, H. P. Liddon to A.M.W.C., 10.12.1878, pp. 1, 2, 3.
ll. 31, 38 Letter, same to same, 17.12.1878, pp. 7, 9-10, 11.
p. 208 ll. 7, 10, 13, 23 Letter, E. B. Pusey to A.M.W.C., 24.12.1878, pp. 1, 2-3, 4.
l. 36 Letter, same to same, 1.1.1879, pp. 1, 2.

p. 209 l. 2 Liddon, *op. cit.*, vol. iv, p. 320.
p. 210 ll. 22, 25, 29 *The Oxford Chronicle*, 26.5.1877, p. 7.
p. 211 ll. 6, 9, 11 Letter, 'The Late Canon Christopher', from F. C. T. Jansen, *The Record*, 4.4.1913, p. 306.
ll. 17, 21, 29 Letter, W. G. D. Fletcher to W.H.G.T., 24.11.1920, pp. 4, 2, 3.
l. 35 Cp. Printed invitation cards, Ch. Assocn. meetings, Oxford, 11.9. & 27.11.1877; 24.11.1881; 21.2. & 24.10.1882; printed notices 11.10.1877, 5.3.1883.
p. 212 l. 2 *Reminiscences of an Octogenarian* by E. A. Knox, n.d. (Bodley cat: 1935), p. 112.
l. 16 Cp. *Church Association Monthly Intelligencer*, 1.3.1882, pp. 86-8.
l. 19 Griffith Thomas, ch. vii, p. 32.
p. 213 l. 7 Webster, pp. 1-2.
l. 33 MS. (pp. 4), A.M.W.C., "Before Dr. McCarthy's Lecture", pp. 1-2, 3, 4. (Subsequent inscription by A.M.W.C.: "In 1882, A.M.W.C. in St. Aldate's.")
p. 214 l. 7 Knox, *op. cit.*, p. 115. Cp. *Minutes of the Oxford Diocesan Conference* 1878, pp. 8-9.
l. 26 Draft letter, A.M.W.C. to G. N. Freeling, n.d., pp. 2, 3, 4. (LL no. 32.)
l. 34 Letter, E. P. Hathaway to A.M.W.C., 7.10.1878, pp. 1, 2-3.
p. 215 l. 2 *Ibid.*, p. 3.
ll. 11, 15 Letter, Bp. J. F. Mackarness to A.M.W.C., 18.12.1878, pp. 1, 3.
l.20 *The Founding of Cuddesdon* by W. O. Chadwick (1954), p. 129.
l. 26 *The Life of the Right Reverend Ronald Knox* by E. A. St. J. Waugh (1959), p. 35.
l. 36 *Religion in the Victorian Era* by L. E. Elliott-Binns (reissue of 1953), p. 323.
p. 216 l. 19 *Oxford: Its Social and Intellectual Life* by A. M. M. Stedman (1878), p. 116.
l. 26 Griffith Thomas, ch. vii, p. 34.
p. 220 l. 35 *Ibid.*, ch. vii, pp. 34-7.
p. 221 l. 12 *George Anthony King* by A. R. Buckland (1928), p. 11.
l. 20 *Henry Bazely the Oxford Evangelist* by E. L. Hicks (1886), p. 85.
l. 34 Buckland, *op. cit.*, *ibid.*
p. 222 l. 4 *Memories of Victorian Oxford* by Sir C. W. C. Oman (1941), p. 80.
l. 18 Griffith Thomas, ch. vii, between pp. 32 & 34, 3rd inserted pa.
l. 23 n Downer, p. 35.
l. 24 Letter, 'The Late Canon Christopher', from F. C. T. Jansen, *The Record*, 4.4.1913, p. 306.
l. 35 *Francis James Chavasse* by J. B. Lancelot (1929), p. 85; letter, Bp. C. M. Chavasse to J.S.R., 12.7.1958, pp. 1-2. Cp. *The Chavasse Twins* by S. Gummer (1963), p. 19.
p. 223 l. 3 Ingham, p. 4.
l. 5 Griffith Thomas, ch. x, p. 39.

ll. 8, 14 *An Oxford Parish Priest* (W. B. Duggan) by G. Lewis, n.d., (Bodley cat: [1905]), p. 107.
p. 224 l. 16 Letter, W. B. Duggan to A.M.W.C., 9.1.1881, p.1.
p. 225 l. 2 *Dawn of Day,* 'St. Paul's, Oxford, Parochial Page,' 1.1.1881, p. iv.
l. 11 Copy of letter, A.M.W.C. to W. B. Duggan, 19.1.1881, pp. 1-4, 1. (LL no. 42.)
ll. 27, 34 Griffith Thomas, ch. vii, p. 48; cp. *Francis James Chavasse,* as cited, p. 76.
p. 226 l. 11 *Should the Church Association be dissolved or strengthened by those who value the English Reformation and the Gospel Truth identified with it?* Church Assocn. Tract lxxix, n.d., p. 1.
l. 14 C. A. *Tract lxxix,* as cited, p. 3. Cp. *Essays on the Re-Union of Christendom,* ed. F. G. Lee (1867), p. 180.
l. 23 C. A. *Tract lxxix,* as cited, *ibid.*

CHAPTER XII 1882-90

p. 227 l. 15 *The Life of Dwight L. Moody* by W. R. Moody, n.d. (Bodley cat: [1900]), pp. 312-3.
l. 18 *The Official Report of the Church Congress* . . . 1883, ed. C. Dunkley (1883), p. 329.
p. 228 l. 3 Preachers' Book, St. Aldate's, Oxford, vol. iii, 12. 2. 1871.
l. 24 Webster, p. 1.
l. 25 Cox, p. 4.
l. 33 Webster, *ibid.*
p. 229 l. 4 Cox, *ibid.*
l. 13 *St. Aldate's with St. Matthew's Parish Magazine,* July 1894, p. 3.
l. 26 Webster, *ibid.*
p. 230 l. 10 *Ibid.,* p. 2.
l. 20 *The Early Days of the Church Army 1883-1886,* anon. (1891), p. 26.
l. 32 Webster, pp. 2-3.
p. 231 l. 1 *Wilson Carlile and the Church Army* by E. Rowan (1905), p. 189.
ll. 9, 23 *Ibid.,* pp. 189-90, 191.
l. 27 *Wilson Carlile and the Church Army,* as cited, p. 193.
p. 232 ll. 9, 14 *St. Aldate's Church, Oxford, Parish Magazine,* March 1889, p. 2.
p. 233 l. 11 *The Church Army: Its Doings in 1885,* anon., n.d., pp. 30-31.
l. 18 Webster, p. 3.
l. 25 Personal recollection, Miss E. C. Christopher, 1957. Cp. letter, Bp. C. M. Chavasse to J.S.R., 12.7.1958, pp. 2-3.
l. 29 Webster, *ibid.*
l. 36 Cox, p. 8.
p. 234 l. 3 Letter, 'The Late Canon Christopher', from F. C. T. Jansen, *The Record,* 4.4.1913, p. 306.
l. 26 Letter, Bp. J. Fraser to A.M.W.C., 12.4.1883.
p. 235 l. 9 Letter, Bp. J. C. Ryle to A.M.W.C., 19.1.1883, pp. 1-8.
l. 16 Letter, from same to same, 6.1.1883, pp. 2, 3-4.

l. 33 Griffith Thomas, ch. vii, pp. 40-1; cp. MS., in A.M.W.C's hand, for use at diocesan conference, pp. 1, 3, 2, 4.
p. 236 l. 6 Letter, C. J. Goodhart to A.M.W.C., 15.1.1883, pp. 1-2.
l. 12 Letter, H. Law to A.M.W.C., 12.1.1883, pp. 1-3.
l. 25 Letter, J. B. Whiting to A.M.W.C., 12.1.1883, pp. 1-4.
p. 237 l. 2 II Cor. 5. 8.
l. 15 *Henry Bazely the Oxford Evangelist* by E. L. Hicks (1886), pp. 312-4.
l. 36 *Oxford: Its Life and Schools*, ed. A. M. M. Stedman (1887), p. 131.
p. 238 l. 19 *The Heart of the Lord Jesus Christ towards the Lost* by A.M.W.C. (1883), p. 10. (STL no. 56.)
p. 239 ll. 16, 24, 32 *The Official Report of the Church Congress . . . 1883*, ed. C. Dunkley (1883), pp. 331-2.
p. 240 l. 10 *Ibid.*, p. 332.
p. 241 l. 29 *The Oxford Chronicle*, 8.3.1884, p. 8.
p. 242 l. 10 'To the Rev. A. M. W. Christopher, M.A.', printed letter, 10.3.1884; cp. MS. portion, Plate 53.
ll. 20, 26, 37 *The Oxford Chronicle*, 15.3.1884, p. 8.
p. 243 l. 4 Allan Smith, p. 3.
l. 7 *The Oxford Chronicle*, 22.3.1884, p. 8.
ll. 11, 16 Printed memorial, 'To the Reverend the Proctors', Oxford, Feb. 1845: in fact issued shortly *before* the decisive convocation of 13 Feb.
l. 19 Letter, R. B. Girdlestone to W.H.G.T., 25.11.1910, pp. 2-3.
l. 24 Griffith Thomas, ch. vii, p. 51.
l. 38 *The Oxford Chronicle*, 26.4.1884, p. 8.
p. 244 ll. 18, 22 Griffith Thomas, ch. vii, p. 43.
l. 27 *Ibid.*, p. 53. Cp. MS. copy of address dated 1.1.1885, pp. 1, [1909.]
l. 28 *The Oxford Chronicle*, 17.1.1885, p. 5.
l. 31 Griffith Thomas, *ibid.*
p. 245 l. 14 Letter, 'The Late Canon Christopher', from F. C. T. Jansen, *The Record*, 4.4.1913, p. 306.
l. 20 *Home Words*, ed. C. Bullock, 1884, 'The Rev. A. M. W. Christopher, M.A.', p. 16.
l. 36 *The Life of Henry Drummond* by G. A. Smith (1899), pp. 307-8.
p. 246 ll. 6,8,10 *Ibid.*, pp. 309, 311.
p. 247 l. 3 Cox, pp. 1-2.
l. 19 n Preachers' Book, St. Aldate's, Oxford, vol. v, 13.11.1887.
p. 248 l. 7 Cox, pp. 8-11.
l. 19 *Oxford: Its Life and Schools*, ed. A. M. M. Stedman (1887), p. 153.
l. 27 n Downer, p. 30.
l. 33 Cox, pp. 6-7.
l. 37 Newspaper cutting, 'Sleeplessness: A Prescription' by A.M.W.C., 1898.

p. 249 ll. 2, 3, 9, 10, 12, 15 *Ibid.*
l. 34 *Our Father; or The Lord's Prayer Expanded in the Words of Holy Scripture*, anon. (1886), pp. v-vi.

p. 250 l. 9 Cox, p. 12.
l. 14 n Griffith Thomas's source was probably the Revd. H. Grey, Principal of Wycliffe Hall. Cp. *The Oxford Chronicle*, 14.3.1913, p. 7.
l. 14 MS. 'Index to the Clergy . . . of the Diocese of Oxford . . . to . . . July 1908' by W. J. Oldfield (1915), vol. 1, f. 73.
l. 21 Downer, p. 30.

p. 251 l. 16 Griffith Thomas, chap. viii, pp. 3-4.
ll. 25, 31 *Union of Heart amongst Christians Essential to the Evangelization of the World* by A.M.W.C. (1886), pp. 6, 11. (STL no. 65.)

p. 252 l. 2 *Ibid.*, p. 12.
l. 27 *Saving Gospel Truth; and Uniting Christian Love* by A.M.W.C. n.d. (Bodley cat: [1890]), pp. 17, 18. (STL no. 87.)
l. 36 *The Church Army: Its Doings in 1885*, anon., n.d., p. 30.

p. 253 l. 7 *St. Aldate's Church, Oxford, Parish Magazine*, Jan. 1888, p. 1.
l. 23 n Account book, Oxford Fund, kept by E. P. Hathaway, 1857-95, p. 3 from end.
l. 24 *St. Aldate's Church, Oxford, Parish Magazine*, Dec. 1888, p. 1.
l. 26 n *Church Association Monthly Intelligencer*, 1.11.1883, p. 321.

p. 254 l. 4 Griffith Thomas, ch. viii, p. 21.
l. 6 St. Aldates' return, Oxford episcopal visitation, 1893. (O.D.P. c. 359. f. 307 r.)
l. 14 Personal recollection, M. R. Lawrence, 1963.
ll. 17, 21 *St. Aldate's Church, Oxford, Parish Magazine*, Feb. 1889, p. 1; March 1889, p. 1.
l. 28 Ibid., March 1889, p. 2.
l. 33 Letters, A.M.W.C. to W.H.G.T., *e.g.* 13.5. (p. 1), 18.5. (p. 1), 24.8. (p. 1) 1911. (LL nos. 188, 189, 194.)

p. 255 l. 16 Letter, same to same, 2.7.1888 (2), pp. 5-6. (LL no. 51.)
l. 18 Letter, same to T. Redfern, 7.7.1888, p. 2. (LL no. 52.)
l. 27 Letter, same to W.H.G.T., 3.1.1889, p. 1. (LL no. 57.)
l. 38 Letter, same to same, 8.1.1889, pp. 2, 3-4. (LL no. 58).

p. 256 l. 21 Letter, same to same, 23.5.1889, pp. 3-4. (LL no. 70.)
l. 26 Letter, same to same, 3.8.1889, p. 2. (LL no. 73.)
l. 31 Letter, same to same, 15.8.1889, p. 4. (LL no. 76.)
ll. 32, 33 Letter, same to same, 21.8.1889 (1), pp. 1, 2. (LL no. 77.)

p. 257 l. 1 *Ibid.*, pp. 3-4.
ll. 3, 4, 7 Letter, same to same, 2.9.1889, pp. 1, 4. (LL no. 81.)
l. 12 *Reminiscences of an Octogenarian* by E. A. Knox, n.d. (Bodley cat: 1935), p. 108.

p. 258 l. 17 *The Life and Correspondence of Thomas Valpy French* by H. Birks (1895), vol. i, p. 362.
l. 31 *Ibid.*, vol. ii, p. 179.

p. 259 l. 8 'Church Missionary Society. Breakfast at Oxford. February 17th. 1886' (reprinted from *The Oxford Times*, 20.2.1886), pp. 1-2.
l. 10 Committee Minutes, C.M.S., vol. 52 (1887-88), p. 577 (26.4.1888).
p. 261 l. 3 'The Work of the Church Association', printed letter, A.M.W.C. to H. Miller (Sec., C.A.), 5.11.1889, pp. 1-2. (LL no. 83.)

CHAPTER XIII 1890-96

p. 263 l. 2 'An Appeal for Help towards the Building of a Church for the New Suburb of Grandpont in the Parish of St. Aldate's, Oxford' (1889). (STL no. 82.)
l. 2 n 'An Appeal for Help . . .' title as above (1891). (STL no. 96.)
l. 6 'St. Matthew's Church, Grandpont, Oxford' (1890). (STL no. 91.)
l. 16 n 'Minute Book of Rators in Vestry', St. Aldate's, Oxford, (1782-1865); 'St. Aldate's Parish Minute Book' (1865-1928).
l. 21 Griffith Thomas, ch. viii, p. 6. Cp. letter, E. P. Hathaway to A.M.W.C., 22.4.1891, p. 3.
l. 28 *St. Matthew's Church, Grandpont, St. Aldate's, Oxford, Building Fund Account* (1895), pp. 8-41. (STL no. 117.)
p. 264 l. 9 *St. Aldate's and Grandpont (Oxford) Schools Building Fund* (1896), p. 2. (STL no. 122.)
l. 19 'An Appeal for Help', as cited, (1889), p. 1. (STL no. 82.)
l. 30 St. Aldates' return, Oxford episcopal visitation, 1890. (O.D.P. c. 356. f. 295 v.)
p. 265 ll. 2, 9 Griffith Thomas, ch. viii, p. 21.
l.15 n Personal recollection, M. R. Lawrence, 1963.
l. 24 Copy of letter, A.M.W.C. to E. P. Hathaway, 20.4.1891, p. 2. (LL no. 86.) Cp. Appendix III.
p. 266 l. 3 Personal recollection, M. R. Lawrence, 1963.
l. 34 Griffith Thomas, ch. x, p. 19.
l. 35 St. Aldates' returns, Oxford episcopal visitations, 1893, 1896. (O.D.P. c. 359. f. 307 v., c. 362. f. 298 v.)
p. 267 l. 2 *Ibid.*, 1890. (O.D.P. c. 356. f. 295 v.)
l. 20 *The Record*, 28.2.1890, p. 209. Cp. Reprint, 'A National Protestant Congress'. (STL no. 90.)
p. 268 l. 1 n Letter, 'The late Canon Christopher', from F. C. T. Jansen, *The Record*, 4.4.1913, p. 306.
l. 19 *The Church Intelligencer*, June 1890, p. 89.
l. 33 Griffith Thomas, ch. viii, p. 9.
l. 35 *The Guardian*, 18.4.1906, 'Clerical Changes at Oxford', p. 659.
p. 269 l. 5 *The Church Intelligencer*, June 1892, p. 95.
l. 11 Griffith Thomas, ch. viii, pp. 2-3.
l. 18 *Ibid.*, ch. viii, p. 3.
l. 20 Letter, E. P. Hathaway to A.M.W.C., n.d. [1892], p. 2.
l. 28 Letter, J. E. Matthews to A.M.W.C., 24.2.1892, pp. 1-2.
l. 34 Griffith Thomas, ch. viii, p. 10.

p. 270 l. 8 — *The Church Intelligencer*, as cited, p. 95.
l. 15 — Copy of letter, in A.M.W.C's hand, Sir W. Odling to A.M.W.C., 3.7.1902, p. 1.
ll. 25, 30, 34 — *A Short Memoir of the Rev. Thomas Chamberlain* by A. B. Simeon (1892), pp. 3, 28, 27.

p. 271 l. 2 n — *In West Oxford*, ed. T. W. Squires (1928), pp. 18-26.
l. 9 — *The Christian*, 17.11.1892, p. 19. (Quoted *via* a misleading transcription.)
ll. 16, 24 — *Ibid.*, 24.11.1892, p. 16.
l. 36 — *Memories of Victorian Oxford* by Sir C. W. C. Oman (1941), p. 133.

p. 272 l. 24 — *Things I Have Seen* by Sir C. W. C. Oman (1933), pp. 90-1. Cp. *Anatomy of Oxford*, compiled C. D. Lewis and C. Fenby (1938), pp. 96-7.
l. 26 — *The Oxford Times*, 1.4.1893, p. 6; *The Oxford Chronicle*, 1.4.1893, p. 7.

p. 273 l. 2 — 'The Rector of St. Aldate's Address at the Easter Vestry Meeting, on April 4, 1893.' (STL no. 105.)
ll. 5, 9 — *St. Aldate's with St. Matthew's Parish Magazine*, Sept. 1893, p. 5; Aug. 1894, pp. 1-2.

p. 274 l. 26 — *The Evangelical Teaching of Today* by A.M.W.C. (1893), pp. 3, 4. (STL no. 106.)

p. 275 l. 11 — Downer, p. 115; 'The Evangelical Pastorate for Undergraduates at Oxford' [1895], p. 2.
l. 28 — *St. Aldate's with St. Matthew's Parish Magazine*, Oct. 1893, p. 2.

p. 276 l. 3 — Personal recollection, Miss E. C. Christopher, 1957.
l. 35 — *St. Aldate's with St. Matthew's Parish Magazine*, July 1894, pp. 3-4; cp. MS. copy of address, pp. 2 [1909].

p. 277 l. 15 — Letter, H. Miller to A.M.W.C., 1894.

p. 278 l. 2 — Letter, E. P. Hathaway to A.M.W.C., 1894.
l. 8 — *The Record*, 16.11.1894, p. 1132.
l. 13 — Letter, E. P. Hathaway to A.M.W.C., 24.11.1894, p. 2.
l. 21 — Butler, p. 21. Cp. letter, G. W. Butler to W.H.G.T., 10.9.1910, p. 1.
l. 35 — Letter, G. L. Davey to A.M.W.C., undated ("ans. 10.11.1898" in A.M.W.C's hand), pp. 2-3.

p. 279 l. 12 — *The Record*, 19.9.1941, 'Jubilee of St. Matthew's, Oxford', by H. J. Colclough, p. 343.
l. 15 — Terminal cards, O.I.C.C.U., Oct. 1890, Oct. 1896, Oct. 1898, Oct. 1899; University Missionary Union card, undated [1890-2].
l. 19 — Personal recollection, Dr. J. H. Oldham, 1963.

p. 280 l. 22 — *The Dial*, vol. i, no. 8, Aug. 1913, p. 316.
l. 30 — 'An Appeal for a School for Grandpont, St. Aldate's, Oxford' (1893), p. 2. (STL no. 107.)
l. 36 — 'St. Aldate's Schools Minute Book' (1866-1904), 21.12.1891; 14, 21.3.1892; 19.2, 21.6, 20.9, 20.11.1895.

p. 281 l. 9. — *The Oxford Times*, 31.8.1895, p. 3. Cp. *ibid.*, 24.8, p. 6; 7.9, p. 6; 14.9, p. 8; 21.9, pp. 3, 5, 8; 28.9, p. 8.

l. 13 *The Oxford Chronicle,* 12.10.1895, p. 6.
l. 19 Letter, E. P. Hathaway to A.M.W.C., 13.9.1895, p. 1.
l. 21 *The Oxford Chronicle,* 5.10.1895, p. 8.
l. 30 *The Oxford Times,* 26.10.1895, p. 7; *The Oxford Chronicle* 26.10.1895, p. 7.
p. 282 l. 8 *Ibid.*
l. 15 *St. Aldate's with St. Matthew's Parish Magazine,* Oct. 1895, p. 8.
l. 33 Cp. *ibid.*, Nov. 1895, p. 7; Aug. 1896, p. 5.
l. 33 n 2 'St. Matthew's Church, Grandpont. Minute Book' (1897-1952), mem., p. 1.
p. 283 l. 14 Griffith Thomas, ch. x, p. 20.
ll. 20, 23 *St. Aldate's, Oxford, Parish Magazine,* May 1896, pp. 4, 5-6.
l. 24 St. Aldates' returns, Oxford episcopal visitations, 1893, 1896, *etc.* (O.D.P. c. 359 f. 307v v., *et seq.*)
l. 33 *St. Aldate's with St. Matthew's Parish Magazine,* Sept. 1907, p. 2.
p. 284 l. 4 *Ibid.*, p. 3.
l. 10 Griffith Thomas, *ibid.*
l. 11 'National Club. General Committee Minute Book' (1895-1905), p. 34 (14.1.1896).
l. 12 *Ibid.*, p. 59 (printed list); 'National Club. General Committee Minute Book' (1906-17), p. 20 (29.5.1906).
l. 22 'National Club. General Committee Minute Book (1895-1905), pp. 101-2 (8.6.1897); *ibid.* (1906-17), p. 226 (24.9.1912).
l. 37 Griffith Thomas, ch. viii, MS. insertion, pp. 26-7.

CHAPTER XIV 1896-1900

p. 285 l. 9 *St. Aldate's, Oxford, Parish Magazine,* May 1896, p. 4.
l. 13 Written reminiscence, G. Foster-Carter, 17.7.1960.
p. 286 l. 3 Collecting card (No. 14), Bp. Hannington Memorial Hall, Oxford, n.d. [1896].
l. 6 Letter, E. P. Hathaway to A.M.W.C., 6.10.1895, p. 2.
l. 8 Copy of letter, A.M.W.C. to ?, 5.1.1903, p. 2. (LL no. 108.)
l. 26 Griffith Thomas, ch. vi, pp. 34-5.
l. 28 *St. Aldate's with St. Matthew's Parish Magazine,* Nov. 1895, p. 2.
p. 287 l. 14 Cp. *ibid.*, June 1896, pp. 4-5.
l. 20 Cp. *ibid.*, March 1903, p. 2.
l. 33 *The History of the Church Missionary Society* by E. Stock (1899), vol. iii, p. 790.
l. 36 Griffith Thomas, ch. viii, p. 12.
p. 288 ll. 10, 12 *My Recollections* by E. Stock (1909), p. 247.
ll. 16, 19 Ingham, p. 6.
ll. 29, 30, 31, 32, 33, 35 Preachers' Books, St. Aldate's, Oxford, vols. v (2.2.1890); vii (11.5.1902); vi (10.2.1901); vii (1.6.1902; 12.2.1905); vi. (10.2.1895; 4.2. & 10.6.1894; 29.10-1.11.1895).

p. 289 ll. 1, 2, 11 *Ibid.*, vols. vii (10.4.1904; 10.4.1905); vi (10.6.1894); vii (26.2.1905).
l. 28 *Report of the Islington Clerical Meeting 1897*, (1897), p. 14.
l. 33 *Ibid.*, pp. 83-4.
p. 290 l. 14 Griffith Thomas, ch. x, additional sheet 3, between pp. 16-7.
l. 19 Letter, E. P. Hathaway to A.M.W.C., n.d. [1892], p. 1.
l. 34 Letter, same to same, 13.11.1894, pp. 1-2.
p. 291 l. 4 Letter, same to same, 24.11.1894, p. 1.
l. 9 Letter, same to same, 13.9.1895, pp. 1-2.
p. 292 l. 19 Letter, same to same, 19.5.1896, pp. 1-3.
l. 21 Account book, Oxford Fund, kept by E. P. Hathaway, 1857-95; annual printed balance sheets, Oxford Fund, 1857-96.
l. 23 n Cp. Printed letter, 'Oxford Fund', over names of E. Auriol and E. P. Hathaway, dated from St. Ebbes' Rectory, Oxford, 1873.
l. 27 Cp. *The Story of a Quiet Work for God*, revised version of Oxford Fund statement of 1897, over names of W. H. Barlow and W. H. Griffith Thomas, n.d. [1903].
p. 293 l. 6 Letter, A.M.W.C. to W.H.G.T., 24.8.1896, p. 1. (LL no. 100.)
l. 10 *Home Words*, ed. C. Bullock, 1897, art. 'The Late Rev. E. Penrose Hathaway, M.A.', by C. B(ullock), p. 177.
l. 15 Cp. *The Church Intelligencer*, June 1890, p. 89.
l. 25 Letter, A.M.W.C. to W.H.G.T., 24.8.1896, p. 3. (LL no. 100.)
p. 294 l. 6 *Ibid.*, pp. 1-3.
l. 20 n 3 Cp. Facsimile letter, unsigned, dated 22 June [1853], as cited (*re* p. 84.)
l. 30 Letter, A.M.W.C. to W.H.G.T., 24.8.1900, pp. 1-2, 4-5, 7. (LL no. 105.)
p. 295 l. 10 Cp. *The Record*, 9.5.1913, p. 421.
l. 28 Letter, Miss L. Harvey to W.H.G.T., n.d. [1913], pp. 1-3.
p. 296 l. 5 Downer, p. 35. Cp. *The Churchman*, ed. W. H. Griffith Thomas, vol. xxiv, no. 57, New Series, Sept. 1910, p. 689.
p. 297 l. 13 'The Rev. C. H. H. Wright, D.D. and the Protestant Reformation Society' (1903), p. 3.
l. 29 *Ibid.*, pp. 2, 3.
l. 37 Copy of letter, Lord Harrowby to A.M.W.C., 31.1.1898, p. 1.
p. 298 l. 3 *Ibid.*
l. 7 Griffith Thomas, ch. viii, p. 20.
l. 12 *Ibid.*, ch. xi, p. 256.
ll. 23, 30 Memorandum by A.M.W.C., 24.8.1900, *re* course of evangelicalism at Oxford 1856-1900, p. 7.
p. 299 l. 1 *Ibid.*
l. 11 *D.N.B. 1931-40* (1949), art. by Sir G. G. A. Murray, p. 599.
l. 14 *Monument Facts and Higher Critical Fancies* by A. H. Sayce (1904), p. 5.
l. 22 *D.N.B., 1931-40* (1949), art. by G. B. Gunn, p. 787.
l. 29 *The Fullness of God and Other Addresses* by M. Rainsford (1898), p. viii.
ll. 32, 38 *Ibid.*, p. vii.

p. 300 l. 12 Letters, A.M.W.C. to W.H.G.T., 22.7.1899, p. 4 (LL no. 102b) & 1.9.1906, p. 4 (LL no. 155.)
l. 25 *St. Aldate's, Oxford, Parish Magazine,* April 1897, p. 5.
l. 33 *Ibid.,* July 1897, p. 5.
p. 301 l. 4 Griffith Thomas, ch. x, p. 21.
l. 16 Personal recollection, Mrs. A. Barnes-Griggs, 1962.
l. 26 *St. Aldate's, Oxford, Parish Magazine,* Nov. 1898, p. 4.
l. 33 *Not Only a Dean* by D. H. S. Cranage (1952), p. 62.
l. 35 *In Memoriam. Thomas Augustus Nash,* ed. A. M. W. Christopher, n.d. [1898], p. 8. (STL no. 129.)
p. 302 l. 20 Letter, W. H. Ward to J.S.R., 27.7.1961, pp. 1-2.
p. 304 l. 7 *The Guardian,* 18.4.1906, pp. 659-60.
l. 21 Memorandum by A.M.W.C., 24.8.1900, as cited, p. 3.
l. 27 *The Christian Portrait Gallery,* n.d. (Bodley accession stamp 1890), p. 73.

CHAPTER XV 1900-1905

p. 305 l. 11 *La Martinière Chronicle,* Centenary Number, 1900, p. 22.
l. 21 'Scheme to Provide Funds for the Purpose of Founding Exhibitions at Wycliffe Hall, Oxford, and Ridley Hall, Cambridge, to be known as the "Christopher Exhibitions"' (1901), p. 2.
p. 306 ll. 7, 13, 21, 26, 35 *Ibid.,* pp. 3, 4, 5, 6.
p. 307 ll. 8, 20 *Ibid.,* p. 7.
l. 26 *The Times,* 26.12.1901, 'Candidates for Holy Orders', p. 3.
p. 308 l. 20 Letter, J. Hewetson to A.M.W.C., 6.10.1902, pp. 1-3.
l. 27 *Distinguished Churchmen* by C. H. Dant (1902), p. 34.
p. 309 l. 4 Letter, R. Roberts to A.M.W.C., 18.7.1904, pp. 1-3.
l. 9 Griffith Thomas, ch. viii, p. 8.
l. 19 *Ibid.,* ch. x, between pp. 16, 17, pp. 1, 2.
l. 26 *Ibid.,* p. 22.
p. 310 l. 16 *Ibid.,* between pp. 16, 17, pp. 2, 3.
l. 21 *Ibid.,* ch. xi, p. 256.
l. 25 Personal recollection, Miss C. Brown, 1961.
l. 33 Griffith Thomas, ch. viii, p. 31.
p. 311 l. 2 Letter, Sir D. L. Savory to J.S.R., 1957.
l. 10 Letter, Sir H. L. W. Verney to J.S.R., 19.1.1964, p. 1.
l. 32 Copy of letter, W. W. Jackson to A.M.W.C., 20.8.1902, in A.M.W.C's hand, dated 25.8.1902.
l. 36 *The Oxford Magazine,* vol. xxi, no. 17, 24 April 1913, p. 281.
p. 312 l. 34 Letter, T. W. H. Hunt to A.M.W.C., 20.6.1903, pp. 1-2, 4, 9-10, 11-13, 16-18.
p. 313 l. 14 *Forgotten Heroes* by C. J. Casher (1900), p. iii.
l. 23 *The Church and the Children* by A. Smellie and others, n.d. (B.M. cat: [1902]), p. iii.
p. 314 l. 11 *The Christian Leaders of England in the Eighteenth Century* by J. C. Ryle (1902), preface, pp. 1, 2-3 (not numbered, and not according with pagination beginning at p. iii).
l. 28 *The Record,* 6.6.1902, p. 550.

p. 315 l. 2 *Ibid.*
ll. 24, 26 *Ibid.*, 13.6.1902, p. 567.
p. 316 l. 22 *Church News, St. Aldate's, Oxford,* No. 52, April 1958, p. 6.
l. 31 Letter, A.M.W.C. to W.H.G.T., 14.6.1904 (1), p. 3. (LL no. 137.)
l. 38 *The Oxford Times,* 17.1.1903, p. 10, quoting letter, A.M.W.C. to F. Pilcher.
p. 317 l. 5 *The Oxford Chronicle,* 16.1.1903, p. 11.
l. 7 *The Oxford Times,* 17.1.1903, 'Passing Notes', p. 7.
l. 14 *The Oxford Chronicle,* 16.1.1903, p. 11; cp. p. 6.
l. 34 *St. Aldate's with St. Matthew's Parish Magazine,* Feb. 1903, pp. 3-4.
ll. 35, 36 *The Times,* 15.1.1903, p. 4; *The Daily Telegraph,* 15.1.1903, p. 10; *The Guardian,* 21.1.1903, p. 80.
p. 318 l. 10 Copy of letter, Bp. F. J. Chavasse to A.M.W.C., 12.1.1903, in 'My Mother', album compiled by A. C. Seton-Christopher, n.d. [1903], p. 25.
l. 17 Copy of letter, Mrs. L. H. Liddell to A.M.W.C., 13.1.1903, *ibid.*, pp. 31-2.
l. 22 Copy of letter, Mrs. S. D. Miller to A.M.W.C., 12.1.1903, *ibid.*, pp. 29-30.
l. 27 *The Record,* 16.1.1903, p. 54.
l. 37 Letter, Mrs. M. Warner to A.M.W.C., 15.11.1904, pp. 1-2.
p. 319 l. 4 Personal recollection, Miss C. Brown, 1961.
l. 9 Personal recollection, Miss E. M. Davenport, 1963.
l. 11 Letter, A.M.W.C. to B.F.B.S. Secs., 7.11.1903, p. 5. (LL no. 124.)
l. 12 Letter, same to same, 28.11.1903, p. 4. (LL no. 126.)
l. 14 Letter, same to J. H. Ritson, 29.6.1903, p. 2. (LL no. 116.)
l. 16 Personal recollection, G. Foster-Carter, 1961. Cp. Griffith Thomas, ch. x, p. 19.
l. 22 St. Aldates' returns, Oxford episcopal visitations, 1860-87. (O.D.P. d. 180. f. 852 v.—c. 353. f. 317 v.)
l. 23 Preachers' Books, St. Aldate's, Oxford, vols. v, vi, vii: Easter 1890, 1893, 1896, 1899-1905.
l. 31 Service registers, St. Matthew's, Grandpont, Oxford, Easter 1892-1905.
l. 33 See note in Appendix VII, p. 463.
p. 320 l. 7 Cp. *Christ and the Colleges,* ed. F. D. Coggan (1934), p. 59.
l. 8 St. Aldates' return, Oxford episcopal visitation, 1869. (O.D.P. c. 335. f. 282 v.)
l. 14 *Ibid.*, 1881. (O.D.P. c. 347. f. 301 v.)
l. 26 Letter, Bp. C. M. Chavasse to J.S.R., 12.7.1958, p. 2.
l. 27 Sharp, p. 2.
p. 321 ll. 5, 9 Copy of letter, W. E. Sherwood to A.M.W.C., 5.1.1904, p. 1.
l. 19 Griffith Thomas, ch. viii, copy of letter, A.M.W.C. to W. E. Sherwood, 9.1.1904, between pp. 5, 6, inserted pp. 4-5, (LL no. 131.)

p. 322 ll. 3, 18, 33 *The Oxford Times,* 20.9.1913, letter A.M.W.C. to H. G. Grey, 20.8.1904, p. 10. (LL no. 140.) Cp. reprint, from *Oxford Times*' correspondence, 'Oxford Parishes Rearrangement Scheme', n.d., p. 3 (STL no. 178); 'Abridgement of a Letter . . . ' (1904), pp. 3, 3-4, 4. (STL no. 156.)

p. 323 l. 7 *Ibid.* ('Abridgement of a Letter . . . ', p. 4.)

p. 324 l. 31 *Ibid.* ('Abridgement of a Letter . . . ', pp. 4-6.)

p. 325 l. 15 *The Oxford Times,* 20.9.1913, letter, F. Pilcher to A.M.W.C., 14.9.1904, p. 10.

l. 18 Letter, A.M.W.C. to W.H.G.T., 9.6.1904 (2), p. 1. (LL no. 136.)

l. 19 Letters, Messrs. Stone, Simpson and Mason, solicitors, to W.H.G.T., 24, 30.6.1909.

ll. 37, 38 Letter, A.M.W.C. to H. G. Grey, 20.8.1904, as cited, (LL no. 140); letter A.M.W.C. to W.H.G.T., 9.6.1904 (1), p. 2, (LL no. 135.)

p. 326 l. 2 Letter, same to W.H.G.T., 9.6.1904 (2), p. 1. (LL no. 136.)

l. 18 Letter, same to same, 9.6.1904 (1), pp. 3-4. (LL no. 135.)

l. 21 Letter, same to same, 14.6.1904 (1), p. 5. (LL no. 137.)

l. 23 Letter, same to same, 16.6.1904 p. 4. (LL no. 139.)

l. 36 Letter, same to same, 9.6.1904 (2), p. 2. (LL no. 136.)

p. 327 ll. 7, 20, 22 Letter, same to F. Burden, 20.8.1904, pp. 1, 2-3. (LL no. 141.)

l. 16 n Personal recollection, the Misses Burden, 1963.

p. 328 l. 25 Letter, A.M.W.C. to F. Burden, *ibid.,* pp. 7-8, 9, 12, 13-15. (LL no. 141.)

l. 30 Griffith Thomas, ch. viii, p. 32. Cp. *The Oxford Times,* 29.10.1904, p. 12; *The Oxford Chronicle,* 28.10.1904, p. 12; *St. Aldate's with St. Matthew's Parish Magazine,* Feb. 1905, p. 3.

p. 329 l. 18 Letter, Bp. F. Paget to A.M.W.C., 11.11.1904, pp. 1-2.

l. 23 Griffith Thomas, ch. viii, between pp. 33, 34, inserted pa. 1.

p. 330 l. 27 *Ibid.,* inserted pp. 2-3.

l. 30 n Telegram, A.M.W.C. to ? Lay Sec., B.F.B.S., 3.4.1905 (LL no. 142); letter, A.M.W.C. to same, 3.4.1905 (LL no. 143); *St. Aldate's with St. Matthew's Parish Magazine,* May 1905, p. 1. Cp. letter, J. Hewetson to A.M.W.C., 15.3.1905, p. 9.

p. 331 ll. 2, 10 MS. 'Letter accompanying Testimonial to Canon Christopher', June 1905, signed W. J. Thornton, Frank Burden, A. Martin. Cp. *St. Aldate's with St. Matthew's Parish Magazine,* Aug. 1905, p. 1.

l. 19 'Extract from Minutes of Meeting held November 24th, 1904', typed, signed by chairman, clerical superintendent (Dr. C. H. H. Wright), and secretary. Cp. Griffith Thomas, ch. viii, p. 35.

l 38 Letter, A. C. Downer to A.M.W.C., 23.11.1904, pp. 1-2, 3-5.

p. 332 ll. 6, 7 II Tim. 4. 7.

l. 13 *The Dial,* vol. i, no. 8, Aug. 1913, 'Canon Christopher' by G. Foster-Carter, p. 315.

CHAPTER XVI 1905-10

p. 334 l. 12 *The Dial,* as cited, p. 317.
ll. 15, 20 Personal recollection, Miss E. C. Christopher, 1957.
l. 21 Cp. letter, A.M.W.C. to W.H.G.T., 5.1.1898, p. 1. (LL no. 101.)
p. 335 l. 1 n For period 1905-13, letter from Mr. N. A. Garrard, Bursar of St. John's Coll., to J.S.R., 6.5.1964, p. 1.
l. 11 Griffith Thomas, ch. ix, p. 1.
l. 17 n Minute Book, Wycliffe Hall Council (1877-1933), pp. 298, 299.
l. 22 Printed letter, 29.6.1905. (G. A. Oxon. b. 151. f. 1.)
ll. 26, 30 Same, over signature of W. W. Jackson, 12.6.1906, pp. 2, 3. (G. A. Oxon. b. 151. f. 1.)
p. 336 l. 2 Cp. letter, A.M.W.C. to W.H.G.T., 14.9.1910, p. 1. (LL no. 178.)
l. 4 Letter, W. W. Jackson to W.H.G.T., 2.7.1909, p. 1.
l. 5 Printed letter, over name of W. W. Jackson, Jan. 1912, p. 3. (G. A. Oxon. b. 151. f. 1.)
l. 6 n Will, A.M.W.C., proved London 5.5.1913. (Principal Registry, 1913-705.)
l. 7 Will, M. F. Christopher, proved London 7.3.1903. (Principal Registry, 1903-308.)
l. 10 MS. 'Index to the Clergy . . . of the Diocese of Oxford . . . to . . . July 1908' by W. J. Oldfield (1915), vol. i, f. 73 (30 Sept.)
l. 27 *The Dial,* as cited, pp. 316-7.
l. 31 Griffith Thomas, ch. ix, p. 13.
p. 337 l. 5 *The Acts of the Apostles, Outline Studies in Primitive Christianity* by W. H. Griffith Thomas (1905), p. 4 (fly-leaf).
l. 7 Letter, C. B. Heberden to A.M.W.C., 25.5.1907, pp. 1, 2.
l. 27 *The Record,* 17.8.1906, p. 718. Cp. reprint 'Orr's Problem of the Old Testament.' (STL no. 169.)
l. 36 Letter, A. R. Buckland to A.M.W.C., 5.9.1907, pp. 1, 2.
p. 338 l. 14 *Essays in Ecclesiastical Biography* by J. Stephen, 3rd. edn. (1853), vol. ii, p. 145.
p. 339 l. 2 Letter, A.M.W.C. to (?) W.H.G.T., 6.8.1906, pp. 1-3. (LL no. 153.)
l. 14 Letter, J. W. Tapper to A.M.W.C., 19.2.1906, pp. 1-3.
ll. 22, 36, 38 Letter, A.M.W.C. to W.H.G.T., 9.10.1905, p. 1. (LL no. 150.)
p. 340 l. 2 Article XXV.
l. 33 *Quousque? Whereunto are we drifting?* ed. A.M.W.C. and J. C. Sharpe (1908), t.-p. (STL no. 173).
p. 341 l. 10 *Anglo-Catholic Principles Vindicated,* ed. J. C. S(harpe), (1877), t.-p.
p. 342 l. 2 *Quousque?,* as cited, pp. 1-2.
l. 23 Letter, F. F. Grensted to A.M.W.C., 16.2.1907, p. 2.
l. 32 Letter, A.M.W.C. to F. F. Grensted, 19.2.1907 (1), pp. 1, 2, 3-4. (LL no. 158.)
p. 343 l. 4 Letter, F. F. Grensted to A.M.W.C., 21.2.1907, pp. 1, 3.
l. 14 Copy of letter, E. Stock to A.M.W.C., 26.11.1910, in (incomplete) letter, A.M.W.C. to W.H.G.T., surviving 2 pp. (LL no. 182.)

l. 30 Letter, Bp. E. G. Ingham to A.M.W.C., 19.11.1907, pp. 1-2.
l. 33 Letter, same to same, 24.12.1908, p. 2.
p. 344 l. 4 Letter, G. Quick to A.M.W.C., 15.12.1908, p. 1.
l. 12 Sturdy, p. 8.
l. 27 *The Guardian*, 20.3.1913, p. 369.
l. 34 *Do You Believe? or, Aids to Faith* by R. C. Burr, n.d. ("20th Thousand"), preface, opposite t.-p.
l. 38 Printed card, Jan. 1908. (STL no. 174.)
p. 346 l. 10 *The Dial*, as cited, p. 317.
l. 13 Personal recollection, M. R. Lawrence, 1963.
l. 20 *T. E. Lawrence by his Friends*, ed. A. W. Lawrence (1937), p. 27.
l. 22 *The Home Letters of T. E. Lawrence and His Brothers* (1954), pp. 4, 100, 124, 159, 174, 202, 212, 400, 421, 425, 432.
l. 33 Letter, A.M.W.C. to M. R. Lawrence, 11.10.1910, pp. 3-4. (LL no. 180.)
l. 38 Letter, same to same, 12.7.1911, pp. 2-3. (LL no. 190.)
p. 347 l. 17 Letter, W. T. Evans to A.M.W.C., 23.11.1910, pp. 1-2.
l. 25 Letter, C. H. Townson to same, 26.7.1911, pp. 2-3.
ll. 27, 28 Letter, W. A. Frogley to same, 26.7.1911, pp. 4, 1.
p. 348 l. 2 Letter, I. Williams to same, 25.7.1911, pp. 2, 3-4.
l. 7 Griffith Thomas, ch. x, p. 18.
l. 22 *Ibid.*, between pp. 15, 16, inserted p. 1.
p. 349 l. 14 Letter, W. N. Carter to W.H.G.T. (first pa., ? with date, missing), surviving pp. 1-2.
l. 17 Griffith Thomas, ch. ix, p. 6.
l. 18 n Letter, W. N. Carter to J.S.R., 7.3.1963, p. 4.
l. 22 Letter, A.M.W.C. to W.H.G.T., 18.5.1911, p. 12. (LL no. 189.)
l. 29 Letter, C. C. Williams to A.M.W.C., 5.8.1910, pp. 1-2.
l. 36 Letter, J. F. W. Deacon to A.M.W.C., 7.9.1910, pp. 1, 2.
p. 350 l. 10 Letter, Bp. E. G. Ingham to A.M.W.C., 9.9.1910, pp. 1, 2, 4.
l. 27 Griffith Thomas, ch. ix, between pp. 6, 7, inserted pa.
l. 32 Fly-leaves of *God's Way of Peace* by H. Bonar, n.d., copy belonging to Miss A. D. Bridge.
p. 351 l. 15 Letter, W. N. Carter to A.M.W.C., n.d., pp. 1-4; cp. letter, W. N. Carter to W.H.G.T., 10.9.1910, pp. 1-2.
l. 18 Letter, W. N. Carter to J.S.R., 7.3.1963, pp. 1-2.
l. 32 Letter, F. K. Aglionby to W.H.G.T., 6.9.1910, pp. 1-3.

CHAPTER XVII 1910-13

p. 353 ll. 11, 19 Letter, A.M.W.C. to W.H.G.T., 18.5.1911, pp. 10-11, 12, 9-10. (LL no. 189.)
l. 30 Copy of letter, Sir J. H. Kennaway to Dowager Lady Buxton, 16.2.1911, pp. 1-2.
l. 34 Letter, Miss A. C. Buxton to A.M.W.C., 19.2.1909, p. 2.
p. 354 l. 3 *The Record*, 19.2.1909, p. 197; letter, A.M.W.C. to W.H.G.T., 24.8.1911, p. 8. (LL no. 194.)
l. 19 Copy of letter, A.M.W.C. to Mrs. L. P. Pelham, 6.3.1912, p. 1. (LL no. 203.)

p. 355 l. 29 *The Oxford Chronicle*, 7.2.1913, p. 5.
l. 34 Griffith Thomas, ch. ix, p. 5.
p. 356 l. 2 *The Oxford Magazine*, vol. xxxi, no. 17, 24 April 1913, p. 285.
l. 11 Letter, Bp. F. Paget to A.M.W.C., 23.2.1911, pp. 2-3.
l. 18 Letter, W .W. Jackson to same, 15.3.1911, p. 1.
l. 25 Letter, W. H. Findlay to same, 13.3.1911, p. 2.
l. 28 Letter, W. W. Jackson to same, as cited, pp. 1-2.
l. 34 Letter, G. A. Cooke to same, "Easter Even" 1910.
p. 357 l. 2 Letter, A.M.W.C. to W.H.G.T., 10.9.1910, p. 4. (LL no. 176b.)
l. 9 Letter, same to same, 14.9.1910, pp. 3-4. (LL no. 178.)
l. 21 Griffith Thomas, ch. ix, p. 3.
ll. 32, 33, 37 Letter, R. L. Ottley to A.M.W.C., 2.1.1912, pp. 2, 1-2.
p. 358 ll. 9, 11, 13, 28 Letter, A.M.W.C. to W.H.G.T., 11.5.1911, pp. 4, 1-2. (LL no. 187.)
l. 33 Letter, same to Mrs. A. Griffith Thomas, 24.(8.)1911, pp. 2-3. (LL no. 193.)
p. 359 ll. 10, 19 Letter, same to W.H.G.T., 18.5.1911, pp. 1-2, 5. (LL no. 189.)
l. 24 *The Record*, 16.5.1913, p. 451.
p. 360 l. 6 Letter, H. S. Christopher to W.H.G.T., 29.5.1910, pp. 1-2.
l. 10 Letter, Bp. F. Paget to A.M.W.C., 24.2.1911, p. 1.
l. 17 *The Family of Christopher and Some Others*, anon. (by A. C. Seton-Christopher) (1933), p. 132.
p. 361 l. 6 Copy of letter, A.M.W.C. to Mrs. Tonge, 15.1.1911, pp. 1-2. (LL no. 185.)
ll. 11, 13, 14, 20 Copy of letter, same to Archd. T. H. Archer-Houblon, 3.8.1911, pp. 1, 2-4. (LL no. 191.)
ll. 24, 28 *The Record*, 21.2.1913, 'In Memoriam, Francis Pilcher', p. 171.
l. 34 Letter, Bp. E. A. Knox to A.M.W.C., 17.6.1911, p. 1.
p. 362 l. 2 Letter, same to same, 20.6.1911, pp. 1, 2.
l. 7 Letter, A.M.W.C. to W.H.G.T., 1.2.1912, p. 4. (LL no. 200.)
l. 18 Letter, same to R. J. Benson, 24.2.1912, pp. 2, 3, 7-8. (LL no. 201; cp. Plate 83.)
l. 25 Griffith Thomas, ch. ix, p. 14.
l. 32 Letter, W. N. Carter to W.H.G.T. (first pa., ? with date, missing), surviving p. 2.
p. 363 l. 1 Letter, Miss E. J. Christopher to Mrs. A. Griffith Thomas, 13.2.1912, pp. 1-2.
l. 7 Downer, p. 33. Cp. *The Oxford Times*, 7.2.1914, p. 16.
ll. 9, 16 *The Oxford Chronicle*, 21.3.1913, p. 7.
p. 364 l. 17 *The Oxford Times*, 22.3.1913, p. 7.
l. 27 *The Record*, 20.3.1913, p. 271.
p. 365 l. 5 *Ibid*.
p. 367 ll. 31, 38 *The Oxford Chronicle*, 21.3.1913, p. 7; *The Oxford Times*, 22.3.1913, p. 7; contemporary note-book, M. R. Lawrence, pp. 74-86.
p. 368 l. 17 *Ibid*. Cp. *The Record*, 20.3.1913, pp. 272-3.
l. 36 *The Oxford Times*, 22.3.1913, p. 7.
p. 369 l. 3 *The Oxford Diocesan Magazine*, April 1913, p. 51. Cp. *The Record*, 4.4.1913, p. 306.

	l. 17	*The Oxford Times,* 22.3.1913, p. 7.
	l. 34	*The Oxford Chronicle,* 21.3.1913, p. 7.
p. 370	l. 13	*The Oxford Times,* 22.3.1913, p. 7.
	ll. 20, 35	*The Oxford Chronicle,* 21.3.1913, p. 7.
p. 371	l. 12	*The Leamington Spa Courier and Warwickshire Standard,* 21.3.1913, p. 6.
	ll. 18, 22	*The Oxford Chronicle,* 14.3.1913, p. 7.
	l. 24	*The Times,* 12.3.1913, p. 11: cp. reprint, 'Canon Christopher', 1913; *The Guardian,* 14.3.1913, p. 333; *The Eagle* (magazine of St. John's Coll., Cambridge), vol. xxxv, no. clxiii, March 1914, pp. 215-7.
	l. 27	*The Record,* 14.3.1913, p. 247. Cp. *ibid.,* 20.3.1913, pp. 271-2.
	l. 29	*The Christian,* 27.3.1913, p. 17.
	ll. 33, 37	*The Oxford Magazine,* vol. xxxi, no. 17, 24 April 1913, p. 285.
p. 372	l. 14	*The Oxford Times,* 15.3.1913, p. 9.
	l. 25	Committee Minutes, C.M.S., vol. 78 (1913-14), p. 90 (8.4.1913.) Cp. Griffith Thomas, ch. x, p. 2.
	l. 35	'Memorial to the late Canon Christopher', May 1913, p. 2.
p. 373	l. 2	'Memorial to the late Canon Christopher,' Oct. 1913.
	l. 16	Cp. *Oxford Journal Illustrated,* 11.12.1914, p. 6, with illustration; *The Family of Christopher and Some Others,* anon. (by A. C. Seton-Christopher) (1933), p. 131.
	ll. 24, 28	*The Oxford Times,* 7.2.1914, p. 16.
p. 374	ll. 3, 18	*Ibid.*
	l. 27	*Ibid.,* 6.6.1914, p. 13; Griffith Thomas, ch. x, between pp. 2, 3, inserted pa.
	l. 32	*The Record,* 18.4.1913, p. 361.
	l. 38	*The Family of Christopher and Some Others,* anon. (by A. C. Seton-Christopher) (1933), p. 132.
p. 375	ll. 6, 8	*The Oxford Times,* 18.3.1916, p. 8; *Oxford Journal Illustrated,* 22.3.1916, p. 9, with illustration; Griffith Thomas, ch. x, p. 21.
	l. 15	Matthews, p. 1.
	l. 18	*The Oxford Pastorate* by G. I. F. Thomson (1946), p. 64.
	l. 24	Downer, p. 33.
	l. 36	*The Guardian,* 20.3.1913, p. 369.

Appendix V

CANON A. M. W. CHRISTOPHER

SHORT-TITLE LIST OF PUBLICATIONS, INCLUDING EPHEMERAE, 1847-1920

By far the most extensive collection of Christopher's printed works is in the Bodleian Library, Oxford. Items represented there are not specifically located below. For the remainder, one location only has been listed. More than a third of the total exist only as apparently unique copies. Letters written to and published in newspapers are not included, unless reprinted separately. LL=Letter List (Appendix VI).

1847

1 "The Head Master's Report, for the Year ending September 1847", *Report of La Martinière Institution, from 1st March to 1st September,* 1847, pp. 20-39. (Printed Carey & Mendes, Calcutta). Extracts from A.M.W.C.'s reports Sept. 1845, March & Sept. 1846, & March 1847, are given there in Appendix, pp. i-iii.

Copy: India Office Library, London. There appear to be no other copies of any reports of La Martinière in England. According to *La Martinière Chronicle,* Centenary Number (1900), p. 21, none existed in Calcutta earlier than 1848; but Mr. R. J. Fearn, during his principalship of La Martinière, Calcutta (1935-48), "collected, indexed, and annotated" a complete set of annual reports from 1836. (Letter to J.S.R. dated 1.3.1961, p. 1).

1849

2 "The Gospel in Bengal. A Visit to Mogra Hât". Letter, dated from Richmond 6.9.1849, in *Quarterly Paper*, Society for the Propagation of the Gospel in Foreign Parts, No. 51, Oct. 1849, pp. 1-5. (LL no. 1).

Copy: S.P.G. Library, London.

1854

3 Introduction by A.M.W.C. as editor (pp. vii-xxii) to *Memoir of the Rev. John James Weitbrecht,* compiled by his widow. London, James Nisbet.

Copy: 1st edn., C.M.S. Library, London.

4 Second edn. of no. 3.

5 *Look and Live: Being Thoughts on John 1.29.* London, Wertheim & Mackintosh. n.d. (but see p. 18: "During the past year, 1853 . . . ") pp. 23. See also nos. 87, 88, 162.

1857

6 "New edn." of no. 3. See *English Catalogue of Books, 1835-1863,* p. 816.

No copy known.

1859

7 Preface (pp. iii-xv) to English edn. of *Living for Christ: A Memoir of Virginia Hale Hoffman* by G. D. Cummins. (London, Seeley, Jackson & Halliday).

1862

8 'St. Aldate's Church and Schools, Oxford'. Appeal by A.M.W.C. (pp. 1-2), commended by Bp. S. Wilberforce (p. 3). Dated Feb. 1862. pp. 4.

9 Reissue of no. 8, with additional matter, including list of subscribers, dated March 1862.

10 Broadsheet *re* church services during closure of St. Aldate's, Oxford. Over A.M.W.C.'s name. Dated 28.6.1862. cm. 31 × 19.

11 'Information with Respect to La Martinière, Calcutta'. anon. (published and evidently written by A.M.W.C.), dated July 1862. Printed Lewis, Portsmouth. Inviting applications for principalship, to be sent to A.M.W.C. pp. 4.
Copy: J.S.R.

1863

12 'Re-opening of St. Aldate's Church, Oxford'. Over names of A.M.W.C. and churchwardens. Dated 16.4.1863. pp. 4.

1864

13 (No t.-p.) Appeal for St. Aldates' schools, with commendatory letter by Bp. S. Wilberforce (pp. 1-2), and list of subscribers. anon. (Two paragraphs—p. 2—and ed. apparently by A.M.W.C.) pp. 4.

14 'A Review of *God's Way of Holiness* by H. Bonar'. Letter, dated 23.11.1864, reprinted from *The Record* 5 & 7.12.1864, p. 4 & p. 4. London, Nisbet; Oxford, Slatter & Rose. pp. 24.

1865

15 *Address to the Citizens of Oxford, and especially to Working Men, on the Propriety of Closing Public Houses and Beer Shops on the Lord's Day.* Oxford, Slatter & Rose. pp. 10 + x.

1866

16 (No t.-p.) Appeal for St. Aldates' schools. pp. 1-2, & ed. presumably, by A.M.W.C. dated 18.1.1866. pp. 4.

1868

17 *A Few Thoughts on the Best Means of Fortifying the Minds of Educated Young Men against Infidelity and Popery.* London, W. Hunt; Oxford, Slatter & Rose. pp. 12.
Abstract of a paper read at the annual conference of the Clerical and Lay Association for the Maintenance of Evangelical Principles (Midland District), at Derby.

1869

18 *How May the Clergy Further the Supply of Suitable Candidates for the Ministry?* London, W. Hunt; Oxford, Slatter & Rose. pp. 22.
A paper read at the annual clerical meeting, Southport, 7.4.1869.

1870

19 *A Sermon, preached in St. Aldate's Church . . . on July 3rd, 1870.* Printed at *The Oxford Times'* office. pp. 12.
After a fatal fire in St. Aldates' parish.

1871

20 'Report', *Forty Sixth Report of the Association for Oxford and Its Vicinity in aid of the Church Missionary Society*, pp. 5-11. (Printed E. Baxter, Oxford). The 'Report', read by A.M.W.C. at the annual meeting, appears to have been written by him.

1872

21 Cp. no. 20,—*Forty Seventh Report.*
No copy known.

22 Address by A.M.W.C., *The Mildmay Conference 1872*, pp. 126-35.

23 Preface, dated 14.12.1872, in 1873 edn. (9th: incorrectly called "12th" in reissue of 1915) of *Christ Our Example* by C. Fry (first published 1832), pp. v-x. (London, Hatchard). See also nos. 139, 172, 180.

24 Extract from no. 23. Single sheet, dated 31.12.1872. cm. 19 × 12.
Copy: J.S.R.

1873

25 'A Review . . . of *A Memoir of the Rev. John James Weitbrecht*, abridged by his widow'. pp. 10. Cp. nos. 3, 4 & 6.

26 *The Missionary of Burdwan.* London, Nisbet. pp. 32. Another edn. of no. 25.

27 'St. Aldate's Parish. Come to the Mission in Your Parish Church'. n.d. Single sheet. A.M.W.C.'s name printed at foot. cm. 12 × 14.

28 'Special Mission Services. St. Aldate's, Oxford'. n.d. Single sheet. A.M.W.C.'s name printed at foot. cm. 21 × 14.

29 'Special Services. St. Aldate's Church'. (W. H. M. H. Aitken, P. C. Christ Church, Everton, missioner). Feb. 16-23. Printed Hall, Oxford. pp. 4.

30 Printed letter over names of H. Linton (St. Peter-le-Bailey), A.M.W.C., E. P. Hathaway (St. Ebbe's), S. Linton (Holy Trinity), dated 17.2.1873. To mistresses of households *re* attendance of their female servants at mission. pp. 2.

31 Printed letter, over same names and dated as no. 30, for enclosure with same. To female servants. Single sheet. cm. 17 × 11.

32 'Mission beginning February 16th, 1873. St. Aldate's Parish'. Printed over A.M.W.C.'s name. pp. 4.

33 Cp. no. 20,—*Forty Eighth Report*, pp. 5-11.

1874

34 Cp. no. 20,—*Forty Ninth Report.*
No copy known.

1875

35 Cp. no. 20,—*Fiftieth Report.*
No copy known.

36 Contribution to *Account of the Union Meeting for the Promotion of Scriptural Holiness held at Oxford August 29 to September 7, 1874*—p. 28. (London, S. W. Partridge; Morgan & Scott).

37 *The Supply of Clergy*. London, Hatchard. pp. 8.
A paper read at the Church Congress, Stoke-upon-Trent, 7.10.1875.

38 'The Supply of Clergy' (as no. 37), *Authorised Report of the Church Congress 1875*, pp. 417-24.

39 Speech, 'Recent Legislation and Religious Instruction in our Universities' *Authorised Report of the Church Congress 1875*, pp. 353-4.

1876

40 Cp. no. 20,—*Fifty First Report*, pp. 5-14.

ANTE 1877

41 *Baptismal Regeneration*. Extracted by A.M.W.C. from *The Primitive Doctrine of Baptismal Regeneration* and *A Review of the Baptismal Controversy* by J. B. Mozley. Printed Hall, Oxford; obtainable Hatchard, London. n.d. pp. 8. See also nos. 44, 71.
This tract was published between 1871 and 1877, while Dr. Mozley was Regius Professor of Divinity, as he is so described in A.M.W.C.'s introductory paragraph.

1877

42 'Parsonage House for St. Aldate's, Oxford'. Appeal by A.M.W.C. (pp. 1-2), with list of subscribers to date (p. 3). pp. 4.
The Bodleian copy is dated in A.M.W.C.'s hand 21 March [1877], and has a short personal note by him to Prof. J. O. Westwood written on it.

43 Cp. no. 20,—*Fifty Second Report*.
No copy known.

POST 1877

44 Second edn. of no. 41. See also no. 71.
In A.M.W.C.'s introductory paragraph Dr. Mozley, who died in 1877, is described as "the late Regius Professor of Divinity".

1878

45 Cp. no. 20,—*Fifty Third Report*.
No copy known.

1879

46 Cp. no. 20,—*Fifty Fourth Report*, pp. 5-12.

1880

47 Cp. no. 20,—*Fifty Fifth Report*, pp. 5-7.

48 Address, *China's Millions*, ed. J. Hudson Taylor, May 1880, pp. 64-5. Given at valedictory meeting, Oxford, 9.3.1880, for C.I.M. missionaries: R. J. Landale (Exeter Coll.), Dr. R. H. A. Schofield (Linc. Coll.) and Mrs. R. H. A. Schofield. See also no. 60.

49 Speech, *China's Millions*, ed. J. Hudson Taylor, July & Aug. 1880, pp. 102-4.
Made at C.I.M. anniversary meeting, Mildmay Park, London, 26.5.1880.

50 Extract from no. 49, "reprinted by permission". Single sheet. cm. 22 × 13.
Copy: J.S.R.

ANTE 1881

51 *Salvation in the Lord Jesus, from the Dominion of Sin*, n.d. pp. 32. An address, commended by Dr. H. Law, Dean of Gloucester, who died in 1884. A reference to it implicit in A.M.W.C.'s letter to Capt. Archer, 17.12.1880 (LL no. 41), p. 8. See also nos. 81, 165, 179.
No early copy known.

1881

52 Cp. no. 20,—*Fifty Sixth Report,* pp. 5-6.

1882

53 Cp. no. 20,—*Fifty Seventh Report.*
No copy known.

54 Speech, *Should the Church Association be Dissolved or Strengthened by those who value the English Reformation and the Truth identified with it?*, pp. 1-3. (London. Church Assocn. Tract 79. "8th thousand.") Made at Oxford Diocesan Conference, 6.10.1882.
Copy: J.S.R.

1883

55 Cp. no. 20,—*Fifty Eighth Report.*
No copy known.
In addition to contributing as hitherto, these reports were probably edited by A.M.W.C. from this date, when Prof. Gandell resigned as senior secretary of the Oxford association. This is also suggested from no. 59 onwards by stylistic evidence.

56 *The Heart of the Lord Jesus Christ towards the Lost.* Assize Sermon. Oxford, J. Vincent. pp. 10.
Preached at the University church, Oxford, 6.7.1883.

57 Speech, 'The Church and the Universities', *The Official Report of the Church Congress 1883,* ed. C. Dunkley, pp. 331-3.

1884

58 'The Word of God and Its Power. III Canada Again.' Article, dated 5.1.1884, *The Fireside News.*
Copy (cutting): J.S.R. There appears to be no copy of *The Fireside News* extant before Nov. 1884 (cp. *British Union Catalogue of Periodicals,* vol. ii (1956), p. 192), though publication apparently began in November 1883. (Cp. cutting from *The Fireside News,* dated 23.11.1883, preserved by Dr. W. H. Griffith Thomas, — including commendatory letter from A.M.W.C. dated 19.11.1883.)

59 Cp. no. 55,—*Fifty Ninth Report.*

1885

60 Letter, pp. 30-2 (LL no. 49), & speeches, pp. 124-6, 127-8, *Memorials of R. Harold A. Schofield* by A. T. Schofield. (London, Hodder & Stoughton.) Second item in part reproduces no. 48. See also no. 130.

61 Cp. no. 55,—*Sixtieth Report.*
The Bodleian copy has 'Rev. A. Clark' (Vicar of All Saints', Oxford, 1884-5, & Fellow of Linc. Coll.) in A.M.W.C's hand on t.-p.

62 'News from the Field.—St. Aldate's, Oxford,' *The Church Army: Its Doings in 1885,* pp. 30-1.
Copy: Church Army Headquarters, London.

ANTE 1886

63 *"Saved by His Life."* London, Morgan & Scott. pp. 15.
From an address. After 1883, as Assize Sermon (no. 56) advertised. "Twentieth Thousand." A.M.W.C. described as 'Rector of St. Aldate's'

but not as hon. canon of Ch. Ch. as in later reissues. See also nos. 64, 72, 166.

64 Another issue of no. 63. "Twenty-Fifth Thousand". See also nos. 72, 166.

1886

65 *Union of Heart among Christians Essential to the Evangelisation of the World.* London, Evangelical Alliance. pp. 12.
Address given at Ryde Conference, Evangelical Alliance.

66 Introduction to *Our Father; or the Lord's Prayer Expanded in the Words of Holy Scripture,* compiled by a Mother for the use of her Sons, pp. iii-viii. (London, Elliot Stock.)
A 'Note' is initialled "C.H.W." (? Dr. C. H. Waller, Principal of St. John's Hall, Highbury, whose mother was a daughter of Lucy Lyttelton Cameron (*D.N.B.*), writer of religious tales for children.)

67 Contributions to *Henry Bazely: The Oxford Evangelist* by E. L. Hicks, pp. 101-2, 312-4. (London, Macmillan.)

68 Speech, *Church Missionary Society. Breakfast at Oxford,* Feb. 17th, 1886, pp. 1-2. Reprinted from *The Oxford Times* 20.2.1886, p. 7, by Oxford Times Coy. Ltd.

69 Cp. no. 55,—*Sixty First Report.*

70 Speech, *The Church of England Scriptural in Her Teaching and therefore Protestant* (Church Assocn. lecture, Oxford, 1.3.1886, by C. H. Wainwright, Vicar of Christ Church, Blackpool), pp. 1-2. Reprinted from *The Oxford Times* 6.3.1886, p. 8.
Copy: J.S.R.

POST 1886

71 Third edn. of no. 41. London, John F. Shaw. Printed W. Brendon, Plymouth. pp. 15. See also no. 44.
Published after A.M.W.C. had become hon. canon of Ch.Ch., as he is so described on t.-p.

72 Reissue of no. 63. T.-p. differently printed. "Thirtieth Thousand." A.M.W.C. described as 'Rector of St. Aldate's', and 'Hon. Canon of Christ Church Cathedral'. Bodl. acc. stamp 1889. See also nos. 64, 166.

1887

73 Speech, *The Anniversary of the Church Missionary Society at Oxford,* Feb. 1887, p. 4. Reprinted from *The Oxford Times,* 19.2.1887, p. 7, by The Oxford Times Coy. Ltd.
Copy: J.S.R.

74 Cp. no. 55,—*Sixty Second Report.*

1888

75 Occasional contributions, each month, to *St. Aldate's Church, Oxford, Parish Magazine.* Usually of parochial interest, over A.M.W.C's name, unsigned paragraphs being identifiable by style. See also nos. 98, 150.
Copies, 1888-1905: St. Aldate's.

76 Speech, *The Dangers and Difficulties which beset the Church of England* (Church Assocn. lecture, Oxford, 23.4.1886, by A. A. Isaacs, Vicar of Christ Church, Leicester), pp. 1-5.
Copy: J.S.R.

77 Cp. no. 55,—*Sixty Third Report.*

1889

78 Cp. no. 75.

79 Cp. no. 55,—*Sixty Fourth Report.*

80 *An Apostolic Entreaty Earnestly Repeated.* London, Hatchard. pp. 16. See also no. 177.
One of the Bodleian copies headed, in unknown hand, "From the writer, May 1889."

81 Reissue of no. 51. London, Morgan & Scott. pp. 32. "Eightieth Thousand". Envelope Series. See also nos. 165, 179.

82 'An Appeal for Help towards the Building of a Church for the New Suburb of Grandpont in the Parish of St. Aldate's, Oxford.' dated 25.4.1889. pp. 4. See also nos. 87, 96.
Letters from Bp. W. Stubbs & Archd. E. Palmer (p. 2) List of subscribers (pp. 3-4.)

83 'The Work of the Church Association.' Letter to Church Assocn. Sec. (H. Miller), London, Church Assocn. "75th Thousand." Single sheet. cm. 22 × 14. Accepting office of vice-president.
Copy: J.S.R.

84 'Account of the Income and Expenditure of the St. Aldate's Parochial Schools for the Year ending September 30, 1889.' Over A.M.W.C's name. Single sheet. cm. 22 × 28.

1890

85 Cp. no. 75.

86 Cp. no. 55,—*Sixty Fifth Report.*
No copy known.

87 *Saving Gospel Truth; and Uniting Christian Love.* London, Hunt. pp. 24. See also nos. 5, 88, 162.
Two sermons, the first based on no. 5.
On back cover: 'An Appeal for Help towards the Building of a Church in the New Suburb of Grandpont, in the Parish of St. Aldate's, Oxford.' See nos. 82, 96.

88 *Saving Gospel Truth.* London, Hunt, n.d. pp. 15.
As first part of no. 87—based on no. 5. See also no. 162.
Bodl. copy has M.S. note (in hand of F. Madan, Sub-Librarian, Bodleian Library & Fellow of B.N.C.): "Given out to those who were returning from the Eights on May 28, 1890." Also a note: "current 1890."

89 *Sowing to the Flesh, And its Consequences; Sowing to the Spirit and its Reward.* London, Hunt. n.d; Bodl. cat: [1890]. pp. 16.

90 'A National Protestant Congress.' Letter. Off-print from *The Record,* 28.2.1890, p. 209. Single sheet. cm. 32 × 12.

91 'St. Matthew's Church, Grandpont, Oxford.' Printed letter of appeal, over A.M.W.C.'s name, dated 4.6.1890. cm. 34 × 22.

92 Speech, *The Church Intelligencer,* June 1890, pp. 89-90. Moving acceptance of annual report of Church Assocn.
Copy: B.M.

93 Notice, for college boards, over A.M.W.C's name, announcing laying of foundation stone, St. Matthew's church, Grandpont. (June 1890). Single sheet. cm. 13 × 21.

1891

94 Cp. no. 75.

95 Cp. no. 55,—*Sixty Sixth Report.*
No copy known.

96 'An Appeal for Help towards the Building of a Church for the New Suburb of Grandpont, in the Parish of St. Aldate's, Oxford.' Reissue of no. 82, with additions, including statement by A.M.W.C. dated 10.3.1891. pp. 4. See also no. 87.

97 Printed invitation card, from Canon & Mrs. Christopher, to luncheon (attended by Bp. W. Stubbs) after consecration of St. Matthew's, Grandpont, 29.10.1891. cm. 8 × 11.
The Bodleian copy invited F. Madan, Fellow of B.N.C., Bodley's Librarian 1912-19.

1892

98 Cp. no. 75,—*St. Aldate's with St. Matthew's Parish Magazine.* (St. Matthew's, Grandpont, had been built in St. Aldates' parish in 1891.)

99 Cp. no. 55,—*Sixty Seventh Report.*

100 *Strength Perfect in Weakness.* London, Hunt. n.d; Bodl. cat: 1892. pp. 16.

101 *The Word that Judgeth.* London, Hunt. n.d; Bodl. cat: [1892]. pp. 16.

102 Speech, *The Church Intelligencer,* June 1892, pp. 94-5. Proposing vote of thanks.
Copy: B.M.

1893

103 Cp. no. 98.

104 Cp. no. 55,—*Sixty Eighth Report.*

105 'The Rector of St. Aldate's Address at the Easter Vestry Meeting, on April 4, 1893.' published A.M.W.C. pp. 2.
Copy: J.S.R.

106 *The Evangelical Teaching of Today.* London, Hunt. pp. 32.
A paper read at Cheltenham.

107 'An Appeal for a School for Grandpont, St. Aldate's, Oxford'. dated 9.5.1893. Over A.M.W.C's name. pp. 4.
Letters from Bp. W. Stubbs & Archd. E. Palmer (p. 2). List of subscribers (pp. 3-4.)

108 *Pentecost Repeated.* Sermon outline. Worcester Tract Soc. pp. 4.
Preached in St. Aldate's for Worcester Tract Soc., 29.10.1893.

1894

109 Cp. no. 98.

110 Cp. no. 55,—*Sixty Ninth Report.*

111 *Personal Experience.* London, Hunt. pp. 16.

112 *Reconciliation.* London, Hunt. pp. 16. See also nos. 142, 163.

113 Chap. ix (pp. 59-70) in *What is the Gospel?* by H. C. G. Moule (Principal of Ridley Hall, Cambridge) & others. n.d; Bodl. cat: [1894]. London, *Home Words.*

1895

114 Cp. no. 98.
115 Cp. no. 55,—*Seventieth Report.*
116 *An Unanswerable Question.* London, Hunt, pp. 16.
117 *St. Matthew's Church, Grandpont, St. Aldate's, Oxford, Building Fund Account.* Over A.M.W.C's name, with introductory statement by him. Oxford, Baxter's Press. pp. 44.
Copy: J.S.R.

1896

118 Cp. nos. 75, 98, 150,—*St. Aldate's, Oxford, Parish Magazine.* 'St. Matthew's', omitted from the title probably to emphasize that it remained part of St. Aldates' parish. Cp. p. 282.
119 Cp. no. 55,—*Seventy First Report.*
No copy known.
120 *Dead Unto Sin: Alive Unto God.* London, Hunt, pp. 14.
Date p. 14: "May 1896."
121 *What is Faith?* London, Hunt. pp. 16.
Date p. 16: "May 1896." See also no. 157.
122 *St. Aldate's and Grandpont (Oxford) Schools Building Fund.* Over A.M.W.C's name. pp. 27.
Copy: J.S.R.

1897

123 Cp. no. 118.
124 Cp. no. 55,—*Seventy Second Report.*
125 *Thirst.* London, Hunt. n.d; Bodl. cat: [1897]. pp. 16.

1898

126 Cp. no. 118.
127 Cp. no. 55,—*Seventy Third Report.*
No copy known.
128 Preface (pp. vii-x) to *The Fullness of God and Other Addresses* by M. Rainsford. (London, Partridge.)
129 *In Memoriam. Thomas Augustus Nash.* ed., & pp. 1-8, 17, by A.M.W.C. Reprinted from *The Record* 15.4.1898, pp. 342-3, by Bemrose, Derby & London. pp. 17.
Copy: Mr. H. D. W. Lees, Lowestoft.
130 Second edn. of no. 60. Letter, pp. 29-31 (LL no. 49), speeches pp. 111-3, 114-5.
Cp. no. 48.

1899

131 Cp. no. 118.
132 Cp. no. 55,—*Seventy Fourth Report.*
No copy known.
133 *The Love of God.* London, Nisbet. Printed Ballantyne Press, London. pp. 16.
134 *The Late General Sir Arthur Cotton, R.E., K.C.S.I.* Reprinted from *The Record,* 18 & 25.8.1899, pp. 818, 838. London, *The Record.* pp. 8.

1900

135 Cp. no. 118.

136 Cp. no. 55,—*Seventy Fifth Report.*
No copy known.

137 Introduction (pp. i-xiii) to *Forgotten Heroes* by C. J. Casher (London, Thynne.) See also nos. 138, 164.

138 As no. 137, but in booklet form. Advertised in no. 137.
No copy known.

139 New edn. of no. 23. Preface pp. v-x. (London, Thynne.) "Twenty-Fifth Thousand." See also nos. 172, 180.

1901

140 Cp. no. 118.

141 Cp. no. 55,—*Seventy Sixth Report.*
The Bodleian copy inscribed in A.M.W.C.'s hand: "A. J. Whitwell, Esq., 70, Banbury Rd."

142 Second edn. of no. 112. London, Thynne. pp. 24. See also no. 163.

143 Contribution (pp. 38-9) to *Sir Arthur T. Cotton, R.E., K.C.S.I.,* by H. Morris. (Christian Literature Soc for India: London & Madras.) See also no. 171.

1902

144 Cp. no. 118.

145 Cp. no. 55,—*Seventy Seventh Report.*

146 Preface (pp. i-iv) to *The Christian Leaders of the Eighteenth Century* by J. C. Ryle (1st. Bp. of Liverpool) (London, Thynne.) Posthumous edn. (retitled) of Ryle's *The Christian Leaders of the Last Century* (first published in book form, 1869.)

147 Preface (pp. iii-v) to *The Church and The Children* by various contributors, including W. H. Griffith Thomas. (London, Morgan & Scott.) n.d; B.M. cat: [1902].
B.M. cat. gives A.M.W.C. as editor of this booklet; but there seems to be no evidence for this.

148 'Appeal for St. Aldate's, Oxford, Parochial Schools.' Over A.M.W.C's name. Single sheet. cm. 23 × 8.

149 'Account of the Income and Expenditure of the St. Aldate's Parochial Schools for the Year ending September 30, 1902.' Over A.M.W.C's name. Single sheet. cm. 22 × 29.

1903

150 Cp. no. 118,—*St. Aldate's with St. Matthew's Parish Magazine*. See also nos. 75, 98.
Probably with success of reintegration policy (p. 282), 'St. Matthew's' was restored to the title.

151 Cp. no. 55,—*Seventy Eighth Report.*

152 Reissue (apparently promoted by A.M.W.C.—see note by him, p. 13 n.) of *We Have an Altar* by E. B. Elliott (Vicar of St. Mark's, Brighton, 1853-75.) (London, Seeley.)

153 Letter (p. 3) in 'The Rev. C. H. H. Wright, D.D., and the Protestant Reformation Society'. (London, Protestant Reformation Soc.) LL no. 127. An appeal for stipend to continue Dr. Wright's services as superintendent of the society.

1904

154 Cp. no. 149.

155 Cp. no. 55,—*Seventy Ninth Report.*

156 (No. t.-p.) Abridgement of a Letter, dated August 20, 1904 . . . Canon Christopher . . . to the Rev. H. G. Grey . . . in reply to a proposed "Scheme" for . . . Amalgamation of St. Aldate's and Holy Trinity parishes, Oxford; and . . . of St. Peter-le-Bailey and St. Ebbe's parishes, Oxford . . . ' pp. 3-6. See also no. 178 & LL no. 140.
Copy: St. Peter's Coll., Oxford (*Records and Papers,* St. Peter-le-Bailey, Oxford, p. 46.)

157 Third edn. of no. 121. London, Thynne. printed W. Hart, Oxford. n.d. Bodl. accession stamp: 1904.

ANTE 1905

158 *Fruitful in Every Good Work.* Advertised in nos. 162, 163, 177.
No copy known.

159 *Unity Through Love.* Advertised in nos. 162, 163, 177.
No copy known.

1905

160 Cp. no. 149, to June 1905.

161 Cp. no. 55,—*Eightieth Report.*

162 Third edn. of no. 88. "Ninth Thousand". pp. 32. See also nos. 5, 87.

163 Third printing of no. 112, as no. 142. Printed Wright, Beverley.

164 Second edn. of no. 137.

POST 1905

165 Reissue of no. 81. "Eighty-Seventh Thousand". A.M.W.C. described as 'late Rector of St. Aldate's', 'Hon. Canon of Christ Church Cathedral.' See also nos. 51, 179.
Copy: J.S.R.

166 Reissue of no. 63. "Forty-Second Thousand". Envelope Series. A.M.W.C. described as in no. 165. See also nos. 64, 72.
Copy: J.S.R.

1906

167 Cp. no. 55,—*Eighty First Report.*
No copy known.

168 *An Example from India.* London, Elliot Stock. printed Baxter's Press, Oxford. "Fourth Thousand." pp. 24.

169 *Orr's 'Problem of the Old Testament'.* Letter. Off-print from *The Record,* 17.8.1906, p. 718. Single sheet. cm. 30 × 5.

1907

170 Cp. no. 55,—*Eighty Second Report.* There is insufficient evidence to assume that the printed reports, if any, of 1908 and 1909 were edited by A.M.W.C., although he remained one of the Oxford secretaries of C.M.S.

171 Second edn. of no. 143. A.M.W.C's contribution, pp. 36-7.

172 Preface, dated 26.3.1907 (pp. v-vii), preceding former preface (pp. ix-xiii), to new edn. of no. 23. (London, Thynne.) "Twenty-Seventh Thousand." See also nos. 139, 180.
26,000 copies sold since 1872. (See p. v.)

1908

173 *Quousque? Whereunto Are We Drifting?* ed. A.M.W.C. & J. C. Sharpe. Joint introducn: pp. 1-6. Oxford, Parker; London, Simpkin Marshall. pp. 156. See also nos. 176, 181.

174 Printed card recommending *The Glories of Jesus*, "Sent, in his 88th year, by Canon A. M. W. Christopher, Oxford . . . "
Copy: J.S.R.

175 Printed card, giving notice of Sunday afternoon Bible Reading at 3.30 p.m. at 4, Norham Road, Oxford, and A.M.W.C's subject, 24.5.1908.
Copy: J.S.R.

1909

176 Second edn. of no. 173, with preface by Dr. H. Wace, Dean of Canterbury. See also no. 181.

ANTE 1910

177 Third edn. of no. 80. London, Thynne. Printed Wright & Hoggard, Beverley. pp. 24.
The Bodleian copy has note on cover in A.M.W.C's hand: "See page 23." Printed insertion p. 23 refers to A.M.W.C's ninetieth birthday (1910).

1913

178 Letter (p. 3) dated 20.8.1904, in 'Oxford Parishes Rearrangement Scheme', correspondence reprinted from *The Oxford Times*, 13.9.1913, p. 10; 29.9.1913, p. 10 (including A.M.W.C's letter); 27.9.1913, p. 11. See also no. 156. LL no. 140.
Copy: J.S.R.

179 Reissue of no. 81. "Ninety-Fifth Thousand." n.d; Bodl. cat: 1913. See also nos. 51, 165.

1915

180 Reissue of no. 172. See also nos. 23, 139.

1920

181 Third edn. of no. 173, with new preface by Dr. H. Wace, Dean of Canterbury. London, Church Book Room. See also no. 176.

Appendix VI

CANON A. M. W. CHRISTOPHER

LETTERS, 1849-1912

Where no location is given, the originals are, at present, in the author's possession. Those elsewhere are preserved in the archives of the British and Foreign Bible Society (B.S.), the Church Missionary Society (C.M.), (in both cases some relevant records are uncalendared), the diocese of Oxford (O.D.), and St. Aldates' parish (St. A.) Letters written to and published in newspapers (unless reprinted separately), and appeals which appeared in letter form, are not included; nor are annual New Year messages to all parishioners, printed as letters in St. Aldate's Church, Oxford, Parish Magazine. *The contents of letters of trivial interest are not described, but these are marked with an asterisk. Christopher normally wrote on paper approximately 7″ × 4½″; conspicuous exceptions to this are noted. STL=Short-Title List (Appendix V.) b.e.=black-edged.*

Until 1859, written from 'Richmond', unless otherwise stated.

1. 1849 *Sept. 6:* describing visit by A.M.W.C. to Barripur and Mogra Hât, Bengal. printed in *SPG Quarterly Paper,* No. 51, Oct. 1849, pp. 1-5. (STL no. 2.)
2. 1853 *March 11:* from St. John's Parsonage, Richmond: to "My dear Sir", requesting Bible Soc. literature. pp. 4. (B.S.)
3. 1854 *March 23:* from St. John's Parsonage, Richmond: to "Gentlemen", *re* his report of Bible Soc. local auxiliary. pp. 2. (B.S.)
4. 1855 *March 19:* from St. John's Parsonage, Richmond: to H. Venn (Hon. Sec., C.M.S.), accepting association secretaryship. pp. 1. (C.M.)
5. *June 16:* no address: to C.M. accountant. pp. 2.* (C.M.)
6. *June 19:* to "Dear Sir". pp. 3*. (C.M.)
7. *Sept. 21:* no address: to Secretaries, B.F.B.S.,—"Gentlemen",—asking for Bibles for 3 "masters" going to Calcutta, to distribute on voyage. pp. 3. (B.S.)
8. 1856 *July 5:* to "Dear Mr. Edwards" (Revd. A. T. Edwards, B.F.B.S. District Sec., Middx., 1853-7) declining invitation to speak: too busy with C.M.S. work. pp. 2. (B.S.)
9. *Aug. 11:* from Guernsey: to "My dear Sir" (?J. M. Strachan, of C.M.S. Committee). pp. 3.* (C.M.)
10. *Aug. 15:* c/o Mrs. Harvey, Morland Hs., Nelson St., Ryde, I.oW.: to J. M. Holl (Asst. Lay Sec., C.M.S.). pp. 2½.* (C.M.)
11. *Sept. 6:* from Quenington Rectory, Glos.: to J. M. Holl. pp. 3.* (C.M.)
12. 1857 *June* [3]: no address: to C. J. Glyn (Rector of Witchampton, Dorset, 1830-97), declining secretaryship of B.F.B.S. holograph copy (1896), included in no. 98, pp. 2, 3.
13. *July 7:* to J. M. Holl. pp. 3.* (C.M.)
14. *Nov. 14:* to "Dear Sir". pp. 2.* (C.M.)
15. 1858 *June 24:* from Yorkshire: to J. M. Strachan (of C.M.S. Committee). Unwell. Doing lighter exchange work. pp. 4. (C.M.)

16. Sept. 21: from Weymouth (reply to be directed c/o Revd. E. Forbes, Douglas (p.c. St. George's 1847-58), I.o.M.): to J. M. Holl. pp. 4.* (C.M.)

17. *Nov. 4:* to J. M. Holl. pp. 2.* (C.M.)

18. 1859 *Aug. 2:* from Whippingham Rectory, I.o.W.: to J. M. Holl. Refers to royal party at church. pp. 2. (C.M.)

Until 1905, written from 'St. Aldate's Rectory, Oxford', unless otherwise stated.

19. 1861 *Aug. 5:* from Southsea: to "Dear Friends" (C.M.S. Secretaries), *re* C.M. affairs at Marlborough. pp. 4. b.e. (C.M.)

20. 1862 *March 27:* no address: to Col. M. Dawes (Lay Sec., C.M.S., 1859-66), *re* balance, Oxford auxiliary, at Parsons' (Old) Bank. pp. 3. b.e. (C.M.)

21. *April 1:* to J. Davenport (Diocesan Registrar, Oxford), *re* St. Aldates' rebuilding. pp.2. (O.D.)

22. *April 5:* to same, same topic. pp. 1. (3″ × 5″). (O.D.)

23. 1863 *March 30:* from 'Oxford' (Union Soc.): to "Dear Friends" (C.M.S. Secretaries), *re* remittance to headquarters, from Parsons' Bank, from Oxford auxiliary. pp. 1. b.e. (C.M.)

24. *April 9:* from 'Oxford' (Union Soc.): to J. M. Holl, *re* remittance overpaid. pp. 1. b.e. (C.M.)

25. *June 27:* c/o Capt. (T. B.) Christopher, R.N., Castletown, I.o.M.: to same,—about to go on holiday to I.o.M.,—*re* debt on St. Aldate's, Oxford, and H. Linton's (Rector of St. Peter-le-Bailey, 1856-77) help. Asks for subscribers' lists, etc. pp. 3. b.e. (C.M.)

26. 1864 *March 29:* from 'Oxford': to same, *re* smaller remittance to headquarters for Oxford auxiliary. Refers to "dear Mrs. Symons'" bazaar at Wadham Coll. (Dr. B. P. Symons, Warden) and to T. A. Nash as sec. of coll. assocns. pp. 8. b.e. (C.M.)

27. *June 6:* from 'Oxford': to same, *re* collections remitted. pp. 2. (C.M.)

28. *Aug. 13:* from 'Oxford': to "My dear friend" (E. P. Hathaway, Lincoln's Inn): *re* Diocesan Conference. pp. 6.

29. 1865 *March 31:* from London: to J. M. Holl, *re* remittance from Oxford Old Bank to Williams Deacons'. Refers to delay in coll. collections, and local report. pp. 2. b.e. (C.M.)

30. 1870 *April 9:* to T. Chamberlain (Vicar of St. Thomas's, Oxford, and Student of Ch. Ch.) *re* Oseney Cemetery. Copy, St. Aldate's Parish Minute Book (vestry meetings, 1865-1928). (St. A.)

31. 1872 *July 15:* to C. C. Cole (headmaster, St. Aldates' boys school 1872-93) *re* appointment as head. Copy, in Cole's hand, *c.* 1894. (pp. 2).

32. [1878] n.d.: to G. N. Freeling (Vicar of St. Cross, Oxford, 1871-91, & Fellow of Merton Coll.) *re* E. A. Knox, Fellow of Merton, speaking at Diocesan Conference. Draft reply, with emendations in hand of E. P. Hathaway. pp. 4.

33. 1878 *Nov. 27:* to H. P. Liddon (Canon of St. Paul's, and Student of Ch. Ch.). holograph copy. "No. 1". (This, and nos. 34-36, num-

bered by A.M.W.C.). pp. 4. Nos. 33 to 37 concern a Church Assocn. lecture at Oxford, and are printed in full in Appendix II.

34. *Dec. 2:* to same, same topic. holograph draft. "No. 2". pp. 4.

35. *Dec. 6:* to same, same topic. holograph copy. "No. 3". pp. 4.

36. *Dec. 9:* to same, same topic. holograph copy. "No. 4". pp. 4.

37. *Dec. 14:* to same, same topic. copy in (?) M. F. Christopher's hand. pp. 3.

38. *Dec. 19:* to Bp. (Mackarness) of Oxford, *re* Cuddesdon Coll. memorial. holograph copy. "No. 1". pp. 4.

39. *Dec. 21:* to same, same topic. holograph copy (Union Soc., Oxon., letterhead). "No. 2". pp. 4.

40. 1879 *Nov. 24:* to H. E. Campbell (Chaplain, Bp. (Hill) of Sodor & Man), *re* mission at Oxford of W. H. M. H. Aitken (Gen. Supt., Ch. Parochial Missions Soc.) typed copy, *c.* 1916. (Griffith Thomas, ch. vii, pp. 34-7).

41. 1880 *Dec. 17:* to Capt. Archer, *re* 'ritualist' controversy. Ref. to *Salvation in the Lord Jesus* (STL no. 51), p.8. holograph draft. (Union Soc., Oxon., letterhead). pp. 8.

42. 1881 *Jan. 19:* to W. B. Duggan (Vicar of St. Paul's, Oxford, 1871-1904), *re* Ch. Assocn. etc. pp. 4.

43. [1881] n.d.: to "My dear—" (W. B. Duggan), *re* evidence for married clergy from early Christian tombstones. holograph copy, and later notes by A.M.W.C., both dated 27.8.1906. pp. 6 (foolscap).

44. 1881 *Feb. 3:* to H. P. Liddon, *re* letter to *The Times.* Draft, holograph copy dated 3.9.1906. pp. 2.

45. 1883 *Dec. 7:* to W. Ring (asst. master, St. Aldates' boys' school, 1884), *re* appointment as teacher. holograph copy, St. Aldates' Schools Minute Book (1866-1904). (St. A.)

46. 1884 *Jan. 30:* to J. H. Salter, *re* not holding a political meeting in St. Aldates' schools. holograph copy, St. Aldates' Schools Minute Book (1866-1904). (St. A.)

47. *Jan. 30:* to G. D. D. Dudley (solicitor), *re* salary of P. A. Bolton (pupil-teacher, St. Aldates' boys' school, 1881-83). holograph copy, St. Aldates' Schools Minute Book (1866-1904). (St. A.)

48. *Feb. 16:* to same, same topic, holograph copy, St. Aldates' Schools Minute Book (1866-1904). (St. A.)

49. [1884] n.d.: no address: ? to Dr. A. T. Schofield, reminiscences of R. H. A. Schofield. Printed in *Memorials of R. Harold A. Schofield* by A. T. Schofield (1885), pp. 30-32; edn. of 1898, pp. 29-31. (STL nos. 60, 130)

50. 1888 *July 2:* to W. H. Griffith Thomas (curate of St. Peter's, Clerkenwell), *re* St. Aldates' curacy. pp. 4.

51. *July 2:* to same, *re* Oxford degree. pp. 8.

52. *July 7:* to T. Redfern (Vicar of Holy Trinity, Oswestry, 1887-1907), *re* W. H. Griffith Thomas, and former curates. pp. 4.

53. *July 12:* to W. H. Griffith Thomas, *re* St. Aldates' curacy. pp. 2.

54. *July 13:* to same, same topic. pp. 4.

55. *July 17:* to same, same topic, and *re* C. J. Casher (hon. curate, St. Aldate's, 1888-1905). pp. 4.

56. *Aug. 1:* to same, same topic. pp. 4.
57. 1889 *Jan. 3:* to same, same topic. pp. 3.
58. *Jan. 8:* to same, same topic. pp. 4 (incomplete).
59. *Jan. 21:* to same, same topic, and *re* lodgings. pp. 3.
60. *Jan. 23:* to same, *re* lodgings. pp. 4.
61. *Jan. 23:* to same, same topic. (another). pp. 4.
62. *Jan. 23:* to same, *re* testimonials. pp. 2.
63. *Jan. 23:* to same, *re* lodgings. (another). pp. 4.
64. *Jan. 25:* to same, *re* licensing. pp. 3.
65. *Jan. 30:* to same, *re* speaking engagements. pp. 3.
66. *Jan. 30:* to same, *re* final arrangements. pp. 4.
67. *Feb. 15:* to same, as curate of St. Aldate's. pp. 4.
68. *March 12:* to T. Hutton of Ormskirk (author of *The Voice of the Church*), *re* his pamphlet, (which has proved untraceable), thanks and approval. holograph draft. pp. 12.
69. *May 22:* to W. H. Griffith Thomas, as curate of St. Aldate's. Refers to publication of *An Apostolic Entreaty Earnestly Repeated*. (STL no 80). pp. 4.
70. *May 23:* to same. pp. 4.*
71. *May 28:* to same. Refers to corrections of (?) *An Apostolic Entreaty Earnestly Repeated,* & J. O. West (curate of St. Ebbe's, Oxford, 1884-6).
72. *June 5:* from 1, Widcombe Terrace, Bath: to same, *re* speaking at Bath Clerical and Lay Conference, and at Monkton Combe School. pp. 4.
73. *Aug. 3:* from Castletown, I.o.M.: to same, *re* holiday events, etc. pp. 4.
74. *Aug. 8:* from Castletown, I.o.M.: to same. Refers to need for visiting in Grandpont. pp. 8.
75. *Aug. 14:* from Castletown, I.o.M.: to same. pp. 4.*
76. *Aug. 15:* from Castletown, I.o.M.: to same: partly *re* Grandpont contributions, and R. J. Rowton (Vicar of Eynsham, Oxon., 1888-93). pp. 4.
77. *Aug. 21:* from Castletown, I.o.M.: to same. pp. 4.
78. *Aug. 21:* from Castletown, I.o.M.: to same, *re* A. F. L. and E. C. Christopher attending Oxford High School. pp. 4.
79. *Aug. 23:* from Castletown, I.o.M.: to same, *re* St. Aldate's Ch. Army coy.'s alleged intrusion into Holywell parish, Canon G. N. Freeling's. (cp. no. 32).
80. *Aug. 29* (dated Sept., apparently incorrectly): from Castletown, I.o.M.: to same, *re* Freeling's complaint unjustified. Refers to a good attendance at W. H. Griffith Thomas's (St. Aldate's) Bible class, and Mr. and Mrs. Williams (p. 284 & n) at Industrial School.
81. *Sept. 2:* from Castletown, I.o.M.: to same. pp. 4.*
82. *Sept. 12:* from Castletown, I.o.M., 3 a.m.: to same, partly *re* Oxford politics. pp. 4.
83. *Nov. 5:* to H. Miller (Sec., Ch. Assocn., 1887-1909), accepting Ch. Assocn. vice-presidency. printed. pp. 2. (STL no. 83).

84. 1891 *Jan. 2:* to "Dear Friends" (C.M.S. Secretaries), *re* Archd. Palmer of Oxford as friend of C.M.S. Includes extract from letter to Palmer. pp. 4.

85. *Jan. 9:* to F. E. Wigram (Hon. Sec., C.M.S., 1880-95), *re* views of Revd. S. Bickersteth (Vicar of Lewisham, 1891-1905). pp. 4. (C.M.)

86. *April 20:* to "Dear brother" (E. P. Hathaway, Rector of Holbrook, Suffolk, 1885-92). *re* singing psalms. copy in hand of W. H. Griffith Thomas (pp. 4). This and no. 87 are printed in full in Appendix III.

87. [1891] n.d.: to same. holograph draft reply to Hathaway's answer (see Appendix III) to no. 86, with note to W. H. Griffith Thomas. pp. 4.

88. *July 28:* to T. M. Davenport (Deputy Diocesan Registrar, Oxford), *re* St. Matthew's, Grandpont, and H. J. Colclough's licence thereto. pp. 4. (O.D.)

89. *July 29:* to Bp. (Stubbs) of Oxford, *re* sermon at St. Matthews' consecration, and *re* H. J. Colclough. pp. 4. (O.D.)

90. *Oct. 5:* to T. M. Davenport, *re* consecration of St. Matthew's, Grandpont. pp. 4. (O.D.)

91. *Oct. 27:* to same, same topic. pp. 2. (O.D.)

92. *Nov. 4:* to same, acknowledging subscription towards St. Matthew's, Grandpont. pp. 3. (O.D.)

93. *Dec. 15:* to Secretary, Charity Commissioners, *re* St. Aldates' Church Charity. Printed in 'The Rector of St. Aldate's Address at the Easter Vestry Meeting, on April 4, 1893'. (STL no. 105).

94. 1893 *Jan. 2:* to F. E. Wigram (Hon. Sec., C.M.S., 1880-95), "My dear Friend"), *re* speakers for C.M.S. meetings. pp. 4. (C.M.)

95. *July 8:* to H. Miller (Sec., Ch. Assocn., 1887-1909), *re* inscription on Ch. Assocn. van, and Tn. Hall meeting of 26.1.1892. notes Oxford Tn. Hall & Corn Exchange "now being pulled down". holograph draft. pp. 8.

96. 1894 *Jan. 1:* from Oxford: to Sydney, Duchess of Manchester, *re* Sir S. A. Blackwood and the Barnet Conference of 1862. Printed in *Some Records of the Life of Stevenson Arthur Blackwood*, compiled by a Friend (1896), pp. 350-51.

97a. *Sept. 17:* from Oxford: to W. H. Griffith Thomas, *re* C. C. Cole (St. Aldates' schoolmaster, 1872-93). pp. 8.

97b. 1895 *June 12:* from 37, Grosvenor Place, Bath: to same, inviting him to call, & encouraging him, after taking final schools. pp. 3.

98. 1896 *March 10:* to same: including transcription of letter from C. J. Glyn (Rector of Witchampton, Dorset, 1830-97), *re* secretaryship of Bible Society, dated 2.6.1857, and copy of no. 12. pp. 4.

99. *Aug. 22:* from Castletown, I.o.M.: to same, *re* anecdote for own biography. pp. 2.

100. *Aug. 24:* from Castletown, I.o.M.: to same, *re* information about 'Oxford Fund' history, and for own biography, including copy of letter from E. P. Hathaway (now retired) dated 17.8.1896. pp. 4.

101. 1898 *Jan. 5:* to same, *re* same topic. refers to diary. pp. 2 (incomplete.)

102a. 1899 *July 20:* to same, *re* possible appointments for him (W. H. Griffith Thomas). pp. 4.

102b. *July 22:* to same, *re* principalship of C.M. Coll., Islington, the Keswick Convention, Mrs. Christopher's health & their Boars Hill holiday, etc. Notes Bp. S. Wilberforce instituted A.M.W.C. at Cuddesdon, 1859. pp. 4.

103. *Oct. 9:* to H. Miller (Sec., Ch. Assocn., 1887-1909), recommending Bp. J. C. Ryle's lecture on Bp. Hooper of Gloucester. (Letter returned at A.M.W.C.'s request). pp. 4.

104. 1900 *Jan. 1:* to T. R. Lawrence, Oxford: acknowledging additional gift towards a church collection. pp. 3.

105. *Aug. 24:* from Castletown, I.o.M.: to W. H. Griffith Thomas, *re* obtaining historical information from Dr. J. Allan Smith (Chancellor of St. David's, 1897-1903) and Mrs. Hathaway (widow of E. P. Hathaway), *re* 'Oxford Fund'. Refers to his son born 7.9.1847. pp. 8.

106. *Feb. 24:* as no. 104: acknowledging gift for parish needs. pp. 3.

107. 1902 *Aug. 26:* from Castletown, I.o.M.: to W. H. Griffith Thomas, *re* fire in Pembroke St., St. Aldate's, Feb. 1902, and holiday events. pp. 4.

108. 1903 *Jan. 5:* to "My dear ——": *re* Hannington Hall, Oxford. holograph copy. pp. 4.

109. *March 31:* to W. P. Wakelin (accountant, B.F.B.S.): sending cheque for cash received from W. A. Prideaux, C.C.C., Oxon. pp. 4. b.e. (B.S.)

110. *April 2:* to "My dear Friends" (Secs., B.F.B.S.), *re* sums sent from Oxford for Centenary Fund. pp. 3. b.e. (B.S.)

111. *April 7:* to W. P. Wakelin: same topic. mentions R. W. Livingstone, New Coll. pp. 3. b.e. (B.S.)

112. *April 13:* as no. 104: *re* eldest son's confirmation. pp. 4. b.e.

113. *June 3:* to J. Sharp (Editorial Supt., B.F.B.S., 1901-8), (first known to A.M.W.C. when undergraduate of Queen's Coll., 1859-60): *re* Oxford auxiliary annual meeting. pp. 3. b.e. (B.S.)

114. *June 8:* to "My dear Friends" (Secs., B.F.B.S.), *re* same topic. pp. 4. b.e. (B.S.)

115. *June 18:* to Revd. A. Taylor (Sec., B.F.B.S., 1901-18), *re* same topic. Mentions Revd. G. B. Durrant (Foreign Sec., C.M.S., 1898-1913), known to A.M.W.C. as undergraduate of Oriel Coll., 1868-71. pp. 4. (B.S.)

116. *June 29:* to Revd. J. H. Ritson (Sec., B.F.B.S., 1899-1931), *re* speakers. pp. 3. b.e. (B.S.)

117. *Aug. 27:* from Castletown, I.o.M.: to H. O. Barratt (curate of St. Aldate's, 1899-1907), *re* St. Matthew's, Grandpont, endowment. pp. 4.

118. *Sept. 5:* from Castletown, I.o.M.: to Preb. (E. A. Eardley-Wilmot, Vicar of St. Jude's, S. Kensington, 1892-1919), *re* same topic. Refers to circumstances of own appointment to St. Aldate's. fair, holograph, copy. ? incomplete. pp. 4. foolscap.

119. *Oct. 15:* from Oxford: to "Dear Friends" (Secs., B.F.B.S.), *re* Oxford auxiliary annual report (printed). pp. 1. b.e. (B.S.)

120. *Oct. 17:* telegram: to B.F.B.S. Secretaries, *re* tracts to accompany report above. (B.S.)

121. *Oct. 19:* to "Dear Friends" (Secs., B.F.B.S.), *re* same topic. pp. 2. b.e. (B.S.)

122. *Oct. 19:* to same, *re* important tract omitted. pp. 3. b.e. (B.S.)

123. *Oct. 27:* to same, *re* no socinians on B.F.B.S. Committee, for Oxford R.D. Chapter. pp. 4. ($6'' \times 3\frac{7}{8}''$). b.e. (B.S.)

124. *Nov. 7:* to same, *re* Oxford R.D. Chapter meeting and B.F.B.S. pp. 12. ($6'' \times 3\frac{7}{8}''$). b.e. (B.S.)

125. *Nov. 22:* to same, *re* tracts for undergraduates. pp. 4. b.e. (B.S.)

126. *Nov. 28:* to same, *re* same topic. pp. 4. (B.S.)

127. [1903] n.d.: to ? Sec., Protestant Reformation Soc., *re* financing Dr. C. H. H. Wright's services. printed in 'The Rev. C. H. H. Wright, D.D. and the Protestant Reformation Society' [1903]. (STL no. 153). pp. 3.

128. *Dec. 14:* to "Dear Friends" (Secs., B.F.B.S.), *re* P. W. G. Filleul (Rector of St. Ebbe's, Oxford, 1901-9) and Bibles for his schools. pp. 3. b.e. (B.S.)

129. *Dec. 21:* to Revd. J. H. Ritson (Sec., B.F.B.S., 1899-1931), thanking for grant, to Filleul above, for Bibles. pp. 2. b.e. (B.S.)

130. 1904 *Jan. 8:* to Revd. S. Harvey Gem (Oxford sec., S.P.C.K.), thanking for letter *re* C.M.S. & S.P.G. typed copy. (pp. 1).

131. *Jan. 9:* to W. E. Sherwood (Vicar of Sandford-on-Thames, Oxon., 1901-10), *re* Oxford Missionary Festival. (Griffith Thomas, ch. viii, after p. 5, inserted pp. 4 & 5).

132. *Feb. 16:* to "Dear Friends" (Secs., B.F.B.S.), *re* Balliol chapel collection. pp. 3. (B.S.)

133. *Feb. 29:* to F. W. Challis, Oriel Coll. pp. 2.*

134. *April 6:* to W. P. Wakelin (Accountant, B.F.B.S.). pp. 1. b.e.* (B.S.)

135. *June 9:* to W. H. Griffith Thomas, *re* successor as rector of St. Aldate's. pp. 4.

136. *June 9* (another): to same, *re* income of St. Aldates' living. Refers to own appointment 1859, when metropolitan assocn. sec., C.M.S. pp. 3 (foolscap).

137. *June 14:* to same, *re* own resignation. pp. 8.

138. *June 14* (another): to same, same topic. pp. 4.

139. *June 16:* to same, *re* income of St. Aldates' living. pp. 4.

140. *Aug. 20:* from Castletown, I.o.M.: to H. G. Grey (Principal of Wycliffe Hall, Oxford), *re* proposed scheme for amalgamating Oxford (evangelical) parishes. Reprinted from *The Oxford Times,* 20.9.1913, p. 10. (STL nos. 156 & 178).

141. *Aug. 20:* from Castletown, I.o.M., to F. Burden (churchwarden, St. Aldate's), *re* fall down steps of (Castletown) Town Hall, illness at Richmond 1854, and successor at St. Aldate's. pp. 15. (Plate 77).

142. 1905 *April 3:* telegram, to Lay Sec., B.F.B.S. refers to own illness. (B.S.)

143. *April 3:* to "Dear Friend" (? Lay Sec., B.F.B.S.). refers to C.M.S. breakfast. (B.S.)

144. *April 4:* to "Dear Brothers" (Secs., B.F.B.S.), *re* unpaid bills. pp. 4. b.e. (B.S.)

145. *April 5:* to W.P.Wakelin, *re* same topic. pp. 1. (B.S.)

146. [1905] n.d. [April ? 25]: to "Dear Friend", *re* enforced absence from Easter vestry, St. Aldate's, 1905, nominating F. Burden as churchwarden. Printed, *St. Aldate's with St. Matthew's, Oxford, Parish Magazine,* May 1905, pp. 1, 2. (St. A.)

147. *May 30:* to "My dear Friends": his last message as rector of St. Aldate's. Printed, *St. Aldate's with St. Matthew's, Oxford, Parish Magazine,* June 1905, pp. 1, 2. (St. A.)

148. [1905] n.d. [June ? 25]: to "My dear Churchwardens (W. J. Thornton and F. Burden) and my dear Mr. Martin" (sec., presentation fund), thanking for letter and cheque. Printed, *St. Aldate's with St. Matthew's, Oxford, Parish Magazine,* Aug. 1905. pp. 1, 2. (St. A.)

Written from '4, Norham Road, Oxford', unless otherwise stated.

149. *Oct. 8:* to Dr. C. R. D. Biggs (Vicar of St. Philip's & St. James's, Oxford, 1900-23), *re* receiving sacrament from W. H. Griffith Thomas (Principal of Wycliffe Hall, Oxford) and others. holograph copy. pp. 2 (foolscap).

150. *Oct. 9:* to W. H. Griffith Thomas, same topic. pp. 1 (attached to no. 149).

151. *Oct. 20:* to F. W. Challis, Oriel Coll., *re* W. H. Griffith Thomas's Bible readings in Hannington Hall, Oxford. pp. 3. (Plate 80).

152. *Oct. 21:* to same, *re* same topic. pp. 4.

153. 1906 *Aug. 6:* to (?) W. H. Griffith Thomas. Refers to M. F. Christopher, A. C. Macnutt (Vicar, Holy Trinity, Oxford, 1905-9), and Bp. A. Pearson of Burnley (Rector, St. Ebbe's, Oxford, 1877-80). pp. 4. ($9'' \times 7\frac{1}{2}''$).

154. *Aug. 30:* from 'Oxford': to H. G. Grey: *re* Indian memories. pp. 4-14, 29-32 only. Printed in full, *The Punjab Mission News,* 15.12.1906, pp. 5-6: copy preserved by W.H.G.T. with annotations by A.M.W.C.

155. *Sept. 1:* to W. H. Griffith Thomas, *re* Gen. Sir A. T. Cotton; and C. Millard. pp. 12.

156. *Sept. 3:* to same. p. 4.*

157. [1906] n.d.: to same, *re* La Martinière experiences. pp. 10 (incomplete).

158. 1907 *Feb. 19:* to Revd. F. F. Grensted (Diocesan Inspector of Education, Liverpool, 1895-1920), *re Baptismal Regeneration* (STL no. 41). refers to Grensted's son, afterwards Prof. L. W. Grensted. pp. 62. This and no. 159 are in the possession of the Rt. Revd. F. E. Lunt.

159. *Feb. 20:* to same, same topic. pp. 12.

160. *Feb. 20:* to W. H. Griffith Thomas, enclosing note from M. J. Sutton of Reading (to whom "some of my most interesting biographical letters have been written"). pp. 2.

161. *Aug. 26:* to "Dear Friends" (parishioners of St. Aldate's), *re* late Miss A. Cutler. Printed, *St. Aldate's with St. Matthew's, Oxford, Parish Magazine,* Sept. 1907, pp. 2-4. (St. A.)

162. 1908 *Jan. 13:* to W. H. Griffith Thomas, with message to conference. Refers to Revd. Sparks Byers, *c.* 1838 (John Sparks Byers, Vicar of St. Mary's, Fulham, 1838-56, brother of J. B. Byers, Vicar of Lamphey, Pembs., 1824-67 (p. 152.) Cp. *Alumni Cantabrigienses,* ed. J. & J. A. Venn, pt. ii, vol. i (1940), p. 484); his curates, especially T. A. Nash; and E. P. Hathaway. pp. 8.

163. *Jan. 21:* to J. M. W. Brooke, Queen's Coll. (card).*

164. *Feb. 8:* to same. (card.)*

165. *Sept. 1:* to W. H. Griffith Thomas, enclosing STL no. 50. pp. 2.

166. 1909 *Jan. 22:* to J. M. W. Brooke, Queen's Coll., *re* C.M.S. breakfast, and his Sunday Bible readings. pp. 2. b.e.

167. *May 5:* to same, *re* latter topic. pp. 1.

168. *June 2:* to W. H. Griffith Thomas, *re* latter's prospects, and his own connection with Cheam School, when metropolitan assocn. sec., C.M.S. pp. 8.

169. *June 16:* to J. M. W. Brooke, Queen's Coll., *re Christ Our Example*. pp. 1.

170. *Aug. 25:* to M. R. Lawrence, St. John's Coll. pp. 4.

171. 1910 *Jan. 6:* to W. H. Griffith Thomas, *re* his *Christianity is Christ.* pp. 4.

172. *Feb. 8:* to A. Warrack (nonconformist minister). Refers to having been hon. sec., Richmond auxiliary B.F.B.S. typed copy, incomplete. pp. 1.

173. *March 23:* as no. 170. pp. 3.

174. *Aug. 23:* to St. Aldates' congregation, *re* 90th birthday. typed copy, Griffith Thomas, ch. ix, between pp. 6 & 7, inserted pa.

175. *Aug. 25:* to Mrs. Lawrence, Oxford. pp. 4.

176a. *Sept. 1:* to W. H. Griffith Thomas, *re* art., 'Evangelical Religion at Oxford in the Later Sixties' by A. C. Downer, *The Churchman,* Sept. 1910, & Town Hall meetings for working men *c.* 1868. (cp. p. 163.) pp. 4. (incomplete.)

176b. *Sept. 10:* to same, *re* farewells, etc., enclosing letter from W. N. Carter, Wycliffe Hall. pp. 4.

177. *Sept. 13:* to same, *re* a meeting. pp. 4.

178. *Sept. 14:* to same, acknowledging £30 from 'Pension Fund'. Refers to J. H. (incorrectly named E. J.) Mortimer (Vicar of Marston, Oxford, 1905-51). pp. 4.

179. *Sept. 18:* to same, including copy of letter from J. C. Hirst (curate, St. Luke's, Wallsend, 1910-12), *re* Griffith Thomas as principal of Wycliffe Hall, Oxford. pp. 9.

180. *Oct. 11:* as no. 170. pp. 4.

181. *Nov. 7:* as no. 175. Refers to Sir S. A. Blackwood. pp. 16.

182. [1910] n.d. [Nov.]: to W. H. Griffith Thomas: mainly copy of letter of E. Stock (Editorial Sec., C.M.S. 1875-1902) to A.M.W.C. 26.11.1910, *re* omission of ref. to J. B. Mozley & Gorham judgment, in his *Recollections*. incomplete. pp. 2.

183. *Dec. 14:* to J. S. Rimmer, (curate, St. Athanasius, Kirkdale, 1909-12), *re* latter's ensuing ordination. pp. 3. Cp. list of illustrations, no. 78 (p. xxiii).

184. *Dec. 27:* to Mrs. A. Griffith Thomas, *re* her husband's Stone lectures, etc. pp. 12.

185. 1911 *Jan. 15:* to Mrs. Tonge (widow of G. Tonge, Lincoln Coll., 1856-60; curate, St. Peter-le-Bailey, Oxford, 1864-7), commiserating on husband's death. typed copy. (pp. 2).

186. *March 9:* from 'Oxford', to W. H. Griffith Thomas. pp. 2. ($5\frac{1}{4}'' \times 3\frac{1}{2}''$).*

187. *May 11:* to same, *re* Paley's *Evidences*, etc. pp. 28. b.e.

188. *May 13:* from 'Oxford': to same, partly *re* same topic. pp. 8. (incomplete) b.e.

189. *May 18:* to same, including copy of letter sent with Bp. J. C. Ryle's *Are You Forgiven?* and *re* C.M.S. breakfast. pp. 16. b.e.

190. *July 12:* as no. 170. pp. 4. b.e.

191. *Aug. 3:* to Archd. (Archer-Houblon, 1903-21) of Oxford, *re* death of Bp. (Paget, 1901-11) of Oxford. holograph copy. pp. 4. b.e.

192. *Aug. 22:* as no. 175. Refers to Dowager Lady Buxton (1813-1911) and missionary breakfasts. pp. 4. b.e.

193. [1911 Aug.] *24* (misdated 1910): to Mrs. Griffith Thomas, thanking for birthday letter. pp. 4. b.e.

194. *Aug. 24:* to W. H. Griffith Thomas, same topic, and *re* C.M.S. breakfast. pp. 8. b.e.

195. [1911 Aug.]: to 'Sister Ruth', *re* Dowager Lady Buxton (1813-1911) and missionary breakfasts. pp. 2 (incomplete).

196. [1911] n.d. (*post* Oct.): to ?: *re* his sister I. F. Christopher. refers to death of Julia Christopher (29.10.1911). pp. 1 (incomplete).

197. *Dec 2:* to G. Foster-Carter (Rector of St. Aldate's, Oxford, 1905-13), *re* infant son. pp. 3. b.e.

198. [1911] n.d.: to ? pp. 4. (incomplete).

199. 1912 *Jan. 4:* to W. H. Griffith Thomas, *re* own health, C.M.S. breakfast, etc. pp. 8. b.e.

200. *Feb. 1:* to same, *re* own health and book distribution. pp. 6. b.e. (incomplete).

201. *Feb. 24:* to R. J. Benson, Pembroke Coll., *re* prayer for Oxford, etc. pp. 4. b.e. (Plate 83).

202. *March 6:* to W. H. Griffith Thomas, *re* book distribution and missionary breakfast, including copy of letter from Mrs. L. P. Pelham (widow of Dr. H. Pelham, President of Trin. Coll., Oxford, 1897-1907) dated 3.3.1912. pp. 2 (foolscap). (? incomplete).

203. March 6: to Mrs. L. P. Pelham, in reply to above. holograph copy, p.3. of no. 202.

Appendix VII

ADDITIONS AND CORRECTIONS, Chapters I – XVII

p. 3 l. 1 No. 14 Coram Street was demolished in 1966.

p. 4 l. 25 Christopher's mother was the elder daughter of Captain Thomas Ashington, R.N., who died in 1810. (Soc. of Genealogists' Library, D.MSS., Christopher.) His portrait, and that of his wife Margaret Cleghorn, formerly in the possession of Major-General L. W. Christopher (*The Family of Christopher and Some Others,* anon, (by A. C. Seton-Christopher) (1933), p. 76), has not been preserved by the latter's descendants. Those of Christopher's paternal grandparents, however, (*ibid.,* facing p. 28), remain in the safe keeping of Colonel J. R. C. Christopher.

p. 7 l. 34 An incomplete letter, in the possession of Miss M. C. L. Christopher, dated, from St. Aldates' Rectory, 10 Oct. [1902], and written, probably in the last year of her life, by Mrs. M. F. Christopher (the Canon's wife), to her daughter-in-law, Mrs. Henry Christopher, speaks of "one of Uncle M[illard]'s relatives, he [apparently Millard] was a *very* reserved man".

p. 9 l. 32 Foster, however, inclined to unorthodox views.

p. 12 l. 14 J. C. Miller, afterwards Rector of Birmingham, a friend of Christopher, and a preacher at St. Aldate's, Oxford, was ordained as curate of Bexley in 1837.

p. 16 l. 3 A valuable commentary on the early development of St. Marys', Castle Street, up to the date (1836) of its being licensed as an episcopal chapel, is given by Canon Smyth in his *Simeon and Church Order* (1940), pp. 234-6. The significance which lies in its continuing history is exemplified by the enduring influence exercised on Christopher at this important stage in his life.

p. 16 l. 14 In 1912–13 Park Chapel was rebuilt as St. Andrew's, Chelsea.

p. 17 l. 18 A diary kept by Margaret Ashington Christopher from October to December 1825, describing a journey to co. Durham, is printed in *The Christopher Family and Some Others,* anon. (by A. C. Seton-Christopher) (1933), pp. 135-51. The original is no longer in the possession of the Christopher family, and seems to have disappeared. With it has apparently gone the possibility of recovering any further portions, which may have dealt with the home life at Chiswick.

p. 21 l. 29 The College Register shows (16.10.1840) that on admission, Christopher's college tutor was the Revd. Thomas Gaskin, F.R.S., second wrangler in 1831, "a distinguished mathematician and a good classical scholar" (*Alumni Cantabrigienses,* ed. J. and J. A. Venn, pt. ii, vol. iii (1947), p. 23). Gaskin, however, resigned his fellowship in 1842, and it may possibly have been on this account that Christopher put himself under Hopkins.

l. 36 In spite of Dr. Griffith Thomas's circumstantial statement (ch. ii, p.11), based on Christopher's own assertion (Notes, A.M.W.C., n.d.) that he became a scholar of Jesus, this has proved difficult to verify. His name, while duly appearing in the College Register from 1840 to 1843, does not occur as elected to a scholarship; nor in the Scholarship Book as receiving payment as a scholar. But after 1700 foundation scholarships of Jesus, owing to their negligible emoluments, ceased to attract candidates, and it became customary to elect to them some who had been chosen for more valuable ones. To none of the latter, however, is Christopher recorded as having been elected. But the Steward's Book, of accounts, which includes a record of payments on behalf of all foundation scholars, shows regular disbursements (apparently augmented) to Christopher, in this capacity, from June 1841 to March 1844. It would therefore seem that his election was accidentally omitted from the College Register; and his benefits, being in kind, would not have been entered in the Scholarship Book. (Cp. letters from Mr. F. K. Jones, Assistant Archivist, Jesus College, Cambridge, 14 & 18.6.1965; 5 & 25.10.1965.)

p. 32 l. 5 For 'santification' read 'sanctification'.

p. 35 l. 31 For '1899' read '*c.* 1906'.

p. 40 l. 8 Some pages of notes, kindly extracted from the school records in Calcutta by a friend, the Revd. K. C. Cooper, then (1965) Vicar of Cumnor, Berkshire, unhappily disappeared before they reached the author's hands.

p. 46 l. 30 For 'Kapasdanga' read 'Kafasdanga'.

p. 49 l. 2 f. Closer examination of Dr. Griffith Thomas's account (ch. iii, pp. 32, 47) suggests that in fact Christopher travelled in three stages, first, by P. & O. steamer from Calcutta to Suez, then presumably overland (the Suez Canal was not opened until twenty years later), and finally, on the *Ripon* (also P. & O.), under Captain Moresby, from Alexandria to Southampton.

p. 50 l. 21 Bishop Sumner's carefully considered opinion was that for the sake of the candidates it was desirable to hold ordinations in the quietness of his little chapel rather than as public services in his cathedral or elsewhere. (*Life of Charles Richard Sumner, D.D.* by G. H. Sumner (1876), pp. 141-2.) It is evident that, in contrast to some of a rather earlier period, they were far from perfunctory occasions. "None . . . can have been present at the ordinations conducted by the Bishop, without feeling that all was done that could be done . . . to solemnise the hearts of those most deeply concerned in the service . . ." (*Ibid.*, p. 142.) Above all, he always impressed on his candidates the necessity of 'preaching Christ,'—"preach nothing but Christ." (*Ibid.*, p. 143.) Thus Christopher had the advantage of a thoroughly spiritual and evangelical beginning to his ministry. Others have testified to feeling that it was impossible that "any of the candidates could ever forget the simple solemnity of the occasion, or the paternal tenderness and wisdom of him who bore himself among us as a true father in God"; to "the deep impression made . . . by the paternal welcome

. . . the godly counsels of the Bishop . . . and the admirable arrangements on these solemn occasions." (*Ibid.*, pp. 144, 147-8.) See also pp. 53 l. 36 – 54 l. 6.

p. 63 l. 28 For 'Glynn' read 'Glyn'.

p. 64 l. 26 For 'Vicar' (so *D.N.B.*, vol. vi (1886), p. 320) read 'Rector'.

p. 69 ll. 3-4 For 'Dr. Handley Moule . . . 1886' read 'Dr. George Moule.'

p. 70 l. 4 For 'Ainsley' read 'Anstey'.

p. 78 l. 9 Hanbury was brother-in-law to William Yeadon of All Saints. (*The Hanbury Family* by A. A. Locke (1916), vol. ii, pp. 334, 342.)

p. 79 n. For 'Moncrieff' read 'Moncreiff'.

p. 85 n. Hathaway was several years senior to Thorold, and was not his contemporary at Oxford.

p. 87 l. 22 That Penson was non-resident at Brize Norton in that year, as stated by Canon W. J. Oldfield in his 'Index to the Muniments at Cuddesdon Palace as far as they relate only to individual parishes in the original Diocese of Oxford' is a mistake due to a misreading of Bodl. O.D.P. c. 658 f. 74, which in fact relates to Brightwell Baldwin. Cp. Residence returns, Brize Norton 1812-13 (O.D.P. d. 705 f. 49), St. Peter-le-Bailey, Oxford, 1812-13 (O.D.P. d. 705 f. 219.)

p. 94 l. 14 This arrangement, contrary to the opinion of the late Alderman H. S. Rogers (typescript, 'St. Aldate's, Church, Oxford. Description of Plans.' n.d.), in fact appears to have dated from 1843. (Church plan, St. Aldate's, showing addition of 1843 at north-east angle, n.d. Cp. Churchwardens' Accounts, St. Aldate's, Oxford (1815–1927), 16.5.1844.)

p. 95 l. 28 For '1602' read '1600'.

l. 32 Hall was instituted to St. Aldate's in 1667/8.

p. 96 l. 6 Canon Venables substituted (*D.N.B.*, vol. xxiv (1890), p. 73) 'theology' for 'catechism'.

l. 23 For 'bequeated' read 'bequeathed'.

p. 98 l. 20 Another contributor to this exchange was Christopher's friend Henry Barne, Vicar of Faringdon. Cp. *A Letter addressed to the Rev. A. P. Cust . . . on the State of the Diocese of Oxford* by H. Barne (3rd edn. 1859).

p. 99 l. 1 Christopher was instituted at Cuddesdon. (Letter, A.M.W.C. to W.H.G.T., 22.7.1899, p. 1.–LL no. 102b).

p. 100 l. 24 For 'Water Shelford' (so *D.N.B.*, vol. v (1886), p. 441) read 'Water Stratford'.

p. 104 l. 17 In the 'seventies there was a St. Aldates' branch of the Church of England Temperance Society, with Christopher as president. ('Church of England Temperance Society, St. Aldates' Branch' (187–), p. 2: Bodl. G.A. Oxon. b. 151 f. 10.)

p. 106 l. 9 Miss M. C. L. Christopher has three letters relating to this period: one from Mrs. M. F. Christopher (the Canon's wife), to her son Alfred, from Dartmouth, dated (in pencil, ? by the latter) Oct. 1864; and two from H. S. Christopher to his mother, the first from H.M.S. *Caledonia,* near Naples, dated 15.8. [1865], saying that he had been up Vesuvius, the second from H.M.S. *Gibraltar*, off Naples, undated, reporting worship of the Virgin Mary, and wishing he could leave the service, which he did not like. He had entered H.M.S. *Britannia* as one of the first batch of cadets at Dartmouth in January 1864, and passed his examination March 1865. (Letter, Lt. Com. D. V. Dawe, R.N., to J.S.R., 31.7.1965, p. 1). According to his brother, he left the Navy in February 1867. (*The Family of Christopher* by A. C. Seton-Christopher (1933), p. 58).

l. 21 Sharp, a descendant of John Sharp, Archbishop of York, was maternally a great-grandson of Thomas Scott 'the Commentator,' a writer particularly esteemed by Christopher for his *Force of Truth*. (*History of the British and Foreign Bible Society* by W. Canton, vol. iii (1910), p. 30.)

p. 110 l. 28 For 'Rupertsland' read 'Rupert's Land'.

p. 112 l. 7 Chavasse's biographer quotes extensively from a diary which F. J. Chavasse kept before and while he was an undergraduate, 1862-67 (*Francis James Chavasse* by J. B. Lancelot (1929), pp. 9-13 *passim*, with several references to Christopher.) This is not to be found among the numerous Chavasse papers preserved at St. Peter's College, Oxford, nor is its whereabouts known to the Chavasse family. But a note-book of the future bishop survives, in the college collection, which includes sermons preached in St. Aldate's by the Hon. and Rt. Revd. S. Waldegrave, 3.6.1866 (pp. 14-18; and see p. 21), and J. C. Ryle, 10.6.1866 (pp. 9-13); also notes of addresses in Oxford or the vicinity by C. J. Goodhart (1866, 1869), Canon W. W. Champneys (1868), W. Cadman (1869), E. P. Hathaway (1869), and H. E. Fox (1869).

p. 115 l. 32 A comparable later inscription (1894) is to be seen on a fly-leaf of *The Place of Christ in Modern Theology* by A. M. Fairbairn, in the library of Dallas Theological Seminary, Texas, U.S.A.

p. 116 l. 34 In 1862 Samuel Garratt was Perpetual Curate of Holy Trinity, Lincoln's Inn Fields. He moved to Ipswich five years later.

p. 121 l. 20 For 'W. H. Hooper' read 'W. Hooper'.

l. 24 There does not seem to be any connection between this incident and the contemporary disturbance caused by the publication of *Essays and Reviews*.

p. 125 l. 6 Compulsory church rates were not abolished until 1868; but after 1853 they frequently could not, in practice, be enforced in town parishes.

l. 15n It is clear from a vestry minute book which came to light subsequent to the printing of ch. viii, that additional seating capacity was not the only major motive for rebuilding. In 1848 the condition of the tower and spire was already bad, and in the case of the spire, reconstruction was recommended. Ten years later, in 1858, the fabric of the church was said to have been for a long time in an "unsound state," a report having been asked for in September 1857. ('Minute Book of Rators in Vestry', St. Aldate's, Oxford, (1782-1865), 16.4.1848, 16.4.1858.) Cp. p. 130n.

p. 127 l. 18 For 'afterward' read 'afterwards'.

p. 128 l. 6 At an earlier stage, Dr. Wilberforce had objected to galleries as a method of enlarging the seating accommodation. On 28 October 1861, he wrote privately to Christopher from Bishopthorpe Palace, Yorks.: "I rejoice unfeignedly in the acceptance of your Ministry which makes the enlargement of your Church desirable & in the munificence of Spirit which leads you to undertake the task. There is only this question of the Galleries. Now you must not my dear Friend ask me to accede to them . . . I feel sure that an Architect capable of drawing these plans would find for you some other way of enlarging the room of the Church . . ." (Bodl. Dep. d. 210 / f. 206; pp. 189-90, typed copy.) It had evidently been considered that enlargement of the building itself would be difficult in view of adjoining burial places and the proximity of the Master of Pembroke's lodgings. (*Ibid.*, ff. 207-8; pp. 190-91.)

p. 133 n 2 From 1868, "voluntary church rates have . . . been generally superceded by pew rents and voluntary contributions." (*A Dictionary of English Church History*, ed. S. L. Ollard and G. Crosse (1912), p. 117.) See also note, p. 125 l. 6 above.

p. 138 l. 2 For 'President' read 'a member of the General Council'.

p. 145 l. 13 For 'Vicar' read 'Rector'.

p. 150 l. 26 For 'nearly a year' read 'six months'.

l. 35 Christopher continued in this capacity until 1909. (*Proceedings of the Church Missionary Society 1909–10* (1910), p. 172.)

p. 159 ll. 6, 7 Cp. correction, p. 85 n. above.

p. 160 l. 27 For 'Aluredus Gulielmus Christopher' read 'Aluredus Millard Gulielmus Christopher'.

p. 161 l. 16 The contractor was Joseph Castle.

p. 166 l. 25 For 'Chaundy' read 'Chandler'.

p. 168 l. 17 For 'Aquila' read 'Aguilar'. So also p. 257, l. 25.

p. 170 l. 26 Some further details about these visits (to Belleville, Galt, and Knowlton) may be found in a letter [1873] from Christopher printed in *God's Answers: A Record of Miss Annie Macpherson's Work* by C. M. S. Lowe (1882), pp. 89–93.

p. 172 l. 23 It is a curious fact that this lady, Catherine Louisa Hathaway, *née* Legh, was a maternal second cousin, three times removed, of Canon Christopher's great-granddaughter, Miss M. C. L. Christopher, who is now his only living descendant. (Burke's *Landed Gentry* (1914), pp. 1699, 1700, art. 'Shaw of Bishopswood'; *The Evangelicals at Oxford 1735-1871* by J. S. Reynolds (1953), p. 171.)

p. 173 l. 12 For 'Keable' read 'Keeble'.

p. 180 l. 6 For 'Sir Thomas Beauchamp' read 'Sir Thomas Proctor-Beauchamp'.

p. 184 l. 30 It has been doubtfully suggested that Christopher had some slight connection with this revival. Cp. *The Second Evangelical Awakening in Britain* by J. E. Orr (1949), pp. 118-9.

p. 192 l. 30 For 'is' read 'it'.

p. 193 l. 19 For 'his' read 'a recent'.

p. 196 ll. 8,9 For 'Payne-Smith' read 'Payne Smith'.

p. 201 l. 31 For 'World's Evangelical Alliance' read 'Evangelical Alliance (British Organisation)'.

p. 207 l. 8 For 'ἒλεγξον' read 'ἔλεγξον'.

p. 215 l. 36 This quotation, modified from the text of 1936, represents almost the only revision which Dr. Elliott-Binns was able to make in his second edn., 1946. (See p. 10 of that edn., of which the reissue of 1953 was a reprint.)

p. 222 l. 9 It is likely that a little later another sympathiser was Edwin Kempson, scholar of Christ Church, who took a 'double first' in mathematics, and became curate to F. J. Chavasse at St. Peter-le-Bailey 1886-7, Principal of King William's College, Isle of Man, 1899-1912, when Christopher probably renewed contact with him, and finally Bishop of Warrington 1920-28.

p. 225 l. 6 For 'criticisim' read 'criticism'.

p. 230 l. 34 The Victoria Theatre was situated behind Magdalen Street and George Street, with entrances from both thoroughfares. (Bodl. MS. Top. Oxon. d. 500 f. 13.)

p. 239 l. 4 For 'A. J. Lyttleton' read 'A. T. Lyttleton'.

l. 9 Cp. correction, p. 138 l. 2 above.

p. 241 l. 17 For 'not prosecute' read 'not to prosecute'.

l. 30 For 'but no one' read 'but as no one'.

p. 242 l. 1 For 'Dr. B. Jowett' read 'the Revd. B. Jowett'.

l. 6 Cp. correction, p. 138 l. 2 above. (Also p. 239 l. 9 above).

p. 243 l. 26 Mr. Justice Lopes afterwards became Baron Ludlow.

p. 244 l. 34 A portrait at La Martinière, Calcutta, made in 1961 from a photograph of Christopher evidently taken in later middle life, is not a recognisable likeness, as is shown by a photograph kindly obtained for the author by his friend Mr. T. L. F. Royle, while in Calcutta in 1965.

l. 34n For 'Bishops'' read 'Bishop's'.

p. 245 l. 20 This article is illustrated by an engraving from a photograph by T. Shrimpton & Son, Oxford, apparently portraying Christopher as he was in the mid-'seventies, a copy of which is not known to have survived. (*Home Words* 1884, ed. C. Bullock, p. 16.)

p. 245 l. 21 For 'Edinburgh' read 'Glasgow'.

p. 251 l. 18 Cp. correction, p. 201 l. 31 above.

p. 254 l. 4 When Wheelhouse died in 1901, he was buried close to H. C. B. Bazely in St. Sepulchre's Cemetary, Walton Street, and ultimately, therefore, near Christopher. His tombstone recounts the circumstances of his conversion.

l. 9 A sermon preached by Casher at St. Aldates' in Advent 1895 was published under the title *The Rapture of the Saints at the Second Coming of Christ.*

p. 257 l. 12 A. S. Christopher had gone up to Christ Church from Magdalen College School (MS. notebook (1855-75), unfoliated, Dean H. G. Liddell, Ch. Ch. Cp. *The Magdalen College School Journal* 23.3.1873; 21.3.1874; 22.6.1874; Feb. 1875; *The Lily*, Nov. 1886.)

p. 265 n 2 For 'Christopher Hathaway' read 'Christopher and Hathaway'.

p. 267 l. 29 For 'Leighton' read 'Lighton'.

p. 269 l. 34 Dr. V. H. H. Green, in *Religion at Oxford and Cambridge* (1964), p. 314, seems to go too far in describing Ince as "a man of evangelical leanings."

p. 273 l. 28 *The Love of God* was published by Nisbet.

p. 279 l. 9 Nor in *Fraser of Trinity and Achimota* by W. E. F. Ward (1965).

l. 24 Mr. Foster-Carter died in 1966.

p. 281 l. 14 For '15 September' read '16 September'.

p. 283 n. For 'W. R. Enraght' read 'R. W. Enraght'.

p. 284 l. 4 Mrs. B. V. England of Abingdon Road, South Oxford, recalls that in the 'nineties, Christopher often paid a morning visit to her uncle's confectionary shop, Viner's in Cornmarket, to talk pastorally to Miss Kate Spencer, afterwards Mrs. Wilson, another Sunday School teacher, who worked there, and that while doing so he would frequently have a glass of ginger beer and a piece of ginger bread. The bread rolls for the missionary breakfasts at the Clarendon Hotel opposite were supplied by Mr. Viner.

p. 289 l. 17 For 'Westmoreland' read 'Westmorland'.

n. For 'Streatfield' read 'Streatfeild'; for 'Emmanuel' read 'Immanuel'.

p. 295 l. 35 For 'Indo-China' read 'Cochin China'.

p. 296 l. 2 The officiating minister was Dr. W. J. Butler, Dean of Lincoln, who as Vicar of Wantage had trained, among other curates, Christopher's Oxford neighbours, H. P. Liddon and M. H. Noel. (Marriage Register, St. Peter's, Eaton Square, London, 7.7.1892.)

p. 300 l. 10 For 'Boar's Hill' read 'Boars Hill'.

p. 301 l. 6 For '1899' read '1901'.

l. 12 The living of Portland being in the gift of the Bishop of Oxford.

l. 13 Mrs. Barnes-Griggs died in 1966.

p. 303 n 4 For 'Dr. E. Talbot' read 'Dr. E. S. Talbot'.

p. 304 l. 23 For 'a year or two before' read 'some ten years before'.

p. 307 l. 29 This letter is interesting as showing Christopher's spiritually-minded attitude towards contemporary social ideals of the ministry. It also throws sympathetic light on the author of the letter quoted pp. 307-8.

p. 316 l. 23 A few of Mrs. Christopher's latest letters, each written from St. Aldates' Rectory, Oxford, are in the possession of Miss M. C. L. Christopher, viz. i. 1 Feb [1902] to H. S. Christopher; ii. part of another [Feb. 1902] to same; iii. 10 Oct. [1902] to Mrs. Hy. Christopher; iv. 15 Nov. [1902] to same—all these concern heirlooms or relations; v. 24 Dec. 1902 to A. C. Seton-Christopher — perhaps her last to him — reporting "The Father fairly well."

p. 319 l. 33 These approximations, taken or made from visitation returns, Oxford Fund papers, and other casual references, reflect an inconsistent picture which is not made clearer by the parish being divided between Oxfordshire and Berkshire, some figures perhaps referring to the former portion alone. A more exact account of population, however, may be obtained from the census returns. These show that in fact the total population of the ecclestiastical parish of St. Aldate's remained stationary during Christopher's early years, even diminishing, only rising appreciably during his later ministry. In 1851, the registered population amounted to 1891, in 1861 to 1810, in 1871 to 1808, in 1881 to 1533, in 1891 to 2,861, in 1901 to 3,365. (*Census of England and Wales 1861,* vol. i (1862), p. 304; *ibid., 1871,* vol. i (1872), p. 300; *ibid., 1881,* vol. i (1883), p. 306; *ibid., 1891,* vol. i (1893), p. 294; *Index to the Population Tables for England and Wales in the County Volumes of the Census Report, 1901* (1903), p. 189.)

p. 320 ll. 7, 12 Dr. V. H. H. Green, in his *Religion at Oxford and Cambridge* (1964), is incorrect in implying that throughout his incumbency Christopher "attracted an increasing number of undergraduates" (p. 218) to St. Aldate's.

p. 321 l. 36 An abridged version of this letter had been printed by Christopher for circulation in 1904. (Cp. STL no. 156.)

p. 324 l. 32 For '1877' read '1878'.

p. 325 l. 23 For '1914' read '1913'.

p. 327 n 2 For 'North Oxford' read 'Headington'.

p. 328 l. 28 Even at this time, Christopher himself continued active in sacred study. On 8 October 1904 he began to annotate the sermons of a distinguished Irish evangelical, Dr. J. T. O'Brien, formerly Bishop of Ossory. (See MS. notebook, partly in A.M.W.C.'s hand (pp. 1-40, 44-48, Oct.-Nov. 1904), in the possession of Dr. M. R. Lawrence, with loose page of holograph notes of address by Christopher, Saturday, 21 January 1905, on 'The Holy Ghost the Comforter'.)

p. 335 l. 20 For 'theological' read 'theology'.

l. 25 For 'house' read 'home'.

n. 1 For 'Petit Trianion' read 'Petit Trianon'.

p. 336 l. 10 For 'October' read 'September'.

p. 347 l. 25 For 'Arthur' read 'William'.

p. 350 l. 28 For 'Miss S. Bridge' read 'Miss D. Bridge'.

p. 355 l. 6 For 'Rhys' read 'Rhŷs'.

p. 359 l. 13 For 'father' read 'uncle'.

p. 362 ll. 8, 9 Mr. Benson resigned Pulverbatch in 1964.

p. 363 l. 9 The cause of death, as certified by H. P. Symonds, F.R.C.S., was "Dilatation of the heart 20 years, Exhaustion 1 year". (Certified copy, 25.9.1964, entry, Register of Deaths, Headington, Oxon., A. M. W. Christopher, 15.3.1913.)

p. 364 l. 18 For 'Seton Ker' read 'Seton-Karr'.

l. 20 For 'Mendelsohn' read 'Mendelssohn'.

p. 375 ll. 6, 8 A further, parochial memorial included oak choir stalls.

p. 413 l. 34 For '1880' read '1881'.

p. 451 ll. 29, 30 R. W. Livingstone became President of C.C.C., 1933–50.

Index